Reading

Grade 2, Unit 5

Responsibility

PEARSON

Scott
Foresman

scottforesman.com

Editorial Offices: Glenview, Illinois • Parsippany, New Jersey • New York, New York
Sales Offices: Boston, Massachusetts • Duluth, Georgia • Glenview, Illinois
Coppell, Texas • Sacramento, California • Mesa, Arizona

We dedicate Reading Street to
Peter Jovanovich.

His wisdom, courage,
and passion for education
are an inspiration to us all.

Accelerated Reader®

Cover Scott Gustafson

About the Cover Artist
When Scott Gustafson was in grade school, he spent most of his spare time drawing pictures. Now he gets to make pictures for a living. Before he starts a painting, he photographs his family, pets, or friends posing as characters that will appear in the illustration. He then uses the photos to inspire the finished picture.

ISBN-13: 978-0-328-24371-6
ISBN-10:   0-328-24371-x

Copyright © 2008 Pearson Education, Inc.

All Rights Reserved. Printed in the United States of America. This publication is protected by Copyright, and permission should be obtained from the publisher prior to any prohibited reproduction, storage in a retrieval system, or transmission in any form by any means, electronic, mechanical, photocopying, recording, or likewise. For information regarding permission(s), write to: Permissions Department, Scott Foresman, 1900 East Lake Avenue, Glenview, Illinois 60025.

Many of the designations used by manufacturers and sellers to distinguish their products are claimed as trademarks. Where those designations appear in this book, and Scott Foresman was aware of a trademark claim, the designations have been printed with initial capitals and in cases of multiple usage have also been marked with either ® or ™ where they first appear.

2 3 4 5 6 7 8 9 10 V064 16 15 14 13 12 11 10 09 08 07

CC: N1

Reading STREET

Where the Love of Reading Begins

Reading Street Program Authors

Peter Afflerbach, Ph.D.
Professor, Department of
Curriculum and Instruction
University of Maryland at
College Park

Camille L.Z. Blachowicz, Ph.D.
Professor of Education
National-Louis University

Candy Dawson Boyd, Ph.D.
Professor, School of Education
Saint Mary's College of California

Wendy Cheyney, Ed.D.
Professor of Special Education
and Literacy, Florida
International University

Connie Juel, Ph.D.
Professor of Education, School of
Education, Stanford University

Edward J. Kame'enui, Ph.D.
Professor and Director, Institute for
the Development of Educational
Achievement, University of Oregon

Donald J. Leu, Ph.D.
John and Maria Neag Endowed
Chair in Literacy and Technology
University of Connecticut

Jeanne R. Paratore, Ed.D.
Associate Professor of Education
Department of Literacy
and Language Development
Boston University

P. David Pearson, Ph.D.
Professor and Dean,
Graduate School of Education
University of California, Berkeley

Sam L. Sebesta, Ed.D.
Professor Emeritus,
College of Education,
University of Washington, Seattle

Deborah Simmons, Ph.D.
Professor, College of Education
and Human Development
Texas A&M University
(Not pictured)

Sharon Vaughn, Ph.D.
H.E. Hartfelder/Southland
Corporation Regents Professor
University of Texas

Susan Watts-Taffe, Ph.D.
Independent Literacy Researcher
Cincinnati, Ohio

Karen Kring Wixson, Ph.D.
Professor of Education
University of Michigan

Components

Student Editions (1–6)

Teacher's Editions (PreK–6)

Assessment
Assessment Handbook (K–6)
Baseline Group Tests (K–6)
DIBELS™ Assessments (K–6)
ExamView® Test Generator CD-ROM (2–6)
Fresh Reads for Differentiated
Test Practice (1–6)
Online Success Tracker™ (K–6)*
Selection Tests Teacher's Manual (1–6)
Unit and End-of-Year
Benchmark Tests (K–6)

Leveled Readers
Concept Literacy Leveled Readers (K–1)
Independent Leveled Readers (K)
Kindergarten Student Readers (K)
Leveled Reader Teaching Guides (K–6)
Leveled Readers (1–6)
Listen to Me Readers (K)
Online Leveled Reader Database (K–6)*
Take-Home Leveled Readers (K–6)

Trade Books and Big Books
Big Books (PreK–2)
Read Aloud Trade Books (PreK–K)
Sing with Me Big Book (1–2)
Trade Book Library (1–6)

Decodable Readers
Decodable Readers (K–3)
Strategic Intervention
Decodable Readers (1–2)
Take-Home Decodable Readers (K–3)

Phonics and Word Study
Alphabet Cards in English and Spanish
(PreK–K)
Alphabet Chart in English and Spanish
(PreK–K)
Animal ABCs Activity Guide (K)
Finger Tracing Cards (PreK–K)
Patterns Book (PreK–K)
Phonics Activities CD-ROM (PreK–2)*
Phonics Activities Mats (K)
Phonics and Spelling Practice Book (1–3)
Phonics and Word-Building Board and Letters
(PreK–3)
Phonics Songs and Rhymes Audio CD (K–2)
Phonics Songs and Rhymes Flip Chart (K–2)
Picture Word Cards (PreK–K)
Plastic Letter Tiles (K)
Sound-Spelling Cards and Wall Charts (1–2)
Strategies for Word Analysis (4–6)
Word Study and Spelling Practice Book (4–6)

Language Arts
Daily Fix-It Transparencies (K–6)
Grammar & Writing Book and
Teacher's Annotated Edition, The (1–6)
Grammar and Writing Practice Book
and Teacher's Manual (1–6)
Grammar Transparencies (1–6)
Six-Trait Writing Posters (1–6)
Writing Kit (1–6)
Writing Rubrics and Anchor Papers (1–6)
Writing Transparencies (1–6)

Practice and Additional Resources
AlphaBuddy Bear Puppet (K)
Alphasaurus Annie Puppet (PreK)
Amazing Words Posters (K–2)
Centers Survival Kit (PreK–6)
Graphic Organizer Book (2–6)
Graphic Organizer Flip Chart (K–1)
High-Frequency Word Cards (K)
Kindergarten Review (1)
Practice Book and Teacher's Manual (K–6)
Read Aloud Anthology (PreK–2)
Readers' Theater Anthology (K–6)
Research into Practice (K–6)

Retelling Cards (K–6)
Scott Foresman Research Base (K–6)
Skill Transparencies (2–6)
Songs and Rhymes Flip Chart (PreK)
Talk with Me, Sing with Me Chart (PreK–K)
Tested Vocabulary Cards (1–6)
Vocabulary Transparencies (1–2)
Welcome to Reading Street (PreK–1)

ELL
ELL and Transition Handbook (PreK–6)
ELL Comprehensive Kit (1–6)
ELL Posters (K–6)
ELL Readers (1–6)
ELL Teaching Guides (1–6)
Ten Important Sentences (1–6)

Digital Components
AudioText CDs (PreK–6)
Background Building Audio CDs (3–6)
ExamView® Test Generator
CD-ROM (2–6)
Online Lesson Planner (K–6)
Online New Literacies Activities (1–6)*
Online Professional Development (1–6)
Online Story Sort (K–6)*
Online Student Editions (1–6)*
Online Success Tracker™ (K–6)*
Online Teacher's Editions (PreK–6)
Phonics Activities CD-ROM (PreK–2)*
Phonics Songs and Rhymes
Audio CD (K–2)
Sing with Me/Background Building
Audio CDs (PreK–2)
Songs and Rhymes Audio CD (PreK)

My Sidewalks Early Reading Intervention (K)

My Sidewalks Intensive Reading Intervention (Levels A–E)

Reading Street for the Guided Reading Teacher (1–6)

v

Grade 2
Priority Skills

Priority skills are the critical elements of reading—phonemic awareness, phonics, fluency, vocabulary, and text comprehension—as they are developed across and within grades to assure that instructional emphasis is placed on the right skills at the right time and to maintain a systematic sequence of skill instruction.

Key

● = Taught/Unit priority
◐ = Reviewed and practiced
○ = Integrated practice

	UNIT 1		UNIT 2	
	Weeks		**Weeks**	
	1–2	**3–5**	**1–2**	**3–5**
Phonemic Awareness	Appears in Strategic Intervention lessons (pp. DI•14–DI•64)			
Phonics				
Know letter-sound relationships	●	●	●	●
Blend sounds of letters to decode				
Consonants	●	◐	○	◐
Consonant blends and digraphs	●	●	◐	◐
Short Vowels	●	◐	◐	◐
Long Vowels	●	◐	◐	◐
r-Controlled Vowels			●	●
Vowel Digraphs				●
Diphthongs				
Other vowel patterns	●	◐	◐	○
Phonograms/word families	●	●	○	○
Decode words with common word parts				
Base words and inflected endings		●	◐	
Contractions			●	◐
Compounds				
Suffixes and prefixes				
Blend syllables to decode multisyllabic words	◐	◐	●	●
Fluency				
Read aloud with accuracy, comprehension, and appropriate rate	●	●	●	○
Read aloud with expression		●	●	●
Attend to punctuation and use appropriate phrasing		●	●	●
Practice fluency in a variety of ways, including choral reading, paired reading, and repeated oral reading	●	●	●	●
Work toward appropriate fluency goals	50–60 WCPM	50–60 WCPM	58–68 WCPM	58–68 WCPM
Vocabulary				
Read high-frequency words and lesson vocabulary automatically	●	●	●	●
Develop vocabulary through direct instruction, concrete experiences, reading, and listening to text read aloud	●	●	●	●
Use word structure to figure out word meaning				
Use context clues to determine word meaning of unfamiliar words, multiple-meaning words, homonyms, homographs				●
Use grade-appropriate references sources to learn word meanings			●	○
Use new words in a variety of contexts	○	○	○	○
Use graphic organizers to group, study, and retain vocabulary	●	●	●	●
Classify and categorize words				
Understand antonyms and synonyms		●		
Examine word usage and effectiveness	●	●		

	UNIT 3		UNIT 4		UNIT 5		UNIT 6	
	Weeks		Weeks		Weeks		Weeks	
	1–2	3–5	1–2	3–5	1–2	3–5	1–2	3–5

	UNIT 3		UNIT 4		UNIT 5		UNIT 6	
	66–76 WCPM	66–76 WCPM	74–84 WCPM	74–84 WCPM	82–92 WCPM	82–92 WCPM	90–100 WCPM	90–100 WCPM

Grade 2
Priority Skills

● = Taught/Unit priority
◑ = Reviewed and practiced
○ = Integrated practice

	UNIT 1 Weeks		UNIT 2 Weeks	
	1–2	3–5	1–2	3–5
Text Comprehension				
Strategies				
Preview the text	○	○	○	○
Set and monitor purpose for reading	○	○	○	○
Activate and use prior knowledge			●	○
Make and confirm predictions	●	○	●	○
Monitor comprehension and use fix-up strategies		●	○	○
Use graphic organizers to focus on text structure, to represent relationships in text, or to summarize text	○	○	○	○
Answer questions	○	○	○	○
Generate questions				
Recognize text structure: story and informational	●	●	◑	●
Summarize text by retelling stories or identifying main ideas	○	○	○	●
Visualize; use mental imagery				●
Make connections: text to self, text to text, text to world	○	○	○	○
Use parts of a book to locate information		●	●	○
Skills				
Author's purpose	◑	○	○	●
Cause and effect				
Compare and contrast		◑	○	○
Draw conclusions				●
Fact and opinion				
Graphic sources (charts, diagrams, graphs, maps, tables)			●	○
Main idea and supporting details	●	●	○	○
Realism/fantasy		●	●	◑
Sequence of events			●	●
Literary Elements				
Character (Recognize characters' traits, actions, feelings, and motives)	●	●	◑	○
Plot and plot structure				
Setting	●	●	◑	○
Theme				

	UNIT 3		UNIT 4		UNIT 5		UNIT 6	
	Weeks		Weeks		Weeks		Weeks	
	1–2	3–5	1–2	3–5	1–2	3–5	1–2	3–5
	○	○	○	○	○	○	○	○
	○	○	○	○	○	○	○	○
	○	○	○	○	○	●	○	●
	○	●	○	○	○	○	○	○
	○	●	○	○	○	●	●	○
	○	○	○	●	●	○	○	●
	○	○	○	○	○	○	○	○
			●	●	○	●	○	○
	●	○	●	○	●	○	○	○
	○	○	○	●	○	○	○	●
	●	○	○	○	○	○	●	○
	○	○	○	○	○	○	○	○
	●	○	○	○	○	○	○	○
	●	○	○	○	◐	●	○	○
		●	○	○	○	○	○	●
	○	○	●	●	○	○	●	○
	●	◐	○	◐	○	○	○	●
			●	●	○	○	●	◐
	●	●	●	●	●	●	●	●
	○	○	○	◐	●	○	◐	○
	○	○	○	○	○	●	○	○
	◐	○	○	○	●	◐	○	○
	○	○	◐	○	○	○	○	●
		●	○	●	◐	●	○	●
	○	○	◐	○	○	○	○	●
		●	○	●	◐	●	○	○

UNIT

5

You Are Here

U.S. COAST GUARD

255018

Unit 3
Creative Ideas

Unit 4
Our Changing World

Responsibility

What does it mean to be responsible?

Firefighter!

Firefighters have an important job in the community.

NARRATIVE NONFICTION

connect to SOCIAL STUDIES

One Dark Night

A boy takes care of a stray cat and her kittens.

REALISTIC FICTION

connect to SCIENCE

Bad Dog, Dodger!

Sam is responsible for his pet's behavior.

REALISTIC FICTION

connect to SOCIAL STUDIES

Horace and Morris but mostly Dolores

Good friends take care of their friendship.

FANTASY

connect to SOCIAL STUDIES

The Signmaker's Assistant

A young signmaker takes responsibility for his actions.

HUMOROUS FICTION

connect to SOCIAL STUDIES

Unit 5
Skills Overview

WEEK 1

158–177

Firefighter!/
Firefighting Teamwork

NARRATIVE
NONFICTION

WEEK 2

184–205

One Dark Night/
Adoption/
The Stray Cat

REALISTIC FICTION

		WEEK 1	WEEK 2
Oral Language		*Why is it important to do a good job?*	*Why should we take care of animals?*
Word Work	Phonics	T 💿 Suffixes -ly, -ful, -er, -or T REVIEW Vowels oo, ue, ew, ui	T 💿 Prefixes un-, re-, pre-, dis- T REVIEW Suffixes -ly, -ful, -er, -or
	Spelling	T Words with Suffixes -ly, -ful, -er, -or	T Words with Prefixes un-, re-, pre-, dis-
	Lesson Vocabulary	T station, building, roar, masks, quickly, tightly, burning	T pours, lightning, thunder, storm, flashes, pounds, rolling
Reading	Comprehension	T 💿 **Skill** Main Idea/Supporting Details 💿 **Strategy** Text Structure REVIEW **Skill** Author's Purpose	T 💿 **Skill** Sequence 💿 **Strategy** Graphic Organizer REVIEW **Skill** Plot and Theme
	Vocabulary	**Skill** Suffix -ly T **Strategy** Word Structure	**Skill** Unfamiliar Words; Classify/Categorize T **Strategy** Context Clues
	Fluency	Read Silently with Fluency and Accuracy	Read with Accuracy and Appropriate Pace/Rate
Language Arts	Writing	**Weekly Writing** Persuasive Letter **Unit Process Writing**	**Weekly Writing** Persuasive Letter **Unit Process Writing**
	Grammar	T Pronouns	T Pronouns for One and More Than One
	Speaking, Listening, Viewing	Look for Main Idea	Telephone and Voice Mail
	Research/Study Skills	Glossary: Word Meaning and Pronunciation Key	Bar Graph
Integrate Science and Social Studies Standards		Time for SOCIAL STUDIES — Job Responsibility, Job Training, Tools/Equipment, Service, Teamwork	TIME FOR Science — Living Things, Shelter/Survival, Growth and Change, Thunderstorms

💿 Target Skill   T Tested Skill

 **Big Idea** *What does it mean to be responsible?*

WEEK 3	WEEK 4	WEEK 5
212–231	**238–261**	**268–289**
Bad Dog, Dodger!/ How to Train Your Puppy — REALISTIC FICTION	**Horace and Morris but mostly Dolores/ Good Kicking** — FANTASY	**The Signmaker's Assistant/ Helping Hand** — HUMOROUS FICTION
How can we be responsible family members?	*What do good friends and neighbors do?*	*What happens when we do the wrong thing?*
T ◉ Silent Consonants **T** REVIEW Prefixes *un-, re-, pre-, dis-*	**T** ◉ *ph, gh/f/* **T** REVIEW Silent Consonants *kn, wr, gn, mb*	**T** ◉ Vowels *aw, au, augh, al* **T** REVIEW *ph, gh/f/*
T Words with Silent Consonants	**T** Words with the *ph, gh/f/*	**T** Words with Vowels *aw, au, augh, al*
T practice, grabbed, chewing, chased, treat, wagged, dripping	**T** adventure, climbed, greatest, truest, clubhouse, exploring, wondered	**T** idea, important, blame, signmaker, townspeople, afternoon
T ◉ **Skill** Theme and Plot ◉ **Strategy** Prior Knowledge REVIEW **Skill** Sequence	**T** ◉ **Skill** Author's Purpose ◉ **Strategy** Ask Questions REVIEW **Skill** Theme and Plot	**T** ◉ **Skill** Realism and Fantasy ◉ **Strategy** Monitor and Fix Up: Reread REVIEW **Skill** Author's Purpose
Skill Endings *-ed* and *-ing*; Classify/ Categorize **T Strategy** Word Structure	**Skill** Ending *-est* **T Strategy** Word Structure	**Skill** Compound Words **T Strategy** Word Structure
Read with Expression	Express Characterization	Read with Appropriate Phrasing
Weekly Writing Persuasive Letter **Unit Process Writing**	**Weekly Writing** Persuasive Letter **Unit Process Writing**	**Weekly Writing** Persuasive Letter **Unit Process Writing**
T Using *I* and *Me*	Different Kinds of Pronouns	Contractions
Retell a Movie or Play	Contribute to Discussions	Understanding Advertising
Encyclopedia	Table	Evaluate Online Sources
Citizenship, Family, Rules, Pets	Friendship, Groups, Community Services, Exploration, Fairness and Respect	Rights and Responsibilities, Laws, Goods and Services, Technology/Communication

Unit 5
Monitor Progress

Predictors of Reading Success		WEEK 1	WEEK 2	WEEK 3	WEEK 4
Word Reading	**Phonics**	🌐 🎯 **Suffixes** *-ly, -ful, -er, -or*	🌐 🎯 **Prefixes** *un-, re-, pre-, dis-*	🌐 🎯 **Silent Consonants**	🌐 🎯 *ph, gh/f/*
WCPM	**Fluency**	Read Silently with Fluency and Accuracy 82–92 WCPM	Read with Accuracy and Appropriate Pace/Rate 82–92 WCPM	Read with Expression/ Intonation 82–92 WCPM	Express Characterization 82–92 WCPM
Vocabulary	**Lesson Vocabulary**	🌐 building 🌐 burning 🌐 masks 🌐 quickly 🌐 roar 🌐 station 🌐 tightly	🌐 flashes 🌐 lightning 🌐 pounds 🌐 pours 🌐 rolling 🌐 storm 🌐 thunder	🌐 chased 🌐 chewing 🌐 dripping 🌐 grabbed 🌐 practice 🌐 treat 🌐 wagged	🌐 adventure 🌐 climbed 🌐 clubhouse 🌐 exploring 🌐 greatest 🌐 truest 🌐 wondered
Oral Vocabulary	**Vocabulary/ Concept Development** (assessed informally)	caretaker community instrument lug operation responsible supplies teamwork	concern fragile growth litter pellets pollute protection release	behavior companion confident consider cooperate obedient properly reprimand	advantage appreciate communicate defiant demand ferocious firmly respect
Retelling	**Text Comprehension**	🌐 🎯 **Skill** Main Idea/ Supporting Details 🎯 **Strategy** Text Structure	🌐 🎯 **Skill** Sequence 🎯 **Strategy** Graphic Organizer	🌐 🎯 **Skill** Theme and Plot 🎯 **Strategy** Prior Knowledge	🌐 🎯 **Skill** Author's Purpose 🎯 **Strategy** Ask Questions

152e Responsibility   🎯 Target Skill   🌐 SuccessTracker/Unit 5 Benchmark Tested Skills

Make Data-Driven Decisions

Data Management	Classroom Management
• Assess	• Monitor Progress
• Diagnose	• Group
• Prescribe	• Differentiate Instruction
• Disaggregate	• Inform Parents

ONLINE CLASSROOM

WEEK 5

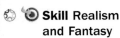 Vowels *aw, au, augh, al*

Read with Appropriate Phrasing

82–92 WCPM

- afternoon
- blame
- idea
- important
- signmaker
- townspeople

apologize
citizen
hoard
interrupt
judgment
protest
scold
troublemaker

Skill Realism and Fantasy

Strategy Monitor and Fix Up

Manage Data

- Assign the Unit 5 Benchmark Test for students to take online.
- SuccessTracker records results and generates reports by school, grade, classroom, or student.

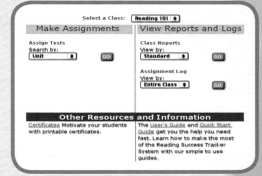

- Use reports to disaggregate and aggregate Unit 5 skills and standards data to monitor progress.
- Based on class lists created to support the categories important for adequate yearly progress (AYP, i.e., gender, ethnicity, migrant education, English proficiency, disabilities, economic status), reports let you track AYP every six weeks.

Group

- Use results from Unit 5 Benchmark Tests taken online through SuccessTracker to regroup students.
- Reports in SuccessTracker suggest appropriate groups for students based on test results.

Individualize Instruction

- Tests are correlated to Unit 5 tested skills and standards so that prescriptions for individual teaching and learning plans can be created.
- Individualized prescriptions target instruction and accelerate student progress toward learning outcome goals.
- Prescriptions include resources to reteach Unit 5 skills and standards.

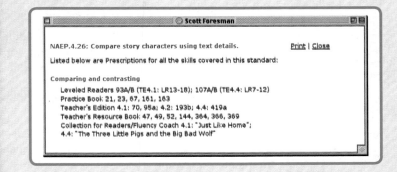

NAEP.4.26: Compare story characters using text details.   Print | Close

Listed below are Prescriptions for all the skills covered in this standard:

Comparing and contrasting
    Leveled Readers 93A/B (TE4.1: LR13-18); 107A/B (TE4.4: LR7-12)
    Practice Book: 21, 23, 67, 161, 163
    Teacher's Edition 4.1: 70, 95a; 4.2: 193b; 4.4: 419a
    Teacher's Resource Book: 47, 49, 52, 144, 364, 366, 369
    Collection for Readers/Fluency Coach 4.1: "Just Like Home";
    4.4: "The Three Little Pigs and the Big Bad Wolf"

STEP 1

Diagnose and Differentiate

Diagnose

To make initial grouping decisions, use the Baseline Group Test or another initial placement test. Depending on children's ability levels, you may have more than one of each group.

Differentiate

If... a child's performance is **Below-Level** **then...** use the regular instruction and the daily Strategic Intervention, pp. DI·14–DI·62.

If... a child's performance is **On-Level** **then...** use the regular instruction for On-Level learners throughout each week.

If... a child's performance is **Advanced** **then...** use the regular instruction and the daily instruction for Advanced learners, pp. DI·9–DI·63.

Group Time

On-Level

- Explicit instructional routines teach core skills and strategies.
- Ample practice for core skills.
- Independent activities provide practice for core skills.
- Leveled readers (LR1–48) and decodable readers provide additional reading and practice with core skills and vocabulary.

Strategic Intervention

- Daily Strategic Intervention provides more intensive instruction, more scaffolding, more practice with critical skills, and more opportunities to respond.
- Decodable readers practice word reading skills.
- Reteach lessons (DI·64–DI·68) provide additional instructional opportunities with target skills.
- Leveled readers (LR1–48) build background for the selections and practice target skills and vocabulary.

Advanced

- Daily Advanced lessons provide compacted instruction for accelerated learning, options for independent investigative work, and challenging reading content.
- Leveled readers (LR1–48) provide additional reading tied to lesson concepts.

Additional opportunities to differentiate instruction:
- Reteach Lessons, pp. DI·64–DI·68
- Leveled Reader Instruction and Leveled Practice, LR1–48
- My Sidewalks on Scott Foresman Reading Street Intensive Reading Intervention Program

Monitor Progress

STEP 2

- **Monitor Progress boxes** to check word reading, lesson vocabulary, retelling, and fluency
- **Weekly Assessments** on Day 5 for phonics, lesson vocabulary, comprehension, fluency, and retelling
- **Guiding comprehension questions** and skill and strategy instruction during reading
- **Practice Book** pages at point of use
- **Weekly Selection Tests** or **Fresh Reads for Differentiated Test Practice**

Assess and Regroup

STEP 3

- **Day 5 Assessments** Record results of weekly Day 5 assessments for phonics, lesson vocabulary, and fluency (pp. WA18–WA19) to track children's progress.
- **Unit 5 Benchmark Test** Administer this test to check mastery of unit skills.
- Use weekly assessment information, Unit Benchmark Test performance, and the Unit 5 Assess and Regroup (p. WA20) to make regrouping decisions. See the time line below.

YOU ARE HERE
Begin Unit 5

SCOTT FORESMAN ASSESSMENT

	Group Baseline Group Test		Regroup Units 1 and 2		Regroup Unit 3		Regroup Unit 4		Regroup Unit 5	

| Week | 1 | | 5 | | 10 | | 15 | | 20 | | 25 | | 30 |

OUTSIDE ASSESSMENT

Initial placement — Outside assessment for regrouping — Outside assessment for regrouping

END OF YEAR

Outside assessments (e.g., DIBELS) may recommend regrouping at other times during the year.

Summative Assessment

STEP 4

- **Benchmark Assessment** Use to measure a child's mastery of each unit's skills.
- **End-of-Year Benchmark Assessment** Use to measure a child's mastery of program skills covered in all six units.

Unit 5
Theme Launch

Discuss the Big Idea

Read and discuss the theme question. Explain

- people have different responsibilities at home and at school (helping with the dishes, feeding and caring for pets, completing schoolwork, respecting classmates)

- people have responsibilities to others in the community (being kind, taking care of friendships, keeping the town and streets safe and clean)

- many people in your community are responsible for taking care of others (firefighters, nurses, veterinarians, teachers, police officers, mail carriers)

Have children use the pictures along the side of the page to preview the selections in this unit. Read the titles and captions together. Ask children how each selection might be about what it means to be responsible.

Read Aloud

Read the big book *Animal Hospital*.

- How did Jack and Luke take responsibility in this book?

- How do vets help animals in the animal hospital?

- Why do people take responsibility for helping animals?

- How does an animal hospital help the people in a community?

For more read alouds related to the theme, see the *Read Aloud Anthology*.

UNIT
5

Read
Onlir
PearsonSuccessN

Responsibility

What does it mean to be responsible?

152

CONNECTING CULTURES

You can use the following selections to help children learn about their own and other cultures and explore common elements of culture.

Firefighter! Communities all over the world have firefighters to help keep people safe. Have children from different cultures tell what kind of services people in other countries have, including nurses, firefighters, police officers, and other public servants.

Firefighter!

Firefighters have an important job in the community.

NARRATIVE NONFICTION

Paired Selection

Firefighting Teamwork

PLAY

One Dark Night

A boy takes care of a stray cat and her kittens.

REALISTIC FICTION

Paired Selection

"Adoption" and "The Stray Cat"

POETRY

Bad Dog, Dodger!

Sam is responsible for his pet's behavior.

REALISTIC FICTION

Paired Selection

How to Train Your Puppy

HOW-TO ARTICLE

Horace and Morris but mostly Dolores

Good friends take care of their friendship.

FANTASY

Paired Selection

Good Kicking

NEWSPAPER ARTICLE

The Signmaker's Assistant

A young signmaker takes responsibility for his actions.

HUMOROUS FICTION

Paired Selection

Helping Hand

ONLINE REFERENCE SOURCE

153

Unit Inquiry Project

Research Responsible Acts

Children can work individually or in groups to research ways that people are responsible in the community.

PROJECT TIMETABLE

WEEK	ACTIVITY/SKILL CONNECTION
1	**BRAINSTORM** Children can brainstorm different community workers and their jobs.
2	**INTERVIEW AND RESEARCH** Children work in small groups and choose a responsible community member. Have groups interview people in the school, community, or at home about their jobs. They can also refer to books in the library or research helping out online.
3	**ORGANIZE INFORMATION** Children organize information into different categories, such as duties, equipment, and special training.
4	**WRITE AND ILLUSTRATE** Children draw illustrations on a poster to show responsible community workers and label each drawing.
5	**PRESENT** Children present their posters to the class or other classes.

An assessment rubric can be found on p. 292a. Rubric 4 3 2 1

CONCEPT DEVELOPMENT

Unit 5
Responsibility

CONCEPT QUESTION

What does it mean to be responsible?

Expand the Concept
What happens when we do the wrong thing?

Connect the Concept

Literature

Develop Language
apologize, citizen, hoard, interrupt, judgment, protest, scold, troublemaker

Teach Content
Rights and Responsibilities
Laws
Goods and Services
Technology and Communication

Writing
A Sign

Week 4

Expand the Concept
What do good friends and neighbors do?

Connect the Concept

Literature

Develop Language
advantage, appreciate, communicate, defiant, demand, ferocious, firmly, respect

Teach Content
Friendship
Groups
Community Services
Exploration
Fairness and Respect

Writing
Advice

Week 3

Expand the Concept
How can we be responsible family members?

Connect the Concept

Literature

Develop Language
behavior, companion, confident, consider, cooperate, obedient, properly, reprimand

Teach Content
Citizenship
Family Responsibility
Rules
Pet Care

Writing
Rules

Week 1

Expand the Concept
Why is it important to do a good job?

Connect the Concept

Literature

Develop Language
caretaker, community, instrument, lug, operation, responsible, supplies, teamwork

Teach Content
Job Responsibility
Job Training
Tools/Equipment
Service
Teamwork

Writing
A Report

Week 2

Expand the Concept
Why should we take care of animals?

Connect the Concept

Literature

Develop Language
concern, fragile, growth, litter, pellets, pollute, protection, release

Teach Content
Living Things
Shelter/Survival
Growth and Change
Thunderstorms

Writing
Reasons

Illinois

Planning Guide for Performance Descriptors

Fire Fighter!

Reading Street Teacher's Edition pages	Grade 2 English Language Arts Performance Descriptors
Oral Language Build Concepts: 154l, 156a, 172a, 174a, 178a Share Literature: 154m, 156b, 172b, 174b, 178b	**1A.Stage B.5.** Use letter-sound knowledge and sight vocabulary to read orally and silently/whisper read age-appropriate material. **2B.Stage B.1.** Investigate self-selected/teacher-selected literature (e.g., picture books, nursery rhymes, fairy tales, poems, legends) from a variety of cultures.
Word Work **Phonics** Suffixes *-ly, -ful, -er, -or:* 154n–154p, 156c–156d, 172c–172d, 174c–174d, 178c–178f **Spelling:** 154p, 156d, 172d, 174d, 178d	**1A.Stage B.1.** Use phonics to decode simple words in age-appropriate material. **3A.Stage B.5.** Use correct spelling of high frequency words. **3A.Stage B.6.** Use phonemic clues, phonetic and/or developmental spelling to spell unfamiliar words.
Reading **Comprehension** Main Idea and Supporting Details: 154r–155, 158–171a, 172g, 174–177, 178e Text Structure: 154r–155, 158–171, 172g **Vocabulary** Word Structure: 156–157 Suffix-*ly*: 156–157, 172e, 174–175, 178b **Fluency** Oral Rereading: 154q Silent Reading: 172f Reader's Theater: 177a **Self-Selected Reading:** LR1–9, TR16–17 **Literature** Genre—Narrative Nonfiction: 158–159 Reader Response: 172g–172h	**1A.Stage B.5.** Use letter-sound knowledge and sight vocabulary to read orally and silently/whisper read age-appropriate material. **1B.Stage B.1.** Read fiction and non-fiction materials for specific purposes. **1B.Stage B.3.** Recognize informational text structure (e.g., sequence, list/example) before and during reading. **1B.Stage B.9.** Demonstrate creative responses to text such as dramatizations, oral presentations, or "make believe" play after reading. **1C.Stage B.1.** Respond to analytical and interpretive questions based on information in text. **1C.Stage B.6.** Identify the author's purpose and the main idea. **2A.Stage B.3.** Define unfamiliar vocabulary.
Language Arts **Writing** Report, Poster, Respond to Literature, List: 155a, 171b, 172g, 177b, 178–179 **Six-Trait Writing** Word Choice: 173a, 178–179 **Grammar, Usage, and Mechanics** Nouns: 155b, 171c, 173b, 177c, 178–179 **Speaking/Viewing** Look for Main Idea: 177d **Research/Study** Glossary: 179a	**3A.Stage B.2.** Use correct subject/verb agreement. **3B.Stage B.5.** Elaborate and support written content with facts, details, and description. **4A.Stage B.14.** Begin to distinguish between main ideas and details that are heard. **5A.Stage B.6.** Use text aids (e.g., table of contents, glossary, index, alphabetical order) to locate information in a book.
Unit Skills **Writing** Persuasive Letter: WA2–9 **Project/Wrap-Up:** 292–293	**2A.Stage B.7.** Recognize a regular beat and similarities of sound (rhythm and rhyme) in poetry. **3C.Stage B.2.** Use available technology to plan, compose, revise and edit written work.

This Week's Leveled Readers

Below-Level

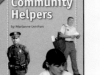

1B.Stage B.6. State facts and details of text during and after reading.

2B.Stage B.4. Make a reasonable judgment with support from the text.

Nonfiction

On-Level

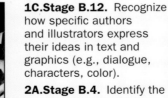

1C.Stage B.12. Recognize how specific authors and illustrators express their ideas in text and graphics (e.g., dialogue, characters, color).

2A.Stage B.4. Identify the topic or main idea (theme).

Nonfiction

Advanced

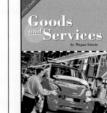
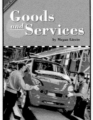

1C.Stage B.5. Use self-monitoring to solve problems in meaning to achieve understanding of a broad range of reading materials.

4A.Stage B.14. Begin to distinguish between main ideas and details that are heard.

Nonfiction

Content-Area Illinois Performance Descriptors in This Lesson

Social Studies

14A.Stage B.4. Produce new rules that could apply to students' lives at home or school.

14C.Stage B.1. Discuss a situation in their home or school that illustrates people being responsible in their duties or job.

14F.Stage B.1. Identify an example of behavior that shows someone showing good citizenship (e.g., recycling, being honest when being questioned).

15C.Stage B.1. Explain that people who make goods and services are producers.

15E.Stage B.1. Identify public goods and services that students or families use.

17A.Stage B.4. Observe and suggest reasons for the locations of stop signs, stoplights, fire hydrants, and other human-made features in the area around the school.

Science

12C.Stage B.2. Apply scientific inquiries or technological designs to compare qualitative and quantitative properties of matter: identifying component materials in objects.

12E.Stage B.2. Apply scientific inquiries or technological designs to examine the natural processes that change Earth's surface.

13A.Stage B.1. Apply the appropriate principles of safety: mapping pathways to leave classroom or home in case of fire or severe weather situations.

Math

7B.Stage B.2. Estimate standard measurements of length, weight, and capacity.

10B.Stage B.1. Gather data by creating and using interview questions.

ILLINOIS FUN FACTS
Did You Know?

- In northern Illinois, temperatures can fall below freezing more than one hundred times per year.

- In 1942 scientists at the University of Chicago set off the world's first controlled atomic chain reaction.

- The Chicago Board of Trade is the largest commodities exchange in the world. Traders buy and sell contracts for corn, soybeans, and other commodities, or goods.

Children can . . .
Make a list of real or imaginary things they would like to trade with someone. Have them exchange lists with a partner to see if they can trade any of their goods for new ones.

A FAMOUS ILLINOISAN
Richard J. Daley

Richard J. Daley (1902–1976) was born and raised in Chicago. He became a lawyer in 1933. Before becoming mayor of Chicago, Daley served in the Illinois General Assembly as a representative and a senator. As mayor, he was reelected every fourth year from 1955 through 1975 and became known as "the last of the big-city bosses." Daley was also powerful in national Democratic party politics.

Children can . . .
Learn about what a mayor does. Ask children to describe how the roles of a mayor and a school principal are alike and how they are different.

A SPECIAL ILLINOIS PLACE
Wabash River

The Wabash River forms two hundred miles of the boundary between Illinois and Indiana. During the 1700s the French used the river as a transportation link between Louisiana and Quebec. The name *Wabash* comes from a Native American word that means "shining white" or "white over white stones." The Wabash River is the second largest tributary of the Ohio River.

Children can . . .
Draw an outline map of Illinois and use a blue crayon or marker to draw the path of the Wabash River.

Unit 5
Responsibility

CONCEPT QUESTION

What does it mean to be responsible?

EXPAND THE CONCEPT
Why is it important to do a good job?

CONNECT THE CONCEPT

▶ **Build Background**

caretaker	lug	supplies
community	operation	teamwork
instrument	responsible	

A Good Job

▶ **Social Studies Content**
Job Responsibility, Job Training, Tools/
Equipment, Service, Teamwork

▶ **Writing**
A Report

Preview Your Week

Why is it important to do a good job?

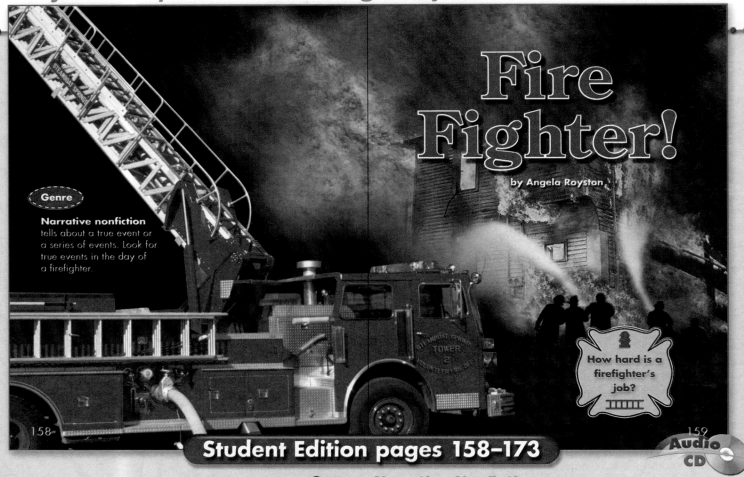

Student Edition pages 158–173

Genre Narrative Nonfiction

Phonics Suffixes -ly, -ful, -er, -or

Vocabulary Strategy Word Structure

Comprehension Skill Main Idea and Supporting Details

Comprehension Strategy Text Structure

Paired Selection

Reading Across Texts
Compare Jobs

Genre
Play

Text Features
Character Names
Stage Directions

Time for SOCIAL STUDIES

Drama in Reading

Play

Genre
- A play is a story that is acted out.
- A play has characters who each have their own speaking parts.

Text Features
- A character's name appears before each speaking part.
- Directions to the actors sometimes appear in parentheses. These tell the actors how to move, where to go, or what to do.

Link to Reading
Use the library to find other plays to read. Choose one or two to read together as a Readers' Theater.

FIRE FIGHTING TEAMWORK
a play by Connie Carpenter

CHARACTERS:
Firefighter Kelly (FF KELLY)
Firefighter Sanchez (FF SANCHEZ)
Firefighter Johnson (FF JOHNSON)
Chief
Three or Four Council Members

Scene: A firehouse.
(One firefighter is sweeping. Another is washing dishes. Another is sleeping.)

FF KELLY: *(sweeping)* Boy, is this fire station dirty!

FF SANCHEZ: *(washing dishes)* Yeah, we all have to clean up the mud and dirt we tracked in. That last fire was a mess!

FF KELLY: I think Johnson worked really hard. He had to roll up that hose almost all by himself. That was hard work! He's probably upstairs taking a nap.
(Telephone rings.)

FF KELLY: *(stops sweeping)* I'll get that. *(picks up phone)* Firefighter Kelly here.

CHIEF: *(voice from off stage)* Firefighter Kelly, this is the Chief.

FF KELLY: Yes, Chief. What is it?

CHIEF: We're having an inspection by the city council today. Is everything in shape?

FF KELLY: It will be, Chief. With teamwork we should be able to get things in tip-top shape for the inspection.

CHIEF: Good! I'll bring the council right over.

FF KELLY: Right! Good-by, Chief! *(hangs up phone)* We've got big trouble!

Student Edition pages 174–177

Read It
ONLINE
PearsonSuccessNet.com
- Student Edition
- Leveled Readers
- Decodable Reader

Leveled Readers

⊙ **Skill** Main Idea and Supporting Details
⊙ **Strategy** Text Structure
Lesson Vocabulary

Below-Level

On-Level

Advanced

E L L Reader
- Concept Vocabulary
- Text Support
- Language Enrichment

At the Fire Station

Decodable Reader

Apply Phonics
- *Hobbies*

Decodable Reader 21
Hobbies
Written by Donna Michaels
Illustrated by Tom Hurst

Phonics Skill

Time for
SOCIAL STUDIES

Integrate Social Studies Standards
- Job Responsibility
- Job Training
- Tools/Equipment
- Service
- Teamwork

✓ **Read**

Firefighter! pp. 158–173

"Fire Fighting Teamwork" pp. 174–177

✓ **Read**
Leveled Readers

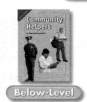 

Below-Level **On-Level** **Advanced**

- Support Concepts
- Develop Concepts
- Extend Concepts
- Social Studies Extension Activity

✓ **Read**
E L L Reader

At the Fire Station

✓ **Build Concept Vocabulary**
Responsibility, p. 154m

✓ **Teach Social Studies Concepts**
Firefighting Tools, p. 162–163
Economic Resources, p. 166–167

✓ **Explore Social Studies Center**
Make an Illustrated Job Manual, p. 154k

Weekly Plan

READING

90–120 minutes

TARGET SKILLS OF THE WEEK

Phonics
Suffixes *-ly, -ful, -er, -or*

Comprehension Skill
Main Idea and Supporting Details

Comprehension Strategy
Text Structure

Vocabulary Strategy
Word Structure

DAY 1   PAGES 154l–155b

Oral Language

QUESTION OF THE WEEK, 154l
Why is it important to do a good job?

Oral Vocabulary/Share Literature, 154m
Sing with Me Big Book, Song 21
Amazing Words *community, responsible, teamwork*

Word Work

Phonics, 154n–154o
Introduce Suffixes *-ly, -ful, -er, -or* **T**

Spelling, 154p
Pretest

Comprehension/Vocabulary/Fluency

Read Decodable Reader 21

Grouping Options 154f–154g

Review High-Frequency Words
Check Comprehension
Reread for Fluency
Comprehension Skill/Strategy Lesson, 154r–155
Main Idea and Supporting Details **T**
Text Structure

DAY 2   PAGES 156a–171c

Oral Language

QUESTION OF THE DAY, 156a
How hard is a firefighter's job?

Oral Vocabulary/Share Literature, 156b
Big Book *Animal Hospital*
Amazing Word *operation*

Word Work

Phonics, 156c–156d
Review Suffixes *-ly, -ful, -er, -or* **T**

Spelling, 156d
Dictation

Comprehension/Vocabulary/Fluency

Build Background, 156e
Firehouse

Lesson Vocabulary, 156f
Introduce *building, burning, masks, quickly, roar, station, tightly* **T**

Vocabulary Strategy Lesson, 156–157a
Word Structure **T**

Read *Firefighter!*, 158–171a

Grouping Options 154f–154g

Main Idea and Supporting Details **T**
Text Structure
REVIEW Author's Purpose **T**
Reread for Fluency

LANGUAGE ARTS

20–30 minutes

Trait of the Week

Word Choice

Shared Writing, 155a
Report

Grammar, 155b
Introduce Pronouns **T**

Interactive Writing, 171b
Poster

Grammar, 171c
Practice Pronouns **T**

DAILY JOURNAL WRITING

Day 1 *List people who do jobs for the community.*

Day 2 *Write about a time when you have seen firefighters at work.*

DAILY SOCIAL STUDIES CONNECTIONS

Day 1 A Good Job Concept Web, 154m

Day 2 Time for Social Studies: Firefighting Tools, 162–163; Economic Resources, 166–167

DAILY SUCCESS PREDICTORS
for Adequate Yearly Progress

Monitor Progress and Corrective Feedback

Phonics
Check Word Reading, *154o*
Spiral REVIEW Phonics

Fluency
Check Lesson Vocabulary, *156f*
Spiral REVIEW High-Frequency Words

Grouping Options for Differentiated Instruction

Turn the page for the small group lesson plan.

DAY 3 PAGES 172a–173b

Oral Language

QUESTION OF THE DAY, 172a
What else do they use to do their job?

Oral Vocabulary/Share Literature, 172b
Big Book *Animal Hospital*
Amazing Word *instrument*

Word Work

Phonics, 172c
REVIEW Vowel Patterns *oo, ue, ew, ui* **T**

Lesson Vocabulary, 172d
Practice *building, burning, mask, quickly, roar, station, tightly* **T**

Spelling, 172d
Practice

Comprehension/Vocabulary/Fluency

Vocabulary, 172e
Suffix *-ly*

Read *Firefighter!,* 158–173

Grouping Options
154f–154g

Fluency, 172f
Read Silently with Fluency and Accuracy

Reader Response, 172g

Trait of the Week, 173a
Introduce Word Choice

Grammar, 173b
Write with Pronouns **T**

Day 3 *Write about a job you would like to have and the responsibilities necessary for people to have it.*

Day 3 Let's Talk About the Concept, 173b

DAY 4 PAGES 174a–177d

Oral Language

QUESTION OF THE DAY, 174a
What jobs do you have at home?

Oral Vocabulary/Share Literature, 174b
Read Aloud Anthology "Ahmed, the Boab's Son"
Amazing Words *caretaker, lug, supplies*

Word Work

Phonics, 174c–174d
REVIEW Sentence Reading **T**

Spelling, 174d
Partner Review

Comprehension/Vocabulary/Fluency

Read "Fire Fighting Teamwork," 174–177
Leveled Readers

Grouping Options
154f–154g

Suffix *-ly*

Reading Across Texts

Fluency, 177a
Read Silently with Fluency and Accuracy

Writing Across the Curriculum, 177b
List

Grammar, 177c
Review Pronouns **T**

Speaking and Viewing, 177d
Look for Main Idea

Day 4 *Write a paragraph about teamwork.*

Day 4 Time for Social Studies: Teamwork, 174–175;
Transportation, 176–177

DAY 5 PAGES 178a–179b

Oral Language

QUESTION OF THE DAY, 178a
Why is it important to do a good job?

Oral Vocabulary/Share Literature, 178b
Read Aloud Anthology "Ahmed, the Boab's Son"
Amazing Words Review

Word Work

Phonics, 178c
🎯 Review Suffixes *-ly, -ful, -er, -or* **T**

High-Frequency Words, 178c
Review *building, burning, mask, quickly, roar, station, tightly* **T**

Spelling, 178d
Test

Comprehension/Vocabulary/Fluency

Read Leveled Readers

Grouping Options 154f–154g

Monitor Progress, 178e–178g
Read the Sentences
Read the Story

Writing and Grammar, 178–179
Develop Word Choice
Use Pronouns **T**

Research/Study Skills, 179a
Glossary

Day 5 *Write about a responsible person.*

Day 5 Revisit the A Good Job Concept Web, 179b

KEY 🎯 = Target Skill **T** = Tested Skill

Comprehension Check Retelling, *172g*

Fluency Check Fluency WCPM, *177a*
Spiral REVIEW Phonics, High-Frequency Words

Oral Vocabulary Check Oral Vocabulary, *178b*
Assess Phonics, Lesson Vocabulary, Fluency, Comprehension, *178e*

SUCCESS PREDICTOR

Small Group Plan for Differentiated Instruction

Daily Plan AT A GLANCE

Reading

Whole Group
- Oral Language
- Word Work
- Comprehension/Vocabulary

Group Time

Meet with small groups to provide:
- Skill Support
- Reading Support
- Fluency Practice

Read

This week's lessons for daily group time can be found behind the Differentiated Instruction (DI) tab on pp. DI·14–DI·23.

Whole Group
- Comprehension/Vocabulary
- Fluency

Language Arts
- Writing
- Grammar
- Speaking/Listening/Viewing
- Research/Study Skills

Use My Sidewalks on Reading Street for Tier III intensive reading intervention.

DAY 1

On-Level	Strategic Intervention	Advanced
Teacher-Led *Page 154q*	**Teacher-Led** *Page DI · 14*	**Teacher-Led** *Page DI · 15*
• **Read** Decodable Reader 21	• Blend Words with *-ly, -ful, -er, -or*	• Extend Word Reading
• **Reread** for Fluency	• **Read** Decodable Reader 21	• **Read** Advanced Selection 2
	• **Reread** for Fluency	• Introduce Concept Inquiry

ⓘ Independent Activities
While you meet with small groups, have the rest of the class...

- Reread for fluency
- Write in their journals
- Read self-selected reading
- Visit the Word Work Center
- Complete Practice Book 2.2, pp. 53–54

DAY 2

On-Level	Strategic Intervention	Advanced
Teacher-Led *Pages 158–171*	**Teacher-Led** *Page DI · 16*	**Teacher-Led** *Page DI · 17*
• **Read** *Firefighter!*	• Blend Words with *-ly, -ful, -er, -or*	• **Read** *Firefighter!*
• **Reread** for Fluency	• **Read** SI Decodable Reader 21	• Continue Concept Inquiry
	• **Read** or Listen to *Firefighter!*	

ⓘ Independent Activities
While you meet with small groups, have the rest of the class...

- Read self-selected reading
- Write in their journals
- Visit the Listening Center
- Complete Practice Book 2.2, pp. 55–57

DAY 3

On-Level	Strategic Intervention	Advanced
Teacher-Led *Pages 158–173*	**Teacher-Led** *Page DI · 18*	**Teacher-Led** *Page DI · 19*
• **Reread** *Firefighter!*	• **Reread** *Firefighter!*	• Self-Selected Reading
	• Read Words and Sentences	• Continue Concept Inquiry
	• Review Main Idea and Details and Text Structure	
	• **Reread** for Fluency	

ⓘ Independent Activities
While you meet with small groups, have the rest of the class...

- Read self-selected reading
- Write in their journals
- Visit the Writing Center
- Complete Practice Book 2.2, pp. 58–59

① Begin with whole class skill and strategy instruction.

② Meet with small groups to provide differentiated instruction.

③ Gather the whole class back together for fluency and language arts.

DAY 4

On-Level
Teacher-Led
Pages 174–177, LR4–LR6

- **Read** "Firefighting Teamwork"
- Practice with On-Level Reader *Who Can Help?*

Strategic Intervention
Teacher-Led
Pages DI·20, LR1–LR3

- **Read** or Listen to "Firefighting Teamwork"
- **Reread** for Fluency
- Build Concepts
- Practice with Below-Level Reader *Community Helpers*

Advanced
Teacher-Led
Pages DI·21, LR7–LR9

- **Read** "Firefighting Teamwork"
- Extend Vocabulary
- Continue Concept Inquiry
- Practice with Advanced Reader *Goods and Services*

ⓘ Independent Activities

While you meet with small groups, have the rest of the class...

- Reread for fluency
- Write in their journals
- Read self-selected reading
- Review spelling words with a partner
- Visit the Listening and Social Studies Centers

DAY 5

On-Level
Teacher-Led
Pages 178e–178g, LR4–LR6

- Sentence Reading, Set B
- Monitor Comprehension
- Practice with On-Level Reader *Who Can Help?*

Strategic Intervention
Teacher-Led
Pages DI·22, LR1–LR3

- Practice Word Reading
- Sentence Reading, Set A
- Monitor Comprehension
- Practice with Below-Level Reader *Community Helpers*

Advanced
Teacher-Led
Pages DI·23, LR7–LR9

- Sentence Reading, Set C
- Share Concept Inquiry
- Monitor Fluency and Comprehension
- Practice with Advanced Reader *Goods and Services*

ⓘ Independent Activities

While you meet with small groups, have the rest of the class...

- Reread for fluency
- Write in their journals
- Read self-selected reading
- Visit the Technology Center
- Complete Practice Book 2.2, p. 60

ELL

Grouping Place English language learners in the groups that correspond to their reading abilities in English.

Use the appropriate Leveled Reader or other text at children's instructional level.

TiP Send home the appropriate Multilingual Summary of the main selection on Day 1.

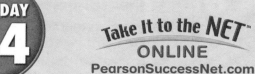
Take It to the NET™ ONLINE
PearsonSuccessNet.com

Sharon Vaughn
For ideas for ELL students, see the article "Effectiveness of Supplemental Reading Instruction ..." by S. Linan-Thompson, Scott Foresman author S. Vaughn, and others.

TEACHER TALK

Structural analysis is the process of using knowledge of base words, endings, and affixes to decode words.

Be sure to schedule time for children to work on the unit inquiry project "Research Responsible Acts." This week children should brainstorm different community workers and their jobs.

Looking Ahead

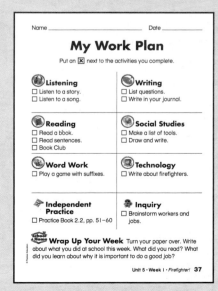

Name _____ Date _____

My Work Plan
Put an ☒ next to the activities you complete.

Listening
☐ Listen to a story.
☐ Listen to a song.

Writing
☐ List questions.
☐ Write in your journal.

Reading
☐ Read a book.
☐ Read sentences.
☐ Book Club

Social Studies
☐ Make a list of tools.
☐ Draw and write.

Word Work
☐ Play a game with suffixes.

Technology
☐ Write about firefighters.

Independent Practice
☐ Practice Book 2.2, pp. 51–60

Inquiry
☐ Brainstorm workers and jobs.

Wrap Up Your Week Turn your paper over. Write about what you did at school this week. What did you read? What did you learn about why it is important to do a good job?

Unit 5 · Week 1 · Firefighter! **37**

▲ **Group-Time Survival Guide** p. 37, Weekly Contract

☑ Customize Your Plan *by Strand*

ORAL LANGUAGE

Concept Development

Why is it important to do a good job?

 *Amazing Words* to build oral vocabulary

caretaker	community	instrument
lug	operation	responsible
supplies	teamwork	

BUILD

❑ **Question of the Week** Use the Morning Warm-Up! to introduce and discuss the question of the week. This week children will talk, sing, read, and write about responsibility. **DAY 1** *154l*

❑ **Sing with Me Big Book** Sing a song about firefighters working as a team. Ask children to listen for the concept-related Amazing Words *community, responsible, teamwork.* **DAY 1** *154m*

Sing with Me Big Book

❑ **Build Background Responsibility** Remind children of the question of the week. Then create a concept chart for children to add to throughout the week. **DAY 1** *154m*

DEVELOP

❑ **Question of the Day** Use the questions in the Morning Warm-Ups! to discuss lesson concepts and how they relate to the unit theme, Responsibility. **DAY 2** *156a,* **DAY 3** *172a,* **DAY 4** *174a,* **DAY 5** *178a*

❑ **Share Literature** Read big books and read aloud selections that develop concepts, language, and vocabulary related to the lesson concept and the unit theme. Continue to develop this week's Amazing Words. **DAY 2** *156b,* **DAY 3** *172b,* **DAY 4** *174b,* **DAY 5** *178b*

CONNECT

❑ **Wrap Up Your Week!** Revisit the Question of the Week. Then connect concepts and vocabulary to next week's lesson. **DAY 5** *179b*

CHECK

❑ **Check Oral Vocabulary** To informally assess children's oral vocabulary, ask individuals to use some of this week's Amazing Words to tell you about the concept of the week—Responsibility. **DAY 5** *178b*

PHONICS

◐ **SUFFIXES -LY, -FUL, -ER, -OR** Prefixes, suffixes, and some inflected endings usually form separate syllables from the base word.

TEACH

❑ **Suffixes -ly, -ful, -er, -or** Introduce the blending strategy for words ending in suffixes *-ly, -ful, -er, -or.* Then have children blend and build words by adding the suffix to each base word, read the new word, and supply its meaning. **DAY 1** *154n-154o*

❑ **Fluent Word Reading** Use the Fluent Word Reading Routine to develop children's word reading fluency. Use the Phonics Songs and Rhymes Chart for additional word reading practice. **DAY 2** *156c-156d*

Phonics Songs and Rhymes Chart 21

PRACTICE/APPLY

❑ **Decodable Reader 21** Practice reading words with suffixes *-ly, -ful, -er, -or* in context. **DAY 1** *154q*

❑ *Firefighter!* Practice decoding words in context. **DAY 2** *158-171*

Decodable Reader 21

❑ **Homework** Practice Book 2.2 p. 53. **DAY 1** *154o*

❑ **Word Work Center** Practice suffixes *-ly, -ful, -er, -or.* **ANY DAY** *154j*

Main Selection—Nonfiction

RETEACH/REVIEW

❑ **Review** Review words with this week's phonics skills. **DAY 5** *178c*

❑ **Reteach Lessons** If necessary, reteach suffixes *-ly, -ful, -er, -or.* **DAY 5** *DI-64*

❑ **Spiral REVIEW** Review previously taught phonics skills. **DAY 1** *154o,* **DAY 3** *172c,* **DAY 4** *174c*

ASSESS

❑ **Sentence Reading** Assess children's ability to read words with suffixes *-ly, -ful, -er, -or.* **DAY 5** *178e-178f*

SPELLING

SUFFIXES -LY, -FUL, -ER, -OR   Suffixes and some inflected endings usually form separate syllables from the base word.

TEACH

☐ **Pretest** Before administering the pretest, model how to segment word endings with suffixes *-ly, -ful, -er, -or,* to spell them. Dictate the spelling words, segmenting them if necessary. Then have children check their pretests and correct misspelled words.   **DAY 1** *154p*

PRACTICE/APPLY

☐ **Dictation** Have children write dictation sentences to practice spelling words.   **DAY 2** *156d*

☐ **Write Words** Have children practice writing the spelling words by writing and unscrambling sentences that use spelling words.   **DAY 3** *172d*

☐ **Homework** Phonics and Spelling Practice Book pp. 81–84.   **DAY 1** *154p,*   **DAY 2** *156d,*   **DAY 3** *172d,*   **DAY 4** *174d*

RETEACH/REVIEW

☐ **Partner Review** Have pairs work together to read and write the spelling words.   **DAY 4** *174d*

ASSESS

☐ **Posttest** Use dictation sentences to give the posttest for words with suffixes *-ly, -fl, -er, -or.*   **DAY 5** *178d*

Spelling Words

Suffixes -ly, -ful, -er, -or

1. cheerful
2. visitor
3. slowly*
4. weekly
5. teacher
6. helper
7. hardly*
8. graceful
9. yearly
10. quickly*
11. fighter*
12. sailor

Challenge Words

13. gardener
14. competitor
15. extremely

* Words from the Selection

VOCABULARY

STRATEGY WORD STRUCTURE   When you come to a word you don't know, see if the word has a suffix that can help you figure out its meaning.

LESSON VOCABULARY

building	burning	masks	quickly
roar	station	tightly	

TEACH

☐ **Words to Know** Introduce and discuss this week's lesson vocabulary.   **DAY 2** *156f*

☐ **Vocabulary Strategy Lesson** Use the lesson in the Student Edition to introduce/model *word structure.*   **DAY 2** *156-157a*

Vocabulary Strategy Lesson

PRACTICE/APPLY

☐ **Words in Context** Read the lesson vocabulary in context.   **DAY 2** *158-171,*   **DAY 3** *158-173*

☐ **Lesson Vocabulary** Practice lesson vocabulary.   **DAY 3** *172d*

☐ **Leveled Text** Read the lesson vocabulary in leveled text.   **DAY 4** *LR1-LR9,*   **DAY 5** *LR1-LR9*

☐ **Homework** Practice Book 2.2 pp. 56, 59.   **DAY 2** *156f,*   **DAY 3** *172d*

Main Selection—Nonfiction

Leveled Readers

RETEACH/REVIEW

☐ **Suffix -ly** Discuss the suffix *-ly.* Have children find and explain sentences using *tightly, quickly, tight,* and *quick.*   **DAY 3** *172e*

☐ **Review** Review this week's lesson vocabulary words.   **DAY 5** *178c*

ASSESS

☐ **Selection Test** Use the Selection Test to determine children's understanding of the lesson vocabulary words.   **DAY 3**

☐ **Sentence Reading** Assess children's ability to read this week's lesson vocabulary words.   **DAY 5** *178e-178f*

HIGH-FREQUENCY WORDS

RETEACH/REVIEW

☐ **Spiral REVIEW** Review previously taught high-frequency words.   **DAY 2** *156f,*   **DAY 4** *174c*

COMPREHENSION

🎯 **SKILL MAIN IDEA AND SUPPORTING DETAILS** The main idea is the most important idea in a selection. Supporting details tell more about the main idea.

🎯 **STRATEGY TEXT STRUCTURE** Text structure is the way in which a selection is organized.

TEACH

☐ **Skill/Strategy Lesson** Use the skill/strategy lesson in the Student Edition to introduce *main idea and supporting details* and *text structure.* DAY 1 *154r–155*

Skill/Strategy Lesson

PRACTICE/APPLY

☐ **Skills and Strategies in Context** Read *Firefighter!,* using the Guiding Comprehension questions to apply *main idea and supporting details* and *text structure.* DAY 2 *158–171*

Main Selection—Nonfiction

☐ **Reader Response** Use the questions on Student Edition p. 172 to discuss the selection. DAY 3 *172g–173*

☐ **Skills and Strategies in Context** Read "Fire Fighting Teamwork," guiding children as they apply skills and strategies. DAY 4 *174–177*

Paired Selection— Drama

☐ **Leveled Text** Apply *main idea and supporting details* and *text structure* to read leveled text. DAY 4 *LR1–LR9,* DAY 5 *LR1–LR9*

Leveled Readers

☐ **Homework** Practice Book 2.2 pp. 54, 55. DAY 1 *154–155,* DAY 2 *156e*

ASSESS

☐ **Selection Test** Determine children's understanding of the main selection and assess their ability to identify the *main idea and supporting details.* DAY 3

☐ **Story Reading** Have children read the passage "Happy Campers at Bat." Ask questions that require them to identify the *main idea and supporting details.* Then have them retell. DAY 5 *178e–178g*

RETEACH/REVIEW

☐ **Reteach Lesson** If necessary, reteach *main idea and supporting details.* DAY 5 *DI·64*

FLUENCY

SKILL READ SILENTLY WITH FLUENCY/ACCURACY When you read, try not to change any words or leave any words out. Read at a pace like you are speaking.

REREAD FOR FLUENCY

☐ **Oral Rereading** Have children read orally from Decodable Reader 21 or another text at their independent reading level. Listen as children read and provide corrective feedback regarding their oral reading and their use of the blending strategy. DAY 1 *154q*

☐ **Paired Reading** Have pairs of children read orally from the main selection or another text at their independent reading level. Listen as children read and provide corrective feedback regarding their oral reading and their use of the blending strategy. DAY 2 *171a*

TEACH

☐ **Model** Use passages from *Firefighter!* to model reading with fluency and accuracy. DAY 3 *172f,* DAY 4 *177a*

PRACTICE/APPLY

☐ **Silent Reading** Have children practice reading a short passage from *Firefighter!* silently, then aloud to you. Monitor progress and provide feedback regarding children's fluency and accuracy. DAY 3 *172f*

☐ **Readers' Theater** Have groups read parts from "*Fire Fighting Teamwork,*" with you and independently. Monitor progress, provide feedback, and then have the groups perform. DAY 4 *177a*

☐ **Listening Center** Have children follow along with the AudioText for this week's selections. **ANY DAY** *154j*

☐ **Reading/Library Center** Have children build fluency by rereading Leveled Readers, Decodable Readers, or other text at their independent level. **ANY DAY** *154j*

☐ **Fluency Coach** Have children use Fluency Coach to listen to fluent reading or to practice reading on their own. **ANY DAY**

ASSESS

☐ **Story Reading** Take a one-minute timed sample of children's oral reading. Use the passage "Happy Campers at Bat." DAY 5 *178e–178g*

❶ Use assessment data to determine your instructional focus.

❷ Preview this week's instruction by strand.

❸ Choose instructional activities that meet the needs of your classroom.

WRITING

Trait of the Week

WORD CHOICE Good words make your writing more interesting. Using exact nouns, strong verbs, and exciting adjectives will make your work interesting, clear, and lively.

TEACH

❑ **Write Together** Engage children in writing activities that develop language, grammar, and writing skills. Include independent writing as an extension of group writing activities.

> **Shared Writing** DAY 1 155a
> **Interactive Writing** DAY 2 171b
> **Writing Across the Curriculum** DAY 4 177b

❑ **Trait of the Week** Introduce and model *word choice*. DAY 3 173a

PRACTICE/APPLY

❑ **Write Now** Examine the model on Student Edition pp. 178–179. Then have children write reports. DAY 5 178-179

Write Now

> **Prompt** *Firefighter!* tells about an important community job. Think about other jobs in your community. Now write a report about one or more of those jobs.

❑ **Daily Journal Writing** Have children write about concepts and literature in their journals. EVERY DAY 154d-154e

❑ **Writing Center** Have children write a list of questions they would like to ask a firefighter. ANY DAY 154k

ASSESS

❑ **Scoring Rubric** Use a rubric to evaluate reports. DAY 5 178-179

RETEACH/REVIEW

❑ **The Grammar and Writing Book** Use pp. 170–175 of The Grammar and Writing Book to extend instruction. ANY DAY

The Grammar and Writing Book

SPEAKING AND VIEWING

TEACH

❑ **Look for Main Idea** Model identifying the main idea of a news story using photographs. Have children create captions that tell the main idea. DAY 4 177d

GRAMMAR

SKILL PRONOUNS A pronoun is a word that takes the place of a noun or nouns. The words *he, she, it, we, you,* and *they* are pronouns.

TEACH

❑ **Grammar Transparency 21** Use Grammar Transparency 21 to teach *pronouns*. DAY 1 155b

Grammar Transparency 21

PRACTICE/APPLY

❑ **Develop the Concept** Review the concept of *pronouns* and provide guided practice. DAY 2 171c

❑ **Apply to Writing** Have children use pronouns in writing. DAY 3 173b

❑ **Define/Practice** Review *pronouns*. Then have children underline the pronoun or pronouns in each sentence. DAY 4 177c

❑ **Write Now** Discuss the grammar lesson on Student Edition p. 179. Have children use pronouns in their report. DAY 5 178-179

Write Now

❑ **Daily Fix-It** Have children find and correct errors in grammar, spelling, and punctuation. DAY 1 155a, DAY 2 171c, DAY 3 173a, DAY 4 177c, DAY 5 178-179

❑ **Homework** The Grammar and Writing Practice Book pp. 81–84. DAY 2 171c, DAY 3 173b, DAY 4 177c, DAY 5 178-179

RETEACH/REVIEW

❑ **The Grammar and Writing Book** Use pp. 170–173 of The Grammar and Writing Book to extend instruction. ANY DAY

The Grammar and Writing Book

RESEARCH/INQUIRY

TEACH

❑ **Glossary** Discuss how to use a glossary. Have partners look in the glossary for entry words. DAY 5 179a

❑ **Unit Inquiry Project** Allow time for children to brainstorm different community workers and their jobs. ANY DAY 153

Resources for Differentiated Instruction

LEVELED READERS

▶ **Comprehension**
  ◎ **Skill** Main Idea/
              Supporting Details
  ◎ **Strategy** Text Structure

▶ **Lesson Vocabulary**
  ◎ **Word Structure**

station
building
roar
masks
quickly
tightly
burning

▶ **Social Studies Standards**
  • Job Responsibility
  • Job Training
  • Tools/Equipment
  • Service
  • Teamwork

Leveled Reader Database ONLINE
PearsonSuccessNet.com

Use the Online Database of over 600 books to
• Download and print additional copies of this week's leveled readers
• Listen to the readers being read online
• Search for more titles focused on this week's skills, topic, and content

---

On-Level

Social Studies
Who Can Help?
by Donna Foley

On-Level Reader

Main Idea
Read the paragraph below.

> Emergency line operators, or 911 operators, answer phone calls from people in danger. They keep the caller calm and ask the right questions. They make sure help gets sent out quickly. The 911 operators make sure that other people in the emergency team know everything they need to know to help.

What is the main idea of this paragraph? **Write** your ideas below.

911 operators help people in danger.

On-Level Practice TE p. LR5

Vocabulary
The paragraph below tells about an emergency, but some words are missing. **Read** the paragraph and fill in the correct missing words from the box.
Hint: The part of speech has been given to help you.

Words to Know
buildings	burning	masks	quickly
roar	station	tightly	

A fire erupted last night at the Townville apartment (noun) **buildings**. Firefighters (adverb) **quickly** responded to the call from the emergency operators. They could hear the (noun) **roar** of the fire as they approached. The firefighters pulled their (noun) **masks** over their faces to protect themselves. They then ran toward the (adjective) **burning** buildings, holding (adverb) **tightly** to their hoses. They worked steadily for one hour, and the fire was extinguished. They returned to the fire (noun) **station** weary but glad that no one had been injured.

On-Level Practice TE p. LR6

Strategic Intervention

Social Studies
Community Helpers
by Marianne Lenihan

Below-Level Reader

Main Idea
Read the paragraph below.

> Police officers patrol their communities using cars, bicycles, or horses. They make sure everyone is safe. Some police officers direct traffic. Police officers help the people in a community live together in peace.

What is the main idea of this paragraph? Write your ideas below.

Police officers help the people in a community live together in peace.

Below-Level Practice TE p. LR2

Vocabulary
Choose a word from the box that best fits in each sentence.

Words to Know
buildings	burning	masks	quickly
roar	station	tightly	

1. The alarm went off at the fire **station**
2. The firemen dressed **quickly** and rushed to the fire engine.
3. The fire spread to three apartment **buildings**
4. The firemen wore **masks** on their faces to help them breathe.
5. They gripped the hose **tightly**
6. People could hear the fire **roar**
7. The firemen rushed into the **burning** building.

Below-Level Practice TE p. LR3

Advanced

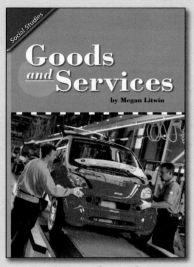

Advanced Reader

Main Idea

Read the paragraphs below.

> Sometimes we don't need to buy something, but we need to pay someone to help us get something done. If you need a haircut, you might go to a hairdresser. You wouldn't ask the baker who sold you banana bread to cut your hair! You would want help from someone who knows how to cut hair. When a person with special training gives you help, it is called a service.
>
> Goods and services are similar. The people who provide services are also producers. The people who pay for their services are consumers.

What is the main idea of this paragraph? **Write** your ideas below.

<u>A service is when a person</u>
<u>with special training gives</u>
<u>you help.</u>

Advanced Practice TE p. LR8

Vocabulary

Choose a word from the Word Box that best fits in each sentence.

Words to Know
community consumers goods producers responsible service teamwork

1. <u>Goods</u> are things that people buy. Which do you like? Which would you try?

2. <u>Producers</u> make the things we need. Like clothes and books and cars with speed.

3. <u>Consumers</u> buy what a producer makes. Like shoes and cookies, freshly baked.

4. Need a haircut? Get one here!
We provide <u>service</u> throughout the year.

5. Consumers, producers, services, too.
Are in your <u>community</u> to help you.

Advanced Practice TE p. LR9

ELL

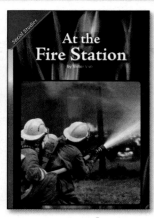

ELL Reader

ELL Poster 21

Teacher's Edition Notes

ELL notes throughout this lesson support instruction and reference additional resources at point of use.

ELL Teaching Guide pp. 141–147, 252–253

- Multilingual summaries of the main selection
- Comprehension lesson
- Vocabulary strategies and word cards
- ELL Reader 21 lesson

ELL and Transition Handbook

Ten Important Sentences

- Key ideas from every selection in the Student Edition
- Activities to build sentence power

More Reading

Readers' Theater Anthology

- Fluency practice
- Five scripts to build fluency
- Poetry for oral interpretation

Leveled Trade Books

- Extend reading tied to the unit concept
- Lessons in Trade Book Library Teaching Guide

Homework

- Family Times Newsletter
- ELL Multilingual Selection Summaries

Take-Home Books

- Decodable Readers
- Leveled Readers

Firefighter! **154i**

Literacy Centers

 Listening

Let's Read Along

MATERIALS `SINGLES`
CD player, headphones, print copies of recorded pieces

LISTEN TO LITERATURE As children listen to the following recordings, have them follow along or read along in the print version.

AudioText
Firefighter!
"Firefighting Teamwork"

Sing with Me/Background Building Audio
"The Firefighting Team"

Phonics Songs and Rhymes Audio
"On the Job"

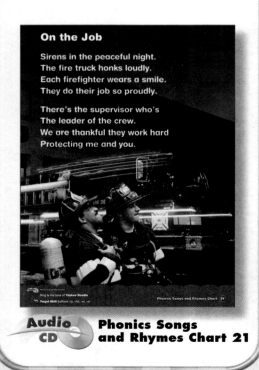

On the Job

Sirens in the peaceful night.
The fire truck honks loudly.
Each firefighter wears a smile.
They do their job so proudly.

There's the supervisor who's
The leader of the crew.
We are thankful they work hard
Protecting me and you.

Audio CD **Phonics Songs and Rhymes Chart 21**

 Reading/Library

Read It Again!

MATERIALS `SINGLES` `PAIRS` `GROUPS`
collection of books for self-selected reading, reading logs

REREAD BOOKS Have children select previously read books from the appropriate book box and record titles of books they read in their logs. Use these previously read books:

- Decodable Readers
- Leveled Readers
- ELL Readers
- Stories written by classmates
- Books from the library

TEN IMPORTANT SENTENCES Have children read the Ten Important Sentences for *Firefighter!* and locate the sentences in the Student Edition.

BOOK CLUB Encourage a group to discuss *Firefighter!* Were they surprised by the different things firefighters do during the day?

 Word Work

Great Endings

MATERIALS `PAIRS` `GROUPS`
20 index cards

SUFFIXES -ly, -ful, -er, -or Have two to four children play a game using words with suffixes.

1. Write a suffix on each of four cards. Place the cards facedown in a pile.
2. Place sixteen cards with base words such as *cheer, play, quick, tight, sudden* facedown in another pile.
3. Children take turns picking a card from each pile and reading the base word and suffix. If the cards make a word, the child keeps the base word card.
4. Play continues until the base word pile is exhausted.

Phonics Activities CD This interactive CD provides additional practice.

thank **ful**

act **or**

play **er**

Scott Foresman Reading Street Centers Survival Kit

Use the *Firefighter!* materials from the Reading Street
Centers Survival Kit to organize this week's centers.

Writing

Ask a
Firefighter

MATERIALS [SINGLES]
paper, pencils

WRITE QUESTIONS Recall that Liz, Dan, and Anthony are firefighters.

1. **Have children discuss things that firefighters do.**
2. **Then children make a list of questions they'd like to ask a firefighter.**

LEVELED WRITING Encourage children to write at their own ability level. Some may have unclear questions. Others will present questions that are sometimes unclear. Your best writers' work will contain clear questions.

Questions for a Firefighter

• Why did you want to be a firefighter?
• Do you get scared?
• Have you ever saved a pet?

Social Studies

A Student's
Job

MATERIALS [SINGLES]
paper, pencils, construction paper, markers

MAKE A BOOKLET Discuss why it is important to have the right tools to do a job.

1. **Have individuals make a list of the tools and equipment they need for their job as a student.**
2. **Then have them draw one tool or piece of equipment and write about how it is used.**
3. **Children's illustrated pages can be bound into a booklet.**

My book bag is a piece of equipment that I put my tools in. I have pencils, markers, and scissors in my book bag.

Technology

Community
Heroes

MATERIALS [SINGLES] [PAIRS]
computer, printer, pencils, markers

USE A WORD PROCESSING PROGRAM Have individuals or pairs of children write a short story.

1. **Have children open a word processing program.**
2. **Have them write a three- or four-sentence story about firefighters.**
3. **Then have them print out their story, illustrate it, and share it.**

Firefighters save people. They put out fires. They are brave.

ALL CENTERS

Oral Vocabulary
"The Firefighting Team" 21

Phonics and Spelling
Suffixes -ly, -ful, -er, -or

Spelling Pretest: Words With Suffixes

Read Apply Phonics

Group Time < Differentiated Instruction

Comprehension
Skill Main Idea/Supporting Details

Strategy Text Structure

Shared Writing
Report

Grammar
Pronouns

Materials

- *Sing with Me Big Book*
- Letter Tiles
- Decodable Reader 21
- Student Edition 154–155
- Graphic Organizer 14
- Skill Transparency 21
- Writing Transparency 21
- Grammar Transparency 21

Take It to the NET™
ONLINE

Professional Development
To learn more about repeated reading, go to PearsonSuccessNet.com and read the article "The Method of Repeated Readings" by S. J. Samuels.

Morning Warm-Up!

**Everybody has a job to do.
Mine is to teach.
Yours is to learn.
Why is it important
to do a good job?**

QUESTION OF THE WEEK Tell children they will talk, sing, read, and write about Responsibility. Write and read the message and discuss the question.

CONNECT CONCEPTS Ask questions to connect to Unit 4 selections.

- Did Annie in *Helen Keller and the Big Storm* do a good job teaching Helen? What did she do?

- Did the mothers in *The Quilt Story* do a good job of being a mom? Why or why not?

REVIEW HIGH-FREQUENCY WORDS

- Circle the high-frequency words *everybody* and *learn* in the message.

- Have children say and spell each word as they write it in the air.

Build Background Use the Day 1 instruction on ELL Poster 21 to assess knowledge and develop concepts.

ELL Poster 21

Oral Vocabulary

SHARE LITERATURE Display p. 21 of the *Sing with Me Big Book.* Tell children that the class is going to sing a song about firefighters working as a team. Divide the class into three teams, and assign each team one Amazing Word (**community, responsible,** or **teamwork**). Ask each team to listen for its Amazing Word as you sing the song. Tell them to jump to their feet when they hear it. Then help each team explain what their Amazing Word means, and encourage the team to sing along with the verse in which the word appears. Then sing the whole song as a class.

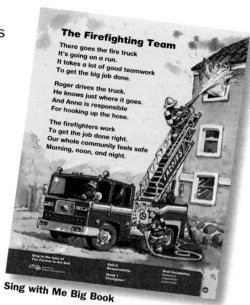

The Firefighting Team

There goes the fire truck
It's going on a run.
It takes a lot of good teamwork
To get the big job done.

Roger drives the truck.
He knows just where it goes.
And Anna is responsible
For hooking up the hose.

The firefighters work
To get the job done right.
Our whole community feels safe
Morning, noon, and night.

Sing with Me Big Book

Sing with Me/
Background Building Audio

BUILD BACKGROUND Remind children of the question of the week.

• Why is it important to do a good job?

Draw a simple web or use Graphic Organizer 14. Write *A Good Job* in the center of the web. Help children brainstorm reasons for doing a good job. Encourage them to use the Amazing Words. Display the web for use throughout the week.

• What could it mean to do a good job? (to be responsible, to help your community)

• When do we use teamwork in our classroom?

A Good Job

▲ **Graphic Organizer 14**

Amazing Words to build oral vocabulary

MONITOR PROGRESS

community responsible teamwork operation instrument caretaker lug supplies	**If…** children lack oral vocabulary experiences about the concept Responsibility, **then…** use the Oral Vocabulary Routine below to teach *community*.

Oral Vocabulary ROUTINE

1 Introduce the Word Relate the word *community* to the song. Supply a child-friendly definition. Have children say the word. Example: You, your family, and all the people who live around you are your *community*.

2 Demonstrate Provide an example to show meaning. The *community* pitched in to clean up the empty lot.

3 Apply Have children demonstrate their understanding. Your *community* includes which of the following: the president of Mexico or your next-door neighbor?

4 Display the Word/Word Parts Write the word on a card. Display it. Run your hand under the word parts *com-mu-ni-ty* as you read the word. See p. DI·3 to teach *responsible* and *teamwork*.

Build Oral Vocabulary Help children understand the words *fire truck, drives,* and *hose.* Have children play firefighters getting into a truck, driving to the scene, unloading a hose, and putting out a fire.

1

OBJECTIVE

- Blend, read, and build words with suffixes *-ly, -ful, -er, -or.*

Skills Trace

◎ Suffixes *-ly, -ful, -er, -or*

Introduce/Teach	TE: 2.5 154n–o
Practice	TE: 2.5 154p, 156c–d; PB: 2.2 53; DR21
Reteach/Review	TE: 2.5 178c, 202c, DI·64; PB: 2.2 68
Test	TE: 2.5 178e–g; Benchmark Test: Unit 5

Generalization

Suffixes *-ly, -ful, -er, -or* Prefixes, suffixes, and some inflected endings usually form separate syllables from the base word.

Strategic Intervention

Use **Monitor Progress,** p. 154o, during Group Time after children have had more practice with suffixes *-ly, -ful, -er, -or.*

Advanced

Use **Monitor Progress,** p. 154o, as a preassessment to determine whether this group of children would benefit from this instruction on suffixes.

Support Phonics The suffix *-ly* is used in the same way as the suffix *-mente* in Spanish. For Spanish speakers, offer examples of parallel words: *slowly/lentamente; rapidly/rápidamente; completely/completamente.*

In Spanish, *er* is pronounced like *air* in English. Spanish speakers may pronounce words like *teacher* and *sailor* as *tea-chair* and *sai-lair.*

See the Phonics Transition Lessons in the ELL and Transition Handbook.

◎Suffixes *-ly, -ful, -er, -or*

TEACH/MODEL

Blending Strategy

ROUTINE

1 **Connect** Write *quickly, joyful, painter,* and *actor.* What do you know about reading these words? (They have a base word and an ending.) Today we'll learn about adding suffixes *-ly, -ful, -er,* and *-or* to the end of words. Each suffix has a special meaning:

- *-ly*   in a _____ way
- *-ful*   full of
- *-er, -or*   a person who _____

2 **Model** Write *quickly.* This is a two-syllable word formed from the base word *quick* and the suffix *-ly.* You can cover the suffix, read the base word, and then blend the base word and the suffix to read the whole word. This is how I blend this word. First, I chunk the word into its parts—the base word *quick* and the suffix *-ly.* **Cover the suffix to read the base word; uncover and read the ending. Blend the two parts.** Let's blend this word together:

/kwik/ /lē/ What is the word? *(quickly)* What does it mean? *(in a quick way).* Repeat with *joyful, painter,* and *actor.*

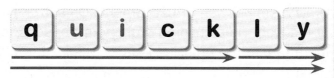

3 **Group Practice** First, I chunk the word into its parts—the base word and the suffix. Then I read the base word, read the suffix, and blend the two parts. **Continue with** *closely, helpful, reader, inventor.*

4 **Review** What do you know about reading words with suffixes? Chunk the word into its parts. **Read the base word, read the suffix, and then blend the two parts.**

BLEND WORDS

INDIVIDUALS BLEND WORDS Call on individuals to chunk and blend the words *wonderful, gently, actor, teacher, farmer, graceful, lightly, editor.* Have them tell what they know about each word before reading it. (Suffixes form separate syllables that are added to the end of base words.) For feedback, refer to step four of the Blending Strategy Routine.

BUILD WORDS

READ LONGER WORDS Write the suffixes *-ly, -ful, -er,* and *-or* as headings for a four-column chart. Write several base words in each column. Have children add the suffix to each base word, read the new word, and supply its meaning.

-ly	-ful	-er	-or
quietly	peaceful	fighter	actor
clearly	hopeful	player	sailor
gladly	helpful	singer	visitor

Vocabulary Tip

You may wish to explain the meanings of these words.

editor   someone who fixes writing to make it better

graceful   full of grace or charm

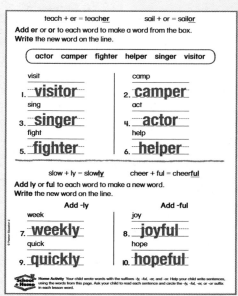

▲ **Practice Book 2.2** p. 53, Suffixes *-ly, -ful, -er, -or*

Monitor Progress   Check Word Reading Suffixes *-ly, -ful, -er, -or*

Write the following words and have individuals read them.

slowly	quietly	wonderful	graceful	closely
helper	dancer	visitor	reader	editor
fullest	joyful	bravest	clearly	softer

If... children cannot blend suffixes at this point,

then... continue to monitor their progress using other instructional opportunities during the week so that they can be successful with the Day 5 Assessment. See the Skills Trace on p. 154n.

SUCCESS PREDICTOR

Spiral REVIEW

● Row 3 contrasts comparative endings *-er* and *-est.*

▶ **Day 1 Check Word Reading**

Day 2 Check Lesson Vocabulary/High-Frequency Words

Day 3 Check Retelling

Day 4 Check Fluency

Day 5 Assess Progress

Word Reading

SUCCESS PREDICTOR

OBJECTIVES

- Segment sounds and word parts to spell words.
- Spell words with suffixes *-ly, -ful, -er, -or*

Spelling Words

Suffixes *-ly, -ful, -er, -or*

1. cheerful
2. visitor
3. slowly*
4. weekly
5. teacher
6. helper
7. hardly*
8. graceful
9. yearly
10. quickly*
11. fighter*
12. sailor

Challenge Words

13. gardener
14. competitor
15. extremely

* Words from the Selection

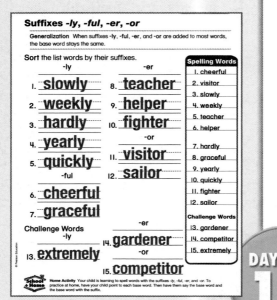

Suffixes *-ly, -ful, -er, -or*

Generalization When suffixes -ly, -ful, -er, and -or are added to most words, the base word stays the same.

Sort the list words by their suffixes.

-ly
1. slowly
2. weekly
3. hardly
4. yearly
5. quickly

-ful
6. cheerful
7. graceful

Challenge Words
-ly
13. extremely

-er
8. teacher
9. helper
10. fighter

-or
11. visitor
12. sailor

-er
14. gardener

-or
15. competitor

Spelling Words
1. cheerful
2. visitor
3. slowly
4. weekly
5. teacher
6. helper
7. hardly
8. graceful
9. yearly
10. quickly
11. fighter
12. sailor

Challenge Words
13. gardener
14. competitor
15. extremely

Home Activity Your child is learning to spell words with the suffixes -ly, -ful, -er, and -or. To practice at home, have your child point to each base word. Then have them say the base word and the base word with the suffix.

▲ **Spelling Practice Book** p. 81

ELL

Support Spelling Before giving the spelling pretest, clarify the meaning of each spelling word with examples, such as saying *slowly* while walking slowly across the room and pointing to yourself to illustrate *teacher.*

Spelling

PRETEST Suffixes *-ly, -ful, -er, -or*

MODEL WRITING FOR WORD PARTS Each spelling word ends with a suffix. Before administering the spelling pretest, model how to segment suffixes to spell them.

- You can spell words with suffixes by thinking about the base word and the suffix. What base word and suffix make up *sweetly?* (*sweet* and *-ly*)
- Start with the sounds in the base word: *sweet.* What letters spell /sweet/? Write *sweet.*
- Now add the suffix *-ly.* Add *ly.*
- Now spell *sweetly.*
- Repeat with *harmful, waiter, actor.*

PRETEST Dictate the spelling words. Segment the words for children if necessary. Have children check their pretests and correct misspelled words.

HOMEWORK Spelling Practice Book, p. 81

Group Time

Teamwork Works

"Class," said Mrs. Landers, "here is our job for Community Day. We must pack twenty boxes of food for poor families. We must also make twenty lunches for the drivers who will deliver the food."

Mrs. Landers divided the class into teams. Five children would make the lunches. The other twenty children would pack the boxes.

DAY 1

On-Level	Strategic Intervention	Advanced
Read Decodable Reader 21.	**Read** Decodable Reader 21.	**Read** Advanced Selection 21.
• Use p. 154q.	• Use the **Routine** on p. DI·14.	• Use the **Routine** on p. DI·15.

ELL Place English language learners in the groups that correspond to their reading abilities in English.

(i) Independent Activities

Fluency Reading Pair children to reread Leveled Readers or the ELL Reader from the previous week or other text at children's independent level.

Journal Writing List people who do jobs for the community. Share writing.

Independent Reading See p. 154j for Reading/Library activities and suggestions.

Literacy Centers To practice suffixes *-ly, -ful, -er, -or* you may use Word Work, p. 154j.

Practice Book 2.2 Suffixes *-ly, -ful, -er, -or,* p. 53; Main Ideas and Details, p. 54

Break into small groups after Spelling and before the Comprehension lesson.

Apply Phonics

⊙ PRACTICE Suffixes

HIGH-FREQUENCY WORDS Review *anything, colors,* and *something.*

READ DECODABLE READER 21

- Pages 42–43 Read aloud quietly with the group.
- Pages 44–45 Have the group read aloud without you.
- Pages 46–48 Select individuals to read aloud.

CHECK COMPREHENSION AND DECODING Ask children the following questions about Hobbies:

- What does Janet like to do? (She likes to tend plants in her garden.)
- What hobby does Kelvin have? (He is a painter.)
- What do Kerry and Ben have in common? (They are both storytellers.)

Then have children locate words with suffixes *-ly, -ful, -er,* and *-or* in the story. Review *-ly, -ful, -er,* and *-or* spelling patterns. Sort words according to their spelling patterns.

-ly	*-ful*	*-er*	*-or*
boldly	boastful	gardener	actor
bravely	peaceful	hiker(s)	
gladly	playful	painter	
weekly	restful	storyteller	
		teacher	

HOMEWORK Take-Home Decodable Reader 21

REREAD FOR FLUENCY

Oral Rereading

ROUTINE

1 **Read** Have children read the entire story orally.

2 **Reread** To achieve optimal fluency, children should reread the text three or four times.

3 **Provide Feedback** Listen as children read and provide corrective feedback regarding their oral reading and their use of the blending strategy.

Monitor Progress

Decoding

If...	then... prompt
children have difficulty decoding a word,	them to blend the word. • What is the new word? • Is the new word a word you know? • Does it make sense in the story?

Access Content
Beginning Preview the book *Hobbies,* identifying each character and naming his or her hobby.

Intermediate Preview *Hobbies,* explaining the meanings of adjectives such as *boastful, boldly,* and *bravely.* Facilitate a discussion, using these words to build conversational fluency.

Advanced After reading *Hobbies,* have children discuss their favorite hobbies.

Main Idea and Details
 # Text Structure

TEACH/MODEL

OBJECTIVES

 Recognize the main idea and supporting details.

Use chronological order and sequence.

Skills Trace

Main Idea/Supporting Details

Introduce/Teach	TE: 2.1 43a–b, 44e, 97a–b, 98e; 2.5 154r, 154–155
Practice	TE: 2.1 102–103; 2.5 160–161; PB: 2.1 14–15, 34–35; 2.2 54–55
Reteach/Review	TE: 2.1 32–33, DI-65, DI-67; 2.4 132–133; 2.5 DI-64; 2.6 338–339; PB: 2.1 7; 2.2 47, 117
Test	TE: 2.1 66e–g, 126e–g; 2.5 178e–g; Selection Tests: 2.1 5–8, 13–16; 2.5 81–84; Benchmark Test: Units 1, 3–6

INTRODUCE MAIN IDEA AND SUPPORTING DETAILS Recall *Helen Keller and the Big Storm*. Have students tell the main idea of the story. (Possible response: Helen learned something about the power of weather and friendship.)

- When would it be helpful to be able to tell the main idea of a story?

Read p. 154. Explain the following:

- The topic of a story is what the story is about. The topic can be said in one or two words. The main idea is the most important idea about the topic. Smaller facts make up the details.

- The way in which a selection is organized is called the text structure. Sometimes a selection can be written in the order that things happen. The main idea can be given at the beginning, middle, or end of the selection.

Use Skill Transparency 21 to teach main idea and supporting details and text structure.

SKILL Use paragraph one to model finding the main idea.

> **Think Aloud** **MODEL** I know the main idea is often given in a sentence at the beginning, middle, or end of a selection. I can read the first paragraph to look for the main idea and some details about it. **Read the paragraph aloud.** I think the main idea is *My Uncle Ernie is a firefighter in our town.*

STRATEGY Continue with paragraphs two and three to model text structure.

> **Think Aloud** **MODEL** I will read to find out the way in which this selection is organized. I see the clue words *one morning* and *next*. This tells me the selection is written in the order things happen.

My Uncle, the Firefighter

My Uncle Ernie works hard as a firefighter in our town. He puts out brush fires and house fires. He helps at car wrecks. He saves people.

One morning, Uncle Ernie took me to the fire station. I saw the hose truck and the ladder truck. Uncle Ernie and the other firefighters had a drill. They practiced with the hoses.

Next, Uncle Ernie let me try on his heavy coat, helmet, and boots. I got to stand on the back of the fire truck!

I had a great time. My Uncle Ernie is good at his job. He is a great firefighter.

Skill Here's the main idea of this paragraph. What is it? Read on to find some details.

Strategy How is this selection organized? In what order did things happen?

Unit 5 Fire Fighter   Skill Transparency 21

▲ **Skill Transparency 21**

ELL

Access Content

Beginning/Intermediate For a Picture It! lesson on main idea and supporting details, see the ELL Teaching Guide, pp. 141–142.

Advanced Before children read "My Uncle, the Firefighter" make sure they know the meanings of *firefighter, wrecks,* and *drill.*

Comprehension

Skill
Main Idea

Strategy
Text Structure

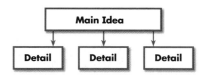

Main Idea

- The main idea is the most important idea in a selection.
- The main idea is often stated near the beginning of a selection.
- Details tell more about the main idea.

Main Idea

Detail	Detail	Detail

Strategy: Text Structure

Text structure is the way a selection is organized. A selection can be organized in the order in which things happen. Noticing the organization can help you find the main idea.

Write to Read

1. Read "My Uncle, the Firefighter." Find the main idea and at least three details.

2. Make a graphic organizer like the one above. Fill it in with the main idea and details you found.

154

My Uncle, the Firefighter

My Uncle Ernie works hard as a firefighter in our town. He puts out brush fires and house fires. He helps at car wrecks. He saves people.

One morning, Uncle Ernie took me to the fire station. I saw the hose truck and the ladder truck. Uncle Ernie and the other firefighters had a drill. They practiced with the hoses.

Next, Uncle Ernie let me try on his heavy coat, helmet, and boots. I got to stand on the back of the fire truck!

I had a great time. My Uncle Ernie is good at his job. He is a great firefighter.

Skill Here's the main idea of this paragraph. What is it? Read on to find some details.

Strategy How is this selection organized? In what order did things happen?

155

PRACTICE

WRITE Work with children to complete the steps in the Write activity. Have children use the completed graphic organizer to describe the main idea and three details in "My Uncle, the Firefighter."

Monitor Progress	**Main Idea and Supporting Details**
If… children are unable to complete Write on p. 154,	**then…** use Practice Book 2.2, p. 54, for additional practice.

CONNECT TO READING Encourage children to ask themselves these questions when they read.

- Do I know how the selection is organized?
- Do I know the order in which things happen?

Read the paragraph. Follow the directions.

Fire moves quickly. That is why each family member needs to know what to do in a fire. If a smoke alarm rings, get out. Make sure someone helps any young children or older people. Once you get out, stay out. Call for help after you get outside.

1. **Circle** the answer below that tells what the paragraph is about.
   using smoke alarms   (what to do in a fire)   calling for help

2. **Circle** the answer below that tells the most important idea about the paragraph.
   (Each family member needs to know what to do in a fire)
   Once you get out, stay out.
   Call for help after you get outside.

3. **Underline** the sentence in the paragraph that tells what to do if a smoke alarm rings.

4. **Circle** the sentence in the paragraph that tells when to call for help.

5. **Write** a title for this paragraph.
   <u>Sample answer: What to</u>
   <u>Do in a Fire</u>

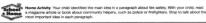 **Home Activity** Your child identified the main idea in a paragraph about fire safety. With your child, read a magazine article or book about community helpers, such as police or firefighters. Stop to talk about the most important idea in each paragraph.

▲ **Practice Book 2.2** p. 54, Main Idea and Supporting Details

DAILY FIX-IT

1. I witsh i saw the fire truck.
   I wi<u>sh</u> <u>I</u> saw the fire truck.

2. Those trucks is red
   Those trucks <u>are</u> red<u>.</u>

This week's practice sentences appear on Daily Fix-It Transparency 21.

Strategic Intervention

Have children who are not able to write independently dictate a sentence or two about community workers. Write the sentences on the board and have children copy them.

Advanced

Have children write a report about other people who work in the community, such as grocers, auto mechanics, and dentists.

ELL

Support Writing Before children begin writing independently, reread the report from the Shared Writing activity. Then have children orally share their ideas about community workers to help them prepare for writing their ideas.

▲ **The Grammar and Writing Book**
For more instruction and practice, use pp. 170–175.

Shared Writing

WRITE Report

GENERATE IDEAS Read aloud each group of community workers on the page. Ask children to explain what each group does to help people in the community.

WRITE A REPORT Explain that the class will write a report about several kinds of community workers and their jobs and then summarize what these workers do for the community.

COMPREHENSION SKILL Explain to children that a main idea ties many details together. Have children come up with a main idea that tells something important about what community workers do. (They help the community.)

- Display Writing Transparency 21 and read the title.
- Ask children to think about community workers they see around their neighborhood and the kinds of activities these people do.
- Read the names of the different community workers.
- As children tell what each group of workers does, record their responses.

HANDWRITING While writing, model the letter forms as shown on pp. TR14–17.

READ THE REPORT Have children read the completed report aloud as you track the print.

In Our Community
Possible answers:

Police officers **protect us and solve crimes**

Firefighters **put out fires and help keep us safe**

Mail carriers **bring us letters and packages**

Teachers **help us learn about many things**

Librarians **help us find books and other sources of information**

These people **are all workers who help**

people in the community

Unit 5 Fire Fighter!   Writing Model **21**

▲ **Writing Transparency 21**

INDEPENDENT WRITING

WRITE REPORT Have children write their own report about community workers. Encourage them to use words from the Word Wall and the Amazing Words board. Let children illustrate their writing. You may display children's work on a bulletin board in the classroom.

ADDITIONAL PRACTICE For additional practice, use pp. 170–175 in the Grammar and Writing Book.

Grammar

TEACH/MODEL Pronouns

REVIEW NOUNS Remind children that a noun is a word that names a person, place, animal, or thing.

IDENTIFY PRONOUNS Display Grammar Transparency 21. Read the definition aloud.

- *Sue Kresky* is a person's name, so it is a noun. Instead of using the noun *Sue Kresky,* we can use a pronoun.

- *Sue Kresky* is a woman's name. That tells us to choose the pronoun *she.*

Continue modeling with items 2–5.

PRACTICE

FIND PRONOUNS Write several sentences on the board. Use pronouns in some of the sentences. Read each sentence aloud and have children decide if it contains a pronoun.

- Firefighters work hard.
- They rescue people and put out fires.
- I want to be a firefighter.
- Bob wants to be a firefighter too.

Pronouns

A pronoun is a word that takes the place of a noun or nouns. The words **he, she, it, we, you,** and **they** are pronouns.

Rosa is a doctor. **She** helps people. **She** takes the place of the noun Rosa.

Dan and Marie are nurses. **They** help people too. **They** takes the place of the nouns Dan and Marie.

Write the pronoun that can take the place of the underlined word or words. Use *he, she, it, we,* or *they.*

1. <u>Sue Kresky</u> talks to the children at school. ____ **She**

2. <u>The children</u> listen to the police officer. ____ **They**

3. <u>Juan and I</u> want to be police officers. ____ **We**

4. <u>Juan</u> asks Officer Kresky many questions. ____ **He**

5. Someday <u>the dream</u> will come true. ____ **it**

Unit 5 Fire Fighter!   Grammar **21**

▲ **Grammar Transparency 21**

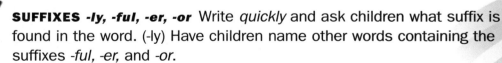

Wrap Up Your Day!

✓ **SUFFIXES -ly, -ful, -er, -or** Write *quickly* and ask children what suffix is found in the word. (-ly) Have children name other words containing the suffixes *-ful, -er,* and *-or.*

✓ **SPELLING WORDS WITH SUFFIXES -ly, -ful, -er, -or** Have children spell the word *fight* and write it on the board. Ask: How do we make the word *fighter,* as in *firefighter*? Continue with *nicely* and *thankful.*

✓ **MAIN IDEA** To review the concept of main idea, ask: What is the main idea of "My Uncle the Firefighter"? How can you tell?

LET'S TALK ABOUT IT Recall what children read about firefighters in "My Uncle the Firefighter." What did you learn about what firefighters do from this story?

HOMEWORK Send home this week's Family Times newsletter.

PREVIEW Day 2

Tell children that tomorrow the class will read about a day at a fire station.

Share Literature
Animal Hospital

Phonics and Spelling
Suffixes *-ly, -ful, -er, -or*
Spelling: Words with Suffixes

Build Background
A Day in a Firehouse

Lesson Vocabulary
station   building   roar   masks
quickly   tightly   burning
More Words to Know
fireproof   hydrant   outriggers

Vocabulary
Skill Suffix *-ly*
Strategy Word Structure

Read

Group Time < Differentiated Instruction

Firefighter!

Interactive Writing
Poster

Grammar
Pronouns

Materials

- *Sing with Me Big Book*
- Big Book *Animal Hospital*
- Phonics Songs and Rhymes Chart 21
- Background Building Audio
- Graphic Organizers 2, 26
- Student Edition 158–171

Morning Warm~Up!

Today we will read about
helpful firefighters.
They work calmly and quickly.
How hard is a firefighter's job?

QUESTION OF THE DAY Encourage children to sing "The Firefighting Team" from the *Sing with Me Big Book* as you gather. Write and read the message and discuss the question.

REVIEW SUFFIXES

- Read the message again. Have children raise their hands when they hear a word with the suffix *-ly* or *-ful*. (*helpful, calmly, quickly*)

- Ask children to tell you what each word is without the suffix. (*help, calm, quick*) Review that adding the suffix to these words helps describe firefighters and how they work.

ELL

Build Background Use the Day 2 instruction on ELL Poster 21 to preview lesson vocabulary words.

ELL Poster 21

Share Literature

BUILD CONCEPTS

NARRATIVE NONFICTION Tell children that you are going to read a book called *Animal Hospital.* Explain that the book is narrative nonfiction. This means that even though it's told as a story, it tells about real animal doctors.

BUILD ORAL VOCABULARY Ask children what they know about animal doctors. Introduce the Amazing Word **operation**. Explain that it means cutting into a sick or hurt part of a body to make it better. People might have an operation, but an animal can too. Suggest that as you read, children listen to find out what operation the animal doctor does.

Big Book

MONITOR LISTENING COMPREHENSION

- Which animal needed an operation and why? (The dog needed an operation because it had a broken leg.)

- What is another word for "animal doctor"? (vet)

- What animals does the vet take care of in the story? (duck, goose, rabbit, kittens, dog, horse)

- Do you think animal doctors have a hard job? Explain your answer. (Children will probably agree that animal doctors have a hard job because they need to know a lot about all different kinds of animals.) Remind children of the words *calmly* and *quickly* from the morning message. Ask them if it is important for a vet to work this way too.

OBJECTIVES

- Discuss characteristics of narrative nonfiction.
- Set purpose for listening.
- Build oral vocabulary.

Amazing Words
to build oral vocabulary

MONITOR PROGRESS

community	**If...** children lack oral vocabulary experiences about the concept Responsibility,
responsible	
teamwork	
operation	
instrument	
caretaker	**then...** use the Oral Vocabulary Routine. See p. DI·3 to teach *operation.*
lug	
supplies	

Build Concepts Help children understand the idea of an animal doctor. Ask them why they visit a doctor. (they don't feel well, they've had an accident, they need a check-up, they need shots) Explain that animals visit doctors, too, for the same reasons. Ask children to find situations in the story that are similar to what happens when they visit the doctor.

2

Suffixes -ly, -ful, -er, -or

TEACH/MODEL

Fluent Word Reading

ROUTINE

1 **Connect** Write *lovely*. You can read this word because you know how to read words with suffixes. What base word and suffix form *lovely*? (*love* and -*ly*) Do the same with *faithful, driver,* and *creditor*.

2 **Model** When you come to a word with a suffix, look at the base word and suffix and blend the two word parts together to read it. **Model reading *wonderful, teacher, inventor, cheerful,* and *gardener*.** When you come to a new word, what are you going to do?

3 **Group Practice** Write *quickly, painter, competitor, eventful, reader.* Read these words. Look at the word, say the word to yourself, and then read the word aloud. **Allow 2–3 seconds previewing time.**

WORD READING

PHONICS SONGS AND RHYMES CHART 21 Frame each of the following words on Phonics Songs and Rhymes Chart 21. Call on individuals to read them. Guide children in previewing.

loudly	**proudly**	**peaceful**	**thankful**
firefighter	**leader**	**supervisor**	

Sing "On the Job" to the tune of "Yankee Doodle," or play the CD. Have children follow along on the chart as they sing. Then have individuals take turns underlining and reading words with suffixes on the chart.

 Phonics Songs and Rhymes Audio

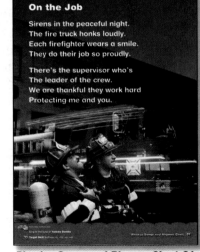

On the Job

Sirens in the peaceful night.
The fire truck honks loudly.
Each firefighter wears a smile.
They do their job so proudly.

There's the supervisor who's
The leader of the crew.
We are thankful they work hard
Protecting me and you.

Phonics Songs and Rhymes Chart 21

SORT WORDS

INDIVIDUALS SORT WORDS WITH SUFFIXES -ly, -ful, -er, -or Write suffixes
-ly, -ful, -er, and -or spelling patterns as headings. Have individuals write words
with suffixes -ly, -ful, -er, and -or from the Phonics Chart under the appropriate
headings and circle the suffixes. Have all children complete the activity on
paper. Ask individuals to read the words. Provide feedback as necessary.

-ly	-ful	-er	-or
loudly	peaceful	fire fighter	supervisor
proudly	thankful	leader	

Spelling

PRACTICE Suffixes -ly, -ful, -er, -or

WRITE DICTATION SENTENCES Have children write these sentences. Repeat
words slowly, allowing children to hear each sound. Children may use the Word
Wall to help with spelling high-frequency words. **Word Wall**

> **My teacher has a weekly helper.**
> **I like to skate slowly and look graceful.**
> **The firefighter quickly put out the fire.**
> **He was a cheerful visitor.**

HOMEWORK Spelling Practice Book, p. 82

Spelling Words

Suffixes -ly, -ful, -er, -or

1. cheerful	7. hardly*
2. visitor	8. graceful
3. slowly*	9. yearly
4. weekly	10. quickly*
5. teacher	11. fighter*
6. helper	12. sailor

Challenge Words

13. gardener
14. competitor
15. extremely

* Words from the Selection

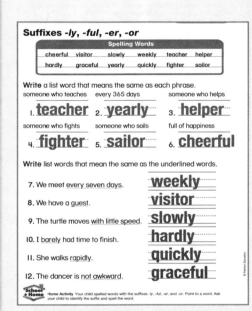

▲ **Spelling Practice Book** p. 82

Look at the picture. **Read** the paragraph. **Follow** the directions.

Forest fires burn quickly when it is windy and dry. Firefighters try to keep the fire from growing. Sometimes planes drop water on the fire. Firefighters also chop down trees and grass around the fire. This takes away the dry plants that feed the fire.

1. What do you think the picture is mostly about?
   Circle your answer below.
   (forest fires)   planes   trees

2. **Pick** the best title for the paragraph. **Circle** your answer below.
   How to Cut Down Trees
   Water Puts Out Fires
   (Fighting Forest Fires)

3. **Draw** a picture to show a detail of what the paragraph is about.
   Children's artwork should show a detail related to fighting forest fires, such as a plane dropping water onto a forest fire or firefighters removing trees and brush to create a fire break.

4. **Write** a sentence that tells about the detail in your picture.
   _____
   Children's sentence should tell about the detail they drew.
   _____

 Home Activity Your child identified the main idea and important details in a paragraph about forest fires. Read a story or nonfiction selection to your child. Ask your child to draw a picture that shows the main idea of the text.

▲ **Practice Book 2.2** p. 55,
  Main Idea and Supporting Details

ELL

Activate Prior Knowledge Define the word *fire* and have students say it in their home language. Then have them explain the terms *fire truck*, *firefighter*, and *firehouse*.

Build Background

DISCUSS A FIREHOUSE If available, display a picture of a local firehouse. Initiate discussion by asking children if they have ever visited a firehouse.

- What did you see and hear?
- What are firehouses for?

BACKGROUND BUILDING AUDIO Have children listen to the CD and share the new information they learned about a day in a firehouse.

Audio CD   Sing with Me/
                Background Building Audio

STORY PREDICTION FROM VOCABULARY Draw or display Graphic Organizer 2. Have students read the selection title. Write the following vocabulary words in the upper box: *station, building, roar, masks, quickly, tightly,* and *burning*. Have children think about the title and vocabulary words as they predict what the selection might be about. Remind them to use personal experiences and what they know about the vocabulary words as they make predictions.

After children have read the selection, have them discuss the accuracy of their predictions. Have them draw a picture in the lower box that shows what the selection is about.

> **Title and Story Words**
>
> Read the title and the story words.
> What do you think a problem in the story might be?
> I think a problem might be _____
> After reading _____
> draw a picture of one of the problems in the story.

▲ Graphic Organizer 2

CONNECT TO SELECTION Connect background information to *Firefighter!*

Firefighters fight fires, but did you know that they are also responsible for saving lives? We're going to read a story about firefighters who are worried that there might be a little boy in a burning house. We'll find out how they use teamwork to fight the fire and whether the boy is rescued.

Vocabulary

LESSON VOCABULARY

WORD MEANING CHART Draw a three-column chart or use Graphic Organizer 26. Have children list words and their meanings and use each word in a sentence.

Word	Definition	Sentence
station	a building where a service takes place	The firefighers drove out of the fire station.

▲ Graphic Organizer 26

WORDS TO KNOW

T **station** a building where a service takes place
T **building** a place with walls and a roof
T **roar** a loud, deep noise
T **masks** coverings for the face
T **quickly** in a fast way
T **tightly** fitting in a close way
T **burning** hurting or harming someone or something by fire

MORE WORDS TO KNOW

fireproof something made to resist burning easily
hydrant a metal structure connected to a water supply for use on fires
outriggers leg-like structures that hold a fire truck steady

T = Tested Word

- Children should be able to decode all words except *station*. To read *station*, divide the word into syllables (*sta/tion*) and have children blend them.

Pick a word from the box to match each clue.
Write the word on the line.

> building   burning   masks   quickly
> roar   station   tightly

1.
   masks

2.
   building

3. firmly
   tightly

4. on fire
   burning

5. not slowly
   quickly

6. where firefighters work
   station

7. a loud, deep sound
   roar

Home Activity Your child used clues to identify and write words that he or she learned to read this week. Work with your child to write a story about firefighters, using as many of the listed words as possible.

▲ **Practice Book 2.2** p. 56, Lesson Vocabulary

Monitor Progress | Check Lesson Vocabulary

Write these words and have individuals read them.

station	building	roar	masks	quickly	tightly
burning	enough	finally	ladder	someone	special

If... children cannot read these words,

then... have them practice in pairs with word cards before reading the selection. Monitor their fluency with these words during reading, and provide additional practice opportunities before the Day 5 Assessment.

SUCCESS PREDICTOR

Spiral REVIEW

● Reviews previously taught high-frequency words and lesson vocabulary.

Day 1 Check Word Reading
▶**Day 2** Check Lesson Vocabulary/High-Frequency Words
Day 3 Check Retelling
Day 4 Check Fluency
Day 5 Assess Progress

Word Reading

SUCCESS PREDICTOR

Words to Know

| station |
| quickly |
| tightly |
| masks |
| burning |
| building |
| roar |

Remember

Try the strategy. Then, if you need more help, use your glossary or a dictionary.

Vocabulary Strategy
for Suffixes

Word Structure Sometimes when you are reading, you may come across a word you don't know. Look closely at the word. Does it have *-ly* at the end? When the suffix *-ly* is added to a word, it usually makes the word mean "in a ___ way." For example, *kindly* means "in a kind way." Use the *-ly* suffix to help you figure out the meaning of the word.

1. Put your finger over the *-ly* suffix.

2. Look at the base word. Put the base word in the phrase "in a ___ way."

3. Try that meaning in the sentence. Does it make sense?

Read "A Trip to the Fire Station." Look for words that end with *-ly*. Use the suffix to help you figure out the meanings of the words.

A Trip to the Fire Station

Carlos is a firefighter. Some children are at his fire station for a tour. He points out where the firefighters sleep and eat. Carlos slides down the fire pole. "That is how we quickly get from our beds to the trucks," he says.

"We use hoses to spray water on a fire," he says. "Fire hoses can be very heavy when they are filled with water. We have to grip the hoses tightly."

"Fires give off a lot of smoke," Carlos tells the children. "We must wear air tanks and masks if we go into a fire. We use masks to breathe clean air."

Carlos shows the children his thick clothes, heavy boots, and hard helmet. "These keep me safe from the things that can fall from or in a burning building."

Suddenly, the fire alarm goes off! Carlos tells the children good-bye. He puts on his gear and climbs onto the fire truck. With a loud roar, the fire truck races off.

Words to Write

What might happen to Carlos next? Write more of the story. Use words from the Words to Know list.

156

157

OBJECTIVE

◉ Use word structure (suffix *-ly*) to determine the meaning of unfamiliar words.

ELL

Access Content Use ELL Poster 21 to preteach the lesson vocabulary. Reinforce the words with the vocabulary activities and word cards in the ELL Teaching Guide, pp. 143–144. Choose from the following to meet children's language proficiency levels.

Beginning Use the list of Multilingual Lesson Vocabulary in the ELL Teaching Guide, pp. 272–283, and other home-language resources to provide translations of the tested words.

Intermediate Return to the Word Meaning chart from the Introduce Vocabulary page. Have children add information they have learned.

Advanced Have children determine whether lesson vocabulary words have cognates in their home languages.

Vocabulary Strategy

TEACH/MODEL Word Structure

CONNECT Remind children of strategies to use when they come across words they don't understand.

- Sometimes we can figure out a word's meaning from word parts. We may understand the two shorter words in a compound (*snowman, a man made of snow*), or we can check to see if *-s, -ed,* or *-ing* have been added to a verb to change the tense.

- We can look in a dictionary or glossary.

- We can look for the suffixes in the unknown word. Today we will learn more about using the suffix *-ly*.

INTRODUCE THE STRATEGY

- Read and discuss the steps for using word structure on p. 156.
- Have children read "A Trip to the Fire Station," paying attention to words that end with -ly.
- Ask children if those words have base words they know. Then ask how the added ending changes the meaning of the word.
- Model using word structure -ly to determine the meaning of quickly.

> **Think Aloud**
>
> **MODEL** The word quickly has an -ly ending. If I cover the -ly, I see the word quick. By adding -ly, the word's meaning changes to "in a quick way." The sentence says, "That is how we quickly get from our beds to the trucks." It makes sense that firefighters get to the trucks in a quick way.

PRACTICE

- Have children find the highlighted words in "A Trip to the Fire Station" and explain how the -ly suffix helps them determine the words' meanings.
- Remind children they can cover the -ly suffix with their fingers to find the base word. If they don't know the base word, they can use the glossary or a dictionary, then put the base word in the phrase "in a _____ way."

WRITE Children's writing should include lesson vocabulary to tell what might happen to Carlos next.

CONNECT TO READING Encourage children to use these strategies to determine the meaning of an unknown word.

- Look for the suffix -ly in an unknown word. Put the base word in the phrase "in a _____ way."
- Use the glossary or a dictionary.

Group Time

DAY 2

ⓘ Independent Activities

Independent Reading See p. 154j for Reading/Library activities and suggestions.

Journal Writing Write about a time when you have seen firefighters at work. Share writing.

Literacy Centers To provide experiences with Firefighter!, you may use the Listening and Writing Centers on pp. 154j and 154k.

Practice Book 2.2 Main Idea, p. 55; Lesson Vocabulary, p. 56; Author's Purpose, p. 57

Break into small groups after Vocabulary and before Writing.

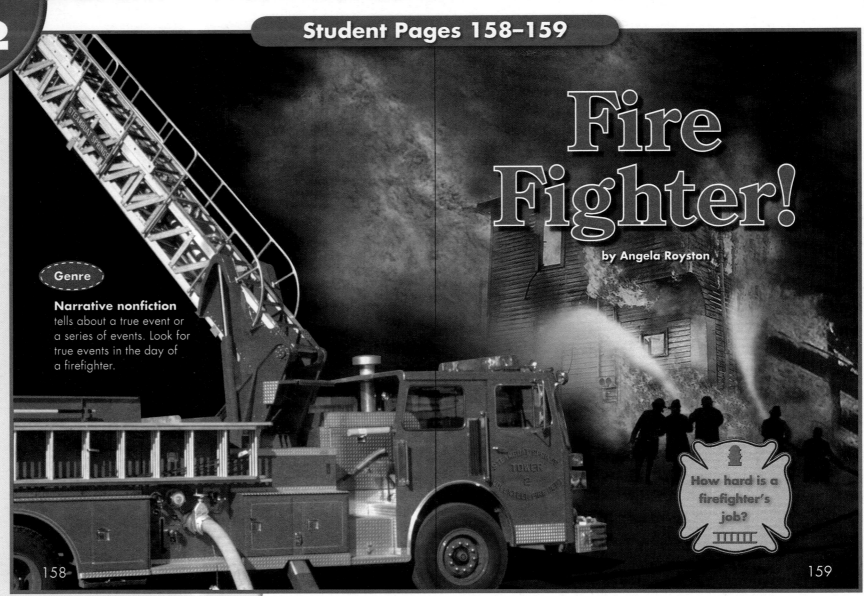

Genre

Narrative nonfiction
tells about a true event or
a series of events. Look for
true events in the day of
a firefighter.

Fire Fighter!
by Angela Royston

How hard is a firefighter's job?

158   159

AudioText

Read
Prereading Strategies

PREVIEW AND PREDICT Have children read the title. Make sure children recognize that the people in the photographs are firefighters. Identify the author. Have children preview the selection by studying the photographs and discuss what the selection may be about.

DISCUSS NARRATIVE NONFICTION Ask children if they think this true selection is about real firefighters. Help children understand that the selection tells about what real firefighters do. Remind children that selections that give facts about a topic are nonfiction. Read the definition of narrative nonfiction on p. 158 of the Student Edition.

SET PURPOSE Read the question on p. 159. Ask children what they would like to find out about firefighters and their jobs when they read the selection.

ELL

Access Content Before reading, review the story summary in English and/or the home language. See the ELL Teaching Guide, pp. 145–147.

____ Suffixes -ly, -ful, -er, -or   ☐ lesson/tested vocabulary

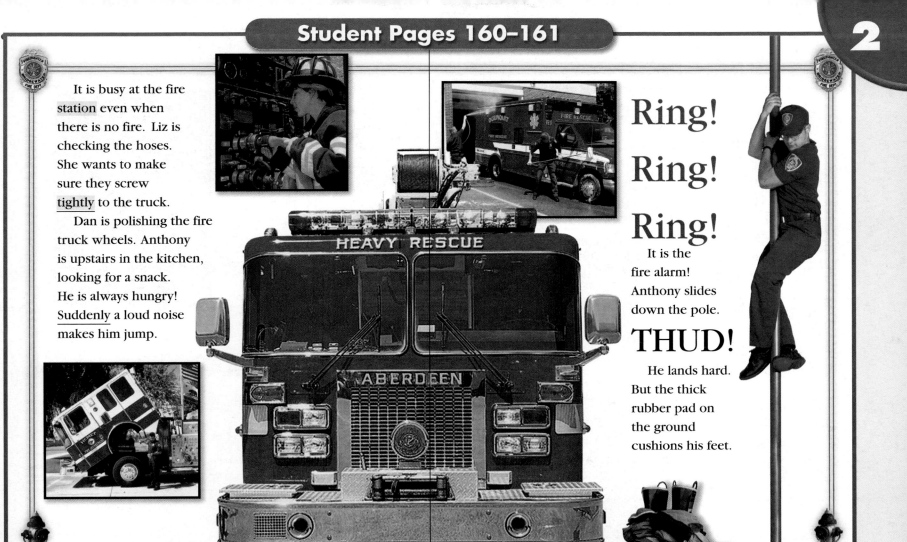

It is busy at the fire station even when there is no fire. Liz is checking the hoses. She wants to make sure they screw tightly to the truck.

Dan is polishing the fire truck wheels. Anthony is upstairs in the kitchen, looking for a snack. He is always hungry! Suddenly a loud noise makes him jump.

HEAVY RESCUE

ABERDEEN

Ring!

Ring!

Ring!

It is the fire alarm! Anthony slides down the pole.

THUD!

He lands hard. But the thick rubber pad on the ground cushions his feet.

160

161

Skills in Context

⊙ MAIN IDEA

• **What is the most important idea on these pages? Where can we find this main idea?**

The main idea is that a fire station is a busy place. The first sentence gives the main idea.

Monitor Progress	⊙ **Main Idea**
If... children are unable to identify the main idea,	**then...** model how to use the text and photographs to determine the main idea.

Think Aloud

MODEL This first sentence says that it is busy at the fire station. The other sentences and the photographs explain what everyone is doing; they tell more about the fire station being busy. The first sentence must be the main idea.

ASSESS Have children complete a Main Idea/Supporting Details Chart.

▲ **Pages 160–161**
Have children study the photographs and read to find out what happens at the fire station.

Monitor Progress	
Read New Words	
If... children come to a word they don't know,	**then...** remind them to: 1. Blend the word. 2. Decide if the word makes sense. 3. Look in a dictionary for more help.

Liz jumps into her boots and pulls up her fireproof pants. She checks the computer. It shows the fire is at 7 Oak Lane. In the truck Liz grabs the walkie-talkie. "Chief Miller! We're on our way!"

"Right!" says the fire chief.

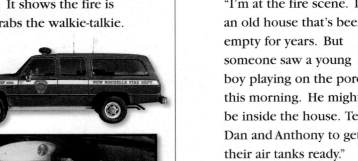

He has gone ahead in a special fast car. "I'll meet you there."

Liz starts the engine as the firefighters jump in. She flips on the sirens and lights and drives out of the fire house. The truck speeds toward the fire.

Cars and buses stop and wait when they hear the siren coming.

The fire chief calls Liz. "I'm at the fire scene. It's an old house that's been empty for years. But someone saw a young boy playing on the porch this morning. He might be inside the house. Tell Dan and Anthony to get their air tanks ready."

"Okay, Chief," says Liz. "I can see the smoke from here. We'll be there in two minutes."

162

163

▲ **Pages 162–163**
Have children read to find out what problem the firefighters might have at the fire scene.

Firefighting Tools

Time for SOCIAL STUDIES

Before the invention of firefighting tools such as fire hydrants and hoses, people transported water to fire scenes by forming lines and passing along buckets of water. They also used poles, hooks, and axes to chop and tear away parts of the burning building so the fire would not spread.

Guiding Comprehension

Draw Conclusions • Inferential

- *Text to World* **Why does Liz turn on the sirens and lights? What have you seen people do when they see a fire truck with sirens and lights on?**
  The sirens and lights warn cars that the fire truck is coming. People stop and wait for fire trucks to pass.

Draw Conclusions • Inferential

- **Why may Dan and Anthony need their air tanks?**
  They may have to go inside the house to find the boy.

Sequence • Literal

- **What does Liz do before she gets in the fire truck?**
  She puts on her boots and fireproof pants. She also calls Chief Miller to say that they are on their way.

_____ Suffixes *-ly, -ful, -er, -or*   ☐ lesson/tested vocabulary

Liz turns the corner into Oak Lane. Flames cover the top of the house.

The fire is spreading quickly. There's no time to lose! Liz hooks a hose from the truck to the nearest fire hydrant. A pump on the truck pulls water from the hydrant to another hose. Liz and another firefighter point the hose at the flames. "Ready!" calls Liz.

WHOOSH!

They hold on tight as the water shoots out. It comes out of a fire hose hard enough to knock a person down.

164

165

Guiding Comprehension

Make Judgments • Critical

• *Text to World* Drivers are not allowed to park their cars in front of fire hydrants. Do you think this is a good idea? Why or why not?

Possible response: It is a good idea because a parked car would make it hard for firefighters to get to the hydrant.

Author's Purpose • Inferential

• *Question the Author* Why do you think the author wrote *WHOOSH* in big capital letters?

Possible response: to show that the water was coming out of the hose fast and hard.

Summarize • Inferential

• **What has happened in the selection so far?**

The fire alarm went off, and the firefighters hurried to the fire. They hooked the hose to a hydrant and then sprayed water on the fire.

▲ **Pages 164–165**
Have children read to find out what happens when the firefighters get to the fire.

Strategy Self-Check

Have children ask themselves these questions to check their reading.

Vocabulary Strategy

• Do I look for the suffix *-ly* in an unknown word?

• Do I look for antonyms near a difficult word?

• Do I use the glossary or a dictionary?

Text Structure

• Do I know how the selection is organized?

• Do I know the order in which things happen?

166

Anthony and Dan are ready to search the burning building. They have put on their air tanks and face masks. Each tank holds 40 minutes of air. That's not much time!

"The boy's name is Luke," the chief tells them.

"Right," says Anthony. He grabs a hose.

"Let's put the wet stuff on the red stuff!" says Dan.

Dan and Anthony run to the back of the house. The fire is not as bad here. Dan feels the back door. If it is hot, flames could leap out. "It's cold," says Dan. They step inside.

Thick black smoke is everywhere. Anthony shines his flashlight around. "Luke! Luke!" he calls. No one answers.

"I can hear fire upstairs," says Dan.

The fire has damaged the staircase. It could fall down at any time. They climb up the steps very slowly.

167

▲ **Pages 166–167**
Have children read to find out what the firefighters do inside the house.

Monitor Progress

Lesson Vocabulary

| **If**...children have a problem reading a new lesson vocabulary word, | **then**...use the Lesson Vocabulary Routine on p. 156f to reteach the problematic word. |

Economic Resources

Time for **SOCIAL STUDIES**

Community workers—such as firefighters, police officers, and doctors—serve the people of their communities. Have children discuss the ways these workers serve.

Strategies in Context

⊙ TEXT STRUCTURE

- **What are the steps Anthony and Dan take to search the house safely?**
  They put on air tanks and masks, grab the hose, feel the door to see if it is hot, shine the flashlight around, and slowly go up the steps.

Monitor Progress	**Text Structure**
If... children have difficulty recalling the sequence of events,	**then**... model how to determine what happens first, next, and so on.

Think Aloud **MODEL** First, I read that Anthony and Dan put on their air tanks and face masks. Next, Anthony grabbed the hose. As I read, I noticed that the author listed other things the firefighters did, in the order in which they did them.

ASSESS Provide children with a time line and have them list the steps Anthony and Dan take.

_____ Suffixes -ly, -ful, -er, -or ☐ lesson/tested vocabulary

Outside, the <u>outriggers</u> are set down on the ground. <u>Outriggers</u> are like legs. They keep the truck steady as the ladder is raised. The ladder goes up like a telescope to the top of the house. A hose runs up the side. The <u>firefighter</u> on the ladder shoots water down on the fire. The flames crackle and hiss. They get smaller, then <u>suddenly</u> jump even higher.

Inside the house, the fire rages. It is hot enough to melt glass. Anthony sprays water on the flames. Fire has made the house weak.

"It could come down any second," says Dan. "We must find Luke."

BOOM! A beam crashes down near them. But their helmets protect their heads. CRASH!

"Quick!" says Anthony. "We're running out of time."

They come to another door. But it will not open. Dan swings his ax at the door. Once. Twice. Three times. "It's jammed!" shouts Dan. The <u>roar</u> of the fire is so loud they can <u>hardly</u> hear. "We'll have to use the electric saw."

168

169

Skills in Context

REVIEW AUTHOR'S PURPOSE

- **Why do you think the author wrote this selection?**
  Children might say the author wrote this selection to explain how important the work is that a firefighter does.

Monitor Progress	**Author's Purpose**
If... children have difficulty understanding the author's purpose,	**then...** model how to discover the reason an author wrote a selection.

Think Aloud **MODEL** To find out the reason the author wrote this selection, I think about what the author wrote. This selection is full of facts about firefighters. I think the author wrote this selection to explain what firefighters do and how important their job is to the community.

ASSESS Ask children what they think the author thinks about firefighters.

▲ **Pages 168–169**
Have children look at the photograph and set their own purposes for reading.

Read the paragraph. **Follow** the directions.

Fire Safety
by Liz Stone

One way to fight fires is with fire safety. Firefighters sometimes visit(schools)to talk to children. They show what to do if there is a fire. They teach how to keep fires from starting. They also remind people to use <u>smoke alarms</u>.

1. Write the author's name. __Liz Stone__

2. Circle the word below that tells what the paragraph is all about.
(safety)   smoke   school

3. Underline the name of something in the paragraph that firefighters want people to use.

4. Circle a word in the paragraph that tells where firefighters might talk to children.

5. Write a sentence that tells why you think the author wrote this paragraph.
__The author wrote it to tell the reader how firefighters teach fire safety.__

School + Home Home Activity Your child answered questions about nonfiction text and explained why the author wrote it. Write a list of fire safety rules for your home and family. Help your child read the rules. Ask your child to explain why you wrote these rules.

Practice Book Unit 5   **Comprehension** Author's Purpose Review **57**

▲ **Practice Book 2.2** p. 57,
Author's Purpose

Firefighter! **168–169**

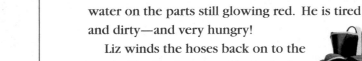

Anthony switches on the saw. WHRRR! He cuts a hole in the door big enough to climb through.

"Luke!" calls Dan. "Luke?" But the room is empty.

<u>Suddenly</u> the chief calls. "Get out now! The roof is coming down!"

Dan and Anthony race downstairs. They get out just as the roof falls in. "We didn't find Luke!" yells Dan.

"He's okay," says the chief. "We just found him up the block."

"Whew!" says Dan. "Good news!"

Hours later the flames are out. Anthony sprays water on the parts still glowing red. He is tired and dirty—and very hungry!

Liz winds the hoses back on to the truck. <u>Finally</u> she rests. She is tired too. Back at the station Anthony sits down to eat. "At last!" he says.

<u>Suddenly</u> a loud noise makes him jump.

"Dinner will have to wait!" laughs Dan.

Ring! Ring! Ring!

Practice E.D.I.T.H.—Exit Drills in the Home

Do you know what to do if a fire starts in your home? Don't wait until it happens:

- Sit down with your family now.
- Talk about how you would get out of the house.
- Plan at least two ways out of every room.
- Decide where you will all meet once you get outside.

A fire drill now could save lives later!

170

171

▲ **Pages 170–171**
Have children read to find out what happens to the missing boy.

EXTEND SKILLS

Details

For instruction in identifying details, discuss the following:

- Details are small pieces of information that tell more about the main idea.
- Details help us picture and understand what we read.

Assess Have children identify other details that tell more about what firefighters do.

Access Content Help children understand that the word *winds* on p. 171 means "twists up," not "blowing air."

Guiding Comprehension

Main Idea • Inferential
- **What is the main idea of this selection?**
The selection is about what firefighters do when there is a fire.

Draw Conclusions • Inferential
- **Why does Dan say "Good news!"**
Dan was afraid that Luke was trapped in the house when the roof fell down. He is happy when he finds out that the boy is safe.

Prior Knowledge • Inferential
- *Text to World* **Have you ever seen firefighters working in your community? What were they doing that showed teamwork?**
Children might say they saw firefighters putting out a fire or helping at the scene of a car accident.

Fluency

REREAD FOR FLUENCY

Paired Reading

ROUTINE

1 **Reader 1 Begins** Children read the entire book, switching readers at the end of each page.

2 **Reader 2 Begins** Have partners reread; now the other partner begins.

3 **Reread** For optimal fluency, children should reread three or four times.

4 **Provide Feedback** Listen to children read and provide corrective feedback regarding their oral reading and their use of the blending strategy.

OBJECTIVES

- Write a poster.
- Identify pronouns.
- Use pronouns.

Strategic Intervention

Give children extra phonics support as they write, helping them sound out unfamiliar words.

Advanced

Have children who are able to write complete sentences independently write their own persuasive poster about other community heroes.

Support Writing Before children begin writing, reread the class poster. Point out important words, such as *save* or *fire*, that children might want to use in their own writing.

Beginning Provide children with a word bank drawn from the word web responses to help them in their writing.

Intermediate Have small groups of children discuss ideas for their writing. Suggest that they take notes and use the notes as they write.

Advanced Review children's writing. Point out places where they can add more details or where they are not using conventional English.

Support Grammar Ask children if they can write anyone's name in their home languages. Use examples to show that, in English and some other languages, people names begin with capital letters. See the Grammar Transition lessons in the ELL and Transition Handbook.

Interactive Writing

WRITE Poster

MAKE A WEB Use the selections "A Trip to the Fire Station" and *Firefighter!* to encourage a discussion about firefighters. Ask students to describe the work firefighters do. Use their responses to create a web on the board.

SHARE THE PEN Have children participate in writing a persuasive poster. The poster will focus on why firefighters are community heroes. First, have a volunteer make a statement about firefighters. Have the class repeat it. As you write the statement on the board, invite children to write familiar letter-sounds, word parts, and high-frequency words. Ask questions such as:

- What is the first sound you hear in the word *quickly*? (/kw/)
- What letters stand for that sound? *(qu)* Have a volunteer write *qu.*
- What is the second sound you hear in the word *quickly*? (/i/)
- What letter stands for that sound? *(i)*

Continue to have individuals make contributions. Frequently reread what has been written while tracking the print.

READ THE POSTER Read the completed poster aloud, having children echo you.

Firefighters Are Heroes

Firefighters put out fires quickly.

They save the lives of people and animals.

They have to work very hard.

Firefighters are heroes in our community.

INDEPENDENT WRITING

WRITE A POSTER Have children write their own poster about firefighters. Let children illustrate their writing.

Grammar

DEVELOP THE CONCEPT Pronouns

IDENTIFY PRONOUNS Write *Mary* and *she* on the board. Point to each word as you read it. Ask children to identify the pronoun. *(she)* Continue with *he* and *David.*

A pronoun is a word that takes the place of a noun or nouns. Why might you want to use a pronoun instead of a noun? (You might not want to keep repeating the noun.)

PRACTICE

CHOOSE PRONOUNS Display pictures of people shopping, gardening, or doing other activities. Model using nouns and pronouns.

MODEL This is Mrs. Potter. The name *Mrs. Potter* is a noun. **Write** *Mrs. Potter.* Mrs. Potter is shopping. Mrs. Potter wants to buy some oranges. If I don't want to say *Mrs. Potter* over and over, I can also say *She is shopping.* **Write** *She. She* is a pronoun. It takes the place of the noun *Mrs. Potter.*

As you show children the other pictures, give names to the people in the pictures. Have children use pronouns to tell what the people are doing. You might also identify some objects in the pictures and have children use pronouns as they describe the objects.

DAILY FIX-IT

3. The cherful boy worked quicklie.
The <u>cherful</u> boy worked <u>quickly</u>.

4. where is the fire!
<u>W</u>here is the fire<u>?</u>

Pronouns

A **pronoun** is a word that takes the place of a noun or nouns. The words **he, she, it, we, you,** and **they** are pronouns.

Carlos is a vet. **He** helps animals. **He** takes the place of the noun **Carlos.**

Keesha and Paul are zookeepers. **They** also help animals. **They** takes the place of the nouns **Keesha** and **Paul.**

Write the pronoun that can take the place of the underlined word or words. **Use** *he, she, it, we,* or *they.*

1. <u>Len Smith</u> has a sick dog. — **He**
2. <u>Len and I</u> will take the pet to the vet. — **We**
3. <u>People</u> are waiting for the doctor. — **They**
4. <u>Gina Jones</u> helps the vet. — **She**
5. "Put <u>the dog</u> on the table," said Gina. — **it**
6. <u>Carlos Lopez</u> helped the dog. — **He**

▲ **Grammar and Writing Practice Book** p. 81

Wrap Up Your Day!

 LESSON VOCABULARY Write the following sentences. *I walk quickly past the store. I hold my umbrella tightly.* Ask children to read the sentences and identify the words with suffixes. *(quickly, tightly)* Write sentences for the other vocabulary words. Have children identify each word.

 TEXT STRUCTURE To help children recognize text structure, say: Think about all the things that happen in "A Trip to the Fire Station." **Ask:** How did the author tell the story? (in the order in which things happened)

LET'S TALK ABOUT IT Recall *Animal Hospital.* Have children discuss the best and worst things about being a vet.

PREVIEW Day 3

Tell children that tomorrow they will hear about two boys and the animals they help.

Day 3
AT A GLANCE

Materials

- *Sing with Me Big Book*
- Big Book *Animal Hospital*
- Graphic Organizer 27
- Student Edition 172–173

Morning Warm-Up!

Today we will read about an animal doctor. Animal doctors are responsible. They work hard to help our community. They use teamwork to do a good job. What else do they use to do their job?

QUESTION OF THE DAY Encourage children to sing "The Firefighting Team" from the *Sing with Me Big Book* as you gather. Write and read the message and discuss the question.

REVIEW ORAL VOCABULARY

- Read the message again. Ask children to raise their hand if they hear any of the Amazing Words they have learned in the past two days. *(responsible, community, teamwork)*

- Ask volunteers to say one of the Amazing Words and tell you what it means.

ELL

Build Background Use the Day 3 instruction on ELL Poster 21 to support children's use of English to communicate about lesson concepts.

ELL Poster 21

Share Literature

LISTEN AND RESPOND

USE ILLUSTRATIONS AS A FIX-UP STRATEGY Recall what *Animal Hospital* is about. Ask children to look at the picture on p. 16. Explain that pictures can help readers understand hard words in a story. Ask children what hard word is explained by the picture of Dr. Corby and the cat on p. 16. *(stethoscope)*

BUILD ORAL VOCABULARY Review that yesterday the class read to find out what operation the vet does. Introduce the Amazing Word **instrument** and explain that it is a tool used to do an operation. Ask that children listen today to find out what instruments Dr. Corby uses to do her job.

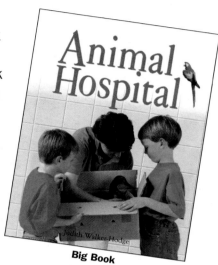

Big Book

MONITOR LISTENING COMPREHENSION

• What instrument did Dr. Corby use to check each kitten's heart and lungs?
(a stethoscope)

• What instrument did she use to clip the rabbit's teeth? (a pair of special scissors)

• What other things help the vet do her job? (X-rays, shots, bandages, Andrew the nurse)

• Why do you think Dr. Corby and Andrew work in an animal hospital? (Possible response: They work in an animal hospital because they love animals and want to help them get better.)

OBJECTIVES

● Use illustrations as a fix-up strategy.
● Set purpose for listening.
● Build oral vocabulary.

Amazing Words to build oral vocabulary

	MONITOR PROGRESS
community responsible teamwork operation instrument caretaker lug supplies	**If...** children lack oral vocabulary experiences about the concept Responsibility, **then...** use the Oral Vocabulary Routine. See p. DI·3 to teach *instrument*.

ELL

Listen and Respond Help children understand some of the verbs in *Animal Hospital*. Discuss the meaning of verbs *rushed, listened, waddling, quacking, nodded,* and *scrubbed.* Then, as you call out each word, have children act it out to show their understanding.

Review Phonics

3

OBJECTIVES

- Review vowels *oo, ue, ew,* and *ui.*
- Blend, read, and sort *oo, ue, ew, ui* words.
- Recognize lesson vocabulary.
- Spell words with suffixes *-ly, -ful, -er, -or.*

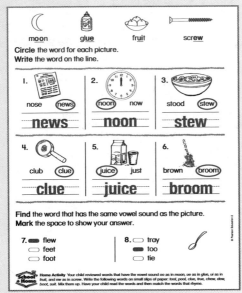

▲ **Practice Book 2** p. 58,
Vowel Patterns *oo, ue, ew, ui*

REVIEW **VOWEL PATTERNS *oo, ue, ew, ui***

READ *oo, ue, ew, ui* WORDS Write *spoon, clue, new,* and *suit.* Look at these words. You can read these words because you know how to read words that have the sound /ü/. What sound do *oo, ue, ew,* and *ui* stand for in these words? (/ü/) What are the words?

SORT WORDS Write the words below in random order. Then write *oo, ue, ew,* and *ui* as headings for a four-column chart or use Graphic Organizer 27. Have children read each word and write it under the appropriate heading.

oo	*ue*	*ew*	*ui*
spoon	due	flew	cruise
cool	true	drew	fruit
shampoo	blue	threw	juice

Lesson Vocabulary

PRACTICE

IDENTIFY MEANING Write lesson vocabulary on the board. Ask children to answer questions by reading and using the lesson vocabulary words.

• Which word is a place where firefighters live and work? **(station)**

• Which word is something that has been built? **(building)**

• Which word is a kind of loud noise? **(roar)**

• Which word is something that covers a face? **(mask)**

• Which word means moving in a fast way? **(quickly)**

• Which word means fitting closely? **(tightly)**

• Which word describes something that is on fire? **(burning)**

Spelling

PRACTICE Suffixes *-ly, -ful, -er, -or*

UNSCRAMBLE SENTENCES Have children practice by writing and unscrambling sentences that use spelling words.

• Have children write sentence strips that use spelling words. Ask children to cut the sentences apart and put the words for each sentence in envelopes.

• Ask children to trade envelopes and unscramble the sentences.

HOMEWORK Spelling Practice Book, p. 83

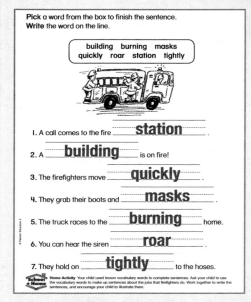

Pick a word from the box to finish the sentence. **Write** the word on the line.

> building   burning   masks
> quickly   roar   station   tightly

1. A call comes to the fire _____ **station** _____.
2. A _____ **building** _____ is on fire!
3. The firefighters move _____ **quickly** _____.
4. They grab their boots and _____ **masks** _____.
5. The truck races to the _____ **burning** _____ home.
6. You can hear the siren _____ **roar** _____.
7. They hold on _____ **tightly** _____ to the hoses.

Home Activity Your child used lesson vocabulary words to complete sentences. Ask your child to use the vocabulary words to make up sentences about the jobs that firefighters do. Work together to write the sentences, and encourage your child to illustrate them.

▲ **Practice Book 2.2** p. 59, Lesson Vocabulary

Spelling Words

Suffixes *-ly, -ful, -er, -or*

1.	cheerful	7.	hardly*
2.	visitor	8.	graceful
3.	slowly*	9.	yearly
4.	weekly	10.	quickly*
5.	teacher	11.	fighter*
6.	helper	12.	sailor

Challenge Words

13. gardener
14. competitor
15. extremely

* **Words from the Selection**

Suffixes *-ly, -ful, -er, -or*

Spelling Words					
cheerful	visitor	slowly	weekly	teacher	helper
hardly	graceful	yearly	quickly	fighter	sailor

Read about Tracy's job. **Circle** three spelling mistakes. **Write** the words correctly. Then write the last sentence using correct grammar.

Frequently Misspelled Words
beautiful
through

> I am the music (helpar) We have music class weekly. I help the (teecher) pass out song sheets and instruments. I put things away when we are (threw) I works quickly.

1. **helper**   2. **teacher**   3. **through**
4. **I work quickly.**

Circle the word that is spelled correctly.

5. I can get ready _____.   (quickly)   quickle
6. Who was your _____?   visiter   (visitor)
7. The _____ cleaned the deck.   (sailor)   sailer
8. It _____ ever snows there.   (hardly)   hardlie
9. We saw a _____ plane.   fightor   (fighter)
10. This is a _____ room.   cheerfull   (cheerful)

Home Activity Ask your child to name the three words they find the most difficult. Have your child divide each word and spell the base word and the suffix separately.

▲ **Spelling Practice Book** p. 83

Firefighter!   **172d**

Vocabulary

SUFFIX -ly

DISCUSS THE SUFFIX -ly Have children recall p. 160, when Anthony was looking for a snack. Point to the following sentence: "Suddenly a loud noise makes him jump." If I look at the word *suddenly,* I see the root word *sudden,* and the suffix -ly. Knowing the parts of a word helps me figure out what the word means. I know that *sudden* means "unexpected." The suffix -ly means "in a certain way." Knowing the root word and the suffix, I can figure out that the loud noise happened unexpectedly.

EXPAND SELECTION VOCABULARY Help children find sentences that contain words with the suffix -ly in the reading. They should find the words *tightly* (p. 160) and *quickly* (p. 164). Discuss what those words mean. Then have them find sentences that have the words *tight* (p. 164) and *quick* (p. 168). Challenge volunteers to rewrite the sentences, adding -ly to the words *tight* and *quick.*

Strategic Intervention

Ask children to write their own sentences using *quickly* and *tightly.* Have them illustrate their sentences.

Advanced

Have children scan the reading for root words to which they can add the suffix -ly. Have them write sentences using those words. Have volunteers share their sentences.

ELL

Extend Language Help children see how they can add the suffix -ly to the end of words. Write the words *tightly* and *quickly* on the board. Have volunteers come to the board to erase the -ly from each word. Ask other volunteers to come to the board to add the suffix back again.

Group Time

DAY 3

On-Level	Strategic Intervention	Advanced
Read *Firefighter!*	**Read** or listen to *Firefighter!*	**Read** Self-Selected Reading.
• Use pp. 158–173.	• Use the Routine on p. DI·18.	• Use the Routine on p. DI·19.

 ELL Place English language learners in the groups that correspond to their reading abilities in English.

(i) Independent Activities

Independent Reading See p. 154j for Reading/Library activities and suggestions.

Journal Writing Write about a job you would like to have and the responsibilities necessary for people who have it. Share writing.

Literacy Centers To provide experiences with *Firefighter!,* you may use the Writing Center on p. 154k.

Practice Book 2.2 Vowel Patterns, p. 58; Lesson Vocabulary, p. 59

Break into small groups after Vocabulary and before Writing.

Fluency

READ SILENTLY WITH FLUENCY/ACCURACY

MODEL READING SILENTLY WITH FLUENCY AND ACCURACY Use *Firefighter!*

- Point to the big, bold words with exclamation points on p. 161. There is a lot of action in this story. It would be easy for me to read fast. But when I read fast, I make mistakes. When I read, I want to make as few mistakes as possible. If I find that I am reading too fast, I will correct myself and make an effort to slow down.

- Ask children to follow along as you model how to read the page with fluency and accuracy and self-correct when reading.

- Have children read the page after you. Encourage them to read silently, self-correcting themselves when making mistakes. Continue in the same way with pp. 162–163.

REREAD FOR FLUENCY

Silent Reading

ROUTINE

1 **Select a Passage** For *Firefighter!,* use p. 167.

2 **Assign** Assign each child a short passage of text.

3 **Practice** Have children read their assigned passage 3–5 times silently.

4 **Independent Readings** Have children read aloud to you. Monitor progress and provide feedback. For optimal fluency, children should read at an appropriate pace.

Monitor Progress	**Fluency**
If... children have difficulty reading with appropriate phrasing,	**then...** prompt: • Are there exclamation marks? • Is there a lot of action? • Try to slow down and read as if you are speaking.
If... the class cannot read fluently without you,	**then...** continue to have them read along with you.

Options for Oral Reading

Use *Firefighter!* or one of the following Leveled Readers.

On-Level

Who Can Help?

Strategic Intervention

Community Helpers

Advanced

Goods and Services

E L L

Model reading "At the Fire Station" or *Firefighter!* with fluency and accuracy, self-correcting as you read. Have English language learners reread the passage several times at the same rate of speed.

 Fluency Coach CD To develop fluent readers, use Fluency Coach.

Reader Response

Retelling Plan

☑ **This week assess Strategic Intervention students.**

☐ Week 2 assess Advanced students.

☐ Week 3 assess Strategic Intervention students.

☐ Week 4 assess On-Level students.

☐ Week 5 assess any students you have not yet checked during this unit.

Look Back and Write

Point out information from the text that answers the question. Then have children write a response to the question. For test practice, assign a 10–15 minute time limit. For assessment, see the Scoring Rubric at the bottom of this page.

Assessment Allow children to listen to other retellings before attempting their own. For more ideas on assessing comprehension, see the ELL and Transition Handbook.

OPEN FOR DISCUSSION Model a response. I smell burning wood. I hear water whooshing out of the hose. I see the water putting out the flames of the fire.

1. RETELL Have children use the retelling strip in the Student Edition to retell the selection.

Monitor Progress | **Check Retelling** Rubric 4 3 2 1

Have children retell *Firefighter!*

If... children have difficulty retelling the story,

then... use the Retelling Cards and the Scoring Rubric for Retelling on pp. 172–173 to help them move toward fluent retelling.

SUCCESS PREDICTOR

| **Day 1** Check Word Reading | **Day 2** Check Lesson Vocabulary/High-Frequency Words | ▶ **Day 3 Check Retelling** | **Day 4** Check Fluency | **Day 5** Assess Progress |

2. **MAIN IDEA** Model a response. I'll look back at pages 162–163 and read that part of the selection again. The main idea is how the firefighters respond quickly to a fire. I think a good headline would be "Firefighters Act Quickly to Save Lives."

3. **TEXT STRUCTURE** Model a response. The order of events helped me understand everything that happens when firefighters fight a fire—what they do first, next, and so on.

 LOOK BACK AND WRITE Read the writing prompt on p. 172 and model your thinking. I'll look back through the selection and see what kinds of equipment the firefighters use. I'll look for at least ten things. Then I'll write my response. **Have children write their responses.**

Scoring Rubric | **Look Back and Write**

Top-Score Response A top-score response will use details from the selection to name ten pieces of equipment used by firefighters.

Example of a Top-Score Response

1. hoses	5. fireproof pants	8. fast car
2. truck	6. computer	9. sirens and lights
3. pole	7. walkie-talkie	10. fire hydrant
4. boots		

For additional rubrics, see p. WA10.

Reader Response

Open for Discussion Firefighter Dan says, "Let's put the wet stuff on the red stuff!" Pretend you are there. Tell everything you hear, smell, and see.

1. Use the photographs below to retell how the firefighters respond to a fire alarm. Retell

2. Reread pages 162–163. Write a headline that expresses the main idea on those pages. Main Idea

3. The author wrote about an actual fire. How did the order of events the author told about help you understand the information? Text Structure

Look Back and Write Firefighters need equipment—things to help them fight fires. Look through the story. Find at least ten pieces of equipment used by firefighters. Write them in a list.

Meet the Author

Angela Royston

Read two more books by Angela Royston.

Angela Royston writes books about all sorts of things. She has written about animals, plants, ships, trains, trucks, cars, and science. Royston was born in England and studied many different things at school. "I feel able to tackle almost any subject," she says. "I most like to work on books that are fun." She likes to read all she can about something before she writes about it.

Life Cycle of a Kangaroo

Strange Plants

Retelling Strip

172

173

Scoring Rubric — Expository Retelling

Rubric 4 3 2 1	4	3	2	1
Connections	Makes connections and generalizes beyond the text	Makes connections to other events, texts, or experiences	Makes a limited connection to another event, text, or experience	Makes no connection to another event, text, or experience
Author's Purpose	Elaborates on author's purpose	Tells author's purpose with some clarity	Makes some connection to author's purpose	Makes no connection to author's purpose
Topic	Describes the main topic	Identifies the main topic with some details early in retelling	Identifies the main topic	Retelling has no sense of story
Important Ideas	Gives accurate information about ideas using key vocabulary	Gives accurate information about ideas with some key vocabulary	Gives limited or inaccurate information about ideas	Gives no information about ideas
Conclusions	Draws conclusions and makes inferences to generalize beyond the text	Draws conclusions about the text	Is able to tell some learnings about the text	Is unable to draw conclusions or make inferences about the text

Use the Retelling Chart on p. TR21 to record retelling.

Selection Test To assess with *Firefighter!*, use Selection Tests, pp. 81–84.

Fresh Reads for Differentiated Test Practice For weekly leveled practice, use pp. 121–126.

Retelling

SUCCESS PREDICTOR

OBJECTIVE

● Recognize and use good word choice in writing.

DAILY FIX-IT

5. Fire Fighters use many tules.
   Firefighters use many tools.

6. They carries walkie-talkies
   They carry walkie-talkies.

Connect to Unit Writing

Writing Trait

Have students use strategies for developing **word choice** when they write a persuasive letter in the Unit Writing Workshop, pp. WA2–WA9.

Word Choice Pair an English learner with a proficient English speaker to discuss pictures in books or magazines. Have them list colorful words from the discussion to use in writing, such as *sticky, butterfly, smash, thunderstorm,* and *fluffy.*

Writing Trait of the Week

INTRODUCE Word Choice

TALK ABOUT WORD CHOICE Explain to children that they should choose words carefully to add style to their writing. Using exact nouns, strong verbs, and exciting adjectives will make their work clear and lively. Ask them to think about some words the author of *Firefighter!* uses to make the story lively and vivid. Then model your thinking.

Think Aloud **MODEL** *Firefighter!* tells what firefighters do. The article describes people's actions, so I think strong action words would make the story vivid. Let's find sentences on page 168 with strong action verbs.

The firefighter on the ladder shoots water down on the fire. The flames crackle and hiss. They get smaller, then suddenly jump even higher.

Which action verb in these sentences vividly describes the firefighter's actions? **(shoots)** Which words describe the sounds the fire makes? **(crackle, hiss)** What action verb is in the last sentence? **(jump)**

STRATEGY FOR DEVELOPING WORD CHOICE On the board, write sentences without verbs, such as those below. Then ask children to brainstorm several vivid action verbs to complete each sentence.

Firefighters _____ to the fire. (race, speed)

The trucks' sirens _____. (wail, howl)

Smoke _____ from a burning house. (billows, pours)

Part of the roof _____ to the ground. (crashes, falls)

PRACTICE

APPLY THE STRATEGY Ask children to brainstorm actions that firefighters do during a day. Have them suggest vivid verbs to describe the actions. *(scramble, slide, battle, rescue)* Then have children use several of the words to write a description of a firefighter's job.

Grammar

APPLY TO WRITING Pronouns

IMPROVE WRITING WITH PRONOUNS Write *Firefighters need equipment to fight fires. How do they use each piece of equipment?* Circle the word *they.* Explain that writers use pronouns instead of repeating the same noun many times. Add that using the same noun over and over can make sentences awkward or confusing. Remind children to use pronouns in their own writing.

Ask volunteers to read some types of equipment from their list. Work with children to create sentences, using pronouns, that describe how the equipment is used. Circle the pronouns.

It helps firefighters get water onto the fire. (hose)

They are very loud. They let people know there's a fire.
(sirens)

PRACTICE

WRITE WITH PRONOUNS Call on individuals to name kinds of equipment they use in their own lives. Then have volunteers write sentences that use pronouns and describe how they use a piece of equipment. Have other volunteers circle the pronouns.

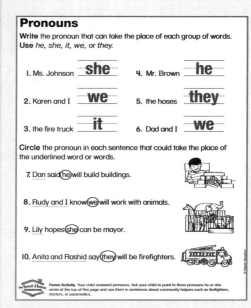

Pronouns

Write the pronoun that can take the place of each group of words. Use *he, she, it, we,* or *they.*

1. Ms. Johnson	**she**	4. Mr. Brown	**he**
2. Karen and I	**we**	5. the hoses	**they**
3. the fire truck	**it**	6. Dad and I	**we**

Circle the pronoun in each sentence that could take the place of the underlined word or words.

7. Dan said (he) will build buildings.

8. Rudy and I know (we) will work with animals.

9. Lily hopes (she) can be mayor.

10. Anita and Rashid say (they) will be firefighters.

Home Activity Your child reviewed pronouns. Ask your child to point to three pronouns he or she wrote at the top of this page and use them in sentences about community helpers such as firefighters, doctors, or paramedics.

▲ **Grammar and Writing Practice Book** p. 82

Wrap Up Your Day!

 MAIN IDEA Have children recall the main idea of *Firefighter!* (Firefighters work hard.) What details tell me more about the main idea?

 FLUENCY Have children practice reading sentences from *Firefighter!* silently.

LET'S TALK ABOUT IT Ask children to recall the search for Luke in *Firefighter!* Remind them that he was finally found down the street. Should the firefighters have tried so hard to find him in the house? Why or why not? (Yes, because they didn't know whether he was in there or not.) Have children discuss how the story relates to the week's question: Why is it important to do a good job?

PREVIEW Day 4

Tell children that tomorrow they will read about other kinds of work firefighters do.

Day 4

AT A GLANCE

Share Literature
"Ahmed, the Boab's Son"

Phonics and Spelling
Suffixes -ly, -ful, -er, -or

Read
 **Group Time** < Differentiated Instruction

"Firefighting Teamwork"

Fluency
Read Silently with Fluency and Accuracy

Writing Across the Curriculum
List

Grammar
Pronouns

Viewing and Speaking
Look for Main Idea

Materials

- *Sing with Me Big Book*
- *Read Aloud Anthology*
- Student Edition 174–177

Morning Warm~Up!

Today we will read about three firefighters. They work hard to clean the fire station. They work together to do a good job. What jobs do you have at home?

QUESTION OF THE DAY Encourage children to sing "The Firefighting Team" from the *Sing with Me Big Book* as you gather. Write and read the message and discuss the question.

REVIEW PRONOUNS

- Ask children how many pronouns they see in the message. Have them hold up that many fingers. *(four: we, they, they, you)*
- Ask children to tell you which pronoun refers to the firefighters and which pronoun refers to the class. *(they, we)*

Extend Language Use the Day 4 instruction on ELL Poster 21 to extend and enrich language.

ELL Poster 21

Share Literature

CONNECT CONCEPTS

ACTIVATE PRIOR KNOWLEDGE Recall Dr. Corby and the firefighters and what a good job they do. Explain that you will read another story about someone who does a good job—"Ahmed, the Boab's Son" by Andy Entwistle.

BUILD ORAL VOCABULARY Introduce the Amazing Words **caretaker, lug,** and **supplies.** Tell the class that if someone lugged something, they pulled something heavy, and that supplies are things needed to do a job. Explain that a boab is the same as a caretaker: they both are people who take care of a building. Ask children to listen to find out more about what a caretaker might do.

Read Aloud Anthology
Ahmed, the Boab's Son

REVIEW ORAL VOCABULARY After reading, review all the Amazing Words for the week. Have children take turns using them in sentences that tell about the concept for the week. Then talk about Amazing Words they learned in other weeks and connect them to the concept, as well. For example, ask:

- Have you ever been in a **situation** when you had to **assist** a friend or family member with a **project?** How did you help?

- What sorts of chores do you perform that **contribute** to the household?

- How do you feel after you have **accomplished** a **tough** task?

MONITOR LISTENING COMPREHENSION

- Name two things a caretaker does for the people in his building. (washes the floors and washes the cars)

- Why do the cars need to be washed every day? (Every night dust blows into the city from the desert.)

- What did Ahmed do before he started washing the cars? (He got the cleaning supplies out and lugged them to the curb.)

- Do you think Ahmed will help his father again? Explain. (Possible responses: Yes, because now he knows how hard his father's job is; because now he knows that hard work earns money.)

to build oral vocabulary

	MONITOR PROGRESS
community responsible teamwork operation instrument caretaker lug supplies	**If...** children lack oral vocabulary experiences about the concept Responsibility, **then...** use the Oral Vocabulary Routine. See p. DI·3 to teach *caretaker, lug,* and *supplies.*

Connect Concepts Help children understand the process Ahmed goes through to wash the cars. Reread the last paragraph on p. 111 and the first paragraph on p. 112. Explain the words *pail, hose,* and *sponge.* Show children the motions of "back and forth, up and down." Have them imitate moving a sponge back and forth and up and down across a wall or tall object in the room.

Spiral REVIEW

- Reviews high-frequency words *break, family, heard, listen, once, pull.*
- Reviews vowel diphthongs *oi, oy* /oi/ and *ou, ow* /ou/.

Sentence Reading

REVIEW WORDS IN CONTEXT

READ DECODABLE AND HIGH-FREQUENCY WORDS IN CONTEXT Write these sentences. Call on individuals to read a sentence. Then randomly point to words and have children read them. To help you monitor word reading, high-frequency words are underlined and decodable words are circled.

I (enjoy) how (peaceful) it is when I am with my <u>family</u> (around) the (house.)

<u>Once</u> Uncle (Howard) was (employed) as an (inspector) at an (oil) company.

Watch the (gardener) (slowly) <u>pull</u> the weeds (out) of the (soil.)

I like to <u>listen</u> to the (sounds) and (noises) of the sea on this (wonderful) (voyage.)

I <u>heard</u> the (loud) (voices) of the (singers) and (actors.)

(Now) you must <u>break</u> the (oyster) shells in half and (broil) them.

Monitor Progress	Word Reading
If... children are unable to read an underlined word,	**then**... read the word for them and spell it, having them echo you.
If... children are unable to read a circled word,	**then**... have them use the blending strategy they have learned for that word type.

Support Phonics For additional review, see the phonics activities in the ELL and Transition Handbook.

Spelling

PARTNER REVIEW Suffixes *-ly, -ful, -er, -or*

READ AND WRITE Supply pairs of children with index cards on which the spelling words have been written. Have one child read a word while the other writes it. Then have children switch roles. Have them use the cards to check their spelling.

HOMEWORK Spelling Practice Book, p. 84

Group Time

On-Level	Strategic Intervention	Advanced
Read "Firefighting Teamwork."	**Read** or listen to "Firefighting Teamwork."	**Read** "Firefighting Teamwork."
• Use pp. 174–177.	• Use the Routine on p. DI·20	• Use the Routine on p. DI·21.

 Place English language learners in the groups that correspond to their reading abilities in English.

ⓘ Independent Activities

Fluency Reading Pair children to reread *Firefighter!*

Journal Writing Write a paragraph telling why teamwork is important. Share writing. Spelling: Partner Review

Independent Reading See p. 154j for Reading/Library activities and suggestions.

Literacy Centers To provide listening opportunities, you may use the Listening Center on p. 154j. To extend social studies concepts, you may use the Social Studies Center on p. 154k.

Break into small groups after Spelling and before Fluency.

OBJECTIVE

● Spell words with suffixes *-ly, -ful, -er, -or.*

Spelling Words

Suffixes *-ly, -ful, -er, -or*

1.	cheerful	7.	hardly*
2.	visitor	8.	graceful
3.	slowly*	9.	yearly
4.	weekly	10.	quickly*
5.	teacher	11.	fighter*
6.	helper	12.	sailor

Challenge Words

13. **gardener**
14. **competitor**
15. **extremely**

* Words from the Selection

Suffixes *-ly, -ful, -er, -or*

Spelling Words					
cheerful	visitor	slowly	weekly	teacher	helper
hardly	graceful	yearly	quickly	fighter	sailor

Use the base word and the new suffix to write a list word.

1. Change **slower** to a word that ends with -ly — 1. **slowly**
2. Change **helpful** to a word that ends with -er. — 2. **helper**
3. Change **quickest** to a word that ends with -ly. — 3. **quickly**
4. Change **harder** to a word that ends with -ly. — 4. **hardly**
5. Change **sailing** to a word that ends in -or. — 5. **sailor**
6. Change **teaching** to a word that ends in -er. — 6. **teacher**

Write the list words in the box in ABC order.

7. **cheerful** 8. **fighter**
9. **graceful** 10. **visitor**
11. **weekly** 12. **yearly**

graceful
visitor
cheerful
yearly
fighter
weekly

Home Activity: Your child has been learning to spell words with the suffixes -ly, -ful, -er, and -or. Look through printed material to find other words with these suffixes.

▲ **Spelling Practice Book 2.2** p. 84

DAY 4

Drama in Reading

N°3 FIRE STATION N°3

FIRE FIGHTING TEAMWORK

a play by Connie Carpenter

Play

Genre
- A play is a story that is acted out.
- A play has characters who each have their own speaking parts.

Text Features
- A character's name appears before each speaking part.
- Directions to the actors sometimes appear in parentheses. These tell the actors how to move, where to go, or what to do.

Link to Reading
Use the library to find other plays to read. Choose one or two to read together as a Readers' Theater.

CHARACTERS:

Firefighter Kelly (FF KELLY)
Firefighter Sanchez (FF SANCHEZ)
Firefighter Johnson (FF JOHNSON)
Chief
Three or Four Council Members

Scene: A firehouse.
(One firefighter is sweeping. Another is washing dishes. Another is sleeping.)

FF KELLY: *(sweeping)* Boy, is this fire station dirty!

FF SANCHEZ: *(washing dishes)* Yeah, we all have to clean up the mud and dirt we tracked in. That last fire was a mess!

FF KELLY: I think Johnson worked really hard. He had to roll up that hose almost all by himself. That was hard work! He's probably upstairs taking a nap.
(Telephone rings.)

FF KELLY: *(stops sweeping)* I'll get that. *(picks up phone)* Firefighter Kelly here.

CHIEF: *(voice from off stage)* Firefighter Kelly, this is the Chief.

FF KELLY: Yes, Chief. What is it?

CHIEF: We're having an inspection by the city council today. Is everything in shape?

FF KELLY: It will be, Chief. With teamwork we should be able to get things in tip-top shape for the inspection.

CHIEF: Good! I'll bring the council right over.

FF KELLY: Right! Good-by, Chief! *(hangs up phone)* We've got big trouble!

Main Idea Sum up the main idea so far.

174   175

AudioText

Read
Drama in Reading

PREVIEW AND PREDICT Read the title and author's name. Have children preview the play and discuss the illustrations. Ask children to predict what this play will be mostly about. Have children read to find out what jobs the firefighters do.

PLAYS Review that a play is a story that is acted out. Plays have characters who speak. The text shows each character's speaking parts with the character's name in front of the words she or he will say.

VOCABULARY/SUFFIX -ly Remind children that the word part -ly can be added to the end of words to mean "in a ____ way." Have children locate *slowly* on p. 177. Take away the word part -ly. What is the word? What does *slowly* mean?

Teamwork

Time for **SOCIAL STUDIES**

Ask children to brainstorm a list of activities that firefighters do at the firehouse that require teamwork, for example, preparing meals and eating together. To help children start the list, ask them to think about tasks that would need to be done each day similar to those in a home.

Nº 3 FIRE STATION Nº 3

FF SANCHEZ: What? Is it a fire? an accident?

FF KELLY: No! The Chief is bringing over the city council for an inspection.

FF SANCHEZ: Uh-oh! We'd better hurry!

FF KELLY: What about our beds?

FF SANCHEZ: Johnson is up there. Do you think he made them?

FF KELLY: We'd better get up there and check! *(Both firefighters run up the stairs. Firefighter Johnson is lying on bed, snoring.)*

FF KELLY: *(looks at beds)* Just as I thought! Unmade!

FF SANCHEZ: Johnson, wake up!

FF JOHNSON: What? What is it? *(wakes up and rises)* What's happening?

FF SANCHEZ: *(begins making bed)* We have to hurry. The Chief is bringing the city council over for an inspection.

FF JOHNSON: Inspection! Oh, no! Let's get this place cleaned up. *(begins making bed)*

FF KELLY: I'll get the broom. This place needs sweeping. I'll use the pole. It's faster. *(slides down pole)*

Main Idea What main idea is the author trying to get across?

176

(Fire alarm rings.)

FF JOHNSON: The alarm!

FF SANCHEZ: This cleaning will have to wait. *(Firefighters slide down pole and put on their gear. Firefighter Sanchez checks fireboard for location of fire and turns off alarm.)*

FF SANCHEZ: There! I've turned off the alarm. The fire is at 422 East Jay Street. Let's go! *(Firefighters exit; fire truck siren slowly fades away.)* *(Chief and council members arrive.)*

CHIEF: *(looking around)* This place looks great! Kelly, Johnson, Sanchez? *(Chief looks at fireboard to find out where the firefighters have gone. He turns to council members.)* It looks like they've gone to another fire. Well, that's our fire department. They're hard workers, both in the fire station and in the community.

Reading Across Texts
Each selection told of certain jobs firefighters must do. What did you learn about the jobs? Which job do you think is most important?

Writing Across Texts
Write a brief paragraph to explain your answer.

177

BUILD CONCEPTS

Cause and Effect • Inferential

- **How does the council visit affect the firefighters?**
  The city council visit makes the firefighters work together to clean the fire station.

Main Idea/Supporting Details • Critical

- **Why is the last thing the Chief says a good ending for the play?**
  The sentence tells the main idea of the play—the firefighters are hard workers.

CONNECT TEXT TO TEXT

Help children make a list of jobs in each selection and compare the two. Encourage them to evaluate which job is more important and to give reasons for their choice.

Direct children to begin their paragraph by identifying the job they think is most important. Suggest that they use words such as *because* or *the reason why* to explain their choice.

Transportation

Pose questions about fire trucks, such as *Why are they red? Why do they have sirens? Ladders? Hoses?* To help answer the questions, remind children that firefighters often must travel through traffic to reach the fire, so fire trucks must be easy to see. They must warn people to get out of the way. The equipment is on the truck to help firefighters fight fires.

Activate Prior Knowledge Call attention to the phrase *city council*. Make sure children understand that a city council is a group of city leaders that work together.

OBJECTIVE
● Read silently with fluency and accuracy.

Options for Oral Reading

Use *Firefighter!*, "Firefighting Teamwork," or one of the following Leveled Readers.

On-Level

Who Can Help?

Strategic Intervention

Community Helpers

Advanced

Goods and Services

Read interesting sentences aloud to English language learners frequently, adding think-aloud comments to explain how cues such as letter patterns in words, phrases or other "chunks" of words, and punctuation can help you understand and read fluently.

To develop fluent readers, use Fluency Coach.

Fluency

READ SILENTLY WITH FLUENCY AND ACCURACY

MODEL READING WITH FLUENCY AND ACCURACY Use *Firefighter!*

• Direct children to p. 168. There are a lot of words on this page. When I read silently, I might make a few mistakes. It's important for me to self-correct myself as I read to make sure I understand what I'm reading.

• Ask children to follow along as you read the page with fluency and accuracy.

• Have children read the page silently after you. Encourage them to read carefully to avoid mistakes. Continue in the same way with pp. 168–171.

REREAD FOR FLUENCY

Readers' Theater

ROUTINE

1 **Select a Passage** For "Firefighting Teamwork," use pp. 175–177.

2 **Divide into Groups** Assign each group parts to read. For this play, the parts include Firefighters Kelly, Sanchez, and Johnson and the Chief.

3 **Model** Have children track the print as you read. Model reading with fluency and accuracy.

4 **Practice and Feedback** Have children read their parts along with you and independently. Monitor progress and provide feedback. For optimal fluency, children should read three to four times.

5 **Performance** Have the groups perform a Readers' Theater. Invite another group of children to attend the performance.

Monitor Progress | Check Fluency WCPM

As children reread, monitor their progress toward their individual fluency goals. Current Goal: 82–92 words correct per minute. End-of-Year Goal: 90 words correct per minute.

If... children cannot read fluently at a rate of 82–92 words correct per minute,

then... make sure children practice with text at their independent level. Provide additional fluency practice, pairing nonfluent readers with fluent readers.

If... children already read at 90 words correct per minute,

then... they do not need to reread three to four times.

SUCCESS PREDICTOR

Day 1 Check Word Reading	Day 2 Check Lesson Vocabulary/High-Frequency Words	Day 3 Check Retelling	▶ Day 4 Check Fluency	Day 5 Assess Progress

Writing Across the Curriculum

WRITE List

DISCUSS Have children discuss some of the ways the firefighters in *Firefighter!* and "Firefighting Teamwork" worked together as a team. Then have them discuss how they and their classmates might use teamwork in the classroom.

SHARE THE PEN Have children participate in creating a list of suggestions for teamwork in the classroom. Explain that creating a list can help them check to see if they are following good teamwork practices. First, work with children to create a title for the list. Then call on individuals to state a suggestion, based on the class discussion. Write the suggestion and number it, inviting individuals to help by writing familiar letter-sounds. Ask questions, such as the following:

- How do I start each sentence? (with a capital letter)
- How do I end each sentence? (with an end mark)
- Should I use any exclamation points? If so, when would I use them? (Children might suggest that exclamation marks should be used for very important items, such as items having to do with classroom safety.)

Continue having individuals contribute to the list. After writing each suggestion, have children read the suggestion aloud.

Teamwork in Our Classroom

1. **We should give everyone a chance to answer questions.**
2. **We should take turns caring for the class pet.**
3. **Everyone should help keep the classroom clean.**
4. **If you see a spill, tell the teacher!**

Words Correct Per Minute

SUCCESS PREDICTOR

Grammar

7. Bill and i went skating
   Bill and <u>I</u> went skating<u>.</u>

8. We am not very gracefull.
   We <u>are</u> not very graceful<u>.</u>

Pronouns

Mark the letter of the pronoun that can take the place of the underlined word or words.

1. What do <u>Carla and Denny</u> want to be?
   ○ A he
   ○ B she
   ⊗ C they

2. <u>Carla</u> wants to be a teacher.
   ○ A He
   ⊗ B She
   ○ C You

3. <u>Denny</u> wants to be a pilot.
   ⊗ A He
   ○ B She
   ○ C We

4. <u>The job</u> would be fun and exciting.
   ○ A You
   ⊗ B It
   ○ C They

5. <u>Juan and I</u> want to write books.
   ○ A You
   ○ B She
   ⊗ C We

6. <u>Paul, Beth, and Ryan</u> are not sure.
   ⊗ A They
   ○ B You
   ○ C He

 Home Activity Your child prepared for taking tests on pronouns. Ask your child to write sentences about one or more people and then to replace their names with the pronouns *he, she, it, we, you,* or *they.*

▲ **Grammar and Writing Practice Book** p. 83

REVIEW Pronouns

DEFINE PRONOUNS

- What word takes the place of a noun or nouns? (pronoun)
- What pronouns can you name? *(he, she, it, we, you, they)*

PRACTICE

IDENTIFY PRONOUNS Write the following sentences on the board. Have individuals underline the pronoun or pronouns in each sentence.

> Yesterday I ran in a long race.
> Then we all went out for pizza.
> It had lots of cheese and sauce.
> I think you would have liked this treat.

Viewing and Speaking

LOOK FOR MAIN IDEA

DEMONSTRATE VIEWING AND SPEAKING Explain to children that photographs, such as those that accompany news stories, can add to a reader's understanding of text. Point out that photographs, especially those taken on the scene of a news story, may contain details that aren't very important. When you look at photographs, ask yourself, "What is the most important thing the photographer wanted to tell me?" Look at the photo. Who or what is closest to the center of the photo? Which parts of the photo are clearest? Is there any action taking place? What is the setting in the photograph? Answering these questions can help you tell the main idea of a photograph. Then ask children to think about these questions as they look at photographs clipped from a newspaper.

CREATE CAPTIONS Have children come up with captions that tell the main idea of each photograph. Ask each child to orally present one caption to the class.

Firefighters battle a fire in a skyscraper.

Wrap Up Your Day!

✓ **MAKING CONNECTIONS: TEXT TO SELF** Write "Teamwork is important." Remind children that the firefighters they read about practiced good teamwork. Then ask them to recount their own experiences with teamwork and tell why it was important.

LET'S TALK ABOUT IT Use the text from "Firefighting Teamwork" as a springboard for a discussion of the week's question: "Why is it important to do a good job?" Ask students to recall the tasks the firefighters did in the play. Then ask children if they think it is important to do these tasks well. Have them explain their opinion.

PREVIEW Day 5

Tell children that tomorrow they will hear about a boy who does a good job.

Share Literature

"Ahmed, the Boab's Son"

Phonics and Spelling

 REVIEW Suffixes -ly, -ful, -er, -or

Lesson Vocabulary

station   building   roar   masks
quickly   tightly   burning
More Words to Know
fireproof   hydrant   outriggers

Monitor Progress

Spelling Test: Words with Suffixes

Group Time < Differentiated Assessment

Writing and Grammar

Trait: Word Choice
Pronouns

Research and Study Skills

Glossary: Word Meaning and Pronunciation Key

Materials

- *Sing with Me Big Book*
- *Read Aloud Anthology*
- Reproducible Pages TE 178f–178g
- Student Edition 178–179
- Graphic Organizer 14

Morning Warm~Up!

This week we read about responsible people in our community. To do a good job, they use teamwork, instruments, and supplies.
Why is it important to do a good job?

QUESTION OF THE DAY Encourage children to sing "The Firefighting Team" from the *Sing with Me Big Book* as you gather. Write and read the message and discuss the question.

REVIEW ORAL VOCABULARY Have children explain what *responsible*, *community*, and *teamwork* mean.

Then have children name

- the responsible people they read about this week (firefighters, vets, caretakers)

- the instruments or supplies these people use

ELL

Assess Vocabulary Use the Day 5 instruction on ELL Poster 21 to monitor children's progress with oral vocabulary.

ELL Poster 21

Share Literature

LISTEN AND RESPOND

USE PRIOR KNOWLEDGE Review that yesterday the class listened to "Ahmed, the Boab's Son" to find out more about what a caretaker does. Suggest that today the class listen to find out if Ahmed did a good job as a caretaker.

MONITOR LISTENING COMPREHENSION

- Did Ahmed finish washing all eight cars? (No, he only finished four cars.)

- Why did Mr. Naguib give Ahmed money? (Even though Ahmed didn't work as fast as his father, he did a good job and he tried hard.)

- What do you think is the main idea of this story? (Possible response: It's important to do a good job because people are counting on you.)

Read Aloud Anthology
Ahmed, the Boab's Son

BUILD ORAL VOCABULARY

GENERATE DISCUSSION Recall that, although Ahmed was not able to wash as many cars as his father, he worked hard and did the best he could. He was rewarded for his efforts. Ask children to discuss a time when they worked as hard as they could on a project and how they felt about doing the best they could. Have children use some of this week's Amazing Words as they share their stories.

Monitor Progress | Check Oral Vocabulary

Remind children of the unit concept—Responsibility. Ask them to tell you about the concept using some of this week's Amazing Words: *community, responsible, teamwork, operation, instrument, caretaker, lug,* and *supplies.*

If... children have difficulty using the Amazing Words,

then... ask more questions about the Read Aloud selection or the concept using the Amazing Words. Note which questions children can respond to. Reteach unknown words using the Oral Vocabulary Routine on p. DI·1.

SUCCESS PREDICTOR

Day 1 Check
Word Reading

Day 2 Check
Lesson Vocabulary
High-Frequency
Words

Day 3 Check
Retelling

Day 4 Check
Fluency

▶**Day 5** Check
Oral Vocabulary/
Assess Progress

Amazing Words to build oral vocabulary

community	instrument
responsible	caretaker
teamwork	lug
operation	supplies

Extend Language Write the following words: *silly, lily,* and *jolly.* Have children try to guess what word the ending *-ly* was added to. Tell them that the ending *-ly* is not always a suffix. Sometimes it is a part of the word. Challenge the class to think of other non-suffixed words that end in *-ly.*

Oral Vocabulary

SUCCESS PREDICTOR

OBJECTIVES

- Review words with suffixes *-ly, -ful, -er, -or.*
- Review lesson vocabulary.

Suffixes *-ly, -ful, -er, -or*

REVIEW

IDENTIFY WORDS WITH SUFFIXES *-ly, -ful, -er, -or* Write these sentences. Have children read each one aloud. Call on individuals to name and underline the words with suffixes and identify the base word and suffix in each.

The <u>actor</u> spoke his lines <u>quickly</u> and <u>quietly</u>.

My <u>teacher</u> said, "Today is a <u>wonderful</u> day!"

Mom was <u>cheerful</u> when her <u>supervisor</u> spoke <u>highly</u> of her.

The <u>painter</u> <u>gladly</u> moved the paint can away from the <u>lovely</u> rug.

Lesson Vocabulary

REVIEW

MEANING CLUES Read the following clues aloud. Have children write a review word from p. 156 for each clue. Then reread clues and answers.

This word means the opposite of slowly. **(quickly)**

This word means the opposite of loosely. **(tightly)**

This is the sound a lion makes. **(roar)**

This is a word that has to do with fire. **(burning)**

This place is a police or fire _____. **(station)**

This place has apartments in it. **(building)**

These are things you wear on your face at a costume party. **(masks)**

Vocabulary For additional practice with lesson vocabulary, use the vocabulary strategies and word cards in the ELL Teaching Guide, pp. 143–144.

SPELLING TEST Suffixes *-ly, -ful, -er, -or*

DICTATION SENTENCES Use these sentences to assess this week's spelling words.

1. We walked <u>slowly</u> down the steps.
2. I love to watch the <u>graceful</u> skaters.
3. Pete had a <u>visitor</u> come to his home.
4. I love our <u>yearly</u> trip to the beach.
5. My friend Rosa wants to be a <u>fighter</u> pilot.
6. The <u>sailor</u> wore a white hat.
7. The children were <u>cheerful</u> on their day off.
8. We like the <u>weekly</u> trip to the store with Mom.
9. We ran to the park as <u>quickly</u> as we could.
10. I <u>hardly</u> had time to do my homework.
11. My <u>teacher</u> will take our class to the zoo.
12. Mom said I am her good <u>helper</u>!

CHALLENGE WORDS

13. This is an <u>extremely</u> warm time of year.
14. Each <u>competitor</u> wore a number in the race.
15. The <u>gardener</u> planted the flowers.

ASSESS

● Spell words with suffixes *-ly, -ful, -er, -or.*

Spelling Words

Suffixes *-ly, -ful, -er, -or*

1. **cheerful**
2. **visitor**
3. **slowly***
4. **weekly**
5. **teacher**
6. **helper**
7. **hardly***
8. **graceful**
9. **yearly**
10. **quickly***
11. **fighter***
12. **sailor**

Challenge Words

13. **gardener**
14. **competitor**
15. **extremely**

* Words from the Selection

Group Time

On-Level

Read Set B Sentences.

● Use pp. 178e–178g.

Strategic Intervention

Read Set A Sentences.

● Use pp. 178e–178g.

● Use the Routine on p. DI·22.

Advanced

Read Set C Sentences and the Story.

● Use pp. 178e–178g.

● Use the Routine on p. DI·23.

DAY 5

 Place English language learners in the groups that correspond to their reading abilities in English.

(i) Independent Activities

Fluency Reading Children reread selections at their independent level.

Journal Writing Write about a responsible person in a community. Share writing.

Independent Reading See p. 154j for Reading/Library activities and suggestions.

Literacy Centers You may use the Technology Center on p. 154k to support this week's concepts and reading.

Practice Book 2.2 Glossary: Word Meaning and Pronunciation Key, p. 60

5

ASSESS

- ◉ Decode suffixes -ly, -ful, -er, -or.
- ● Read lesson vocabulary.
- ● Read aloud with appropriate speed and accuracy.
- ◉ Recognize main idea and supporting details.
- ● Retell a story.

Differentiated Assessment

On-Level
Set B

Strategic Intervention
Set A

Advanced
Set C

Fluency Assessment Plan

☑ **This week assess Advanced students.**

☐ Week 2 assess Strategic Intervention students.

☐ Week 3 assess On-Level students.

☐ Week 4 assess Strategic Intervention students.

☐ Week 5 assess any students you have not yet checked during this unit.

Set individual fluency goals for children to enable them to reach the end-of-year goal.

- Current Goal: 82–92 wcpm
- End-of-Year Goal: 90 wcpm
- **ELL** Oral fluency depends not only on reading without halting but also on word recognition. After children read passages aloud for assessment, help them recognize unfamiliar English words and their meanings. Focus on each child's progress.

SENTENCE READING

ASSESS SUFFIXES -ly, -ful, -er, -or AND LESSON VOCABULARY Use one of the reproducible lists on p. 178f to assess children's ability to read words with suffixes -ly, -ful, -er, -or and lesson vocabulary. Call on individuals to read two sentences aloud. Have each child in the group read different sentences. Start over with sentence one if necessary.

RECORD SCORES Use the Sentence Reading Chart for this unit on p. WA19.

Monitor Progress	Suffixes -ly, -ful, -er, -or
If… children have trouble reading suffixes,	**then…** use the Reteach Lessons on p. DI·64.
Lesson Vocabulary	
If… children cannot read a lesson vocabulary word,	**then…** mark the missed words on a lesson vocabulary list and send the list home for additional word reading practice or have the child practice with a fluent reader.

FLUENCY AND COMPREHENSION

ASSESS FLUENCY Take a one-minute sample of children's oral reading. See Monitoring Fluency, p. WA17. Have children read "Happy Campers at Bat," the on-level fluency passage on p. 178g.

RECORD SCORES Record the number of words read correctly in a minute on the child's Fluency Progress Chart.

ASSESS COMPREHENSION Have the child read to the end of the passage. (If the child had difficulty with the passage, you may read it aloud.) Ask what the main idea and supporting details are and have the child retell the passage. Use the Narrative Retelling Rubric on p. 202–203 to evaluate the child's retelling.

Monitor Progress	Fluency
If… a child does not achieve the fluency goal on the timed reading,	**then…** copy the passage and send it home with the child for additional fluency practice, or have the child practice with a fluent reader.
Main Idea and Supporting Details	
If… a child cannot recognize the main idea/supporting details,	**then…** use Reteach Lesson on p. DI·64.

READ THE SENTENCES

Set A

1. The bus driver slowly left the station.
2. The worker sadly looked at the burning building.
3. Face masks are helpful to firefighters.
4. The roar of thunder woke the campers nightly.
5. The hopeful sailor quickly jumped on the boat.
6. The graceful rider held tightly to the horse.

Set B

1. The deadly tiger's roar made the trainer fearful.
2. The cheerful actors wore funny masks backstage.
3. The ranchers made a brightly burning campfire.
4. The painters quickly finished the beautiful building.
5. The skillful player held on tightly to the football.
6. The ticket seller at the station was friendly.

Set C

1. The train conductor at the railroad station was helpful to us when we traveled through the terminal.
2. The batter held onto the bat tightly and was thankful to get a grand slam hit.
3. The singer quickly stopped the roar of the crowd as she began singing the words of a peaceful song.
4. Doctors and nurses wear masks so they don't spread harmful germs to their patients.
5. The candles were burning, and music was playing softly as the visitors ate dinner.
6. The window washers cleaned the filthy panes of glass on the buildings on a weekly basis.

© Pearson Education

Monitor Progress | Suffixes *-ly, -ful, -er, -or* Lesson Vocabulary

SUCCESS PREDICTOR

Happy Campers at Bat

The Happy Campers had a skillful baseball   7
team. Their trainer had trained them well. Emma   15
was the pitcher. She had a good arm for throwing.   25
The catcher was Megan. She was great at getting   34
runners out at home plate. The team gladly played   43
every day so they would be the best.   51

Today was the last game of the summer. If the   61
Happy Campers won, they would be champs.   68
Many visitors were there to watch. They cheered   76
loudly.   77

It was the last inning. There were two outs. The   87
pitcher threw a fastball. Megan bravely swung the   95
bat. She missed!   98

Megan sadly walked to the bench. She thought   106
her friends would be upset. But good friends are   115
helpful to each other. The players gathered   122
around her.   124

"It's all right," said Emma sweetly. "We know   132
you did the best you could. We are still hopeful.   142
Maybe next year we'll be the champs." Megan felt   151
better.   152

See also Assessment Handbook, p. 346 • REPRODUCIBLE PAGE

Monitor Progress   Fluency Passage

SUCCESS PREDICTOR

Write Now
Writing and Grammar

Report

Prompt

Firefighter! tells about an important community job.
Think about other jobs in your community.
Now write a report about one or more of those jobs.

Writing Trait

Precise **word choice** makes writing clear and interesting.

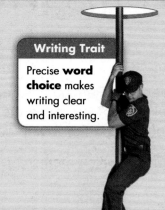

Student Model

Writer gives details about jobs.

Word choice includes strong verbs and exact nouns.

> Community workers are important helpers. Police officers are helpers. They protect people. Mail carriers are helpers. They deliver letters and packages. Teachers are helpers. They educate students. These workers help our community.

Ending restates main idea.

178

Writer's Checklist

- **Focus** Do sentences tell about one or more workers?
- **Organization** Is there a beginning, middle, and end?
- **Support** Do details describe what the workers do?
- **Conventions** Are pronouns used correctly?

Grammar

Pronouns

A **pronoun** is a word that takes the place of a noun or nouns. The words **he, she, it, we, you,** and **they** are pronouns.

Liz starts the engine. **She** flips on the sirens and lights.

She takes the place of the noun **Liz.**

. . . .

Look at the report. Write the pronouns. Write the nouns that the pronouns replace.

179

Writing and Grammar

LOOK AT THE PROMPT Read p. 178 aloud. Have children select and discuss key words or phrases in the prompt. *(other jobs in your community, report, one or more of those jobs)*

STRATEGIES TO DEVELOP WORD CHOICE Have children

- brainstorm community jobs and details about the jobs, using clear, interesting words.
- look at the nouns and verbs in their report and replace weak verbs with stronger verbs.
- eliminate wordiness by rewriting sentences that contain unnecessary words.

See Scoring Rubric on p. WA11. **Rubric 4 3 2 1**

HINTS FOR BETTER WRITING Read p. 179 aloud. Use the checklist to help children revise their reports. Discuss the grammar lesson. (Answers: *They,* police officers; *They,* mail carriers; *They,* teachers) Have children use pronouns correctly in their reports.

DAILY FIX-IT

9. Wee have weekly fire drils.
   We have weekly fire drills.

10. I thnk it is great idea.
    I think it is a great idea.

Pronouns

Write the pronoun that can take the place of each group of words. Use *he, she, it, we,* or *they.*

1. Ms. Johnson **she**	4. Mr. Brown **he**
2. Karen and I **we**	5. the hoses **they**
3. the fire truck **it**	6. Dad and I **we**

Circle the pronoun in each sentence that could take the place of the underlined word or words.

7. Dan said (he) will build buildings.

8. Rudy and I know (we) will work with animals.

9. Lily hopes (she) can be mayor.

10. Anita and Rashid say (they) will be firefighters.

Home Activity Your child reviewed pronouns. Ask your child to point to three pronouns he or she wrote at the top of this page and use them in sentences about community helpers such as firefighters, doctors, or paramedics.

▲ **Grammar and Writing Practice Book** p. 84

Firefighter! **178–179**

OBJECTIVE

- Use glossary: word meaning and pronunciation key.

Read the Glossary and **answer** the questions.

Glossary

able · button

Aa able (AY bul) If you have the power or skill to do something, you are **able.**
Tom was **able** to lift the heavy box. *ADJECTIVE*

add (ad) If you join one thing to another, you **add.**
Mom will **add** some apples to the bowl of oranges. *VERB*

Bb buried (BAIR eed) Something that is **buried** is hidden or covered up.
The dog **buried** the bone. *VERB*

button (BUT un) You use a round, flat object called a **button** on clothes to hold parts together.
Jodi lost a **button** on her skirt. *NOUN*

1. Which word is an adjective? __**able**__
2. Which word could describe a hidden treasure?
__**buried**__
3. Which word is a noun? __**button**__
4. Circle the one that has the same vowel sound in *able*.
a as in hat　(a as in age)　a as in far
5. Circle the one that matches the vowel sound in *button*.
(u as in cup)　u as in put　u as in huge

Home Activity Your child learned how to use a Glossary. Ask your child to read each word and its definition. Then have your child make up a sentence, using each word.

▲ **Practice Book 2.2** p. 60, Glossary

Access Content Explain to English language learners that a glossary is like a dictionary at the end of a book. Point out each part of the glossary and show how it is like a dictionary. Make sure that children understand and know how to use guide words, pronunciation keys, and the parts of an entry.

Research/Study Skills

TEACH/MODEL Glossary

MODEL USING A GLOSSARY Remind children that glossaries give information about words. Model how to determine the correct meaning of a word. Then explain what a pronunciation key is and demonstrate its use.

Model how to determine which meaning is correct.

Think Aloud

MODEL I can use the glossary to learn the meaning of the word *special* on p. 162: He has gone ahead in a special fast car. First, I use the guide words to find the entry. Then I see that *special* has more than one meaning. To figure out which is correct, I try each definition. The sentence *He has gone ahead in a TV show fast car* does not make sense. The other meaning does make sense: He has gone ahead in an unusual fast car. The pronunciation key helps me know how to pronounce *special*. The large letters tell me to say that part of the word with more force than the other part.

CHOOSE CORRECT MEANING Draw attention to this sentence near the end of p. 170: *We just found him up the block.* Read aloud the three definitions of block in the glossary. Ask individuals to try using each meaning in the sentence. Have them tell which meaning is correct and how they know this.

PRACTICE

DEMONSTRATE USING A GLOSSARY Have partners look in the glossary for entry words that have more than one meaning. Have them tell at least one meaning of the word and use it in a sentence.

Wrap Up Your Week!

LET'S TALK ABOUT Responsibility

QUESTION OF THE WEEK Recall this week's question.

• Why is it important to do a good job?

Display Graphic Organizer 14 or the web you drew earlier. Have children name several kinds of workers, such as store clerks, doctors, and carpenters. Have them then give one example of that worker doing a good job. For example, a store clerk might add up a bill correctly or help a customer find an item.

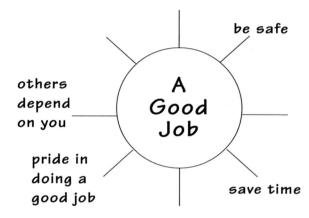

CONNECT Use questions such as these to prompt a discussion.

• Who in your community is responsible for keeping people safe? Why is teamwork so important to them?

• Why are supplies so important during an operation? Who do you think is responsible for supplying and cleaning these things?

• Which people in your community are caretakers? Which people in your home are caretakers?

ELL

Build Background Use ELL Poster 22 to support the Preview activity.

You've learned	You've learned
008 Amazing Words	**169** Amazing Words
this week!	so far this year!

PREVIEW Tell children that next week they will read about a boy who takes care of a stray cat that has a special reason to come in from a storm.

PREVIEW Next Week

Assessment Checkpoints *for the Week*

Selection Assessment

Use pp. 81–84 of Selection Tests to check:

 Selection Understanding

 Comprehension Skill *Main Idea and Details*

 Selection Vocabulary

building
burning
masks
quickly
roar
station
tightly

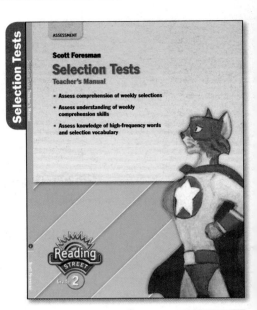

Leveled Assessment

Use pp. 121–126 of Fresh Reads for Differentiated Test Practice to check:

 Comprehension Skill *Main Idea and Details*

 REVIEW Comprehension Skill *Author's Purpose*

 Fluency *Words Correct Per Minute*

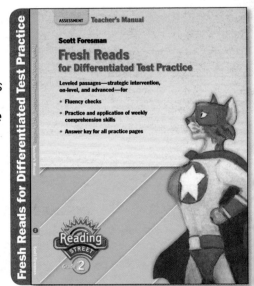

Managing Assessment

Use Assessment Handbook for:

 Weekly Assessment Blackline Masters for Monitoring Progress

 Observation Checklists

 Record-Keeping Forms

 Portfolio Assessment

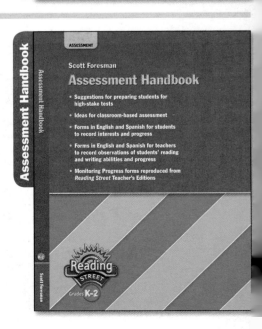

Illinois

Planning Guide for Performance Descriptors

One Dark Night

Reading Street Teacher's Edition pages	Grade 2 English Language Arts Performance Descriptors
Oral Language Build Concepts: 180l, 182a, 202a, 204a, 206a Share Literature: 180m, 182b, 202b, 204b, 206b	**1A.Stage B.4.** Use a variety of decoding strategies (e.g., phonics, word patterns, structural analysis, context clues) to recognize new words when reading age-appropriate material. **2B.Stage B.3.** Re-enact and retell selections (e.g., stories, songs, poems).
Word Work **Phonics** Prefixes *un-, re-, pre-, dis-*: 180n–180q, 182c–182d, 202c–202d, 204c–204d, 206c–206f **Spelling:** 180p, 182d, 202d, 204d, 206d	**1A.Stage B.2.** Use phonological awareness knowledge (e.g., isolate, blend, substitute, manipulate letter sounds) to identify phonetically regular one and two syllable words. **3A.Stage B.5.** Use correct spelling of high frequency words.
Reading **Comprehension** Sequence: 180r–181, 184–201a, 202g, 204–205, 206e Graphic Organizer: 180r–181, 184–201, 202g **Vocabulary** Context Clues: 182–183 Classify/Categorize: 202e, 204e, 206b **Fluency** Paired Reading: 180q, 201a Choral Reading: 202f, 205a **Self-Selected Reading:** LR10–18, TR16–17 **Literature** Genre—Realistic Fiction: 184–185 Reader Response: 202g–202h	**1A.Stage B.5.** Use letter-sound knowledge and sight vocabulary to read orally and silently/whisper read age-appropriate material. **1B.Stage B.3.** Recognize informational text structure (e.g., sequence, list/example) before and during reading. **1C.Stage B.1.** Respond to analytical and interpretive questions based on information in text. **2A.Stage B.3.** Define unfamiliar vocabulary. **2A.Stage B.5.** Distinguish between "make believe" and realistic narrative. **2B.Stage B.1.** Investigate self-selected/teacher-selected literature (e.g., picture books, nursery rhymes, fairy tales, poems, legends) from a variety of cultures. **5A.Stage B.4.** Use aids (e.g., KWL, webs, graphic organizers, technology) to locate and present information.
Language Arts **Writing** Reasons, Suspense, Respond to Literature, Outline: 181a, 201b, 202g, 205b, 206–207 **Six-Trait Writing** Voice: 203a, 206–207 **Grammar, Usage, and Mechanics** Singular and Plural Nouns: 181b, 201c, 203b, 205c, 206–207 **Speaking/Listening** Use Telephone and Voice Mail: 205d **Research/Study** Bar Graph: 207a	**3A.Stage B.6.** Use phonemic clues, phonetic and/or developmental spelling to spell unfamiliar words. **3C.Stage B.4.** Experiment with different forms of writing (e.g., song, poetry, short fiction, recipes, diary, journal, directions). **4B.Stage B.1.** Demonstrate awareness of situation and setting for the oral message. **4B.Stage B.10.** Contribute relevant, appropriate information to discussions. **5C.Stage B.8.** Develop ideas by using details from pictures, diagrams, maps, and other graphic organizers.
Unit Skills **Writing** Persuasive Letter: WA2–9 **Project/Wrap-Up:** 292–293	**1B.Stage B.4.** Develop familiarity with poetry (e.g., choral reading to develop fluency). **3B.Stage B.1.** Use appropriate prewriting strategies (e.g., drawing, brainstorming, idea mapping, graphic organizers) to generate and organize ideas with teacher assistance.

This Week's Leveled Readers

Below-Level

1B.Stage B.7. Locate answers to age-appropriate questions, before, during, and after reading, to clarify understanding.

3B.Stage B.4. Organize the picture(s) and text to tell the story in proper order.

Nonfiction

On-Level

1C.Stage B.10. Recognize and discuss the structure of a story in sequential order.

4A.Stage B.8. Use question-building words appropriately (e.g., what, when, how, why, could, should, did).

Nonfiction

Advanced

A Day in the Life of a Vet
by Kristin Cashore
illustrated by Aleksey Ivanov

1B.Stage B.3. Recognize informational text structure (e.g., sequence, list/example) before and during reading.

1C.Stage B.4. Use information in text or illustrations to generate questions about the cause of a specific effect.

Nonfiction

Content-Area Illinois Performance Descriptors in This Lesson

Science

12A.Stage B.1. Apply scientific inquiries or technological designs to explore common and diverse structures and functions of living things: categorizing animals by structures for food-getting and movement; comparing how plants and animals live and reproduce.

12B.Stage B.1. Apply scientific inquiries or technological designs to explore the impact of plants and animals in their changing environments: matching plant and animal adaptations to changing seasons or climatic changes.

12E.Stage B.2. Apply scientific inquiries or technological designs to examine the natural processes that change Earth's surface: identifying water cycle in local weather conditions and features.

13A.Stage B.1. Apply the appropriate principles of safety: mapping pathways to leave classroom or home in case of fire or severe weather situations.

Math

6A.Stage B.1. Count with understanding, including skip counting from any number by 2's and 10's.

6A.Stage B.3. Describe numeric relationships using comparison notation.

10A.Stage B.2. Make predictions from simple data.

10C.Stage B.1. Identify and discuss likely, unlikely, and impossible probability events.

10C.Stage B.2. Communicate and display results of probability events in order to make predictions of future events.

Social Studies

17D.Stage B.1. Describe daily changes in the weather and changes in the seasons in the local community.

18B.Stage B.2. Explain how contact with others shapes peoples' lives.

Illinois!

A FAMOUS ILLINOISAN
Michael Jordan

Michael Jordan (1963–) is one of the most accomplished basketball players in history. As a rookie he was among the top scorers in the NBA. Jordan guided the Chicago Bulls to six NBA titles. He was also a member of the U.S. men's Olympic basketball teams that won gold medals in 1984 and 1992. In 1996 he starred in *Space Jam,* a movie in which his co-stars were Daffy Duck and Bugs Bunny.

Children can . . .
Learn more about Michael Jordan. Have students make a fact card about Michael Jordan with his picture on one side and information about his basketball career on the other.

A SPECIAL ILLINOIS PLACE
Bishop Hill

Bishop Hill is located in Henry County in the northwestern part of the state. The village was founded in 1846 by Swedish immigrants. Their leader, Erik Jansson, brought them to the United States so they could be free to practice their religious beliefs. The people of Bishop Hill were talented carpenters who built several buildings that still stand today. The village is now known for its agriculture and coal mining.

Children can . . .
Learn more about Bishop Hill. Have them use craft sticks, with an adult's help, to construct a building that might have been built by the original settlers of Bishop Hill.

ILLINOIS FUN FACTS
Did You Know?

- Writer Carl Sandburg nicknamed Chicago "the city of big shoulders."

- Products manufactured in Illinois include machinery, chemicals, fabricated metal products, computer and electronic products, and printed materials.

- In the west central part of the state, the Spoon River Trail winds through the area made famous by poet Edgar Lee Masters in *Spoon River Anthology.*

Children can . . .
Think of a title for a poem about a place in their community. Working with a partner, have children write four rhyming verses for the poem.

Unit 5
Responsibility

CONCEPT QUESTION
What does it mean to be responsible?

Week 1
Why is it important to do a good job?

Week 2
Why should we take care of animals?

Week 3
How can we be responsible family members?

Week 4
What do good friends and neighbors do?

Week 5
What happens when we do the wrong thing?

Week 2

EXPAND THE CONCEPT
Why should we take care of animals?

CONNECT THE CONCEPT

▶ Build Background

concern	*litter*	*protection*
fragile	*pellets*	*release*
growth	*pollute*	

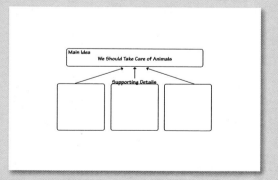

▶ Social Studies Content
Living Things, Shelter/Survival, Growth and Change, Thunderstorms

▶ Writing
Reasons

Preview Your Week

One Dark Night

by Hazel Hutchins

illustrated by Susan Kathleen Hartung

Genre Realistic fiction tells about events that could happen in real life. Could this story really happen?

What can happen on a rainy, dark night?

184   185

Audio CD

Student Edition pages 184–203

Genre	Realistic Fiction
Phonics	Prefixes *un-, re-, pre-, dis-*
Vocabulary Strategy	Context Clues
Comprehension Skill	Sequence
Comprehension Strategy	Graphic Organizer

Paired Selection

Reading Across Texts
Finding a Pet

Genre
Poetry

Text Features
Lines That Rhyme and Have Rhythm

TIME FOR Science

Poetry

Genre
• Poetry often has a rhythm or a beat. Listen for the beat as you read these poems.
• Sometimes poetry rhymes, but not always.
• Each stanza of "Adoption" has two rhyming lines. "The Stray Cat" uses rhyming words in different places throughout the poem.
• A poet often tries to create clear images with as few words as possible.

Link to Writing
Write your own poem about a cat. Use rhyme and rhythm in your poem. Share it with your classmates.

Adoption
Isabel Joshlin Glaser

I found a kitten
At the city pound,
A tiny creature
My hands wrapped around.

I held it up
Against my cheek
And I could feel
Its wild heartbeat.

It touched me
With its icy nose–
We liked each other
From head to toes.

The Stray Cat
Eve Merriam

It's just an old alley cat
that has followed us all the way home.

It hasn't a star on its forehead,
or a silky satiny coat.

No proud tiger stripes, no dainty tread,
no elegant velvet throat.

It's a splotchy, blotchy
city cat, not pretty cat,
a rough little tough little bag of old bones.

"Beauty," we shall call you.
"Beauty, come in."

Reading Across Texts
The cats in *One Dark Night* and in these two poems are homeless. Where was each cat was found?
Writing Across Texts Write a sentence welcoming each cat to its new home.

Visualize As you read, create a picture of these cats in your mind.

204

Student Edition pages 204–205

Audio CD

Read It
ONLINE
PearsonSuccessNet.com

- Student Edition
- Leveled Readers
- Decodable Reader

Leveled Readers

○ **Skill** Sequence

○ **Strategy** Graphic Organizer

Lesson Vocabulary

Below-Level

On-Level

Advanced

ELL Reader

- Concept Vocabulary
- Text Support
- Language Enrichment

Decodable Reader

Apply Phonics

· In the Woods

Integrate Science Standards

- Living Things
- Shelter/Survival
- Growth and Change
- Thunderstorms

✓ **Read**

One Dark Night pp. 184–203

"The Stray Cat"/"Adoption" pp. 204–205

✓ **Read**

Leveled Readers

Below-Level   On-Level   Advanced

- Support Concepts
- Develop Concepts
- Extend Concepts
- Science Extension Activity

✓ **Read**

ELL Reader

✓ **Build Concept Vocabulary**
Responsibility, p. 180m

✓ **Teach Science Concepts**
Weather, p. 186–187
Shelter, p. 200–201
Change and Growth, p. 204–205

✓ **Explore Science Center**
Design a Home for a Pet, p. 180k

Weekly Plan

READING

90–120 minutes

TARGET SKILLS OF THE WEEK

Phonics
Prefixes *un-, re-, pre-, dis-*

Comprehension Skill
Sequence

Comprehension Strategy
Graphic Organizers

Vocabulary Strategy
Context Clues

DAY 1 — PAGES 180l–181b

Oral Language

QUESTION OF THE WEEK, 180l
Why should we take care of animals?

Oral Vocabulary/Share Literature, 180m
Sing with Me Big Book, Song 22
Amazing Words *concern, growth, protection*

Word Work

Phonics, 180n–180o
Introduce Prefixes *un-, re-, pre-, dis-* **T**

Spelling, 180p
Pretest

Comprehension/Vocabulary/Fluency

Read Decodable Reader 22

Grouping Options 180f–180g

Review High-Frequency Words
Check Comprehension
Reread for Fluency

Comprehension Skill/Strategy Lesson,
180r–181
Sequence **T**
Graphic Organizers

DAY 2 — PAGES 182a–201c

Oral Language

QUESTION OF THE DAY, 182a
What do animals need for growth and well-being?

Oral Vocabulary/Share Literature, 182b
Big Book *Animal Hospital*
Amazing Word *fragile*

Word Work

Phonics, 182c–182d
Review Prefixes *un-, re-, pre-, dis-* **T**

Spelling, 182d
Dictation

Comprehension/Vocabulary/Fluency

Build Background, 182e
Pets

Lesson Vocabulary, 182f
Introduce *flashes, lightning, pounds, pours, rolling, storm, thunder* **T**

Vocabulary Strategy Lesson, 182–183a
Context Clues **T**

Read *One Dark Night,* 184–201a

Grouping Options
180f–180g

Sequence **T**
Graphic Organizers
REVIEW Plot and Theme **T**
Reread for Fluency

LANGUAGE ARTS

20–30 minutes

Trait of the Week

Voice

Shared Writing, 181a
Reasons

Grammar, 181b
Introduce Singular and Plural Pronouns **T**

Interactive Writing, 201b
Suspense

Grammar, 201c
Practice Singular and Plural Pronouns **T**

DAILY JOURNAL WRITING

Day 1 *Write about a concern you have.*

Day 2 *Write about an animal you have helped or seen during a storm.*

DAILY SCIENCE CONNECTIONS

Day 1 Take Care of Animals Concept Chart, 180m

Day 2 Time for Science: Weather, 186–187; Shelter, 200–201

DAILY SUCCESS PREDICTORS
for Adequate Yearly Progress

Monitor Progress and Corrective Feedback

Phonics
Check Word Reading, *180o*
Spiral REVIEW Phonics

Fluency
Check Lesson Vocabulary, *182f*
Spiral REVIEW High-Frequency Words

Grouping Options for Differentiated Instruction

Turn the page for the small group lesson plan.

DAY 3 PAGES 202a–203b

Oral Language

QUESTION OF THE DAY, 202a
What would you like to study?

Oral Vocabulary/Share Literature, 202b
Big Book *Animal Hospital*
Amazing Word *pellets*

Word Work

Phonics, 202c
REVIEW Suffixes *-ly, -ful, -er, -or* **T**

Lesson Vocabulary, 202d
Practice *flashes, lightning, pounds, pours, rolling, storm, thunder* **T**

Spelling, 202d
Practice

Comprehension/Vocabulary/Fluency

Vocabulary, 202e
Classify/Categorize **T**

Read *One Dark Night,* 184–203

Grouping Options
180f–180g

Fluency, 202f
Read with Accuracy and Appropriate Pace/Rate

Reader Response, 202g

Trait of the Week, 203a
Introduce Voice

Grammar, 203b
Write with Singular and Plural Pronouns **T**

Day 3 *Write about a time that you experienced bad or scary weather.*

Day 3 Let's Talk About the Concept, 203b

DAY 4 PAGES 204a–205d

Oral Language

QUESTION OF THE DAY, 204a
How can we show an animal that we love it?

Oral Vocabulary/Share Literature, 204b
Read Aloud Anthology "Bringing Back Salmon"
Amazing Words *litter, pollute, release*

Word Work

Phonics, 204c–204d
REVIEW Sentence Reading **T**

Spelling, 204d
Partner Review

Comprehension/Vocabulary/Fluency

Read "Adoption"/"The Stray Cat," 204–205
Leveled Readers

Grouping Options
180f–180g

Classify
Reading Across Texts

Fluency, 205a
Read with Accuracy and Appropriate Pace/Rate

Writing Across the Curriculum, 205b
Outline

Grammar, 205c
Review Singular and Plural Pronouns **T**

Speaking and Viewing, 205d
Telephones and Voice Mail

Day 4 *Write about a puppy with a growth spurt.*

Day 4 Time for Science: Growth and Change, 204–205

DAY 5 PAGES 206a–207b

Oral Language

QUESTION OF THE DAY, 206a
Why is it important to care for animals?

Oral Vocabulary/Share Literature, 206b
Read Aloud Anthology "Bringing Back Salmon"
Amazing Words Review

Word Work

Phonics, 206c
Review Prefixes *un-, re-, pre-, dis-* **T**

Lesson Vocabulary, 206c
Review *flashes, lightning, pounds, pours, rolling, storm, thunder* **T**

Spelling, 206d
Test

Comprehension/Vocabulary/Fluency

Read Leveled Readers

Grouping Options 180f–180g

Monitor Progress, 206e–206g
Read the Sentences
Read the Story

Writing and Grammar, 206–207
Develop Voice
Use Singular and Plural Pronouns **T**

Research/Study Skills, 207a
Bar Graph

Day 5 *Write about a thunderstorm.*

Day 5 Revisit the Take Care of Animals Concept Chart, 207b

KEY ◎ = Target Skill **T** = Tested Skill

Check Retelling, *202g*

Check Fluency wcpm, *205a*
Spiral REVIEW Phonics, High-Frequency Words

Check Oral Vocabulary, *206b*
Assess Phonics, Lesson Vocabulary, Fluency, Comprehension, *206e*

SUCCESS PREDICTOR

Small Group Plan *for Differentiated Instruction*

Daily Plan AT A GLANCE

Reading
Whole Group
- Oral Language
- Word Work
- Comprehension/Vocabulary

Group Time

Meet with small groups to provide:
- Skill Support
- Reading Support
- Fluency Practice

Read

This week's lessons for daily group time can be found behind the Differentiated Instruction (DI) tab on pp. DI·24–DI·33.

Whole Group
- Comprehension/Vocabulary
- Fluency

Language Arts
- Writing
- Grammar
- Speaking/Listening/Viewing
- Research/Study Skills

Use *My Sidewalks on Reading Street* for Tier III intensive reading intervention.

DAY 1

On-Level	Strategic Intervention	Advanced
Teacher-Led *Page 180q*	**Teacher-Led** *Page DI·24*	**Teacher-Led** *Page DI·25*
• **Read** Decodable Reader 22 • **Reread** for Fluency	• Blend Words with Prefixes *un-, re-, pre-, dis-* • **Read** Decodable Reader 22 • **Reread** for Fluency	• Extend Word Reading • **Read** Advanced Selection 2 • Introduce Concept Inquiry

ⓘ Independent Activities

While you meet with small groups, have the rest of the class...

- Reread for fluency
- Write in their journals
- Read self-selected reading
- Visit the Word Work Center
- Complete Practice Book 2.2, pp. 63–64

DAY 2

On-Level	Strategic Intervention	Advanced
Teacher-Led *Pages 184–201*	**Teacher-Led** *Page DI·26*	**Teacher-Led** *Page DI·27*
• **Read** *One Dark Night* • **Reread** for Fluency	• Blend Words with Prefixes *un-, re-, pre-, dis-* • **Read** SI Decodable Reader 22 • **Read** or Listen to *One Dark Night*	• **Read** *One Dark Night* • Continue Concept Inquiry

ⓘ Independent Activities

While you meet with small groups, have the rest of the class...

- Read self-selected reading
- Write in their journals
- Visit the Listening Center
- Complete Practice Book 2.2, pp. 65–67

DAY 3

On-Level	Strategic Intervention	Advanced
Teacher-Led *Pages 184–203*	**Teacher-Led** *Page DI·28*	**Teacher-Led** *Page DI·29*
• **Reread** *One Dark Night*	• **Reread** *One Dark Night* • Read Words and Sentences • Review Sequence and Graphic Organizer • **Reread** for Fluency	• Self-Selected Reading • Continue Concept Inquiry

ⓘ Independent Activities

While you meet with small groups, have the rest of the class...

- Read self-selected reading
- Write in their journals
- Visit the Writing Center
- Complete Practice Book 2.2, pp. 68–69

① Begin with whole class skill and strategy instruction.

② Meet with small groups to provide differentiated instruction.

③ Gather the whole class back together for fluency and language arts.

On-Level

Teacher-Led
Pages 204–205, LR13–LR15

- **Read** "Adoption" and "The Stray Cat"
- Practice with On-Level Reader *Animal Shelters*

Strategic Intervention

Teacher-Led
Pages DI · 30, LR10–LR12

- **Read** or Listen to "Adoption" and "The Stray Cat"
- **Reread** for Fluency
- Build Concepts
- Practice with Below-Level Reader *Horse Rescue!*

Advanced

Teacher-Led
Pages DI · 31, LR16–LR18

- **Read** "Adoption" and "The Stray Cat"
- Extend Vocabulary
- Continue Concept Inquiry
- Practice with Advanced Reader *A Day in the Life of a Vet*

DAY 4

ⓘ Independent Activities

While you meet with small groups, have the rest of the class...

- Reread for fluency
- Write in their journals
- Read self-selected reading
- Review spelling words with a partner
- Visit the Listening and Science Centers

On-Level

Teacher-Led
Pages 206e–206g, LR13–LR15

- Sentence Reading, Set B
- Monitor Comprehension
- Practice with On-Level Reader *Animal Shelters*

Strategic Intervention

Teacher-Led
Pages DI · 32, LR10–LR12

- Practice Word Reading
- Sentence Reading, Set A
- Monitor Comprehension
- Practice with Below-Level Reader *Horse Rescue!*

Advanced

Teacher-Led
Pages DI · 33, LR16–LR18

- Sentence Reading, Set C
- Share Concept Inquiry
- Practice with Advanced Reader *A Day in the Life of a Vet*

DAY 5

ⓘ Independent Activities

While you meet with small groups, have the rest of the class...

- Reread for fluency
- Write in their journals
- Read self-selected reading
- Visit the Technology Center
- Complete Practice Book 2.2, p. 70

Grouping Place English language learners in the groups that correspond to their reading abilities in English.

Use the appropriate Leveled Reader or other text at children's instructional level.

TiP Send home the appropriate Multilingual Summary of the main selection on Day 1.

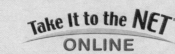

Take It to the NET™ ONLINE
PearsonSuccessNet.com

Deborah Simmons and Edward Kame'enui
For research on word recognition and diverse learners, see the article "Understanding the Primary Role of Word Recognition . . . " by D. Chard and Scott Foresman authors D. Simmons and E. Kame'enui.

TEACHER TALK

Text written at a child's **independent reading level** is text in which no more than about 1 in 20 words is difficult for the child to read.

Be sure to schedule time for children to work on the unit inquiry project "Research Responsible Acts." This week children should work in small groups, choose a responsible community member, and do research to gather information about the person.

Looking Ahead

Name _____ Date _____

My Work Plan

Put an ☒ next to the activities you complete.

Listening
- ☐ Listen to a story.
- ☐ Listen to a song.

Writing
- ☐ Make a flyer.
- ☐ Write in your journal.

Reading
- ☐ Read a book.
- ☐ Read sentences.
- ☐ Book Club

Science
- ☐ Draw a picture.

Word Work
- ☐ Play phonics football with prefixes.

Technology
- ☐ Search for cat books online.
- ☐ Make a list.

Independent Practice
- ☐ Practice Book 2.2, pp. 61–70

Inquiry
- ☐ Interview or research.

Wrap Up Your Week Turn your paper over. Write about what you did at school this week. What did you read? What did you learn about animal responsibilities?

38 Unit 5 · Week 2 · *One Dark Night*

▲ **Group-Time Survival Guide**
p. 38, Weekly Contract

One Dark Night 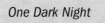 **180g**

☑ Customize Your Plan *by Strand*

ORAL LANGUAGE

Concept Development

Why should we take care of animals?

concern   fragile   growth   litter
pellets   pollute   protection   release

BUILD

❑ **Question of the Week** Use the Morning Warm-Up! to introduce and discuss the question of the week. This week children will talk, sing, read, and write about responsibility. DAY 1 *180l*

❑ **Sing with Me Big Book** Sing a song about taking care of animals. Ask children to listen for the concept-related Amazing Words *concern, growth, protection*. DAY 1 *180m*

Sing with Me Big Book

❑ **Build Background** Remind children of the question of the week. Then create a concept chart for children to add to throughout the week. DAY 1 *180m*

DEVELOP

❑ **Question of the Day** Use the questions in the Morning Warm-Ups! to discuss lesson concepts and how they relate to the unit theme, Responsibility. **DAY 2** *182a*, **DAY 3** *202a*, **DAY 4** *204a*, **DAY 5** *206a*

❑ **Share Literature** Read big books and read aloud selections that develop concepts, language, and vocabulary related to the lesson concept and the unit theme. Continue to develop this week's Amazing Words. **DAY 2** *182b*, **DAY 3** *202b*, **DAY 4** *204b*, **DAY 5** *206b*

CONNECT

❑ **Wrap Up Your Week!** Revisit the Question of the Week. Then connect concepts and vocabulary to next week's lesson. **DAY 5** *207b*

CHECK

❑ **Check Oral Vocabulary** To informally assess children's oral vocabulary, ask individuals to use some of this week's Amazing Words to tell you about the concept of the week—Responsibility. **DAY 5** *206b*

PHONICS

PREFIXES *UN-, RE-, PRE-, DIS-* Prefixes, suffixes, and some inflected endings usually form separate syllables from the base word.

TEACH

❑ **Prefixes *un-, re-, pre-, dis-*** Introduce the blending strategy for words beginning with the prefixes *un-, re-, pre-, dis-*. Then have children blend and build words by adding the prefix to each base word, reading the new word, and supplying its meaning. DAY 1 *180n–180o*

❑ **Fluent Word Reading** Use the Fluent Word Reading Routine to develop children's word reading fluency. Use the Phonics Songs and Rhymes Chart for additional word reading practice. **DAY 2** *182c–182d*

Phonics Songs and Rhymes Chart 22

PRACTICE/APPLY

❑ **Decodable Reader 22** Practice reading words with prefixes *un-, re-, pre-, dis-* in context. DAY 1 *180q*

❑ *One Dark Night* Practice decoding words in context. **DAY 2** *184–201*

Decodable Reader 22

❑ **Homework** Practice Book 2.2 p. 63. DAY 1 *180o*

❑ **Word Work Center** Practice prefixes *un-, re-, pre-, dis-*. **ANY DAY** *180j*

Main Selection—Fiction

RETEACH/REVIEW

❑ **Review** Review words with this week's phonics skills. **DAY 5** *206c*

❑ **Reteach Lessons** If necessary, reteach prefixes *un-, re-, pre-, dis-*. **DAY 5** *DI·65*

❑ **Spiral REVIEW** Review previously taught phonics skills. DAY 1 *180o*, **DAY 3** *202c*, **DAY 4** *204c*

ASSESS

❑ **Sentence Reading** Assess children's ability to read words with prefixes *un-, re-, pre-, dis-*. **DAY 5** *206e–206f*

❶ Use assessment data to determine your instructional focus.

❷ Preview this week's instruction by strand.

❸ Choose instructional activities that meet the needs of your classroom.

SPELLING

PREFIXES *UN-, RE-, PRE-, DIS-*   Prefixes usually form separate syllables from the base word.

TEACH

☐ **Pretest** Before administering the pretest, model how to segment words beginning with prefixes *un-, re-, pre-,* and *dis-* to spell them. Dictate the spelling words, segmenting them if necessary. Then have children check their pretests and correct misspelled words. **DAY 1** *180p*

PRACTICE/APPLY

☐ **Dictation** Have children write dictation sentences to practice spelling words. **DAY 2** *182d*

☐ **Write Words** Have children practice writing the spelling words by writing sentences or pairs of sentences that include both a spelling word and its base word. **DAY 3** *202d*

☐ **Homework** Phonics and Spelling Practice Book pp. 85–88. **DAY 1** *180p*, **DAY 2** *182d*, **DAY 3** *202d*, **DAY 4** *204d*

RETEACH/REVIEW

☐ **Partner Review** Have pairs work together to read and write the spelling words. **DAY 4** *204d*

ASSESS

☐ **Posttest** Use dictation sentences to give the posttest for words with prefixes *un-, re-, pre-, dis-*. **DAY 5** *206d*

Spelling Words

Prefixes *un-, re-, pre-, dis-*

1. unsafe
2. preheat
3. rerun
4. disappear*
5. unlock
6. retie
7. rewind
8. unpack
9. unplug
10. regroup
11. preschool
12. disagree

Challenge Words

13. prehistoric
14. unfortunate
15. reunion

* Words from the Selection

VOCABULARY

🔘 **STRATEGY CONTEXT CLUES**   When you come to a word you don't know, look for clues around the word to help you figure out what it means.

LESSON VOCABULARY

flashes	lightning	pounds	pours
rolling	storm	thunder	

TEACH

☐ **Words to Know** Introduce and discuss this week's lesson vocabulary. **DAY 2** *182f*

☐ **Vocabulary Strategy Lesson** Use the lesson in the Student Edition to introduce/model *context clues*. **DAY 2** *182–183a*

Vocabulary Strategy Lesson

PRACTICE/APPLY

☐ **Words in Context** Read the lesson vocabulary in context. **DAY 2** *184–201,* **DAY 3** *184–203*

☐ **Lesson Vocabulary** Have children complete sentences with vocabulary words. **DAY 3** *202d*

Main Selection—Fiction

☐ **Leveled Text** Read the lesson vocabulary in leveled text. **DAY 4** *LR10–LR18,* **DAY 5** *L10–LR18*

☐ **Homework** Practice Book 2.2 pp. 66, 69. **DAY 2** *182f,* **DAY 3** *202d*

Leveled Readers

RETEACH/REVIEW

☐ **Classify/Categorize** Model classifying related words and phrases. Have children classify words. **DAY 3** *202e*

☐ **Review** Review this week's lesson vocabulary words. **DAY 5** *206c*

ASSESS

☐ **Selection Test** Use the Selection Test to determine children's understanding of the lesson vocabulary words. **DAY 3**

☐ **Sentence Reading** Assess children's ability to read this week's lesson vocabulary words. **DAY 5** *206e–206f*

HIGH-FREQUENCY WORDS

RETEACH/REVIEW

☐ **Spiral REVIEW** Review previously taught high-frequency words. **DAY 2** *182f,* **DAY 4** *204c*

COMPREHENSION

🔄 **SKILL SEQUENCE** Sequence is the order of events in a story.

🔄 **STRATEGY GRAPHIC ORGANIZERS** A graphic organizer is a picture that can help you organize information as you read. Recording events of a story on a graphic organizer helps you remember the correct order of events in a story.

TEACH

☐ **Skill/Strategy Lesson** Use the Skill/Strategy Lesson in the Student Edition to introduce *sequence* and *graphic organizers.* **DAY 1** *180r–181*

Skill/Strategy Lesson

PRACTICE/APPLY

☐ **Skills and Strategies in Context** Read *One Dark Night,* using the Guiding Comprehension questions to apply *sequence* and *graphic organizers.* **DAY 2** *184–201a*

Main Selection—Fiction

☐ **Reader Response** Use the questions on Student Edition p. 202 to discuss the selection. **DAY 3** *202g–203*

☐ **Skills and Strategies in Context** Read the poems, guiding children as they apply skills and strategies. **DAY 4** *204e–205*

Paired Selection— Poetry

☐ **Leveled Text** Apply *sequence* and *graphic organizers* to read leveled text. **DAY 4** *LR10–LR18,* **DAY 5** *LR10–LR18*

☐ **Homework** Practice Book 2.2 pp. 64, 65. **DAY 1** *180–181,* **DAY 2** *182e*

Leveled Readers

ASSESS

☐ **Selection Test** Determine children's understanding of the main selection and assess their ability to identify *sequence.* **DAY 3**

☐ **Story Reading** Have children read the passage "Doghouse Redo." Ask questions that require them to *sequence.* Then have them retell. **DAY 5** *206e–206g*

RETEACH/REVIEW

☐ **Reteach Lesson** If necessary, reteach *sequence.* **DAY 5** *D1-65*

FLUENCY

SKILL READ WITH ACCURACY AND APPROPRIATE PACE/RATE When you read, try not to change any words or leave any words out. Read at the pace you use when you are speaking.

REREAD FOR FLUENCY

☐ **Paired Reading** Have children read orally from Decodable Reader 22 or another text at their independent reading level. Listen as children read and provide corrective feedback regarding their oral reading and their use of the blending strategy. **DAY 1** *180q*

☐ **Paired Reading** Have pairs of children read orally from the main selection or another text at their independent reading level. Listen as children read and provide corrective feedback regarding oral reading and their use of the blending strategy. **DAY 2** *201a*

TEACH

☐ **Model** Use passages from *One Dark Night* to model reading with accuracy and appropriate pace/rate. **DAY 3** *202f,* **DAY 4** *205a*

PRACTICE/APPLY

☐ **Choral Reading** Have groups choral read parts from *One Dark Night,* "Adoption" and "The Stray Cat." Monitor progress and provide feedback regarding children's accuracy and pace/rate. **DAY 3** *202f,* **DAY 4** *205a*

☐ **Listening Center** Have children follow along with the AudioText for this week's selections. **ANY DAY** *180j*

☐ **Reading/Library Center** Have children build fluency by rereading Leveled Readers, Decodable Readers, or other text at their independent level. **ANY DAY** *180j*

☐ **Fluency Coach** Have children use Fluency Coach to listen to fluent reading or to practice reading on their own. **ANY DAY**

ASSESS

☐ **Story Reading** Take a one-minute timed sample of children's oral reading. Use the passage "Doghouse Redo." **DAY 5** *206e–206g*

① Use assessment data to determine your instructional focus.

② Preview this week's instruction by strand.

③ Choose instructional activities that meet the needs of your classroom.

WRITING

Trait of the Week

VOICE Voice tells how the writer feels and thinks about a topic.

TEACH

☐ **Write Together** Engage children in writing activities that develop language, grammar, and writing skills. Include independent writing as an extension of group writing activities.

> **Shared Writing** DAY 1 *181a*
> **Interactive Writing** DAY 2 *201b*
> **Writing Across the Curriculum** DAY 4 *205b*

☐ **Trait of the Week** Introduce and model the Trait of the Week, *voice.* DAY 3 *203a*

PRACTICE/APPLY

☐ **Write Now** Examine the model on Student Edition pp. 206–207. Then have children write reasons. DAY 5 *206–207*

> **Prompt** In *One Dark Night,* a cat has reasons for braving a storm. Think about something you think people should do. Now write reasons to convince them.

Write Now

☐ **Daily Journal Writing** Have children write about concepts and literature in their journals. **EVERY DAY** *180d–180e*

☐ **Writing Center** Create a flyer to convince people to help animals. **ANY DAY** *180k*

ASSESS

☐ **Scoring Rubric** Use a rubric to evaluate reasons. DAY 5 *206–207*

RETEACH/REVIEW

☐ **The Grammar and Writing Book** Use pp. 176–181 of The Grammar and Writing Book to extend instruction. **ANY DAY**

The Grammar and Writing Book

SPEAKING AND LISTENING

TEACH

☐ **Use Telephones and Voice Mail** Demonstrate how to use a telephone and voice mail. Then have partners practice appropriate speaking and listening behaviors on the phone. DAY 4 *205d*

GRAMMAR

SKILL PRONOUNS *He, she,* and *it* are pronouns that name only one. *We* and *they* are pronouns that name more than one.

TEACH

☐ **Grammar Transparency 22** Use Grammar Transparency 22 to teach *pronouns.* DAY 1 *181b*

Grammar Transparency 22

PRACTICE/APPLY

☐ **Develop the Concept** Review the concept of *pronouns* and provide guided practice. DAY 2 *201c*

☐ **Apply to Writing** Have children use pronouns in writing. DAY 3 *203b*

☐ **Define/Practice** Review the definition of *pronouns.* Then have children write a paragraph describing what happens, using pronouns for one and more than one. DAY 4 *205c*

☐ **Write Now** Discuss the grammar lesson on Student Edition p. 207. Have children use singular and plural pronouns in their reasons. DAY 5 *206–207*

Write Now

☐ **Daily Fix-It** Have children find and correct errors in grammar, spelling, and punctuation.
DAY 1 *181a,* DAY 2 *201c,* DAY 3 *203a,* DAY 4 *205c,* DAY 5 *206–207*

☐ **Homework** The Grammar and Writing Practice Book pp. 85–88.
DAY 2 *201c,* DAY 3 *203b,* DAY 4 *205c,* DAY 5 *206–207*

RETEACH/REVIEW

☐ **The Grammar and Writing Book** Use pp. 176–179 of The Grammar and Writing Book to extend instruction. **ANY DAY**

The Grammar and Writing Book

RESEARCH/INQUIRY

TEACH

☐ **Bar Graph** Model how to use and read a bar graph. Then as a class, create a bar graph that displays information about the pets they own. DAY 5 *207a*

☐ **Unit Inquiry Project** Allow time for children to work in small groups, choose a responsible community member, and do research to gather information about the person. **ANY DAY** *153*

Resources for
Differentiated Instruction

LEVELED READERS

▶ **Comprehension**
- ◎ **Skill** Sequence
- ◎ **Strategy** Graphic Organizer

▶ **Lesson Vocabulary**
- ◎ **Context Clues**

pours	thunder
lightning	
storm	flashes
pounds	rolling

▶ **Science Standards**
- • Living Things
- • Shelter/Survival
- • Growth and Change
- • Thunderstorms

Leveled Reader Database

ONLINE

PearsonSuccessNet.com

Use the Online Database of over 600 books to
- • Download and print additional copies of this week's leveled readers
- • Listen to the readers being read online
- • Search for more titles focused on this week's skills, topic, and content

On-Level Reader

Sequence
Complete the chart below. Write the animals in the order in which they appeared in the book.

Farm Animal Shelter
1. pigs
2. cows
3. sheep
4. chickens

Wild Animal Shelter
1. bees
2. birds

Shelter for Pets
1. pigs
2. hamsters
3. fish
4. lizard

◎ **On-Level Practice** TE p. LR14

Vocabulary
Finish the poem below. Think about what makes sense and what words rhyme. The words below each rhyme tell you the part of speech.

flashes lightning pounds pours
rolling storm thunder

Lightning **flashes** **Thunder** pounds.
(verb)   (noun)

Rain **pours** down, and down and down.
(verb)

The **storm** is bursting, all around,
(noun)

Rolling with a scary sound.
(verb)

Think about the words you wrote and their parts of speech. Make any changes. Compare poems with a classmate.

◎ **On-Level Practice** TE p. LR15

Below-Level Reader

Sequence
Number the sentences below from 1 to 7 to show the sequence of the horse rescue.
Hint: Look for clue words, like **first** and **finally**.

4 Next, the Coast Guard lowered a person down to each big horse.

2 Helicopters flew to the place where the horses were last seen.

7 Finally, an animal doctor checked the horses.

3 The Coast Guard loaded the smaller horses onto a boat.

5 Then the person put a sling around the big horse.

1 First, the farmers called the U.S. Coast Guard for help.

6 The helicopters flew the big horses to safety.

◎ **Below-Level Practice** TE p. LR11

Vocabulary
Find these words in the puzzle. They can be across, up, or down.

| flashes | lightning | pounded | poured |
| rolling | storm | thunder | |

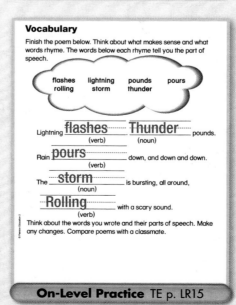

Now write the leftover letters in order on the lines below to reveal a secret message.

L o o k   a t   t h e   s k y !   H o r s e s   f l y !

◎ **Below-Level Practice** TE p. LR12

Advanced

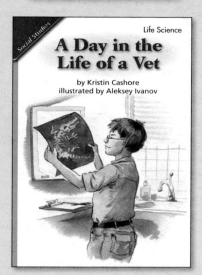

Advanced Reader

Life Science
A Day in the Life of a Vet
by Kristin Cashore
illustrated by Aleksey Ivanov

Sequence
Write the names of the vets in the box in the order in which we met them in the book.

Dr. Billings and Dr. Mor—Wildlife Vets
Dr. Hopkins—A Small Animal Vet
Dr. Jung—A Zoo Vet
Dr. Martinez—A Large Animal Vet

1. **Dr. Hopkins**   3. **Dr. Billings, Dr. Mor**
2. **Dr. Martinez**   4. **Dr. Jung**

Choose one of the vets from *A Day in the Life of a Vet*.
Fill in the schedule below to show the order in which he or she examined patients. **Responses will vary.**

First patient: _____
Second patient: _____
Third patient: _____
Last patient: _____

Advanced Practice TE p. LR17

Vocabulary
Read the report below. It was written by an animal doctor.
Complete the report with the missing words from the box.

| Words to Know |
| growth   llama   protect   survive   yak   veterinarian |

January 14
I have completed my morning rounds. I checked on the
growth of a newborn giraffe. I had a report that
something was tangled around a **yak** 's horns.
I also stopped by the pen of a **llama** whose
nails were recently trimmed. I am worried about our newest
addition, a crocodile. If the crocodile is to **survive**
the winter, we'll need to **protect** it from cold
weather. Ah! The job of a **veterinarian** is never done.

What kind of vet wrote this report? Write your idea below.

A zoo vet wrote the report.

Advanced Practice TE p. LR18

ELL

ELL Reader

ELL Poster 22

Teacher's Edition Notes
ELL notes throughout this lesson support instruction and reference additional resources at point of use.

ELL Teaching Guide pp. 148–154, 254–255
- Multilingual summaries of the main selection
- Comprehension lesson
- Vocabulary strategies and word cards
- ELL Reader 22 lesson

ELL and Transition Handbook

Ten Important Sentences
- Key ideas from every selection in the Student Edition
- Activities to build sentence power

More Reading

Readers' Theater Anthology
- Fluency practice
- Five scripts to build fluency
- Poetry for oral interpretation

Leveled Trade Books

- Extend reading tied to the unit concept
- Lessons in Trade Book Library Teaching Guide

Homework
- Family Times Newsletter
- ELL Multilingual Selection Summaries

Take-Home Books
- Decodable Readers
- Leveled Readers

Literacy Centers

Let's Read Along

MATERIALS `SINGLES`
CD player, headphones, print copies of recorded pieces

LISTEN TO LITERATURE As children listen to the following recordings, have them follow along or read along in the print version.

AudioText
One Dark Night
"Stray Cat" and "Adoption"

Sing with Me/Background Building Audio
"Love, Love Animals"

Phonics Songs and Rhymes Audio
"Kitten Rescue"

Kitten Rescue

Little kitty sat up in a tree,
Looking as unhappy as can be.
"Mew!" cried the kitten.
"Yowl!" cried the kitten.
"This displeases me!"

I refilled her dish so she could eat.
I gave her a preview of her treat.
"Purr," mewed the kitten.
"Yay," mewed the kitten.
She came back to me.

Audio CD **Phonics Songs and Rhymes Chart 22**

Read It Again!

MATERIALS `SINGLES` `PAIRS` `GROUPS`
collection of books for self-selected reading, reading logs

REREAD BOOKS Have children select previously read books from the appropriate book box and record titles of books they read in their logs. Use these previously read books:

- **Decodable Readers**
- **Leveled Readers**
- **ELL Readers**
- **Stories written by classmates**
- **Books from the library**

TEN IMPORTANT SENTENCES Have children read the Ten Important Sentences for *One Dark Night* and locate the sentences in the Student Edition.

BOOK CLUB Encourage a group to discuss the genre of realistic fiction. What about this story could happen in real life? Invite the group to read other realistic fiction.

Phonics Football

MATERIALS `PAIRS`
football field game board, 15 prefix word cards, 10 suffix word cards, game markers

PREFIXES *un-, re-, pre-, dis-* Have two children play a phonics football game using words with prefixes.

1. **Make a football field game board and write words with prefixes such as *unable, replace, precut, discount* on each of 15 index cards. On the remaining 10 cards, write words with suffixes such as *spoonful, butcher, lovely*.**
2. **Stack the cards facedown on the fifty-yard line.**
3. **Play begins on the fifty-yard line. Children take turns picking a card and reading the word. If the word has a prefix, the child advances ten yards towards the end zone.**
4. **Play continues until someone reaches the opposite end zone.**

Phonics Activities CD This interactive CD provides additional practice.

disappear

Scott Foresman Reading Street Centers Survival Kit
Use the *One Dark Night* materials from the Reading Street
Centers Survival Kit to organize this week's centers.

Writing

Helping
STRAYS

MATERIALS `SINGLES`
paper, pencils, crayons,
markers

CREATE A PERSUASIVE FLYER Recall
that three kittens and one stray
cat stayed safe with Jonathan
during the storm.

1. Have children think about what people should do to help stray animals.
2. Ask children to create a flyer to convince people to help stray animals.
3. Then have children illustrate their
   flyers.
4. Display the flyers in the classroom.

LEVELED WRITING Encourage
children to write at their own ability
level. Some will have no sense
of audience or purpose. Others'
writing may sometimes suit
audience or purpose. Your best
writers' work will have an engaging
voice well suited to the purpose
and audience.

Please Help Stray Cats.

People get rid of cats
they don't want. These cats
need our help. They need
food and clean water. If
you see a stray cat, call a
vet or shelter.

Science

Home Sweet
Home

MATERIALS `PAIRS`
construction paper, markers,
books, pet supply catalogs
and/or magazines about cats

MAKE A HOME Children make a
good home for a cat.

1. Pairs talk about what they would
   need to take care of a cat.
2. Then they draw a picture of the
   things they would provide.
3. Partners can explain their choices to
   others.

Technology

Books
Galore

MATERIALS `PAIRS`
computer with Internet access,
paper, pencils

USE A SEARCH ENGINE Have pairs
of children research books about
cats online.

1. Have children search for books about
   cats that they would like to read.
2. Then have them make a list of at
   least three books that sound interesting to them. They should organize
   their lists beginning with their first
   choice.

Search Engine

1. Cat Heaven
2. Jenny and the Cat Club
3. The Cat in the Hat Comes Back

ALL CENTERS

Oral Vocabulary
"Love, Love Animals" 22

Phonics and Spelling
Prefixes *un-, re-, pre-, dis-*
Spelling Pretest: Words
   with Prefixes

Read Apply Phonics **Word Wall**

Group Time < Differentiated Instruction

Listening Comprehension
Skill Sequence
Strategy Graphic Organizer

Shared Writing
Reasons

Grammar
Singular and Plural Pronouns

Materials

- *Sing with Me Big Book*
- Letter Tiles
- Decodable Reader 22
- Student Edition 180–181
- Tested Word Cards
- Graphic Organizer 16
- Skill Transparency 22
- Writing Transparency 22
- Grammar Transparency 22

Take It to the NET
ONLINE
Professional Development
To learn more about oral language, go to PearsonSuccessNet.com and read "Listening and Reading" by T. Sticht and J. James.

Morning Warm-Up!

**Some animals live with our family.
Other animals are wild.
We should be kind to all animals.
Why should we take care of animals?**

QUESTION OF THE WEEK Tell children they will talk, sing, read, and write about Responsibility. Write and read the message and discuss the question.

CONNECT CONCEPTS Ask questions to connect to other Unit 5 selections.

- Who did the firefighters in *Firefighter!* take care of? Do you think firefighters might take care of animals too?

- Firefighters Kelly, Sanchez, and Johnson cleaned the firehouse. How can we keep our animals' houses clean?

REVIEW HIGH-FREQUENCY WORDS

- Ask a volunteer to circle the high-frequency words *animals* and *live* in the message.

- Have children say and spell each word as they write it in the air.

Build Background Use the Day 1 instruction on ELL Poster 22 to assess knowledge and develop concepts.

ELL Poster 22

Oral Vocabulary

SHARE LITERATURE Display p. 22 of the *Sing with Me Big Book.* Tell children that the class is going to sing a song about taking care of animals. Ask the class to listen for the Amazing Words **concern, growth,** and **protection** as you sing. Then ask for volunteers to create a sentence using one of the words. Prompt children to think about what they have concern for, what shows growth, and what needs protection (besides animals). Then encourage the class to sing the song with you.

 **Sing with Me/ Background Building Audio**

Love, Love Animals

Oh, animals need
Help from us to succeed,
So we give them protection and care.
We need to protect
And also respect
Each rabbit, dog, tiger, and bear.

Love, love animals,
The tame and the wild ones both.
We all need to learn
To show our concern.
Protection and care help their growth.

Sing with Me Big Book

BUILD BACKGROUND Remind children of the question of the week.

* Why should we take care of animals?

Draw a main idea chart or use Graphic Organizer 16. Write *We Should Take Care of Animals* in the main idea box. Help children come up with reasons that support the main idea. Encourage them to use the Amazing Words. (Animals need protection; animals need food for growth.) Display the diagram for use throughout the week.

* How can we show concern for animals? (We can provide them with a safe, warm place to sleep, give them water and healthy food for their growth, and offer them protection.)

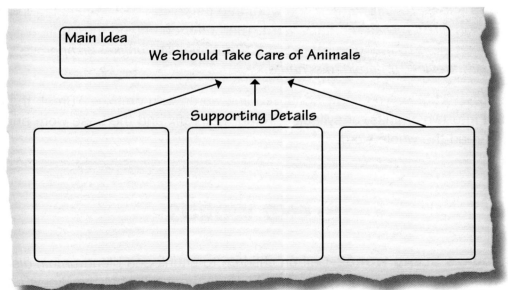

▲ **Graphic Organizer 16**

OBJECTIVE
* Build oral vocabulary.

Amazing Words to build oral vocabulary

MONITOR PROGRESS

concern
growth
protection
fragile
pellets
litter
pollute
release

If... children lack oral vocabulary experiences about the concept Responsibility,

then... use the Oral Vocabulary Routine below to teach *concern.*

Oral Vocabulary ROUTINE

1. **Introduce the Word** Relate the word *concern* to the song. Supply a child-friendly definition. Have children say the word. **Example:** When you have a reason to worry, you have *concern.*

2. **Demonstrate** Provide an example to show meaning. Mom is *concerned* about us walking to school alone.

3. **Apply** Have children demonstrate their understanding. Which would you have *concern* about—your puppy getting out of the yard or your excellent report card?

4. **Display the Word/Letter-Sounds** Write the word on a card. Display it. Point out the hard and soft *c* in *concern.* See p. DI·4 to teach *growth* and *protection.*

E L L

Build Oral Vocabulary Help children understand the words *tame* and *wild.* Ask which of these groups is *tame* and which is *wild:* pet cats, dogs, and farm horses, bears, tigers, and hawks.

OBJECTIVES

- Use structural cues to decode words with prefixes *un-, re-, pre-, dis-.*
- Blend, read, and build words with prefixes *un-, re-, pre-, dis-.*

Skills Trace

Prefixes

Introduce/Teach	TE: 2.5 180n–o, 182c–d
Practice	TE: 2.5 180q, 202d; PB: 2.2 63
Reteach/Review	TE: 2.5 204d, DI·65
Assess/Test	TE: 2.5 206e–g Benchmark Test: Unit 5

Generalization

Prefixes Prefixes, suffixes, and some inflected endings usually form separate syllables from the base word.

Strategic Intervention

Use **Monitor Progress,** p. 180o, during Group Time after children have had more practice with prefixes.

Advanced

Use **Monitor Progress,** p. 180o, as a preassessment to determine whether this group of children would benefit from this instruction on prefixes.

Support Phonics Prefixes are common in various European languages. Invite children or their family members to share examples of words with prefixes in their home languages. If possible, show these words in written form and divide them between the prefix and the base word. Examples in Spanish include *desagradable (disagreeable)* and *infeliz (unhappy).*

See the Phonics Transition Lessons in the ELL and Transition Handbook.

Prefixes *un-, re-, pre-, dis-*

TEACH/MODEL

Blending Strategy
ROUTINE

1 Connect Write *quickly* and *wonderful.* You studied words like this already. What do you know about reading them? **(They all contain suffixes that are separate syllables from the base word.)** Today we'll learn about adding prefixes *un-, re-, pre-,* and *dis-* to the beginning of words. Each prefix has a specific meaning:

- *un-, dis-*   not
- *re-*   again
- *pre-*   before

2 Model Write *restart.* This is a two-syllable word formed from the base word *start* and the prefix *re-.* You can chunk the word into its parts—the prefix and the base word. Then cover the prefix, read the base word, and then blend the prefix and the base word to read the whole word. What is the word? *(restart)* What does it mean? *(to start again)* Let's blend this word together: /restärt/ Repeat with *unreal, disallow,* and *prepay.*

3 Group Practice First, chunk the word into its parts—the prefix and the base word. Then read the base word. Then read and blend the prefix and the base word to read the whole word. **Continue with *unlike, disapprove, reapply, preview, unafraid, discharge.***

4 Review What do you know about reading words with prefixes? Break the word into two chunks, or syllables. Read the prefix and the base word and then read the whole word.

BLEND WORDS

INDIVIDUALS BLEND WORDS Call on children to chunk and blend *unfair, disloyal, recount, prefix, unmark, dismount, redo.* Have them tell what they know about each word before reading it. (Prefixes form separate syllables that are added to the beginning of base words.) For feedback, refer to step four of the Blending Strategy Routine.

BUILD WORDS

READ LONGER WORDS Write the prefixes *un-, re-, pre-,* and *dis-* as headings for a four-column chart or use Graphic Organizer 27. Write several base words in each column. Have children add the prefix to each base word, read the new word, and supply its meaning.

un-	re-	pre-	dis-
unmade	reread	preheat	disorder
unclear	recook	preprint	dislike
untie	reload	prepress	disown

Vocabulary TiP

You may wish to explain the meanings of these words.

resend   to send again
distaste   a feeling of dislike
reprints   copies of pictures of prints

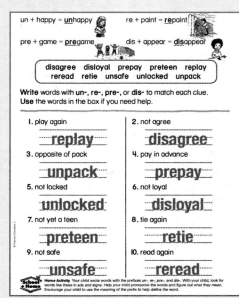

▲ **Practice Book 2.2** p. 63, Prefixes

Monitor Progress   Check Word Reading Prefixes *un-, re-, pre-, dis-*

Write the following words and have individuals read them.

unglue	resend	replace	undress	redo
preview	disagree	preheat	distaste	preschool
rereading	unloading	dislikes	reprints	prewriting

If...children cannot blend suffixes at this point,

then... continue to monitor their progress using other instructional opportunities during the week so that they can be successful with the Day 5 Assessment. See the Skills Trace on p. 180n.

SUCCESS PREDICTOR

Spiral REVIEW

● Row 3 contrasts *un-, re-, pre-, dis-* with inflected endings.

▶ **Day 1 Check** Word Reading

Day 2 Check Lesson Vocabulary/High-Frequency Words

Day 3 Check Retelling

Day 4 Check Fluency

Day 5 Assess Progress

Word Reading

SUCCESS PREDICTOR

OBJECTIVES

- Segment sounds and word parts to spell words.
- Spell words with prefixes *un-, re-, pre-, dis-*.

Spelling Words

Prefixes *un-, re-, pre-, dis-*

1. unsafe
2. preheat
3. rerun
4. disappear*
5. unlock
6. retie
7. rewind
8. unpack
9. unplug
10. regroup
11. preschool
12. disagree

Challenge Words

13. prehistoric
14. unfortunate
15. reunion

* Word from the Selection

Prefixes *un-, re-, pre-, dis-*

Generalization When prefixes un-, re-, pre-, and dis- are added to most words, the base word stays the same.

Sort the list words by their prefixes.

un-	pre-	**Spelling Words**
1. unsafe	9. preheat	1. unsafe
2. unlock	10. preschool	2. preheat
3. unpack	dis-	3. rerun
4. unplug	11. disappear	4. disappear
re-	12. disagree	5. unlock
5. rerun		6. retie
6. retie	**Challenge Words**	7. rewind
7. rewind	un-	8. unpack
8. regroup	13. unfortunate	9. unplug
	pre-	10. regroup
	13. prehistoric	11. preschool
	re-	12. disagree
	15. reunion	**Challenge Words**
		13. prehistoric
		14. unfortunate
		15. reunion

Home Activity Your child is learning to spell words with the prefixes un-, re-, pre-, and dis-. To practice at home, have your child look at the word, say it, spell it, and identify the base word.

▲ **Spelling Practice Book** p. 85

ELL

Support Spelling Before giving the spelling pretest, clarify the meaning of each spelling word with examples, such as saying *unplug* while unplugging a cord and *unlock* while unlocking a door.

Spelling

PRETEST Prefixes *un-, re-, pre-, dis-*

MODEL WRITING FOR WORD PARTS Each spelling word begins with a prefix. Before administering the spelling pretest, model how to segment prefixes to spell them.

- You can spell words with prefixes by thinking about the prefix and the base word. What prefix and base word make up *prepay*? (*pre-* and *pay*)
- Start with the sounds in the base word: *pay*. What letters spell /pā/? Write *pay*.
- Now add the prefix *pre-*. Add *pre-*.
- Now spell *prepay*.
- Repeat with *unreal, redraw, disassemble*.

PRETEST Dictate the spelling words. Segment the words for children if necessary. Have children check their pretests and correct misspelled words.

HOMEWORK Spelling Practice Book, p. 85

Group Time

On-Level	**Strategic Intervention**	**Advanced**
Read Decodable Reader 22.	**Read** Decodable Reader 22.	**Read** Advanced Selection 22
• Use pp. 180q.	• Use the **Routine** on p. DI·24.	• Use the **Routine** on p. DI·25.

ELL Place English language learners in the groups that correspond to their reading abilities in English.

ⓘ Independent Activities

Fluency Reading Pair children to reread Leveled Readers or the ELL Reader from the previous week or other text at children's independent level.

Journal Writing Write about a concern you have. Share writing.

Independent Reading See p. 180j for Reading/Library activities and suggestions.

Literacy Centers To practice prefixes, you may use Word Work, p. 180j.

Practice Book 2.2 Prefixes p. 63; Sequence, p. 64

Break into small groups after Spelling and before the Comprehension lesson.

Apply Phonics

⊙ PRACTICE Prefixes *un-, re-, pre-, dis-*

Decodable Reader 22
In the Woods
Written by Paula Bilika
Illustrated by Chip Mitchell

Phonics Skill
Prefixes un-, re-, pre-, dis-

HIGH-FREQUENCY WORDS Review *come, family,* and *water.*

READ DECODABLE READER 22

• Pages 50–51 Read aloud quietly with the group.
• Pages 52–53 Have the group read aloud without you.
• Pages 54–56 Select individuals to read aloud.

CHECK COMPREHENSION AND DECODING Have children retell the story to include characters, setting, and plot. Then have children locate words with prefixes *un-, re-, pre-,* and *dis-* in the story. Review *un-, re-, pre-, and dis-* spelling patterns. Sort words according to their spelling patterns.

un-	*re-*	*dis-*	*pre-*
unhooks	relight	dislikes	precooked
unload	repack		
unlocks			
unpacks			
unrolls			
unsafe			
unties			

HOMEWORK Take-Home Decodable Reader 22

REREAD FOR FLUENCY

Paired Reading

ROUTINE

Reader 1 Begins Children read the entire story, switching readers at the end of each page.

Reader 2 Begins Have partners reread; now the other partner begins.

Reread For optimal fluency, children should reread three or four times.

Provide Feedback Listen to children read and provide corrective feedback regarding their oral reading and their use of the blending strategy.

Monitor Progress

Decoding

If... children have difficulty decoding a word,	**then...** prompt them to blend the word.
	• What is the new word?
	• Is the new word a word you know?
	• Does it make sense in the story?

Access Content

Beginning Preview *In the Woods,* identifying tents, backpacks, and lake in the pictures and print.

Intermediate Preview *In the Woods,* explaining the meanings of verbs *unload, relight,* and *repack.* Have children point out where characters are performing these actions in the pictures.

Advanced After reading *In the Woods,* have partners take turns retelling the first few pages of the story.

OBJECTIVES

- Recognize sequence.
- Use graphic organizers.

Skills Trace

Sequence

Introduce/Teach	TE: 2.2 163a–b, 164e, 219a–b, 220e; 2.5 180r, 180–181
Practice	TE: 2.2 174–175, 234–235; 2.5 194–195; PB: 2.1 54–55, 74–75; 2.2 64–65
Reteach/Review	TE: 2.2 204–205, DI·64 DI·66; 2.3 330–331; 2.5 216–217, DI·65; PB: 2.1 67, 107; 2.2 77
Test	TE: 2.2 188e–g, 250e–g; 2.5 206e–g; Selection Tests: 2.2 21–24, 29–32; 2.5 85–88; Benchmark Test: Units 2, 3, 5

When a Thunderstorm
Strikes

A thunderstorm can happen even on a nice day. First, you may see big dark clouds in the distance. They were not there an hour ago. You also see that the clouds are moving toward you.

The next thing you know—flash! Lightning streaks from the clouds to the ground. Then—boom! Thunder rumbles. You can tell how far away the storm is. Just count the seconds between the flash and the boom. Every five seconds is one mile. So, if you count five seconds, the storm is one mile away.

Now the storm is moving closer. When you count fewer than five seconds between lightning and thunder, the storm is less than a mile away.

Finally, you can't count even one full second. The storm is here!

Skill Here's a clue word. *First* tells you that events are beginning to happen.

Strategy If you made a graphic organizer, use the clue word in this sentence to add more information to it.

Unit 5 One Dark Night   Skill Transparency 22

▲ Skill Transparency 22

Access Content

Beginning/Intermediate For a Picture It! lesson on Sequence, see the ELL Teaching Guide, pp. 148–149.

Advanced Before children read "When a Thunderstorm Strikes," make sure they know the meanings of *rumble, lightning,* and *mile.*

❖ Sequence
❖ Graphic Organizer

TEACH/MODEL

INTRODUCE Recall *Firefighter!* Have students tell, in order, three things that happen in that selection. (Possible response: The firefighters race to the fire; they look for Luke as they put out the fire; they find Luke up the street.)

- Could the last thing have happened first? Why not?

Read p. 180 with children. Explain the following:

- Good readers pay attention to the order of events in a story. Sometimes there are helpful clue words, such as *first, next,* and *finally,* to tell the sequence. Sometimes there aren't.

- We can keep track of sequence by using a graphic organizer to record events as we read. This helps us remember the correct order of events in a story.

Use Skill Transparency 22 to teach sequence and graphic organizers.

SKILL Use paragraph one to model using clue words to identify sequence.

 MODEL I know I should keep track of the sequence of events as I read. This selection has some clue words to help me. The clue word *first* tells me that the first thing you might notice about a thunderstorm is dark clouds in the distance.

STRATEGY Continue with paragraphs one and two to model using a graphic organizer.

 MODEL Under the heading *First* on my graphic organizer, I will write *dark clouds in the distance.* I continue reading, and I spot the clue word *next.* It tells me that next you might see lightning streaking from the clouds, so I write that under the heading *Next.*

One Dark Night

Comprehension

Skill
Sequence

Strategy
Graphic Organizers

🎯 Sequence

- Sequence is the order of events in a story.
- Clue words such as *first, next, then, now,* and *finally* will help you figure out and remember the order of events.

🎯 Strategy: Graphic Organizers

A graphic organizer is a picture that can help you organize information as you read. You can make a graphic organizer like this one to show the order of events in a story.

| First: |
| Next: |
| Then: |
| Now: |
| Finally: |

Write to Read ✏️

1. Read "When a Thunderstorm Strikes." Write down some clue words that tell the order of events.

2. Make a graphic organizer like the one above. Fill in your chart to show the order of events as you read.

180

When a Thunderstorm Strikes

A thunderstorm can happen even on a nice day. First, you may see big dark clouds in the distance. They were not there an hour ago. You also see that the clouds are moving toward you.

The next thing you know—flash! Lightning streaks from the clouds to the ground. Then—boom! Thunder rumbles. You can tell how far away the storm is. Just count the seconds between the flash and the boom. Every five seconds is one mile. So, if you count five seconds, the storm is one mile away.

Now the storm is moving closer. When you count fewer than five seconds between lightning and thunder, the storm is less than a mile away.

Finally, you can't count even one full second. The storm is here!

Skill Here's a clue word. *First* tells you that events are beginning to happen.

Strategy If you made a graphic organizer, use the clue word in this sentence to add more information to it.

181

PRACTICE

WRITE Work with children to complete the steps in the Write activity. Have children use the completed graphic organizer to retell the events in "When a Thunderstorm Strikes."

Monitor Progress	**Sequence**
If... children are unable to complete Write on p. 180,	**then...** use Practice Book 2.2, p. 64, for additional practice.

CONNECT TO READING Encourage children to ask themselves these questions when they read.

- Do I look for clue words that help me understand the order of events in a story?
- Do I make a graphic organizer to show the order of events in a story?

Look at the pictures.
Write the words **first, second, third,** and **last** to show the correct order of events.

second

last

first

third

Write a sentence about what might happen next.

Possible answer: The boy takes his dog for a walk.

Home Activity Your child identified the order of events in a picture story about a boy and his dog. Have your child draw four or five pictures that tell a different story about a child and pet. Ask your child to label the pictures to show the order of events.

▲ **Practice Book 2.2** p. 64, Sequence

OBJECTIVE

⬤ Write reasons.

DAILY FIX-IT

1. she will un lock the doors.
   She will <u>unlock</u> the doors.

2. She well unpack her groceries?
   She <u>will</u> unpack her groceries<u>.</u>

This week's practice sentences appear on Daily Fix-It Transparency 22.

Strategic Intervention

Children who are not able to write independently may copy one or more of the reasons for helping animals and add an illustration.

Advanced

Have children write a list of reasons it is important to help people who are less fortunate.

Support Writing Before writing reasons why people should help animals, have children work in pairs to tell each other what they are planning to write about.

▲ **The Grammar and Writing Book**
For more instruction and practice, use pp. 176–181.

Shared Writing

WRITE Reasons

GENERATE IDEAS Ask children to think of reasons why people should help animals. Write children's suggestions on the board. Have them put their reasons in order from the most important to the least important.

WRITE REASONS Explain that the class will make a list of reasons why people should help animals and rank the reasons from most important (#1) to least important (#5).

COMPREHENSION SKILL Have children think about the reasons they should help animals.

- Display Writing Transparency 22 and read the title.
- Ask children to think about a time when they had to help an animal and why it was important to help that animal.
- Then ask children to name reasons why it is important to help animals.
- As children name reasons, record their thoughts. Before recording, inquire as to whether the suggestion is a very important reason or a less important reason. Record reasons in sequence— from most important to least important.

HANDWRITING While writing, model the letter forms as shown on pp. TR14–17.

READ THE REASONS Have children read the completed list of reasons aloud as you track the print.

> ### A List of Reasons
>
> **Why People Should Help Animals**
> **Possible answers:**
>
> 1. <u>It is the right thing to do.</u>
>
> 2. <u>Animals are living things.</u>
>
> 3. <u>People are smarter than animals.</u>
>
> 4. <u>Animals help people.</u>
>
> 5. <u>Animals provide food for people.</u>
>
> Unit 5 One Dark Night   Writing Model **22**

▲ **Writing Transparency 22**

INDEPENDENT WRITING

WRITE A LIST OF REASONS Have children write their own list of reasons why they think it is important to help animals. Encourage them to use words from the Word Wall and the Amazing Words board. Let children illustrate their writing. You may gather children's work to save in their portfolios.

ADDITIONAL PRACTICE For additional practice, use pp. 176–181 in the Grammar and Writing Book.

Grammar

TEACH/MODEL Pronouns

REVIEW PRONOUNS Remind children that a pronoun is a word that takes the place of a noun or nouns.

IDENTIFY PRONOUNS FOR ONE AND MORE THAN ONE Display Grammar Transparency 22. Read the definition aloud.

- *Dad* and *Mom* name two nouns. When more than one person is being talked about, you can use the pronoun *they.*

- *A cat* names only one thing. The pronoun *it* can be used to name the cat.

Continue modeling with the rest of the paragraph.

PRACTICE

FIND PRONOUNS Have children suggest several more sentences to continue the story. Record these sentences on the board. Then reread the sentences and find singular and plural pronouns.

- Where do we use a pronoun that names only one?
- Where do we use a pronoun that names more than one?

Pronouns for One and More Than One

He, she, and it are pronouns that name only one.
We and they are pronouns that name more than one.

Mom helps animals. She works for a vet.
She is a pronoun that names one person—Mom.

Sometimes Dad and I help. We feed the animals.
We is a pronoun that names more than one—Dad and I.

Circle the pronouns that name only one.
Underline the pronouns that name more than one.

Dad and Mom were driving home last night. They saw

a cat. It was sitting by the side of the road. "We should stop,"

Mom said. Dad pulled over. He got a blanket out of the trunk.

He wrapped the blanket around the cat. Mom held the cat.

She said, "Drive to Dr. Klute's." They took the cat to the vet.

Unit 5 One Dark Night   Grammar 22

▲ **Grammar Transparency 22**

Wrap Up Your Day!

 PREFIXES un-, re-, pre-, dis- Write *disappear* and ask children what prefix is found in the word. *(dis-)* Have children name other words with prefixes.

 SPELLING WORDS WITH PREFIXES Have children name the letters for the prefix in *preheat.* Write the letters as children write them in the air. Continue with *preschool* and other words with prefixes.

 SEQUENCE To help children identify the sequence of the story, ask: What happened first in the story? What happened in the middle? What happened at the end?

LET'S TALK ABOUT IT Recall that there are events that warn you about a storm. What are some words that tell the order of events? (first, next, then, finally)

 HOMEWORK Send home this week's Family Times newsletter.

PREVIEW Day 2

Tell children that tomorrow the class will read about how a boy and his grandfather help some stray animals.

Day 2

AT A GLANCE

Share Literature
Animal Hospital

Phonics and Spelling
Prefixes *un-, re-, pre-, dis-*
Spelling: Words with Prefixes *un-, re-, pre-, dis-*

Build Background
How Children Acquired Their Pets

Lesson Vocabulary
pours   lightning thunder storm
flashes pounds   rolling
More Words to Know
stray   nudging   brooding

Vocabulary
Skill Unfamiliar Words
Strategy Context Clues

Read

 Group Time < Differentiated Instruction

One Dark Night

Interactive Writing
Suspense

Grammar
Pronouns for One and More Than One

Materials

- *Sing with Me Big Book*
- Big Book *Animal Hospital*
- Phonics Songs and Rhymes Chart 22
- Background Building Audio CD
- Graphic Organizer 26
- Tested Word Cards
- Student Edition 182–201

Morning Warm~Up!

Today we will read about Jonathan.
He shows concern for a family of cats.
They need protection from a storm.
What do animals need for growth
and well-being?

QUESTION OF THE DAY Encourage children to sing "Love, Love Animals" from the *Sing with Me Big Book* as you gather. Write and read the message and discuss the question.

REVIEW ORAL VOCABULARY

- Read the message again and ask children to raise their hands when they hear any of the Amazing Words from yesterday (*concern, protection, growth*).

- Ask volunteers to define the three Amazing Words.

Build Background Use the Day 2 instruction on ELL Poster 22 to preview high-frequency words.

ELL Poster 22

Share Literature

BUILD CONCEPTS

CALL-OUT BOXES Recall the book *Animal Hospital*. Point out the call-out boxes on pp. 6–7. Discuss with children why these boxes appear in the book. Point out that the text in the boxes is not meant to be read as part of the story about Jack and Luke, but that they give extra information about things in the story.

Big Book

BUILD ORAL VOCABULARY Introduce the Amazing Word **fragile.** Explain that it means "easily breakable." Suggest that as you read, children listen to find out what parts of an animal are fragile.

● What are some things that are fragile in this room?

MONITOR LISTENING COMPREHENSION

● What things in the story are fragile? (Wing bones are fragile.)

● What animal had a hurt wing? How did the vet help the animal? (The duck was hurt and the vet strapped its wing to its body with a bandage.)

● What other parts of animals do you think are fragile and why? (Possible responses: a rabbit's teeth because they can be cut with scissors; a dog's bones because they break easily; a duck's feet because they crack if they get too dry; a horse's feet because horses have to wear special shoes to protect their feet)

to build oral vocabulary

	MONITOR PROGRESS
concern growth protection fragile pellets litter pollute release	**If…** children lack oral vocabulary experiences about the concept Responsibility, **then…** use the Oral Vocabulary Routine. See p. DI·4 to teach *fragile.*

Build Concepts Help children understand what happens when the dog arrives at the animal hospital. Ask them if they have ever seen an *ambulance* or heard a *siren*. Explain that an ambulance brings a hurt animal to the vet as fast as possible, and that a siren lets everyone know they have to act quickly. Help children understand that the expression *right away* means "now."

OBJECTIVES

◉ Review words with prefixes *un-, re-, pre-, dis-.*

● Sort and read words with prefixes *un-, re-, pre-, dis-.*

Strategic Intervention

Use **Strategic Intervention Decodable Reader 22** for more practice with prefixes *un-, re-, pre-, and dis-.*

ELL

Support Phonics Invite children to use gestures and facial expressions to act out *unhappy, refilled, preview,* and *displeases* as you replay the Phonics Songs and Rhymes Audio CD.

◉Prefixes *un-, re-, pre-, dis-*

TEACH/MODEL

Fluent Word Reading

ROUTINE

1 **Connect** Write *replay.* You can read this word because you know how to read words with prefixes. What prefix and base word form *replay? (re-* and *play)* Do the same with *unwrap, preview,* and *disagree.*

2 **Model** When you come to a word with a prefix, look at the word and then read it. Model reading *unclasp, rework, predate, disapprove, rethink, undisturbed.* When you come to a new word, what are you going to do?

3 **Group Practice** Write *unglue, pretest, rethink, disprove, unlatch, rewrite.* Read these words. Look at the word, say the word to yourself, and then read the word aloud. **Allow 2–3 seconds previewing time.**

WORD READING

PHONICS SONGS AND RHYMES CHART 22 Frame each of the following words on Phonics Songs and Rhymes Chart 22. Call on individuals to read them. Guide children in previewing.

unhappy	**refilled**
preview	**displeases**

Sing "Kitten Rescue" to the tune of "Kookaburra," or play the CD. Have children follow along on the chart as they sing. Then have individuals take turns circling the words with prefixes on the chart.

Audio CD **Phonics Songs and Rhymes Audio**

Kitten Rescue

Little kitty sat up in a tree,
Looking as unhappy as can be.
"Mew!" cried the kitten.
"Yowl!" cried the kitten.
"This displeases me!"

I refilled her dish so she could eat.
I gave her a preview of her treat.
"Purr," mewed the kitten.
"Yay," mewed the kitten.
She came back to me.

Phonics Songs and Rhymes Chart 22

SORT WORDS

INDIVIDUALS SORT WORDS WITH PREFIXES *un-, re-, pre-, dis-* Write prefixes *un-, re-, pre-,* and *dis-* as heads for four columns. Have individuals write words with prefixes *un-, re-, pre-,* and *dis-* under the appropriate headings and circle the prefixes. Have all children complete the activity on paper. Ask individuals to read the words. Provide feedback as necessary.

un-	*re-*	*pre-*	*dis-*
unhappy	rethink	preheat	disagree
unfold	repaint	preview	displace
unseen	react	prepaid	displease

Spelling

PRACTICE Prefixes *un-, re-, pre-, dis-*

WRITE DICTATION SENTENCES Have children write these sentences. Repeat words slowly, allowing children to hear each sound. Children may use the Word Wall to help with spelling high-frequency words. **Word Wall**

Will you rewind the rerun of that show?

Do not disappear before it is time to unpack.

The preschool children learn to retie their laces.

It is unsafe to preheat the oven while you are gone.

HOMEWORK Spelling Practice Book, p. 86

Spelling Words

Prefixes *un-, re-, pre-, dis-*

1. unsafe
2. preheat
3. rerun
4. disappear*
5. unlock
6. retie
7. rewind
8. unpack
9. unplug
10. regroup
11. preschool
12. disagree

Challenge Words

13. prehistoric
14. unfortunate
15. reunion

* Word from the Selection

Prefixes *un-, re-, pre-, dis-*
Write the list word.

not safe — 1. **unsafe**   wind again — 2. **rewind**

opposite of pack — 3. **unpack**   group in a new way — 4. **regroup**

Spelling Words	
unsafe	rewind
preheat	unpack
rerun	unplug
disappear	regroup
unlock	preschool
retie	disagree

Read the sentence. Make a list word by adding a prefix to the underlined word.

5. Did you plug the lamp? **unplug**
6. I agree with that idea. **disagree**
7. Let's run those home movies. **rerun**
8. Eddie started school this year. **preschool**
9. Be sure to lock the door. **unlock**
10. My cat seems to appear at night. **disappear**
11. Please tie your shoes. **retie**
12. Did you heat the oven? **preheat**

School + Home Home Activity Your child spelled words with the prefixes *un-, re-, pre-,* and *dis-*. Have your child explain how the new word changes the meaning of the sentences in Exercises 5 to 12 above.

▲ Spelling Practice Book p. 86

Build Background

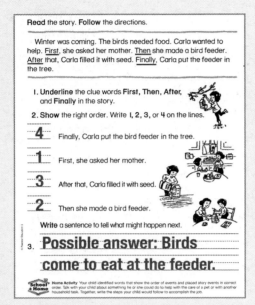

▲ **Practice Book 2.2** p. 65, Sequence

Activate Prior Knowledge Draw simple pictures of a dog, a cat, and a fish inside the outline of a house. Ask children to name the animals in their home language and say the words in English.

DISCUSS PETS Write *pets* on the chalkboard. Display pictures of possible family pets. Initiate discussion by asking children what pets they have.

● What kind of pet do you have?
● Where or how did you get your pet?

BACKGROUND BUILDING AUDIO Have children listen to the CD and share the new information they learned about acquiring pets.

 **Sing with Me/ Background Building Audio**

MAKE PREDICTIONS Draw a three-column chart or use Graphic Organizer 26. Have children read the selection title and preview the illustrations. Encourage children to think about the title and pictures as they predict what might happen in the story. Remind them to use what they already know as they write predictions in column one. Help students think about what clues they used to make their predictions. Have them write the clues in column two. After children have finished the story, have them write what actually happened in the story in column three. Then have them compare what happened with what they predicted might happen.

Predictions	Clues	What Actually Happened
A boy cares for kittens caught in a storm.	There are pictures of a storm, a cat carrying a kitten, and kittens sleeping next to the boy.	

▲ **Graphic Organizer 26**

CONNECT TO SELECTION Connect background information to *One Dark Night*.

Thunderstorms can be loud and frightening. People and animals look for shelter from the rain, winds, and lightning. Jonathan is a character In this story who is watching a storm. Suddenly he spots a cat carrying something small and fragile. Concerned for the cat's safety, Jonathan tries to offer protection. We'll find out how Jonathan helps the cat and her little family.

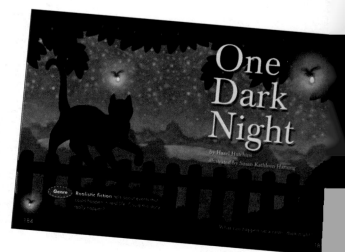

One Dark Night
by Hazel Hutchins
illustrated by Susan Kathleen Hartung

Vocabulary

LESSON VOCABULARY

DISCUSS THE VOCABULARY Share the lesson vocabulary with children. Have children locate each word in their glossaries and note its pronunciation and meaning.

WORDS TO KNOW

T pours rains heavily

T lightning a flash of light in the sky during a storm

T thunder a loud sound in the sky that comes after a flash of lightning

T storm heavy rain, snow, or hail

T flashes moves quickly by

T pounds hits with noise and force

T rolling making a loud, deep sound

MORE WORDS TO KNOW

stray lost

nudging giving a small push

brooding worrying or thinking hard

T = Tested Word

- Children should be able to decode all words.

- Encourage children to use the words in personal contexts. Have children talk about a time they were in a thunderstorm. Have them use the words *thunder* and *storm* when they tell about it.

- Then direct children to use the words *lightning, pours, flashes, pounds,* and *rolling* as they continue to tell about their experiences with thunderstorms.

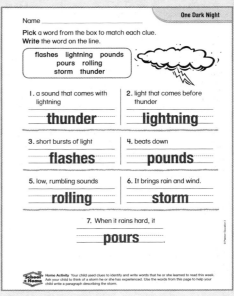

Name	One Dark Night

Pick a word from the box to match each clue.
Write the word on the line.

flashes lightning pounds
pours rolling
storm thunder

1. a sound that comes with lightning	2. light that comes before thunder
thunder	**lightning**
3. short bursts of light	4. beats down
flashes	**pounds**
5. low, rumbling sounds	6. It brings rain and wind.
rolling	**storm**

7. When it rains hard, it

pours

Home Activity Your child used clues to identify and write words that he or she learned to read this week. Ask your child to think of a storm he or she has experienced. Use the words from this page to help your child write a paragraph describing the storm.

▲ **Practice Book 2.2** p. 66, Lesson Vocabulary

Monitor Progress | Check Lesson Vocabulary

Point to the following words and have individuals read them.

lightning	thunder	storm	flashes	rolling	pounds	pours
angry	door	second(s)	watch(ing)	warm(ing)	water	

If... children cannot read these words,

then... have them practice in pairs with word cards before reading the selection. Monitor their fluency with these words during reading, and provide additional practice opportunities before the Day 5 Assessment.

SUCCESS PREDICTOR

Spiral **REVIEW**

- Reviews previously taught high-frequency words and lesson vocabulary.

Day 1 Check Word Reading

▶**Day 2** Check Lesson Vocabulary/High-Frequency Words

Day 3 Check Retelling

Day 4 Check Fluency

Day 5 Assess Progress

Word Reading

SUCCESS PREDICTOR

Words to Know

lightning
thunder
storm
flashes
rolling
pounds
pours

Remember

Try the strategy. Then, if you need more help, use your glossary or a dictionary.

Vocabulary Strategy
For Unfamiliar Words

Context Clues Sometimes as you read, you may not know the meaning of a word. What can you do? You can look at the words and sentences around the word. These are called **context clues**. They can help you figure out the meaning of the word you don't know.

1. Read the words and sentences around the word you don't know. Sometimes the author tells you what the word means.

2. Use the words and sentences to predict a meaning for the word.

3. Try that meaning in the sentence. Does it make sense?

Read "Some Like It Stormy." Use context clues to help you understand the meanings of the vocabulary words.

Some Like It Stormy

My cat Trevor is afraid of noises. He hates lightning and thunder. Whenever there is a storm, he hides in my bedroom closet. I usually go into the closet with him. I do that to keep him company, not because I am afraid. Only babies—and Trevor—are afraid of storms.

In fact, I like a good storm. I like the way lightning flashes and crackles like fireworks. It makes loud noises that boom in my ears. I like the way thunder crashes and rumbles. It sounds like rolling bowling balls. I like the way rain pounds on the ground and pours off the roofs of the houses. After the storm, the whole world smells fresh and new.

But try telling Trevor that. I have tried to explain storms to him. He always listens and seems to understand. But then the next time there is a storm, there he is, back in the closet again!

Words to Write

Do you like storms? Write about how you feel about storms. Use words from the Words to Know list.

182

183

OBJECTIVE

● Use context clues to determine the meaning of unfamiliar words.

ELL

Access Content Use ELL Poster 22 to preteach the lesson vocabulary. Reinforce the words with the vocabulary activities and word cards in the ELL Teaching Guide, pp. 150–151. Choose from the following to meet children's language proficiency levels.

Beginning If children are unfamiliar with the words *lightning, thunder,* and *flashes,* point out the context clues in the second paragraph.

Intermediate After reading, children can use vocabulary words in a Venn diagram showing *Things You Hear in a Storm, Things You See in a Storm,* and both.

Advanced Teach the lesson on pp. 182–183. Have children draw pictures of a thunderstorm and use five vocabulary words in their descriptions.

Vocabulary Strategy

TEACH/MODEL Context Clues

CONNECT Remind children of strategies to use when they come across words they don't understand.

● Sometimes we can get the meaning from word parts. We may understand the base word and suffix (*teacher, a person who teaches*) or the two shorter words in a compound (*raindrop, a drop of rain*).

● We can look in a dictionary or glossary.

● We can look for context clues in the words and sentences around the unknown word. Today we will learn more about using context clues.

INTRODUCE THE STRATEGY

- Read and discuss the steps for using context clues on p. 182.
- Have children read "Some Like It Stormy," paying attention to context clues to determine the meaning of highlighted words.
- Model using context clues to determine the meaning of *thunder*.

Think Aloud **MODEL** I'm not sure what *thunder* is. The second paragraph tells me that thunder crashes and rumbles and sounds like rolling bowling balls. *Thunder* must be the loud crashing sound that comes after lightning in a storm.

PRACTICE

- Have children determine the meanings of highlighted words in "Some Like It Stormy" and explain the context clues they used.
- Point out that context doesn't work with every word, and they may have to use the glossary or a dictionary to find the meaning of some words.

WRITE Children's writing should include lesson vocabulary in a description of a storm they remember.

CONNECT TO READING Encourage children to use these strategies to determine the meaning of an unknown word.

- Look for context clues in nearby words or sentences.
- Use word structure.
- Use the glossary or a dictionary.

Group Time

On-Level	Strategic Intervention	Advanced
Read *One Dark Night.*	**Read** SI Decodable Reader 22.	**Read** *One Dark Night.*
• Use pp. 184–201.	• Read or listen to *One Dark Night.*	• Use the Routine on p. DI·27.
	• Use the Routine on p. DI·26.	

DAY 2

ELL Place English language learners in the groups that correspond to their reading abilities in English.

Independent Activities

Independent Reading See p. 180j for Reading/Library activities and suggestions.

Journal Writing Write about an animal you have helped or seen during a storm. Share writing.

Literacy Centers To provide experiences with *One Dark Night,* you may use the Listening and Writing Centers on pp. 180j and 180k.

Practice Book 2.2 Sequence, p. 65; Lesson Vocabulary, p. 66; Plot and Theme, p. 67

Break into small groups after Vocabulary and before Writing.

2

One Dark Night

by Hazel Hutchins

illustrated by Susan Kathleen Hartung

Genre **Realistic fiction** tells about events that could happen in real life. Could this story really happen?

What can happen on a rainy, dark night?

184

185

AudioText

ELL

Access Content Before reading, review the story summary in English and/or the home language. See the ELL Teaching Guide, pp. 152–154.

Read
Prereading Strategies

PREVIEW AND PREDICT Have children read the title. Identify the author and illustrator. Do a picture walk of pp. 184–187. Discuss what an approaching storm feels and sounds like. Ask children what they think this story will be about.

DISCUSS REALISTIC FICTION Ask if a storm is something that could really happen. Help children understand that this story is fiction because it comes from the author's imagination. However, it is a story that could happen in real life. Remind them that an imaginary story that could really happen is a special kind of fiction called realistic fiction. Read the definition of realistic fiction on p. 184 of the Student Edition.

SET PURPOSE Read the question on p. 185. Ask children to make predictions about what might happen on a rainy, dark night.

_____ Prefixes *un-, re-, pre-, dis-*   ☐ lesson/tested vocabular

One dark night, lightning flashes.
Count the seconds before the thunder rolls.
One, two, three, four, five, six, seven, eight,
nine, ten.

Baroom!

A summer storm is two miles away and
coming closer.

Jonathan looks into the night.
Something small and dark is looking
back at him.

186

187

Guiding Comprehension

Detail • Literal

- **How does Jonathan know a storm is coming?**
He sees lightning and hears thunder.

Prior Knowledge • Inferential

- **Why does Jonathan count the seconds between the lightning and thunder?**
It tells him how far away the storm is.

Predict • Inferential

- **What do you think the small, dark something might be?**
Children might say a dog, a cat, or a raccoon.

▲ **Pages 186–187**
Have children read to find out what the boy in the picture sees and hears.

TIME FOR Science

Weather
You can measure the distance between yourself and an approaching thunderstorm by counting the seconds between the lightning flash and the thunder clap. Divide the number of seconds by five and you will know how many miles you are from the storm.

He races downstairs and throws open the screen door. "The stray cat's afraid of the thunder!" he tells his grandparents.

"Stray cats aren't afraid of storms," says Grandfather.

"Look out! I think she's got a mouse!" cries Grandmother. But stray cat is already inside and laying her prize on the rug.

"It's a kitten!" says Jonathan. One small kitten–soft as whispers, gray as dawn.

188   189

▲ **Pages 188–189**
Have children read to find out what Jonathan saw.

EXTEND SKILLS

Simile

For instruction in simile, discuss the following:

- Sometimes authors compare two unlike things that are alike in at least one way. An author uses words such as *like* or *as* to draw this comparison.
- Look on p. 188 to find two similes.
- The phrases "soft as whispers, gray as dawn" are the similes. How are the objects similar?

Assess Read some more similes and ask children to describe the comparison being made.

Guiding Comprehension

Confirm Predictions • Inferential
- **What is the small, dark something that Jonathan sees?**
  It is the stray cat and her kitten.

Draw Conclusions • Critical
- **Why do you think the stray cat wants to come inside?**
  Possible response: She wants protection from the storm for her kitten.

Predict • Inferential
- **What do you think will happen next?**
  Possible response: Jonathan will take care of the cat and kitten.

____ Prefixes *un-, re-, pre-, dis-*   ☐ lesson/tested vocabulan

Lightning spills into the room. Count the seconds before the thunder rolls. One, two, three, four, five. . .

BAROOM!

The storm is one mile away and coming closer. Stray cat disappears into the night.

"Come back!" calls Jonathan. He steps into the brooding dark, but Grandfather gently draws him inside and pulls the screen door shut.

190   191

Guiding Comprehension

▲ **Pages 190–191**
Have children read to find out what the stray cat does next.

🌀 **Sequence • Literal**
- **What does the stray cat do next?**
  The cat goes back outside.

Draw Conclusions • Inferential
- **How does Jonathan know the storm is coming closer?**
  He counts only five seconds between the lightning and thunder.

Predict • Inferential
- **Why do you think the stray cat goes back outside?**
  Possible response: She has another kitten to bring inside.

Monitor Progress

Read New Words	
If... children come to a word they don't know,	**then...** remind them to: 1. Blend the word. 2. Decide if the word makes sense. 3. Look in a dictionary for more help.

Jonathan lays his bathrobe on the rug.
He snuggles the kitten within its folds.
"We'll take care of it, won't we?" he asks.
"As ever best we can," says Grandmother.
But how can they take care of anything so small?

192   193

▲ **Pages 192–193**
Have children read to find out what Jonathan does with the kitten.

Strategy Self-Check

Have children ask themselves these questions to check their reading.

Vocabulary Strategy

• Do I look for context clues in nearby words or sentences?

• Do I use word structure, such as Greek or Latin roots?

• Do I use the glossary or a dictionary?

Graphic Organizer

• Do I look for a mark like an apostrophe that helps me understand the word?

• Do I reread to be sure the new word makes sense in the story?

Guiding Comprehension

Draw Conclusions • Inferential

• **Why do you think Jonathan puts the kitten in his bathrobe?**
Children may respond that he is concerned about the kitten and wants to keep it warm.

Prior Knowledge • Inferential

• *Text to World* **What will Jonathan and his grandparents have to do to care for the kitten?**
They will have to feed it and keep it warm.

Summarize • Inferential

• **What has happened so far in the story?**
A storm is coming, so the stray cat brings her kitten into Jonathan's house. Then the stray cat runs back outside, and Jonathan snuggles the kitten.

____ Prefixes *un-, re-, pre-, dis-*   ☐ lesson/tested vocabular

A scratching at the door.
Two green eyes peer in at them.
"She's back! She's back!"
cries Jonathan and races to the door.
Stray cat enters, carrying a second
kitten–soft as stuffing, white as snow.
Lightning flashes. Count the seconds
before the thunder rolls. One, two, thr–

BARRROOOMMM!
The storm is half a mile away
and coming closer. Stray cat darts into
the night before the last echo fades.

194

195

Skills in Context

⟳ SEQUENCE

- **Which happens first: the stray cat goes back outside, or the noise of the thunder ends?**

The stray cat goes back outside.

Monitor Progress	Sequence
If... children are unable to identify the order of events,	**then...** model how to use clue words to determine the sequence.

Think Aloud

MODEL When I read the last sentence on p. 194, I see the word *before*. This clue word helps me figure out the order of events. It tells me that the cat goes out before the thunder ends.

ASSESS Have children contribute to an ordered list of events that take place on p. 194 of the story.

▲ **Pages 194–195**
Have children read to find out what happens when the stray cat comes back.

EXTEND SKILLS

Onomatopoeia

For instruction in onomatopoeia, discuss the following:

- Sometimes authors choose words that sound like what they are describing. For example, the word *purr* sounds like the noise that a cat makes.
- Look on p. 194 to find a word that sounds like what it is describing.
- How is the noise *BARRROOOMMM* like the noise it describes?

Assess Have children find other examples of onomatopoeia in the selection.

Outside a great wind whips the trees
and hurtles single drops of rain.

Splat! Splat!
Jonathan warms the kittens in their bed
and looks into the night. Watching. Waiting.
This time when the lightning comes
it splits the sky with wild, white brightness.
There is no time to count before the
thunder cracks.

BAAAARRRROOOOM!
A hard rain drums the roof and pounds into
the grass like something angry.
"There she is!" cries Jonathan.

196   197

▲ **Pages 196–197**
Have children read to find out more plot details.

Read the story. Follow the directions.

Rob wanted a pet more than anything. He begged for a dog. His mom said, "No." Dogs need a yard. Rob begged for a cat. His mom said, "No." Cats make her nose itch. He asked for a fish. This time she said, "Yes." Later that day Rob picked out a big, beautiful fish. It was just the right pet for him.

Circle the sentence below that tells the big idea of this story.

Dogs need space to run.

Cats make some people sick.

A pet must be right for your family.

Write 1, 2, or 3 on the lines to show the right order.

2 Rob's mom said, "No."

3 Rob got a fish.

1 Rob begged for a dog.

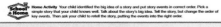

Home Activity Your child identified the big idea of a story and put story events in correct order. Pick a simple story that your child knows well. Talk about the story's big idea. Tell the story, but change the order of key events. Then ask your child to retell the story, putting the events into the right order.

▲ **Practice Book 2.2** p. 67,
Plot and Theme

Skills in Context

(REVIEW) PLOT AND THEME

• **What is the plot of this story? What is the theme of the story?**
The plot is a series of events that happen during a storm. The theme is the importance of helping each other during a storm.

Monitor Progress	Plot and Theme
If... children have difficulty answering the question,	**then...** model how to identify plot and theme.

Think Aloud **MODEL** The plot is what happens. I know that Jonathan and his family provide protection for the mother cat and her kittens during the storm. The theme is the "big idea," or what the story is trying to teach me. I think the story is trying to teach me the importance of helping one another.

ASSESS Have children find text to support the theme of this story.

_____ Prefixes *un-, re-, pre-, dis-*   ☐ lesson/tested vocabular

The next moment he is outside too,
to help them battle through the rain.
One boy, one cat, and a third small kitten—
wet as water, black as night. The rain pours.
Jonathan drips puddles on the floor.
"Are there any more?" he asks stray cat.
"Do we need another trip?"

198

199

Strategies in Context

⊙ GRAPHIC ORGANIZER

- **What are the important things that happen in this story?**
  A storm is coming. The stray cat brings a kitten inside, and Jonathan and his grandparents take care of it. Then the cat goes back outside two more times to get two more kittens.

Monitor Progress	Graphic Organizer
If... children have difficulty recalling the sequence of events of the story,	**then...** model how to use a story sequence chart to recall story events.

Think Aloud

MODEL As I read, I picture what is happening to see if the order of events makes sense. I can use a story sequence chart to help me remember the story. I write the most important things that happened in each part of the story.

ASSESS Have children contribute details to the story sequence chart.

▲ **Pages 198–199**
Have children read to find out what Jonathan does next.

One Dark Night **198–199**

But stray cat climbs into the bathrobe,
licking, nudging, and arranging her family.
    They are all here.
One stray cat
and three small kittens,
safe from the rain and the wind
and the rolling thunder,
safe with Jonathan,
safe with his grandparents,
one dark night.

200

201

▲ **Pages 200–201**
Have children read to find out what happens to Jonathan, the cat, and her kittens.

Shelter

TIME FOR Science

A basic need of animals is shelter. Humans need special shelters to protect themselves when storms hit. Some people build safe rooms, or places where the walls are made of such strong concrete and metal that nothing can break through, even objects blown by strong storm winds. Often these safe rooms are built underground.

____ Prefixes *un-, re-, pre-, dis-*   ☐ lesson/tested vocabular

Guiding Comprehension

Draw Conclusions • Inferential
- **Why does the stray cat climb into the bathrobe?**
She has brought all her kittens to safety and is taking care of them now.

Prior Knowledge • Inferential
- *Text to Self* **When are some times when you have taken care of an animal? What would you do if you saw an animal that was hurt or sick?**
Children might talk about a time when they rescued or helped a hurt stray animal or when they cared for a pet. They might suggest finding a parent or other adult to help take the animal to a vet.

REREAD FOR FLUENCY

Paired Reading

ROUTINE

1 Reader 1 Begins Children read the entire book, switching readers at the end of each page.

2 Reader 2 Begins Have partners reread; now the other partner begins.

3 Reread For optimal fluency, children should reread three or four times.

4 Provide Feedback Listen to children read and provide corrective feedback regarding their oral reading and their use of the blending strategy.

OBJECTIVES

- Write suspense.
- Identify pronouns for one and more than one.

Strategic Intervention

Have children copy two suspenseful phrases or sentences from the story and illustrate their writing.

Advanced

Have children who are able to write complete sentences independently write their own suspenseful story.

Writing Support Before writing, children might share ideas in their home languages.

Beginning Pair children with more proficient English speakers. A more proficient speaker can help the partner write a suspenseful sentence.

Intermediate Help children orally practice sentences before they write them.

Advanced Encourage children to write and read aloud their stories.

Interactive Writing

WRITE Suspense

BRAINSTORM Use the Student Selection *One Dark Night* to encourage a discussion about suspenseful writing. Review the book and ask children to identify phrases or words that add uncertainty about what might happen in the story.

SHARE THE PEN Have children participate in writing a suspenseful story. To begin, have a child give an opening sentence. Write the sentence, inviting individuals to write familiar letter-sounds, word parts, and high-frequency words. Ask questions such as:

- What is the first sound you hear in the word *night*? *(/n/)*
- What letter stands for that sound? *(n)* Have a volunteer write *n*.
- What is the second sound you hear in the word *night*? *(/ī/)*
- What letters stand for that sound? *(igh)* Have a volunteer write *igh*.

Continue to have individuals make contributions. Frequently reread what has been written while tracking the print.

READ THE LIST Read the completed story, having children echo you.

A Blizzard

One cold, dark night the snow fell quickly. Before long, it was a blizzard. Our car got stuck on the way home from the store. It was cold out. We were in big trouble!

INDEPENDENT WRITING

WRITE A SUSPENSEFUL STORY Have children organize and write a composition of one or more paragraphs about a blizzard or another weather event they know about. Remind them to build the story around a central idea and to include a beginning, middle, and end. Let children illustrate their writing.

Support Grammar Ask children to orally identify singular or plural pronouns in several sentences you say aloud. See the Grammar Transition lessons in the ELL and Transition Handbook.

Grammar

DEVELOP THE CONCEPT Pronouns

IDENTIFY PRONOUNS FOR ONE AND MORE THAN ONE Write *it* and *they* on the board. Point to each word as you read it. Ask children to identify the pronoun that names only one. *(it)* Then have children identify the pronoun that names more than one. *(they)*

Singular pronouns name one. Plural pronouns name more than one. Name another singular pronoun. *(he)* Name another plural pronoun. *(we)*

PRACTICE

THINK ALOUD AND MODEL Gather pictures of single objects and groups of objects. Display a picture. Model giving a sentence that uses the appropriate pronoun, singular or plural.

Think Aloud

MODEL This is a cat. If I used a pronoun to name the word *cat,* I would use the pronoun *it. It* is a singular pronoun; it names only one. These are two cats. If I used a pronoun to name the cats, I would use *they. They* is a plural pronoun and names more than one.

Have children suggest appropriate pronouns for the other pictures. Write the pronouns for each picture.

DAILY FIX-IT

3. the movie was a reerun.
   The movie was a <u>rerun</u>.

4. She will unplug the Light
   She will unplug the <u>light</u>.

Pronouns for One and More Than One

He, she, and it are pronouns that name only one.
We and they are pronouns that name more than one.

Dale likes to read. He has a library card.
He is a pronoun that names one person—Dale.
Dale and Jen are friends. They will go to the library.
They is a pronoun that names more than one—Dale and Jen.

Circle the pronouns that name only one. Underline the pronouns that name more than one. Write the pronouns in the chart.

Dale and Jen walked to the library. Suddenly they heard a tiny whine. "We should see what the noise is," Jen said. She went over to a bush. A puppy was caught. Dale pulled it free. He set the puppy down. The puppy ran to a boy nearby.

Pronouns That Name Only One	Pronouns That Name More Than One
She it He	they We

Home Activity Your child learned about pronouns for one and more than one. Ask your child to read aloud the story on this page. Have him or her continue the story by telling what happened next. Remind your child to use *he, she, it, we,* and *they.*

▲ **Grammar and Writing Practice Book** p. 85

Wrap Up Your Day!

☑ **VOCABULARY WORDS** Write the following sentences. *A storm is rolling in. It will bring lightning and thunder with it.* Ask children to read the sentences and identify the vocabulary words *storm, lightning,* and *thunder.*

☑ **GRAPHIC ORGANIZER** Tell children that a list is one kind of graphic organizer. Ask: When might it be helpful to use a list? (when they need to order information in a logical way)

LET'S TALK ABOUT IT Recall the Student Selection *One Dark Night.* Ask: What is one way Jonathon helped the kittens? (He took them inside.) Encourage children to tell about a time when they helped an animal.

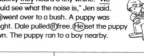
PREVIEW Day 3

Tell children that tomorrow they will hear about a doctor who helps animals.

Share Literature
Animal Hospital

Phonics and Spelling
REVIEW Suffixes *-ly, -ful, -er, -or*

Spelling: Words with Prefixes *un-, re-, pre-, dis-*

Vocabulary
Skill Classify/Categorize

Fluency
Read with Accuracy and Appropriate Pace/Rate

Writing Trait
Voice

Grammar
Pronouns for One and More Than One

Materials

- *Sing with Me Big Book*
- Big Book *Animal Hospital*
- Student Edition 202–203

Morning Warm~Up!

Today we will read more about animal doctors.
They attend school for a long time.
They study veterinary medicine.
What would you like to study?

QUESTION OF THE DAY Encourage children to sing "Love, Love Animals" from the *Sing with Me Big Book* as you gather. Write and read the message and discuss the question.

REVIEW UNFAMILIAR WORDS

- Ask children to point to words they don't recognize in the message. (Possible responses: *attend, study, veterinary, medicine*)

- Review with the class what to do when they see an unfamiliar word. Help them use the context clues in the message to figure out what each unfamiliar word means.

Build Background Use the Day 3 instruction on ELL Poster 22 to support children's use of English to communicate about lesson concepts.

ELL Poster 22

Share Literature

LISTEN AND RESPOND

BUILD ORAL VOCABULARY Review that yesterday the class listened to *Animal Hospital* to find out which parts of an animal are fragile. Introduce the Amazing Word **pellets** and explain that they are small balls of food. Ask that children listen today to find out which animal eats pellets.

MONITOR LISTENING COMPREHENSION

- What does the nurse put on the ground for Jemima the duck? **(some pellets and fresh water)**

- Why did Alice bring her rabbit to the vet? **(because it wasn't eating)**

- Do you think Luke and Jack would be good pet owners? How do you know? **(Children will probably agree that they would be because they show concern for animals, they visit Jemima, and they're interested in what the vet does.)**

Big Book

Amazing Words
to build oral vocabulary

	MONITOR PROGRESS
concern **growth** **protection** **fragile** **pellets** **litter** **pollute** **release**	**If...** children lack oral vocabulary experiences about the concept Responsibility, **then...** use the Oral Vocabulary Routine. See p. DI·4 to teach *pellets*.

Listen and Respond Teach children about the different kinds of animal feet. Review that in the book *Animal Hospital*, they learned that ducks have *webbed* feet and horses have *hooves*. Have children find pictures of these in the book. Then discuss other animals that have hooves (*cows, sheep, pigs*), and what dogs and cats have for feet *(paws)*. Finally, name an animal discussed above and have children respond with the kind of feet it has.

3

OBJECTIVES

- Review suffixes *-ly, -ful, -er,* and *-or.*
- Build, blend, and read *-ly, -ful, -er, -or* words.
- Recognize lesson vocabulary.
- Spell words with prefixes *un-, re-, pre-, dis-.*

Pick a word from the box to match each clue.
Write the letters of the word in each puzzle.

| harmful | inventor | painter | softly | useful | yearly |

1. not loudly
2. artist
3. every summer
4. bad for you
5. of help
6. a person who makes up something new

1.	s	o	f	t	l	y
2.	p	a	i	n	t	e	r
3.	y	e	a	r	l	y
4.	h	a	r	m	f	u	l
5.	u	s	e	f	u	l
6.	i	n	v	e	n	t	o	r

Put these letters in order to write a word.
HINT: The circled letters in the words above spell the new word.

rerfam _____**farmer**_____

School + Home **Home Activity** Your child reviewed words with the suffixes -ly, -ful, -er, and -or. Help your child write a story using some of this lesson's words. Encourage your child to include other words with suffixes. Have your child circle each -ly, -ful, -er, and -or suffix and read the story aloud.

▲ **Practice Book 2.2** p. 68, Suffixes *-ly, -ful, -er, -or*

Review Phonics

REVIEW SUFFIXES *-ly, -ful, -er, -or*

READ WORDS WITH SUFFIXES Write *slowly, cheerful, teacher,* and *actor.* Look at these words. You can read these words because you know how to read words with suffixes. You can cover the suffix, read the base word, and then blend the base word and the suffix to read the whole word. What are the words? Remind children of the meaning of each suffix and have them provide meanings for *slowly, cheerful, teacher,* and *actor.*

- *-ly*   in a _____ way
- *-ful*   full of _____
- *-er, -or*   a person who_____

BUILD WORDS Write the suffixes *-ly, -ful, -er,* and *-or* as headings for a four-column chart or use Graphic Organizer 27. Write several base words in each column. Have children add the suffix to each base word, read the new word, and supply its meaning.

-ly	*-ful*	*-er*	*-or*
quickly	wonderful	helper	editor
stupidly	graceful	dancer	sailor
closely	helpful	reader	visitor

Lesson Vocabulary

PRACTICE

COMPLETE SENTENCES Provide sentences such as the following. Have children write the word that completes each sentence. Children can refer to the list of words on p. 182 of the Student Edition.

- When there is a _____, we have to bring our toys in from the yard. (storm)
- Water _____ from the faucet into the sink. (pours)
- My bedroom light _____ when I flip the switch on and off and on and off. (flashes)
- The dark sky was lit up by _____. (lightning)
- I covered my ears when I heard the loud _____. (thunder)
- The hammer _____ the nail to push it into the wood. (pounds)
- The _____ waves kept sweeping over the beach. (rolling)

Spelling

PRACTICE Prefixes *un-, re-, pre-, dis-*

WRITE WITH WORDS AND BASE WORDS Have children practice spelling words by writing sentences or pairs of sentences that include both a spelling word and its base word. For example:

- We agree that beans are good to eat, but we disagree about how to cook them.

  Children go to preschool before they go to school.

- We unlock the door when we come home and lock it when we leave.

  Ask children to exchange sentences, underline the base words, and circle the spelling words.

HOMEWORK Spelling Practice Book, p. 87

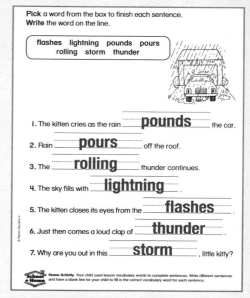

Pick a word from the box to finish each sentence. Write the word on the line.

> flashes lightning pounds pours
> rolling storm thunder

1. The kitten cries as the rain **pounds** the car.
2. Rain **pours** off the roof.
3. The **rolling** thunder continues.
4. The sky fills with **lightning**.
5. The kitten closes its eyes from the **flashes**.
6. Just then comes a loud clap of **thunder**.
7. Why are you out in this **storm**, little kitty?

Home Activity Your child used lesson vocabulary words to complete sentences. Write different sentences and have a blank line for your child to fill in the correct vocabulary word for each sentence.

▲ **Practice Book 2.2** p. 69, Lesson Vocabulary

Spelling Words

Prefixes *un-, re-, pre-, dis-*

1. unsafe
2. preheat
3. rerun
4. disappear*
5. unlock
6. retie
7. rewind
8. unpack
9. unplug
10. regroup
11. preschool
12. disagree

Challenge Words

13. prehistoric
14. unfortunate
15. reunion

* Word from the Selection

Prefixes *un-, re-, pre-, dis-*
Read Denny's note. Circle three spelling mistakes. Write the words correctly. Write the word that needs a capital letter.

Spelling Words	
unsafe	rewind
preheat	unpack
rerun	unplug
disappear	regroup
unlock	preschool
retie	disagree

Hey, I found out where your dogs go when they (disapear) I saw them when I was riding my bike. they were playing with the boys at the (preskool) I (sed) I'd find out, and I did!
Denny

1. **disappear** 2. **preschool**
3. **said** 4. **They**

Frequently Misspelled Words
upon
said
was

Circle the word that is spelled correctly. Write it.

5. (unpack) inpack — 5. **unpack**
6. perheet (preheat) — 6. **preheat**
7. disagre (disagree) — 7. **disagree**
8. (regroup) rigroup — 8. **regroup**
9. unsav (unsafe) — 9. **unsafe**
10. (rewind) rewine — 10. **rewind**

Home Activity Your child identified misspelled words with the prefixes un-, re-, pre-, and dis-. Pronounce a list word. Ask your child to identify the prefix and spell the word.

▲ **Spelling Practice Book** p. 87

One Dark Night **202d**

OBJECTIVES

- Discuss classifying/categorizing words.
- Classify/categorize words from the story.

Strategic Intervention

Have children choose one of the weather categories: lightning, thunder, or storm. Then ask them to write at least three other words or phrases that they could use to further classify it.

Advanced

Have children think of other categories of weather that they could add to the list they have already developed.

Extend Language Help children practice classifying words. Write each lesson vocabulary word on an index card. Give each child one card. Then challenge children to physically group themselves by type of weather.

Vocabulary

CLASSIFY/CATEGORIZE

DISCUSS CLASSIFYING/CATEGORIZING WORDS Have children recall that *One Dark Night* is about a cat and her kittens. Explain that to help them understand what they read, they can classify, or group, related words and phrases. In this story, the author uses words and phrases to describe the cat and kittens. By grouping these words together, children can picture what the cat and kittens look like. Ask them to find words and phrases that describe the cat or kittens, such as *small, dark, stray, soft as whispers, gray as dawn.* Explain that they can further classify these words by grouping them into words about the cat and words about the kittens.

EXPAND SELECTION VOCABULARY Tell children that this story is also about the weather. Work as a group to classify words the author uses to describe the weather. Write their responses on the board. Be sure they include *lightning, thunder, storm, pours, flashes, pounds,* and *rolling.*

Group Time

On-Level

Read *One Dark Night.*
- Use pp. 184–203.

Strategic Intervention

Read or listen to *One Dark Night.*
- Use the **Routine** on p. DI·28.

Advanced

Read Self-Selected Reading.
- Use the **Routine** on p. DI·29.

E L L Place English language learners in the groups that correspond to their reading abilities in English.

(i) Independent Activities

Independent Reading See p. 180j for Reading/Library activities and suggestions.

Journal Writing Write a journal entry about a time that you experienced bad or scary weather. Share writing.

Literacy Centers To provide experiences with *One Dark Night,* you may use the Writing Center on p. 180k.

Practice Book 2.2 Suffixes, p. 68; Lesson Vocabulary, p. 69

Break into small groups after Vocabulary and before Writing.

Fluency

READ WITH ACCURACY AND APPROPRIATE PACE/RATE

MODEL READING WITH ACCURACY AND APPROPRIATE PACE/RATE Use *One Dark Night.*

- Point to the word *Baroom!* on p. 186. Before I read, I scan for unfamiliar words. When I find a word I do not know, I look up its meaning and pronunciation. This helps me read with accuracy because I avoid mistakes as I read. And in that way, I can read as if I am speaking.

- Ask children to follow along as you read the page with accuracy and appropriate pace/rate.

- Have children read the page after you. Encourage them to read at the same pace that you did and to be careful to not make mistakes. Continue in the same way with pp. 188–191.

REREAD FOR FLUENCY

Choral Reading   ROUTINE

1 **Select a Passage** For *One Dark Night,* use pp. 193–199.

2 **Divide into Groups** Assign each group a part to read. For this story, use these parts: the narrator, Grandmother, and Jonathan. You may want someone to do the sound effects too.

3 **Model** Have children track the print as you read.

4 **Read Together** Have children read along with you.

5 **Independent Readings** Have the groups read aloud without you. Monitor progress and provide feedback. For optimal fluency, children should reread three to four times.

Monitor Progress	Fluency
If... children have difficulty reading with accuracy,	**then...** prompt: • Are there unfamiliar words? • Are you reading at an appropriate pace? • Try to scan the reading for unfamiliar words and learn their meanings and pronunciations so that you do not make mistakes when you see them.
If... the class cannot read fluently without you,	**then...** continue to have them read along with you.

Retelling Plan

☑ Week 1 assess Strategic Intervention students.

☑ **This week assess Advanced students.**

☐ Week 3 assess Strategic Intervention students.

☐ Week 4 assess On-Level students.

☐ Week 5 assess any students you have not yet checked during this unit.

Look Back and Write

Point out information from the text that answers the question. Then have children write a response to the question. For test practice, assign a 10–15 minute time limit. For assessment, see the Scoring Rubric at the bottom of this page.

Assessment Before retelling, help children name the characters and items shown. For more ideas on assessing comprehension, see the ELL and Transition Handbook.

Reader Response

OPEN FOR DISCUSSION Model a response. I picked the part when lightning flashes and thunder rolls.

1. **RETELL** Have children use the retelling strip in the Student Edition to retell the selection.

Monitor Progress [Rubric 4 3 2 1] **Check Retelling**

Have children retell *One Dark Night.*

If... children have difficulty retelling the story,

then... use the Retelling Cards and the Scoring Rubric for Retelling on p. 202–203 to help them move toward fluent retelling. [Rubric 4 3 2 1]

 SUCCESS PREDICTOR

| **Day 1** Check Word Reading | **Day 2** Check Lesson Vocabulary/High-Frequency Words | ▶ **Day 3** Check Retelling | **Day 4** Check Fluency | **Day 5** Assess Progress |

---

2. **SEQUENCE** Model a response. First he noticed the lightning, and then he counted the seconds until the thunder rolled. When he counted again, he noticed that the storm was coming closer.

3. **GRAPHIC ORGANIZERS**

Seconds	Miles
15	3
10	2
5	1

▲ Graphic Organizer 25

LOOK BACK AND WRITE Read the writing prompt on p. 202 and model your thinking. I'll look back at page 188 and read what each of the characters says. I'll think about what information could help them understand what is happening. Then I'll write my response. Have children write their responses.

Scoring Rubric | Look Back and Write

Top-Score Response A top-score response will use details from p. 188 of the selection to explain what Jonathan, Grandfather, and Grandmother say about the stray cat and whether or not they are right.

Example of a Top-Score Response Grandfather may be right that stray cats aren't afraid of storms, but Jonathan sees that she is afraid for her kittens. Grandmother thinks the stray cat has a mouse. It is really one of her kittens. She is bringing it inside.

For additional rubrics, see p. WA10.

Reader Response

Open for Discussion A storm can be terrible or exciting! Read an exciting part aloud. Make your reading exciting! Tell why you picked that part.

1. Use the pictures below to retell the story. Then draw a picture to show what might happen the next morning. **Retell**

2. How did Jonathan know that the storm was getting closer? What was the first thing he noticed about the thunder and lightning? What did he notice next? after that? **Sequence**

3. Make a chart showing how far away the storm is when you can count fifteen, ten, and five seconds between the lightning flash and the sound of thunder. **Graphic Organizers**

 Look Back and Write On page 188, Jonathan, Grandfather, and Grandmother each say something about the stray cat. Are they right? Explain your answer.

Meet the Author

Hazel Hutchins

Read two more books by Hazel Hutchins.

One Duck

Two So Small

Hazel Hutchins lives in Canada. She wanted to be an author from the time she was ten years old. Now, she has written more than 25 books!

How did she get the idea for *One Dark Night?* Ms. Hutchins says, "People often tell me stories about their pets. Over the years, I have been told at least three stories about mother cats moving their kittens to a house or porch when threatened by a storm. I have always been touched by the stories as they express the safety we all seek for our loved ones at times of danger."

Ms. Hutchins loves to read books and write stories.

Retelling Strip

202

203

Scoring Rubric — Narrative Retelling

Rubric 4 3 2 1	4	3	2	1
Connections	Makes connections and generalizes beyond the text	Makes connections to other events, stories, or experiences	Makes a limited connection to another event, story, or experience	Makes no connection to another event, story, or experience
Author's Purpose	Elaborates on author's purpose	Tells author's purpose with some clarity	Makes some connection to author's purpose	Makes no connection to author's purpose
Characters	Describes the main character(s) and any character development	Identifies the main character(s) and gives some information about them	Inaccurately identifies some characters or gives little information about them	Inaccurately identifies the characters or gives no information about them
Setting	Describes the time and location	Identifies the time and location	Omits details of time or location	Is unable to identify time or location
Plot	Describes the events in sequence, using rich detail	Tells the plot with some errors in sequence that do not affect meaning	Tells parts of plot with gaps that affect meaning	Retelling has no sense of story

Use the Retelling Chart on p. TR20 to record retelling.

Selection Test To assess with *One Dark Night*, use Selection Tests, pp. 85–88.

Fresh Reads for Differentiated Test Practice For weekly leveled practice, use pp. 127–132.

Retelling

SUCCESS PREDICTOR

DAILY FIX-IT

5. Jamal herd a cat out side.
   Jamal h<u>ea</u>rd a cat <u>outside</u>.

6. He unlocked the dor .
   He unlocked the d<u>oor</u>.

Connect to Unit Writing

Writing Trait

Have children use strategies for developing **voice** when they write a persuasive letter in the Unit Writing Workshop, pp. WA2–WA9.

Voice Show pictures that convey people's feelings, such as being proud or frightened. Model discussion of these feelings: *The girl is frightened of the huge dog.* Explain that *frightened* tells a feeling. Remind language learners to show their feelings when they write.

Writing Trait of the Week

INTRODUCE Voice

TALK ABOUT VOICE Remind children that voice shows how a writer feels about a topic. A writer's voice may show fear, pride, joy, anger, or any number of other feelings. Ask children to think about how the characters in the story feel about the kittens. Then model your thinking.

MODEL In *One Dark Night*, Jonathan and his grandparents aren't expecting to find kittens during the storm. As the story begins, I wonder how they will feel about the kittens. Here is a sentence from the story.

One small kitten—soft as whispers, gray as dawn.

After I read this sentence, I have a better idea of how the characters feel about the kitten. The author's voice is caring. The words "soft as whispers, gray as dawn" show good feelings toward the kitten. I will read another sentence from the story.

Stray cat enters, carrying a second kitten—soft as stuffing, white as snow.

Ask children to find words that express the author's caring, kind voice. *(soft as stuffing, white as snow)* Ask what Jonathan does in the story to show that he cares about the cat and her kittens. *(He snuggles a kitten in his bathrobe, warms the kittens, and goes outside to help the mother and her kitten.)*

STRATEGY FOR DEVELOPING VOICE Write the sentences below. Read each sentence in the voice indicated in parentheses. Work with children to describe the voice expressed in each sentence.

Sid shivered as he crept down the dark tunnel. *(scary)*
My story won the first prize. *(proud, excited)*
How could anyone dance with a pig? *(funny)*

PRACTICE

APPLY THE STRATEGY Ask children to brainstorm a list of animals they would describe as scary, funny, or amazing. Then have them use an appropriate voice to write a description of one of the animals on their list.

Grammar

APPLY TO WRITING Pronouns

IMPROVE WRITING WITH PRONOUNS FOR ONE AND MORE THAN ONE Write *The cat wants to bring her kittens inside. She thinks they will be safe there.* Circle *She* and *they.* Ask who *she* is. (the mother cat) Ask who *they* are. (the kittens) Point out that *she* is a pronoun for one and *they* is a pronoun for more than one. Explain that these number clues help readers know whom you are talking about when you use pronouns. Remind children to use pronouns for one and more than one correctly in their own writing.

Write *he, she, it, we,* and *they.* Have children think of nouns that could be replaced by each pronoun.

he	she	it	we	they
Ben	Emily	the desk	Bob and I	the stars
Dad	my sister	dog	our class	Jill and Sam

PRACTICE

WRITE SENTENCES WITH PRONOUNS FOR ONE AND MORE THAN ONE Call on individuals to come up with pairs of sentences, one using a noun from the list and one using the appropriate pronoun. Continue until three or four examples have been written for each pronoun.

OBJECTIVE

● Use pronouns for one and more than one in writing.

Pronouns for One and More Than One

Circle the pronoun in ( ) that can take the place of the underlined word or words.

1. <u>Gina</u> found a lost kitten. (They, **She**)
2. <u>Leroy</u> helped his neighbor carry groceries. (We, **He**)
3. <u>The firefighters</u> rescued a family. (**They**, He)
4. <u>Kelly and I</u> raked leaves for Grandpa. (**We**, She)

Tell about a time you and someone else helped someone or something. **Write** about who or what you helped and what you did. **Use** *he, she, it, we,* or *they* in some of your sentences.

Possible answer: We helped Mrs. Slaney. She likes to plant flowers. We dug a hole. She put a flower in it. We planted many flowers.

Home Activity Your child learned how to use pronouns for one and more than one in writing. Have your child read his or her story on this page. Ask your child to circle the pronouns that he or she used.

▲ **Grammar and Writing Practice Book** p. 86

Wrap Up Your Day!

 SEQUENCE Lead the class in retelling the story *One Dark Night.* Encourage children to use words such as *first, next, then,* and *finally* to show the order of events in the story.

 FLUENCY Read the last page of *One Dark Night* aloud. Read with accuracy and at the appropriate pace and rate. Did I make any mistakes? Did I read too fast or too slow? Call on children to read this page with accuracy and at the appropriate pace and rate.

LET'S TALK ABOUT IT Do you think the family in *One Dark Night* did the right thing when they took in the family of cats during the storm? Have students use the story to discuss the Question of the Week: Why should we take care of animals?

PREVIEW Day 4

Tell children that tomorrow they will read two poems about people who decide to give some cats a home.

Day 4

Share Literature
"Bringing Back Salmon"

Phonics and Spelling

Prefixes *un-, re-, pre-, dis-*
Spelling: Words with Prefixes *un-,
re-, pre-, dis-*

Read

Group Time < Differentiated
Instruction

"Adoption" and "The Stray Cat"

Fluency
Read with Accuracy and
Appropriate Pace/Rate

Writing Across
the Curriculum
Outline

Grammar
Pronouns for One and More
Than One

Speaking and Listening
Telephone and Voice Mail

Materials
- *Sing with Me Big Book*
- *Read Aloud Anthology*
- Student Edition 204–205

Morning Warm~Up!

Today we will read two poems about
some unloved cats who find a home.
They are reassured that someone
loves them. How can we show an
animal that we love it?

QUESTION OF THE DAY Encourage children to sing "Love, Love Animals"
from the *Sing with Me Big Book* as you gather. Write and read the
message and discuss the question.

REVIEW PREFIXES

- Ask children how many words with prefixes they see in the message.
  (two: *unloved, reassured*)

- Review that adding *un-* to a word turns the word into its opposite. Ask
  them to explain the word *unloved.*

- Review that adding *re-* to a word makes it mean "to do again." Tell the
  class that *to assure* means "to make someone sure of something."
  Help them understand what *reassured* means.

E L L

Extend Language Use the Day 4
instruction on ELL Poster 22 to extend
and enrich language.

ELL Poster 22

Share Literature

CONNECT CONCEPTS

ACTIVATE PRIOR KNOWLEDGE Recall Jonathan and Luke and Jack and how they took care of animals. Explain that they will listen to another story about people who take care of animals—"Bringing Back Salmon" by Jeffrey Rich.

BUILD ORAL VOCABULARY Introduce the Amazing Words **litter, pollute,** and **release.** Explain that *litter* is trash, *pollute* means "to make dirty," and *release* means "to let go." Ask children to listen to find out what the people release in the story and why.

Read Aloud Anthology
Bringing Back Salmon

- What kinds of things make litter?

REVIEW ORAL VOCABULARY After reading, review all the Amazing Words for the week. Have children take turns using them in sentences that tell about the concept for the week. Then talk about Amazing Words they learned in other weeks and connect them to the concept, as well. For example, ask:

- Have you ever worked on any **research projects** that help animals? What did you do?

- Can you name other ways people can help **wildlife** that **struggle** for **survival?**

MONITOR LISTENING COMPREHENSION

- What do the students release into the water and why? **(They release baby salmon because the water is cleaner now and the salmon will come back when they are ready to have babies.)**

- Why were there no salmon in the river for 50 years? **(because the river was polluted)**

- What effect did the polluted water have on salmon? **(The salmon weren't able to survive, and they all died.)**

- How do you think salmon know their way back to where they were born?

to build oral vocabulary

	MONITOR PROGRESS
concern growth protection fragile pellets litter pollute release	**If...** children lack oral vocabulary experiences about the concept Responsibility, **then...** use the Oral Vocabulary Routine. See p. DI·4 to teach *litter, pollute,* and *release.*

Connect Concepts Help children understand the concept of a fish hatchery. First tell children that *to hatch* means "to be born out of an egg." Explain that a *hatchery* is a place where scientists keep a lot of fish eggs and take care of them so they will grow into healthy fish. Tell them that when the fish are old enough, many hatcheries release them into the water so they can grow into adults.

Spiral REVIEW

- Reviews vowel patterns *oo, ue, ew, ui.*
- Reviews vowel patterns *oo, u.*
- Reviews high-frequency words *certainly, either, great, laugh, second, worst, you're.*

Sentence Reading

REVIEW WORDS IN CONTEXT

READ DECODABLE AND HIGH-FREQUENCY WORDS IN CONTEXT Write these sentences. Call on individuals to read a sentence. Then randomly point to words and have children read them. To help you monitor word reading, high-frequency words are underlined and decodable words are circled.

I ⟨disagree⟩–this <u>certainly</u> does not ⟨look⟩ like a ⟨full⟩⟨moon⟩.

<u>You're</u> going to want to ⟨reread⟩ this ⟨great⟩⟨new⟩⟨book⟩.

He was <u>either</u> the first or <u>second</u> ⟨blue⟩ ribbon winner at the ⟨preschool⟩.

Is it ⟨unfair⟩ to say this is the <u>worst</u> ⟨juice⟩ I have ever had.

Will you ⟨replay⟩ the tape of the ⟨cook⟩ in the funny ⟨suit⟩ that made me <u>laugh</u>?

The ⟨food⟩ is <u>great</u> but do not ⟨reheat⟩ any more because I am ⟨full⟩.

Monitor Progress	Word Reading
If... children are unable to read an underlined word,	**then...** read the word for them and spell it, having them echo you.
If... children are unable to read a circled word,	**then...** have them use the blending strategy they have learned for that word type.

Support Phonics For additional review, see the phonics activities in the ELL and Transition Handbook.

Spelling

PARTNER REVIEW Prefixes *un-, re-, pre-, dis-*

READ AND WRITE Supply pairs of children with index cards on which the spelling words have been written. Have one child read a word while the other writes it. Then have children switch roles. Have them use the cards to check their spelling.

HOMEWORK Spelling Practice Book, p. 88

Group Time

On-Level

Read "Adoption" and "The Stray Cat."

• Use pp. 204–205.

Strategic Intervention

Read or listen to "Adoption" and "The Stray Cat."

• Use the Routine on p. DI·30.

Advanced

Read "Adoption" and "The Stray Cat."

• Use the Routine on p. DI·31.

DAY 4

E L L Place English language learners in the groups that correspond to their reading abilities in English.

(*i*) Independent Activities

Independent Reading Pair children to reread *One Dark Night*.

Journal Writing Write about a puppy that had an incredible growth spurt. Share writing.

Spelling Partner Review

Independent Reading See p. 180j for Reading/Library activities and suggestions.

Literacy Centers To provide listening opportunities, you may use the Listening Center on p. 180j. To extend science concepts, you may use the Science Center on p. 180k.

Break into small groups after Spelling and before Fluency.

AudioText

Read
Poetry

OBJECTIVES

● Respond to poems read aloud.
● Recognize characters in a poem.

Pets

Time for **SOCIAL STUDIES**

Lead children in a discussion to compare stray animals and pets. Help children with the comparison by listing their responses on a Venn diagram. You may want to guide the discussion with questions such as, *Does a stray animal have a home? Does a pet have a home? Does a stray animal need food and shelter? Does a pet need those things?*

EXTEND SKILLS

Rhythm in Poetry

For instruction in rhythm in poetry, discuss the following:

• *Rhythm* is the pattern, or beat, that is created in writing.
• Poetry often has a rhythm to it, which can be heard clearly when it is read aloud.
• Rhythm in poetry is often created by adjusting the number of syllables in different lines of the poem.
• Listen for the rhythm in this popular nursery rhyme.

Recite the first verse of "Mary Had a Little Lamb," enunciating the rhythm by clapping.

• As you read the next two poems, listen for the rhythm in each one.

Assess Have children write rhyming poems about something they love, such as a relative or a pet. Encourage them to be aware of the rhythm they create with their words.

PREVIEW AND PREDICT Read the title and poet's name for each poem. Have children preview the poems and describe what they see in the illustration. Then ask them to predict whether the cats in both poems will find a new home. Have children read to find out how the speakers in the poems feel about these cats.

POETRY Remind children that poems are written in a special way—with lines and stanzas. Point out that the words of a poem often form a beat, and sometimes the words rhyme. Ask children to listen for rhyme and rhythm as they listen to the poems.

VOCABULARY/CLASSIFY Remind children that words can be put together in groups that are alike in some way. Write the following words from p. 204 on the board: *hands, cheek, nose, head, toes.* What is a good name for this group of words?

Poetry

Genre

- Poetry often has a rhythm or a beat. Listen for the beat as you read these poems.

- Sometimes poetry rhymes, but not always.

- Each stanza of "Adoption" has two rhyming lines. "The Stray Cat" uses rhyming words in different places throughout the poem.

- A poet often tries to create clear images with as few words as possible.

Link to Writing

Write your own poem about a cat. Use rhyme and rhythm in your poem. Share it with your classmates.

204

Adoption

Isabel Joshlin Glaser

I found a kitten
At the city pound,
A tiny creature
My hands wrapped around.

I held it up
Against my cheek
And I could feel
Its wild heartbeat.

It touched me
With its icy nose—
We liked each other
From head to toes.

The Stray Cat

Eve Merriam

It's just an old alley cat
that has followed us all the way home.

It hasn't a star on its forehead,
or a silky satiny coat.

No proud tiger stripes, no dainty tread,
no elegant velvet throat.

It's a splotchy, blotchy
city cat, not pretty cat,
a rough little tough little bag of old bones.

"Beauty," we shall call you.
"Beauty, come in."

Reading Across Texts

The cats in *One Dark Night* and in these two poems are homeless. Where was each cat found?

Writing Across Texts Write a sentence welcoming each cat to its new home.

Visualize | As you read, create a picture of these cats in your mind.

205

BUILD CONCEPTS

◎ Sequence • Inferential

- **In the first poem, what did the kitten do after the person held it up?**
The kitten touched the person with its icy nose.

Draw Conclusions • Inferential

- **In the second poem, will the person keep the cat? How do you know?**
The person is going to keep the cat. The person gives the cat a name and tells it to come in. Those are things a person does with their own pet.

CONNECT TEXT TO TEXT

Have children review *One Dark Night* and the two poems to find out where each cat was found.

Have children make a list of words that are commonly used to welcome someone. Ask children what punctuation mark they can use to show excitement in their sentences. (exclamation mark)

Growth and Change

Lead children in a discussion about how baby animals are different from adults. Then write a list of baby animal names such as the following, and ask children to provide the corresponding adult names: *kid (goat); fawn (deer); calf (cow); cub (bear); duckling (duck).* Give assistance as needed.

ELL

Access Content Call attention to the phrase *little bag of old bones.* Explain to children that the saying *bag of bones* means that something is very thin.

Options for Oral Reading

Use *One Dark Night,* "Adoption," "The Stray Cat," or one of the following Leveled Readers.

On-Level

Animal Shelters

Strategic Intervention

Horse Rescue!

Advanced

A Day in the Life of a Vet

For English language learners, reading aloud song lyrics, poems, and very short, engaging stories provides good opportunities to increase oral reading fluency.

 To develop fluent readers, use Fluency Coach.

Fluency

READ WITH ACCURACY AND APPROPRIATE PACE/RATE

MODEL READING WITH ACCURACY Use *One Dark Night.*

- Remind children to read with accuracy. Before I read, I scan the passage for unfamiliar words. When I find one, I figure out its meaning and how to pronounce it. This helps me avoid making mistakes as I read.

- Ask children to follow along as you read p. 197 with accuracy and appropriate pace/rate.

- Have children read the page after you. Encourage them to read with accuracy and at your same rate. Continue in the same way with p. 200.

REREAD FOR FLUENCY

Choral Reading

ROUTINE

1 **Select a Passage** For "Adoption" and "The Stray Cat," use pp. 204–205.

2 **Divide into Groups** Assign each group a part to read. For these poems, assign each group a stanza.

3 **Model** Have children track the print as you read.

4 **Read Together** Have children read along with you.

5 **Independent Readings** Have the groups read aloud without you. Monitor progress and provide feedback. For optimal fluency, children should reread three to four times.

Monitor Progress | Check Fluency wcpm

As children reread, monitor their progress toward their individual fluency goals. Current Goal: 82–92 words correct per minute. End-of-Year Goal: 90 words correct per minute.

If... children cannot read fluently at a rate of 82–92 words correct per minute,

then... make sure children practice with text at their independent level. Provide additional fluency practice, pairing nonfluent readers with fluent readers.

If... children already read at 90 words correct per minute,

then... they do not need to reread three to four times.

SUCCESS PREDICTOR

Day 1 Check Word Reading

Day 2 Check Lesson Vocabulary/High-Frequency Words

Day 3 Check Retelling

▶ **Day 4 Check Fluency**

Day 5 Assess Progress

Writing Across the Curriculum

WRITE Outline

Advanced

Encourage children to create a more detailed outline that tells about the needs of a specific kind of animal.

Home Language Connection
Invite children to create a multilingual outline by finding out how to describe the needs of pets in their home languages. Resources for home-language words may include parents, bilingual staff members, or bilingual dictionaries.

BRAINSTORM Have children recall how the family in *One Dark Night* helped the cat and her kittens. Then have them discuss other kinds of things pets need to stay safe and healthy.

SHARE THE PEN Provide a simple outline form or display Graphic Organizer 30. Start the outline by writing *A.* and *B.* Under each letter, write *1.* and *2.*, leaving space for additional letters and numbers. Explain that an outline is a way of organizing information. Explain that main ideas are listed beside letters and details are listed beside numbers. Call on an individual to suggest a word or phrase for the outline, inviting individuals to help spell the word by writing familiar letter-sounds. Ask questions, such as the following:

- Is *Diet* a main idea or a detail? (main idea)
- Where should I write the word *Diet*? (After the *A.*)
- Is *Food* a main idea or a detail? (detail)
- Where should I write the word *Food*? (Under *Diet* and after the number 1.)

Continue having individuals contribute to the outline. If children disagree about where an item should be listed, have them explain their reasoning and ask the class to decide.

> **Pet Needs**
>
> **A. Diet**
>   **1. Food**
>   **2. Water**
> **B. Shelter**
>   **1. Protection from weather**
>   **2. Protection from other animals**
> **C. Health**
>   **1. Daily care**
>   **2. Exercise**
>   **3. Visits to vet**

SUCCESS PREDICTOR

Words Correct Per Minute

OBJECTIVE

● Use pronouns for one and more than one.

DAILY FIX-IT

7. Mom get a new bed for hour cat.

   Mom <u>got</u> a new bed for <u>our</u> cat.

8. The ole one was unsaif.

   The ol<u>d</u> one was unsa<u>fe</u>.

Pronouns for One and More Than One

Mark the letter of the pronoun that can take the place of the underlined word or words.

1. <u>Greg</u> thinks strange things happen in our house.
   - ⊗ A He
   - ○ B They
   - ○ C We

2. One dark night, <u>my sister</u> saw a window pop open.
   - ○ A they
   - ○ B we
   - ⊗ C she

3. One stormy night, <u>Cara and I</u> heard the steps creak.
   - ○ A he
   - ⊗ B we
   - ○ C she

4. One bright morning Dad said, "<u>Our house</u> is old."
   - ⊗ A It
   - ○ B They
   - ○ C We

5. One sunny day Mom said, "<u>The sounds</u> are not strange."
   - ○ A It
   - ○ B She
   - ⊗ C They

6. "<u>The house</u> is just stretching."
   - ○ A We
   - ⊗ B It
   - ○ C They

Home Activity Your child prepared for taking tests on pronouns for one and more than one. Ask your child to make up sentences about what family members like to do and then to change the names to the pronouns he, she, we, or they.

▲ **Grammar and Writing Practice Book** p. 87

Grammar

REVIEW Pronouns for One and More Than One

DEFINE PRONOUNS

● What are pronouns? (words that can take the place of nouns)
● Which pronouns name more than one person, place, or thing? (*we* and *they*)

PRACTICE

USE PRONOUNS FOR ONE AND MORE THAN ONE Ask children to suppose they and some friends found a box with some baby birds inside. Have children write a paragraph describing what happens, using pronouns for one and more than one. When they are finished, have volunteers share their work with the class.

> **Jenny and I went for a walk. We saw a box. It made a peeping sound. Jenny asked, "What is in the box?" She looked inside. "There are baby birds inside! Why aren't they in a nest?" she asked.**

Speaking and Listening

USE TELEPHONES AND VOICE MAIL

DEMONSTRATE SPEAKING AND LISTENING Remind children of appropriate listening and speaking behaviors for communicating by telephone and voice mail. Then ask them to think about these behaviors as they practice leaving and retrieving messages. Have a volunteer demonstrate how to use a telephone directory.

Speakers	Listeners
• Speak slowly and clearly.	• Listen carefully.
• Give complete, accurate information.	• Write down the message.
• Be polite.	• Deliver the message.
• Stay on the topic. Don't ramble.	

LEAVE MESSAGES Have children suppose they are answering an ad about a kitten who has been lost or found. Have pairs practice conversing as if they are on the telephone. You might use a tape recorder to have them practice leaving and retrieving voice messages.

Mary Cartland found Peaches!
Call her after 7:00 tonight.
(555) 123-4567

Wrap Up Your Day!

✓ **MAKING CONNECTIONS: TEXT TO TEXT** Remind children that the cats in the story and the cats in the poems have something in common— they are homeless. Do you think the people in the story and the people in the poems might have something in common too? (Children may suggest that they all love animals and that they are all kind.)

LET'S TALK ABOUT IT Ask children to describe the cat in the poem, "The Stray Cat." This cat isn't very pretty. Why do you think someone would give it a home? Remind them of the Question of the Week, "Why should we take care of animals?" Have them discuss whether people should take care of *all* animals.

PREVIEW Day 5

Remind children that they read poems about cats who find a new home. Tell them that tomorrow they will hear again about what happens during the storm.

Share Literature
"Bringing Back Salmon"

Phonics and Spelling

Review Prefixes *un-, re-, pre-, dis-*

Lesson Vocabulary
pours   lightning   thunder   storm
flashes   pounds   rolling
More Words to Know
stray   nudging   brooding

Monitor Progress
Spelling Test: Words with Prefixes

Group Time < Differentiated Assessment

Writing and Grammar
Trait: Voice
Pronouns for One and
    More Than One

Research and Study Skills
Bar Graph

Materials

- *Sing with Me Big Book*
- *Read Aloud Anthology*
- Reproducible Pages TE 206f–206g
- Student Edition 206–207

Morning Warm~Up!

This week we read about showing concern for animals. We can do many things to look after them. Why is it important to care for animals?

QUESTION OF THE DAY Encourage children to sing "Love, Love Animals" from the *Sing with Me Big Book* as you gather. Write and read the message and discuss the question.

REVIEW ORAL VOCABULARY Have children name people from this week's readings who showed concern for animals. Then have them offer a sentence for each of these Amazing Words: *concern, growth, protection, fragile, pellets, pollute, release,* and *litter.*

Draw a T-chart with the headings "Why" and "How." Say each of the following words: **concern, growth, protection, fragile, pellets, pollute, release, litter.** For each one, have children say whether it is more about *why* we should care for animals or *how* we can care for them. For example, **growth** is more about *why* because animals won't grow if we don't care for them. Write each word under the appropriate heading.

ELL

Assess Vocabulary Use the Day 5 instruction on ELL Poster 22 to monitor children's progress with oral vocabulary.

ELL Poster 22

Share Literature

LISTEN AND RESPOND

USE PRIOR KNOWLEDGE Review that yesterday the class listened to "Bringing Back Salmon" to find out what the students release and why. Suggest that today the class listen to find out if the students' actions are a success.

MONITOR LISTENING COMPREHENSION

- What happened first in the story? (People polluted the river and all the salmon died.)

- What did the students hope would happen to the salmon they released? (They would grow into adults and return to the creek to have babies.)

- What happened after three years? (The salmon came back to the creek.)

Read Aloud Anthology
Bringing Back Salmon

BUILD ORAL VOCABULARY

GENERATE DISCUSSION Recall how students helped scientists reintroduce salmon to a creek that hadn't had salmon in it for more than 50 years! Invite children to talk about projects they would like to work on that would help protect or save animals. Have children use some of this week's Amazing Words as they share their ideas.

Monitor Progress | Check Oral Vocabulary

Remind children of the unit concept—Responsibility. Ask them to tell you about the concept using some of this week's Amazing Words: *concern, growth, protection, fragile, pellets, litter, pollute,* and *release.*

If... children have difficulty using the Amazing Words,

then... ask more questions about the Read Aloud selection or the concept using the Amazing Words. Note which questions children can respond to. Reteach unknown words using the Oral Vocabulary routine on p. DI·1.

SUCCESS PREDICTOR

Day 1 Check Word Reading	**Day 2** Check Lesson Vocabulary/High-Frequency Words	**Day 3** Check Retelling	**Day 4** Check Fluency	▶**Day 5** Check Oral Vocabulary/ Assess Progress

Amazing Words to build oral vocabulary

concern	pellets
growth	litter
protection	pollute
fragile	release

Extend Language Remind children that we can put things that are alike into categories. For example, salmon, goldfish, and trout could be put in a category called *fish*. Creek, lake, and ocean could be in a category called *bodies of water*. Using these two categories, make a T-chart. Have children add to each category: Fish or Bodies of Water.

Oral Vocabulary

SUCCESS PREDICTOR

Prefixes *un-, re-, pre-, dis-*

REVIEW

IDENTIFY WORDS WITH PREFIXES *un-, re-, pre-, dis-* Write these sentences. Have children read each one aloud. Call on individuals to name and underline the prefixes and base words that make up each word.

I will <u>replay</u> the <u>preview</u> so I can see how the actors <u>react</u>.

Dad has an <u>unpaid</u> ticket that he <u>disagrees</u> with.

Mom says her job will <u>prepay</u> our movers when we <u>relocate</u>.

I will <u>undo</u> this ribbon so you can <u>retie</u> it for me.

Lesson Vocabulary

REVIEW

MEANING CLUES Write the following clues for children. Have children write a review word from p. 182 for each clue. Then reread clues and answers.

This is how rain falls during a storm. **(pours)**

You sometimes see this in the sky. **(lightning)**

Sometimes you can hear a clap of _____ when it rains hard. **(thunder)**

When lightning moves quickly across the sky it does this. **(flashes)**

What someone does when he or she bangs on a door with a fist. **(pounds)**

Grandfather had a _____ laughter. **(rolling)**

This is much more than a light rain. **(storm)**

SPELLING TEST Prefixes *un-, re-, pre-, dis-*

DICTATION SENTENCES Use these sentences to assess this week's spelling words.

1. This show is a <u>rerun</u>.
2. I will <u>preheat</u> the oven before I bake the cake.
3. Will you please <u>unlock</u> that trunk?
4. I have to <u>unpack</u> my bags.
5. Please <u>unplug</u> the lamp and bring it here.
6. The sun's rays <u>disappear</u> at night.
7. The teacher planned to <u>regroup</u> the children.
8. My little brother likes his new <u>preschool</u>.
9. It is <u>unsafe</u> to cross the street without looking.
10. My brother and I often <u>disagree</u>.
11. Please <u>rewind</u> that tape for me.
12. My sister will <u>retie</u> the bow.

CHALLENGE WORDS

13. It is <u>unfortunate</u> that we can't play today.
14. We saw the <u>prehistoric</u> bones on our trip.
15. My family is going to the <u>reunion</u> this year.

Group Time

i Independent Activities

Fluency Reading Children reread selections at their independent level.

Journal Writing Write about something unusual that happens during a thunderstorm. Share writing.

Independent Reading See p. 180j for Reading/Library activities and suggestions.

Literacy Centers You may use the Technology Center on p. 180k to support this week's concepts and reading.

Practice Book 2.2 Bar Graph, p. 70

Break into small groups after Spelling and before Grammar and Writing.

SENTENCE READING

ASSESS PREFIXES *un-*, *re-*, *pre-*, *dis-* AND LESSON VOCABULARY Use one of the reproducible lists on p. 206f to assess children's ability to read words with prefixes *un-*, *re-*, *pre-*, *dis-* and lesson vocabulary. Call on individuals to read two sentences aloud. Have each child in the group read different sentences. Start over with sentence one if necessary.

RECORD SCORES Use the Sentence Reading Chart for this unit on p. WA19.

Monitor Progress	Prefixes *un-*, *re-*, *pre-*, *dis-*
If... children have trouble reading prefixes,	**then...** use the Reteach Lessons on p. DI·65.
Lesson Vocabulary	
If... children cannot read a lesson vocabulary word,	**then...** mark the missed words on a lesson vocabulary list and send the list home with the child for additional word reading practice, or have the child practice with a fluent reader.

FLUENCY AND COMPREHENSION

ASSESS FLUENCY Take a one-minute sample of children's oral reading. See Monitoring Fluency, p. WA17. Have children read "Doghouse Redo," the on-level fluency passage on p. 206g.

RECORD SCORES Record the number of words read correctly in one minute on the child's Fluency Progress Chart.

ASSESS COMPREHENSION Have the child read to the end of the passage. (If the child had difficulty with the passage, you may read it aloud.) Ask questions about the sequence of events and have the child retell the passage. Use the Expository Retelling Rubric on p. 172–173 to evaluate the child's retelling.

Monitor Progress	Fluency
If... a child does not achieve the fluency goal on the timed reading,	**then...** copy the passage and send it home with the child for additional fluency practice, or have the child practice with a fluent reader.
Sequence	
If... a child cannot recognize the sequence of events,	**then...** use the Reteach Lesson on p. DI·65.

Differentiated Assessment

On-Level
Set B

Strategic Intervention
Set A

Advanced
Set C

Fluency Assessment Plan

- ☑ Week 1 assess Advanced students.
- ☑ **This week assess Strategic Intervention students.**
- ☐ Week 3 assess On-Level students.
- ☐ Week 4 assess Strategic Intervention students.
- ☐ Week 5 assess any students you have not yet checked during this unit.

Set individual fluency goals for children to enable them to reach the end-of-year goal.

- Current Goal: 82–92 wcpm
- End-of-Year Goal: 90 wcpm
- **ELL** Measuring a child's oral reading speed—words per minute—provides a low-stress informal assessment of fluency. Such an assessment should not take the place of more formal measures of words correct per minute.

READ THE SENTENCES

Set A

1. Lightning flashes made us feel unhappy and unsafe.
2. Tad was unable to unload the boat in the storm.
3. Jean is unafraid of thunder, but she dislikes its noise.
4. We had to reload and retie the rolling pipes.
5. Sam preheats the stove and pours the uncooked food.
6. When the rain pounds down, Val is unhappy as she rechecks the roof.

Set B

1. You may have to renail or rebuild your roof if the rain pounds through it during a storm.
2. Thunder makes his dog unfriendly and distrustful.
3. Dad prepaid to have the lightning rods replaced.
4. Unpack and unroll the tent in case it pours.
5. It's unsafe to unlock the door during lightning.
6. He disagrees that you must repaint the flashes.

Set C

1. You may have to recover lost files if you do not unplug the computer before lightning strikes.
2. Replay the pregame tape after the thunderstorm.
3. Tom must repaint the barn because the rain pounds on it and discolored the wood.
4. After the rain pours down the air feels refreshing and the dirt seems to disappear.
5. It is unclear if we will regroup after the storm.
6. Gail rewrapped the food and the repacked picnic basket when she saw lightning in the sky.

Monitor Progress | Prefixes
Lesson Vocabulary

SUCCESS
PREDICTOR

Doghouse Redo

Is your pooch unhappy about a dirty doghouse?   8
Does your dog's house need a redo? It's unkind to   18
make him or her stay in a dirty place. Your dog is   30
unable to fix it, so it's up to you. Follow these   41
steps.   42

First, unload all the bones and toys from the   51
inside of the doghouse. Next, prewash the dog's   59
house with just water from a hose to get the dirt   70
off. Then wash it with soapy water. Watch all that   80
dirt disappear.   82

Is the paint on the outside discolored or   90
chipping? If it is, you will have to repaint the   100
outside. Scrape the wood. After that, recover it   108
with some bright paint. Let it dry.   115
Finally, clean or replace the dog's toys, bowls,   123
and blanket. Refill the dog's bowls with food and   132
water.   133

The dog's home is now clean and refreshed.   141
Your pooch will love you for it!   148

See also Assessment Handbook, p. 348 • REPRODUCIBLE PAGE

Write Now
Writing and Grammar

Reasons

Prompt
In *One Dark Night*, a cat has reasons for braving a storm.
Think about something you think people should do.
Now write reasons to convince them.

Writing Trait

Your **voice** shows how you feel about your topic.

First sentence states main idea.

Sentences give reasons to support main idea.

Voice shows writer feels strongly about topic.

Student Model

> We should help animals. Here's why. Animals are living things. They deserve to be cared for. Some animals provide food. Some animals help people work. We may even use animals to travel to places. Helping animals is the right thing to do.

Writer's Checklist
- **Focus** Do all sentences relate to my belief?
- **Organization** Is the main idea stated at the beginning?
- **Support** Do reasons show my feelings?
- **Conventions** Does each sentence begin with a capital letter?

Grammar

Pronouns for One and More than One
He, she, and **it** are pronouns that name only one. **We** and **they** are pronouns that name more than one.

Jonathan hears thunder.
He races downstairs.

The cat brings three kittens inside.
Now **they** are safe from the rain.

He is a pronoun that names one person—Jonathan.
They is a pronoun that names more than one—the cat and her kittens.

Look at the model. Write the pronouns that name more than one.

206

207

Writing and Grammar

LOOK AT THE PROMPT Read p. 206 aloud. Have children select and discuss key words or phrases in the prompt. *(something you think people should do, reasons to convince them)*

STRATEGIES TO DEVELOP VOICE Have children
- write sentences about who their audience is before they begin writing their main idea and reasons.
- write a list of persuasive words.
- read their reasons aloud to make sure their voice is strong, persuasive, and natural.

See Scoring Rubric on p. WA11. **Rubric 4 3 2 1**

HINTS FOR BETTER WRITING Read p. 207 aloud. Use the checklist to help children revise their reasons. Discuss the grammar lesson. (Answers: *They, We*) Have children use pronouns correctly in their reasons.

DAILY FIX-IT

9. The cat disappaered in the gras.
   (disapp**ea**red, gra**ss**.)

10. They was afraid of dog.
    (**It**, the)

Pronouns for One and More Than One

Circle the pronoun in ( ) that can take the place of the underlined words.

1. An animal shelter takes in lost or unwanted animals. (It, We)
2. Special people care for the animals there. (She, They)
3. You and I can adopt the animals. (We, They)

Write the pronoun that can take the place of the underlined words. Use *he, she, it, we,* or *they.*

4. Roy and Rita are new pet owners.

   They ———————— have a new kitten.

5. The kitten must see the vet.

   It/He/She ———————— will get a checkup.

6. Dr. Maria Green gives the kitten a shot.

   She ———————— checks the kitten's teeth.

▲ **Grammar and Writing Practice Book** p. 88

Research/Study Skills

TEACH/MODEL *Bar Graph*

MODEL USING A BAR GRAPH Draw and label a simple bar graph that compares the adoption of different kinds of animals. Explain that bar graphs help readers compare information. Read the labels and tell children that this bar graph gives information about four different groups: dogs, puppies, cats, and kittens. The bar graph shows how many of each kind of animal were adopted last year.

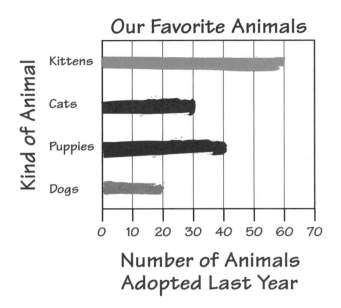

Model how to read the information on a bar graph.

Think Aloud **MODEL** I can tell by the title of this graph and the information at the bottom that I will learn how many animals were adopted from an animal shelter last year. When I see the label *Dogs*, I follow the bar across and see where it ends. It ends on the line 20, so I know that 20 dogs were adopted. I can also use the graph to tell how many dogs were adopted compared to other animals. If I look at each bar, I see that dogs were the least adopted animals.

READ BAR GRAPH Call on individuals to tell how many puppies, cats, and kittens were adopted.

PRACTICE

MAKE A BAR GRAPH First poll the children to find out who has pet cats, pet dogs, other kinds of pets, and no pets. Write the numbers and categories on the board. Then work with the class to create a bar graph that displays this information.

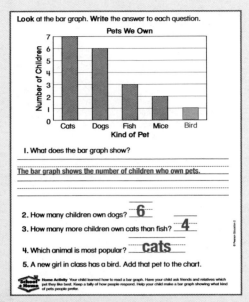

▲ **Practice Book 2.2** p. 70, Bar Graph

Access Content Explain to English language learners that a graph is a kind of diagram or chart that shows information. A bar graph uses bars, or thick lines, to show the amounts of the things listed in the graph.

Wrap Up Your Week!

LET'S TALK ABOUT Responsibility

QUESTION OF THE WEEK Recall this week's question.

• Why should we take care of animals?

Display Graphic Organizer 16 or the simple main idea and details chart you created earlier. Ask children which needs of animals are also needs of people. Have children name at least one other need that humans and animals share (such as medical care or water) and one that they do not share (clothing).

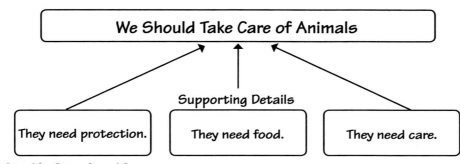

▲ **Graphic Organizer 16**

CONNECT Use questions such as these to prompt a discussion.

• Baby animals are fragile and need protection. How do adult animals show concern for their young?

• Animals need food and water for growth. What happens to animals if the land and water around them gets polluted? How can picking up litter help keep land and water clean?

• No one would release a puppy into traffic because the puppy might get hurt. What other things do people do to take care of a puppy?

ELL

Build Background Use ELL Poster 23 to support the Preview activity.

You've learned	You've learned
008 Amazing Words	**177** Amazing Words
this week!	so far this year!

PREVIEW Tell children that next week they will read about a boy who discovered one of the most important things that puppies need.

PREVIEW Next Week

Assessment Checkpoints *for the Week*

Selection Assessment

Use pp. 85–88 of Selection Tests to check:

 ☑ **Selection Understanding**

 ☑ **Comprehension Skill** *Sequence*

☑ **Selection Vocabulary**
flashes
lightning
pounds
pours
rolling
storm
thunder

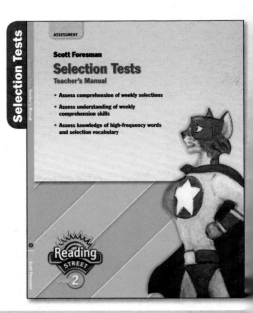

Leveled Assessment

On-Level
Strategic Intervention
Advanced

Use pp. 127–132 of Fresh Reads for Differentiated Test Practice to check:

 ☑ **Comprehension Skill** *Sequence*

 ☑ **REVIEW** **Comprehension Skill** *Plot and Theme*

 ☑ **Fluency** *Words Correct Per Minute*

Managing Assessment

Use Assessment Handbook for:

 ☑ **Weekly Assessment Blackline Masters for Monitoring Progress**

 ☑ **Observation Checklists**

 ☑ **Record-Keeping Forms**

☑ **Portfolio Assessment**

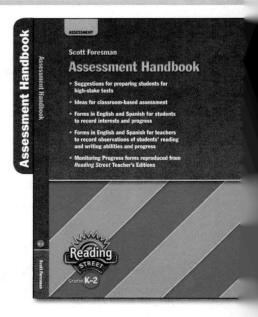

Illinois

Planning Guide for Performance Descriptors

Bad Dog, Dodger!

Reading Street Teacher's Edition pages	**Grade 2 English Language Arts Performance Descriptors**
Oral Language Build Concepts: 208l, 210a, 226a, 228a, 232a Share Literature: 208m, 210b, 226b, 228b, 232b	**1A.Stage B.7.** Use a variety of resources (e.g., context, previous experiences, dictionaries, glossaries, computer resources, ask others) to determine and clarify meanings of unfamiliar words. **2B.Stage B.6.** Make connections from text to text, text to self, text to world.
Word Work **Phonics** Silent Consonants: 208n–208q, 210c–210d, 226c–226d, 228c–228d, 232c–232f **Spelling:** 208p, 210d, 226d, 228d, 232d	**1A.Stage B.4.** Use a variety of decoding strategies (e.g., phonics, word patterns, structural analysis, context clues) to recognize new words when reading age-appropriate material. **3A.Stage B.6.** Use phonemic clues, phonetic and/or developmental spelling to spell unfamiliar words.
Reading **Comprehension** Plot and Theme: 208r–209, 212–225a, 226g, 232e Prior Knowledge: 208r–209, 212–225, 226g **Vocabulary** Word Structure: 210–211 Classify/Categorize: 226e, 228–229 **Fluency** Oral Rereading: 208q Choral Reading: 226f, 231a **Self-Selected Reading:** LR19–27, TR16–17 **Literature** Genre—Realistic Fiction: 212–213 Reader Response: 226g–226h	**1A.Stage B.5.** Use letter-sound knowledge and sight vocabulary to read orally and silently/whisper read age-appropriate material. **1C.Stage B.1.** Respond to analytical and interpretive questions based on information in text. **1C.Stage B.7.** Compare an author's information with the student's knowledge of self, world, and other texts in non-fiction text. **2A.Stage B.3.** Define unfamiliar vocabulary. **2A.Stage B.4.** Identify the topic or main idea (theme). **2A.Stage B.5.** Distinguish between "make believe" and realistic narrative. **2B.Stage B.1.** Investigate self-selected/teacher-selected literature (e.g., picture books, nursery rhymes, fairy tales, poems, legends) from a variety of cultures.
Language Arts **Writing** Rules, Directions, Respond to Literature, List: 209a, 225b, 226g, 231b, 232–233 **Six-Trait Writing** Voice: 227a, 232–233 **Grammar, Usage, and Mechanics** Use *I* and *Me*: 209b, 225c, 227b, 231c, 232–233 **Speaking/Viewing** Retell a Movie or a Play: 231d **Research/Study** Encyclopedia: 233a	**1C.Stage B.9.** Summarize and retell text read or heard. **2B.Stage B.3.** Re-enact and retell selections (e.g., stories, songs, poems). **3A.Stage B.2.** Use correct subject/verb agreement. **3C.Stage B.3.** Begin to rely on text as well as pictures and oral narration to convey meaning. **5A.Stage B.5.** Recognize that information is available through an organizational system (e.g., library, media center, classroom resources, available technology).
Unit Skills **Writing** Persuasive Letter: WA2–9 **Project/Wrap-Up:** 292–293	**3C.Stage B.1.** Use the writing process for a variety of purposes (e.g., narration, exposition).

This Week's Leveled Readers

Below-Level

2A.Stage B.4. Identify the topic or main idea (theme).
2B.Stage B.3. Re-enact and retell selections (e.g., stories, songs, poems).

Fiction

On-Level

1C.Stage B.8. Compare a broad range of books that have the same theme and topic.
2B.Stage B.5. Apply text variations (e.g., change setting, alter a character, rewrite the ending).

Fiction

Advanced

2A.Stage B.4. Identify the topic or main idea (theme).
2B.Stage B.1. Investigate self-selected/teacher-selected literature (e.g., picture books, nursery rhymes, fairy tales, poems, legends) from a variety of cultures.

Fiction

Content-Area Illinois Performance Descriptors in This Lesson

Social Studies

14A.Stage B.2. Name some of the benefits of sharing and taking turns during games and group activities.

14C.Stage B.1. Discuss a situation in their home or school that illustrates people being responsible in their duties or job.

15B.Stage B.2. Identify a choice students have made about the use of time.

17B.Stage B.1. Describe how seasons relate to the ways people dress and seasonal activities they engage in, in different areas of the world using pictures in books and magazines.

18B.Stage B.1. Define social group.

18B.Stage B.2. Explain how contact with others shapes peoples' lives.

18C.Stage B.1. Provide examples of how individuals make choices that affect the group.

Science

12A.Stage B.1. Apply scientific inquiries or technological designs to explore common and diverse structures and functions of living things: describing how plants and animals obtain energy; categorizing animals by structures for food-getting and movement.

12D.Stage B.1. Apply scientific inquiries or technological designs to compare and contrast common forces around us: dramatizing the ways that forces cause action and reaction behaviors of common objects.

12D.Stage B.2. Apply scientific inquiries or technological designs to make connections between the basic concepts of motion to real world applications: demonstrating the rate, time and distance factors and units for speed; describing examples of inertia and momentum in the classroom, playground and at home.

A FAMOUS ILLINOISAN
Vachel Lindsay

The poet Vachel Lindsay (1879–1931) was born in Springfield. His work was first published in 1913 in *Poetry* magazine. Lindsay's subjects included William Booth, founder of the Salvation Army, and Johnny Appleseed. Lindsay believed that poetry should not simply be read, but performed, and he did so with powerful rhythms and vivid images.

Children can . . .
Practice reading a poem with expression. Have children select a favorite poem and read it aloud to the class.

A SPECIAL ILLINOIS PLACE
Fort de Chartres

Fort de Chartres was the last of three forts built by the French near Prairie du Rocher. It was a massive stone fort, with walls fifteen feet high and three feet thick. Today visitors can see a partial reconstruction of the fort at Fort de Chartres State Historic Site. Each June the site hosts the largest get-together in the Midwest. More than one thousand people participate in a re-enactment of the traditional French fur trappers' annual gathering.

Children can . . .
Study pictures of Fort de Chartres. Have them build a model fort of their own design using natural materials such as rocks and twigs, with the help of an adult.

ILLINOIS FUN FACTS
Did You Know?

• The Northern Cross Railroad was the first railroad in Illinois, covering a distance of twelve miles from Meredosia to Morgan City.

• Richard M. Daley, son of Richard J. Daley, became mayor of Chicago in 1989 and was reelected in 1991, 1995, 1999, and 2003.

• The Chicago Jazz Festival attracts thousands of music lovers to Grant Park every year.

Children can . . .
Listen to jazz music. Have them write words or draw and color shapes in response to the music.

Bad Dog, Dodger!

Unit 5
Responsibility

CONCEPT QUESTION

What does it mean to be responsible?

Week 1

Why is it important to do a good job?

Week 2

Why should we take care of animals?

Week 3

How can we be responsible family members?

Week 4

What do good friends and neighbors do?

Week 5

What happens when we do the wrong thing?

Week 3

EXPAND THE CONCEPT
How can we be responsible family members?

CONNECT THE CONCEPT

▶ **Build Background**

behavior	*consider*	*properly*
companion	*cooperate*	*reprimand*
confident	*obedient*	

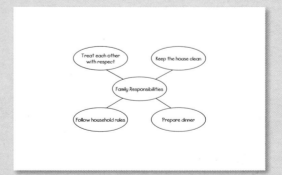

▶ **Social Studies Content**
Citizenship, Family Responsibility, Rules, Pet Care

▶ **Writing**
Rules

Preview Your Week

How can we be responsible family members?

Bad Dog, Dodger!

by Barbara Abercrombie • Illustrated by Laura Ovresat

Genre

Realistic fiction means a story is possible. Look for things that could really happen to a boy and his dog.

Do the things that Dodger does make him a bad dog?

212   213

Student Edition pages 212–227

Audio CD

Genre	Realistic Fiction
Phonics	Silent Consonants
Vocabulary Strategy	Word Structure
Comprehension Skill	Plot and Theme
Comprehension Strategy	Prior Knowledge

Paired Selection

Reading Across Texts

Compare Pet Training

Genre

How-to Article

Text Features

Numbered Steps
Photos

Time for SOCIAL STUDIES

Science in Reading

How-to Article

Genre

• How-to articles explain how to do something one step at a time.

Text Features

• This how-to article has numbered steps that give examples to help you train your puppy.

• Photos also help explain what to do.

Link to Science

Use the library or the Internet to find out more about training other types of animals. Make a poster with steps to show how to do it. Tell the class about your poster.

How to Train Your Puppy

by L.B. Coombs

Have you ever tried to make a puppy behave? Training a puppy means making it do the same thing over and over again. You can train a puppy, or most any pet, too. Here's how.

• Begin training when your puppy is very young.

• Teach your puppy to do only one new thing at a time.

• Pick one word as the command for each new thing you want the puppy to learn, but don't repeat the command too many times.

The words and pictures that follow will help you train your puppy.

1 First, let your puppy get to know you. Let him sniff your hand. He will learn to know you by your smell.

2 When you want your puppy to bark, say "Speak." Don't say "Talk" one day and "Bark" the next. Use the same word every time.

Speak!

Prior Knowledge What do you know about dogs that helps you understand this?

228

Student Edition pages 228–231

Audio CD

Read It
ONLINE
PearsonSuccessNet.com
• **Student Edition**
• **Leveled Readers**
• **Decodable Reader**

Leveled Readers

🎯 **Skill** Plot and Theme

🎯 **Strategy** Prior Knowledge

Lesson Vocabulary

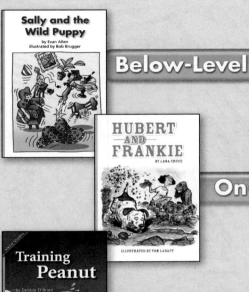

Below-Level

On-Level

Advanced

ELL Reader

· **Concept Vocabulary**
· **Text Support**
· **Language Enrichment**

Decodable Reader

Apply Phonics

· *Penpals*

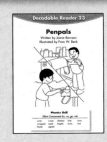

Integrate Social Studies Standards

• **Citizenship**
• **Family Responsibility**
• **Rules**
• **Pet Care**

✓ **Read**

Bad Dog, Dodger! pp. 212–227

"How to Train Your Puppy" pp. 228–231

✓ **Read**

Below-Level   **On-Level**   **Advanced**

• **Support Concepts**   • **Develop Concepts**   • **Extend Concepts**
• **Social Studies Extension Activity**

✓ **Read**

✓ **Build Concept Vocabulary**
Responsibility, p. 208m

✓ **Teach Social Studies Concepts**
Citizenship, p. 222–223
Government, p. 224–225
Pets, p. 228–229

✓ **Explore Social Studies Center**
Classroom Rules, p. 208k

Weekly Plan

READING

90–120 minutes

TARGET SKILLS OF THE WEEK

- **Phonics**
  Silent Consonants
- **Comprehension Skill**
  Plot and Theme
- **Comprehension Strategy**
  Prior Knowledge
- **Vocabulary Strategy**
  Word Structure

DAY 1 — PAGES 208l–209b

Oral Language

QUESTION OF THE WEEK, 208l
How can we be responsible family members?

Oral Vocabulary/Share Literature, 208m
Sing with Me Big Book, Song 23
Amazing Words *behavior, cooperate, obedient*

Word Work

Phonics, 208n–208o
Introduce Silent Consonants **T**

Spelling, 208p
Pretest

Comprehension/Vocabulary/Fluency

Read Decodable Reader 23

Grouping Options 208f–208g

Review High-Frequency Words
Check Comprehension
Reread for Fluency

**Comprehension Skill/Strategy
Lesson,** 208r–209
Plot and Theme **T**
Prior Knowledge

DAY 2 — PAGES 210a–225c

Oral Language

QUESTION OF THE DAY, 210a
How do we know right from wrong?

Oral Vocabulary/Share Literature, 210b
Read Aloud Anthology "Zooks"
Amazing Words *companion, consider*

Word Work

Phonics, 210c–210d
Review Silent Consonants **T**

Spelling, 210d
Dictation

Comprehension/Vocabulary/Fluency

Build Background, 210e
Training Pets

Lesson Vocabulary, 210f
Introduce *chased, chewing, dripping, grabbed, practice, treat, wagged* **T**

Vocabulary Strategy Lesson, 210–211a
Word Structure **T**

Read *Bad Dog, Dodger!,* 212–225a

Grouping Options
208f–208g

Plot and Theme **T**
Prior Knowledge
REVIEW Sequence **T**
Reread for Fluency

LANGUAGE ARTS

20–30 minutes

Trait of the Week

Voice

Shared Writing, 209a
Rules

Grammar, 209b
Introduce *I* and *Me* **T**

Interactive Writing, 225b
Directions

Grammar, 225c
Practice *I* and *Me* **T**

DAILY JOURNAL WRITING

Day 1 *List ways people can cooperate with each other.*

Day 2 *Write about a time when you saw a dog doing something funny.*

DAILY SOCIAL STUDIES CONNECTIONS

Day 1 Family Responsibilities Concept Web, 208m

Day 2 Time for Social Studies: Citizenship, 222–223; Government, 224–225

DAILY SUCCESS PREDICTORS

for Adequate Yearly Progress

Monitor Progress and Corrective Feedback

Phonics
Check Word Reading, *208o*
Spiral REVIEW Phonics

Fluency
Check Lesson Vocabulary, *210f*
Spiral REVIEW High-Frequency Words

RESOURCES FOR THE WEEK

- Practice Book 2.2, *pp. 71–80*
- Phonics and Spelling Practice Book, *pp. 89–92*
- Grammar and Writing Practice Book, *pp. 89–92*
- Selection Test, *pp. 89–92*

- Fresh Reads for Differentiated Test Practice, *pp. 133–138*
- Phonics Songs and Rhymes Chart 23
- The Grammar and Writing Book, *pp. 182–187*

Grouping Options for Differentiated Instruction

Turn the page for the small group lesson plan.

DAY 3 · PAGES 226a–227b

Oral Language

QUESTION OF THE DAY, 226a
What kind of animal do you love best?

Oral Vocabulary/Share Literature, 226b
Read Aloud Anthology "Zooks"
Amazing Word *reprimand*

Word Work

Phonics, 226c
REVIEW Prefixes *un-, re-, pre-, dis-* **T**

Lesson Vocabulary, 226d
Practice *chased, chewing, dripping, grabbed, practice, treat, wagged* **T**

Spelling, 226d
Practice

Comprehension/Vocabulary/Fluency

Vocabulary, 226e
Classify/Categorize

Read *Bad Dog, Dodger!,* 212–227

Grouping Options
208f–208g

Fluency, 226f
Read with Expression/Intonation

Reader Response, 226g

Trait of the Week, 227a
Introduce Voice

Grammar, 227b
Write with *I* and *Me* **T**

Day 3 *Write about a pet behaving badly or doing something impressive.*

Day 3 Let's Talk About the Concept, 227b

DAY 4 · PAGES 228a–231d

Oral Language

QUESTION OF THE DAY, 228a
How do you think dogs are trained?

Oral Vocabulary/Share Literature, 228b
Read Aloud Anthology "Me and My Pet Dog"
Amazing Words *confident, properly*

Word Work

Phonics, 228c–228d
REVIEW Sentence Reading **T**

Spelling, 228d
Partner Review

Comprehension/Vocabulary/Fluency

Read "How to Train Your Puppy," 228–231
Leveled Readers

Grouping Options
208f–208g

Classify/Categorize Words
Reading Across Texts

Fluency, 231a
Read with Expression and Intonation

Writing Across the Curriculum, 231b
List

Grammar, 231c
Review *I* and *Me* **T**

Speaking and Listening, 231d
Retell a Movie or a Play

Day 4 *Write about a puppy who learns to obey.*

Day 4 Time for Social Studies: Pets, 228–229

DAY 5 · PAGES 232a–233b

Oral Language

QUESTION OF THE DAY, 232a
In what other ways can we be responsible family members?

Oral Vocabulary/Share Literature, 232b
Read Aloud Anthology "Me and My Pet Dog"
Amazing Words Review

Word Work

Phonics, 232c
◎ Review Silent Consonants **T**

Lesson Vocabulary, 232c
Review *chased, chewing, dripping, grabbed, practice, treat, wagged* **T**

Spelling, 232d
Test

Comprehension/Vocabulary/Fluency

Read Leveled Readers

Grouping Options 208f–208g

Monitor Progress, 232e–232g
Read the Sentences
Read the Story

Writing and Grammar, 232–233
Develop Voice
Use *I* and *Me* **T**

Research/Study Skills, 233a
Encyclopedia

Day 5 *Write about a pet that is silly.*

Day 5 Revisit the Family Responsibilities Concept Chart, 233b

---

KEY ◎ = Target Skill **T** = Tested Skill

Comprehension Check Retelling, *226g*

Fluency Check Fluency WCPM, *231a*
Spiral REVIEW Phonics, High-Frequency Words

Oral Vocabulary Check Oral Vocabulary, *232b*
Assess Phonics, Lesson Vocabulary, Fluency, Comprehension, *232e*

SUCCESS PREDICTOR

Small Group Plan *for Differentiated Instruction*

Daily Plan
AT A GLANCE

Reading
Whole Group
- Oral Language
- Word Work
- Comprehension/Vocabulary

Group Time

Meet with small groups to provide:
- Skill Support
- Reading Support
- Fluency Practice

Read

This week's lessons for daily group time can be found behind the Differentiated Instruction (DI) tab on pp. DI·34–DI·43.

Whole Group
- Comprehension/Vocabulary
- Fluency

Language Arts
- Writing
- Grammar
- Speaking/Listening/Viewing
- Research/Study Skills

Use *My Sidewalks on Reading Street* for Tier III intensive reading intervention.

DAY 1

On-Level
Teacher-Led
Page 208q
- **Read** Decodable Reader 23
- **Reread** for Fluency

Strategic Intervention
Teacher-Led
Page DI · 34
- Blend Words with Silent Consonants
- **Read** Decodable Reader 23
- **Reread** for Fluency

Advanced
Teacher-Led
Page DI · 35
- Extend Word Reading
- **Read** Advanced Selection 23
- Introduce Concept Inquiry

(i) Independent Activities
While you meet with small groups, have the rest of the class...
- Reread for fluency
- Write in their journals
- Read self-selected reading
- Visit the Word Work Center
- Complete Practice Book 2.2, pp. 73–74

DAY 2

On-Level
Teacher-Led
Pages 212–225
- **Read** *Bad Dog, Dodger!*
- **Reread** for Fluency

Strategic Intervention
Teacher-Led
Page DI · 36
- Blend Words with Silent Consonants
- **Read** SI Decodable Reader 23
- **Read** or Listen to *Bad Dog, Dodger!*

Advanced
Teacher-Led
Page DI · 37
- **Read** *Bad Dog, Dodger!*
- Continue Concept Inquiry

(i) Independent Activities
While you meet with small groups, have the rest of the class...
- Read self-selected reading
- Write in their journals
- Visit the Listening Center
- Complete Practice Book 2.2, pp. 75–77

DAY 3

On-Level
Teacher-Led
Pages 212–227
- **Reread** *Bad Dog, Dodger!*

Strategic Intervention
Teacher-Led
Page DI · 38
- **Reread** *Bad Dog, Dodger!*
- Read Words and Sentences
- Review Prior Knowledge
- **Reread** for Fluency

Advanced
Teacher-Led
Page DI · 39
- Self-Selected Reading
- Continue Concept Inquiry

(i) Independent Activities
While you meet with small groups, have the rest of the class...
- Read self-selected reading
- Write in their journals
- Visit the Writing Center
- Complete Practice Book 2.2, pp. 78–79

① Begin with whole class skill and strategy instruction.

② Meet with small groups to provide differentiated instruction.

③ Gather the whole class back together for fluency and language arts.

On-Level

Teacher-Led
Pages 228–231, LR22–LR24

- **Read** "How to Train Your Puppy"
- Practice with On-Level Reader *Hubert and Frankie*

Strategic Intervention

Teacher-Led
Pages DI · 40, LR19–LR21

- **Read** or Listen to "How to Train Your Puppy"
- **Reread** for Fluency
- Build Concepts
- Practice with Below-Level Reader *Sally and the Wild Puppy*

Advanced

Teacher-Led
Pages DI · 41, LR25–LR27

- **Read** "How to Train Your Puppy"
- Extend Vocabulary
- Continue Concept Inquiry
- Practice with Advanced Reader *Training Peanut*

 DAY 4

ⓘ Independent Activities

While you meet with small groups, have the rest of the class...

- Reread for fluency
- Write in their journals
- Read self-selected reading

- Review spelling words with a partner
- Visit the Listening and Social Studies Centers

On-Level

Teacher-Led
Pages 232e–232g, LR22–LR24

- Sentence Reading, Set B
- Monitor Fluency and Comprehension
- Practice with On-Level Reader *Hubert and Frankie*

Strategic Intervention

Teacher-Led
Pages DI · 42, LR19–LR21

- Practice Word Reading
- Sentence Reading, Set A
- Monitor Comprehension
- Practice with Below-Level Reader *Sally and the Wild Puppy*

Advanced

Teacher-Led
Pages DI · 43, LR25–LR27

- Sentence Reading, Set C
- Monitor Comprehension
- Share Concept Inquiry
- Practice with Advanced Reader *Training Peanut*

DAY 5

ⓘ Independent Activities

While you meet with small groups, have the rest of the class...

- Reread for fluency
- Write in their journals
- Read self-selected reading

- Visit the Technology Center
- Complete Practice Book 2.2, p. 80

ELL

Grouping Place English language learners in the groups that correspond to their reading abilities in English.

Use the appropriate Leveled Reader or other text at children's instructional level.

TIP Send home the appropriate Multilingual Summary of the main selection on Day 1.

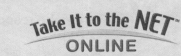
Take It to the NET™ ONLINE
PearsonSuccessNet.com

Connie Juel
For research on word identification, see the article "The Role of Orthographic Redundancy . . . " by Scott Foresman author Connie Juel along with R. L. Solso.

TEACHER TALK

Text written at a child's **instructional reading level** is text in which no more than about 1 in 10 words is difficult for the child to read.

Be sure to schedule time for children to work on the unit inquiry project "Research Responsible Acts." This week children should organize information into different categories, such as duties, equipment, and special training.

Looking Ahead

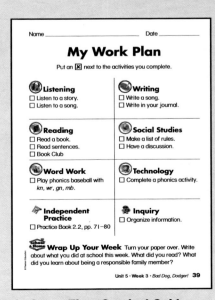

Name _____ Date _____

My Work Plan

Put an ☒ next to the activities you complete.

Listening
☐ Listen to a story.
☐ Listen to a song.

Writing
☐ Write a song.
☐ Write in your journal.

Reading
☐ Read a book.
☐ Read sentences.
☐ Book Club

Social Studies
☐ Make a list of rules.
☐ Have a discussion.

Word Work
☐ Play phonics baseball with *kn, wr, gn, mb.*

Technology
☐ Complete a phonics activity.

Independent Practice
☐ Practice Book 2.2, pp. 71–80

Inquiry
☐ Organize information.

Wrap Up Your Week Turn your paper over. Write about what you did at school this week. What did you read? What did you learn about being a responsible family member?

Unit 5 · Week 3 · *Bad Dog, Dodger!* **39**

▲ **Group-Time Survival Guide**
p. 39, Weekly Contract

Bad Dog, Dodger! **208g**

☑ Customize Your Plan *by Strand*

ORAL LANGUAGE

Concept Development

How can we be responsible family members?

 to build oral vocabulary

behavior	companion	confident
consider	cooperate	obedient
properly	reprimand	

BUILD

❑ **Question of the Week** Use the Morning Warm-Up! to introduce and discuss the question of the week. This week children will talk, sing, read, and write about responsibility. DAY 1 *208l*

❑ **Sing with Me Big Book** Sing a song about training a puppy. Ask children to listen for the concept-related Amazing Words *behavior, cooperate, obedient.* DAY 1 *208m*

❑ **Build Background** Remind children of the question of the week. Then create a concept chart for children to add to throughout the week. DAY 1 *208m*

Sing with Me Big Book

DEVELOP

❑ **Question of the Day** Use the questions in the Morning Warm-Ups! to discuss lesson concepts and how they relate to the unit theme, Responsibility. DAY 2 *210a*, DAY 3 *226a*, DAY 4 *228a*, DAY 5 *232a*

❑ **Share Literature** Read big books and read aloud selections that develop concepts, language, and vocabulary related to the lesson concept and the unit theme. Continue to develop this week's Amazing Words. DAY 2 *210b*, DAY 3 *226b*, DAY 4 *228b*, DAY 5 *232b*

CONNECT

❑ **Wrap Up Your Week!** Revisit the Question of the Week. Then connect concepts and vocabulary to next week's lesson. DAY 5 *233b*

CHECK

❑ **Check Oral Vocabulary** To informally assess children's oral vocabulary, ask individuals to use some of this week's Amazing Words to tell you about the concept of the week—Responsibility. DAY 5 *232b*

PHONICS

🔊 **SILENT CONSONANTS** When a word begins with *kn*, the *k* is silent; with *wr*, the *w* is silent; with *gn*, the *g* is silent.

TEACH

❑ **Silent Consonants** Introduce the blending strategy for words with silent consonants. Then have children blend and build words by adding the missing letters to make each word and read the completed lists. DAY 1 *208n-208o*

❑ **Fluent Word Reading** Use the Fluent Word Reading Routine to develop children's word reading fluency. Use the Phonics Songs and Rhymes Chart for additional word reading practice. DAY 2 *210c-210d*

Phonics Songs and Rhymes Chart 23

PRACTICE/APPLY

❑ **Decodable Reader 23** Practice reading words with silent consonants in context. DAY 1 *208q*

❑ *Bad Dog, Dodger!* Practice decoding words in context. DAY 2 *212-225*

❑ **Homework** Practice Book 2.2 p. 73. DAY 1 *208o*

❑ **Word Work Center** Practice silent consonants. ANY DAY *208j*

Decodable Reader 23

Main Selection—Fiction

RETEACH/REVIEW

❑ **Review** Review words with this week's phonics skills. DAY 5 *232c*

❑ **Reteach Lessons** If necessary, reteach silent consonants. DAY 5 *D1·66*

❑ **Spiral REVIEW** Review previously taught phonics skills. DAY 1 *208o*, DAY 3 *226c*, DAY 4 *228c*

ASSESS

❑ **Sentence Reading** Assess children's ability to read words with silent consonants. DAY 5 *232e-232f*

SPELLING

SILENT CONSONANTS When a word begins with *kn*, the *k* is silent; with *wr*, the *w* is silent; with *gn*, the *g* is silent.

TEACH

☐ **Pretest** Before administering the pretest, model how to segment words beginning with silent consonants to spell them. Dictate the spelling words, segmenting them if necessary. Then have children check their pretests and correct misspelled words. **DAY 1** *208p*

PRACTICE/APPLY

☐ **Dictation** Have children write dictation sentences to practice spelling words. **DAY 2** *210d*

☐ **Write Words** Have children practice spelling words by writing the spelling words that match the clues. **DAY 3** *226d*

☐ **Homework** Phonics and Spelling Practice Book pp. 89–92. **DAY 1** *208p*, **DAY 2** *210d*, **DAY 3** *226d*, **DAY 4** *228d*

RETEACH/REVIEW

☐ **Partner Review** Have pairs work together to read and write the spelling words. **DAY 4** *228d*

ASSESS

☐ **Posttest** Use dictation sentences to give the posttest for words beginning with silent consonants. **DAY 5** *232d*

Spelling Words

Silent Consonants

1. knock*	7. wrap
2. sign	8. wren
3. knee	9. gnat
4. wrong	10. lamb
5. write	11. comb
6. climb	12. knob

Challenge Words

13. knuckle	15. wrestle
14. plumber	

* Words from the Selection

VOCABULARY

STRATEGY WORD STRUCTURE Recognizing endings such as *-ed* or *-ing* can help you with a word's meaning.

LESSON VOCABULARY

chased	chewing	dripping	grabbed
practice	treat	wagged	

TEACH

☐ **Words to Know** Introduce and discuss this week's lesson vocabulary. **DAY 2** *210f*

☐ **Vocabulary Strategy Lesson** Use the lesson in the Student Edition to introduce/model *word structure*. **DAY 2** *210-211a*

Vocabulary Strategy Lesson

PRACTICE/APPLY

☐ **Words in Context** Read the lesson vocabulary in context. **DAY 2** *212-225*, **DAY 3** *212-227*

Main Selection—Fiction

☐ **Lesson Vocabulary** Have children complete each sentence. **DAY 3** *226d*

☐ **Leveled Text** Read the lesson vocabulary in leveled text. **DAY 4** *LR19-LR27*, **DAY 5** *LR19-LR27*

Leveled Readers

☐ **Homework** Practice Book 2.2 pp. 76, 79. **DAY 2** *210f*, **DAY 3** *226d*

RETEACH/REVIEW

☐ **Classify/Categorize** Model classifying words related to a topic. Have children list story words related to baseball. **DAY 3** *226e*

☐ **Review** Review this week's lesson vocabulary words. **DAY 5** *232c*

ASSESS

☐ **Selection Test** Use the Selection Test to determine children's understanding of the lesson vocabulary words. **DAY 3**

☐ **Sentence Reading** Assess children's ability to read this week's lesson vocabulary words. **DAY 5** *232e-232f*

HIGH-FREQUENCY WORDS

RETEACH/REVIEW

☐ **Spiral REVIEW** Review previously taught high-frequency words. **DAY 2** *210f*, **DAY 4** *228c*

☑ Customize Your Plan *by Strand*

COMPREHENSION

◎ SKILL PLOT AND THEME What happens in the beginning, middle, and end of a story makes up the plot. A theme is the big idea in a story.

◎ STRATEGY PRIOR KNOWLEDGE Prior knowledge is what you already know. Use prior knowledge to figure out different parts of the story.

TEACH

❑ **Skill/Strategy Lesson** Use the skill/strategy lesson in the Student Edition to introduce *plot and theme* and *prior knowledge*. DAY 1 *208r–209a*

Skill/Strategy Lesson

PRACTICE/APPLY

❑ **Skills and Strategies in Context** Read *Bad Dog, Dodger!* using the Guiding Comprehension questions to apply *plot and theme* and *prior knowledge.* DAY 2 *212–225a*

Main Selection—Fiction

❑ **Reader Response** Use the questions on Student Edition p. 226 to discuss the selection. DAY 3 *226g–227*

❑ **Skills and Strategies in Context** Read "How to Train Your Puppy," guiding children as they apply skills and strategies. DAY 4 *228–231*

Paired Selection— Nonfiction

❑ **Leveled Text** Apply *plot and theme* and *prior knowledge* to read leveled text. DAY 4 *LR19–LR27*, DAY 5 *LR19–LR27*

Leveled Readers

❑ **Homework** Practice Book 2.2 pp. 74, 75. DAY 1 *208–209*, DAY 2 *210e*

ASSESS

❑ **Selection Test** Determine children's understanding of the main selection and assess their ability to identify *plot and theme*. DAY 3

❑ **Story Reading** Have children read the passage "Needles or Knots." Ask questions that require them to identify the *plot and theme*. Then have them retell. DAY 5 *232e–232g*

RETEACH/REVIEW

❑ **Reteach Lesson** If necessary, reteach *plot* and *theme*. DAY 5 *DI·66*

FLUENCY

SKILL READ WITH EXPRESSION/INTONATION Reading with expression means reading the words as if you were the character. Intonation means that you use different tones of voice and pitch as you read.

REREAD FOR FLUENCY

❑ **Oral Rereading** Have children read orally from Decodable Reader 23 or another text at their independent reading level. Listen as children read and provide corrective feedback regarding their oral reading and their use of the blending strategy. DAY 1 *208q*

❑ **Paired Reading** Have pairs of children read orally from the main selection or another text at their independent reading level. Listen as children read and provide corrective feedback regarding their oral reading and their use of the blending strategy. DAY 2 *225a*

TEACH

❑ **Model** Use passages from *Bad Dog, Dodger!* to model reading with expression/intonation. DAY 3 *226f*, DAY 4 *231a*

PRACTICE/APPLY

❑ **Choral Reading** Have groups choral read parts from *Bad Dog, Dodger!* and "How to Train Your Puppy." Monitor progress and provide feedback regarding children's expression and intonation. DAY 3 *226f*, DAY 4 *231a*

❑ **Listening Center** Have children follow along with the AudioText for this week's selections. ANY DAY *208j*

❑ **Reading/Library Center** Have children build fluency by rereading Leveled Readers, Decodable Readers, or other text at their independent level. ANY DAY *208j*

❑ **Fluency Coach** Have children use Fluency Coach to listen to fluent reading or to practice reading on their own. ANY DAY

ASSESS

❑ **Story Reading** Take a one-minute timed sample of children's oral reading. Use the passage "Needles or Knots." DAY 5 *232e–232g*

❶ Use assessment data to determine your instructional focus.

❷ Preview this week's instruction by strand.

❸ Choose instructional activities that meet the needs of your classroom.

WRITING

Trait of the Week

VOICE Voice is the way a writer feels and thinks about a topic.

TEACH

❑ **Write Together** Engage children in writing activities that develop language, grammar, and writing skills. Include independent writing as an extension of group writing activities.

  Shared Writing DAY 1 *209a*
  Interactive Writing DAY 2 *225b*
  Writing Across the Curriculum DAY 4 *231b*

❑ **Trait of the Week** Introduce and model the Trait of the Week, *voice.* DAY 3 *227a*

PRACTICE/APPLY

❑ **Write Now** Examine the model on Student Edition pp. 232–233. Then have children write rules. DAY 5 *232-233*

  Prompt In *Bad Dog, Dodger!*, both Dodger and Sam learn rules. Think about something you do that could have rules. Now write rules for that activity.

Write Now

❑ **Daily Journal Writing** Have children write about concepts and literature in their journals. **EVERY DAY** *208d-208e*

❑ **Writing Center** Have children write a song about a pet. **ANY DAY** *208k*

ASSESS

❑ **Scoring Rubric** Use a rubric to evaluate rules. DAY 5 *232-233*

RETEACH/REVIEW

❑ **The Grammar and Writing Book** Use pp. 182–187 of The Grammar and Writing Book to extend instruction. **ANY DAY**

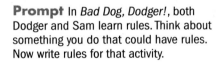
The Grammar and Writing Book

GRAMMAR

SKILL PRONOUNS *I* AND *ME* The pronouns *I* and *me* take the place of your name. Use *I* in the subject of a sentence. Use *me* after an action verb.

TEACH

❑ **Grammar Transparency 23** Use Grammar Transparency 23 to teach pronouns *I* and *me.* DAY 1 *209b*

Grammar Transparency 23

PRACTICE/APPLY

❑ **Develop the Concept** Review the concept of pronouns *I* and *Me* and provide guided practice. DAY 2 *225c*

❑ **Apply to Writing** Have children use pronouns *I* and *me* in writing. DAY 3 *227b*

❑ **Define/Practice** Review the pronouns *I* and *me.* Then have children write a paragraph using *I* and *me.* DAY 4 *231c*

❑ **Write Now** Discuss the grammar lesson on Student Edition p. 233. Have children use the pronouns *I* and *me* in their rules for an activity. DAY 5 *232-233*

Write Now

❑ **Daily Fix-It** Have children find and correct errors in grammar, spelling, and punctuation. DAY 1 *209a*, DAY 2 *225c*, DAY 3 *227a*, DAY 4 *231c*, DAY 5 *232-233*

❑ **Homework** The Grammar and Writing Practice Book pp. 89–92. DAY 2 *225c*, DAY 3 *227b*, DAY 4 *231c*, DAY 5 *232-233*

RETEACH/REVIEW

❑ **The Grammar and Writing Book** Use pp. 182–185 of The Grammar and Writing Book to extend instruction. **ANY DAY**

The Grammar and Writing Book

SPEAKING AND LISTENING

TEACH

❑ **Retell a Movie or Play** Remind children of appropriate listening and speaking behaviors. Have children retell the story of a movie or play that the class has seen. DAY 4 *231d*

RESEARCH/INQUIRY

TEACH

❑ **Encyclopedia** Model how to use an encyclopedia. Then have partners practice using an encyclopedia. DAY 5 *233a*

❑ **Unit Inquiry Project** Allow time for children to organize information into different categories. **ANY DAY** *153*

Resources for
Differentiated Instruction

LEVELED READERS

▶ **Comprehension**
- 🎯 **Skill** Plot and Theme
- 🎯 **Strategy** Prior Knowledge

▶ **Lesson Vocabulary**
- 🎯 Word Structure

practice	chewing
grabbed	
chased	treat
wagged	dripping

▶ **Social Studies Standards**
- • Citizenship
- • Family Responsibility
- • Rules
- • Pet Care

Leveled Reader Database ONLINE

PearsonSuccessNet.com

Use the Online Database of over 600 books to
- • Download and print additional copies of this week's leveled readers
- • Listen to the readers being read online
- • Search for more titles focused on this week's skills, topic, and content

On-Level Reader

Theme and Plot
Hubert and Frankie is all about learning the rules. Circle the three events from the story that best relate to learning and the rules. Then write "beginning," "middle," or "end" next to the circled events to tell when they happened in the story.

middle ① Hubert taught Frankie to listen and what the words *no* and *stop* meant.

beginning ② Madeline tried and tried to teach Frankie to sit, but he would not listen.

3. Hubert had lived with the Kent family for a long time and Frankie was the new puppy.

4. Hubert thought Frankie was trouble.

end ⑤ Frankie showed the Kents that he knew how to sit.

🎯 **On-Level Practice** TE p. LR23

Vocabulary
Choose a word from the Word Box that best fits in each sentence.

Words to Know			
chased	chewing	dripping	grabbed
practice	treat	wagged	

1. To show he was happy, Frankie **wagged** his tail.

2. Frankie **grabbed** the baseball glove.

3. Frankie liked **chewing** on bones.

4. After splashing in the puddle, Frankie was **dripping** wet.

5. Hubert helped Frankie **practice** how to behave.

6. Both Frankie and Hubert got a **treat** when they were good.

7. Frankie still **chased** the cat sometimes.

🎯 **On-Level Practice** TE p. LR24

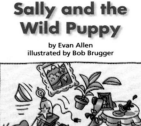 
Sally and the Wild Puppy
by Evan Allen
illustrated by Bob Brugger

Below-Level Reader

Theme and Plot
Sally and the Wild Puppy is all about training a puppy. Circle the three events from the story that best relate to training a puppy. Then write "beginning," "middle," or "end" next to the circled events to tell when they happened in the story.

end ① Sparks learned to obey and became a good listener.

2. Grandma gave Sally a puppy.

beginning ③ Sparks made a big mess.

middle ④ Sally practiced with Sparks.

5. Sally was happy to get a puppy.

In the space below, draw a picture that shows the theme of *Sally and the Wild Puppy*.

🎯 **Below-Level Practice** TE p. LR20

Vocabulary
Choose a word from the box that best fits in each sentence.

Words to Know			
chased	chewing	dripping	grabbed
practice	treat	wagged	

1. Grandma said she had a special **treat** for Sally.

2. Sally's puppy was **chewing** everything in sight.

3. The puppy's tail **wagged** so hard that it was blurry.

4. Sally wanted Sparks to **practice** to become the perfect puppy.

5. Sparks **chased** after Sally.

6. Sally **grabbed** Sparks as he ran out the door.

7. Sparks liked to give sloppy, **dripping** licks.

🎯 **Below-Level Practice** TE p. LR21

Advanced

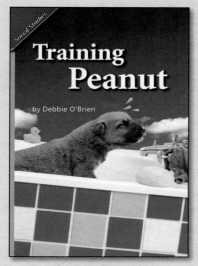

Advanced Reader

Theme and Plot
The theme of *Training Peanut* is that training a puppy takes work but is worthwhile. Then write "beginning," "middle," or "end" next to the circled events to tell when they happened in the story.

end ⑴ When the puppy training course was over, Peanut had learned how to behave better. The family decided to take her to the advanced course for more training.

2. Tomás and Sofía wanted a puppy more than anything else and asked Mom every day about getting one.

beginning ⑶ At the first puppy training class, Mom, Sofía, and Tomás learned how to give the sit command. They practiced all week with Peanut.

middle ⑷ In a few weeks, Mr. Sanders taught the puppies how to lie down, stay, and heel. He told the families to go on many walks with their puppies to practice these commands.

5. The family plans to take other classes at the community center too. Sofía and Tomás might even take swimming lessons.

Advanced Practice TE p. LR26

Vocabulary
Draw a line to match each word with its meaning.

1. behavior — a. behaving badly
2. command — b. to do what you are told
3. naughty — c. the way someone or something acts
4. obey — d. word or acts that show approval
5. patient — e. to be calm and wait
6. praise — f. an order

Advanced Practice TE p. LR27

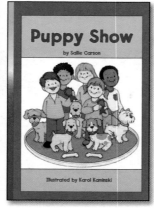

ELL Reader

ELL Poster 23

Teacher's Edition Notes
ELL notes throughout this lesson support instruction and reference additional resources at point of use.

ELL Teaching Guide pp. 155–161, 256–257
- Multilingual summaries of the main selection
- Comprehension lesson
- Vocabulary strategies and word cards
- ELL Reader 23 lesson

ELL and Transition Handbook

Ten Important Sentences
- Key ideas from every selection in the Student Edition
- Activities to build sentence power

More Reading

Readers' Theater Anthology
- Fluency practice
- Five scripts to build fluency
- Poetry for oral interpretation

Leveled Trade Books

- Extend reading tied to the unit concept
- Lessons in Trade Book Library Teaching Guide

School + Home

Homework
- Family Times Newsletter
- ELL Multilingual Selection Summaries

Take-Home Books
- Decodable Readers
- Leveled Readers

Literacy Centers

Listening

Let's Read
Along

MATERIALS `SINGLES`
CD player, headphones, print copies of recorded pieces

LISTEN TO LITERATURE As children listen to the following recordings, have them follow along or read along in the print version.

AudioText
Bad Dog, Dodger!
"How to Train Your Puppy"

Sing with Me/Background Building Audio
"I'm Just a New Puppy"

Phonics Songs and Rhymes Audio
"Obedience School"

I'm Just a New Puppy

I'm just a new puppy.
I haven't lived long,
And sometimes I do things
That I know are wrong.

I wrestle with sweaters,
Knock over knickknacks.
I jump on your kneecaps
And chew socks for snacks.

I climb in the bathtub
And gnaw on a log.
But after I'm trained,
I'll be such a good dog.

Audio CD **Phonics Songs and Rhymes Chart 23**

Reading/Library

Read It
Again!

MATERIALS `SINGLES` `PAIRS` `GROUPS`
collection of books for self-selected reading, reading logs

REREAD BOOKS Have children select previously read books from the appropriate book box and record titles of books they read in their logs. Use these previously read books:

- **Decodable Readers**
- **Leveled Readers**
- **ELL Readers**
- **Stories written by classmates**
- **Books from the library**

TEN IMPORTANT SENTENCES Have children read the Ten Important Sentences for *Bad Dog, Dodger!* and locate the sentences in the Student Edition.

BOOK CLUB Have children discuss *Bad Dog, Dodger!* Have them tell what they liked and did not like about the story.

Word Work

Phonics
Baseball

MATERIALS `PAIRS` `GROUPS`
baseball diamond game board, 20 word cards, game markers

SILENT CONSONANTS kn, wr, gn, mb Have two to four children play a phonics baseball game using words with silent consonants.

1. Make a baseball diamond game board and write a word with a silent consonant such as *knob, wrestle, gnaw, comb* on each of twelve index cards. On the other eight cards, write words without silent consonants.
2. Stack the cards facedown on the pitcher's mound.
3. Children take turns picking a card and reading the word. If the word has a silent consonant, the child advances one base.
4. Play continues until everyone reaches home.

 This interactive CD provides additional practice.

Scott Foresman Reading Street Centers Survival Kit

Use the *Bad Dog, Dodger!* materials from the Reading Street Centers Survival Kit to organize this week's centers.

Writing

Can I Keep Him?

MATERIALS
paper, pencils, crayons

`SINGLES`

WRITE A SONG Recall that Dodger is a dog that gets into a lot of trouble.

1. Ask children if they have or know pets that also get into trouble.
2. Children use a familiar or made up tune to write a song about their own pet or a make-believe pet that gets into trouble.
3. Then have them draw a picture to accompany their writing.

LEVELED WRITING Encourage children to write at their own ability level. Some may write only one or two lines. Others will be able to write a simple song with some attention to mechanics and spelling. Your best writers will write a song with greater detail and attention to mechanics and spelling.

My doggie digs holes in the garden.
My doggie chews socks on my feet.
My doggie gets mud on the carpet.
Oh please train my doggie for me.

Social Studies

Follow the Rules

MATERIALS
paper, pencils

`PAIRS`

CLASSROOM RULES Remind children that classroom rules help keep order and keep people safe.

1. Have pairs write a list of classroom rules.
2. Children can discuss what would happen if each rule were not obeyed.

Class Rules

1 Walk.

2 Work quietly.

3 Raise your hand.

Technology

Focus on Phonics

MATERIALS
computer, Phonics Practice Activities CD-ROM

`PAIRS`

USE A CD-ROM Have pairs of children use a CD-ROM.

1. Have children turn on the computer and open the Phonics Practice Activities CD-ROM.
2. Pairs complete one of the CD-ROM activities.

Phonics Activities CD

ALL CENTERS

Oral Vocabulary
"Obedience School" 23

Phonics and Spelling
Silent Consonants

Spelling Pretest: Words with Silent Consonants

  **Read** Apply Phonics **Word Wall**

Group Time < Differentiated Instruction

Comprehension
Skill Plot and Theme

Strategy Prior Knowledge

Shared Writing
Rules

Grammar
Using *I* and *Me*

Materials

- *Sing with Me Big Book*
- Letter Tiles
- Decodable Reader 23
- Student Edition 208–209
- Tested Word Cards
- Graphic Organizer 15
- Skill Transparency 23
- Writing Transparency 23
- Grammar Transparency 23

Take It to the NET
ONLINE

Professional Development
To learn more about reading failure, go to PearsonSuccessNet.com and read "Matthew Effects in Reading" by Keith Stanovich.

Morning Warm~Up!

We know what the word *responsible* means. It means to do what you're supposed to do. How can we be responsible family members?

QUESTION OF THE WEEK Tell children they will talk, sing, read, and write about Responsibility. Write and read the message and discuss the question.

CONNECT CONCEPTS Ask questions to connect to other Unit 5 selections.

- How was the stray cat in *One Dark Night* a responsible member of her family?

- The vet in *Animal Hospital* takes care of sick animals. If someone in your family got sick, how could you be a responsible family member?

REVIEW HIGH-FREQUENCY WORDS

- Circle the high-frequency words *great* and *word* in the message.

- Have volunteers write the words on the board, and then have the class say the words aloud.

Build Background Use the Day 1 instruction on ELL Poster 23 to assess knowledge and develop concepts.

ELL Poster 23

Oral Vocabulary

SHARE LITERATURE Display p. 23 of the *Sing with Me Big Book.* Tell children that the class is going to sing a song about training a puppy. Ask the class to listen for the Amazing Words **behavior, cooperate,** and **obedient** as you sing. Then ask for volunteers to retell what happens in the song using the Amazing Words. Encourage the class to sing the song with you.

Obedience School

I just got a brand new puppy.
He is really great.
But he has a little problem—
He won't cooperate!

I can change that dog's behavior.
I'll take him to school.
Then he'll be obedient and
Follow every rule.

Sing with Me Big Book

**Sing with Me/
Background Building Audio**

BUILD BACKGROUND Remind children of the question of the week.

• How can we be responsible family members?

Tell children that the class has been discussing how pets can show good behavior, cooperate, and be obedient. Draw a web or use Graphic Organizer 15. Label the center circle Family Responsibilites and ask children to name responsible behaviors for family members. Fill in the chart with their suggestions. Draw more circles as necessary. Display the web for use throughout the week.

• What are some ways that family members can cooperate? (work together to keep the house clean or prepare dinner)

• What are some ways that family members show responsible behavior? (follow the household rules, treat each other with respect)

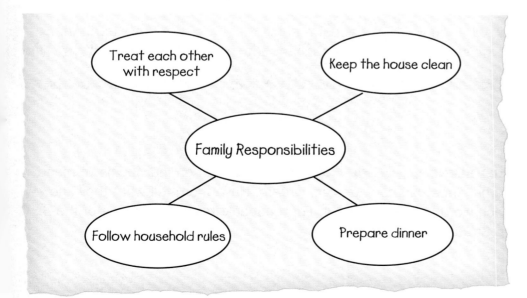

Treat each other with respect

Keep the house clean

Family Responsibilities

Follow household rules

Prepare dinner

▲ **Graphic Organizer 15**

OBJECTIVE

● Build oral vocabulary.

Amazing Words to build oral vocabulary

MONITOR PROGRESS

behavior cooperate obedient companion consider reprimand confident properly	**If...** children lack oral vocabulary experiences about the concept Responsibility, **then...** use the Oral Vocabulary Routine below to teach *behavior*.

Oral Vocabulary ROUTINE

1 **Introduce the Word** Relate the word *behavior* to the song. Supply a child-friendly definition. Have children say the word. **Example:** The way someone acts or behaves is their *behavior.*

2 **Demonstrate** Provide an example to show meaning. The dog's *behavior* improved after we trained her.

3 **Apply** Have children demonstrate their understanding. Which of the following describes *behavior*—a bookshelf or sharing your toys?

4 **Display the Word/Word Parts** Write the word on a card. Display it. Point out the word *behave* in *behavior*. See p. DI·5 to teach *cooperate* and *obedient.*

ELL

Access Content Show children that *behavior* is related to *behave* and *obedient* is related to *obey*. Help them understand these words.

Silent Consonants

TEACH/MODEL

Blending Strategy **ROUTINE**

1 **Connect** Write *knew.* You can read this word. What sound do you hear at the beginning? /k/ What do you know about the beginning sound of this word? (The letters *kn* stand for /n/.) The *k* is silent. Today we'll learn other words that have silent letters.

2 **Use Sound-Spelling Card** Display Card 20. This is a *nurse.* The letter *n* in *nurse* stands for the sound /n/. Say it with me: /n/. The letters *kn* and *gn* can also stand for /n/.

m

kn

Sound-Spelling Card 19

Sound-Spelling Card 20

3 **Model** Write *knot.* The letters *kn* stand for /n/ in *knot.* Listen as I blend this word. **Blend the sounds continuously across the word.** Let's blend this word together: /n/, /o/, /t/, *knot.* Have children compare initial consonant sounds in *not* and *knot.*

Model blending with *gnaw, lamb,* and *wrong.* Point out that when a word begins or ends with *gn,* the *g* is silent; when a word begins with *wr,* the *w* is silent; when a word ends with *mb,* the *b* is silent.

r

Sound-Spelling Card 30

4 **Group Practice** Blend these words together. Continue with *knit, comb, knife, gnat, write, sign.*

5 **Review** What do you know about reading these words? The letters *kn, wr, gn,* and *mb* can stand for the consonant sounds /n/, /r/, /n/, and /m/.

BLEND WORDS

INDIVIDUALS BLEND *kn, wr, gn,* AND *mb* WORDS Call on individuals to blend *wrinkle, gnu, knee, plumber, design, wreath.* Have them tell what they know about each word before reading it. For feedback, refer to step five of the Blending Strategy Routine.

BUILD WORDS

INDIVIDUALS MAKE *kn, wr, gn,* AND *mb* WORDS Write *kn, wr, gn,* and *mb* as headings on a four-column chart or use Graphic Organizer 27. Below each letter pair, write several words with those letters omitted. For example, for *knee,* write ___*ee.* Have children add the missing letters to make each word and then have children read the completed lists.

kn	*wr*	*gn*	*mb*
knee	wreck	gnu	comb
knew	wriggle	gnat	limb
knock	wreath	design	dumb

Vocabulary TiP

You may wish to explain the meanings of these words.

wren	a kind of bird
gnat	a kind of bug
knight	a person who protected a king or queen from long ago

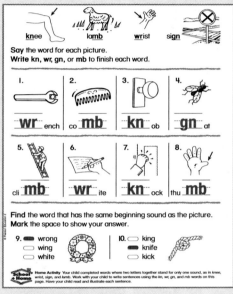

▲ **Practice Book 2.2** p. 73, Silent Consonants

Monitor Progress **Check Word Reading** Silent Consonants

Write the following words and have individuals read them.

knock	knee	wren	knuckle	wrote
lamb	limb	comb	gnome	gnat
knight	write	sign	climb	knife

If... children cannot blend words with *kn, wr, gn,* and *mb* at this point,

then... continue to monitor their progress using other instructional opportunities during the week so that they can be successful with the Day 5 Assessment. See the Skills Trace on p. 208n.

SUCCESS PREDICTOR

Spiral REVIEW

● Row 3 reviews long *i* words with other words that contain silent consonants.

▶ **Day 1 Check Word Reading** **Day 2** Check Lesson Vocabulary/High-Frequency Words **Day 3 Check** Retelling **Day 4 Check** Fluency **Day 5 Assess** Progress

Word Reading

SUCCESS PREDICTOR

OBJECTIVES

- Segment sounds to spell words.
- Spell words with silent consonants *kn, wr, gn,* and *mb.*

Spelling Words

Silent Consonants

1. **knock***   7. **wrap**
2. **sign**   8. **wren**
3. **knee**   9. **gnat**
4. **wrong**   10. **lamb**
5. **write**   11. **comb**
6. **climb**   12. **knob**

Challenge Words

13. **knuckle**   15. **wrestle**
14. **plumber**

* Word from the Selection

Words with kn, wr, gn, mb

Generalization Sometimes two letters together stand for only one sound: **knee,** **write, sign,** and **comb.**

Sort the list words by kn, wr, gn, and mb.

kn	gn
1. knock	7. sign
2. knee	8. gnat
3. knob	**wr**
mb	9. wrong
4. climb	10. write
5. lamb	11. wrap
6. comb	12. wren

Spelling Words
1. knock
2. sign
3. knee
4. wrong
5. write
6. climb
7. wrap
8. wren
9. gnat
10. lamb
11. comb
12. knob

Challenge Words
13. knuckle
14. wrestle
15. plumber

Challenge Words

kn	mb
13. knuckle	14. plumber
	wr
	15. wrestle

Home Activity Your child is learning to spell words with kn, wr, gn, and mb. To practice at home, have your child write the word, say it and then circle the letters that stand together but have one sound.

▲ **Spelling Practice Book** p. 89

ELL

Support Spelling Before giving the spelling pretest, clarify the meaning of each spelling word with examples, such as saying *knee* while pointing to your knee and demonstrating the meaning of *knock* by knocking on a wall or door.

Spelling

PRETEST Silent Consonants

MODEL WRITING FOR SOUNDS Each spelling word has a silent consonant. Before administering the spelling pretest, remind children that the sound /n/ can be spelled *kn* or *gn,* the sound /r/ can be spelled *wr,* and the sound /m/ can be spelled *mb.*

- What sounds do you hear in *knife?* (/n/ /ī/ /f/)
- What are the letters for /n/? Remember that *kn* can spell the sound /n/. Write *kn.* Continue with *i* /ī/, *f* /f/, and silent *e.*
- What letters stand for /n/? *(kn)*
- Repeat with *gnome, wrench,* and *limb.* Remind children that /n/ can be spelled *n, kn,* or *gn,* and tell them that in *gnome,* it is spelled *gn.*

PRETEST Dictate the spelling words. Segment the words for children if necessary. Have children check their pretests and correct misspelled words.

HOMEWORK Spelling Practice Book, p. 89

Group Time

Puppy Kindergarten

On-Level	Strategic Intervention	Advanced
Read Decodable Reader 23.	**Read** Decodable Reader 23.	**Read** Advanced Selection 23.
• Use p. 208q.	• Use the **Routine** on p. DI·34.	• Use the **Routine** on p. DI·35.

ELL Place English language learners in the groups that correspond to their reading abilities in English.

(i) Independent Activities

Fluency Reading Pair children to reread Leveled Readers or the ELL Reader from the previous week or other text at children's independent level.

Journal Writing List ways people can cooperate with each other. Share writing.

Independent Reading See p.208j for Reading/Library activities and suggestions.

Literacy Centers To practice silent consonants, you may use Word Work, p. 208j.

Practice Book 2.2 Silent Consonants, p. 73; Plot and Theme, p. 74

Break into small groups after Spelling and before the Comprehension lesson.

DAY 1

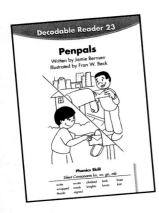

Apply Phonics

PRACTICE Silent Consonants

HIGH-FREQUENCY WORDS Review *brought, grandmother,* and *touch.*

READ DECODABLE READER 23

- Pages 58–59 Read aloud quietly with the group.
- Pages 60–61 Have the group read aloud without you.
- Pages 62–64 Select individuals to read aloud.

CHECK COMPREHENSION AND DECODING Ask children the following questions:

- What are pen pals? (They are friends who keep in touch by writing letters.)
- Who are the pen pals in the story? (Fred and Dan)
- Why did Fred need to stop writing? (His thumb was hurting.)

Then have children locate *kn, wr, gn,* and *mb* words in the story. Review *kn, wr, gn,* and *mb* spelling patterns. Sort words according to their spelling patterns.

kn	wr	gn	mb
knee	wrapped	signed	climbed
knights	write		limb
knit	writing		numb
knots	wrote		thumb

HOMEWORK Take-Home Decodable Reader 23

REREAD FOR FLUENCY

Oral Rereading

ROUTINE

1. **Read** Have children read the entire story orally.

2. **Reread** To achieve optimal fluency, children should reread the text three or four times.

3. **Provide Feedback** Listen as children read and provide corrective feedback regarding their oral reading and their use of the blending strategy.

Monitor Progress

Decoding

If... children have difficulty decoding a word,	then... prompt them to blend the word. • What is the new word? • Is the new word a word you know? • Does it make sense in the story?

Access Content

Beginning Preview the story and encourage children to identify words they are familiar with in the pictures and print.

Intermediate Preview *Penpals,* explaining that *keep in touch* is an expression that means "keep the friendship going" even when two people are separated.

Advanced After reading the first two pages together, explain that *numb* means "hardly any feeling." Ask children why Mom wanted to make Fred's knee numb. (so he wouldn't feel any pain)

OBJECTIVES

- Recognize plot and theme.
- Use prior knowledge.

Skills Trace

Plot and Theme

Introduce/Teach	TE: 2.3 403a–b, 404e; 2.4 96r, 96–97; 2.5 208r, 208–209; 2,6 408r, 408–409
Practice	TE: 2.3 414–415; 2.4 114–115; 2.5 222–223; 2.6 422–423; PB: 2.1 134–135; 2.2 34–35, 74–75, 144–145
Reteach/Review	TE: 2.3 DI·67; 2.4 DI·67; 2.5 196–197, 255a, DI·66; 2.6 DI·68; PB: 2.2 67, 87
Test	TE: 2.3 424e–g; 2.4 122e–g; 2.5 232e–g; Selection Tests: 2.3 53–56; 2.4 73–76; 2.5 85–88, 89–92; 2.6 117–120; Benchmark Test: Units 3–5

Trouble at the Table

Victor set the table for dinner. He did not like this job. Victor set the table for his mom, his sister Sara, and himself.

Dinner was ready. Sara ran into the room and sat in the wrong chair.

"That's my chair," Victor said.

She moved to the next chair. "That's Mom's chair," he said.

Sara sat in her own chair. Mom brought dinner to the table. Sara put her napkin on her head. Mom raised her eyebrows. Victor sighed. Sara put her napkin on her lap.

Mom put salad on the plates. Sara used a spoon to pick up the salad. Most of the lettuce fell off the spoon.

"Why don't you use your fork like us?" Victor asked.

"I am special. I didn't have to set the table," Sara told him.

Sara cut her macaroni and cheese with a knife. Then she tried to eat her pudding with a fork.

Finally Mom had had enough. "Sara," she said, "tomorrow night you can set the table." Sara sighed. Victor smiled. Mom always says stop while you're ahead.

> **Skill** Think about the story's plot. What is happening here at the beginning of the story? You could add it to a graphic organizer.

> **Strategy** Here you can think about the theme. Ask yourself, "Have I kept doing something even though I knew I should stop?" What is the theme of this story?

Unit 5 Bad Dog, Dodger!   *Skill Transparency 23*

▲ Skill Transparency 23

Access Content

Beginning/Intermediate For a Picture It! lesson on plot and theme, see the ELL Teaching Guide, pp. 155–156.

Advanced Before children read "Trouble at the Table," make sure they know the meanings of the phrases *set the table*, *pick up*, and *macaroni and cheese*.

Plot and Theme
Prior Knowledge

TEACH/MODEL

INTRODUCE PLOT AND THEME Recall *One Dark Night*. Have students tell what happened in the story. Then have them tell what they learned about Jonathan. (Possible response: At the beginning, a thunderstorm approaches as Jonathan looks out the window. Then, a mother cat brings her kittens out of the storm to Jonathan. In the end, the cat and all three kittens are safe inside with Jonathan. Children may have learned that Jonathan is a caring and responsible boy.)

- What might have happened if Jonathan had not helped the cat?

Read p. 208 with children. Explain the following: What happens in a story's beginning, middle, and ending is called the plot. The way characters feel can affect how they act, and their actions make up the plot. The theme of a story is the story's "big idea," or what we learn from the story.

- We can use what we already know to draw conclusions about the theme.

Use Skill Transparency 23 to teach plot and theme and prior knowledge.

SKILL Use paragraphs one through five to model identifying the beginning of the plot.

 MODEL After reading the first paragraph, I know Victor has set the table, and he, his mom, and Sara are getting ready to eat dinner. This is the beginning of the plot. I can read to find out what happens in the middle and at the end of the story. I can understand the theme by thinking about the big idea, or what I learned.

STRATEGY Continue with paragraphs six through eleven to model prior knowledge.

 MODEL I can use what I already know to understand the plot. From the title and the first half of the story, I know that Sara is causing trouble by acting silly. I know that I sometimes act silly when I am upset. I wonder if Sara is upset about something.

Comprehension

Skill
Plot and Theme

Strategy
Prior Knowledge

Plot and Theme

- A story's plot is what happens at the beginning, middle, and end of the story.
- A story's theme is the "big idea" that the author is trying to get across. Ask yourself, "What did the characters in the story learn?"

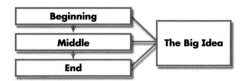

Beginning → Middle → End → The Big Idea

Strategy: Prior Knowledge

Active readers use what they know to understand a story and its plot. Look at the title and pictures of a story. Ask, "What do I think this will be about? Do I know anything about this?"

Write to Read

1. Read "Trouble at the Table." Make a graphic organizer like the one above. In the final box, write the big idea of the story.

2. Choose one thing about "Trouble at the Table" that reminds you of something or someone you know. Write about it.

208

Trouble at the Table

Victor set the table for dinner. He did not like this job. Victor set the table for his mom, his sister Sara, and himself.

Dinner was ready. Sara ran into the room and sat in the wrong chair.

"That's my chair," Victor said.

She moved to the next chair. "That's Mom's chair," he said.

Sara sat in her own chair. Mom brought dinner to the table. Sara put her napkin on her head. Mom raised her eyebrows. Victor sighed. Sara put her napkin on her lap.

Mom put salad on the plates. Sara used a spoon to pick up the salad. Most of the lettuce fell off the spoon.

"Why don't you use your fork like us?" Victor asked.

"I am special. I didn't have to set the table," Sara told him.

Sara cut her macaroni and cheese with a knife. Then she tried to eat her pudding with a fork.

Finally Mom had had enough. "Sara," she said, "tomorrow night you can set the table." Sara sighed. Victor smiled. Mom always says stop while you're ahead.

Skill Think about the story's plot. What is happening here at the beginning of the story? You could add it to a graphic organizer.

Strategy Here you can think about the theme. Ask yourself, "Have I kept doing something even though I knew I should stop?" What is the theme of this story?

209

PRACTICE

WRITE Work with children to complete the steps in the Write activity. Have children use the completed graphic organizer to describe the plot and theme of "Trouble at the Table."

Monitor Progress	**Plot and Theme**
If... children are unable to complete Write on p. 208,	**then...** use Practice Book 2.2, p. 74, for additional practice.

CONNECT TO READING Encourage children to ask themselves these questions when they read.

- Does the story remind me of something I know about?
- Does Sara remind me of someone I know?
- Does the story remind me of another story I have read?

Read the story.
Follow the directions.

Bill had a new puppy. Carmen was going to see it. Then her mom got sick and Carmen had to take care of her little brother. Carmen knew she needed to help out. She asked Bill to bring the puppy to her house. Carmen's mom took a nap. Everybody else had fun in the yard.

1. Underline the sentence that tells about Carmen's problem.

2. Draw two lines under the sentence that tells what Carmen did about her problem.

3. Circle the sentence below that tells how Bill helped Carmen.
   Bill got a new puppy.
   Bill asked Carmen to come to his house.
   Bill took the puppy to Carmen's house.

4. Circle the sentence below that tells the big idea of this story.
   Sometimes people get sick.
   Everyone likes puppies.
   Family members help each other.

5. Circle the parts of the story that helped you tell the big idea.

Home Activity Your child identified the problem, solution, and big idea in a story. Work with your child to come up with an idea you both think is important, such as It's important to try. Help your child write about something that has happened in his or her life that conveys that idea.

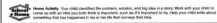
Practice Book 2.2 p. 74, Plot and Theme

OBJECTIVE
● Write rules.

DAILY FIX-IT

1. the rong date is on the sign
<u>T</u>he <u>w</u>rong date is on the sign<u>.</u>

2. The lam scared the wren
away?
The lam<u>b</u> scared the wren away<u>.</u>

This week's practice sentences appear on Daily Fix-It Transparency 23.

Strategic Intervention

Children who are not able to write independently may copy one or more of the pet-care rules and add an illustration.

Advanced

Have children do research to write a list of rules for an unusual pet—for example, a hippo.

Support Writing Before writing pet-care rules, have children work in pairs to tell each other about the pets they have or the pets they'd like to have.

▲ **The Grammar and Writing Book**
For more instruction and practice, use pp. 182–187.

Shared Writing

WRITE Rules

GENERATE IDEAS Discuss with children what people must do to take care of their pets. Have children give their ideas in the form of rules.

WRITE RULES Explain that the class will write rules for taking care of pets.

COMPREHENSION SKILL Tell children that the list of rules they write will have a theme, or big idea. Explain that the theme is "taking care of pets."

- Display Writing Transparency 23 and read the title.
- Ask children to think about rules they need to follow when taking care of pets. Emphasize general rules that apply to a variety of pets rather than specific rules that apply only to certain kinds of pets.
- Read the first rule to children.
- As children suggest other pet-care rules, record their responses.

HANDWRITING While writing, model the letter forms as shown on pp. TR14–17.

READ THE RULES Have children read the completed list of rules aloud as you track the print.

Pet Care Rules

I. Feed your pet.
   Possible answers:
2. <u>Give your pet fresh water.</u>

3. <u>Spend time with your pet.</u>

4. <u>Make sure your pet has a clean, safe home.</u>

5. <u>Take your pet to a vet every year.</u>

Unit 5 Bad Dog, Dodger!   Writing Model **23**

▲ **Writing Transparency 23**

INDEPENDENT WRITING

WRITE SENTENCES Have children write their own list of rules for a pet they have or a pet they would like to have. Children can make this list of rules more specific to the type of pet. Encourage them to use words from the Word Wall and the Amazing Words board. Let children illustrate their writing. You may gather children's work into a class book for self-selected reading.

ADDITIONAL PRACTICE For additional practice, use pp. 182–187 in the Grammar and Writing Book.

Grammar

TEACH/MODEL Pronouns *I* and *Me*

REVIEW PRONOUNS Remind children that a pronoun is a word that takes the place of a noun or nouns.

IDENTIFY PRONOUNS *I* AND *me* Display Grammar Transparency 23. Read the explanation of *I* and *me* aloud.

- Read the first item. *I* names the dog's owner, or the subject of the sentence. Remember that *I* is always written with a capital letter.
- Read the second item. Again, we use *I* because it is the subject of the sentence. *I* comes after the name of the dog because we always name ourselves last.

Continue modeling with items 3–5.

PRACTICE

STATE *I* OR *me* Have children state whether *I* or *me* should be used in the following instances.

- When telling about what you did in school today, what would you say?
- When telling what you and your pet did after school, what would you say?
- Would you say *Mary followed me home* or *Mary followed I home?*

Using *I* and *Me*

The pronouns I and me take the place of your name. Use I in the subject of a sentence. Use **me** after an action verb. Always write I with a capital letter.

    I always wanted a dog.
    My parents gave **me** a dog.

When you talk about yourself and another person, name yourself last. The pronouns I and me take the place of your name.

    The dog and I sing together.
    People are surprised when they hear the dog and **me**.

Write *I* or *me* to complete each sentence.

1. ____**I**____ have a dog named Pepper.

2. Pepper and ____**I**____ are best friends.

3. Pepper sings with ____**me**____.

4. Singing makes Pepper and ____**me**____ happy.

5. Maybe Pepper and ____**I**____ can sing for you.

Unit 5 Bad Dog, Dodger   Grammar **23**

▲ **Grammar Transparency 23**

Wrap Up Your Day!

 SILENT CONSONANTS *kn, wr, gn, mb* Write *lamb* and ask children which letter is silent. (b) Have them name other words with silent consonants.

 SPELLING WORDS WITH SILENT CONSONANTS *kn, wr, gn, mb* Say the word *knee*. Ask children what sounds they hear in the word. Write *knee* and talk about the silent *k*. Continue with *sign, wrap, gnat*.

 PLOT To help children identify plot, ask: What happened in *Trouble at the Table?* How might the story have been different if it had been Sara's turn to set the table?

LET'S TALK ABOUT IT Recall that Sara thought she was special. Do you think she was being a responsible member of her family? Explain. Possible answer: No, because she didn't help out on family chores.

 HOMEWORK Send home this week's Family Times newsletter.

PREVIEW Day 2

Tell children that tomorrow the class will read about a pet that needs to learn how to follow rules.

Day 2
AT A GLANCE

Share Literature
"Zooks"

Phonics and Spelling
Silent Consonants

Spelling: Words with
  Silent Consonants

Build Background
Training Pets

Lesson Vocabulary
practice   grabbed   chewing
chased   treat   wagged
dripping
More Words to Know
bleachers   spectators dugout

Vocabulary
Skill Endings *-ed* and *-ing*
Strategy Word Structure

Read Apply Phonics

Group Time < Differentiated
              Instruction

Bad Dog, Dodger!

Interactive Writing
Directions

Grammar
Using *I* and *Me*

Materials

• *Sing with Me Big Book*
• *Read Aloud Anthology*
• Phonics Songs and Rhymes
  Chart 23
• Background Building Audio
• Student Edition 210–225
• Tested Word Cards

Morning Warm-Up!

Today we will read about Sam
and his dog, Dodger.
Sam must teach Dodger
what's right and what's wrong.
How do we know right from wrong?

QUESTION OF THE DAY Encourage children to sing "Obedience School" from the *Sing with Me Big Book* as you gather. Write and read the message and discuss the question.

REVIEW SILENT CONSONANTS

• Ask children to point out any words in the message that have silent consonants. *(wrong, know)*

• Ask the class to tell you which consonant is silent in each word. *(w, k)* Ask them if they can name any other words with silent consonants.

Build Background Use the Day 2 instruction on ELL Poster 23 to preview high-frequency words.

ELL Poster 23

Share Literature

BUILD CONCEPTS

REALISTIC FICTION Tell the class that you are going to read a story called "Zooks." Explain that "Zooks" is a realistic fiction story. Even though the characters are make-believe, the things that happen in the story could really happen.

BUILD ORAL VOCABULARY Ask children what they know about training a dog. Encourage them to use the Amazing Words they learned yesterday. Introduce the Amazing Words **companion** and **consider.** Tell the class that a *companion* is someone who spends time with you, and *to consider* means "to think about something." Suggest that as you read, children consider whether Eileen is ready to get her own puppy.

Read Aloud Anthology
Zooks

- What do you have to consider when you get a new puppy?
(Possible responses: where he'll sleep, what to feed him, how to train him, who will take him for walks)

MONITOR LISTENING COMPREHENSION

- Why did Eileen want a puppy? (Possible responses: Eileen's friend had one; Eileen was an only child and she thought the puppy would be a good companion.)

- Why does Eileen's mother have to consider letting Eileen have a puppy? (A puppy is a big responsibility, and she doesn't know if Eileen is ready.)

- What does Eileen prove by the end of the story and how? (She proves that she's responsible enough for a puppy because she apologizes for her mistake with Zooks.)

- How else could Eileen have proven she was responsible enough for a new puppy? (Possible responses: She could have walked Zooks every day for Ms. Baxter; she could have taken care of her friend's dog for a few days.)

Amazing Words to build oral vocabulary

	MONITOR PROGRESS
behavior cooperate obedient companion consider reprimand confident properly	**If...** children lack oral vocabulary experiences about the concept Responsibility, **then...** use the Oral Vocabulary Routine. See p. DI·5 to teach *companion* and *consider.*

Build Concepts Help children understand the concept of petsitting. Ask them to tell what they know about babysitting. Explain that, like a babysitter, a petsitter stays with a pet while its owners are busy or away. A petsitter feeds and walks the pet and makes sure it doesn't do anything it's not allowed to do.

Silent Consonants

TEACH/MODEL

Fluent Word Reading

ROUTINE

1 **Connect** Write *knighthood.* You can read this word because you know how to read words with silent consonants that stand for the /n/ sound. What sound do the letters *kn* stand for in this word? (/n/) What's the word? *(knighthood)* Do the same with *gnaw, wreck,* and *lamb.*

2 **Model** When you come to a new word, look at the letters from left to right and think about the consonant sounds. Say the sounds in the word to yourself and then read the word. **Model reading *wriggle, kneepads, design.*** When you come to a new word, what are you going to do?

3 **Group Practice** Write *knickers, gnarl, wristband, signpost, knockout.* Read these words. Look at the letters, think about the consonant sounds, say the sounds to yourself, and then read the word aloud together. **Allow 2–3 seconds previewing time.**

WORD READING

PHONICS SONGS AND RHYMES CHART 23 Frame each of the following words on Phonics Songs and Rhymes Chart 23. Call on individuals to read them. Guide children in previewing.

know	**knock**	**knickknacks**	**kneecaps**
wrong	**wrestle**	**gnaw**	**climb**

Sing "I'm Just a New Puppy" to the tune of "On Top of Old Smokey," or play the CD. Have children follow along on the chart as they sing. Then have individuals take turns locating *kn, wr, gn,* and *mb* words on the chart.

 **Phonics Songs and Rhymes Audio**

I'm Just a New Puppy

I'm just a new puppy.
I haven't lived long,
And sometimes I do things
That I know are wrong.

I wrestle with sweaters,
Knock over knickknacks.
I jump on your kneecaps
And chew socks for snacks.

I climb in the bathtub
And gnaw on a log.
But after I'm trained,
I'll be such a good dog.

Phonics Songs and Rhymes Chart 23

SORT WORDS

INDIVIDUALS SORT _kn, wr, gn,_ AND _mb_ WORDS Distribute word cards with words containing silent consonants _kn, wr, gn,_ and _mb._ Write _kn, wr, gn,_ and _mb_ for four columns. Have children read their words and place their word cards under the appropriate heading. Have all children copy the completed chart and circle the letters that stand for the sounds /n/, /r/, and /m/. Have children use the words in sentences to demonstrate meaning.

_kn_	_wr_	_gn_	_mb_
knuckle	wrestle	gnaw	plumber
knickknack	wrinkle	sign	climb
knothole	wristwatch	gnat	lamb

Spelling

PRACTICE Silent Consonants

WRITE DICTATION SENTENCES Have children write these sentences. Repeat words slowly, allowing children to hear each sound. Children may use the Word Wall to help with spelling high-frequency words. **Word Wall**

If you <u>climb</u> the tree, you can see a <u>wren</u> in a nest.

It is <u>wrong</u> to go inside a house before you <u>knock</u>!

I will <u>sign</u> my name on the card and then <u>wrap</u> the gift.

Let's <u>write</u> about a <u>lamb</u> and a <u>gnat</u> with a <u>comb</u>.

HOMEWORK Spelling Practice Book, p. 90

Spelling Words

Silent Consonants

1.	knock*	7.	wrap
2.	sign	8.	wren
3.	knee	9.	gnat
4.	wrong	10.	lamb
5.	write	11.	comb
6.	climb	12.	knob

Challenge Words

13.	knuckle	15.	wrestle
14.	plumber		

* Words from the Selection

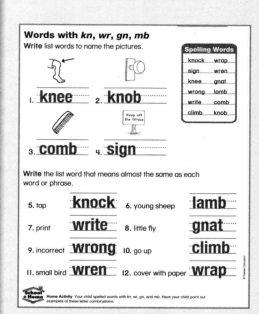

▲ Spelling Practice Book p. 90

OBJECTIVES

● Build background.
● Learn lesson vocabulary.

Read the story. **Follow** the directions.

Maria had a new puppy named Sunny. Sunny chewed Maria's doll. He ate her homework. Maria worked with Sunny. Sunny got better, but he still got into things. Then Maria trained herself. She picked up her toys and papers. Now Sunny no longer eats Maria's things.

I. **Circle** the sentence below that tells the big idea of this story.
Puppies like to chew things.
Ⓐ People and puppies may both need training Ⓑ
Puppies are a lot of work.

2. **Underline two** sentences in the story that show how Maria finally got the puppy to stop eating her things.

Write I, 2, or 3 on the lines to show the right order.

__2__ 3. Sunny chewed Maria's doll.

__1__ 4. Maria had a new puppy named Sunny.

__3__ 5. Now Sunny no longer eats Maria's things.

Write a sentence that tells something that happened in the middle of the story.

Children's sentences should tell something that happened in the
6. middle of the story. Possible answer: Maria worked with Sunny.

Home Activity Your child identified the big idea of a story and put story events in correct order. Read a story aloud to your child. Have your child tell what happened in the beginning, middle, and end of the story. Ask your child what he or she learned from the story.

▲ **Practice Book 2.2** p. 75,
Plot and Theme

Activate Prior Knowledge Invite children to share personal experiences about training their pets. Have them tell the words they use in their home language as well as English.

Build Background

DISCUSS TRAINING PETS Display pictures of cats and dogs being trained to do something. Initiate discussion by asking children what they know about what pets can be trained to do.

● Can pets be trained to act in certain ways?

● Have you ever taught your pet to do something? Explain.

BACKGROUND BUILDING AUDIO Have children listen to the CD and share the new information they learned about things our pets can be trained to do.

Audio CD Sing with Me/
Background Building Audio

COMPLETE A WEB Draw a web or display Graphic Organizer 14. Add circles to the end of the spokes. Write *things dogs can be trained to do* in the center circle. Ask children to suggest things dogs can be trained to do. Write their responses in the circles.

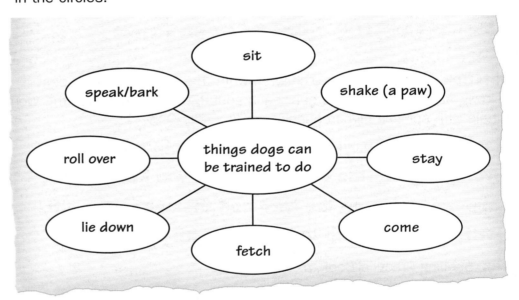

▲ **Graphic Organizer 14**

CONNECT TO SELECTION Connect background information to *Bad Dog, Dodger!*

Dogs are smart pets, and they can be taught to be obedient. In this story, Sam's dog, Dodger, gets into trouble because of his bad behavior. Sam realizes Dodger needs more attention and teaches him some tricks. We'll find out whether Dodger is really a bad dog after all.

Vocabulary

LESSON VOCABULARY

VOCABULARY FRAME Children draw or write an idea or symbol they associate with a given word, write a sentence based on the word's predicted meaning, and then verify the meaning, or use Graphic Organizer 5.

WORDS TO KNOW

T practice to repeat an action in order to improve
T grabbed took hold of something suddenly
T chewing grinding something between your teeth
T chased ran after someone
T treat a special gift, often food
T wagged moved from side to side
T dripping a liquid falling slowly, drop by drop

MORE WORDS TO KNOW

bleachers raised seats on which people sit to watch sports games
spectators people who watch an event
dugout a shelter where baseball players sit when they're waiting to play

T = Tested Word

- Children should be able to decode all words.

- Have children write the word *practice* at the top left side of the paper or graphic organizer. In a box to the right of the word, have them draw or write an idea or symbol they associate with the word.

- Have children predict the word's meaning based on what they already know about it. Students can call on prior knowledge to write a sentence using the word according to their predicted definition.

- Have children verify the word's meaning using the glossary.

- Have children write another sentence reflecting the verified definition.

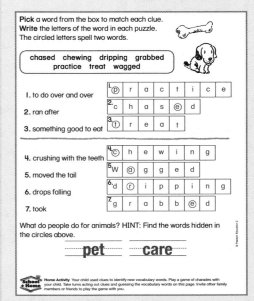

Pick a word from the box to match each clue.
Write the letters of the word in each puzzle.
The circled letters spell two words.

| chased | chewing | dripping | grabbed |
| practice | treat | wagged | |

1. to do over and over — **p r a c t i c e**
2. ran after — **c h a s e d**
3. something good to eat — **t r e a t**

4. crushing with the teeth — **c h e w i n g**
5. moved the tail — **w a g g e d**
6. drops falling — **d r i p p i n g**
7. took — **g r a b b e d**

What do people do for animals? HINT: Find the words hidden in the circles above.

pet **care**

Home Activity Your child used clues to identify new vocabulary words. Play a game of charades with your child. Take turns acting out clues and guessing the vocabulary words on this page. Invite other family members or friends to play the game with you.

▲ **Practice Book 2.2** p. 76, Lesson Vocabulary

Monitor Progress | **Check Lesson Vocabulary**

Write these words and have individuals read them.

| practice | grabbed | chewing | chased | treat | wagged | dripping |
| everybody | laugh | mother | picture | school | pull | parents |

If... children cannot read these words,

then... have them practice in pairs with word cards before reading the selection. Monitor their fluency with these words during reading, and provide additional practice opportunities before the Day 5 Assessment.

SUCCESS PREDICTOR

Spiral REVIEW

- Reviews previously taught high-frequency words and lesson vocabulary.

| **Day 1** Check Word Reading | ▶**Day 2** Check Lesson Vocabulary/High-Frequency Words | **Day 3** Check Retelling | **Day 4** Check Fluency | **Day 5** Assess Progress |

Word Reading

SUCCESS PREDICTOR

2

Words to Know

| treat |
| chewing |
| dripping |
| practice |
| wagged |
| grabbed |
| chased |

Remember 📖

Try the strategy. Then, if you need more help, use your glossary or a dictionary.

Vocabulary Strategy

for Endings

Word Structure Sometimes when you are reading, you may come across a word you don't know. Look closely at the word. Does it have *-ed* or *-ing* at the end? The ending *-ed* or *-ing* is usually added to an action word. You may be able to use the ending to help you figure out the meaning of the word.

1. Put your finger over the *-ed* or *-ing* ending.

2. Look at the base word. (That's the word without the ending.) Do you know what the base word means?

3. Try your meaning in the sentence. Does it make sense?

Read "Rabbit Tricks." Look for words that have the *-ed* or *-ing* ending. Use the endings to help you figure out the meanings of the words.

210

Rabbit Tricks

"You can't teach a rabbit to do tricks," said Eric.

"Why not?" asked Lucy. "Rabbits are smart. I can train Homer. Each time he does what I want, I'll give him a treat."

Eric looked at Homer, who was chewing on a lettuce leaf. He tossed a ball across the room. "Fetch, Homer," he said. Homer sat perfectly still, the lettuce leaf dripping out of his mouth.

Lucy sighed. "Homer won't do dog tricks. He will learn to do rabbit tricks. It will just take some practice."

A week later, Lucy said to Eric, "Come and see what Homer can do." Lucy held a lettuce leaf in front of Homer and asked, "Homer, do you want this lettuce leaf?" She moved the leaf up and down. Homer wagged his head up and down. "See? Homer answered me!" Lucy said.

"He was just following you," said Eric. He grabbed the lettuce leaf and walked out of the room. Homer chased after him.

"See? Now he is playing Follow the Leader," said Lucy.

Eric gave the lettuce to Homer. "Maybe you *can* teach a rabbit to do tricks!"

Words to Write

What would you train Homer to do? Write about it. Use words from the Words to Know list.

211

OBJECTIVE

● Use word endings *-ed* and *-ing* to determine the meaning of unfamiliar words.

ELL

Access Content Use ELL Poster 23 to preteach the lesson vocabulary. Reinforce the words with the vocabulary activities and word cards in the ELL Teaching Guide, pp. 157–158. Choose from the following to meet children's language proficiency levels.

Beginning For the words *chewing, dripping, wagged, grabbed* and *chased,* cover the endings as well as the doubled consonant, and discuss the meanings of the base words.

Intermediate Return to the vocabulary frame from the Introduce Vocabulary page. Have children choose one of the verbs to act out.

Advanced Teach the lesson on pp. 210–211. Have children determine the base word in each verb and write a sentence for each one.

Vocabulary Strategy

TEACH/MODEL Word Structure

CONNECT Remind children of strategies to use when they come across words they don't understand.

● Sometimes we can get the meaning from word parts. We may understand the base word and prefix (*rerun, to run again*) or the base word and suffix (*quickly, in a quick way*).

● We can look in a dictionary or glossary.

● We can look for endings in the unknown word. Today we will learn more about the endings *-ed* and *-ing.*

INTRODUCE THE STRATEGY

- Read and discuss the steps for using word structure on p. 210.
- Have children read "Rabbit Tricks," paying attention to the highlighted words with -*ed* and -*ing* endings.
- Model recognizing the -*ing* ending to help to determine the meaning of *chewing*.

Think Aloud **MODEL** I'm not sure what *chewing* means. I see that it has an -*ing* ending. If I cover up the ending, I see the base word *chew*. I know this word. It means to grind up something in your mouth. When I look at the whole word, *chewing*, I know -*ing* has been added.

PRACTICE

- Have children determine the base words and endings of the highlighted words in "Rabbit Tricks."
- Ask how the added letters change the meanings of the base words.

WRITE Children's writing should include lesson vocabulary in a description of what they would train Homer to do.

CONNECT TO READING Encourage children to use these strategies to determine the meaning of an unknown word.

- Look for endings -*ed* and -*ing* added to words, and see if these words have base words you know.
- Use context clues.
- Use the glossary or a dictionary.

Group Time

On-Level	Strategic Intervention	Advanced
Read *Bad Dog, Dodger!*	**Read** SI Decodable Reader 23.	**Read** *Bad Dog, Dodger!*
• Use pp. 212–225.	• Read or listen to *Bad Dog, Dodger!*	• Use the Routine on p. DI·37.
	• Use the Routine on p. DI·36.	

 Place English language learners in the groups that correspond to their reading abilities in English.

(i) Independent Activities

Independent Reading See p. 208j for Reading/Library activities and suggestions.

Journal Writing Write about a time when you saw a dog do something funny. Share writing.

Literacy Centers To provide experiences with *Bad Dog, Dodger!*, you may use the Listening and Writing Centers on pp. 208j and 208k.

Practice Book 2.2 Plot and Theme, p. 75; Lesson Vocabulary, p. 76; Sequence p.77

Break into small groups after Vocabulary and before Writing.

Bad Dog, Dodger!

by Barbara Abercrombie • illustrated by Laura Ovresat

Genre

Realistic fiction means a story is possible. Look for things that could really happen to a boy and his dog.

Do the things that Dodger does make him a bad dog?

212

213

AudioText

Read
Prereading Strategies

PREVIEW AND PREDICT Have children read the title. Identify Dodger as the dog in the picture. Identify the author and illustrator. Do a picture walk of pp. 212–219. Ask children what they think this story will be about.

DISCUSS REALISTIC FICTION Ask if any children have pets. Help children understand that the story is fiction because it comes from the author's imagination. However, the events in the story could happen in real life because people do have pets that get into trouble. Remind children that an imaginary story that could really happen is called realistic fiction. Read the definition of realistic fiction on p. 212 of the Student Edition.

SET PURPOSE Read the question on p. 213. Ask children what they would like to find out when they read the story.

Access Content Before reading, review the story summary in English and/or the home language. See the ELL Teaching Guide, pp. 159–161.

_____ Silent Consonants   lesson/tested vocabular

Sam wanted a dog.

"If you're a good boy," said his father.

"When you can take care of it yourself," said his mother.

Sam cleaned up his room. He ate carrots and broccoli. He stopped making monster noises at night to scare Molly, his older sister. He hung up his cap after baseball practice.

On the morning of his ninth birthday, Sam found a large box waiting for him. Inside was a puppy. He was black and soft and had big feet. Sam named him Dodger.

The whole family loved Dodger. Dodger licked their faces and curled up on their laps. He nibbled their shoelaces.

214

215

Strategies in Context

⊙ PRIOR KNOWLEDGE

- **What do you think Sam will have to do to take care of Dodger?**
  Children may respond that he will have to feed, walk, and train Dodger.

Monitor Progress	Prior Knowledge
If... children have difficulty activating prior knowledge about pets,	**then...** model using what you know to understand text.

MODEL When I read about Sam's new dog, it reminds me of the dog I got when I was eight. I remember I had to learn how to take care of him and train him to behave. So, I think Sam will have to train and care for Dodger.

ASSESS Have children use what they know about pets to make and record predictions about problems Sam might face as he trains Dodger.

▲ **Pages 214–215**
Have children look at the picture and read to find out about the characters in the story.

Monitor Progress	
Decoding	
If... children come to a word they don't know,	**then...** remind them to:
	1. Blend the word.
	2. Decide if the word makes sense.
	3. Look in a dictionary for more help.

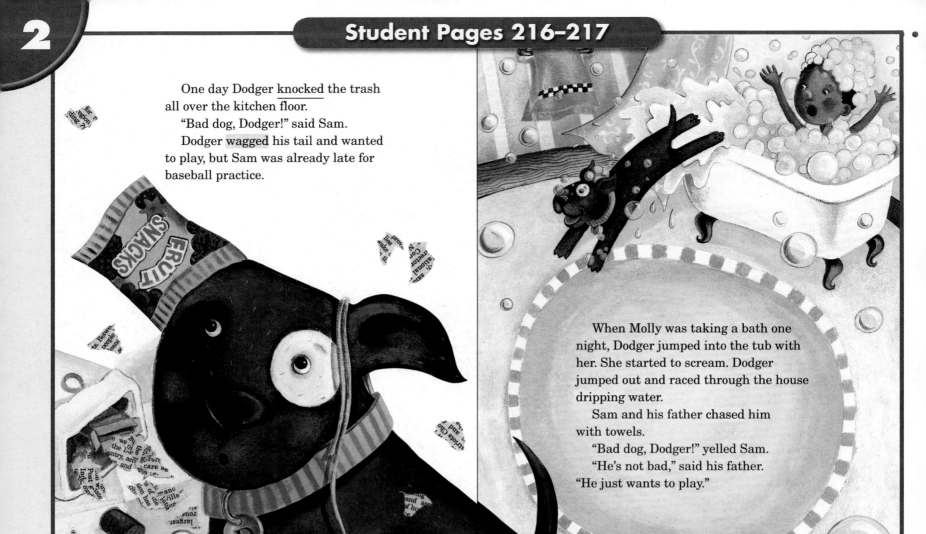

One day Dodger <u>knocked</u> the trash all over the kitchen <u>floor</u>.

"Bad dog, Dodger!" said Sam.

Dodger <u>wagged</u> his tail and wanted to play, but Sam was already late for baseball practice.

216

When Molly was taking a bath one night, Dodger jumped into the tub with her. She started to scream. Dodger jumped out and raced through the house dripping water.

Sam and his father chased him with towels.

"Bad dog, Dodger!" yelled Sam.

"He's not bad," said his father. "He just wants to play."

217

▲ **Pages 216–217**
Have children look at the illustrations and read to see what things Dodger does that get him into trouble.

Look at the pictures.
Write the words first, second, third, and last to show the right order of events.

___third___   1.

___last___   2.

___first___   3.

___second___ 4.

5. Write a sentence about what might happen next.
<u>Possible responses: The mom, the boy, and the dog go inside</u>
<u>and get a snack or the mom and boy play ball with the dog.</u>

Home Activity Your child identified the order of events in a picture story about a boy and his mother working together. Work with your child to write a story about a project you and your child did together. Encourage your child to use words such as first, next, and last to show the sequence of events.

▲ **Practice Book 2.2** p. 77, Sequence

Skills in Context

REVIEW SEQUENCE

• **Tell what things Dodger does in the order he does them.**

First, Dodger knocks trash all over. Then he jumps into the tub with Molly. Sam says he is a bad dog, but his father says he just wants to play.

Monitor Progress	**Sequence**
If... children are unable to tell the order of events,	**then...** model how to use the text and pictures to put events in order.

Think Aloud **MODEL** When I want to see what happened, I look back at the events in order. First I read and see in the picture that Dodger knocked the trash all over. Then I read that Dodger jumped into Molly's tub and raced through the house dripping wet. I can see that in the picture too.

ASSESS Have children use a story sequence chart to record events as they occur.

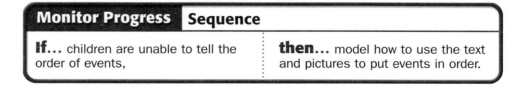

_____ Silent Consonants   ☐ lesson/tested vocabulary

One morning Sam found Dodger chewing his baseball cap. There was a big hole in it. Sam was so mad he almost cried.

They were eating dinner when Dodger pulled down the living room curtains. He wore them into the kitchen. He looked like a bride.

"I've had it," said Sam's mother. "This dog has to live outside."

The next day Dodger jumped over the fence and followed Sam to school and into his classroom.

He knocked over the hamster cage. He ate the cover off a spelling book. Sam's mother had to leave work to take Dodger home.

218

Saturday was Sam's first Little League game. He was up at bat when Dodger came flying onto the field.

The umpire yelled, "Time out!"
The other team booed.
The coach yelled, "Get that dog!"

219

Guiding Comprehension

Cause and Effect • Critical

- **Why do you think Dodger keeps getting into trouble?**
Children may respond that he doesn't know any better or that he isn't getting enough attention.

Summarize • Inferential

- **What has happened in the story so far?**
Sam gets a puppy for his birthday and names him Dodger. Dodger keeps getting into trouble. Sam is mad at Dodger. Sam's mother makes Dodger stay outside, but he gets into trouble there too.

Predict • Inferential

- **What do you think will happen next?**
Children may respond that Sam will have to get rid of Dodger or train him to behave.

▲ **Pages 218–219**
Have children read to find out what kind of trouble Dodger gets into next.

Strategy Self-Check

Have children ask themselves these questions to check their reading.

Vocabulary Strategy

- Do I look for endings -ed and -ing added to words, and see if I know the base words?
- Do I look for context clues?
- Do I use the glossary or dictionary?

Prior Knowledge

- Does the story remind me of something I know about?
- Does Sam remind me of someone I know?
- Does the story remind me of another story I have read?

Dodger grabbed the bat and ran around the field with it. The umpire and the coach ran after him. Sam had to leave the game to take Dodger home.

"We can't go on like this," said Sam's mother. "Maybe Dodger would be better off with somebody who had more time."

Sam knew his mother was right. Dodger needed more attention.

Sam went out and sat in the doghouse with Dodger. "I love you, Dodger." Dodger's tail thumped up and down. "But you need to practice being a good dog."

Suddenly Sam had an idea.

That night he set his alarm to go off half an hour early.

220

The family was still asleep when Sam got up the next morning. In the kitchen he filled his pockets with dog treats.

"Wake up, Dodger!"

Sam pitched a ball to Dodger. Dodger caught it. "Good dog, Dodger!"

Sam waved a treat in the air. "Come!"

Dodger pranced around the yard with the ball in his mouth. "This is training, not a game!" yelled Sam.

Finally Dodger set the ball down at Sam's feet. Sam gave him a treat and said, "Good dog, Dodger!"

221

▲ **Pages 220–221**
Have children read to find out what Sam decides to do about Dodger.

EXTEND SKILLS

Paraphrase

For instruction in paraphrasing, discuss the following:

- Retelling is putting something in your own words.
- When you retell a story, you tell what happened.
- Look at the pictures to help you remember events in order.
- Look at pp. 218–219 as I retell the events that happened on those pages.

Assess Have children contribute to an oral retelling of the story as they look at the pictures on pp. 220–221.

Guiding Comprehension

Draw Conclusions • Inferential
- **What does Sam decide to do about Dodger?**
  Sam decides to spend time with Dodger and train him to be obedient.

Character • Critical
- **What does Sam's decision tell you about him?**
  Possible response: It shows that Sam cares about Dodger or that he wants to do the right thing.

Draw Conclusions • Inferential
- **When does Sam give Dodger a treat?**
  Sam gives Dodger a treat when the dog cooperates and does what he is told to do.

_____ Silent Consonants   [____] lesson/tested vocabular

"Dodger's in spring training," Sam told his parents at breakfast.

Sam pitched balls to Dodger every morning. "Come, Dodger!" he'd shout, waving a treat when Dodger caught the ball.

"Sit!" And Sam would push Dodger's bottom down to show him what sit meant. "Stay!"

After a month of training, Sam decided Dodger was ready to come to a baseball game.

Dodger sat in the bleachers next to Sam's parents.

In the ninth inning, Sam was up at bat with two strikes and the bases loaded. The score was tied. The pitcher wound up to pitch. Everybody held their breath. Sam gripped the bat and hit a fly ball over the bleachers.

"Foul!" yelled the umpire.

Suddenly a flash of black fur leaped into the air to catch the ball.

Oh, no, thought Sam as the umpire called "Time out!" and the game stopped.

"That crazy dog again!" cried the coach. The other team was laughing. Sam's mother was shaking her head.

222

223

Skills in Context

⊙ PLOT AND THEME

- **What is the plot of the story? What is the theme of the story?**
  The plot is what happens to Sam and his dog, Dodger. The theme is how Sam learns to appreciate and take care of Dodger.

Monitor Progress	Plot and Theme
If... children are unable to answer the questions,	**then...** model how to find plot and theme.

Think Aloud

MODEL I know that the plot is what happens to the characters in the story. In this story Sam tries to correct Dodger's behavior. I know that the theme is what the characters learned. In this story, Sam is learning to take care of Dodger because training a dog to be an obedient companion is important.

ASSESS Have children discuss what they think the story is teaching them.

▲ **Pages 222–223**
Have children read to find out if Sam's training is working.

Citizenship *Time for* **SOCIAL STUDIES**
People can do many things to be good citizens. They can train their pets to be well-behaved. They can throw away their trash instead of littering on the ground. They can obey traffic safety laws and walk in crosswalks. Have children discuss these and other ways they can be good citizens.

E L L

Access Content Explain that when the umpire yells, "Foul!" it means that Sam will have another chance to bat.

Dodger trotted toward Sam with the ball in his mouth. He dropped it at Sam's feet.

"Good dog," said Sam.

He walked Dodger to the dugout, "Sit." Dodger sat.

All the spectators grew very quiet. The other team stopped laughing.

"Stay," said Sam.

Dodger stayed.

Sam hit the next pitch right over the fence for a home run. He ran to first, second, third base.

As he reached home plate he called, "Come, Dodger!" and everyone clapped. Even the coach.

224

After the game, the team had their picture taken. Dodger was in the front row and got to wear Sam's baseball cap.

225

▲ **Pages 224–225**
Have children read to find out how the story ends.

Government

Time for **SOCIAL STUDIES**

Discuss how different groups of people make the rules in different settings. For example, in children's homes, parents probably make the rules. In a classroom, the teacher and sometimes the students make the rules. In a community, people join together on a city council or other governing body to make rules. Invite children to discuss times when they have been involved in making rules either at school or at home.

_____ Silent Consonants   ☐ lesson/tested vocabular

Guiding Comprehension

Draw Conclusions • Critical

- **What has Sam taught Dodger? Do you think Sam has done a good job in training Dodger to behave? Why or why not?**
Possible responses: Sam has trained Dodger to come, sit, stay, and drop the ball. Sam has not trained Dodger to behave because Dodger caught the ball at the game.

Cause and Effect • Inferential

- **Why did the spectators grow quiet and the other team stop laughing?**
They were surprised that Dodger caught the ball and brought it to Sam.

Compare and Contrast • Critical

- *Text to Text* **How does the way Sam takes care of Dodger compare to the way Jonathan took care of the stray cat and her kittens in *One Dark Night*?**
Children may say that Jonathan took care of the cats mainly by giving them shelter, while Sam not only gave Dodger food and shelter, but he also trained him to be a good dog.

Fluency

REREAD FOR FLUENCY

Paired Reading

ROUTINE

1. **Reader 1 Begins** Children read the entire book, switching readers at the end of each page.

2. **Reader 2 Begins** Have partners reread; now the other partner begins.

3. **Reread** For optimal fluency, children should reread three or four times.

4. **Provide Feedback** Listen to children read and provide corrective feedback regarding their oral reading and their use of the blending strategy.

OBJECTIVES

- Write directions.
- Identify pronouns *I* and *me*.
- Capitalize pronoun *I*.

Strategic Intervention

Have children copy one of the steps in the directions and illustrate their writing.

Advanced

Have children who are able to write complete sentences independently write their own directions for training an unusual animal to do an unusual thing, such as training an elephant to get books off the high shelf.

Writing Support Before writing, children might share ideas in their home languages.

Beginning Pair children with more proficient English speakers. A more proficient speaker can help the partner choose or write a step in the directions.

Intermediate Help children orally practice the steps for training a dog before they write.

Advanced Encourage children to write and read aloud their directions.

Support Grammar Some languages do not distinguish subject and object pronouns, so children may need extra practice deciding whether to use *I* or *me* in a sentence. See the Grammar Transition lessons in the ELL and Transition Handbook.

Interactive Writing

WRITE Directions

DISCUSS Use *Bad Dog, Dodger!* to encourage a discussion about training dogs. Review pp. 220–222 and have children identify steps that Sam took when training Dodger.

SHARE THE PEN Have children participate in writing directions for training a dog. To begin, have a child give the first step to training a dog. Have the class repeat it. Write the direction, inviting individuals to write familiar letter-sounds, word parts, and high-frequency words. Ask questions such as:

- What is the first sound you hear in the word *first?* (/f/)
- What letter stands for that sound? *(f)* Have a volunteer write *f.*
- What is the second sound you hear in the word *first?* (/er/)
- What letters stand for that sound? *(ir)* Have a volunteer write *ir.*

Continue to have individuals make contributions. Frequently reread what has been written while tracking the print.

READ THE DIRECTIONS Read the directions aloud, having children echo you.

Training a Dog

First, set a time every day for training.

Second, reward your dog with a treat when he does what you ask him to do. For example, when you say "sit," give him a treat when he sits.

Third, practice a lot.

Fourth, teach one trick at a time.

INDEPENDENT WRITING

WRITE DIRECTIONS Have children write their own directions about something they know how to do. Have children illustrate their directions.

ADDITIONAL PRACTICE Have children create a schedule to go along with the directions for training a dog and for their own directions. On a separate sheet of paper, have children make a month-long calendar, including the month, dates, and days of the week. For the dog-training schedule, have children fill in the time they set for training and practice for each day of the month.

Grammar

DEVELOP THE CONCEPT Pronouns

IDENTIFY PRONOUNS *I* AND *ME* Write the following sentences on the board and read them aloud. *My brother and I rode our bikes. My brother followed me everywhere.*

The pronouns *I* and *me* are used to take the place of our names in a sentence. How does the pronoun *I* begin? (with a capital letter) When do we use the pronoun *me?* (when it follows an action word)

PRACTICE

SUGGEST SENTENCES Gather several pictures of people working or playing together. Display a picture. Model giving a sentence to describe the picture using the pronouns *I* and *me.*

Think Aloud

MODEL The mom is reading to the girl. Write *I am reading to my daughter.* If the mom in the picture told me what she was doing, she would say, "I am reading to my daughter." She would use *I* to name herself.

Have children suggest sentences using the pronouns *I* and *me* for the other pictures. Write the sentences children provide. Remind them that the pronoun *I* starts with a capital letter.

DAILY FIX-IT

3. she will com the lamb's wool.
   <u>S</u>he will com<u>b</u> the lamb's wool.

   4. The nat bit the ren.
   The <u>g</u>nat bit the <u>w</u>ren.

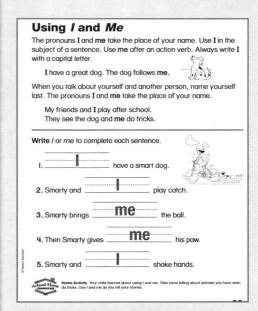

Using *I* and *Me*

The pronouns **I** and **me** take the place of your name. Use **I** in the subject of a sentence. Use **me** after an action verb. Always write **I** with a capital letter.

   I have a great dog. The dog follows **me**.

When you talk about yourself and another person, name yourself last. The pronouns **I** and **me** take the place of your name.

   My friends and **I** play after school.
   They see the dog and **me** do tricks.

Write *I* or *me* to complete each sentence.

1. _____**I**_____ have a smart dog.
2. Smarty and _____**I**_____ play catch.
3. Smarty brings _____**me**_____ the ball.
4. Then Smarty gives _____**me**_____ his paw.
5. Smarty and _____**I**_____ shake hands.

Home Activity Your child learned about using *I* and *me*. Take turns telling about animals you have seen do tricks. Use *I* and *me* as you tell your stories.

▲ **Grammar and Writing Practice Book** p. 89

Wrap Up Your Day!

 LESSON VOCABULARY Write the following sentence. *Dodger chased the baseball, grabbed it, and brought it back to me dripping wet.* Ask children to read the sentence and identify the vocabulary words *chased, grabbed, dripping.*

 THEME AND PLOT Ask children to recall the plot of the story *Bad Dog, Dodger!* (Sam trains his dog to behave himself.) Then have children tell what the author's theme was for the story. (We can be responsible family members by training pets to behave.)

LET'S TALK ABOUT IT Recall the story *Bad Dog, Dodger!* Ask: How did Sam show his family that he could be responsible? (He trained Dodger.) Encourage children to tell about a time when they showed their family that they were responsible.

PREVIEW Day 3

Tell children that they will hear about a girl who learns to be responsible.

Day 3
AT A GLANCE

Share Literature
"Zooks"

Phonics and Spelling
REVIEW Prefixes *un-, re-, pre-, dis-*

Spelling: Words with Silent Consonants

Vocabulary
Skill Classify/Categorize

Fluency
Read with Expression

Writing Trait
Voice

Grammar
Using *I* and *Me*

Materials

- *Sing with Me Big Book*
- *Read Aloud Anthology*
- Student Edition 226–227

Morning Warm~Up!

Today we will read about a dog named Zooks.
Eileen wanted a puppy more than anything. But her mom expected her to do some petsitting first.
What kind of animal do you love best?

QUESTION OF THE DAY Encourage children to sing "Obedience School" from the *Sing with Me Big Book* as you gather. Write and read the message and discuss the question.

REVIEW ENDINGS

- Point to the words ending with *-ed. (named, wanted, expected)* Ask children to name other words with the *-ed* ending.

- Then point to the word ending with *-ing. (petsitting)* Ask children to name other words with the *-ing* ending.

Build Background Use the Day 3 instruction on ELL Poster 23 to support children's use of English to communicate about lesson concepts.

ELL Poster 23

Share Literature

LISTEN AND RESPOND

PARAGRAPH INDENTS Review the first page of "Zooks." Remind students that a paragraph starts with an indent, or a space. A paragraph signals a new idea. It is a way to organize a story.

BUILD ORAL VOCABULARY Introduce the Amazing Word **reprimand**. Explain that a *reprimand* is what someone says to let another person know that he or she has done something wrong. Review that yesterday the class listened to find out if Eileen was ready to get her own puppy. Ask that children listen today to find out whether Eileen gets a reprimand.

Read Aloud Anthology
Zooks

• When might your teacher give you a reprimand? (Possible responses: when you don't clean up, when you take something from someone else)

MONITOR LISTENING COMPREHENSION

• What happens when Eileen watches television at Ms. Baxter's house? (**Zooks goes into the dining room.**)

• What words help you know that Ms. Baxter's guests were not happy to see Zooks? ("**bloodcurdling shriek,**" "**AHHHHHH!**", chaos, confusion, scream)

• Does Eileen get a reprimand from Ms. Baxter? Why or why not? (**no, because she told the truth and because she apologized**)

Amazing Words to build oral vocabulary

	MONITOR PROGRESS
behavior **cooperate** **obedient** **companion** **consider** **reprimand** **confident** **properly**	**If…** children lack oral vocabulary experiences about the concept Responsibility, **then…** use the Oral Vocabulary Routine. See p. DI·5 to teach *reprimand*.

Listen and Respond Help children visualize some of the verbs in "Zooks." Say the words *giggled, waddled, crawled,* and *squirming,* doing an action for each one that helps explain its meaning. Then call out the words and have children demonstrate their understanding by doing the actions.

3

OBJECTIVES

OBJECTIVES

- Review the prefixes *un-*, *re-*, *pre-*, and *dis-*.
- Build, blend, and read *un-*, *re-*, *pre-*, *dis-* words.
- Recognize lesson vocabulary.
- Spell words with silent consonants *kn*, *wr*, *gn*, *mb*.

| un + happy = | pre + game = | re + paint = | dis + appear = |
| **un**happy | **pre**game | **re**paint | **dis**appear |

| dislike | distrust | prepay | pretest |
| remake | rewrite | unlock | unripe |

Pick a word from the box that is the opposite of each word below.
Write the word on the line.

1. like	2. ripe
dislike	**unripe**
3. trust	4. lock
distrust	**unlock**

Pick a word from the box that means the same as each group of words. **Write** the word on the line.

5. make again	6. a test before a big test
remake	**pretest**
7. write again	8. pay ahead of time
rewrite	**prepay**

Home Activity Your child reviewed words with the prefixes *un-*, *re-*, *pre-*, and *dis-*. Work with your child to write a list of words with these prefixes. Have your child read each word and draw a picture to show its meaning.

▲ **Practice Book 2.2** p. 78, Prefixes
un-, *re-*, *pre-*, *dis-*

Review Phonics

REVIEW PREFIXES *un-*, *re-*, *pre-*, *dis-*

READ WORDS WITH PREFIXES Write *unreal, redo, prepay,* and *displease.* Look at these words. You can read these words because you know how to read words with prefixes. You can cover the prefix, read the base word, and then blend the prefix and base word to read the whole word. What are the words?

BUILD WORDS Write the prefixes *un-*, *re-*, *pre-*, and *dis-* as headings for a four-column chart or use Graphic Organizer 27. Write several base words in each column. Have children add the prefix to each base word, read the new word, and supply its meaning.

un-	*re-*	*pre-*	*dis-*
uncover	react	precook	dislike
undo	replay	prepaid	distaste
unlace	reread	pretest	disagree

Lesson Vocabulary

PRACTICE

IDENTIFY EXAMPLES Write lesson vocabulary on the board. Describe two situations for each word and have children identify which is a good example of the word—Situation 1 or Situation 2. Children should write 1 or 2 and then the lesson vocabulary word.

- Which is an example of *practice*—a baseball team gets together to work on playing better, or a baseball team meets with another baseball team to play a game? **(1)**
- Which is an example of something being *grabbed*—a girl handed an apple to her sister or a girl took her sister's apple away from her? **(2)**
- Which is an example of *chewing*—a baby is crushing a blanket with her teeth or a baby is holding a blanket while she sleeps? **(1)**
- Which is an example of something being *chased*—a boy ran after his hat as it blew away in the wind or a boy threw his hat into the air? **(1)**
- Which is an example of getting a *treat*—getting sent to your room or getting a box of candy? **(2)**
- Which is an example of something being *wagged*—a dog moved his tail back and forth or a dog ran after his tail to try to catch it? **(1)**
- Which is an example of someone *dripping*—a girl who just climbed out of a pool or a girl who hasn't gone swimming yet? **(1)**

Spelling

PRACTICE Silent Consonants

GIVE CLUES Have children practice by writing the spelling words that match the clues.

- something a person can read *(sign)*
- a baby sheep *(lamb)*
- a kind of job *(plumber)*
- the opposite of right *(wrong)*
- things people can do *(knock, write, climb, wrap, wrestle)*
- things people use for their hair *(comb)*
- body parts *(knee, knuckle)*
- rhyme with hen, with fat, with cob *(wren, gnat, knob)*

HOMEWORK Spelling Practice Book, p. 91

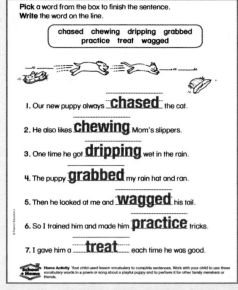

▲ **Practice Book 2.2** p. 79, Lesson Vocabulary

Spelling Words

Silent Consonants

1.	knock*	7.	wrap
2.	sign	8.	wren
3.	knee	9.	gnat
4.	wrong	10.	lamb
5.	write	11.	comb
6.	climb	12.	knob

Challenge Words

13.	knuckle	15.	wrestle
14.	plumber		

* Word from the Selection

▲ **Spelling Practice Book** p. 91

Bad Dog, Dodger!

3

OBJECTIVES

● Discuss classifying/categorizing words.

● Classify/categorize words related to a topic from the story.

Strategic Intervention

Remind children that baseball is a sport. Then challenge them to make a list of all the different sports they can think of.

Advanced

Have children choose another sport instead of baseball. Have them classify words that are related to that sport. They can use books, magazines, or the Internet if they need help. Have children share their lists with the class.

ELL

Extend Language Some children may not know much about the sport of baseball and thus the words used in the story. Hold a discussion about baseball. Talk about how the game is played, the rules, and where it is played.

Vocabulary

CLASSIFY/CATEGORIZE

DISCUSS CLASSIFYING/CATEGORIZING WORDS Have children recall that the title of this story is *Bad Dog, Dodger!* Explain to them that if they want to understand why Dodger is considered a bad dog, they can classify, or group, the things that Dodger does that make people think he is a bad dog. For example, he knocks over the trash, jumps into the bathtub, and chews Sam's baseball cap. Ask volunteers to help you add to your list.

EXPAND SELECTION VOCABULARY Point out to children that *Bad Dog, Dodger!* is also about baseball. Write the word *baseball* on the board. Ask children to help you list all the words in the story that can be classified, or grouped, under the word *baseball.* Be sure they include *bleachers* and *dugout.*

Group Time

DAY 3

On-Level	Strategic Intervention	Advanced
Read *Bad Dog, Dodger!*	**Read** or listen to *Bad Dog, Dodger!*	**Read** Self-Selected Reading.
• Use pp. 212–227.	• Use the Routine on p. DI·38.	• Use the Routine on p. DI·39.

ELL Place English language learners in the groups that correspond to their reading abilities in English.

ⓘ Independent Activities

Independent Reading See p. 208j for Reading/Library activities and suggestions.

Journal Writing Write about a time you saw a pet either behaving badly or doing something impressive, such as doing tricks or helping its owner. Share writing.

Literacy Centers To provide experiences with *Bad Dog, Dodger!,* you may use the Writing Center on p. 208k.

Practice Book 2.2 Prefixes, p. 78; Lesson Vocabulary, p. 79

Break into small groups after Vocabulary and before Writing.

Fluency

READ WITH EXPRESSION/INTONATION

MODEL READING WITH EXPRESSION AND INTONATION Use *Bad Dog, Dodger!*

- Point to the title and question on pp. 212–213. By reading these two pages, I see this is a story about a dog that misbehaves. The exclamation mark tells me I should read the statement "Bad Dog, Dodger!" a little louder than I would read other statements.

- Ask children to follow along as you read the page with expression and intonation.

- Have children read the page after you. Encourage them to read with expression and intonation. Remind them to change the volume of their voice as they read statements with an exclamation mark. Continue in the same way with pp. 214–216.

REREAD FOR FLUENCY

Choral Reading

ROUTINE

1 **Select a Passage** For *Bad Dog, Dodger!*, use pp. 220–222.

2 **Divide into Groups** Assign each group a part to read. For this story, use these parts: the narrator, Sam's mother, and Sam.

3 **Model** Have children track the print as you read.

4 **Read Together** Have children read along with you.

5 **Independent Readings** Have the groups read aloud without you. Monitor progress and provide feedback. For optimal fluency, children should reread three to four times.

Monitor Progress	Fluency
If... children have difficulty reading with accuracy and proper pace,	**then...** prompt: • Are you reading too fast? • Are you making mistakes as you read? • Try to read as if you are speaking to help avoid making mistakes as you read.
If... the class cannot read fluently without you,	**then...** continue to have them read along with you.

Retelling Plan

☑ Week 1 assess Strategic Intervention students.

☑ Week 2 assess Advanced students.

☑ **This week assess Strategic Intervention students.**

☐ Week 4 assess On-Level students.

☐ Week 5 assess any students you have not yet checked during this unit.

Look Back and Write Point out information from the text that answers the question. Then have children write a response to the question. For test practice, assign a 10–15 minute time limit. For assessment, see the Scoring Rubric at the bottom of this page.

Assessment Before retelling, help children name the characters and items shown. For more ideas on assessing comprehension, see the ELL and Transition Handbook.

Reader Response

OPEN FOR DISCUSSION Model a response. Dodger might say that he is glad that Sam now thinks he is a good dog.

1. **RETELL** Have children use the retelling strip in the Student Edition to retell the selection.

Monitor Progress **Check Retelling** [Rubric 4 3 2 1]

Have children retell *Bad Dog, Dodger!*

If... children have difficulty retelling the story,

then... use the Retelling Cards and the Scoring Rubric for Retelling on pp. 226–227 to help them move toward fluent retelling.

SUCCESS PREDICTOR

| **Day 1** Check Word Reading | **Day 2** Check Lesson Vocabulary/High-Frequency Words | ▶ **Day 3** Check Retelling | **Day 4** Check Fluency | **Day 5** Assess Progress |

2. **THEME AND PLOT** Model a response. Sam learned that it was his responsibility to train Dodger.

3. **PRIOR KNOWLEDGE** Model a response. I used treats to teach my parrot to talk. That helps me understand how treats helped Sam train Dodger.

LOOK BACK AND WRITE Read the writing prompt on p. 226 and model your thinking. I'll look back at the story and read the parts that are about the commands Sam teaches Dodger. Then I'll write my response. Have children write their responses.

Scoring Rubric **Look Back and Write**

Top-Score Response A top-score response will use details from p. 222 of the selection to describe the commands and explain why they are important.
Example of a Top-Score Response Sam tells Dodger to come, sit, and stay. It is important for dogs to come when they are called, so they don't get lost. Dogs should learn to sit because they could break things if they run around in some places. They should learn to stay, so they don't scare people by jumping up on them.

For additional rubrics, see p. WA10.

Reader Response

Open for Discussion Sam says, "Bad dog!" Later, Sam says, "Good dog!" If Dodger could talk, what would he say about the two sentences?

1. Use the pictures below to help you retell the story.
Retell

2. What did Sam learn about owning a pet?
Plot/Theme

3. What do you know or what have you read about training a pet? How did that help you understand Sam and Dodger? Prior Knowledge

Look Back and Write Find three commands that Sam uses. List them and write why each command is important for a dog like Dodger to learn to obey.

Meet the Author

Read two more books by Barbara Abercrombie.

Barbara Abercrombie

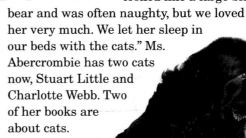

Charlie Anderson

Barbara Abercrombie began writing stories when she was six years old. She likes to write about pets. "When my children were growing up, we had dogs. Our favorite was a Newfoundland named Jennifer. She looked like a large black bear and was often naughty, but we loved her very much. We let her sleep in our beds with the cats." Ms. Abercrombie has two cats now, Stuart Little and Charlotte Webb. Two of her books are about cats.

Michael and the Cats

Retelling Strip

226

227

Scoring Rubric | Narrative Retelling

Rubric 4 3 2 1	4	3	2	1
Connections	Makes connections and generalizes beyond the text	Makes connections to other events, stories, or experiences	Makes a limited connection to another event, story, or experience	Makes no connection to another event, story, or experience
Author's Purpose	Elaborates on author's purpose	Tells author's purpose with some clarity	Makes some connection to author's purpose	Makes no connection to author's purpose
Characters	Describes the main character(s) and any character development	Identifies the main character(s) and gives some information about them	Inaccurately identifies some characters or gives little information about them	Inaccurately identifies the characters or gives no information about them
Setting	Describes the time and location	Identifies the time and location	Omits details of time or location	Is unable to identify time or location
Plot	Describes the events in sequence, using rich detail	Tells the plot with some errors in sequence that do not affect meaning	Tells parts of plot with gaps that affect meaning	Retelling has no sense of story

Use the Retelling Chart on p. TR20 to record retelling.

Selection Test To assess with *Bad Dog, Dodger!* use Selection Tests, pp. 89–92.

Fresh Reads for Differentiated Test Practice For weekly leveled practice, use pp. 133–138.

Retelling

SUCCESS PREDICTOR

OBJECTIVE

● Recognize and use voice in writing.

DAILY FIX-IT

5. The sine said? "Training for dogs."
   The <u>sign</u> said<u>,</u> "Training for dogs."

6. What should i teach my dog.
   What should <u>I</u> teach my dog<u>?</u>

Connect to Unit Writing

Writing Trait

Have children use strategies for developing **voice** when they write a persuasive letter in the Unit Writing Workshop, pp. WA2–WA9.

Voice Encourage English learners to use a bilingual dictionary, if available, to find powerful verbs to express feelings. For example, *shudder* or *twitch* could express fear. See more writing support in the ELL and Transition Handbook.

Writing Trait of the Week

INTRODUCE Voice

TALK ABOUT VOICE Remind children that voice shows how a writer feels and thinks about a topic. The writer's voice may be peaceful, sad, funny, or something else. Explain that the author of *Bad Dog, Dodger!* uses comparisons and words to give the story a funny voice. Model your thinking.

MODEL The story *Bad Dog, Dodger!* made me laugh. Dodger got into all kinds of trouble, and the author uses a funny voice to tell the story. Let me read some sentences from the story.

> **They were eating dinner when Dodger pulled down the living room curtains. He wore them into the kitchen. He looked like a bride.**

These sentences are funny because they help us picture the dog getting into mischief. The author makes the situation funnier with a silly comparison: Dodger looks like a bride. I can just picture how silly Dodger looks wearing the curtains. Let me read some more sentences from the story.

> **Dodger pranced around the yard with the ball in his mouth.**

Which verb shows Dodger's funny action? *(pranced)*

STRATEGY FOR DEVELOPING VOICE Point out that comparisons, such as saying that Dodger looked like a bride, help writers express voice. Help students complete the following comparisons to express a funny voice.

> **He laughed as loud as_____ .** *(thunder, a siren)*
>
> **The puppy was as tiny as a _____.** *(cell phone, peach)*
>
> **His teeth are yellow as _____.** *(lemons, dandelions)*

PRACTICE

APPLY THE STRATEGY Ask children to think of topics for a funny story, such as a soccer game, a trip, or a certain food. Have them brainstorm funny words and comparisons about one of the topics. Then have them use a funny voice to write a description that will make readers laugh.

Grammar

APPLY TO WRITING Pronouns

IMPROVE WRITING BY USING *I* AND *me* Have children consider what Dodger might say about learning commands. Write *I should come to Sam when he calls. Then Sam will always be able to find me.* Underline *I* and *me.* Explain that *I* is the subject of the sentence. It tells who should come to Sam. Explain that *me* comes after the verb *to find.* It tells who Sam will find. Explain that using *I* and *me* correctly helps readers understand who is doing something *(I)* or to whom something is happening *(me).* Remind children to use these pronouns correctly in their own writing.

Write the following on the board.

_____ should get to school on time. (I)

An alarm clock could help _____. (me)

Have volunteers fill in the blanks with *I* or *me* and explain why they chose the pronoun they did.

PRACTICE

WRITE WITH *I* AND *me* Call on individuals to write sentences using *I* and *me*, discussing something they would like to learn. Have the class decide whether the pronouns *I* and *me* were used correctly in each instance.

Using *I* and *Me*

Underline the pronoun in ( ) that completes the sentence.

1. (I, Me) want a rabbit for my birthday.
2. A rabbit will make (I, me) smile.
3. (I, Me) will pet the rabbit's soft fur.
4. Dad got (I, me) a fluffy white rabbit.

Write about a pet you would like to have. Tell what you and the pet would do. Use *I* and *me* in your sentences.

Possible answer:

I would like a hamster. I would

bring it food. It would watch me

put the food in its dish. I would

put a wheel in the cage.

Home Activity Your child learned how to use *I* and *me* in writing. Have your child read his or her story on this page. Ask him or her to circle all the *I*'s and *me*'s. Then tell about a pet you have always wanted.

▲ **Grammar and Writing Practice Book** p. 90

Wrap Up Your Day!

 PLOT AND THEME Have children tell what happened in the beginning, middle, and end of "Bad Dog, Dodger!" (Sam got a dog who began misbehaving. Sam taught him to follow some commands. The dog's obedience impressed everyone at Sam's baseball game.)

 FLUENCY Call on children to select and read a favorite part of "Bad Dog, Dodger!" Remind them to read with expression to make the text come alive for their listeners.

LET'S TALK ABOUT IT Sam took responsibility for his dog's behavior by teaching Dodger to follow commands. What are some other ways he could take responsibility for Dodger's behavior? (Children may suggest that Sam could offer to pay for things Dodger has damaged, keep him on a leash when they go for a walk, and so on.)

PREVIEW Day 4

Tell children that tomorrow they will read about how to train a puppy.

Share Literature
"Oscar the Puppy"

Phonics and Spelling
 Silent Consonants

Spelling: Words with Silent Consonants

Read

Group Time < Differentiated Instruction

"How to Train Your Puppy"

Fluency
Read with Expression

Writing Across the Curriculum
List

Grammar
Using *I* and *Me*

Viewing and Speaking
Retell a Movie or Play

Materials

- *Sing with Me Big Book*
- *Read Aloud Anthology*
- Student Edition 228–231

Morning Warm-Up!

Today we will read more about training a dog. Trained dogs are always on their best behavior.
They are obedient, and they cooperate.
How do you think dogs are trained?

QUESTION OF THE DAY Encourage children to sing "Obedience School" from the *Sing with Me Big Book* as you gather. Write and read the message and discuss the question.

REVIEW ORAL VOCABULARY

- Circle the Amazing Words *behavior, obedient,* and *cooperate.* Review the meaning of each word.

- Ask children to tell you what the second and third sentences mean in their own words.

ELL

Extend Language Use the Day 4 instruction on ELL Poster 23 to extend and enrich language.

ELL Poster 23

Share Literature

CONNECT CONCEPTS

ACTIVATE PRIOR KNOWLEDGE Recall Sam and Eileen and the dogs they had to train. Explain that you will read another story about training a puppy—"Oscar the Puppy" by Julia Nasser.

Read Aloud Anthology
Oscar the Puppy

BUILD ORAL VOCABULARY Explain the Amazing Words **confident** and **properly**. Tell children that *confident* means "sure of yourself" and that *properly* means "in the right way." Ask children to listen to find out how to train a dog properly.

REVIEW ORAL VOCABULARY After reading, review all the Amazing Words for the week. Have children take turns using them in sentences that tell about the concept for the week. Then talk about Amazing Words they learned in other weeks and connect them to the concept, as well. For example, ask:

- Have you ever made a **decision** to help a family member without being asked? How did that make you feel?
- Can you name a time you felt **satisfaction** about being a responsible family member? Explain.
- In what ways do you **participate** as a family member? Is it more fun when you **exhibit** good behavior?

MONITOR LISTENING COMPREHENSION

- What trouble did Manuel's puppy cause? (He chewed on shoes, chased the cat, and went to the bathroom on the kitchen floor.)
- What sorts of things did Manuel do to properly train and care for his puppy? (He took Oscar for walks and trained him to heel. He gave him toys and rawhide to chew on. He asked the veterinarian how he could help Oscar.)
- What helped Manuel and Oscar to be more confident when they went on walks together? (Oscar learned to walk properly on a leash and to follow Manuel's commands.)

OBJECTIVES

- Set purpose for listening.
- Build oral vocabulary.

Amazing Words
to build oral vocabulary

	MONITOR PROGRESS
behavior cooperate obedient companion consider reprimand **confident** **properly**	**If...** children lack oral vocabulary experiences about the concept Responsibility, **then...** use the Oral Vocabulary Routine. See p. DI·5 to teach *confident* and *properly*.

ELL

Connect Concepts Help children understand the importance of keeping a dog on a leash while in public places. Explain what a leash is. Ask children why it might be important to keep a dog on a leash. Encourage such responses as the dog might run away or get lost, it might get hurt or hurt someone else, or it might go somewhere it's not supposed to go.

Spiral REVIEW

● Reviews suffixes *-ly, -ful, -er, -or.*
● Reviews comparative endings *-er, -est.*
● Reviews high-frequency words *enough, toward, above, ago, word,* and *whole.*

Sentence Reading

REVIEW WORDS IN CONTEXT

READ DECODABLE AND HIGH-FREQUENCY WORDS IN CONTEXT Write these sentences. Call on individuals to read a sentence. Then randomly point to words and have them read. To help you monitor word reading, high-frequency words are underlined and decodable words are circled.

A ⟨weekly⟩ ⟨helper⟩ came to our class for the <u>whole</u> day.

I had <u>enough</u> meat to make the ⟨biggest⟩ ⟨fattest⟩ sandwich!

Look <u>above</u> the shelf at the ⟨lovely⟩ gift for my ⟨teacher⟩.

It is the ⟨hardest⟩ <u>word</u> to read since it is ⟨longer⟩ than most.

The story began, "Long <u>ago</u>, there was a ⟨graceful⟩ ⟨dancer⟩."

The ⟨doctor⟩ seems ⟨busiest⟩ <u>toward</u> the end of the day.

Monitor Progress	Word Reading
If... children are unable to read an underlined word,	**then...** read the word for them and spell it, having them echo you.
If... children are unable to read a circled word,	**then...** have them use the blending strategy they have learned for that word type.

Support Phonics For additional review, see the phonics activities in the ELL and Transition Handbook.

Spelling

PARTNER REVIEW Silent Consonants

READ AND WRITE Supply pairs of children with index cards on which the spelling words have been written. Have one child read a word while the other writes it. Then have children switch roles. Have them use the cards to check their spelling.

HOMEWORK Spelling Practice Book, p. 92

OBJECTIVE

● Spell words with *kn, wr, gn, mb*.

Spelling Words

Silent Consonants

1.	knock*	7.	wrap
2.	sign	8.	wren
3.	knee	9.	gnat
4.	wrong	10.	lamb
5.	write	11.	comb
6.	climb	12.	knob

Challenge Words

13.	knuckle	15.	wrestle
14.	plumber		

* Words from the Selection

Group Time

On-Level	Strategic Intervention	Advanced
Read "How to Train Your Puppy."	**Read** or listen to "How to Train Your Puppy."	**Read** "How to Train Your Puppy."
• Use pp. 228–231.	• Use the **Routine** on p. DI·40.	• Use the **Routine** on p. DI·41.

ELL Place English language learners in the groups that correspond to their reading abilities in English.

Words with *kn, wr, gn, mb*

Spelling Words					
knock	knee	write	wrap	gnat	comb
sign	wrong	climb	wren	lamb	knob

Read a clue and write the list word. When you have written all six words, the answer to the riddle will appear in the boxes.

What gets wetter and wetter the more it dries?

1. Wool comes from this animal.   l [a] m b
2. You do this with a pencil.   w r i [t] e
3. You pull this to open a cabinet.   k n [o] b
4. You do this to a gift.   [w] r a p
5. This is part of your leg.   k n [e] e
6. You do this to get up in a tree.   c [l] i m b

Write the list words in the box in ABC order.

7. comb	8. gnat
9. knock	10. sign
11. wren	12. wrong

knock	gnat
sign	wren
wrong	comb

School + Home Home Activity Your child has been learning to spell words with *kn, wr, gn,* and *mb*. Have your child create and write a sentence using two or more of the list words.

DAY 4

▲ **Spelling Practice Book** p. 92

(i) Independent Activities

Fluency Reading Pair children to reread *Bad Dog, Dodger!*

Journal Writing Write a story about a puppy who learns how to be obedient. Share writing.

Spelling Partner Review

Independent Reading See p. 208j for Reading/Library activities and suggestions.

Literacy Centers To provide writing opportunities, you may use the Listening Center on p. 208j. To extend social studies concepts, you may use the Social Studies Center on p. 208k.

Break into small groups after Spelling and before Fluency.

Science
in Reading

How-to Article

Genre
- How-to articles explain how to do something one step at a time.

Text Features
- This how-to article has numbered steps that give examples to help you train your puppy.
- Photos also help explain what to do.

Link to Science
Use the library or the Internet to find out more about training other types of animals. Make a poster with steps to show how to do it. Tell the class about your poster.

228

How to Train Your

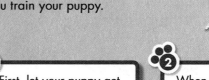
Puppy

by L.B. Coombs

Have you ever tried to make a puppy behave? Training a puppy means making it do the same thing over and over again. You can train a puppy, or most any pet, too. Here's how.

- Begin training when your puppy is very young.
- Teach your puppy to do only one new thing at a time.
- Pick one word as the command for each new thing you want the puppy to learn, but don't repeat the command too many times.

The words and pictures that follow will help you train your puppy.

1 First, let your puppy get to know you. Let him sniff your hand. He will learn to know you by your smell.

2 When you want your puppy to bark, say "Speak." Don't say "Talk" one day and "Bark" the next. Use the same word every time.

Speak!

© Prior Knowledge What do you know about dogs that helps you understand this?

229

AudioText

OBJECTIVE

- Recognize text structure: nonfiction.

Pets

Time for **SOCIAL STUDIES**

Have children write two cards: *good pet* and *not a good pet.* Say a list of animals, such as *cat, gerbil, raccoon, dog, rhinoceros,* and *rabbit.* For each animal, have children hold up a card. Ask volunteers to explain reasons for their choices.

Read
Science in Reading

PREVIEW AND PREDICT Read the title and author's name. Have children preview the article and notice details in the photographs. (puppy sitting, puppy on a leash, puppy treat) Then ask them to predict whether "How to Train Your Puppy" tells a story or provides information. Have children read to learn what is important to remember when training a puppy.

INFORMATIONAL TEXT Review that selections that give information are called nonfiction. Explain that nonfiction can sometimes explain how to do something. Point out that some of the text in this article is presented in numbered steps.

VOCABULARY/CLASSIFY Remind children that words can be put into groups that are alike in some way. Write these words on the board: *speak, no, sit, stay.* These words were all in the article. They are all alike in some way. What is a good name for this group of words?

3 Do not yell at your puppy. This might scare him. Say "No" firmly and in a deep voice. If "No" is the word you want him to remember, use it all the time. Do not say "Stop" or "Don't" when you mean "No."

No!

4 Train your puppy to walk on a leash. Hold your end of the leash loosely. Don't pull your puppy with the leash. Play with your puppy while he is on the leash. It will help him get used to it.

5 After your puppy has done what you ask, tell him he did a good job. Reward him with a treat. Hug and pat your puppy. Training will be fun for both of you.

230

6 You might want to teach your puppy to sit and stay. When your puppy is standing, gently push his bottom to the ground and say "Sit." After your puppy sits, say "Stay." When your puppy sits and stays for a while, praise him and give him a treat.

Sit!

Stay!

It takes time to train a puppy. But if you choose to do it, this training time can be good for both of you. You and your puppy will build a special friendship.

Reading Across Texts
In *Bad Dog, Dodger!*, which rules from "How to Train Your Puppy" did Sam use?

Writing Across Texts
Choose another rule and write a note to Sam explaining why he should follow this rule with Dodger.

 **Prior Knowledge** How does what you already know help you understand this?

231

BUILD CONCEPTS

Draw Conclusions • Critical
- **Why is it important to train a puppy to be obedient?**
A well-trained puppy gets along better in a family and is a better companion. Puppy training can help build a friendship between the owner and the pet.

Draw Conclusions • Inferential
- **Why is it important to use the same word for a command all the time?**
It will help the puppy learn. If you use different words, the puppy may be confused.

CONNECT TEXT TO TEXT

 Discuss Sam's training of Dodger with children. Have them review the rules from "How to Train Your Puppy" that Sam used with Dodger.

 Before children write, you may want to ask them to choose a person the note will be from, such as Sam's mom or dad, Sam's coach, or a dog trainer.

Animal Behavior

TIME FOR Science

Lead children in a discussion about training other types of animals, such as horses, parrots, and seals. Have children list things that these animals can be trained to do. Ask children what they think is the same about training all animals, leading them to conclude that repeating the training many times is important with any type of training.

ELL

Access Content Make sure children understand that in this case *train* means "to teach." List other words in the word family, such as *training, trained,* and *trainer* and discuss their meanings.

Options for Oral Reading

Use *Bad Dog, Dodger!*, "How to Train Your Puppy," or one of the following Leveled Readers.

On-Level

Hubert and Frankie

Strategic Intervention

Sally and the Wild Puppy

Advanced

Training Peanut

Encourage children to repeatedly read aloud texts that they already understand. This extra practice reinforces and improves fluency.

 To develop fluent readers, use Fluency Coach.

Fluency

READ WITH EXPRESSION AND INTONATION

MODEL READING WITH EXPRESSION AND INTONATION Use *Bad Dog, Dodger!*

- Remind children that when they are reading aloud the words a character is saying, they need to make their voices sound the way the characters' voices would.

- Ask children to follow along as you read p. 222. Change your voice to fit what Sam is saying.

- Have children read the page after you. Remind them to read as if they are Sam speaking. Continue in the same way with pp. 223–225.

REREAD FOR FLUENCY

Choral Reading   ROUTINE

1 **Select a Passage** For "How to Train Your Puppy," use pp. 228–231.

2 **Divide into Groups** Assign each group a section to read, switching parts at the top of each page.

3 **Model** Have children track the print as you read.

4 **Read Together** Have children read along with you.

5 **Independent Readings** Have the groups read aloud without you. Monitor progress and provide feedback. For optimal fluency, children should reread three to four times.

Monitor Progress | Check Fluency wCPM

As children reread, monitor their progress toward their individual fluency goals. Current Goal: 82–92 words correct per minute. End-of-Year Goal: 90 words correct per minute.

If... children cannot read fluently at a rate of 82–92 words correct per minute,

then... make sure children practice with text at their independent level. Provide additional fluency practice, pairing nonfluent readers with fluent readers.

If... children already read at 90 words correct per minute,

then... they do not need to reread three to four times.

SUCCESS PREDICTOR

| **Day 1** Check Word Reading | **Day 2** Check Lesson Vocabulary/ High-Frequency Words | **Day 3** Check Retelling | ▶**Day 4 Check Fluency** | **Day 5** Assess Progress |

Writing Across the Curriculum

WRITE List

RECALL Have children look at pp. 221–222. Ask them to tell how Sam trained Dodger. Then have them look at pp. 228–231 and tell how the author of "How to Train Your Puppy" suggests training a dog. Encourage them to use exact words, such as *leash* and *treat.*

SHARE THE PEN Have children participate in creating a list. Explain that the class will work together to create a list of everything they would need to train a puppy. Point out that a list is a way of presenting information very briefly. Guide children to understand that some items on the list will be pieces of equipment, such as *leashes,* and some will not, such as *patience.* Call on an individual to name an item and have the class repeat it. Write the item as part of a numbered list, inviting individuals to help spell the word by writing familiar letter-sounds. Ask questions, such as the following:

- What is the first sound you hear in the word *leash*? (/l/)
- What letter stands for that sound? *(l)* Have a volunteer write *l.*
- What is the second sound you hear in the word *leash*? (/ē/)
- What letters stand for that sound? *(ea)* Have a volunteer write *ea.*

Continue having individuals contribute items to the list. Read back any difficult words, such as *patience.*

1. **Dog**
2. **Treat**
3. **Leash**
4. **Time**
5. **Patience**
6. **Hugs**
7. **Ball**
8. **Space**

- Identify *I* and *me*.

DAILY FIX-IT

7. My cat chewwed my soks.
   My cat che<u>w</u>ed my so<u>ck</u>s.

8. I wish me knew why?
   I wish <u>I</u> knew why<u>.</u>

Using *I* and *Me*

Mark the letter of the word or words that complete the sentence.

1. ___ have a fish named Goldie.
   ⊗ A I
   ○ B Me
   ○ C Mom and me

2. Goldie and ___ watch each other.
   ○ A me
   ⊗ B I
   ○ C Mom and me

3. One day Goldie surprised ___.
   ○ A I
   ⊗ B me
   ○ C Mom and I

4. ___ saw her leap out of her bowl.
   ○ A Me and Mom
   ○ B Me
   ⊗ C I

5. ___ put Goldie back in the bowl.
   ○ A Mom and me
   ⊗ B Mom and I
   ○ C I and Mom

6. Goldie scared ___.
   ⊗ A me
   ○ B I
   ○ C I and Mom

Home Activity Your child prepared for taking tests on using *I* and *me*. Ask your child to read the sentences on this page and to say the word or words that belong in the blank as he or she reads.

▲ **Grammar and Writing Practice Book** p. 91

Grammar

REVIEW Using *I* and *Me*

DEFINE *I* AND *me*

- Which pronouns take the place of your name? (*I* and *me*)
- When you talk about yourself and someone else, who should you name first? (the other person)

PRACTICE

WRITE USING *I* AND *me* Ask children to suppose they have an unusual pet. Have them write a paragraph, using *I* and *me*, telling how they would go about training the pet. Ask volunteers to share their paragraphs with the class.

I would train my whale to do tricks. First, I would teach it to swim to me. It could give me a ride on its back. I would feed it lots of fish as a treat.

Speaking and Listening

RETELL A MOVIE OR A PLAY

OBJECTIVES

● Retell from a movie or a play.
● Listen to follow sequence of events.

DEMONSTRATE SPEAKING Remind children of appropriate listening and speaking behaviors. Then ask them to think about these behaviors as children retell events from a movie or a play.

Speakers	Listeners
• Face the group.	• Sit quietly.
• Speak clearly.	• Face the speaker.
• Speak loudly enough to be heard.	• Listen to what the speaker says.

TELL WHAT HAPPENED Work with children to retell the story of a movie or play that the class has seen. Guide children to make an informal presentation that demonstrates their understanding. Have them begin by telling who the movie or play is about, where it takes place, and what the main character's problem is. If the class has not seen a movie or play together, ask a few volunteers to tell about one they have seen.

Remind children to adjust their tone and volume to suit the purpose (retell a movie or play), audience (classmates), and setting (classroom).

Wrap Up Your Day!

✓ **MAKING CONNECTIONS: _Text to World_** You've read some tips for how to teach a dog something. Do you think you could use any of those tips to teach a friend something? (Children may suggest that using encouraging words, offering rewards, and always teaching something the same way could help a friend learn something too.)

LET'S TALK ABOUT IT Training a puppy can be a big help to family members. Do you think it helps the puppy too? (Children may suggest that the puppy might stop getting in trouble for misbehaving.)

PREVIEW Day 5

Remind children that they read a story about how to train a puppy. Tell them that tomorrow they will hear about more ways to teach a puppy to behave.

Day 5
AT A GLANCE

Share Literature
Oscar the Puppy

Phonics and Spelling
 Review Silent Consonants

Lesson Vocabulary

practice   grabbed   chewing
chased   treat   wagged
dripping

More Words to Know
bleachers   spectators   dugout

Monitor Progress
Spelling Test: Words with
  Silent Consonants

Group Time < Differentiated
Assessment

Writing and Grammar
Trait: Voice
Using *I* and *Me*

Research and Study Skills
Encyclopedia

Materials

- *Sing with Me Big Book*
- *Read Aloud Anthology*
- Reproducible Pages TE 232f–232g
- Student Edition 232–233
- Graphic Organizer 15

Morning Warm~Up!

This week we read about
being responsible by teaching dogs
how to follow the rules.
We must follow rules, too.
In what other ways can we be
responsible family members?

QUESTION OF THE DAY Encourage children to sing "Obedience School" from the *Sing with Me Big Book* as you gather. Write and read the message and discuss the question.

REVIEW ORAL VOCABULARY Encourage children to answer the question in the message, using the Amazing Words learned this week. Say the following words one at a time and ask children to use each in their answer: *behavior, cooperate, obedient, companion, consider, properly.* For example, children could say "We can be responsible family members if we *cooperate* with each other."

ELL

Assess Vocabulary Use the Day 5 instruction on ELL Poster 23 to monitor children's progress with oral vocabulary.

ELL Poster 23

Share Literature

LISTEN AND RESPOND

USE PRIOR KNOWLEDGE Review that yesterday the class listened to find out how to train your puppy properly. Suggest that today the class listen to find out what your dog might do that your family wouldn't like.

MONITOR LISTENING COMPREHENSION

Read Aloud Anthology
Oscar the Puppy

- What might an untrained dog do to the furniture in your house? (It might jump on the furniture or chew the furniture.)

- What other bad behavior might an untrained dog pick up? (It might chew your shoes, chase the cat, or bark or howl.)

- What kind of person does a good dog owner have to be? (Possible responses: responsible, caring, patient, confident, considerate)

BUILD ORAL VOCABULARY

GENERATE DISCUSSION Recall how the authors describe ways to train a pet dog to behave properly. Invite children to discuss ways they have learned new behaviors or taught a pet to be obedient. Have children use some of this week's Amazing Words as they share their stories.

Monitor Progress | Check Oral Vocabulary

Remind children of the unit concept—Responsibility. Ask them to tell you about the concept using some of this week's Amazing Words: *behavior, cooperate, obedient, companion, consider, reprimand, confident,* and *properly.*

If... children have difficulty using the Amazing Words,

then... ask more questions about the Read Aloud selection or the concept using the Amazing Words. Note which questions children can respond to. Reteach unknown words using the Oral Vocabulary routine on p. DI·1.

SUCCESS PREDICTOR

| **Day 1** Check Word Reading | **Day 2** Check Lesson Vocabulary/High-Frequency Words | **Day 3** Check Retelling | **Day 4** Check Fluency | ▶**Day 5** Check Oral Vocabulary/ Assess Progress |

OBJECTIVES

- Set purpose for listening.
- Build oral vocabulary.

Amazing Words
to build oral vocabulary

behavior	consider
cooperate	reprimand
obedient	confident
companion	properly

Extend Language Write *cooperating, considered, reprimanded.* Remind children that, depending on the ending, these things could be happening "Right now" or "Yesterday." For example, children could say, "Right now we are *cooperating.*" "Yesterday my mom *considered* my idea." Add two or three more words to the list. Have children write a Right now and a Yesterday sentence for each one.

Oral Vocabulary

SUCCESS PREDICTOR

OBJECTIVES

- Review *kn, wr, gn,* and *mb* words.
- Review lesson vocabulary.

Silent Consonants

REVIEW

IDENTIFY *kn, wr, gn,* AND *mb* WORDS Write these sentences. Have children read each one aloud. Call on individuals to name and underline the *kn, wr, gn,* and *mb* words and identify the consonant sounds.

> Did you see the <u>wren</u> perch on that <u>limb</u>?
> I will <u>wrap</u> my hurt <u>knee</u> with tape.
> I drew the <u>wrong</u> <u>design</u> on my <u>sign</u>.
> My <u>knit</u> shirt had a <u>wrinkle</u> in it.

Lesson Vocabulary

REVIEW

GIVE CLUES Write the following clues for children. Have children write a word from p. 210 for each clue. Then read clues and answers together.

You must do this to get better at something. **(practice)**

It is a word that means "took quickly." **(grabbed)**

You are doing this before you swallow food. **(chewing)**

It is a word that means *ran after.* **(chased)**

You are happy when you get one of these. **(treat)**

It is the way a happy dog moved its tail. **(wagged)**

It is what water is doing when it comes out in drops. **(dripping)**

Access Content For additional practice with the lesson vocabulary, use the vocabulary strategies and word cards in the ELL Teaching Guide, pp. 157–158.

SPELLING TEST Silent Consonants

DICTATION SENTENCES Use these sentences to assess this week's spelling words.

1. A <u>wren</u> is a small brown bird that eats insects.
2. I do not know why my answer was <u>wrong</u>.
3. Did you read the <u>sign</u> about the school play?
4. Dad put a new <u>knob</u> on the back door.
5. Mom said, "Please <u>comb</u> your hair before you go."
6. I tripped over the step and scraped my <u>knee</u>.
7. Did you see the newborn <u>lamb</u> at the farm?
8. I will <u>write</u> a letter to Grandma this afternoon.
9. Be careful when you <u>climb</u> that big tree.
10. Did you <u>wrap</u> the birthday gift for Mom?
11. That pesty <u>gnat</u> keeps flying around my head!
12. Please <u>knock</u> on my door before you come in.

CHALLENGE WORDS

13. We saw the baby cubs <u>wrestle</u> and play at the zoo.
14. The <u>plumber</u> will come today to fix the sink.
15. The ring would not slide over my <u>knuckle</u>.

ASSESS

● Spell words with *kn, wr, gn, mb.*

Spelling Words

Silent Consonants

1.	knock*	7.	wrap
2.	sign	8.	wren
3.	knee	9.	gnat
4.	wrong	10.	lamb
5.	write	11.	comb
6.	climb	12.	knob

Challenge Words

13.	knuckle	15.	wrestle
14.	plumber		

* Word from the Selection

Group Time

On-Level	Strategic Intervention	Advanced
• Set B Sentences and the Story.	• Set A Sentences.	• Set C Sentences.
• Use pp. 232e–232g.	• Use pp. 232e–232g.	• Use pp. 232e–232g.
	• Use the **Routine** on p. DI·42.	• Use the **Routine** on p. DI·43.

DAY 5

ELL Place English language learners in the groups that correspond to their reading abilities in English.

Independent Activities

Fluency Reading Children reread selections at their independent level.

Journal Writing Write a story about a pet that has silly behavior and makes everyone laugh. Share writing.

Independent Reading See p. 208j for Reading/Library activities and suggestions.

Literacy Centers You may use the Technology Center on p. 208k to support this week's concepts and reading.

Practice Book 2.2 Encyclopedia, p. 80

Break into small groups after Spelling and before Grammar and Writing.

- ◑ Decode silent consonants *kn, wr, gn, mb.*
- ● Read lesson vocabulary.
- ● Read aloud with appropriate speed and accuracy.
- ◑ Recognize story sequence.
- ● Retell a story.

Differentiated Assessment

On-Level
Set B
Strategic Intervention
Set A
Advanced
Set C

Fluency Assessment Plan

- ☑ Week 1 assess Advanced students.
- ☑ Week 2 assess Strategic Intervention students.
- ☑ **This week assess On-Level students.**
- ☐ Week 4 assess Strategic Intervention students.
- ☐ Week 5 assess any students you have not yet checked during this unit.

Set individual fluency goals for children to enable them to reach the end-of-year goal.

- Current Goal: 82–92 wcpm
- End-of-Year Goal: 90 wcpm
- **ELL** Fluency, particularly for English learners reading texts in English, develops gradually through much practice. Focus on each child's improvement rather than solely monitoring the number of words correct per minute.

SENTENCE READING

ASSESS SILENT CONSONANTS AND LESSON VOCABULARY Use one of the reproducible lists on p. 232f to assess children's ability to read words with silent consonants and lesson vocabulary. Call on individuals to read two sentences aloud. Have each child in the group read different sentences. Start over with sentence one if necessary.

RECORD SCORES Use the Sentence Reading Chart for this unit on p. WA19.

Monitor Progress	Silent Consonants
If... children have trouble reading silent consonants,	**then...** use the Reteach Lessons on p. DI·66.
Lesson Vocabulary	
If... children cannot read a lesson vocabulary word,	**then...** mark the missed words on a lesson vocabulary list and send the list home for additional word reading practice or have the child practice with a fluent reader.

FLUENCY AND COMPREHENSION

ASSESS FLUENCY Take a one-minute sample of children's oral reading. See Monitoring Fluency, p. WA17. Have children read "Needles or Knots," the on-level fluency passage on p. 232g.

RECORD SCORES Record the number of words read correctly in a minute on the child's Fluency Progress Chart.

ASSESS COMPREHENSION Have the child read to the end of the passage. (If the child had difficulty with the passage, you may read it aloud.) Ask what the plot and theme of the story are and have the child retell the passage. Use the Retelling Rubric on p. 226–227 to evaluate the child's retelling.

Monitor Progress	Fluency
If... a child does not achieve the fluency goal on the timed reading,	**then...** copy the passage and send it home with the child for additional fluency practice, or have the child practice with a fluent reader.
Plot and Theme	
If... a child cannot recognize plot and theme of the story,	**then...** use the Reteach Lesson on p. DI·66.

READ THE SENTENCES

Set A

1. I knew that the lamb had wagged its tail.
2. Ben knows he has to practice tying the knots.
3. The man knelt by the dripping sign.
4. I chased the cat and hurt my knee and thumb.
5. He grabbed wrapping paper from my knapsack.
6. The knight gave the wren a treat.

Set B

1. Jack grabbed the nasty gnat on his wrist.
2. Kyle will practice making designs for wreaths.
3. A plumber used a wrench to fix the dripping pipes.
4. Ginger wagged her tail when Maria knocked on the wrong door.
5. It is known that the dog grabbed the knob.
6. Mops can wreck a room by chewing signs.

Set C

1. I had to practice knitting scarves before making larger wraps, such as shawls.
2. Meg nicked her knuckle with a knife while cutting a treat.
3. I knelt down and grabbed the dripping towel.
4. In the movie, the gnome with the wrinkled skin chased the elf.
5. The knight's dog wagged its tail as he tried to comb its fur.
6. Fish were chewing on bits of the gnarled wood from the wrecked ship.

REPRODUCIBLE PAGE • See also Assessment Handbook, p. 349

Monitor Progress | Silent Consonants
Lesson Vocabulary

SUCCESS PREDICTOR

Needles or Knots

Grace was kneeling on the floor playing with the   9
cat. Her grandmother was knitting.   14

"Grandma, I want a hobby. I do not know how   24
to do anything. How do you get a hobby?"   33

"Well, first you find something you enjoy. Then   41
you learn how to do it well. I learned to knit a long   54
time ago. Now knitting is my hobby," she said.   63

"But you are so good at it. I always do   73
everything wrong when I try." Grace wrapped   80
some yarn around her wrist and thumb and tied it   90
in knots. The cat climbed on Grace's knee and   99
batted at the yarn.   103

Grace thought about the pretty designs that   110
Grandma made. "I could never knit like you do,"   119
said Grace.   121

"It takes practice. You can't learn something   128
just by wishing for it," said Grandma. "If you want   138
to learn, I will teach you."   144

Grace thought about what her grandma said   151
and knew what to do. She picked up some   160
knitting needles and said, "I'm ready to start."   168

See also Assessment Handbook, p. 350 • REPRODUCIBLE PAGE

Write Now
Writing and Grammar

Rules

Prompt
In *Bad Dog, Dodger!*, both Dodger and Sam learn rules.
Think about something you do that could have rules.
Now write rules for that activity.

Writing Trait
Your **voice** shows how you feel about your topic.

Student Model

Title tells what rules are about.

Numbers keep rules organized and clear.

Voice shows rules are serious.

Dog Care Rules
1. I give Chipper food and fresh water every day.
2. Chipper and I go for a walk twice a day.
3. I brush Chipper every day.
4. I give Chipper a snack when he listens to me.

232

Writer's Checklist
- **Focus** Do all rules tell about one topic?
- **Organization** Are the rules listed clearly?
- **Support** Are rules easy to follow?
- **Conventions** Is the pronoun *I* capitalized?

Grammar

Using I and Me
The pronouns **I** and **me** take the place of your name. Use **I** as the subject of a sentence. Use **me** after an action verb. Always write **I** with a capital letter. When you talk about yourself and another person, name yourself last.

I read a story to Al about a funny dog. The story made Al and **me** laugh.

Look at the model. Write the pronouns that take the place of the writer's name.

233

Writing and Grammar

LOOK AT THE PROMPT Read p. 232 aloud. Have children select and discuss key words or phrases in the prompt. (*something you do that could have rules, rules for that activity*)

STRATEGIES TO DEVELOP VOICE Have children
- listen as you read aloud a list of rules, and then discuss the voice.
- review their purpose for writing and their audience to help them decide what their voice should be.
- use words that show how they feel about the topic.

See Scoring Rubric on p. WA11. **Rubric 4 3 2 1**

_INTS FOR BETTER WRITING Read p. 233 aloud. Use the checklist to help children revise their rules. Discuss the grammar lesson. (Answers: *I, me*) Have children use the pronouns *I* and *me* correctly in their rules.

DAILY FIX-IT

9. My dog listen to Me.
   (listen**s**, **m**e)

10. Then I and Dad comb his hare.
    (Dad and I, ha**i**r)

Using *I* and *Me*
Read the riddle. Write *I* or *me* to complete each sentence. Circle the picture that shows the answer to the riddle.

1. ____I____ am soft and furry.

2. You can hear ___me___ purr.

3. What am ___I___ ?

Underline the word that completes each sentence. Write the word.

4. Mom gave ___me___ a kitten. (I, me)

5. My kitten and ___I___ play with a feather. (I, me)

6. My kitten makes ___me___ laugh. (I, me)

Home Activity Your child reviewed using I and me. Ask your child to make up another riddle. Use the riddle at the top of this page as a model. Remind your child to include the words I and me in the riddle.

▲ **Grammar and Writing Practice Book** p. 92

Bad Dog, Dodger! **232–233**

OBJECTIVE
● Use an encyclopedia.

OBJECTIVE

● Use an encyclopedia.

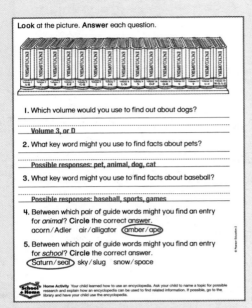

Look at the picture. **Answer** each question.

I. Which volume would you use to find out about dogs?

Volume 3, or D

2. What key word might you use to find facts about pets?

Possible responses: pet, animal, dog, cat

3. What key word might you use to find facts about baseball?

Possible responses: baseball, sports, games

4. Between which pair of guide words might you find an entry for *animal*? **Circle** the correct answer.
acorn/Adler   air/alligator   (amber/ape)

5. Between which pair of guide words might you find an entry for *school*? **Circle** the correct answer.
(Saturn/seal)   sky/slug   snow/space

Home Activity Your child learned how to use an encyclopedia. Ask your child to name a topic for possible research and explain how an encyclopedia can be used to find related information. If possible, go to the library and have your child use the encyclopedia.

▲ **Practice Book 2.2** p. 80, Encyclopedia

Access Content Explain to English language learners that encyclopedias are books with articles arranged in alphabetical order. Encyclopedias are also broken down into different books, or *volumes*. So in order to find a topic, children should first find the correct volume and then use guide words to find the page the topic is on.

Research/Study Skills

TEACH/MODEL Encyclopedia

MODEL USING AN ENCYCLOPEDIA Explain that encyclopedias help people find information about many topics. Encyclopedias contain articles, which are arranged in alphabetical order by topic. Like dictionaries, encyclopedias have guide words and entries. Printed encyclopedias often contain many different books, called *volumes*. The volumes are numbered and have letters on them. Demonstrate how to use the letters on the volumes to find an entry.

Think Aloud **MODEL** I can use an encyclopedia to get more information about dogs. First, I decide what entry word I will look for. I will look for the entry word *dog*. Next I look for the volume that contains entries that begin with *D*. When I find the volume, I look for guide words that begin with the letters *do*. Then I look at the entries on the page until I see the word *dog*.

ALPHABETIZING TO THE SECOND LETTER WITH GUIDE WORDS Write these word pairs on the board in three columns:

Sailing/Seed   Sewing/Snake   Soccer/Submarine

List these words on the board: *Space Exploration, School, Shark, Scotland, Sign, Star.* Ask individuals to determine between which set of guide words each of the encyclopedia subject headings should go. Between which set of guide words might you find an entry for ____? Remind children that since all the words begin with *s*, they need to look at the second letter in each word to find out which set of guide words it should go under. Write the correct word under the column headings.

RECOUNT STEPS IN A PROCESS Call on a series of individuals to tell what steps they would follow to locate information about baseball in the encyclopedia. Have each child take turns telling one step in the process. If the class has a print encyclopedia, demonstrate the steps as the children describe them.

PRACTICE

IDENTIFY CORRECT ENCYCLOPEDIA VOLUMES If the class does not have a set of encyclopedias, draw the spines of six encyclopedia volumes on the board. Have children work with partners. First one partner names a type of pet. Then the other partner must identify the encyclopedia volume that would have an entry about that animal. Partners then switch roles.

Wrap Up Your Week!

LET'S TALK ABOUT Responsibility

QUESTION OF THE WEEK Recall this week's question.

• How can we be responsible family members?

Display Graphic Organizer 15 or the web you drew earlier. Point out that it shows how family members can be responsible. Ask children to explain other things they can do for their families. Fill in the web with their suggestions.

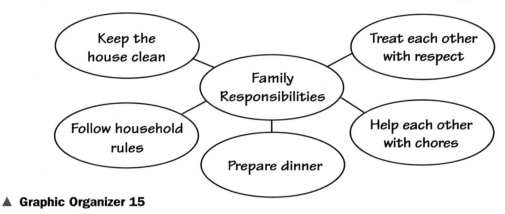

▲ Graphic Organizer 15

CONNECT Use questions such as these to prompt a discussion.

• If you showed good behavior, cooperated, and were obedient, would that make you a good family member and citizen? Give your reasons.

• Would you ever reprimand a pet owner if a pet caused problems? Who is really at fault—the animal or its owner?

• Most people are confident that their friends will always behave like friends. What kinds of situations might make this hard to do?

 **ELL**

Build Background Use ELL Poster 24 to support the Preview activity.

You've learned **008** Amazing Words this week!

You've learned **185** Amazing Words so far this year!

PREVIEW Tell children that next week they will read about friends who have to make a decision that will affect their friendship.

PREVIEW Next Week

Selection Assessment

Use pp. 89–92 of Selection Tests to check:

- ☑ **Selection Understanding**
- ☑ **Comprehension Skill** *Plot and Theme*
- ☑ **Selection Vocabulary**
  chased
  chewing
  dripping
  grabbed
  practice
  treat
  wagged

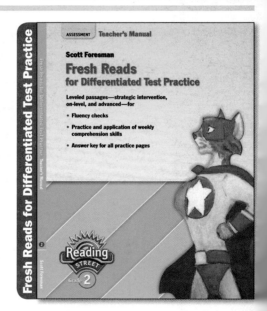

Leveled Assessment

- On-Level
- Strategic Intervention
- Advanced

Use pp. 133–138 of Fresh Reads for Differentiated Test Practice to check:

- ☑ **Comprehension Skill** *Plot and Theme*
- ☑ **REVIEW** **Comprehension Skill** *Sequence*
- ☑ **Fluency** *Words Correct Per Minute*

Managing Assessment

Use Assessment Handbook for:

- ☑ **Weekly Assessment Blackline Masters for Monitoring Progress**
- ☑ **Observation Checklists**
- ☑ **Record-Keeping Forms**
- ☑ **Portfolio Assessment**

Illinois

Planning Guide for Performance Descriptors

Horace and Morris but mostly Dolores

Reading Street Teacher's Edition pages	Grade 2 English Language Arts Performance Descriptors
Oral Language Build Concepts: 234l, 236a, 256a, 258a, 262a Share Literature: 234m, 236b, 256b, 258b, 262b	**1B.Stage B.9.** Demonstrate creative responses to text such as dramatizations, oral presentations, or "make believe" play after reading. **2A.Stage B.3.** Define unfamiliar vocabulary.
Word Work **Phonics** Introduce *ph, gh/f/*: 234n–234q, 236c–236d, 256c–256d, 258c–258d, 262c–262f **Spelling:** 234p, 236d, 256d, 258d, 262d	**1A.Stage B.2.** Use phonological awareness knowledge (e.g., isolate, blend, substitute, manipulate letter sounds) to identify phonetically regular one and two syllable words. **3A.Stage B.5.** Use correct spelling of high frequency words.
Reading **Comprehension** Author's Purpose: 234r–235, 238–255, 256g, 258–261, 262e Ask Questions: 234r–235, 238–255, 256g **Vocabulary** Word Structure: 236–237 Ending -*est*: 256e, 258–259, 262b **Fluency** Paired Reading: 234q, 255a Reader's Theater: 256f, 261a **Self-Selected Reading:** LR28–36, TR16–17 **Literature** Genre—Fantasy: 238–239 Reader Response: 256g–256h	**1B.Stage B.1.** Read fiction and non-fiction materials for specific purposes. **1B.Stage B.9.** Demonstrate creative responses to text such as dramatizations, oral presentations, or "make believe" play after reading. **1C.Stage B.3.** Ask questions to seek clarification of meaning. **1C.Stage B.6.** Identify the author's purpose and the main idea. **2A.Stage B.3.** Define unfamiliar vocabulary. **2B.Stage B.1.** Investigate self-selected/teacher-selected literature (e.g., picture books, nursery rhymes, fairy tales, poems, legends) from a variety of cultures.
Language Arts **Writing** Advice, Problem and Solution, Respond to Literature, Math Story: 235a, 255b, 256g, 261b, 262–263 **Six-Trait Writing** Focus/Ideas: 257a, 262–263 **Grammar, Usage, and Mechanics** Use Different Kinds of Pronouns: 235b, 255c, 257b, 261c, 262–263 **Speaking/Listening** Contribute to Discussions: 261d **Research/Study** Table: 263a	**3A.Stage B.1.** Extend simple sentences (e.g., subject-verb-complement pattern). **3C.Stage B.2.** Use available technology to plan, compose, revise and edit written work. **4B.Stage B.10.** Contribute relevant, appropriate information to discussions. **5C.Stage B.8.** Develop ideas by using details from pictures, diagrams, maps, and other graphic organizers. **5C.Stage B.9.** Explain information using a drawing, graphic aids, oral presentation, available technology, or developmental writing.
Unit Skills **Writing** Persuasive Letter: WA2–9 **Project/Wrap-Up:** 292–293	**3B.Stage B.5.** Elaborate and support written content with facts, details, and description. **3C.Stage B.4.** Experiment with different forms of writing (e.g., song, poetry, short fiction, recipes, diary, journal, directions).

This Week's Leveled Readers

Below-Level

1C.Stage B.2. Select passages in non-fiction materials to answer specific questions.

1C.Stage B.6. Identify the author's purpose and the main idea.

Nonfiction

On-Level

You Can Make A Difference!
by Laura Crawford
Illustrated by Aleksey Ivanov

1C.Stage B.6. Identify the author's purpose and the main idea.

1C.Stage B.7. Compare an author's information with the student's knowledge of self, world, and other texts in non-fiction text.

Nonfiction

Advanced

1C.Stage B.12. Recognize how specific authors and illustrators express their ideas in text and graphics (e.g., dialogue, characters, color).

2A.Stage B.6. Compare different versions of the same story from different cultures and eras.

Nonfiction

Content-Area Illinois Performance Descriptors in This Lesson

Social Studies

14A.Stage B.1. Tell about some rules and responsibilities that students have in school to help promote order and safety.

14F.Stage B.5. State reasons why people benefit from basic rights such as freedom of speech.

15B.Stage B.2. Identify a choice students have made about the use of time.

18B.Stage B.1. Define social group.

18B.Stage B.2. Explain how contact with others shapes peoples' lives.

18B.Stage B.3. Give examples of personality differences.

18C.Stage B.1. Provide examples of how individuals make choices that affect the group.

18C.Stage B.2. Give examples of group decisions that do not please every individual in the group.

Science

11A.Stage B.1. Describe observed science event: sequencing processes or steps; choosing/proposing causes or effects based on observations.

11A.Stage B.2. Begin guided inquiry investigations about objects, events, and/or organisms that can be tested: asking pertinent questions; predicting conditions that can influence change.

11B.Stage B.1. Propose ideas for solutions to technological design problem: asking questions about causes and effects of concept to model or test (e.g., how to test 'if-then' effects of magnets, batteries, sound or buoyancy); identifying criteria for measuring success of design.

Math

6A.Stage B.1. Count with understanding, including skip counting from any number by 2's and 10's.

10A.Stage B.2. Make predictions from simple data.

A FAMOUS ILLINOISAN
David Davis

David Davis (1815–1886) practiced law in Bloomington. He served as an Illinois circuit judge for fourteen years. During that time he became a close friend of Abraham Lincoln. Davis helped Lincoln win his nomination for President of the United States. In 1872 the Labor Reform Convention nominated Davis for President, but he later withdrew.

Children can . . .
Learn more about Abraham Lincoln and David Davis. Have them use construction paper and craft supplies to create top hats like the ones worn by men of Lincoln's and Davis's time.

A SPECIAL ILLINOIS PLACE
De Kalb

De Kalb is the name of a city and a county located along the Kishwaukee River in the north central part of the state. De Kalb County was officially formed in 1837, and the city of De Kalb was established in 1838. Originally called Buena Vista, De Kalb was renamed for Johann Kalb, a Revolutionary War general, in 1856. Northern Illinois University, founded in 1895, is in De Kalb.

Children can . . .
Find out about the mascot of Northern Illinois University. Ask children to write a sentence about their school mascot and draw a picture to go with it.

ILLINOIS FUN FACTS
Did You Know?

• There are more than seventy thousand farms in Illinois. Farmland covers almost three-fourths of the state.

• Oil was discovered in Clark County in 1865. Today Illinois produces close to 1 percent of the nation's crude oil.

• About thirty-five of the state's cities and towns have Amtrak passenger train service.

Children can . . .
Learn more about railroad construction. Have them make a model of train tracks, using craft materials.

Unit 5
Responsibility

CONCEPT QUESTION
What does it mean to be responsible?

Week 4

EXPAND THE CONCEPT
What do good friends and neighbors do?

Time for SOCIAL STUDIES

Horace and Morris **but mostly Dolores**

by James Howe
illustrated by Amy Walrod

Will Horace, Morris, and Dolores remain very good friends?

Genre

Social Studies in Reading

Newspaper Article

Genre
• Newspaper articles may cover news about the city, the nation, or the world.

Text Features
• Newspaper articles usually have catchy headlines that grab the reader's attention.
• Photographs and captions give more information.
• Quotes from a real person help the reader know that the article is true and factual.

Link to Social Studies
Find out more about famous soccer players. Make a poster to report your findings.

Daily Kid News | Sports | Friday, May 3 | 15

Good Kicking

by Rich Richardson
Staff Writer

From spring to fall, you can hear the whoops and hollers of happy children. What's happening? They are playing one of the fastest growing sports around—soccer!

Soccer is played in almost every country in the world. Boys and girls of all ages love this fast-moving sport. Soccer is played in schools and parks across America. Some towns have put together teams of children that play each other.

The small towns around Chicago have some of the best young soccer players. Some children begin playing on teams when they are as young as four or five.

These players chase down the ball.

Good kicking means good foot work.

Ask Questions What question do you have for the writer?

258 | 259

CONNECT THE CONCEPT

▶ **Build Background**

advantage	*defiant*	*firmly*
appreciate	*demand*	*respect*
communicate	*ferocious*	

help each other — respect each other — work out problems — **Good Friends and Neighbors** — say thanks and please — have fun together — appreciate each other — do things together

▶ **Social Studies Content**
Friendship, Groups, Community Services, Exploration, Fairness and Respect

▶ **Writing**
Advice

Preview Your Week

What do good friends and neighbors do?

Horace and Morris but mostly Dolores

by James Howe
illustrated by Amy Walrod

Genre
Fantasies are make-believe stories because they couldn't really happen. What makes this story a fantasy?

Will Horace, Morris, and Dolores remain very good friends?

238 · 239

Student Edition pages 238–257

Genre	Fantasy
Phonics	ph, gh/f/
Vocabulary Strategy	Word Structure
Comprehension Skill	Author's Purpose
Comprehension Strategy	Ask Questions

Paired Selection

Reading Across Texts
Playing for a Coach

Genre
Newspaper Article

Text Features
Headlines

Photographs and Captions

Quotes

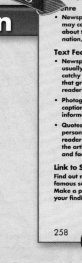

Time for **SOCIAL STUDIES**

Social Studies in Reading

Newspaper Article

Genre
• Newspaper articles may cover news about the city, the nation, or the world.

Text Features
• Newspaper articles usually have catchy headlines that grab the reader's attention.
• Photographs and captions give more information.
• Quotes from a real person help the reader know that the article is true and factual.

Link to Social Studies
Find out more about famous soccer players. Make a poster to report your findings.

Daily Kid News   Sports   Friday, May 2   15

Good Kicking

by Rich Richardson
Staff Writer

From spring to fall, you can hear the whoops and hollers of happy children. What's happening? They are playing one of the fastest growing sports around—soccer!

Soccer is played in almost every country in the world. Boys and girls of all ages love this fast-moving sport. Soccer is played in schools and parks across America. Some towns have put together teams of children that play each other.

The small towns around Chicago have some of the best young soccer players. Some children begin playing on teams when they are as young as four or five.

These players chase down the ball.

Good kicking means good foot work.

Ask Questions What question do you have for the writer?

258

Student Edition pages 258–261

Audio CD

Read It
ONLINE
PearsonSuccessNet.com

- Student Edition
- Leveled Readers
- Decodable Reader

Leveled Readers

⦿ **Skill** Author's Purpose

⦿ **Strategy** Ask Questions

Lesson Vocabulary

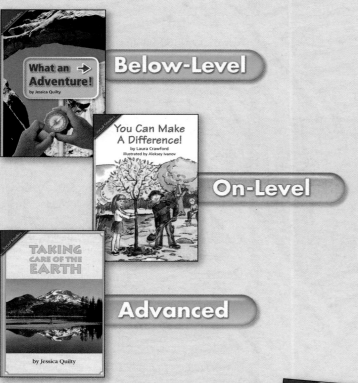

Below-Level

On-Level

Advanced

ELL Reader

- Concept Vocabulary
- Text Support
- Language Enrichment

Decodable Reader

Apply Phonics

- *Phil's Zoo Fun*

Integrate Social Studies Standards

- **Friendship**
- **Groups**
- **Community Services**
- **Exploration**
- **Fairness and Respect**

✓ **Read**

Horace and Morris but mostly Dolores pp. 238–257

"Good Kicking" pp. 258–261

✓ **Read**

Leveled Readers

Below-Level   On-Level   Advanced

- Support Concepts
- Develop Concepts
- Extend Concepts
- Social Studies Extension Activity

✓ **Read**

ELL Reader

✓ **Build Concept Vocabulary**
Responsibility, p. 234m

✓ **Teach Social Studies Concepts**
Groups, p. 248–249
Explorers, p. 252–253
Community Services, p. 260–261

✓ **Explore Social Studies Center**
Make a Card, p. 234k

Horace and Morris **234c**

Weekly Plan

READING

90–120 minutes

TARGET SKILLS OF THE WEEK

- **Phonics**
  ph, gh/f/
- **Comprehension Skill**
  Author's Purpose
- **Comprehension Strategy**
  Ask Questions
- **Vocabulary Strategy**
  Word Structure

DAY 1   PAGES 234l–235b

Oral Language

QUESTION OF THE WEEK, 234l
What do good friends and neighbors do?

Oral Vocabulary/Share Literature, 234m
Sing with Me Big Book, Song 24
Amazing Words *appreciate, communicate, respect*

Word Work

Phonics, 234n–234o
Introduce *ph, gh/f/* **T**

Spelling, 234p
Pretest

Comprehension/Vocabulary/Fluency

Read Decodable Reader 24

Grouping Options 234f–234g

Review High-Frequency Words
Check Comprehension
Reread for Fluency

**Comprehension Skill/Strategy
Lesson,** 234r–235
Author's Purpose **T**
Ask Questions

DAY 2   PAGES 236a–255c

Oral Language

QUESTION OF THE DAY, 236a
What makes a really good friend?

Oral Vocabulary/Share Literature, 236b
Read Aloud Anthology "Bear and Duck on the Run"
Amazing Words *demand, firmly*

Word Work

Phonics, 236c–236d
Review *ph, gh/f/* **T**

Spelling, 236d
Dictation

Comprehension/Vocabulary/Fluency

Build Background, 236e
Making New Friends

Lesson Vocabulary, 236f
Introduce *adventure, climbed, clubhouse, exploring, greatest, truest, wondered* **T**

Vocabulary Strategy Lesson, 236–237a
Word Structure **T**

Read *Horace and Morris but mostly Dolores,* 238–255a

Grouping Options
234f–234g

Author's Purpose **T**
Ask Questions
REVIEW Plot and Theme **T**
Reread for Fluency

LANGUAGE ARTS

20–30 minutes

Trait of the Week

Focus/Ideas

Shared Writing, 235a
Advice

Grammar, 235b
Introduce Different Kinds of Pronouns **T**

Interactive Writing, 255b
Problem and Solution

Grammar, 255c
Practice Different Kinds of Pronouns **T**

DAILY JOURNAL WRITING

Day 1 *List ways you can show family members that you appreciate them.*

Day 2 *Write about a time when you felt left out.*

DAILY SOCIAL STUDIES CONNECTIONS

Day 1 Good Friends and Neighbors Concept Web, 234m

Day 2 Time for Social Studies: Groups, 248–249; Explorers, 252–253

DAILY SUCCESS PREDICTORS →

for Adequate Yearly Progress

Monitor Progress and Corrective Feedback

Phonics
Check Word Reading, *234o*
Spiral REVIEW Phonics

Fluency
Check Lesson Vocabulary, *236f*
Spiral REVIEW High-Frequency Words

RESOURCES FOR THE WEEK

- Practice Book 2.2, *pp. 81–90*
- Phonics and Spelling Practice Book, *pp. 93–96*
- Grammar and Writing Practice Book, *pp. 93–96*
- Selection Test, *pp. 93–96*
- Fresh Reads for Differentiated Test Practice, *pp. 139–144*
- Phonics Songs and Rhymes Chart 24
- The Grammar and Writing Book, *pp. 188–193*

Grouping Options for Differentiated Instruction

Turn the page for the small group lesson plan.

DAY 3 — PAGES 256a–257b

Oral Language

QUESTION OF THE DAY, 256a
Have you ever helped a friend?

Oral Vocabulary/Share Literature, 256b
Read Aloud Anthology "Bear and Duck on the Run"
Amazing Word *advantage*

Word Work

Phonics, 256c
REVIEW Silent Consonants **T**

Lesson Vocabulary, 256d
Practice *adventure, climbed, clubhouse, exploring, greatest, truest, wondered* **T**

Spelling, 256d
Practice

Comprehension/Vocabulary/Fluency

Vocabulary, 256e
Word Ending *-est*

Read *Horace and Morris but mostly Dolores,* 238–257

Grouping Options 234f–234g

Fluency, 256f
Express Characterization

Reader Response, 256g

Trait of the Week, 257a
Introduce Focus/Ideas

Grammar, 257b
Write with Different Kinds of Pronouns **T**

Day 3 *Write about a time you and a friend had a disagreement.*

Day 3 Let's Talk About the Concept, 257b

DAY 4 — PAGES 258a–261d

Oral Language

QUESTION OF THE DAY, 258a
What do you like to do with your friends?

Oral Vocabulary/Share Literature, 258b
Read Aloud Anthology "Eat Your Vegetables"
Amazing Words *defiant, ferocious*

Word Work

Phonics, 258c–258d
REVIEW Sentence Reading **T**

Spelling, 258d
Partner Review

Comprehension/Vocabulary/Fluency

Read "Good Kicking," 258–261
Leveled Readers

Grouping Options 234f–234g

Ending *-est*
Reading Across Texts

Fluency, 261a
Express Characterization

Writing Across the Curriculum, 261b
Math Story

Grammar, 261c
Review Different Kinds of Pronouns **T**

Speaking and Listening, 261d
Contribute to Discussions

Day 4 *List ways you can show fairness and respect.*

Day 4 Time for Social Studies: Community Services, 260–261

DAY 5 — PAGES 262a–263b

Oral Language

QUESTION OF THE DAY, 262a
What does it mean to be a good friend or neighbor?

Oral Vocabulary/Share Literature, 262b
Read Aloud Anthology "Eat Your Vegetables"
Amazing Words Review

Word Work

Phonics, 262c
🎯 Review *ph, gh/f/* **T**

Lesson Vocabulary, 262c
Review *adventure, climbed, clubhouse, exploring, greatest, truest, wondered* **T**

Spelling, 262d
Test

Comprehension/Vocabulary/Fluency

Read Leveled Readers

Grouping Options 234f–234g

Monitor Progress, 262e–262g
Read the Sentences
Read the Story

Writing and Grammar, 262–263
Develop Focus/Ideas
Use Different Kinds of Pronouns **T**

Research/Study Skills, 263a
Table

Day 5 *Write about how to show respect.*

Day 5 Revisit the Good Friends and Neighbors Concept Chart, 263b

---

KEY 🎯 = Target Skill **T** = Tested Skill

Comprehension Check Retelling, *256g*

Fluency Check Fluency WCPM, *261a*
Spiral **REVIEW** Phonics, High-Frequency Words

Oral Vocabulary Check Oral Vocabulary, *262b*
Assess Phonics, Lesson Vocabulary, Fluency, Comprehension, *262e*

SUCCESS PREDICTOR

Small Group Plan *for Differentiated Instruction*

Daily Plan AT A GLANCE

Reading
Whole Group
- Oral Language
- Word Work
- Comprehension/Vocabulary

Group Time

Meet with small groups to provide:
- Skill Support
- Reading Support
- Fluency Practice

Read

This week's lessons for daily group time can be found behind the Differentiated Instruction (DI) tab on pp. DI·44–DI·53.

Whole Group
- Comprehension/Vocabulary
- Fluency

Language Arts
- Writing
- Grammar
- Speaking/Listening/Viewing
- Research/Study Skills

Use *My Sidewalks on Reading Street* for Tier III intensive reading intervention.

DAY 1

On-Level	Strategic Intervention	Advanced
Teacher-Led *Page 234q*	**Teacher-Led** *Page DI·44*	**Teacher-Led** *Page DI·45*
• **Read** Decodable Reader 24 • **Reread** for Fluency	• Blend Words with *ph, gh/f/* • **Read** Decodable Reader 24 • **Reread** for Fluency	• Extend Word Reading • **Read** Advanced Selection 24 • Introduce Concept Inquiry

i Independent Activities

While you meet with small groups, have the rest of the class...

- Reread for fluency
- Write in their journals
- Read self-selected reading
- Visit the Word Work Center
- Complete Practice Book 2.2, pp. 83–84

DAY 2

On-Level	Strategic Intervention	Advanced
Teacher-Led *Pages 238–255*	**Teacher-Led** *Page DI·46*	**Teacher-Led** *Page DI·47*
• **Read** *Horace and Morris but mostly Dolores* • **Reread** for Fluency	• Blend Words with *ph, gh/f/* • **Read** SI Decodable Reader 24 • **Read** or Listen to *Horace and Morris but mostly Dolores*	• **Read** *Horace and Morris but mostly Dolores* • Continue Concept Inquiry

i Independent Activities

While you meet with small groups, have the rest of the class...

- Read self-selected reading
- Write in their journals
- Visit the Listening Center
- Complete Practice Book 2.2, pp. 85–87

DAY 3

On-Level	Strategic Intervention	Advanced
Teacher-Led *Pages 238–257*	**Teacher-Led** *Page DI·48*	**Teacher-Led** *Page DI·49*
• **Reread** *Horace and Morris but mostly Dolores*	• **Reread** *Horace and Morris but mostly Dolores* • Read Words and Sentences • Review Author's Purpose and Ask Questions • **Reread** for Fluency	• Self-Selected Reading • Continue Concept Inquiry

i Independent Activities

While you meet with small groups, have the rest of the class...

- Read self-selected reading
- Write in their journals
- Visit the Writing Center
- Complete Practice Book 2.2, pp. 88–89

DAY 4

On-Level
Teacher-Led
Pages 258–261, LR31–LR33
- **Read** "Good Kicking"
- Practice with On-Level Reader *You Can Make a Difference!*

Strategic Intervention
Teacher-Led
Pages DI·50, LR28–LR30
- **Read** or Listen to "Good Kicking"
- **Reread** for Fluency
- Build Concepts
- Practice with Below-Level Reader *What an Adventure!*

Advanced
Teacher-Led
Pages DI·51, LR34–LR36
- **Read** "Good Kicking"
- Extend Vocabulary
- Continue Concept Inquiry
- Practice with Advanced Reader *Taking Care of the Earth*

ⓘ Independent Activities

While you meet with small groups, have the rest of the class...

- Reread for fluency
- Write in their journals
- Read self-selected reading
- Review spelling words with a partner
- Visit the Listening and Social Studies Centers

DAY 5

On-Level
Teacher-Led
Pages 262e–262g, LR31–LR33
- Sentence Reading, Set B
- Monitor Comprehension
- Practice with On-Level Reader *You Can Make a Difference!*

Strategic Intervention
Teacher-Led
Pages DI·52, LR28–LR30
- Practice Word Reading
- Sentence Reading, Set A
- Monitor Fluency and Comprehension
- Practice with Below-Level Reader *What an Adventure!*

Advanced
Teacher-Led
Pages DI·53, LR34–LR36
- Sentence Reading, Set C
- Monitor Comprehension
- Share Concept Inquiry
- Practice with Advanced Reader *Taking Care of the Earth*

ⓘ Independent Activities

While you meet with small groups, have the rest of the class...

- Reread for fluency
- Write in their journals
- Read self-selected reading
- Visit the Technology Center
- Complete Practice Book 2.2, p. 90

 Grouping Place English language learners in the groups that correspond to their reading abilities in English.

Use the appropriate Leveled Reader or other text at children's instructional level.

TiP Send home the appropriate Multilingual Summary of the main selection on Day 1.

Take It to the NET ONLINE
PearsonSuccessNet.com

P. David Pearson
For research on effective teaching practices, see the article "Looking Inside Classrooms" by B. Taylor, Scott Foresman author P. David Pearson, and others.

TEACHER TALK

Differentiated instruction is instruction tailored to the needs of groups of children, such as struggling children, gifted children, or English language learners.

Looking Ahead

Be sure to schedule time for children to work on the unit inquiry project "Research Responsible Acts." This week children should draw illustrations on a poster to show responsible community workers and label each drawing.

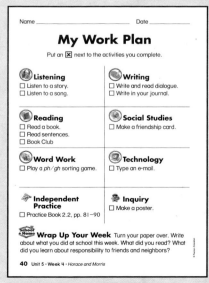

▲ **Group-Time Survival Guide**
p. 40, Weekly Contract

Customize Your Plan *by Strand*

Concept Development

What do good friends and neighbors do?

 *to build oral vocabulary*

advantage	appreciate	communicate
defiant	demand	ferocious
firmly	respect	

BUILD

- ☐ **Question of the Week** Use the Morning Warm-Up! to introduce and discuss the question of the week. This week children will talk, sing, read, and write about what good friends and neighbors do. DAY 1 *234l*

- ☐ **Sing with Me Big Book** Sing a song about what good friends do. Ask children to listen for the concept-related Amazing Words *appreciate, communicate, respect.* DAY 1 *234m*

Sing with Me Big Book

- ☐ **Build Background** Remind children of the question of the week. Then create a concept chart for children to add to throughout the week. DAY 1 *234m*

DEVELOP

- ☐ **Question of the Day** Use the questions in the Morning Warm-Ups! to discuss lesson concepts and how they relate to the unit theme, Responsibility. DAY 2 *236a,* DAY 3 *256a,* DAY 4 *258a,* DAY 5 *262a*

- ☐ **Share Literature** Read big books and read aloud selections that develop concepts, language, and vocabulary related to the lesson concept and the unit theme. Continue to develop this week's Amazing Words. DAY 2 *236b,* DAY 3 *256b,* DAY 4 *258b,* DAY 5 *262b*

CONNECT

- ☐ **Wrap Up Your Week!** Revisit the Question of the Week. Then connect concepts and vocabulary to next week's lesson. DAY 5 *263b*

CHECK

- ☐ **Check Oral Vocabulary** To informally assess children's oral vocabulary, ask individuals to use some of this week's Amazing Words to tell you about the concept of the week—Responsibility. DAY 5 *262b*

 PH, GH/f/ The letters *ph* stand for the sound /f/. The letters *gh* often stand for the sound /f/ when they follow a vowel.

TEACH

- ☐ **ph, gh /f/** Introduce the blending strategy for words with the *ph, gh* /f/ sound. Then have children blend and build words using letter tiles. DAY 1 *234n–234o*

- ☐ **Fluent Word Reading** Use the Fluent Word Reading Routine to develop children's word reading fluency. Use the Phonics Songs and Rhymes Chart for additional word reading practice. DAY 2 *236c–236d*

Phonics Songs and Rhymes Chart 24

PRACTICE/APPLY

- ☐ **Decodable Reader 24** Practice reading words with *ph, gh/f/* in context. DAY 1 *234q*

- ☐ *Horace and Morris but mostly Dolores* Practice decoding words in context. DAY 2 *238–255*

Decodable Reader 24

- ☐ **Homework** Practice Book 2.2 p. 83. DAY 1 *234o*

- ☐ **Word Work Center** Practice consonants *ph, gh/f/.* **ANY DAY** *234j*

 **Main Selection—Fiction**

RETEACH/REVIEW

- ☐ **Review** Review words with this week's phonics skills. DAY 5 *262c*

- ☐ **Reteach Lessons** If necessary, reteach *ph, gh/f/.* DAY 5 *DI-67*

- ☐ **Spiral REVIEW** Review previously taught phonics /skills. DAY 1 *234o,* DAY 3 *256c,* DAY 4 *258c*

ASSESS

- ☐ **Sentence Reading** Assess children's ability to read words with consonants *ph, gh/f/.* DAY 5 *262e–262f*

① Use assessment data to determine your instructional focus.

② Preview this week's instruction by strand.

③ Choose instructional activities that meet the needs of your classroom.

SPELLING

PH, GH/F/ The letters *ph* stand for the sound /f/. The letters *gh* often stand for the sound /f/ when they follow a vowel.

TEACH

☐ **Pretest** Before administering the pretest, model how to segment words with the *ph, gh/f/* consonant sound to spell them. Dictate the spelling words, segmenting them if necessary. Then have children check their pretests and correct misspelled words. DAY 1 *234p*

PRACTICE/APPLY

☐ **Dictation** Have children write dictation sentences to practice spelling words. DAY 2 *236d*

☐ **Write Words** Have children practice the spelling words by writing an adventure story that uses all the words. DAY 3 *256d*

☐ **Homework** Phonics and Spelling Practice Book pp. 93–96. DAY 1 *234p*, DAY 2 *236d*, DAY 3 *256d*, DAY 4 *258d*

RETEACH/REVIEW

☐ **Partner Review** Have pairs work together to read and write the spelling words. DAY 4 *258d*

ASSESS

☐ **Posttest** Use dictation sentences to give the posttest for words with the *ph, gh/f/* consonant sound. DAY 5 *262d*

Spelling Words

ph, gh/f/

1. phone
2. enough
3. stuff
4. laugh
5. puff*
6. giraffe
7. graph
8. tough
9. photo
10. rough
11. cough
12. cliff

Challenge Words

13. dolphin
14. physical
15. autograph

* Words from the Selection

VOCABULARY

STRATEGY WORD STRUCTURE Understanding endings such as *-est* can help you figure out words.

LESSON VOCABULARY

adventure	climbed	clubhouse	exploring
greatest	truest	wondered	

TEACH

☐ **Words to Know** Introduce and discuss this week's lesson vocabulary. DAY 2 *236f*

☐ **Vocabulary Strategy Lesson** Use the lesson in the Student Edition to introduce/model *word structure*. DAY 2 *236-237a*

Vocabulary Strategy Lesson

PRACTICE/APPLY

☐ **Words in Context** Read the lesson vocabulary in context. DAY 2 *238-255*, DAY 3 *238-257*

☐ **Lesson Vocabulary** Have children use vocabulary words and revise sentences. DAY 3 *256d*

Main Selection—Fiction

☐ **Leveled Text** Read the lesson vocabulary in leveled text. DAY 4 *LR28-LR36*, DAY 5 *LR28-LR36*

☐ **Homework** Practice Book 2.2 pp. 86, 89. DAY 2 *236f*, DAY 3 *256d*

Leveled Readers

RETEACH/REVIEW

☐ **Word Ending -est** Discuss the word ending *-est*. Have children write a sentence using the words *truest* or *greatest*. DAY 3 *256e*

☐ **Review** Review this week's lesson vocabulary words. DAY 5 *262c*

ASSESS

☐ **Selection Test** Use the Selection Test to determine children's understanding of the lesson vocabulary words. DAY 3

☐ **Sentence Reading** Assess children's ability to read this week's lesson vocabulary words. DAY 5 *262e-262f*

HIGH-FREQUENCY WORDS

RETEACH/REVIEW

☐ **SPIRAL REVIEW** Review previously taught high-frequency words. DAY 2 *236f*, DAY 4 *258c*

☑ Customize Your Plan *by Strand*

COMPREHENSION

SKILL AUTHOR'S PURPOSE An author has reasons for writing. The author's purpose may be to share important information, explain something, or to tell an interesting story.

STRATEGY ASK QUESTIONS Asking yourself questions before, during, and after reading will help you understand what you just read. This will also help you decide what the author's purpose is.

TEACH

☐ **Skill/Strategy Lesson** Use the Skill/Strategy Lesson in the Student Edition to introduce *author's purpose* and *ask questions*. **DAY 1** *234r–235*

Skill/Strategy Lesson

PRACTICE/APPLY

☐ **Skills and Strategies in Context** Read *Horace and Morris but mostly Dolores*, using the Guiding Comprehension questions to apply *author's purpose* and *ask questions*. **DAY 2** *238-255a*

Main Selection—Fiction

☐ **Reader Response** Use the questions on Student Edition p. 256 to discuss the selection. **DAY 3** *256g-257*

☐ **Skills and Strategies in Context** Read "Good Kicking," guiding children as they apply skills and strategies. **DAY 4** *258-261*

Paired Selection— Nonfiction

☐ **Leveled Text** Apply *author's purpose* and *ask questions* to read leveled text. **DAY 4** *LR28-LR36*, **DAY 5** *LR28-LR36*

Leveled Readers

☐ **Homework** Practice Book 2.2 pp. 84–86. **DAY 1** *234-235*, **DAY 2** *236e, 236f*

ASSESS

☐ **Selection Test** Determine children's understanding of the main selection and assess their ability to recognize *author's purpose*. **DAY 3**

☐ **Story Reading** Have children read the passage "A Dolphin, an Elephant, and a Gopher." Ask questions that require them to recognize the *author's purpose*. Then have them retell. **DAY 5** *262e-262g*

RETEACH/REVIEW

☐ **Reteach Lesson** If necessary, reteach *author's purpose*. **DAY 5** *DI·67*

FLUENCY

SKILL EXPRESS CHARACTERIZATION Expressing characterization means that you read the words as if you are the character.

REREAD FOR FLUENCY

☐ **Paired Reading** Have children read orally from Decodable Reader 24 or another text at their independent reading level. Listen as children read and provide corrective feedback regarding their oral reading and their use of the blending strategy. **DAY 1** *234q*

☐ **Paired Reading** Have pairs of children read orally from the main selection or another text at their independent reading level. Listen as children read and provide corrective feedback regarding their oral reading and their use of the blending strategy. **DAY 2** *255a*

TEACH

☐ **Model** Use passages from *Horace and Morris but mostly Dolores* to model characterization. **DAY 3** *256f*, **DAY 4** *261a*

PRACTICE/APPLY

☐ **Readers' Theater** Have groups read parts from *Horace and Morris but mostly Dolores*. Monitor progress and provide feedback regarding children's expression of characterization. **DAY 3** *256f*, **DAY 4** *261a*

☐ **Listening Center** Have children follow along with the AudioText for this week's selections. **ANY DAY** *234j*

☐ **Reading/Library Center** Have children build fluency by rereading Leveled Readers, Decodable Readers, or other text at their independent level. **ANY DAY** *234j*

☐ **Fluency Coach** Have children use Fluency Coach to listen to fluent reading or to practice reading on their own. **ANY DAY**

ASSESS

☐ **Story Reading** Take a one-minute timed sample of children's oral reading. Use the passage "A Dolphin, an Elephant, and a Gopher." **DAY 5** *262e-262g*

WRITING

Trait of the Week

FOCUS/IDEAS Sentences should focus on a main idea, and give details about the idea. Focus and ideas of sentences have a purpose, which may be to persuade, teach, or entertain.

TEACH

❑ **Write Together** Engage children in writing activities that develop language, grammar, and writing skills. Include independent writing as an extension of group writing activities.

> **Shared Writing** DAY 1 235a
> **Interactive Writing** DAY 2 255b
> **Writing Across the Curriculum** DAY 4 261b

❑ **Trait of the Week** Introduce and model *focus/ideas*. DAY 3 257a

PRACTICE/APPLY

❑ **Write Now** Examine the model on Student Edition pp. 262–263. Then have children write advice. DAY 5 262-263

Write Now

> **Prompt** In *Horace and Morris but mostly Dolores*, Dolores gets upset with her friends. Think about what Dolores should do. Now write advice to her.

❑ **Daily Journal Writing** Have children write about concepts and literature in their journals. **EVERY DAY** 234d-234e

❑ **Writing Center** Have children write a dialogue. **ANY DAY** 234k

ASSESS

❑ **Scoring Rubric** Use a rubric to evaluate advice. DAY 5 262-263

RETEACH/REVIEW

❑ **The Grammar and Writing Book** Use pp. 188–193 of The Grammar and Writing Book to extend instruction. **ANY DAY**

The Grammar and Writing Book

SPEAKING AND LISTENING

TEACH

❑ **Contribute to Discussions** Review appropriate listening and speaking behaviors for a discussion. Have children list things people might want to do when starting a club. DAY 4 261d

GRAMMAR

SKILL DIFFERENT KINDS OF PRONOUNS The pronouns *I, he, she, we,* and *they* are used as subjects. *Me, him, her, us,* and *them* are used after action verbs. *You* and *it* can be used anywhere in a sentence.

TEACH

❑ **Grammar Transparency 24** Use Grammar Transparency 24 to teach *different kinds of pronouns*. DAY 1 235b

Grammar Transparency 24

PRACTICE/APPLY

❑ **Develop the Concept** Review the concept of *different kinds of pronouns* and provide guided practice. DAY 2 255c

❑ **Apply to Writing** Have children use *different kinds of pronouns* in writing. DAY 3 257b

❑ **Define/Practice** Review *different kinds of pronouns*. Have children supply the pronoun they would use as a subject and the one they would use after an action verb. DAY 4 261c

❑ **Write Now** Discuss the grammar lesson on Student Edition p. 263. Have children use pronouns in their advice to Dolores. DAY 5 262-263

Write Now

❑ **Daily Fix-It** Have children find and correct errors in grammar, spelling, and punctuation. DAY 1 235a, DAY 2 255c, DAY 3 257a, DAY 4 261c, DAY 5 262-263

❑ **Homework** The Grammar and Writing Practice Book pp. 93–96. DAY 2 255c, DAY 3 257b, DAY 4 261c, DAY 5 262-263

RETEACH/REVIEW

❑ **The Grammar and Writing Book** Use pp. 188–191 of The Grammar and Writing Book to extend instruction. **ANY DAY**

The Grammar and Writing Book

RESEARCH/INQUIRY

TEACH

❑ **Table** Model how to use and read a table. Then have children gather data and take turns filling in information on a class table. DAY 5 263a

❑ **Unit Inquiry Project** Have children illustrate and label posters showing responsible community workers. **ANY DAY** 153

Resources for Differentiated Instruction

LEVELED READERS

▶ **Comprehension**
- 🎯 **Skill** Author's Purpose
- 🎯 **Strategy** Ask Questions

▶ **Lesson Vocabulary**
- 🎯 Word Structure

adventure climbed greatest truest clubhouse exploring wondered

▶ **Social Studies Standards**
- Friendship
- Groups
- Community Services
- Exploration
- Fairness and Respect

Leveled Reader Database ONLINE
PearsonSuccessNet.com

Use the Online Database of over 600 books to
- Download and print additional copies of this week's leveled readers
- Listen to the readers being read online
- Search for more titles focused on this week's skills, topic, and content

---

On-Level

Social Studies

You Can Make A Difference!
by Laura Crawford
illustrated by Aleksey Ivanov

On-Level Reader

Author's Purpose
Think about why the author wrote *You Can Make A Difference!* Read each question below. Then underline the best answer.

1. Why does the author say that every person needs to think about the environment?
   a. to make us angry
   b. to tell us what she believes
   c. to make us feel ashamed

2. Why does the author describe the EPA?
   a. to explain what the EPA does
   b. to get us to join the EPA
   c. to make us excited

3. Why does the author describe how students helped protect the wetlands?
   a. to compare wetlands to parks
   b. to tell how students can make a difference
   c. to teach us how to plant trees

4. Why does the author list everyday things we can do to make a difference?
   a. to get us to do something
   b. to help us feel good
   c. to fill up the page

5. Why did the author write this book?
   a. to give us a good time
   b. to describe the environment
   c. to get us to make a difference

🎯 **On-Level Practice** TE p. LR32

Vocabulary
Write a word from the box that best fits into each sentence.

Words to Know
adventure climbed clubhouse
exploring greatest truest wondered

1. We built a **clubhouse** for our bird club to meet in.
2. The person who picked up the most litter did the **greatest** job.
3. We **wondered** how many cans we collected.
4. They **climbed** the ladder to the treehouse.
5. Your **truest** friends will help you keep the park clean.
6. Helping on a recycling project can be a big **adventure**.
7. **Exploring** new places can be fun.

🎯 **On-Level Practice** TE p. LR33

Strategic Intervention

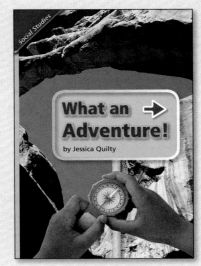

Social Studies

What an Adventure!
by Jessica Quilty

Below-Level Reader

Author's Purpose
Think about why the author wrote *What an Adventure!* Read each question below. Then underline the best answer.

1. Why does the author say that you can join an adventure club?
   a. to get you to do something
   b. to show how to do something
   c. to make you feel good

2. Why does the author show you camping tools?
   a. to get you to buy them
   b. to tell you about camping
   c. to teach you about the tools

3. Why does the author say that sailing is a lot of fun?
   a. to prove that sailing is better than camping
   b. to teach us about sailing
   c. to get us excited about sailing

4. Why does the author describe what adventure clubs do?
   a. to prove they are the best clubs
   b. to teach us about them
   c. to make us feel bad

5. Why did the author write this book?
   a. to get us to try an adventure club
   b. to make us laugh
   c. to help us take a test

🎯 **Below-Level Practice** TE p. LR29

Vocabulary
Draw a line to match each word with its clue.

1. adventure   a. places to meet
2. climbed   b. most loyal
3. clubhouses   c. went up
4. exploring   d. an exciting time
5. greatest   e. had a question
6. truest   f. the most
7. wondered   g. looking for new things

🎯 **Below-Level Practice** TE p. LR30

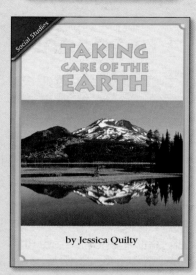

Advanced Reader

Author's Purpose

Think about why the author wrote *Taking Care of the Earth*.
Read each question below. Then underline the best answer.

1. Why does the author say that it is important to protect the environment?
   a. to tell us what she believes
   b. to make us happy
   c. to describe the environment

2. Why does the author say that trash is taken to a landfill?
   a. to explain what landfills are used for
   b. to prove that landfills are bad
   c. to tell us how she feels

3. Why does the author tell us to reduce the amount of plastic we use?
   a. to explain what plastic is
   b. to make us angry
   c. to get us to do something

4. Why does the author list things we can do to respect Earth?
   a. to help us feel good
   b. to get us to do something
   c. to give us something to copy

5. Why did the author write this book?
   a. to explain how to recycle
   b. to show us how to protect the air
   c. to get us to protect the environment

Advanced Practice TE p. LR35

Vocabulary

Write the words from the box to complete the paragraph.

Words to Know

friendships   interests   landfill   litter
pollution   recycle   respect

There are many things you can do to show your
respect for the environment. You can throw
your trash in a garbage can instead of dropping
litter in the street. You can **recycle**
paper, glass, and plastic to keep them from going to a
landfill. When you work with people who share your
interests to help reduce **pollution**,
you may form lasting **friendships**. Then you'll
help both the planet and yourself!

Advanced Practice TE p. LR36

ELL

ELL Reader

ELL Poster 24

Teacher's Edition Notes

ELL notes throughout this lesson support instruction and reference additional resources at point of use.

**ELL Teaching Guide
pp. 162–168, 258–259**

- Multilingual summaries of the main selection
- Comprehension lesson
- Vocabulary strategies and word cards
- ELL Reader 24 lesson

ELL and Transition Handbook

Ten Important Sentences

- Key ideas from every selection in the Student Edition
- Activities to build sentence power

More Reading

Readers' Theater Anthology

- Fluency practice
- Five scripts to build fluency
- Poetry for oral interpretation

Leveled Trade Books

- Extend reading tied to the unit concept
- Lessons in Trade Book Library Teaching Guide

Homework

- Family Times Newsletter
- ELL Multilingual Selection Summaries

Take-Home Books

- Decodable Readers
- Leveled Readers

Literacy Centers

Listening

Let's Read
Along

MATERIALS — SINGLES
CD player, headphones, print copies of recorded pieces

LISTEN TO LITERATURE As children listen to the following recordings, have them follow along or read along in the print version.

AudioText
Horace and Morris but mostly Dolores
"Good Kicking"

Sing with Me/Background Building Audio
"Friendship"

Phonics Songs and Rhymes Audio
"In My Photo Album"

In My Photo Album

In my photo album
This is what you'll see—
Pictures of good pals
Who play and laugh with me.

Sometimes we are quiet,
And sometimes rough and tough.
The time we spend together
Is never long enough.

Audio CD — **Phonics Songs and Rhymes Chart 24**

Reading/Library

Read It
Again!

MATERIALS — SINGLES / PAIRS / GROUPS
collection of books for self-selected reading, reading logs

REREAD BOOKS Have children select previously read books from the appropriate book box and record titles of books they read in their logs. Use these previously read books:

- **Decodable Readers**
- **Leveled Readers**
- **ELL Readers**
- **Stories written by classmates**
- **Books from the library**

TEN IMPORTANT SENTENCES Have children read the Ten Important Sentences for *Horace and Morris but mostly Dolores* and locate the sentences in the Student Edition.

BOOK CLUB Have children write a letter to their pen pals and tell them about *Horace and Morris but mostly Dolores.*

Word Work

Consonant
Clubhouse

MATERIALS — PAIRS
20 index cards, scissors, 2 decorated containers

CONSONANTS *ph, gh* Have two children play a phonics sorting game using words with *ph* and *gh.*

1. Cut index cards into mouse shapes. Write words with *ph* or *gh* on the cards.
2. Label one container "*ph* Clubhouse," the other "*gh* Clubhouse."
3. Lay the cards facedown on the table.
4. Children take turns picking cards and reading the words aloud. Then they place the cards in the proper clubhouse.
5. Play continues until all cards have been sorted.

Phonics Activities CD This interactive CD provides additional practice.

Scott Foresman Reading Street Centers Survival Kit

Use the *Horace and Morris but mostly Dolores* materials
from the Reading Street Centers Survival Kit to
organize this week's centers.

Writing

Social Studies

Technology

He Said, She Said

MATERIALS   **PAIRS**
pencils, sentence strips

WRITE A DIALOGUE Recall that Horace, Morris, and Dolores were friends that liked to go on adventures.

1. Have partners discuss adventures they enjoy.
2. Have them write a dialogue for themselves about what adventure to go on.
3. Then partners take turns reading their dialogue.

LEVELED WRITING Encourage children to write at their own ability level. Some will not be focused on the topic. Others will generally be focused on the topic. Your best writers will be well focused on the topic.

"Let's go hiking in the mountains," said Dan.

"Oh, I thought we could look for lizards in the woods," replied Bobby

Great idea. Count me in!" aimed Dan.

Thanks for Being a Friend

MATERIALS   **SINGLES**
stationery or construction paper, pencils, markers

MAKE A CARD Have children create friendship cards.

1. Have children think of a person that has been a good friend or neighbor.
2. Have them create a card that thanks the person for something that person has done.
3. Ask them to draw a picture to decorate the card.
4. Encourage children to give the card to their friend or neighbor.

April 17
Dear Manuel,
Thank you for coming to my party. I loved the present you gave me.

Your friend,
Luz

E-mail Buddies

MATERIALS   **SINGLES**
computer with Internet access

WRITE AN E-MAIL Have individuals e-mail a friend.

1. Have children write an e-mail to a friend. Encourage them to tell their friend why they are special to them.
2. Have them send the e-mail.
3. Then have them print the e-mail and share it with someone.
4. Be sure to follow classroom rules when using the Internet.

To: brad@abcde.net
From: laura@abcde.net
Subject: Thanks!

Thanks for coming to my party and bringing cookies. They were yummy! You always make me laugh. Bye, Laura

---

ALL CENTERS

Day 1

AT A GLANCE

Oral Vocabulary
"Friendship" 24

Phonics
ph, gh/f/
Spelling Pretest:
    Words with ph, gh/f/

Read Apply Phonics **Word Wall**

(Group Time) < Differentiated Instruction

Comprehension
Skill Author's Purpose
Strategy Ask Questions

Shared Writing
Advice

Grammar
Different Kinds of Pronouns

Materials

- *Sing with Me Big Book*
- Sound-Spelling Card 12
- Letter Tiles
- Decodable Reader 24
- Student Edition 234–235
- Skill Transparency 24
- Grammar Transparency 24
- Writing Transparency 24
- Graphic Organizer 14

Take It to the NET™
ONLINE

Professional Development
To learn about oral vocabulary, go to PearsonSuccessNet.com and read "Taking Delight in Words" by Isabel Beck and others.

Morning Warm~Up!

We live in a world with many people.
Some people are our friends
and our neighbors.
What do good friends
and neighbors do?

QUESTION OF THE WEEK Tell children they will talk, sing, read, and write about what good friends and neighbors do. Write and read the message and discuss the question.

CONNECT CONCEPTS Ask questions to connect to other Unit 5 selections.

- In *Bad Dog, Dodger!,* was Sam a good friend to Dodger? Explain.

- Why would training your dog make you a good neighbor?

REVIEW HIGH-FREQUENCY WORDS

- Read the first sentence of the morning message again. Circle the high-frequency words *world, many,* and *people.*

- Have children say each word as they spell it in the air.

Build Background Use the Day 1 instruction on ELL Poster 24 to assess knowledge and develop concepts.

ELL Poster 24

Oral Vocabulary

SHARE LITERATURE Display p. 24 of the *Sing with Me Big Book.* Tell children that the class is going to sing a song about what good friends do. Ask the class to listen for the Amazing Words **appreciate, communicate,** and **respect** as you sing. Repeat the first verse, asking children to suggest other words for appreciate. Then repeat the first two lines of the second verse and help children define *respect.* Sing the last two lines of the song and ask children to suggest another word for *communicate.* Sing the whole song again, encouraging the class to sing with you.

Sing with Me/
Background Building Audio

Friendship

If you have some friends
That you appreciate,
Never miss a chance
To say that they are great.

Show respect for what they do.
They will do the same for you.
'Cause good friends are people who
Communicate.

Sing with Me Big Book

BUILD BACKGROUND Remind children of the question of the week.

- What do good friends and neighbors do?

Draw a web or use Graphic Organizer 14 and add circles to the end of the spokes. Write *Good Friends and Neighbors* in the center circle. Ask children to describe good friends and neighbors. Suggest that they start with a verb, such as "help" or "say." Encourage children to use the Amazing Words. Draw more circles as necessary. Display the web for use throughout the week.

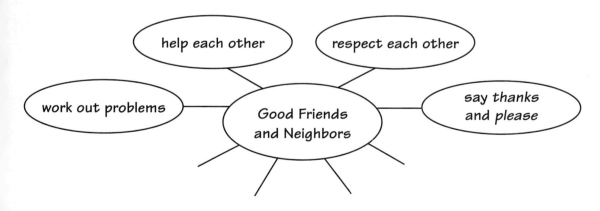

▲ **Graphic Organizer 14**

Amazing Words to build oral vocabulary

	MONITOR PROGRESS
appreciate communicate respect demand firmly advantage defiant ferocious	**If...** children lack oral vocabulary experiences about the concept Responsibility, **then...** use the Oral Vocabulary Routine below to teach *appreciate.*

Oral Vocabulary ROUTINE

1. **Introduce the word** Relate the word *appreciate* to the song. Supply a child-friendly definition. Have children say the word. Example: When you *appreciate* something, you feel grateful for it.

2. **Demonstrate** Provide an example to show meaning. She *appreciates* her best friend and all the fun they have together.

3. **Apply** Have children demonstrate their understanding. Which would you *appreciate,* all your friends coming to your birthday party or losing a favorite toy?

4. **Display the Word/Word Parts** Write the word on a card. Display it. Run your hand under the word parts in *ap-pre-ci-ate.* See p. DI·6 to teach *communicate* and *respect.*

ELL

Build Oral Vocabulary Help children recognize rhymes in "Friendship." Point to and say *appreciate* and *great.* Then point to and say *do* and *you.* Have children repeat the rhyming lines.

TEACH/MODEL

OBJECTIVES

- Associate the sound /f/ with the *ph, gh* spelling patterns.
- Blend, read, and build *ph* and *gh* words.

Skills Trace	
ph, gh/f/	
Introduce/Teach	TE: 2.5 234n–o
Practice	TE: 2.5 234q, 236c–d; PB: 2.2 83; DR24
Reteach/Review	TE: 2.5 262c, 284c, DI-67; PB 2.2 98
Assess/Test	TE: 2.5 262e–g; Benchmark Test: Unit 5

Generalization

ph, gh/f/ The letters *ph* stand for the sound /f/. The letters *gh* often stand for the sound /f/ when they follow a vowel.

Strategic Intervention

Use **Monitor Progress**, p. 234o, during Group Time after children have had more practice with *ph, gh*.

Advanced

Use **Monitor Progress**, p. 234o, as a preassessment to determine whether this group of children would benefit from this instruction on digraphs *ph* and *gh*.

Support Phonics English language learners may need extra support in understanding that *ph* and *gh* can sound like /f/. With Spanish speakers, provide examples of cognates where the letter *f* changes to *ph* or *gh* in English, such as *teléfono/telephone; gráfica/graph; fotografía/photograph.*

See the Phonics Transition Lessons in the ELL and Transition Handbook.

ph, gh/f/

Blending Strategy

1 Connect Write *foam.* What do you know about the sound at the beginning of this word? (The consonant *f* stands for the sound /f/.) Today we will study other spellings for /f/.

2 Use Sound-Spelling Card Display Card 12. This is *fire-fighter.* The sound you hear at the beginning of *firefighter* is /f/. Say it with me, /f/.

3 Model Write *phone.* The letters *ph* stand for the consonant sound /f/ in *phone.* Listen as I blend this word. Blend the sounds across the word in a continuous flow. Let's blend this word together: /fōn/, *phone.* Write *cough.* The letters *gh* stand for the sound /f/ in *cough.* Blend the sounds across the word in a continuous flow. Let's blend this word together: /kôf/, *cough.*

4 Group Practice Continue blending sounds across the word with *photo, laugh, graph, rough, phrase, tough.*

5 Review What do you know about reading these words? The letters *ph* stand for the sound /f/. The letters *gh* often stand for the sound /f/ when they follow a vowel.

Sound-Spelling Card 12

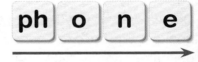

BLEND WORDS

INDIVIDUALS BLEND *ph* AND *gh* WORDS Call on individuals to blend *gopher, enough, phase, orphan.* Have them tell what they know about each word before reading it. For feedback, refer to step five of the Blending Strategy Routine.

BUILD WORDS

INDIVIDUALS MAKE *ph* AND *gh* WORDS Write *phone* and have the class blend it. Have children spell *phone* with letter tiles. Monitor work and provide feedback.

- Change the *on* in *phone* to *as.* What is the new word?

- Add an *r* in *phase* after *ph.* What is the new word?

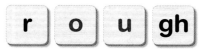

Write *cough* and have the class blend it. Have children spell *cough* with letter tiles. Monitor work and provide feedback.

- Change the *c* in *cough* to *r.* What is the new word?

- Change the *r* in *rough* to *t.* What is the new word?

- Change the *to* in *tough* to *la.* What is the new word?

- Words that have a silent *gh,* such as *dough* and *through,* may be pointed out as exceptions.

Vocabulary TiP

You may wish to explain the meanings of these words.

phrase a short saying
arch a curved structure
ditch a long, narrow hole in the earth

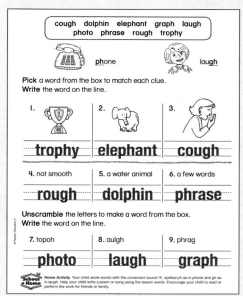

▲ **Practice Book 2.2** p. 83, *ph, gh/f/*

Monitor Progress | Check Word Reading *ph, gh/f/*

Write the following words and have individuals read them.

photo	graph	laugh	enough	phrase
catch	gopher	arch	ditch	cough
when	shot	dolphin	think	tough

If... children cannot blend words with *ph* and *gh* at this point,

then... continue to monitor their progress using other instructional opportunities during the week so that they can be successful with the Day 5 Assessment. See the Skills Trace on p. 234n.

SUCCESS PREDICTOR

Spiral REVIEW

- Row 2 contrasts consonant digraphs *ch* and *tch.*
- Row 3 contrasts digraphs *sh, th, wh.*

▶**Day 1 Check** Word Reading

Day 2 Check Lesson Vocabulary/High-Frequency Words

Day 3 Check Retelling

Day 4 Check Fluency

Day 5 Assess Progress

Word Reading

SUCCESS PREDICTOR

Spelling Words

ph, gh/f/

1. **phone**	7. **graph**
2. **enough**	8. **tough**
3. **stuff**	9. **photo**
4. **laugh**	10. **rough**
5. **puff***	11. **cough**
6. **giraffe**	12. **cliff**

Challenge Words

13. **dolphin**	15. **autograph**
14. **physical**	

*** Word from the Selection**

Consonant Sound /f/

Generalization The consonant sound /f/ can be spelled **ph, gh, ff,** and **ffe:** phone, enough, stuff, and giraffe.

Sort the list words by **ph, gh, ff,** and **ffe.**

ph
1. phone
2. graph
3. photo

ff
4. stuff
5. puff
6. cliff

gh
7. enough
8. laugh
9. tough
10. rough
11. cough

ffe
12. giraffe

Challenge Words

ph
13. dolphin
14. physical
15. autograph

Spelling Words
1. phone
2. enough
3. stuff
4. laugh
5. puff
6. giraffe
7. graph
8. tough
9. photo
10. rough
11. cough
12. cliff
Challenge Words
13. dolphin
14. physical
15. autograph

Home Activity Your child is learning words with the sound of f spelled ph, gh, ff, and ffe. To practice at home, ask your child to write each list word on a piece of paper. Then ask your child to identify the consonants that make the sound of f.

▲ **Spelling Practice Book** p. 93

Support Spelling Before giving the spelling pretest, clarify the meaning of each spelling word with examples, such as coughing for *cough*, and demonstrate the meaning of *photo* by holding up a photograph.

Spelling

PRETEST *ph, gh/f/*

MODEL WRITING FOR SOUNDS Each spelling word has a consonant sound /f/. Before administering the spelling pretest, model how to segment *ph* and *gh* words to spell them.

- What sounds do you hear in *phase?* (/f/ /ā/ /z/)
- What are the letters for /f/? Write *ph.* Continue with the *a/ā/, s/z/,* and silent *e.*
- Repeat with *trough.* Remind children that the letters *gh* stand for /f/.

PRETEST Dictate the spelling words. Segment the words for children if necessary. Have children check their pretests and correct misspelled words.

HOMEWORK Spelling Practice Book, p. 93

Group Time

On-Level	Strategic Intervention	Advanced
Read Decodable Reader 24.	**Read** Decodable Reader 24.	**Read** Advanced Selection 24.
• Use p. 234q.	• Use the **Routine** on p. DI·44.	• Use the **Routine** on p. DI·45.

ELL Place English language learners in the groups that correspond to their reading abilities in English.

ⓘ Independent Activities

Fluency Reading Pair children to reread Leveled Readers or the ELL Reader from the previous week or other text at children's independent level.

Journal Writing List ways you can show family members that you appreciate them. Share writing.

Independent Reading See p. 234j for Reading/Library activities and suggestions.

Literacy Centers To practice consonant sound *ph, gh/f/* you may use Word Work, p. 234j.

Practice Book 2.2 Consonant Sound *ph, gh/f/*, p. 83; Author's Purpose, p. 84

Break into small groups after Spelling and before the Comprehension lesson.

Apply Phonics

⊙ PRACTICE *ph, gh/f/*

HIGH-FREQUENCY WORDS Review *animals, laughs,* and *parents.*

READ DECODABLE READER 24

- Pages 66–67 Read aloud quietly with the group.
- Pages 68–69 Have the group read aloud without you.
- Pages 70–72 Select individuals to read aloud.

CHECK COMPREHENSION AND DECODING Have children retell the story to include characters, setting, and plot. Then have children locate words with *ph*, *gh/f/* in the story. Review *ph* and *gh* spelling patterns. Sort words according to their spelling patterns.

ph	*gh*
dolphin	enough
graph	laughs
Phil	
Phil's	
photos	
phrase	

HOMEWORK Take-Home Decodable Reader 24

REREAD FOR FLUENCY

Paired Reading

ROUTINE

1 **Reader 1 Begins** Children read the entire story, switching readers at the end of each page.

2 **Reader 2 Begins** Have partners reread; now the other partner begins.

3 **Reread** For optimal fluency, children should reread three or four times.

4 **Provide Feedback** Listen to children read and provide corrective feedback regarding their oral reading and their use of the blending strategy.

OBJECTIVES

- Apply knowledge of letter-sounds and word parts to decode unknown words when reading.
- Use context with letter-sounds and word parts to confirm the identification of unknown words.
- Practice fluency in paired reading.

Monitor Progress

Decoding

If... children have difficulty decoding a word,	**then...** prompt them to blend the word.
	• What is the new word?
	• Is the new word a word you know?
	• Does it make sense in the story?

ELL

Access Content

Beginning Preview the story and encourage children to identify words they are familiar with in the pictures and print.

Intermediate Preview *Phil's Zoo Fun* explaining that *dart* means *run* and that a puffer fish is a type of fish that can puff up, or make its body bigger.

Advanced After reading the first two pages together, explain that a petting zoo is a type of zoo where you can pet the animals. Ask children what types of animals people might find at a petting zoo.

Skills Trace

 Author's Purpose

Introduce/Teach	TE: 2.2 253a–b, 254e; 2.3 317a–b, 318e; 2.5 234r, 234–235
Practice	TE: 2.2 258–259; 2.3 326–327; 2.5 252–253; PB: 2.1 84–85, 104–105; 2.2 84–85
Reteach/Review	TE: 2.1 56–57; 2.2 296–297, DI·67; 2.3 362–363, DI·64; 2.5 168–169, 278–279, DI·67; PB: 2.1 97, 177; 2.2 57, 97
Test	TE: 2.2 280e–g; 2.3 342e–g; 2.5 262e–g; Selection Tests: 2.2 33–36; 2.3 41–44; 2.5 93–96; Benchmark Test: Units 1–3, 5

What to Do?

Janet and Erica met after school like they always did. "What do you want to do?" Erica asked. "I really, really want to go to the playground."

Janet said, "I really, really don't. I want to work on our clubhouse."

Erica was surprised. They always wanted to do the same thing. "How about we solve a mystery?" Erica asked.

"No. How about we bother your brother?" Janet replied.

The two friends looked at each other. "Maybe we won't play today," Janet said.

Erica really wanted to play with Janet. She had a thought. "How about today we do what you want to do, and tomorrow we do what I want to do?"

Janet smiled and said, "That's what I would really, really like to do."

Strategy Here's a good spot to ask yourself a question. What is happening between these two characters?

Skill Now that you have read the story, ask yourself, What idea did the author want me to understand?

Unit 5 Horace and Morris but mostly Dolores   Skill Transparency 24

▲ Skills Transparency 24

Access Content

Beginning/Intermediate For a Picture It! lesson on author's purpose, see the ELL Teaching Guide, p. 162–163.

Advanced Before children read "What to Do?" make sure they know the meanings of *playground* and *clubhouse*.

Author's Purpose
Ask Questions

TEACH/MODEL

INTRODUCE Recall *Bad Dog, Dodger!* Have children describe some of the funny things Dodger did. (Possible responses: Dodger tore down the curtains and looked like a bride; Dodger followed Sam into his classroom; Dodger caught a foul ball.)

- Do you think the author wanted to make us laugh?

Read p. 234 with children. Explain the following:

- Authors have reasons for writing what they do. They may want to teach us something, they may want us to believe something, or they may want to make us laugh or imagine.

- Sometimes authors have more than one reason for writing.

- Good readers ask themselves questions before, during, and after reading. Asking questions will help us understand the author's reasons for writing the selection.

Use Skill Transparency 24 to teach author's purpose and asking questions.

STRATEGY Use the first three paragraphs to model asking questions.

Think Aloud **MODEL** From reading the first half of this story, I know it is about two girls who always want to do the same thing. However, on this day, they don't. I wonder why the girls don't agree today.

SKILL Continue with the remaining paragraphs to model author's purpose.

Think Aloud **MODEL** Now that I have finished the story, I wonder whether the author wanted me to learn something about how to work out problems.

Comprehension

Skill
Author's Purpose

Strategy
Ask Questions

Author's Purpose

An author has reasons for writing. The author may want

- to share important information.
- to explain something.
- to tell an interesting story.

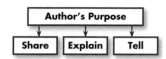

Author's Purpose

| Share | Explain | Tell |

Strategy: Ask Questions

Good readers ask themselves questions before, during, and after they read. This will help you understand what you read. This will also help you decide what the author's purpose is.

Write to Read

1. Read "What to Do?" Think about why the author wrote the story. Use the chart above to help you.

2. As you read, write some questions to ask yourself.

234

What to Do?

Janet and Erica met after school like they always did. "What do you want to do?" Erica asked. "I really, really want to go to the playground."

Janet said, "I really, really don't. I want to work on our clubhouse."

Erica was surprised. They always wanted to do the same thing. "How about we solve a mystery?" Erica asked.

"No. How about we bother your brother?" Janet replied.

The two friends looked at each other. "Maybe we won't play today," Janet said.

Erica really wanted to play with Janet. She had a thought. "How about today we do what you want to do, and tomorrow we do what I want to do?"

Janet smiled and said, "That's what I would really, really like to do."

Strategy Here's a good spot to ask yourself a question. What is happening between these two characters?

Skill Now that you have read the story, ask yourself, What idea did the author want me to understand?

235

PRACTICE

WRITE Work with children to complete the steps in the Write activity. Have children use the completed graphic organizer to discuss the author's purpose in "What To Do?"

Monitor Progress	**Author's Purpose**
If... children are unable to complete **Write** on p. 234,	**then...** use Practice Book 2.2, p. 84, for additional practice.

CONNECT TO READING Encourage children to ask themselves these questions when they read.

- What does the title tell me?
- When I look at the pictures, what do I wonder about?
- If I could talk to the author, what would I ask?

Read the passage. Follow the directions.

A New Park
by Al Turner

Last weekend our neighbors worked together. We turned an empty lot into a park. Everybody helped. I pulled weeds. Nate picked up litter. Mom helped to build the slide. Now we have a great place to play.

1. Circle the name of the author.
2. Circle the answer below that tells what the story is all about.
   Al   a new park   a new slide
3. Circle the words in the story that tell when they made the park.
4. Underline three ways that tell how people worked on the park.
5. Write a sentence that tells why you think the author wrote this story.

Possible answer: The author wrote it to share news about a park he helped build.

Home Activity Your child read and answered questions about a story and told why the author wrote it. Work with your child to write a paragraph about something of interest in your child's life. Have your child read and explain the purpose of the paragraph.

▲ **Practice Book 2.2** p. 84, Author's Purpose

OBJECTIVE
● Write advice.

DAILY FIX-IT

1. It was her fawlt?
   It was her fau**l**t**.**

2. In august they will wak to school.
   In **A**ugust they will wa**l**k to school.

This week's practice sentences appear on Daily Fix-It Transparency 24.

Strategic Intervention

Children who are not able to write independently may illustrate a problem and a solution, adding labels to each picture. .

Advanced

Have children write both a letter that states a problem and a reply letter that states a solution.

Support Writing Before writing about a problem they have with an irresponsible person, have children work in pairs to tell each other about the problem first.

▲ **The Grammar and Writing Book**
For more instruction and practice, use pp. 188–193.

Shared Writing

WRITE Advice

GENERATE IDEAS Read aloud the letter from Puzzled to Advice Person. Ask children to pretend they are Advice Person and have them decide what they would say to Puzzled about the problem with the irresponsible friend.

WRITE ADVICE Explain that the class will answer a letter and give advice about how to deal with a person who is not responsible.

COMPREHENSION SKILL Have children discuss the reasons Puzzled might have written to ask for advice.

- Display Writing Transparency 24 and read the title.
- Read the letter from Puzzled.
- Discuss some possible solutions to Puzzled's problem.
- Using suggestions from children, write a letter to Puzzled that provides solutions to the problem of the irresponsible friend.

HANDWRITING While writing, model the letter forms as shown on pp. TR14–17.

READ THE ADVICE Have children read the completed advice letter aloud as you track the print.

Good Advice

Dear Advice Person,
    My friend borrows my books and toys. Then he never gives them back. What should I do?

                                        Puzzled

Dear Puzzled,   **Possible answer:**
Speak up! Ask your friend
to return all your things.
Maybe he just forgot. Then think
twice before letting him borrow
anything else.
                                Advice Person

Unit 5 *Horace, Morris, but mostly Dolores*   Writing Model **24**

▲ **Writing Transparency 24**

INDEPENDENT WRITING

WRITE A LETTER Have children write their own letter to Advice Person about a problem they are having with an irresponsible friend or family member. Encourage them to use words from the Word Wall and the Amazing Words board. Let children illustrate their writing. You may display children's letters on a bulletin board and have classmates respond.

ADDITIONAL PRACTICE For additional practice, use pp. 188–193 in the Grammar and Writing Book.

Grammar

TEACH/MODEL Different Kinds of Pronouns

REVIEW PRONOUNS Remind children that a pronoun is a word that takes the place of a noun or nouns.

IDENTIFY DIFFERENT KINDS OF PRONOUNS Display Grammar Transparency 24. Read the explanation that tells how pronouns are used differently in sentences. Share the examples with children.

• *Pam* and *I* are the subjects in the sentence. The pronoun *we* can take the place of *Pam* and *I* as the subject.

• *Pam's bike* can be replaced by the pronoun *it*. The pronoun *it* takes the place of the subject, *Pam's bike*.

Continue modeling with items 3–5.

PRACTICE

REPLACING PRONOUNS Have children replace nouns with pronouns in sentences. Write the sentences on the board.

• Name a pronoun that is used as a subject in a sentence.

• What pronouns can be used after action verbs? These pronouns—*me, us, her, him, you, it, them*—depend on what goes before them, or their *antecedents*.

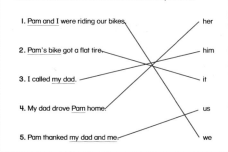

OBJECTIVE

● Identify different kinds of pronouns.

Different Kinds of Pronouns

The pronouns **I, he, she, we,** and **they** are used as subjects of sentences. The pronouns **me, him, her, us,** and **them** are used after action verbs. The pronouns **you** and **it** can be used anywhere in a sentence.

Calvin has a new bike. **He** can't ride **it.**
The pronoun *he* is the subject of a sentence.
The pronoun *it* is used after the action verb *ride*.

Calvin is riding his bike. Angela helped **him.**
The pronoun *him* is used after the action verb *helped*.

Draw lines to match the underlined words to the pronouns.

1. Pam and I were riding our bikes.   her

2. Pam's bike got a flat tire.   him

3. I called my dad.   it

4. My dad drove Pam home.   us

5. Pam thanked my dad and me.   we

▲ **Grammar Transparency 24**

Wrap Up Your Day!

☑ **CONSONANT SOUND /f/** Write *graph* and ask children what letters make the sound /f/. *(ph)* Have children name other words that have the sound /f/ represented by *ph*.

☑ **SPELLING CONSONANT SOUND /f/** Have children name the letters for each sound in *stuff*. Write the letters as children write them in the air. Continue with *giraffe* and *rough*.

☑ **AUTHOR'S PURPOSE** To help children recognize author's purpose, ask: Why did the author tell us about Janet and Erica's problem of deciding what to do together? (to help us understand that people can disagree and find solutions that make them both happy)

LET'S TALK ABOUT IT Recall that Janet and Erica came up with a solution to their problem. What did you think of their solution? (Possible response: I thought it was a good solution because it was fair. Each girl got a turn to do what she wanted.)

HOMEWORK Send home this week's Family Times newsletter.

PREVIEW Day 2

Tell children that tomorrow the class will read about three friends who love to go on adventures together until they are faced with a decision.

Day 2

AT A GLANCE

Share Literature
Bear and Duck on the Run

Phonics and Spelling
🔊 *ph, gh/f/*
Spelling: Words with *ph, gh/f/*

Build Background
How to Make New Friends

Lesson Vocabulary
adventure climbed greatest
truest clubhouse exploring
wondered
More Words to Know
downhearted sewer

Vocabulary
🔊 **Skill** Ending *-est*
🔊 **Strategy** Word Structure

Read

Group Time < Differentiated Instruction

Horace and Morris but mostly Dolores

Interactive Writing
Problem and Solution

Grammar
Different Kinds of Pronouns

Materials

- *Sing with Me Big Book*
- *Read Aloud Anthology*
- Phonics Songs and Rhymes Chart 24
- Background Building Audio
- Graphic Organizers 4, 25
- Student Edition 236–255

Morning Warm~Up!

Today we will read about
Horace and Morris,
but mostly Dolores.

These three mice
are really good friends.

What makes a really good friend?

QUESTION OF THE DAY Encourage children to sing "Friendship" from the *Sing with Me Big Book* as you gather. Write and read the message and discuss the question.

REVIEW SUFFIXES

- Review with children that suffixes come at the end of a word.
- Read the message again and have children raise their hands when they hear a word with the suffix *-ly. (mostly, really)*
- For each word, ask the class to tell you what word the suffix was added to. *(most, real)*

Build Background Use the Day 2 instruction on ELL Poster 24 to preview high-frequency words.

ELL Poster 24

Share Literature

BUILD CONCEPTS

FANTASY Read the title "Bear and Duck on the Run." Ask children if they have ever heard the phrase *on the run* before. Remind them that books about animals doing human things, such as running a race, are called fantasy books.

BUILD ORAL VOCABULARY Introduce the Amazing Words **demand** and **firmly.** Explain that *demand* means "to order" and that *firmly* means "in a determined way." Suggest that as you read, children listen to find out what kind of friend Duck is.

Read Aloud Anthology
Bear and Duck on the Run

MONITOR LISTENING COMPREHENSION

- What does Duck think Bear needs? Why does he think this? (Duck thinks Bear needs exercise because it's good for the heart, and it can help Bear lose weight.)

- What does Duck do with the shorts he bought for Bear? (Duck demands that Bear put the shorts on.)

- Why does Duck speak firmly to Bear? (Possible responses: because Bear is lazy, because Duck cares about Bear, because Bear lied and said he had measles)

- Do you think Duck is a good friend to Bear? Explain. (Children will probably agree that Duck is a good friend to Bear because he tries to help him lose weight and because he doesn't get angry when Bear cheats.)

Amazing Words to build oral vocabulary

	MONITOR PROGRESS
appreciate **communicate** **respect** **demand** **firmly** **advantage** **defiant** **ferocious**	**If**... children lack oral vocabulary experiences about the concept Responsibility, **then**... use the Oral Vocabulary Routine. See p. DI·6 to teach *demand* and *firmly*.

Build Concepts Help children understand what a taxicab is. Explain that Groundhog's job as a taxicab driver is to drive people where they want to go. Explain that *taxi* is short for *taxicab*.

OBJECTIVES

- Review words with *ph, gh*.
- Blend, read, and build words with *ph* and *gh*.

ph, gh/f/

TEACH/MODEL

Fluent Word Reading

ROUTINE

1 **Connect** Write *phone*. You can read this word because you know how to read words with letters that make the consonant sound /f/. What sound do the letters *ph* stand for in this word? (/f/) What's the word? *(phone)* Do the same with *tough*.

2 **Model** When you come to a new word, look at the letters from left to right and think about the consonant sounds. Say the sounds in the word to yourself and then read the word. **Model reading *phase* and *laugh* in this way.** When you come to a new word, what are you going to do?

3 **Group Practice** Write *dolphin, coughing, telegraph, roughly, alphabet.* Read these words. Look at the letters, think about the consonant sounds, say the sounds to yourself, and then read the word aloud together. Allow 2–3 seconds previewing time.

WORD READING

PHONICS SONGS AND RHYMES CHART 24 Frame each of the following words on Phonics Songs and Rhymes Chart 24. Call on individuals to read them. Guide children in previewing.

photo   laugh   rough

tough   enough

Sing "In My Photo Album" to the tune of "Eensy Weensy Spider," or play the CD. Have children follow along on the chart as they sing. Then have individuals take turns locating *ph* and *gh* words on the chart.

In My Photo Album

In my photo album
This is what you'll see—
Pictures of good pals
Who play and laugh with me.

Sometimes we are quiet,
And sometimes rough and tough.
The time we spend together
Is never long enough.

Phonics Songs and Rhymes Chart 24

 **Phonics Songs and Rhymes Audio**

Strategic Intervention

Use **Strategic Intervention Decodable Reader 24** for more practice with *ph, gh/f/*

ELL

Support Phonics Invite children to act out what happens in "In My Photo Album" as you replay the Phonics Songs and Rhymes Audio CD.

BUILD WORDS

INDIVIDUALS MAKE *ph* AND *gh* WORDS Write these sentences. Have children read the sentences and identify the word in each that has the sound /f/. Have them circle the letters that stand for /f/. Then have them choose one of the *ph* or *gh* words from the chart and use it in a sentence.

Coach handed each of us a tro(ph)y.

The sea animal I like best is the dol(ph)in.

Mom asked me if I got enou(gh) to eat.

I asked the basketball player for his autogra(ph).

Please cover your mouth when you cou(gh).

ph	*gh*
dolphin	laugh
gopher	cough
trophy	tough
graphic	enough

Spelling

PRACTICE *ph, gh/f/*

WRITE DICTATION SENTENCES Have children write these sentences. Repeat words slowly, allowing children to hear each sound. Children may use the Word Wall to help with spelling high-frequency words. **Word Wall**

Look at the photo of the giraffe I took at the zoo.

It was tough, but we made it to the top of the cliff.

Do you have enough graph paper for math?

HOMEWORK Spelling Practice Book, p. 94

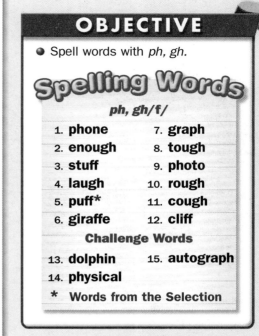

OBJECTIVE

● Spell words with *ph, gh.*

Spelling Words

ph, gh/f/

1. phone
2. enough
3. stuff
4. laugh
5. puff*
6. giraffe
7. graph
8. tough
9. photo
10. rough
11. cough
12. cliff

Challenge Words

13. dolphin
14. physical
15. autograph

* Words from the Selection

Consonant Sound /f/

Write a list word to answer the riddles.
What rhymes with **bone** and starts with ph? 1. phone
What rhymes with **cuff** and starts with p? 2. puff
What rhymes with **bluff** and starts with st? 3. stuff
What rhymes with **stiff** and starts with cl? 4. cliff

Write the list word that means almost the same as each word or phrase.
5. plenty enough 6. chart graph
7. not smooth rough 8. snapshot photo

Write the list word that best fits in each sentence.
9. What questions do you have about a giraffe?
10. This steak is tough.
11. The joke made me laugh.
12. He took medicine for his cough.

▲ **Spelling Practice Book** p. 94

OBJECTIVES

● Build background.
● Learn lesson vocabulary.

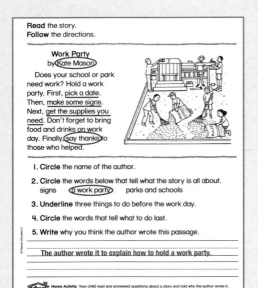

▲ **Practice Book 2.2** p. 85, Author's Purpose

Activate Prior Knowledge Ask students to think about a time when they made a new friend. What did they say and do? Have them tell why they wanted to be friends with this person.

Build Background

DISCUSS HOW TO MAKE NEW FRIENDS Give some examples of how to make new friends, such as asking someone new to play. Initiate discussion by asking children how they make new friends.

● How do you make friends with someone you've just met?
● How did you make friends with the people in this class?

BACKGROUND BUILDING AUDIO Have children listen to the CD and share the new information they learned about how to make new friends.

Audio CD   Sing with Me/
Background Building Audio

COMPLETE A T-CHART Draw a T-chart or display Graphic Organizer 25. Write *Why We Make Friends* above the left column and *How We Make Friends* above the right column. Ask children to give reasons why we like to make friends and write their responses in the first column. Then ask them to think of ways that we can make friends. Write these responses in the second column.

Why We Make Friends	How We Make Friends
someone to talk to	Introduce yourelf.
someone to play with	Talk to them.
someone to help us	Ask them to play.
	Share with them.

▲ **Graphic Organizer 25**

CONNECT TO SELECTION Connect background information to *Horace and Morris but mostly Dolores.*

Even if you already have friends whom you respect and appreciate, it's fun to make new ones. You might make new friends alone or in a group. One way to make friends is to do something together that you both like. In this story Horace, Morris, and Dolores are already friends. But when Horace and Morris want to play without Dolores, she has to find new friends. Let's see how she does that.

Vocabulary

LESSON VOCABULARY

WORD RATING CHART Create word rating charts using the categories *Know, Have Seen,* and *Don't Know,* or use Graphic Organizer 4.

WORDS TO KNOW

T **adventure** an exciting experience
T **climbed** went upward
T **greatest** the best or most wonderful
T **truest** the most real or loyal
T **clubhouse** a house or structure where a group meets
T **exploring** going someplace to discover what it is like
T **wondered** wanted to know more

MORE WORDS TO KNOW

downhearted very sad
sewer underground pipes that carry away waste

T = Tested Word

- Children should be able to decode all words except *adventure.* To read *adventure,* divide the word into syllables. (*ad/ven/ture*) Tell children *ture* has the sound /chər/. Have students blend the syllables together.

- Read each word and have children check one of the three columns: *Know* (know and can use), *Have Seen* (have seen or heard the word; don't know the meaning), *Don't Know.*

- Have children share where they may have seen or heard these words.

- Have children review their charts at the end of the week and make changes to their ratings.

Pick a word from the box to match each clue.
Write the word on the line.

adventure climbed clubhouse exploring greatest truest wondered

1. where the club meets		**clubhouse**
2. the very best		**greatest**
3. an exciting trip or event		**adventure**
4. wanted to know		**wondered**
5. the most loyal		**truest**
6. hiked up		**climbed**
7. looking around a new place.		**exploring**

Home Activity Your child used word clues to practice writing new vocabulary words. Make up a simple crossword puzzle with your child using some of these vocabulary words. Use the clues above or write some of your own.

▲ **Practice Book 2.2** p. 86, Lesson Vocabulary

Monitor Progress | Check Lesson Vocabulary

Point to the following words and have individuals read them.

adventure	climbed	greatest	truest	clubhouse	exploring
wondered	alone	door	friend(s)	love(ed)	their

If... children cannot read these words,

then... have them write each word and practice with a partner. Monitor their fluency with these words during reading, and provide additional practice opportunities before the Day 5 Assessment.

SUCCESS PREDICTOR

Spiral REVIEW

- Reviews previously taught high-frequency words and lesson vocabulary.

Day 1 Check
Word Reading

▶**Day 2**
Check Lesson
Vocabulary/High-
Frequency Words

Day 3 Check
Retelling

Day 4 Check
Fluency

Day 5 Assess
Progress

Word Reading
SUCCESS PREDICTOR

Vocabulary Strategy
for Endings

Words to Know

adventure

wondered

exploring

climbed

clubhouse

greatest

truest

Remember

Try the strategy. Then, if you need more help, use your glossary or a dictionary.

Word Structure As you read, you may see a word you don't know. What can you do? Look at the end of the word. The ending *-est* is often added to a describing word when comparing three or more things, as in *smallest*. You may be able to use the ending to help you figure out the meaning of the word.

1. Put your finger over the ending.

2. Look at the base word. Do you know what the base word means?

3. Try your meaning in the sentence. Does it make sense?

Read "Boris and Cloris." Look for words that have the *-est* ending. Use the ending to help you figure out the meanings.

236

Boris and Cloris

Boris was bored. All he did was eat cheese and scamper across the floor. Boris longed for adventure, something exciting.

At the far end of the backyard was a small building. Boris wondered what was in it.

He asked his friend Cloris to go exploring with him, but she refused. So Boris went alone.

When he got to the building, Boris climbed through a hole in a board. Two girls were sitting on the floor, talking.

"Who will we allow in our clubhouse?" asked one girl.

"Only our best friends, the greatest and the truest of our friends," said the other girl. "But, look! There's a mouse in our clubhouse!"

The two girls jumped up and tried to catch Boris. He raced for the hole, but where was it? "Over here, Boris," Cloris squeaked. Boris jumped through the hole, and they dashed across the backyard.

When they were safe at home, Boris said to Cloris, "Thank you for coming after me. You are the greatest and truest friend." And he never longed for adventure again.

Words to Write

What do you like to do with a friend? Write about your friend. Use the Words to Know list.

237

OBJECTIVE

● Use word ending *-est* to determine the meaning of unfamiliar words.

ELL

Access Content Use ELL Poster 24 and the vocabulary activities and word cards in the ELL Teaching Guide, pp. 164–165. Choose from the following to meet children's language proficiency levels.

Beginning Have children locate the words *greatest* and *truest*. Have them put a finger over the *-est* ending and discuss the meaning of the words *great* and *true*.

Intermediate Have children return to the Word Rating chart they completed for the Introduce Vocabulary page and add information they have learned.

Advanced Teach the lesson on pp. 236–237 and have children use each word in a sentence.

Vocabulary Strategy

TEACH/MODEL Word Structure

CONNECT Remind children of strategies to use when they come across words they don't understand.

● Sometimes we can get the meaning from context clues. Read the words and sentences around the unknown word. Are there other words nearby to help us figure out the meaning?

● We can figure out the meaning of an unfamiliar compound word if we know the meanings of the smaller words.

● We can look for word endings in the unknown word. Today we will learn more about the word ending *-est*.

INTRODUCE THE STRATEGY

- Read and discuss the steps for recognizing word endings on p. 236.

- Have children read "Boris and Cloris," using -*est* endings to help determine the meaning of highlighted words.

- Model using -*est* endings to determine the meaning of *greatest*.

MODEL The word *greatest* describes friends in this selection. If I cover the -*est* ending, I see the word *great*. I know *great* means very, very good. The -*est* ending is used to compare things, so *greatest* must mean *the most great* or *best*. That makes sense in this phrase: "Only our best friends, the greatest and truest of our friends."

PRACTICE

- Have children determine the meanings of the highlighted words in "Boris and Cloris," and explain how -*est* endings helped them recognize the meanings of *greatest* and *truest*.

WRITE Children's writing should include lesson vocabulary in a description of what they like to do with a friend.

CONNECT TO READING Encourage children to use these strategies to determine the meaning of an unknown word.

- Look for the ending -*est* added to words, and see if these words have base words you know.

- Use word parts.

- Use the glossary or a dictionary.

Group Time

On-Level	Strategic Intervention	Advanced
Read *Horace and Morris but mostly Dolores.* • Use pp. 238–255.	**Read** SI Decodable Reader 24. • Read or listen to *Horace and Morris but mostly Dolores.* • Use the Routine on p. DI·46.	**Read** *Horace and Morris but mostly Dolores.* • Use the Routine on p. DI·47.

DAY 2

ELL Place English language learners in the groups that correspond to their reading abilities in English.

(i) Independent Activities

Independent Reading See p. 234j for Reading/Library activities and suggestions.

Journal Writing Write about a time when you felt left out. Share writing.

Literacy Centers To provide experiences with *Horace and Morris but mostly Dolores,* you may use the Listening Center on p. 234j.

Practice Book 2.2 Author's Purpose, p. 85; Lesson Vocabulary, p. 86; Plot and Theme, p. 87

Break into small groups after Vocabulary and before Writing.

Genre

Fantasies are make-believe stories because they couldn't really happen. What makes this story a fantasy?

Horace and Morris but mostly Dolores

by James Howe

illustrated by Amy Walrod

Will Horace, Morris, and Dolores remain very good friends?

238

239

 AudioText

Read
Prereading Strategies

PREVIEW AND PREDICT Have children read the title. Identify Horace, Morris, and Dolores as the three mice in the picture. Identify the author and illustrator. Do a picture walk of pp. 240–245. Ask children what they think this story will be about.

DISCUSS FANTASY Ask if Horace, Morris, and Dolores are real mice. Help children identify the characters as make-believe because real mice don't wear clothing. Remind them that a story about make-believe animals is called fantasy. Read the definition of fantasy on p. 238 of the Student Edition.

SET PURPOSE Read the question on p. 239. Ask children to make predictions about what might happen to the friends.

Access Content Before reading, review the story summary in English and/or the home language. See the ELL Teaching Guide, pp. 166–168.

_____ ph, gh,/f/   ☐ lesson/tested vocabulary

Horace and Morris but mostly Dolores
loved adventure. They sailed the seven sewers.

240

They climbed Mount Ever-Rust. They dared to go where
no mouse had gone before.

241

Guiding Comprehension

Character • Inferential

- **What do you know about Horace, Morris, and Dolores?**
  Children may respond that they are friends who like doing exciting
  things together.

Prior Knowledge • Critical

- *Text to World* **What other things might friends who appreciate adventure
  choose to do?**
  Children may respond that they might go camping or ride bikes.

▲ **Pages 240-241**
Have children read to find out what
the three friends like to do together.

EXTEND SKILLS

Puns and Word Play
For instruction in puns and word play,
discuss the following:

- Sometimes authors play with words
  to create funny names that are
  similar to the real names of things.
- On p. 240, the three mice sail the
  seven sewers. This is a play on
  words because often sailors talk
  about sailing the seven seas.
- Look at the name "Mount Ever-Rust."
  This is a play on the name of Mt.
  Everest.

Assess Have children look for other
examples of word play, such as the
Roque-fort on p. 248.

Horace and Morris but mostly Dolores never said, "This is something we shouldn't do."

They said, "This is something we've *got* to do!" And so there was almost nothing they didn't do.

242 243

▲ **Pages 242–243**
Have children look at the picture and ask themselves what is happening.

Monitor Progress
Decoding

If... children come to a word they don't know,	**then...** remind them to: 1. Blend the word. 2. Decide if the word makes sense. 3. Look in a dictionary for more help.

Strategies in Context

☉ ASK QUESTIONS

- **What are some questions you can ask yourself to help you understand the story better?**

Possible response: What can I learn about Horace, Morris, and Dolores based on how they act? Will they ever find anything they won't do?

Monitor Progress	**Ask Questions**
If... children are unable to generate questions,	**then...** model how to think of questions to increase understanding of the text.

 Think Aloud

MODEL To help myself understand Horace, Morris, and Dolores, I think of questions to ask that begin with words like *who, what, where, when, why,* and *how*. When I read that the mice never said, "This is something we shouldn't do," I asked myself, "When will the mice find something they shouldn't do?"

ASSESS Have children generate *who, what, where, when, why,* and *how* questions and then look for answers.

____ ph, gh/f/   ☐ lesson/tested vocabulary

Horace and Morris and Dolores were friends—the greatest of friends, the truest of friends, the now-and-forever-I'm-yours sort of friends. And then one day . . . Horace and Morris had a decision to make.

They didn't want to do anything without Dolores, but as Horace pointed out, "A boy mouse must do what a boy mouse must do."

"Bet you can't say *that* three times real fast," Dolores said with a smile.

244

Horace and Morris didn't even try. They didn't even smile. "Good-bye, Dolores," they said.

What kind of place doesn't allow girls? Dolores wondered as she watched her friends step through the door of the Mega-Mice clubhouse.

245

Guiding Comprehension

Draw Conclusions • Inferential
- **How does the mice's friendship change?**
Horace and Morris decide they want to join a club that doesn't allow girls.

Character • Inferential
- *Text to Self* **How do you think Dolores feels? How would you feel if you were Dolores?**
Most children will respond that Dolores is sad or angry.

Summarize • Inferential
- **What has happened so far in the story?**
Horace, Morris, and Dolores are good friends who like going on adventures together. Then Horace and Morris decide to join a club that doesn't allow girls. They say good-bye to Dolores.

Make Judgments • Critical
- *Text to Self* **What would you do if your best friend were not allowed to go in someplace where you would like to go?**
Responses will vary. Children should discuss the problem and choose the most appropriate solution.

▲ **Pages 244–245**
Have children read to find out how the mice's friendship changes.

Strategy Self-Check

Have children ask themselves these questions to check their reading.

Vocabulary Strategy
- Do I look for the ending *-est* added to words, and see if I know the base words?
- Do I look for context clues?
- Do I use the glossary or dictionary?

Ask Questions
- What does the title tell me?
- When I look at the pictures, what do I wonder about?
- If I could talk to the author, what would I ask?

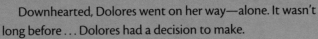

Downhearted, Dolores went on her way—alone. It wasn't long before . . . Dolores had a decision to make.

She didn't really want to do anything without Horace and Morris, but she figured a girl mouse must do what a girl mouse must do. (She said this aloud three times real fast just to prove that she could.)

> A GIRL MOUSE MUST DO WHAT A GIRL MOUSE MUST DO.

246

I'll bet Horace and Morris couldn't do that, she thought. But she wasn't smiling as she stepped through the door of the Cheese Puffs clubhouse.

Day after day, Dolores went to the Cheese Puffs. Day after day, Horace and Morris went to Mega-Mice.

They missed playing with each other, but as they said . . . "A girl mouse must do what a girl mouse must do." "A boy mouse must do what a boy mouse must do."

Horace and Morris and even Dolores were sure their friendship would never be the same. But then one day . . . Dolores made a different decision.

247

▲ **Pages 246–247**
Have children read to find out about the Cheese Puffs and the Mega-Mice.

Guiding Comprehension

Plot • Literal
- **What does Dolores do while the boys go to the Mega-Mice club?**
  She goes to a girls' club called the Cheese Puffs.

Draw Conclusions • Inferential
- **Why do you think Dolores says, "A girl mouse must do what a girl mouse must do"?**
  She is responding to the boys saying, "A boy mouse must do what a boy mouse must do." She wants to remind herself that she can have fun too.

Predict • Inferential
- **What do you think Dolores will do?**
  Possible responses: She will try to have fun with the Cheese Puffs; she will still try to hang out with the boys; she will try to get everyone to do things together.

____ ph, gh/f/

☐ lesson/tested vocabulary

"I'm bored," she announced.

The other girls stared.

"Anybody here want to build a fort? How about a Roque-fort?"

The other girls booed.

"Okay, forget the cheese. I'm sick of making things out of cheese anyway. Let's go exploring."

The other girls gasped.

"Phooey!" said Dolores. "I quit!"

"If you quit, then I quit too!" a small voice said from the back of the room.

TODAY'S TOPIC FOR DISCUSSION: HOW TO GET A FELLA USING MOZZARELLA

248

249

Guiding Comprehension

Draw Conclusions • Inferential

- **Why is Dolores bored with the Cheese Puffs?**

The Cheese Puffs don't do exciting things, such as going exploring.

Sequence • Literal

- **What does Dolores decide to do next?**

Dolores decides to quit the Cheese Puffs.

Draw Conclusions • Critical

- *Text to Self* **Why do you think another girl mouse decides to quit with Dolores? What would you have done?**

The children may say that the other girl mouse is probably bored too.

▲ **Pages 248–249**

Have children read to find out what Dolores decides to do next.

Groups

Time for SOCIAL STUDIES

Explain that there are clubs that do not let in everyone. Discuss what a club that treated everyone fairly would be like. Point out that the Mega-Mice club didn't allow girls to join, and the Cheese Puffs club didn't allow boys to join. Ask if these clubs are fair and, if not, why not.

Outside Dolores introduced herself. "I'm Dolores."
"I'm Chloris," said the girl.

"Now where can we go to have some *real* fun around here?" Dolores thought and thought. "I've got it!" she said at last.

250

251

▲ **Pages 250–251**
Ask children to read to find out what Dolores does after she quits.

Guiding Comprehension

Plot • Critical
• **What do you think Dolores means by "*real* fun"?**
Possible response: Dolores means exploring or having exciting adventures.

Make Predictions • Inferential
• **What do you think Dolores plans to do next?**
Children may respond that Dolores plans to start her own club that will do fun things, not boring things. They may add that Dolores might go to the Mega-Mice Club to see if any of the boys want to join her new club.

_____ ph, gh/f/

lesson/tested vocabular

Skills in Context

⟳ AUTHOR'S PURPOSE

- **Why do you think the author wrote *Horace and Morris but mostly Dolores?***
  Children may respond that the author wanted to tell a funny story about
  friendship.

Monitor Progress	Author's Purpose
If... children are unable to determine the author's purpose,	**then...** model how to use the text and illustrations to determine the purpose.

Think Aloud **MODEL** The things these mice do and say are funny. The mice are also good friends who respect and appreciate one another. I think the author wanted to tell a funny story about friendship.

ASSESS Have children find examples of funny words and pictures.

▲ **Pages 252–253**
Have children look at the illustrations and predict what happens next.

Explorers

Time for **SOCIAL STUDIES**

In the 19th century, Meriwether Lewis and William Clark traveled west of the Mississippi River to explore the land there. Their translator was a Native American woman named Sacagawea, who helped them talk to other Native Americans. They traveled all the way to the Pacific Ocean and returned with stories that made people want to move west. Lewis, Clark, and Sacagawea were explorers like Horace, Morris, and Dolores.

The five friends spent the rest of the day exploring, Chloris and Boris and Horace and Morris... but mostly Dolores...

254

And the next day they built a clubhouse of their own.

255

▲ **Pages 254–255**
Have children read to find out how the plot is resolved.

Name _____

Horace and Morris

Read the story. **Follow** the directions.

Sandy looked outside. All she saw were weeds. Sandy had a plan. We must build a garden! Sandy talked to her neighbors. Soon everyone got to work. By summer they had a beautiful garden. Now people smile when they see what they made together.

1. **Circle** the sentence below that tells the big idea.
Gardens are beautiful.
People can work together to make things better.
Gardens grow in the spring.

2. **Write** 1, 2, or 3 on the lines to show the right order.

_**3**_ They had a beautiful garden.

_**1**_ Sandy talked to her neighbors.

_**2**_ Everyone got to work.

3. **Write** a sentence that tells something that happened in the beginning of the story.

Children's sentence should tell something that happened at the beginning of the story. Possible answers: Sandy looked outside and saw weeds.

School + Home Home Activity Your child identified the big idea of a story and put story events in correct order. Work with your child to write another story about friends or neighbors working together. As you plan your writing, discuss what happens in the *beginning*, *middle*, and *end* of the story.

▲ **Practice Book 2.2** p. 87,
Plot and Theme

Skills in Context

REVIEW PLOT AND THEME

- **What is the plot of this story? What is the theme, or big idea?**
  The plot tells about events in the friendship of Horace, Morris, and Dolores. The big idea is the importance of friendship.

Monitor Progress	Plot and Theme
If… children have difficulty answering the questions,	**then…** model how to identify plot and theme.

Think Aloud **MODEL** I know that the plot is what happens to these three mice as they join separate clubs and come back together to build their own clubhouse. The theme is the big idea the author is trying to express. I think the author wants me to see how the mice learned to appreciate their friendship and then learn to appreciate my own friendships.

ASSESS Have children find details that support the theme.

REREAD FOR FLUENCY

Paired Reading

ROUTINE

1. **Reader 1 Begins** Children read the entire book, switching readers at the end of each page.

2. **Reader 2 Begins** Have partners reread; now the other partner begins.

3. **Reread** For optimal fluency, children should reread three or four times.

4. **Provide Feedback** Listen to children read and provide corrective feedback regarding their oral reading and their use of the blending strategy.

OBJECTIVES

- Write problem and solution.
- Identify different kinds of pronouns.

Strategic Intervention

Have children illustrate a problem and a way to solve that problem. They can label each illustration as "problem" and "solution."

Advanced

Have children who are able to write complete sentences independently write and illustrate a "book" about a problem and solution. The book should include a cover, author page, and several pages with sentences of the story accompanied by pictures.

Writing Support Before writing, children might share ideas in their home languages.

Beginning Pair children with more proficient English speakers. A more proficient speaker can help the partner write about a problem.

Intermediate Help children orally tell about their problem and then write it.

Advanced Encourage children to write and read aloud their problems and the goals they came up with to solve their problems.

Support Grammar Children may confuse subject and object pronouns, using *her* in place of *she* and vice versa. Provide extra practice with subject and object pronouns. See the Grammar Transition lessons in the ELL and Transition Handbook.

Interactive Writing

WRITE Problem and Solution

BRAINSTORM Use *Horace and Morris but mostly Dolores* to encourage a discussion of problems and solutions among friends. Picture walk through the book and ask children to identify the problems Horace, Morris, and Dolores have and the way they solve their problems.

SHARE THE PEN Have children participate in writing about a problem and a solution to that problem. To begin, tell students about a problem many students experience with a friend: deciding which game to play. Write the problem, inviting individuals to write familiar letter-sounds, word parts, and high-frequency words. Ask questions such as:

- What is the vowel sound you hear in the word *play*? (/ā/)
- What letters stand for that sound? *(ay)* Have a volunteer write *ay.*
- How would we write *play*? *(play)* Have a volunteer write *play.*

Continue to have individuals make contributions. Frequently reread what has been written while tracking the print.

READ THE STORY Read the problem and the solution. Have children echo you.

Solving a Problem

One day my friend wanted to play baseball.

I wanted to play soccer.

We decided to play one game of baseball and then one game of soccer.

INDEPENDENT WRITING

WRITE A FRIENDSHIP STORY Have children write about their own problem with a friend and how they solved that problem. Ask children to illustrate their story as well.

Grammar

DEVELOP THE CONCEPT Pronouns

IDENTIFY DIFFERENT KINDS OF PRONOUNS Write the following sentences on the board. *Mrs. Rodriguez brought a book to school. She will read it after lunch.*

Mrs. Rodriguez is the subject in the first sentence. What pronoun took the place of *Mrs. Rodriguez?* *(She)* The noun *book* came after the action verb in the first sentence. What pronoun took the place of *book?* *(it)*

PRACTICE

SUGGEST PRONOUNS Gather pictures of people and animals interacting together. Display a picture. Model replacing each noun in the picture with a pronoun.

 Think Aloud **MODEL** This is Jorge. If Jorge were the subject of the sentence, I would use the pronoun *he* to take the place of his name. **Write he.** This boy is Felix. I would also use the pronoun *he* to take the place of his name. If I were talking about the two boys, I would use *they.* **Write they.** Oscar is catching a football. *It* names the football.

Write *it.* Share other pictures with children and have them suggest other pronouns to replace nouns. Write the pronouns for each picture.

DAILY FIX-IT

3. I will rite a sine.
   I will <u>write</u> a si<u>gn</u>.

4. He laffed on the fone.
   He la<u>ughed</u> on the <u>phone</u>.

Different Kinds of Pronouns

The pronouns **I, he, she, we,** and **they** are used as subjects of sentences. The pronouns **me, him, her, us,** and **them** are used after action verbs. The pronouns **you** and **it** can be used anywhere in a sentence.

Morris has cheese. **He** shares it.
The pronoun *he* is the subject of the sentence.
The pronoun *it* is used after the action verb *shares.*

Morris met Doris. Morris showed **her** the cheese.
The pronoun *her* is used after the action verb *showed.*

Underline the pronoun in ( ) that can take the place of the underlined word or words.

1. "Where did you get cheese?" <u>Doris</u> asked. (<u>she</u>, they)

2. "I bought <u>the cheese</u>," Morris said. (them, <u>it</u>)

3. Morris also gave <u>Horace and Boris</u> cheese. (her, <u>them</u>)

4. <u>Horace, Boris, and Doris</u> thanked Morris. (<u>They</u>, Us)

5. "<u>My friends</u> are welcome," said Morris. (He, <u>You</u>)

Home Activity Your child learned about different kinds of pronouns. Ask your child to make up new sentences using the pronouns he or she wrote on this page.

▲ **Grammar and Writing Practice Book** p. 93

Wrap Up Your Day!

 LESSON VOCABULARY Write the following sentence. *The greatest adventure was when we climbed the mountain.* Ask children to read the sentence and identify the vocabulary words *greatest, adventure, climbed.*

 ASK QUESTIONS Recall with children the question words *who, what, when, where, why,* and *how.* Then have children recall the kinds of questions they asked themselves as they read this story, such as **Who** *are Horace, Morris, and Delores?* and **What** *was their problem?*

LET'S TALK ABOUT IT Recall *Horace and Morris but mostly Dolores.* Ask: How did these good friends solve their problem? (They built a clubhouse for boys and girls.) Encourage children to tell about a time when they had a problem with a friend and how they solved it.

PREVIEW Day 3

Tell children they will hear about Duck and his best friend, Bear.

Share Literature
Bear and Duck on the Run

Phonics and Spelling
REVIEW Silent Consonants
Spelling: Words with *ph, gh*/f/

Vocabulary
Skill Ending *-est*

Fluency
Express Characterization

Writing Trait
Focus/Ideas

Grammar
Different Kinds of Pronouns

Materials

- *Sing with Me Big Book*
- *Read Aloud Anthology*
- Student Edition 256–257

Morning Warm~Up!

**Today we will read about Bear and Duck.
Duck is Bear's greatest and truest friend.**

He makes a decision to help Bear.

Have you ever helped a friend?

QUESTION OF THE DAY Encourage children to sing "Friendship" from the *Sing with Me Big Book* as you gather. Write and read the message and discuss the question.

REVIEW LESSON VOCABULARY

- Circle the words *greatest* and *truest* in the message.
- Review with children the meaning of each word, recalling the story *Horace and Morris but mostly Dolores.*

ELL

Build Background Use the Day 3 instruction on ELL Poster 24 to support children's use of English to communicate about lesson concepts.

ELL Poster 24

Share Literature

LISTEN AND RESPOND

APPROPRIATENESS OF TITLE Recall what "Bear and Duck on the Run" is about. Ask if the title of the story is a good one and why.

BUILD ORAL VOCABULARY Review that yesterday the class listened to find out what kind of friend Duck was. Introduce the Amazing Word **advantage** and explain that it can mean "a better chance of winning." Ask that children listen today to find out who has the advantage in Bear and Duck's race.

MONITOR LISTENING COMPREHENSION

- What happens the first day Bear goes out for a run with Duck? (He only runs for three minutes. Then he stops and eats doughnuts.)

- Why does Bear tell Duck he has measles? (because Bear doesn't want to run again)

- What advantage does Duck give Bear for their race? (Duck says that he will run to the store and back two times, and Bear only has to run there and back once.)

- Why do you think Bear doesn't like running? (Possible responses: because it's hard, because he gets tired, or because he is so big)

Read Aloud Anthology
Bear and Duck on the Run

OBJECTIVES

- Evaluate appropriateness of title.
- Set purpose for listening.
- Build oral vocabulary.

Amazing Words to build oral vocabulary

	MONITOR PROGRESS
appreciate communicate respect demand firmly advantage defiant ferocious	**If...** children lack oral vocabulary experiences about the concept Responsibility, **then...** use the Oral Vocabulary Routine. See p. DI·6 to teach *advantage*.

Listen and Respond Help children understand what kind of character Bear is. Say the words *sleepy, frowned, sighed,* and *moaned.* For each word, do an action or make a sound that helps clarify the word. Then say each word and have children do the appropriate action or make the appropriate sound.

3

▲ **Practice Book 2.2** p. 88,
Silent Consonants

OBJECTIVES

- Review silent consonants *kn, wr, gn,* and *mb.*
- Build, blend, and read *kn, wr, gn, mb* words.
- Recognize lesson vocabulary.
- Spell words with digraphs *ph, gh.*

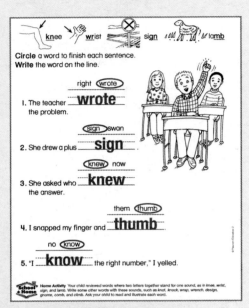

Review Phonics

REVIEW SILENT CONSONANTS

READ *kn, wr, gn, mb* WORDS Write *knee, wren, design,* and *dumb.* Look at these words. You can read these words because you know how to read words with silent consonants. What sound do the letters *kn* stand for at the beginning of a word? /n/ What sound do the letters *wr* stand for? /r/ What sound do the letters *gn* stand for? /n/ What sound do the letters *gn* stand for at the end of a word? /n/ What sound do the letters *mb* stand for? /m/ What are the words?

BUILD WORDS Write *kn, wr, gn,* and *mb* as headings on a four-column chart or use Graphic Organizer 27. Below each pair of letters write several words with those letters omitted. For example, for *know,* write ___*ow.* Have children add the missing letters to each word. Have the completed lists read.

kn	*wr*	*gn*	*mb*
know	write	gnaw	lamb
knife	wrap	gnat	climb
knock	wrong	sign	comb

Lesson Vocabulary

PRACTICE

CHANGE SENTENCES Provide children with sentences that use lesson vocabulary words. Have children read the sentences and tell whether they are true or false. Then have children change the sentences to make them mean the opposite while still using the lesson vocabulary words.

- Watching a boring play is a wonderful *adventure*. (False; Treasure-hunting is a wonderful adventure.)
- If you *climbed* a ladder you would be off the ground. (True; If you climbed a ladder you would be standing on the ground.)
- The *greatest* toy is the one you want to play with all the time. (True; The greatest toy is the one you never play with.)
- When your friend says she will tell you the *truest* thing she knows, she is going to lie to you. (False; When your friend says she will tell you the truest thing she knows, she is not going to lie to you.)
- A *clubhouse* is a good place to buy roller skates. (False; A clubhouse is a good place to meet with other people who like the same things you do.)
- When you go *exploring,* you may find and see new things. (True; When you go exploring, you won't find anything new.)
- If your sister *wondered* if she could learn to roller-skate, she wanted to find out if she could do that. (True; If your sister wondered if she could learn to roller-skate, she knew she could.)

Spelling

PRACTICE *ph, gh/f/*

WRITE AN ADVENTURE STORY Have children practice the spelling words by working together to write an adventure story that uses all the words.

- Divide children into pairs. Tell pairs to think about how Horace, Morris, and mostly Delores loved adventure. Ask pairs to think of an adventure they would like to have.
- Tell one partner to use a spelling word to write the first sentence of their story. Have the second partner write the second sentence using another spelling word. Pairs can reuse the words as needed.

HOMEWORK Spelling Practice Book, p. 95

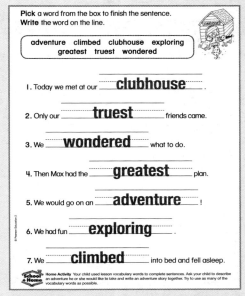

Pick a word from the box to finish the sentence. Write the word on the line.

> adventure   climbed   clubhouse   exploring
> greatest   truest   wondered

1. Today we met at our **clubhouse** .
2. Only our **truest** friends came.
3. We **wondered** what to do.
4. Then Max had the **greatest** plan.
5. We would go on an **adventure** !
6. We had fun **exploring** .
7. We **climbed** into bed and fell asleep.

Home Activity Your child used lesson vocabulary words to complete sentences. Ask your child to describe an adventure he or she would like to take and write an adventure story together. Try to use as many of the vocabulary words as possible.

▲ **Practice Book 2.2** p. 89, Lesson Vocabulary

Spelling Words

ph, gh/f/

1. **phone**	7. **graph**
2. **enough**	8. **tough**
3. **stuff**	9. **photo**
4. **laugh** *	10. **rough**
5. **puff**	11. **cough**
6. **giraffe**	12. **cliff**

Challenge Words

13. **dolphin**
14. **physical**
15. **autograph**

* **Word from the Selection**

Consonant Sound /f/

Read the poem. Circle three spelling mistakes. Write the words correctly. Find a line with a missing end mark. Add the end mark.

Spelling Words
phone   graph
enough   tough
stuff   photo
laugh   rough
puff   cough
giraffe   cliff

> I wrote this poem about the cold
> I caught from my (frend)
> A Cold
> It hurts to laugh.
> My throat feels (puf)
> I have to cough
> I've had (enouff)

Frequently Misspelled Words
different
friend

1. **friend**   2. **rough**
3. **enough**

Circle the word that is spelled correctly.

4. The _____ is ringing.	○ fone	● phone
5. I put your _____ in a box.	○ stuf	● stuff
6. That _____ of wind felt good.	● puff	○ puf
7. The _____ is eating leaves.	○ girafe	● giraffe
8. Did you get _____ to eat?	● enough	○ enouf
9. The joke made me _____.	○ lauff	● laugh
10. I need some _____ paper.	● graph	○ gragh

Home Activity Your child has been learning words with the sound of f spelled ph, gh, ff, and ffe. Ask your child to find examples of these letter combinations in the list words.

▲ **Spelling Practice Book** p. 95

Horace and Morris

OBJECTIVES

- Discuss the word ending -est.
- Use words that end in -est in sentences.

Strategic Intervention

Have children illustrate a pair of words from the lesson: a root word and that word with -est added to it.

Advanced

Point out that in order to add -est to the word *true*, we need to drop one of the e's. Give children a list of other words to which they cannot simply add the ending -est. For example, the words *friendly, big,* and *likely.* Challenge them to figure out which letters to add or drop in order to correctly add the ending -est.

ELL

Extend Language Help children practice adding -est to words. Show them that when you add -est to a word that ends in e, such as *true,* you drop one of the e's. Write a variety of words on the board to which -est can be added. Invite volunteers to come to the board to add -est to each word. Challenge them to read the word and create a sentence using it.

Vocabulary

WORD ENDING -est

DISCUSS THE WORD ENDING -est Have children recall that Horace, Morris, and Dolores were very good friends. Explain that another way to describe people who are very good friends is to say they are "best friends." The word *best* means "most good." Point out that the word *best* can help them remember that the suffix -est means "most." This ending can be added to words to change their meanings. For example, the word *quick* means "very fast." Adding the suffix -est to *quick* to make *quickest* changes its meaning to the "most fast." Ask children to list some other words to which they can add the suffix -est. Write their responses on the board. Challenge them to come up with sentences using those words.

EXPAND LESSON VOCABULARY Challenge children to find words in the story that have the -est suffix. On p. 244, they will find the words *greatest* and *truest.* Discuss what the words *great* and *true* mean. Then talk about what the suffix -est does to change the meaning of those words. Have children write a sentence using the word *truest* or *greatest.* Ask volunteers to share their sentences.

Group Time

DAY 3

On-Level

Read *Horace and Morris but mostly Dolores.*

- Use pp. 238–257.

Strategic Intervention

Read or listen to *Horace and Morris but mostly Dolores.*

- Use the **Routine** on p. DI·48.

Advanced

Read Self-Selected Reading.

- Use the **Routine** on p. DI·49.

 Place English language learners in the groups that correspond to their reading abilities in English.

(i) Independent Activities

Independent Reading See p. 234j for Reading/Library activities and suggestions.

Journal Writing Write about a time you had a disagreement with a friend. Share writing.

Literacy Centers To provide experiences with *Horace and Morris but mostly Dolores,* you may use the Writing Center on p. 234k.

Practice Book 2.2 Silent Consonants, p. 88; Lesson Vocabulary, p. 89

Break into small groups after Vocabulary and before Writing.

Fluency

EXPRESS CHARACTERIZATION

MODEL EXPRESSING CHARACTERIZATION Use *Horace and Morris but mostly Dolores.*

- Point to the three characters and the dialogue on p. 244. I see from the picture that there are at least three characters in this story. As I read the dialogue, I will give each character a slightly different voice. For example, I might read the girl's voice a little higher than the two boys' voices.

- Ask children to follow along as you read p. 244, expressing characterization.

- Have children read the page after you. Encourage them to use different voices for the characters. Continue in the same way with pp. 245–249.

REREAD FOR FLUENCY

Readers' Theater

ROUTINE

1 **Select a Passage** For *Horace and Morris but mostly Dolores,* use pp. 240–245, dividing it into equal sections for the number of groups you have.

2 **Divide into Groups** Assign each person in each group a part to read. For this story, use these parts: narrator, Horace, Morris, Dolores, other mice.

3 **Model** Have children track the print as you read.

4 **Practice and Feedback** Have children read their parts along with you and independently. Monitor progress and provide feedback. For optional fluency, children should reread three to four times.

5 **Performance** Have the groups perform a Readers' Theater. Invite another group of children to attend the performance.

Monitor Progress	Fluency
If... children have difficulty reading dialogue,	**then...** prompt: • Are those sentences inside quotation marks? • Who is speaking? • Try to read the sentences the way the animals might say them.
If... the class cannot read fluently without you,	**then...** continue to have them read along with you.

OBJECTIVE

- Read aloud fluently, expressing characterization.

Options for Oral Reading

Use *Horace and Morris but mostly Dolores* or one of the following Leveled Readers.

On-Level
You Can Make a Difference!

Strategic Intervention
What an Adventure!

Advanced
Taking Care of the Earth

Model expressing characterization by reading *Hello, Friend!* or *Horace, Morris but mostly Dolores.* Have English language learners echo your reading of each character's dialogue.

To develop fluent readers, use Fluency Coach.

Reader Response

Retelling Plan

☑ Week 1 assess Strategic Intervention students.

☑ Week 2 assess Advanced students.

☑ Week 3 assess Strategic Intervention students.

☑ **This week assess On-Level students**.

☐ Week 5 assess any students you have not yet checked during this unit.

Look Back and Write Point out information from the text that answers the question. Then have children write a response to the question. For test practice, assign a 10–15 minute time limit. For assessment, see the Scoring Rubric at the bottom of this page.

OPEN FOR DISCUSSION Model a response. If I am Dolores, things changed because Horace and Morris joined a club I could not join, and I had to make my own club so we could all go exploring together.

1. RETELL Have children use the retelling strip in the Student Edition to retell the selection.

Monitor Progress | **Check Retelling**

Have children retell *Horace and Morris*.

If... children have difficulty retelling the story,

then... use the Retelling Cards and the Scoring Rubric for Retelling on pp. 256–257 to help them move toward fluent retelling.

 SUCCESS PREDICTOR

| **Day 1** Check Word Reading | **Day 2** Check Lesson Vocabulary/High-Frequency Words | ▶**Day 3** Check Retelling | **Day 4** Check Fluency | **Day 5** Assess Progress |

2. 👁 **AUTHOR'S PURPOSE** Model a response. He might be trying to say that clubs are fair when everyone who is interested can join.

3. 👁 **ASK QUESTIONS** Model a response. I was confused about why Horace and Morris would join a club without their friend. So I asked myself why they would do that and how that might make them feel.

 LOOK BACK AND WRITE Read the writing prompt on p. 256 and model your thinking. First I'll look for sentences that are hard to say. I'll think about why they would be hard. Then I'll write my response. Have children write their responses.

Scoring Rubric | **Look Back and Write**

Top-Score Response A top-score response will find two hard-to-say sentences from the selection and use them as a model for two original sentences. **Example of a Top-Score Response** The story says, "A boy mouse must do what a boy mouse must do," and "A girl mouse must do what a girl mouse must do." My sentences are "Bring your sister to Frisky Whisker," and "Wise mice are nice mice!"

For additional rubrics, see p. WA10.

Assessment Before retelling, help children name the characters and items shown. For more ideas on assessing comprehension, see the ELL and Transition Handbook.

Reader Response

Open for Discussion Imagine that you are Horace or Morris or Dolores. Tell how things changed for you in this story.

1. Use the pictures below to retell the story. *Retell*

2. This is a funny, entertaining story. What other message do you think the author might be trying to give you? *Author's Purpose*

3. Did anything in this story confuse you? What questions did you ask yourself as you read? *Ask Questions*

Look Back and Write Find two sentences in the story that would be hard to say three times! Now write two new hard-to-say sentences for the Frisky Whisker Club.

Meet the Author and the Illustrator
James Howe and Amy Walrod

Read two more books by James Howe or illustrated by Amy Walrod.

James Howe began writing stories and plays when he was a boy. Mr. Howe has written more than 70 books about funny characters including Bunnicula and Pinky and Rex. He thinks that the best way to be a good writer is to read— and write, write, write!

Horace and Morris Join the Chorus (but what about Dolores?)

Amy Walrod's first picture book was *Horace and Morris but mostly Dolores.* Ms. Walrod collects toys, lunch boxes, cupcake ornaments, sparkly things, and stuff she finds on the ground. Can you find any of the things she likes to collect in her pictures?

The Little Red Hen Makes a Pizza

Retelling Strip

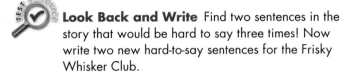

256

257

Scoring Rubric | Narrative Retelling

Rubric 4 3 2 1	4	3	2	1
Connections	Makes connections and generalizes beyond the text	Makes connections to other events, stories, or experiences	Makes a limited connection to another event, story, or experience	Makes no connection to another event, story, or experience
Author's Purpose	Elaborates on author's purpose	Tells author's purpose with some clarity	Makes some connection to author's purpose	Makes no connection to author's purpose
Characters	Describes the main character(s) and any character development	Identifies the main character(s) and gives some information about them	Inaccurately identifies some characters or gives little information about them	Inaccurately identifies the characters or gives no information about them
Setting	Describes the time and location	Identifies the time and location	Omits details of time or location	Is unable to identify time or location
Plot	Describes the events in sequence, using rich detail	Tells the plot with some errors in sequence that do not affect meaning	Tells parts of plot with gaps that affect meaning	Retelling has no sense of story

Use the Retelling Chart on p. TR20 to record retelling.

Selection Test To assess with *Horace and Morris,* use Selection Tests, pp. 93–96.

Fresh Reads for Differentiated Test Practice For weekly leveled practice, use pp. 139–144.

Retelling

SUCCESS PREDICTOR

OBJECTIVE

● Recognize and use focus/ideas in writing.

DAILY FIX-IT

5. Her didn't play to day.
   <u>She</u> didn't play <u>today</u>.

6. She has an rough coufh.
   She has <u>a</u> rough cou<u>gh</u>.

Connect to Unit Writing

Writing Trait

Have children use strategies for developing **focus/ideas** when they write a persuasive letter in the Unit Writing Workshop, pp. WA2–WA9.

Focus/Ideas Write the following sentences on sheets of paper, one to a sheet. Work with English learners to identify the sentence that doesn't belong: *Books can be about anything. Libraries have many books. We will swim after lunch. I read many books this summer.*

Writing Trait of the Week

INTRODUCE Focus/Ideas

TALK ABOUT FOCUS/IDEAS Explain to children that good writers focus on a few ideas and support them with details. All the sentences are about one of these ideas. Have them recall what *Horace and Morris but mostly Dolores* is about. Then model your thinking.

MODEL When I read *Horace and Morris but mostly Dolores*, I learn that these three characters like to explore places and have adventures. I see this idea stated on page 240. Write the sentence below and read it aloud.

Horace and Morris but mostly Dolores loved adventure.

Have volunteers read the second sentence on p. 240 and each sentence on p. 241. Ask after each sentence is read: Does this sentence focus on the idea of the three characters having adventures? *(yes)* Remember that good writers have an idea in mind as they write and produce sentences that focus on that idea.

STRATEGY FOR DEVELOPING FOCUS/IDEAS On the board, write a set of sentences in which all but one tell about the same idea. Work with children to identify and cross out the sentence that does not focus on the idea of the group having adventures.

They sailed the seven sewers.
Outside Dolores introduced herself. (cross out)
They climbed Mount Ever-Rust.
They dared to go where no mouse had gone before.

PRACTICE

APPLY THE STRATEGY Ask children to think of lessons they have learned about getting along with others. Have them write a sentence stating a main idea about a lesson, such as "It is important to share your toys with friends." Then have them add three sentences with details that focus on this idea.

Grammar

OBJECTIVE

● Use pronouns in writing.

APPLY TO WRITING Pronouns

IMPROVE WRITING WITH PRONOUNS Have children recall the names of the mice in the Frisky Whisker Club. Tell children to suppose they wanted to tell a story about Dolores. Ask what pronoun they would use when Dolores is doing something *(she)* and when something is happening *to* Dolores *(her)*. Remind children to use pronouns correctly in their own writing.

Have volunteers give a sentence that tells about something they did with a friend. Write the sentence on the board. Have children decide which pronouns should be used.

> **Bob and I** went to see **the circus.** (We, it)
>
> **Sarah** helped **Jenny and me** make popcorn. (She, us)

PRACTICE

WRITE WITH PRONOUNS Have children write a few sentences telling about something they did with a friend. Tell them to include different kinds of pronouns. Have volunteers read their sentences aloud.

Different Kinds of Pronouns

Circle the pronoun in ( ) that can take the place of the underlined word or words.

1. <u>Zack and Max</u> were cats who loved adventure. (**They**, Them)
2. They climbed <u>the tallest tree.</u> (**it**, him)
3. Only Buster the dog frightened <u>Zack and Max</u>. (they, **them**)
4. Maybe <u>Buster</u> could be a friend. (**he**, him)

Write a make-believe story about two animal friends who have an adventure. Use pronouns from the box in your story.

| I | he | she | we | they | it |
| me | him | her | us | them | you |

Possible answer:

Katie Cat liked adventure. One day Digger
Dog saw **her**. **They** went exploring under a
porch. There were old toys under **it**. **They**
had great adventures playing with **them**.

Home Activity Your child learned how to use different kinds of pronouns in writing. Ask your child to read aloud the story he or she wrote on this page and to circle the pronouns in the story.

▲ **Grammar and Writing Practice Book** p. 94

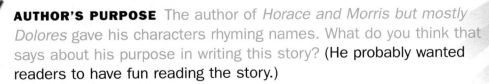

Wrap Up Your Day!

✓ **AUTHOR'S PURPOSE** The author of *Horace and Morris but mostly Dolores* gave his characters rhyming names. What do you think that says about his purpose in writing this story? (He probably wanted readers to have fun reading the story.)

✓ **FLUENCY** Do you think that when Dolores speaks she sounds like the other girls in the Cheese Puffs? (no) How do you think she sounds? (Possible response: She sounds strong and determined.) Have volunteers read p. 248 aloud, paying special attention to how Dolores speaks.

LET'S TALK ABOUT IT Ask children to discuss what it means to be a good friend. Should good friends always do things together? Is it OK for friends to join different clubs or follow different interests sometimes?

PREVIEW Day 4

Tell children that tomorrow they will read about children who play on a soccer team.

Day 4
AT A GLANCE

Share Literature
"Eat Your Vegetables"

Phonics and Spelling

ph, gh/f/
Spelling: Words with *ph, gh*/f/

Read

Group Time < Differentiated Instruction

"Good Kicking"

Fluency
Express Characterization

Writing Across the Curriculum
Math Story

Grammar
Different Kinds of Pronouns

Speaking and Listening
Contribute to Discussions

Materials

• *Sing with Me Big Book*
• *Read Aloud Anthology*
• Student Edition 258–261

Morning Warm-Up!

Today we will read a story about some young soccer players.

The photographs show that they like working and laughing together.

What do you like to do with your friends?

QUESTION OF THE DAY Encourage children to sing "Friendship" from the *Sing with Me Big Book* as you gather. Write and read the message and discuss the question.

REVIEW *ph, gh*/f/

• Read the message again and ask children to raise their hands when they hear /f/. Then ask which words have the /f/ sound in them. *(photographs, laughing)*

• Review that sometimes the /f/ spelling pattern is *ph* or *gh*.

E L L

Extend Language Use the Day 4 instruction on ELL Poster 24 to extend and enrich language.

ELL Poster 24

ORAL LANGUAGE

Share Literature

CONNECT CONCEPTS

ACTIVATE PRIOR KNOWLEDGE Recall Horace, Morris, and Dolores and Bear and Duck. Recall what good friends do for each other. Explain that children will listen to another story about friends helping each other—"Eat Your Vegetables" by James Marshall.

Read Aloud Anthology
Eat Your Vegetables

BUILD ORAL VOCABULARY Introduce the Amazing Words **defiant** and **ferocious.** Explain that if someone is being *defiant,* he or she is not doing what they're told. Tell them that *ferocious* means "wild and dangerous." Ask children to listen to find out who is defiant and who is ferocious in the story.

REVIEW ORAL VOCABULARY After reading, review all the Amazing Words for the week. Have children take turns using them in sentences that tell about the concept for the week. Then talk about Amazing Words they learned in other weeks and connect them to the concept, as well. For example, ask:

- How would you **consider** a good friend or neighbor to act?
- Name ways in which you are a **responsible** or **generous** friend.
- How does **teamwork** and **cooperation** help people to be good friends and neighbors?

MONITOR LISTENING COMPREHENSION

- What kind of animal is eating the owl's tree? (a brontosaurus)
- What kind of jaws does the brontosaurus have? (ferocious)
- What characters in the story are defiant and why? (The owl's friends are defiant because the brontosaurus is eating their friend's house.)
- What words help you imagine how the brontosaurus felt about eating birds? (Possible responses: *Ugh, disgusting, queasy, nauseated, appetite was ruined*)

OBJECTIVES

- Set purpose for listening.
- Build oral vocabulary.

Amazing Words
to build oral vocabulary

	MONITOR PROGRESS
appreciate communicate respect demand firmly advantage defiant ferocious	**If...** children lack oral vocabulary experiences about the concept Responsibility, **then...** use the Oral Vocabulary Routine. See p. DI·6 to teach *defiant* and *ferocious*.

Connect Concepts Define vegetarian for children. Tell them it is a person who does not eat meat. Name some things that a vegetarian would not eat, such as hamburgers, chicken, hotdogs, pepperoni pizza, bacon, and so on. Recall that the brontosaurus is a vegetarian, and help the class understand that he won't eat the birds because the birds are meat.

Sentence Reading

REVIEW WORDS IN CONTEXT

READ DECODABLE AND HIGH-FREQUENCY WORDS IN CONTEXT Write these sentences. Call on individuals to read a sentence. Then randomly point to words and have them read. To help you monitor word reading, high-frequency words are underlined and decodable words are circled.

I (told) Mom I shall (redo) my (graph) even though I (disagree).

Dad said (most) people at the (photo) shoot were pleasant.

I will probably (rewind) the tape so we can (replay) it.

Do you (mind) if we (remount) the sign on a (tough) new post?

A lot of coats are bought and (sold) when it is (cold).

Mom said she would be scared if she saw a (child) try to (preheat) a stove.

Monitor Progress	Word Reading
If... children are unable to read an underlined word,	**then...** read the word for them and spell it, having them echo you.
If... children are unable to read a circled word,	**then...** have them use the blending strategy they have learned for that word type.

Support Phonics For additional review, see the phonics activities in the ELL and Transition Handbook.

Spelling

PARTNER REVIEW *ph, gh/f/*

READ AND WRITE Supply pairs of children with index cards on which the spelling words have been written. Have one child read a word while the other writes it. Then have children switch roles. Have them use the cards to check their spelling.

HOMEWORK Spelling Practice Book, p. 96

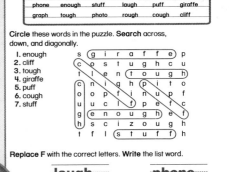

Consonant Sound /f/

Spelling Words					
phone	enough	stuff	laugh	puff	giraffe
graph	tough	photo	rough	cough	cliff

Circle these words in the puzzle. **Search** across, down, and diagonally.

1. enough
2. cliff
3. tough
4. giraffe
5. puff
6. cough
7. stuff

Replace F with the correct letters. **Write** the list word.

8. lauF   **laugh**   9. Fone   **phone**

graF   **graph**   11. rouF   **rough**

Foto   **photo**

Home Activity Your child has been learning words with the sound of *f* spelled *ph, gh, ff,* and *ffe.* Write a list word, omitting these letter combinations. Ask your child to complete the word.

▲ **Spelling Practice Book** p. 96

Group Time

On-Level	Strategic Intervention	Advanced
Read "Good Kicking." • Use pp. 258–261.	**Read** or listen to "Good Kicking." • Use the Routine on p. DI·50.	**Read** "Good Kicking." • Use the Routine on p. DI·51.

DAY 4

ELL Place English language learners in the groups that correspond to their reading abilities in English.

ⓘ Independent Activities

Fluency Reading Pair children to reread *Horace and Morris but mostly Dolores.*

Journal Writing List ways you can show fairness and respect in a club or classroom. Share writing.

Spelling Partner Review

Independent Reading See p.234j for Reading/Library activities and suggestions.

Literacy Centers To provide writing opportunities, you may use the Listening Center on p. 234j. To extend social studies concepts, you may use the Social Studies Center on p. 234k.

Break into small groups after Spelling and before Fluency.

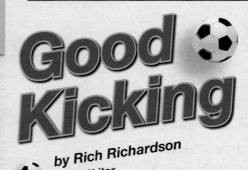

Social Studies in Reading

Newspaper Article

Genre
- Newspaper articles may cover news about the city, the nation, or the world.

Text Features
- Newspaper articles usually have catchy headlines that grab the reader's attention.
- Photographs and captions give more information.
- Quotes from a real person help the reader know that the article is true and factual.

Link to Social Studies

Find out more about famous soccer players. Make a poster to report your findings.

258

Daily Kid News   Sports   Friday, May 2   15

Good Kicking

by Rich Richardson
Staff Writer

From spring to fall, you can hear the whoops and hollers of happy children. What's happening? They are playing one of the fastest growing sports around—soccer!

Soccer is played in almost every country in the world. Boys and girls of all ages love this fast-moving sport. Soccer is played in schools and parks across America. Some towns have put together teams of children that play each other.

The small towns around Chicago have some of the best young soccer players. Some children begin playing on teams when they are as young as four or five.

These players chase down the ball.

Good kicking means good foot work.

Ask Questions What question do you have for the writer?

259

AudioText

OBJECTIVE

- Recognize text structure: nonfiction.

Read
Social Studies in Reading

PREVIEW AND PREDICT Read the title and author's name. Have children preview the article and identify what they see in the photographs. (kids playing soccer; a soccer coach) Then ask them to predict whether "Good Kicking" tells a story or provides information. Have children read to learn about the responsibilities of members of a team.

NEWSPAPER ARTICLE Review that selections about real people doing real things are called nonfiction and that newspaper articles are in this group. Point out that the photographs and captions in this article give additional information.

VOCABULARY/ENDING -est Remind children that the word part -est can be added to the end of some describing words. Tell children that the word part means "most." Call attention to the word *fastest* on p. 259. Take away the ending -est. What is the word? What does *fastest* mean?

"We want everyone to have fun," says Coach Kay of the Goalers, a team of seven-year-olds. "We have a mixed team of boys and girls. They learn to play together as they learn the rules of the game. Most importantly, they learn what it means to be a part of a team."

Trident players chase down the ball for their team.

Anyone who has ever played a team sport knows that each team member is important. Team members have a responsibility to do the best job they can. If each team member does his or her job right, the team has fun and everybody wins.

"It's always nice to win," Coach Kay states.

Two members of the Scooters congratulate each other.

 Author's Purpose Why did the writer write this article?

260

Coach Kay and members of the Goalers relax before a game. "Being part of a team is more than just winning," Coach Kay says.

"But it's also important that children have fun. Being part of a team is more than just winning. It's learning your role as a team member and knowing your responsibility to your fellow teammates. If we all work together, everybody wins."

Coach Kay should know. Her team, the Goalers, has not lost a game all season. The laughter and smiles on the children's faces also show that they have fun.

Reading Across Texts
Do you think Dolores would have liked playing soccer for the Goalers and Coach Kay?

Writing Across Texts
Write a short paragraph telling why you feel as you do.

261

BUILD CONCEPTS

⊙ Author's Purpose • Inferential
- **What is the main message the author wants to share?**
Soccer is a great way to have fun and be a part of a team.

Draw Conclusions • Critical
- **What might Coach Kay say to her team if they lost a game?**
Being a part of a team is more than just winning. It is important to have fun and learn your responsibilities to your team.

CONNECT TEXT TO TEXT

 Have children predict whether Dolores would like the game of soccer and would like to play for the Goalers and Coach Kay. If necessary, remind children that the Goalers is a mixed team of boys and girls.

 Remind children to begin their paragraphs by stating whether or not they think Dolores would like to play soccer with the Goalers. Then have them support their choice with two or three reasons.

Community Services

Time for **SOCIAL STUDIES**

Point out to children that a soccer coach is providing a service. Ask them to list other people in the community who provide a service. If needed, prompt children by asking questions, such as *Who helps people stay well? Who helps people check out books at the library?* Discuss why each service is important.

Extend Language Call attention to the words *whoops* and *hollers* on p. 259 and make sure that children understand their meanings. Elicit synonyms that children may know or supply a list, such as *yells, cheers,* and *screams.*

OBJECTIVE

● Read while expressing characterization.

Options for Oral Reading

Use *Horace and Morris but mostly Dolores,* "Good Kicking," or one of the following Leveled Readers.

On-Level

You Can Make A Difference!

Strategic Intervention

What An Adventure!

Advanced

Taking Care of the Earth

For English language learners, emphasize repeated readings to build fluency with enjoyable passages in English, with as much teacher guidance as feasible.

 **Fluency Coach CD** To develop fluent readers, use Fluency Coach.

Fluency

EXPRESS CHARACTERIZATION

MODEL EXPRESSING CHARACTERIZATION Use *Horace and Morris but mostly Dolores.*

- Point to Dolores's dialogue on p. 248. Dolores's mood changes as she speaks to the other mice in her club. I will change the tone of my voice to show these changes.

- Ask children to follow along as you change your voice to fit Dolores's tone.

- Have children read the page after you. Encourage them to express what a character is feeling. Continue in the same way with pp. 250–253.

REREAD FOR FLUENCY

Readers' Theater

ROUTINE

1 **Select a Passage** For *Horace, Morris, but mostly Dolores,* use pp. 246–255.

2 **Assign** Assign children the roles of Horace, Morris, Dolores, and narrator.

3 **Rehearse** Have children practice their assigned parts silently. For optimal fluency, encourage children to attend to punctuation marks.

4 **Provide Feedback** Suggest ways to improve fluency of reading, emphasizing grouping words.

5 **Performance** Have the groups perform a Readers' Theater. Invite another group of children to attend the performance.

Monitor Progress | Check Fluency WCPM

As children reread, monitor their progress toward their individual fluency goals. Current Goal: 82–92 words correct per minute. End-of-Year Goal: 90 words correct per minute.

If... children cannot read fluently at a rate of 82–92 words correct per minute,

then... make sure children practice with text at their independent level. Provide additional fluency practice, pairing nonfluent readers with fluent readers.

If... children already read at 90 words correct per minute,

then... they do not need to reread three to four times.

SUCCESS PREDICTOR

Day 1 Check Word Reading

Day 2 Check Lesson Vocabulary/High-Frequency Words

Day 3 Check Retelling

▶ **Day 4 Check Fluency**

Day 5 Assess Progress

Writing Across the Curriculum

WRITE Math Story

DISCUSS Ask children to name some clubs, teams, or groups they belong to. Ask questions, such as How many children are on your team? How many games do you play a season? How often do you practice? Then have children discuss ways they could use this kind of information to create math problems.

SHARE THE PEN Have children participate in creating a math story. Call on a volunteer to come up with an idea for a problem. Write the problem first as text, inviting individuals to help by writing familiar letter-sounds and adding appropriate punctuation. Ask questions, such as the following:

- How do you start a proper noun? (with a capital letter)
- How do you start a question? (with a capital letter)
- How do you end a question? (with a question mark)

Continue having individuals contribute to writing the text. When the text problem is finished, have children express the problem numerically and solve the problem.

Our Little Birds troop had six members. Now we have twice as many. How many members do we have now? 6 x 2 = 12

DAILY FIX-IT

7. Jamie and Marge has work too do.
   Jamie and Marge ha<u>ve</u> work <u>to</u> do.

8. Will They work togeter?
   Will <u>t</u>hey work tog<u>eth</u>er?

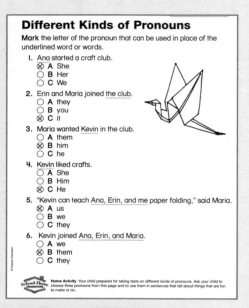

Different Kinds of Pronouns

Mark the letter of the pronoun that can be used in place of the underlined word or words.

1. Ana started a craft club.
   - ⊗ A She
   - ○ B Her
   - ○ C We

2. Erin and Maria joined the club.
   - ○ A they
   - ○ B you
   - ⊗ C it

3. Maria wanted Kevin in the club.
   - ○ A them
   - ⊗ B him
   - ○ C he

4. Kevin liked crafts.
   - ○ A She
   - ○ B Him
   - ⊗ C He

5. "Kevin can teach Ana, Erin, and me paper folding," said Maria.
   - ⊗ A us
   - ○ B we
   - ○ C they

6. Kevin joined Ana, Erin, and Maria.
   - ○ A we
   - ⊗ B them
   - ○ C they

Home Activity Your child prepared for taking tests on different kinds of pronouns. Ask your child to choose three pronouns from this page and to use them in sentences that tell about things that are fun to make or do.

▲ **Grammar and Writing Practice Book** p. 95

Grammar

REVIEW **Different Kinds of Pronouns**

DEFINE DIFFERENT KINDS OF PRONOUNS

● What is the difference between the pronouns *I* and *me*? (*I* is used as the subject of a sentence. *Me* is used after an action verb.)

● Which pronouns are used as subjects of a sentence? (*I*, *he*, *she*, *we*, and *they* are always used as subjects; *you* and *it* may be used as subjects or after an action verb.)

PRACTICE

IDENTIFY DIFFERENT KINDS OF PRONOUNS Write a list of people and things on the board. For each, have children supply the pronoun they would use as a sentence subject and the one they would use after an action verb.

Joann	**(she, her)**
Jeff and Maria	**(they, them)**
Mr. Washington	**(he, him)**
Muhammed and Joe	**(we, us)**
the person to whom you're speaking	**(you, you)**
the race	**(it, it)**

WRITE WITH DIFFERENT KINDS OF PRONOUNS Explain that when a pronoun replaces a noun, the pronoun must agree in number with the noun it replaces (its antecedent). (*Gus used* his *skateboard. Jeff and Maria hiked with* their *parents.*) *His* refers to Gus (singular) and *their* refers to Jeff and Maria (plural).

List several singular and plural nouns (both common and proper) in one column. Randomly list the pronouns that can replace them in another column. Have children write a sentence that uses a noun and its correct pronoun.

Jenny	**their**
The kittens	**her**
Chris and Pat	**his**
The boy	**their**

Speaking and Listening

CONTRIBUTE TO DISCUSSIONS

OBJECTIVES

- Speak to contribute to a discussion.
- Listen to connect experiences and ideas with those of self and others.

DEMONSTRATE SPEAKING AND LISTENING Remind children of appropriate listening and speaking behaviors for a discussion. Then ask them to think about these behaviors as you have a discussion about things club members could do to make a club run smoothly. Choose two or three volunteers to take turns in a discussion leader role.

Speakers	Active Listeners
• Take turns speaking.	• Listen respectfully to other speakers.
• Speak loudly enough to be heard.	• Ask questions to seek information, explanations, and clarification.
• Speak clearly.	
• Support your ideas with facts when you can.	• Respond constructively to ideas of others.

MAKE A LIST Have children create a list of things a group of people might want to do when they start a new club.

1. Set goals for the club.
2. Choose a leader.
3. Choose a time and place for meetings.
4. Decide who can join.
5. Decide how members will share responsibilities.

Wrap Up Your Day!

✓ **MAKING CONNECTIONS: TEXT TO TEXT** Remind children that in "Good Kicking," Coach Kay says team members have a responsibility to other team members. Members of the Cheese Puff Club aren't trying to win games. Do you think they have responsibilities to each other too? What would they be? (Children may suggest that they should respect each other, show up on time, and take part even if they don't like an activity.)

LET'S TALK ABOUT IT Remind children of the Question of the Week, *What do good friends and neighbors do?* How do you think you should act toward teammates if your team loses? How should you act toward members of the other team if you lose? If you win?

PREVIEW Day 5

Remind children that they read a story about children who play on a soccer team. Tell them that tomorrow they will read about the friends again.

Share Literature
"Eat Your Vegetables"

Phonics and Spelling
 Review *ph, gh/f/*

Lesson Vocabulary

adventure   climbed   greatest
truest   clubhouse   exploring
wondered

More Words to Know
downhearted sewer

Monitor Progress

Spelling Test: Words with
  ph, gh/f/

Group Time < Differentiated Instruction

Writing and Grammar

Trait: Focus/Ideas
Different Kinds of Pronouns

Research and Study Skills

Table

Materials

• *Sing with Me Big Book*
• *Read Aloud Anthology*
• Reproducible Pages TE 262f–262g
• Student Edition 262–263

Morning Warm~Up!

This week we read about some characters who worked hard at being good friends.

It's not always easy.
What does it mean to be a good friend or neighbor?

QUESTION OF THE DAY Encourage children to sing "Friendship" from the *Sing with Me Big Book* as you gather. Write and read the message and discuss the question.

REVIEW ORAL VOCABULARY Have children name the characters they read about during the week. Then have them say which ones

• were defiant or ferocious when they stood up for their friends
• appreciated, communicated with, or respected their friends
• acted firmly with their friends

E L L

Assess Vocabulary Use the Day 5 instruction on ELL Poster 24 to monitor children's progress with oral vocabulary.

ELL Poster 24

Share Literature

LISTEN AND RESPOND

USE PRIOR KNOWLEDGE Review that yesterday the class listened to "Eat Your Vegetables" to find out who was defiant and who was ferocious. Suggest that today the class listen to find out what owl's friends did to help her.

MONITOR LISTENING COMPREHENSION

Read Aloud Anthology
Eat Your Vegetables

- What did the owl ask her friends to do? (to stop everything and come to her house at once)

- What did her friends do when they arrived? (They sat on all the branches of the tree so the brontosaurus couldn't eat the branches.)

- Why do you think the author wrote this story? (Possible response: to show what good friends do for each other)

BUILD ORAL VOCABULARY

GENERATE DISCUSSION Recall how the owl's friends and neighbors helped save the owl's home from being eaten by the brontosaurus. Invite children to talk about ways friends or family members have helped them out of a tough situation, or ways in which they have been good friends or neighbors. Have children use some of this week's Amazing Words as they share their stories.

Monitor Progress | Check Oral Vocabulary

Remind children of the unit concept—Responsibility. Ask them to tell you about the concept using some of this week's Amazing Words: *appreciate, communicate, respect, demand, firmly, advantage, defiant,* and *ferocious.*

If... children have difficulty using the Amazing Words,

then... ask more questions about the Read Aloud selection or the concept using the Amazing Words. Note which questions children can respond to. Reteach unknown words using the Oral Vocabulary routine on p. DI·1.

SUCCESS PREDICTOR

Day 1 Check Word Reading	Day 2 Check Lesson Vocabulary/ High-Frequency Words	Day 3 Check Retelling	Day 4 Check Fluency	▶ Day 5 Check Oral Vocabulary/ Assess Progress

ELL

Extend Language Help children with words that are already superlative. Gather a group of 10 pencils. Make one pile with 2 pencils, another pile with 3 pencils, and one pile with 5 pencils. Ask children which pile has the *most* pencils. Remind them that the ending *-est* sometimes means "the most," as in "the *fullest* cup is the *most* full." Then explain that the ending *-est* doesn't need to be added to the word *most.* Do the same kind of activity with the word *best.*

Oral Vocabulary

SUCCESS PREDICTOR

OBJECTIVES

- ⊙ Review *ph* and *gh* words.
- ● Review lesson vocabulary.

ph, gh/f/

REVIEW

IDENTIFY *ph* AND *gh* WORDS Write these sentences. Have children read each one aloud. Call on individuals to name and underline the *ph* and *gh* words and identify the consonant sounds.

I heard you <u>laugh</u> while on the <u>phone</u>.

It is <u>tough</u> to say the al<u>phabet</u> backwards!

I can draw a <u>rough</u> sketch of a <u>dolphin</u>.

He took <u>enough</u> <u>photos</u> of his <u>nephew</u>.

Lesson Vocabulary

REVIEW

COMPLETE THE RHYME Write the rhyme, leaving blanks for missing words. Ask children to complete each line with one of the review words from p. 236. Then read the rhyme together.

Beth _____ to the top of the tree **(climbed)**

And sat in the _____ with me. **(clubhouse)**

We _____ what we should do. **(wondered)**

"An _____!" I said, out of the blue. **(adventure)**

So we packed a bag and went _____. **(exploring)**

Our day was the _____—not boring. **(greatest)**

That is the_____ thing I can say! **(truest)**

Access Content For additional practice with the lesson vocabulary, use the vocabulary strategies and word cards in the ELL Teaching Guide, pp. 164–165.

SPELLING TEST *ph, gh/f/*

DICTATION SENTENCES Use these sentences to assess this week's spelling words.

1. Mom says I have too much <u>stuff</u>!
2. I made a bar <u>graph</u> in class.
3. I will call you on the <u>phone</u> after school.
4. The paper feels <u>rough</u>.
5. Dad and I tell jokes and <u>laugh</u>.
6. The <u>giraffe</u> ate a leaf from the tree.
7. We saw the sun rise over the <u>cliff</u>.
8. The meat was <u>tough</u>.
9. I blew a big <u>puff</u> of air from my straw.
10. I have a <u>photo</u> of my mom.
11. I read <u>enough</u> of my book today.
12. I heard you sneeze and <u>cough</u>.

CHALLENGE WORDS

13. I went to the doctor for a <u>physical</u>.
14. I want her to sign my <u>autograph</u> book.
15. Did you see that <u>dolphin</u> in the waves?

Group Time

On-Level	Strategic Intervention	Advanced
Read Set B Sentences.	**Read** Set A Sentences and the Story	**Read** Set C Sentences.
• Use pp. 262e–262g.	• Use pp. 262e–262g.	• Use pp. 262e–262g.
	• Use the **Routine** on p. DI·52.	• Use the **Routine** on p. DI·53.

DAY 5

 Place English language learners in the groups that correspond to their reading abilities in English.

(i) Independent Activities

Fluency Reading Children reread selections at their independent level.

Journal Writing Write a paragraph about how you can show people that you respect yourself and others. Share writing.

Independent Reading See p. 234j for Reading/Library activities and suggestions.

Literacy Centers You may use the Technology Center on p. 234k to support this week's concepts and reading.

Practice Book 2.2 Table, p. 90

Break into small groups after Spelling and before Grammar and Writing.

5

ASSESS

- Decode *ph, gh/f/*.
- Read lesson vocabulary.
- Read aloud with appropriate speed and accuracy.
- Recognize the author's purpose.
- Retell a story.

Differentiated Assessment

On-Level
Set B

Strategic Intervention
Set A

Advanced
Set C

Fluency Assessment Plan

- ☑ Week 1 assess Advanced students.
- ☑ Week 2 assess Strategic Intervention students.
- ☑ Week 3 assess On-Level students.
- ☑ **This week assess Strategic Intervention students.**
- ☐ Week 5 assess any students you have not yet checked during this unit.

Set individual fluency goals for children to enable them to reach the end-of-year goal.

- Current Goal: 82–92 wcpm
- End-of-Year Goal: 90 wcpm
- **ELL** Measuring a child's oral reading speed—words per minute—provides a low-stress informal assessment of fluency. Such an assessment should not take the place of more formal measures of words correct per minute.

SENTENCE READING

ASSESS *ph, gh/f/* AND LESSON VOCABUARY Use one of the reproducible lists on p. 262f to assess children's ability to read words with *ph, gh/f/* and lesson vocabulary. Call on individuals to read two sentences aloud. Have each child in the group read different sentences. Start over with sentence one if necessary.

RECORD SCORES Use the Sentence Reading Chart for this unit on p. WA19.

Monitor Progress	*ph, gh/f/*
If… children have trouble reading *ph, gh/f/,*	**then…** use the Reteach Lessons on p. DI·67.
Lesson Vocabulary	
If… children cannot read a lesson vocabulary word,	**then…** mark the missed words on a lesson vocabulary list and send the list home for additional word reading practice or have the child practice with a fluent reader.

FLUENCY AND COMPREHENSION

ASSESS FLUENCY Take a one-minute sample of children's oral reading. See Monitoring Fluency, p. WA17. Have children read "A Dolphin, an Elephant, and a Gopher," the on-level fluency passage on p. 262g.

RECORD SCORES Record the number of words read correctly in a minute on the child's Fluency Progress Chart.

ASSESS COMPREHENSION Have the child read to the end of the passage. (If the child had difficulty with the passage, you may read it aloud.) Ask why the author wrote the story and have the child retell the passage. Use the Retelling Rubric on p. 256–257 to evaluate the child's retelling.

READ THE SENTENCES

Monitor Progress	Fluency
If… a child does not achieve the fluency goal on the timed reading,	**then…** copy the passage and send it home with the child for additional fluency practice or have the child practice with a fluent reader.
Author's Purpose	
If… a child cannot recognize the author's purpose,	**then…** use the Reteach Lesson on p. DI·67.

Set A

1. It is tough to phone home while exploring.
2. I wondered if my graph had enough rows.
3. Jake and his truest friend, Phil, always laugh.
4. Her nephew saw an elephant on his adventure.
5. The greatest dolphin was on the rough sea.
6. Ralph took a photo as I climbed the tree.

Set B

1. Which phrase tells about the tough adventure?
2. We had enough time to phone while exploring.
3. I wondered if he got the trophy for his fine photo.
4. Phil began to cough after he ran to the clubhouse.
5. The gopher quickly climbed up the rough hill.
6. Ella laughed when the dolphin made the greatest jump of the day.

Set C

1. Ben took the greatest photo of an elephant on his adventure in Africa.
2. His nephew heard laughter coming from the clubhouse in the backyard.
3. Philip saw horses drinking from a trough while exploring the countryside.
4. The bar graph showed how the numbers of dolphins have climbed into the thousands.
5. I wondered what happened to the mother of the orphaned baby gopher.
6. It was tough when his truest friend moved away, but they talk on the phone often.

Monitor Progress   *ph, gh/f/*
Lesson Vocabulary

SUCCESS PREDICTOR

A Dolphin, an Elephant, and a Gopher

Our teacher asked us to dress up like an animal   10
and give a report. I chose to be a dolphin. My   21
friend Phil wanted to be an elephant, and Ralph   30
decided to be a gopher.   35

Ralph called me on the phone and asked me   44
what sounds gophers make. I said I did not know   54
and told Ralph to read about gophers.   61

On the big day, our teacher took photos of us in   72
our animal suits. My suit was tough to make, but it   83
looked good enough. Phil's suit was really cool.   91
He used sandpaper to make the elephant skin feel   100
rough.   101

After Ralph read his report, he began to cough.   110
He coughed so much that he had to go for some   121
water.   122

After school, I asked Ralph, "Did you ever find   131
out what sounds gophers make?"   136
"No, I still do not know," he said.   144
"Well, I know one thing. Gophers sure do   152
cough a lot!" We laughed all the way home.   161

See also Assessment Handbook, p. 352 • REPRODUCIBLE PAGE

Monitor Progress | Fluency Passage

SUCCESS PREDICTOR

Write Now
Writing and Grammar

Advice

Prompt

In *Horace and Morris but mostly Dolores*, Dolores gets upset with her friends.
Think about what Dolores should do. Now write advice to her.

Writing Trait

Focus on **ideas** that respond to the prompt.

Student Model

Main idea is stated at beginning. →

Advice is stated clearly.

Writer <u>focuses</u> on one <u>idea</u>.

> Dolores, you should do things without Horace and Morris. Give them time to be together. Try to find a new friend. You will enjoy her. Then Horace and Morris will miss you. They will want you as a friend again soon.

262

Writer's Checklist

- **Focus** Are all sentences related to the prompt?
- **Organization** Could I add words such as *then* and *soon* to make order clearer?
- **Support** Does the advice clearly address the problem?
- **Conventions** Are end marks used correctly?

Grammar

Different Kinds of Pronouns

The pronouns **I, he, she, we,** and **they** are used as subjects of sentences. The pronouns **me, him, her, us,** and **them** are used after action verbs. The pronouns **you** and **it** can be used anywhere in a sentence.

Dolores loved adventure. **She** went where no mouse had gone before. There stood Mount Ever-Rust. Dolores climbed **it** quickly.

The pronoun **she** is the subject of the sentence. The pronoun **it** is used after the action verb *climbed*.

· ·

Write the pronouns in the model used as subjects. Then write the pronouns used after action verbs.

263

Writing and Grammar

LOOK AT THE PROMPT Read p. 262 aloud. Have children select and discuss key words or phrases in the prompt. *(Dolores gets upset with her friends, what Dolores should do, advice to her)*

STRATEGIES TO DEVELOP FOCUS/IDEAS Have children

- write a sentence that explains Dolores's problem.
- write as many ideas as they can about what Dolores might do and then choose their best ideas to use in their advice.
- keep their audience in mind as they are writing their advice.

See Scoring Rubric on p. WA11. **Rubric** 4 3 2 1

HINTS FOR BETTER WRITING Read p. 263 aloud. Use the checklist to help children revise their advice. Discuss the grammar lesson. (Answers: Pronouns used as subjects: *you, You, They*; Pronouns used after action verbs: *them, her, you, you*) Have children use pronouns correctly in their advice.

DAILY FIX-IT

9. My phriend call me on the phone. (<u>friend</u>, call<u>ed</u>)

10. Her made me lauff. (<u>She</u>, laugh)

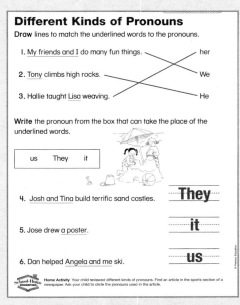

Different Kinds of Pronouns

Draw lines to match the underlined words to the pronouns.

1. My friends and I do many fun things. — her

2. Tony climbs high rocks. — We

3. Hallie taught Lisa weaving. — He

Write the pronoun from the box that can take the place of the underlined words.

| us | They | it |

4. Josh and Tina build terrific sand castles. **They**

5. Jose drew <u>a poster</u>. **it**

6. Dan helped <u>Angela and me</u> ski. **us**

Home Activity Your child reviewed different kinds of pronouns. Find an article in the sports section of a newspaper. Ask your child to circle the pronouns used in the article.

▲ **Grammar and Writing Practice Book** p. 96

Read the table. **Write** the answer to each question.

Family Chores

Person	Job
Stan	Set the table
Nate	Take out the trash
Dean	Wash the dishes
Emmy	Dry the dishes
Mom	Cook Monday–Friday
Dad	Cook Saturday–Sunday

1. What does the table show?

The table shows who does what jobs.

2. What is Nate's job?

Taking out the trash is Nate's job.

3. What is Emmy's job?

Drying the dishes is Emmy's job.

4. Who sets the table? **Stan**

5. Who cooks on the weekends? **Dad**

Home Activity Your child learned how to read a table. Work with your child to make a table of chore assignments. Ask your child to explain the table to others in the household. As household responsibilities change, ask your child to make new tables and explain them.

▲ **Practice Book 2.2** p. 90, Tables

Access Content Explain to English language learners that this kind of table is not like a table that you sit at. This kind of table is a graph that shows information in boxes. Children should start by looking at the title words at the side and across the top of the table to see what kind of information it will show.

Research/Study Skills

TEACH/MODEL Table

MODEL USING A TABLE Draw and label a simple table showing Mouse Club Members. Explain that tables are a way of giving information about a topic. The title tells what the table is about. Tables are shaped like boxes. The boxes contain words or numbers arranged in rows and columns. The words tell what information is being given. Rows go across and columns go up and down.

Model how to use a table.

MODEL I can use this table to figure out how many members each mouse club had at different times. In May, Horace and Morris and Dolores had not joined any club. If I read down, I can see that Mega Mice had 9 members and the Cheese Puffs had 12. Frisky Whiskers had no members that month.

READ TABLE Call on individuals to tell how many members each club had in June.

Mouse Club Members

	May	June	July
Mega Mice	9	7	5
Cheese Puffs	12	9	8
Frisky Whiskers	0	5	8

PRACTICE

CREATE A CLASS TABLE Help children create a 5-column, 3-row table titled *Class Birthdays*. Columns 2–5 should be labeled *Fall, Winter, Spring, Summer*. Rows 2 and 3 should be labeled *Boys* and *Girls*. Draw the table on a large sheet of paper. Then have children gather data and take turns filling in the information.

Wrap Up Your Week!

LET'S TALK ABOUT Responsibility

QUESTION OF THE WEEK Recall this week's question.

• What do good friends and neighbors do?

Display Graphic Organizer 14 or the web you drew earlier. Poll children about which of the items on the web is most important. Ask them to provide examples of general statements, such as "help each other." In other words, have them tell some way one friend might help another.

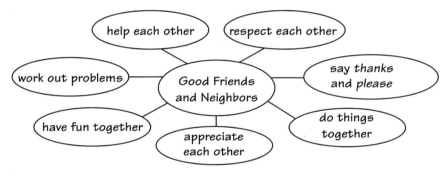

▲ **Graphic Organizer 14**

CONNECT Use questions such as these to prompt a discussion.

• How would people communicate if they did not respect and appreciate each other? How is this different from the way friends communicate?

• If you demanded that someone act a certain way, what do you think the result would be? Would that person be likely to do it or to become defiant and not do it? Give reasons for your answer.

• Why do some people have trouble apologizing for their mistakes? Why can apologizing be good?

ELL

Build Background Use ELL Poster 25 to support the Preview activity.

You've learned	You've learned
008 Amazing Words this week!	**193** Amazing Words so far this year!

PREVIEW Tell children that next week they will read about a boy who was responsible for causing all kinds of trouble.

PREVIEW Next Week

263b

Assessment Checkpoints *for the Week*

Selection Assessment

Use pp. 93–96 of Selection Tests to check:

 Selection Understanding

  Comprehension Skill *Author's Purpose*

 Selection Vocabulary
adventure
climbed
clubhouse
exploring
greatest
truest
wondered

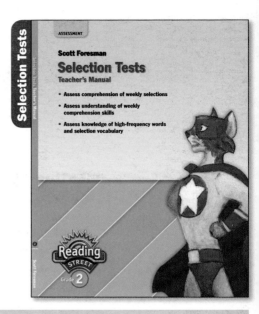

Leveled Assessment

On-Level

Strategic Intervention

Advanced

Use pp. 139–144 of Fresh Reads for Differentiated Test Practice to check:

  Comprehension Skill *Author's Purpose*

 REVIEW Comprehension Skill *Plot and Theme*

 Fluency *Words Correct Per Minute*

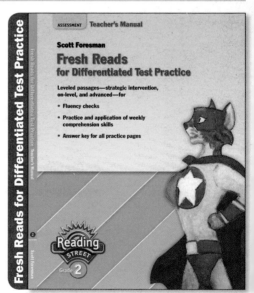

Managing Assessment

Use Assessment Handbook for:

 Weekly Assessment Blackline Masters for Monitoring Progress

 Observation Checklists

 Record-Keeping Forms

 Portfolio Assessment

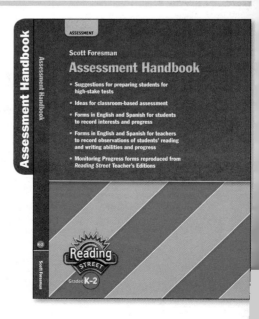

Illinois

Planning Guide for Performance Descriptors

The Signmaker's Assistant

Reading Street Teacher's Edition pages	Grade 2 English Language Arts Performance Descriptors
Oral Language Build Concepts: 264l, 266a, 284a, 286a, 290a Share Literature: 264m, 266b, 284b, 286b, 290b	**1A.Stage B.4.** Use a variety of decoding strategies (e.g., phonics, word patterns, structural analysis, context clues) to recognize new words when reading age-appropriate material. **5C.Stage B.2.** Access and use books and stories to learn something new about a topic.
Word Work **Phonics** Vowels *aw, au, augh, al*: 264n–264q, 266c–266d, 284c–284d, 286c–286d, 290c–290f **Spelling:** 264p, 266d, 284d, 286d, 290d	**1A.Stage B.1.** Use phonics to decode simple words in age-appropriate material. **3A.Stage B.5.** Use correct spelling of high frequency words. **3A.Stage B.6.** Use phonemic clues, phonetic and/or developmental spelling to spell unfamiliar words.
Reading **Comprehension** Realism and Fantasy: 264r–265, 268–283, 284g, 290e Monitor and Fix Up: 264r–265, 268–283, 284g **Vocabulary** Word Structure: 266–267 Compound Words: 266–267, 284e, 290b Suffix-*ly*: 286–287 **Fluency** Oral Reading: 264q Choral Reading: 284f Paired Reading: 289a **Self-Selected Reading:** LR37–45, TR16–17 **Literature** Genre—Humorous Fiction: 268–269 Reader Response: 284g–284h	**1A.Stage B.5.** Use letter-sound knowledge and sight vocabulary to read orally and silently/ whisper read age-appropriate material. **1B.Stage B.1.** Read fiction and non-fiction materials for specific purposes. **1C.Stage B.1.** Respond to analytical and interpretive questions based on information in text. **1C.Stage B.5.** Use self-monitoring (e.g., re-read question, confirm) to solve problems in meaning to achieve understanding of a broad range of reading materials. **2A.Stage B.5.** Distinguish between "make believe" and realistic narrative. **2B.Stage B.1.** Investigate self-selected/teacher-selected literature (e.g., picture books, nursery rhymes, fairy tales, poems, legends) from a variety of cultures.
Language Arts **Writing** Signs, Business Letter, Respond to Literature: 265a, 283a, 284g, 290–291 **Six-Trait Writing** Sentences: 285a, 290–291 **Grammar, Usage, and Mechanics** Contractions: 265b, 283b, 285b, 289c, 290–291 **Speaking/Viewing** Analyze Advertisements: 289d **Research/Study** Evaluate Online Sources: 291a	**1C.Stage B.15.** Develop familiarity with available technology (e.g., computers, copiers, cameras, interactive web sites). **3A.Stage B.6.** Use phonemic clues, phonetic and/or developmental spelling to spell unfamiliar words. **3C.Stage B.1.** Use the writing process for a variety of purposes (e.g., narration, exposition). **4A.Stage B.7.** Demonstrate the ability to listen for different purposes (e.g., entertainment, information, social interaction).
Unit Skills **Writing** Persuasive Letter: WA2–9 **Project/Wrap-Up:** 292–293	**2B.Stage B.1.** Investigate self-selected/teacher-selected literature (e.g., picture books, nursery rhymes, fairy tales, poems, legends) from a variety of cultures. **3B.Stage B.6.** Begin to evaluate and reflect on own writing and that of others.

This Week's Leveled Readers

Below-Level

Fiction

1B.Stage B.1. Read fiction and non-fiction materials for specific purposes.

2A.Stage B.5. Distinguish between "make believe" and realistic narrative.

On-Level

Fiction

1B.Stage B.6. State facts and details of text during and after reading.

2A.Stage B.5. Distinguish between "make believe" and realistic narrative.

Advanced

Fiction

1B.Stage B.9. Demonstrate creative responses to text such as dramatizations, oral presentations, or "make believe" play after reading.

2A.Stage B.5. Distinguish between "make believe" and realistic narrative.

Content-Area Illinois Performance Descriptors in This Lesson

Social Studies

14A.Stage B.1. Tell about some rules and responsibilities that students have in school to help promote order and safety.

14A.Stage B.3. Explain why schools have rules to help students learn.

14A.Stage B.5. Demonstrate examples of honesty and fairness when playing or working with other students.

14A.Stage B.6. Give an example of how governments help people live safely and fairly.

14A.Stage B.7. Identify why people need governments to help organize or protect people.

15A.Stage B.6. Match workers in the community to the goods and services they produce.

15C.Stage B.1. Explain that people who make goods and services are producers.

18B.Stage B.2. Explain how contact with others shapes peoples' lives.

Science

11A.Stage B.1. Describe observed science event: sequencing processes or steps; choosing/proposing causes or effects based on observations.

12B.Stage B.2. Apply scientific inquiries or technological designs to examine how plants and animals (including humans) survive together in their ecosystems.

Math

6A.Stage B.1. Count with understanding, including skip counting from any number by 2's and 10's.

6A.Stage B.3. Describe numeric relationships using comparison notation.

10C.Stage B.1. Identify and discuss likely, unlikely, and impossible probability events.

10C.Stage B.2. Communicate and display results of probability events in order to make predictions of future events.

Illinois!

A FAMOUS ILLINOISAN
Enrico Fermi

Enrico Fermi (1901–1954) was a physicist who was awarded the Nobel Prize in physics in 1938 for his work on nuclear processes. He produced the first nuclear chain reaction in 1942. Born in Rome, Italy, Fermi became a U.S. citizen in 1944. He was a professor of physics at the University of Chicago. Fermi National Accelerator Laboratory, or Fermilab, in Batavia, is named for him.

Children can . . .
Learn more about how scientists use common objects in innovative ways. Have them find an ordinary item, such as a sheet of paper, and construct it into shapes for different purposes; for example, paper can be made into a boat or a hat.

A SPECIAL ILLINOIS PLACE
Illinois River

The Illinois River is the largest and most important river within the state. It is part of the waterway system that connects the Great Lakes with the Gulf of Mexico. The river starts where the Kankakee and Des Plaines Rivers meet, about forty-five miles southwest of Chicago. It flows southwest and empties into the Mississippi River.

Children can . . .
Use a blue crayon or marker to trace the Illinois River on an outline map of the United States and then trace the Mississippi River with a red crayon or marker. Have them place a sticker on the map where the two rivers meet.

ILLINOIS FUN FACTS
Did You Know?

• Peoria is one of the oldest settlements in Illinois.

• Before the American Revoluton (1775–1783), missionaries, fur traders, French and British settlers, and British troops lived in the region that is present-day Illinois.

• Many of the early settlers to the area that is now Illinois built log cabins. Settlers began building homes from bricks and wood frames in the 1800s.

Children can . . .
Look at pictures of log cabins. Ask them to use craft sticks and other art materials to make a model of a log cabin with the help of an adult.

Unit 5
Responsibility

Week 5

CONCEPT QUESTION
What does it mean to be responsible?

EXPAND THE CONCEPT
What happens when we do the wrong thing?

Week 1
Why is it important to do a good job?

Week 2
Why should we take care of animals?

Week 3
How can we be responsible family members?

Week 4
What do good friends and neighbors do?

Week 5
What happens when we do the wrong thing?

CONNECT THE CONCEPT

▶ **Build Background**

apologize	interrupt	scold
citizen	judgment	troublemaker
hoard	protest	

Rules	If We Break the Rules

▶ **Social Studies Content**
Rights and Responsibilities, Laws, Goods and Services, Technology and Communication

▶ **Writing**
A Sign

Preview Your Week

What happens when we do the wrong thing?

Genre

Humorous fiction is a funny story about imaginary people and events. Look for the funny things that happen in this story.

268

THE SIGNMAKER's ASSISTANT

by Tedd Arnold

How will the signmaker's assistant fix the problems he causes?

269

Audio CD

Student Edition pages 268–285

Genre	Humorous Fiction
Phonics	Vowels *aw, au, augh, al*
Vocabulary Strategy	Word Structure
Comprehension Skill	Realism and Fantasy
Comprehension Strategy	Monitor and Fix Up

Time for **SOCIAL STUDIES**

Paired Selection

Reading Across Texts
Volunteering

Genre
Evaluating Sources

Text Features
Text Boxes

Reading Online

Evaluating Sources

Helping Hand

Student Edition pages 286–289

Audio CD

Read It
ONLINE
PearsonSuccessNet.com

- Student Edition
- Leveled Readers
- Decodable Reader

Leveled Readers

◎ **Skill** Realism and Fantasy
◎ **Strategy** Monitor and Fix Up
Lesson Vocabulary

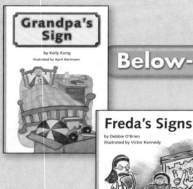

Grandpa's Sign
by Kelly Kong
illustrated by April Hartmann

Below-Level

Freda's Signs
by Debbie O'Brien
illustrated by Victor Kennedy

On-Level

Marty's Job
by Evan Allen

illustrated by Luciana Navarro Alves

Advanced

ELL Reader

- Concept Vocabulary
- Text Support
- Language Enrichment

Three Little Kittens
Learn a Lesson
by Bethany Lyons
Illustrated by Janet Skiles

Decodable Reader

Apply Phonics

- *Fun in the Summer Sun*

Decodable Reader 25
Fun in the Summer Sun
Written by Maggie Yeam
Illustrated by Cherri Britze

Phonics Skill

Time for SOCIAL STUDIES

Integrate Social Studies Standards

- Rights and Responsibilities
- Laws
- Goods and Services
- Technology/ Communication

✓ **Read**

The Signmaker's Assistant
pp. 268–285

"Helping Hand" pp. 286–289

✓ **Read**

Leveled Readers

Grandpa's Sign — Below-Level
Freda's Signs — On-Level
Marty's Job — Advanced

- Support Concepts
- Develop Concepts
- Extend Concepts
- Social Studies Extension Activity

✓ **Read**

ELL Reader

Three Little Kittens
Learn a Lesson

✓ **Build Concept Vocabulary**
Responsibility, p. 264m

✓ **Teach Social Studies Concepts**
Communication, p. 274–275
Goods and Services,
p. 280–281
Internet, p. 286–287

✓ **Explore Social Studies Center**
Make Signs, p. 264k

The Signmaker's Assistant **264c**

Weekly Plan

READING

90–120 minutes

TARGET SKILLS OF THE WEEK

Phonics
Vowels *aw, au, augh, al*

Comprehension Skill
Realism and Fantasy

Comprehension Strategy
Monitor and Fix Up

Vocabulary Strategy
Word Structure

DAY 1 PAGES 264l–265b

Oral Language

QUESTION OF THE WEEK, 264l
What happens when we do the wrong thing?

Oral Vocabulary/Share Literature, 264m
Sing with Me Big Book, Song 25
Amazing Words *apologize, citizen, judgment*

Word Work

Phonics, 264n–264o
Introduce Vowels *aw, au, augh, al* **T**

Spelling, 264p
Pretest

Comprehension/Vocabulary/Fluency

Read Decodable Reader 25

Grouping Options 264f–264g

Review High-Frequency Words
Check Comprehension
Reread for Fluency

Comprehension Skill/Strategy Lesson, 264r–265
Realism and Fantasy **T**
Monitor and Fix Up

DAY 2 PAGES 266a–283b

Oral Language

QUESTION OF THE DAY, 266a
Have you ever caused someone to be upset?

Oral Vocabulary/Share Literature, 266b
Read Aloud Anthology "The Hoot and Holler Hat Dance"
Amazing Word *hoard*

Word Work

Phonics, 266c–266d
Review Vowels *aw, au, augh, al* **T**

Spelling, 266d
Dictation

Comprehension/Vocabulary/Fluency

Build Background, 266e
Signs

Lesson Vocabulary, 266f
Introduce *afternoon, blame, idea, important, signmaker, townspeople* **T**

Vocabulary Strategy Lesson, 266–267a
Word Structure **T**

Read *The Signmaker's Assistant,* 268–283

Grouping Options 264f–264g

Realism and Fantasy **T**
Monitor and Fix Up
REVIEW Author's Purpose **T**
Reread for Fluency

LANGUAGE ARTS

20–30 minutes

Trait of the Week

Sentences

Shared Writing, 265a
Sign

Grammar, 265b
Introduce Contractions **T**

Interactive Writing, 283a
Business Letter

Grammar, 283b
Practice Contractions **T**

DAILY JOURNAL WRITING

Day 1 *Write a paragraph about a time when you had to apologize for something.*

Day 2 *Write about a time when a sign helped you know where to go.*

DAILY SOCIAL STUDIES CONNECTIONS

Day 1 Rules/Break the Rules Concept Chart, 264m

Day 2 Time for Social Studies: Communication, 274–275; Goods and Services, 280–281

DAILY SUCCESS PREDICTORS

for Adequate Yearly Progress

Monitor Progress and Corrective Feedback

Phonics Check Word Reading, *264o*
Spiral **REVIEW** Phonics

Fluency Check Lesson Vocabulary, *266f*
Spiral **REVIEW** High-Frequency Words

RESOURCES FOR THE WEEK

- Practice Book 2.2, *pp. 91–100*
- Phonics and Spelling Practice Book, *pp. 97–100*
- Grammar and Writing Practice Book, *pp. 97–100*
- Selection Test, *pp. 97–100*
- Fresh Reads for Differentiated Test Practice, *pp. 145–150*
- Phonics Songs and Rhymes Chart 25
- The Grammar and Writing Book, *pp. 194–199*

Grouping Options for Differentiated Instruction
Turn the page for the small group lesson plan.

DAY 3 PAGES 284a–285b

Oral Language

QUESTION OF THE DAY, 284a
Why do we have rules to obey?

Oral Vocabulary/Share Literature, 284b
Read Aloud Anthology "The Hoot and Holler Hat Dance"
Amazing Word *scold*

Word Work

Phonics, 284c
REVIEW *ph, gh/f/* **T**

Lesson Vocabulary, 284d
Practice *afternoon, blame, idea, important, signmaker, townspeople* **T**

Spelling, 284d
Practice

Comprehension/Vocabulary/Fluency

Vocabulary, 284e
Compound Words

Read *The Signmaker's Assistant,* 268–285

Grouping Options
264f–264g

Fluency, 284f
Read with Appropriate Phrasing

Reader Response, 284g

Trait of the Week, 285a
Introduce Sentences

Grammar, 285b
Write with Contractions **T**

Day 3 *Write a journal entry about a practical joke you played on someone.*

Day 3 Let's Talk About the Concept, 285b

DAY 4 PAGES 286a–289d

Oral Language

QUESTION OF THE DAY, 286a
How can you make a difference?

Oral Vocabulary/Share Literature, 286b
Read Aloud Anthology "Troublemaker"
Amazing Words *interrupt, protest, troublemaker*

Word Work

Phonics, 286c–286d
REVIEW Sentence Reading **T**

Spelling, 286d
Partner Review

Comprehension/Vocabulary/Fluency

Read "Helping Hand," 286–289
Leveled Readers

Grouping Options
264f–264g

Suffix *-ly*
Reading Across Texts

Fluency, 289a
Read with Appropriate Phrasing

Writing Across the Curriculum, 289b
Signs

Grammar, 289c
Review Contractions **T**

Viewing and Speaking, 289d
Analyze Advertisements

Day 4 *Write about a difficult decision you made.*

Day 4 Time for Social Studies: Internet, 286–287

DAY 5 PAGES 290a–291b

Oral Language

QUESTION OF THE DAY, 290a
What can you do when you make a mistake?

Oral Vocabulary/Share Literature, 290b
Read Aloud Anthology "Troublemaker"
Amazing Words Review

Word Work

Phonics, 290c
🎯 Review Vowels *aw, au, augh, al* **T**

Lesson Vocabulary, 290c
Review *afternoon, blame, idea, important, signmaker, townspeople* **T**

Spelling, 290d
Test

Comprehension/Vocabulary/Fluency

Read Leveled Readers

Grouping Options 264f–264g

Monitor Progress, 290e–290g
Read the Sentences
Read the Story

Writing and Grammar, 290–291
Develop Sentences
Use Contractions **T**

Research/Study Skills, 291a
Evaluate Online Sources

Day 5 *Write about an unusual sign.*

Day 5 Revisit the Rules/Break the Rules Concept Chart, 291b

KEY 🎯 = Target Skill **T** = Tested Skill

Comprehension Check Retelling, *284g*

Fluency Check Fluency wcpm, *289a*
Spiral REVIEW Phonics, High-Frequency Words

Oral Vocabulary Check Oral Vocabulary, *290b*
Assess Phonics, Lesson Vocabulary, Fluency, Comprehension, *290e*

SUCCESS PREDICTOR

Small Group Plan for Differentiated Instruction

Daily Plan AT A GLANCE

Reading
Whole Group
- Oral Language
- Word Work
- Comprehension/Vocabulary

Group Time

Meet with small groups to provide:
- Skill Support
- Reading Support
- Fluency Practice

Read

This week's lessons for daily group time can be found behind the Differentiated Instruction (DI) tab on pp. DI·54–DI·63.

Whole Group
- Comprehension/Vocabulary
- Fluency

Language Arts
- Writing
- Grammar
- Speaking/Listening/Viewing
- Research/Study Skills

Use *My Sidewalks on Reading Street* for Tier III intensive reading intervention.

DAY 1

On-Level	Strategic Intervention	Advanced
Teacher-Led *Page 264q*	**Teacher-Led** *Page DI·54*	**Teacher-Led** *Page DI·55*
• **Read** Decodable Reader 25 • **Reread** for Fluency	• Blend Words with Vowels *aw, au, augh, al* • **Read** Decodable Reader 25 • **Reread** for Fluency	• Extend Word Reading • **Read** Advanced Selection 25 • Introduce Concept Inquiry

ⓘ Independent Activities
While you meet with small groups, have the rest of the class...

- Reread for fluency
- Write in their journals
- Read self-selected reading
- Visit the Word Work Center
- Complete Practice Book 2.2, pp. 93–94

DAY 2

On-Level	Strategic Intervention	Advanced
Teacher-Led *Pages 268–283*	**Teacher-Led** *Page DI·56*	**Teacher-Led** *Page DI·57*
• **Read** *The Signmaker's Assistant* • **Reread** for Fluency	• Blend Words with Vowels *aw, au, augh, al* • **Read** SI Decodable Reader 24 • **Read** or Listen to *The Signmaker's Assistant*	• **Read** *The Signmaker's Assistant* • Continue Concept Inquiry

ⓘ Independent Activities
While you meet with small groups, have the rest of the class...

- Read self-selected reading
- Write in their journals
- Visit the Listening Center
- Complete Practice Book 2.2, pp. 95–97

DAY 3

On-Level	Strategic Intervention	Advanced
Teacher-Led *Pages 268–285*	**Teacher-Led** *Page DI·58*	**Teacher-Led** *Page DI·59*
• **Reread** *The Signmaker's Assistant*	• **Reread** *The Signmaker's Assistant* • Read Words and Sentences • Review Realism/Fantasy and Monitor and Fix Up • **Reread** for Fluency	• Self-Selected Reading • Continue Concept Inquiry

ⓘ Independent Activities
While you meet with small groups, have the rest of the class...

- Read self-selected reading
- Write in their journals
- Visit the Writing Center
- Complete Practice Book 2.2, pp. 98–99

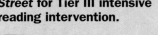

① Begin with whole class skill and strategy instruction.

② Meet with small groups to provide differentiated instruction.

③ Gather the whole class back together for fluency and language arts.

DAY 4

On-Level
Teacher-Led
Pages 286–289, LR40–LR42
- **Read** "Helping Hand"
- Practice with On-Level Reader *Freda's Signs*

Strategic Intervention
Teacher-Led
Pages DI · 60, LR37–LR39
- **Read** or Listen to "Helping Hand"
- **Reread** for Fluency
- Build Concepts
- Practice with Below-Level Reader *Grandpa's Sign*

Advanced
Teacher-Led
Pages DI · 61, LR43–LR45
- **Read** "Helping Hand"
- Extend Vocabulary
- Continue Concept Inquiry
- Practice with Advanced Reader *Marty's Job*

ⓘ Independent Activities

While you meet with small groups, have the rest of the class...

- Reread for fluency
- Write in their journals
- Read self-selected reading
- Review spelling words with a partner
- Visit the Listening and Social Studies Centers

DAY 5

On-Level
Teacher-Led
Pages 290e–290g, LR40–LR42
- Sentence Reading, Set B
- Monitor Fluency and Comprehension
- Practice with On-Level Reader *Freda's Signs*

Strategic Intervention
Teacher-Led
Pages DI · 62, LR37–LR39
- Practice Word Reading
- Sentence Reading, Set A
- Monitor Fluency and Comprehension
- Practice with Below-Level Reader *Grandpa's Sign*

Advanced
Teacher-Led
Pages DI · 63, LR43–LR45
- Sentence Reading, Set C
- Monitor Fluency and Comprehension
- Share Concept Inquiry
- Practice with Advanced Reader *Marty's Job*

ⓘ Independent Activities

While you meet with small groups, have the rest of the class...

- Reread for fluency
- Write in their journals
- Read self-selected reading
- Visit the Technology Center
- Complete Practice Book 2.2, p. 100

Grouping Place English language learners in the groups that correspond to their reading abilities in English.

Use the appropriate Leveled Reader or other text at children's instructional level.

TiP Send home the appropriate Multilingual Summary of the main selection on Day 1.

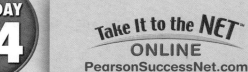

Take It to the NET™ ONLINE
PearsonSuccessNet.com

Deborah Simmons
For research on early intervention, see the article "Effective Academic Interventions . . ." by R. Good, Scott Foresman author D. Simmons, and by S. Smith

TEACHER TALK

Intervention is additional help provided for children who are struggling. It may include reduced group size, increased scaffolding, and more practice.

Be sure to schedule time for children to work on the unit inquiry project "Research Responsible Acts." This week children should present their posters to the class or other classes.

Looking Ahead

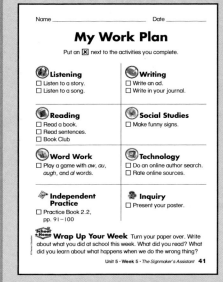

Name _____ Date _____

My Work Plan
Put an ☒ next to the activities you complete.

🎧 Listening
☐ Listen to a story.
☐ Listen to a song.

✏️ Writing
☐ Write an ad.
☐ Write in your journal.

📖 Reading
☐ Read a book.
☐ Read sentences.
☐ Book Club

🌐 Social Studies
☐ Make funny signs.

🔤 Word Work
☐ Play a game with *aw, au, augh,* and *al* words.

💻 Technology
☐ Do an online author search.
☐ Rate online sources.

✍️ Independent Practice
☐ Practice Book 2.2, pp. 91–100

🔎 Inquiry
☐ Present your poster.

Wrap Up Your Week Turn your paper over. Write about what you did at school this week. What did you read? What did you learn about what happens when we do the wrong thing?

Unit 5 · Week 5 · *The Signmaker's Assistant* **41**

▲ **Group-Time Survival Guide**
p. 41, Weekly Contract

☑ Customize Your Plan *by Strand*

Concept Development

What happens when we do the wrong thing?

 to build oral vocabulary ⭐

apologize	citizen	hoard
interrupt	judgment	protest
scold	troublemaker	

BUILD

❑ **Question of the Week** Use the Morning Warm-Up! to introduce and discuss the question of the week. This week children will talk, sing, read, and write about what happens when we do the wrong thing. DAY 1 *264l*

❑ **Sing with Me Big Book** Sing a song about what to do if you've done something wrong. Ask children to listen for the concept-related Amazing Words *apologize, citizen, judgment*. DAY 1 *264m*

Sing with Me Big Book

❑ **Build Background** Remind children of the question of the week. Then create a concept chart for children to add to throughout the week. DAY 1 *264m*

DEVELOP

❑ **Question of the Day** Use the questions in the Morning Warm-Ups! to discuss lesson concepts and how they relate to the unit theme, Responsibility. DAY 2 *266a*, DAY 3 *284a*, DAY 4 *286a*, DAY 5 *290a*

❑ **Share Literature** Read big books and read aloud selections that develop concepts, language, and vocabulary related to the lesson concept and the unit theme. Continue to develop this week's Amazing Words. DAY 2 *266b*, DAY 3 *284b*, DAY 4 *286b*, DAY 5 *290b*

CONNECT

❑ **Wrap Up Your Week!** Revisit the Question of the Week. DAY 5 *291b*

CHECK

❑ **Check Oral Vocabulary** To informally assess children's oral vocabulary, ask individuals to use some of this week's Amazing Words to tell you about the concept of the week—Responsibility. DAY 5 *290b*

🔊 **VOWELS *AW, AU, AUGH, AL*** The letters *aw*, *au*, and *a* followed by *l* or *ll* can stand for the vowel sound in *ball*, /ò/. When *au* is followed by *gh*, *au* may stand for the vowel sound in *ball*, /ò/, and the letters *gh* are silent.

TEACH

❑ **Vowels *aw, au, augh, al*** Introduce the blending strategy for words with the *aw, au, augh, al* sounds. Then have children blend and sort words under the appropriate vowel sound headings. DAY 1 *264n-264o*

❑ **Fluent Word Reading** Use the Fluent Word Reading Routine to develop children's word reading fluency. Use the Phonics Songs and Rhymes Chart for additional word reading practice. DAY 2 *266c-266d*

Phonics Songs and Rhymes Chart 25

PRACTICE/APPLY

❑ **Decodable Reader 25** Practice reading words with vowels *aw, au, augh, al* in context. DAY 1 *264q*

❑ ***The Signmaker's Assistant*** Practice decoding words in context. DAY 2 *268-283*

Decodable Reader 25

❑ **Homework** Practice Book 2.2 p. 93. DAY 1 *264o*

❑ **Word Work Center** Practice vowels *aw, au, augh, al*. ANY DAY *264j*

Main Selection—Fiction

RETEACH/REVIEW

❑ **Review** Review words with this week's phonics skills. DAY 5 *290c*

❑ **Reteach Lessons** If necessary, reteach vowels *aw, au, augh, al*. DAY 5 *Dl· 68*

❑ **Spiral REVIEW** Review previously taught phonics skills. DAY 1 *264o*, DAY 3 *284c*, DAY 4 *286c*

ASSESS

❑ **Sentence Reading** Assess children's ability to read words with vowels *aw, au, augh, al*. DAY 5 *290e-290f*

SPELLING

VOWELS AW, AU, AUGH, AL The letters *aw*, *au*, and *a* followed by *l* or *ll* can stand for the vowel sound in *ball*, /ò/. When *au* is followed by *gh*, *au* may stand for the vowel sound in *ball*, /ò/, and the letters *gh* are silent.

TEACH

❑ **Pretest** Before administering the pretest, model how to segment words with vowels, *aw, au, augh, al*. Dictate the spelling words, segmenting them if necessary. Then have children check their pretests and correct misspelled words. **DAY 1** *264p*

PRACTICE/APPLY

❑ **Dictation** Have children write dictation sentences to practice spelling words. **DAY 2** *266d*

❑ **Write Words** Have children practice writing the spelling words by writing and illustrating sentences. **DAY 3** *284d*

❑ **Homework** Phonics and Spelling Practice Book pp. 97–100. **DAY 1** *264p*, **DAY 2** *266d*, **DAY 3** *284d*, **DAY 4** *286d*

RETEACH/REVIEW

❑ **Partner Review** Have pairs work together to read and write the spelling words. **DAY 4** *286d*

ASSESS

❑ **Posttest** Use dictation sentences to give the posttest for words with vowels *aw, au, aigh, al*. **DAY 5** *290d*

Spelling Words

Vowels aw, au, augh, al

1. talk
2. because
3. August
4. caught
5. draw
6. walk
7. chalk
8. auto
9. taught
10. thaw
11. fault*
12. launch

Challenge Words

13. applause
14. awkward
15. audience

* Words from the Selection

VOCABULARY

👁 **STRATEGY WORD STRUCTURE** A compound word is made from two smaller words. Use the two words to figure out the compound word.

LESSON VOCABULARY

| afternoon | blame | idea | important |
| signmaker | townspeople | | |

TEACH

❑ **Words to Know** Introduce and discuss this week's lesson vocabulary. **DAY 2** *266f*

❑ **Vocabulary Strategy Lesson** Use the lesson in the Student Edition to introduce/model *word structure*. **DAY 2** *266-267a*

Vocabulary Strategy Lesson

PRACTICE/APPLY

❑ **Words in Context** Read the lesson vocabulary in context. **DAY 2** *268-283*, **DAY 3** *268-285*

Main Selection—Fiction

❑ **Lesson Vocabulary** Write questions and answers using lesson vocabulary words. **DAY 3** *284d*

❑ **Leveled Text** Read the lesson vocabulary in leveled text. **DAY 4** *LR37-LR45*, **DAY 5** *LR37-LR45*

Leveled Readers

❑ **Homework** Practice Book 2.2 pp. 96, 99. **DAY 2** 266f, **DAY 3** *284d*

RETEACH/REVIEW

❑ **Compound Words.** Discuss compound words. Then have children create a compound word using two or more listed words. **DAY 3** *284e*

❑ **Review** Review this week's lesson vocabulary words. **DAY 5** *290c*

ASSESS

❑ **Selection Test** Use the Selection Test to determine children's understanding of the lesson vocabulary words. **DAY 3**

❑ **Sentence Reading** Assess children's ability to read this week's lesson vocabulary words. **DAY 5** *290e-290f*

HIGH-FREQUENCY WORDS

RETEACH/REVIEW

❑ **Spiral REVIEW** Review previously taught high-frequency words. **DAY 2** 266f, **DAY 4** *286c*

COMPREHENSION

🎯 **SKILL REALISM AND FANTASY** A realistic story tells about something that could happen in real life. A fantasy is a story that could not happen in real life.

🎯 **STRATEGY MONITOR AND FIX UP** To monitor means to stop occasionally and check to be sure you understand what you are reading. Fix up means to do something if you do not understand or are confused about what you are reading. For example, ask yourself *who, what, where* questions while reading to make sure you understand.

TEACH

❑ **Skill/Strategy Lesson** Use the skill/strategy lesson in the Student Edition to introduce *realism and fantasy* and *monitor and fix up*. DAY 1 *264r-265*

Skill/Strategy Lesson

PRACTICE/APPLY

❑ **Skills and Strategies in Context** Read *The Signmaker's Assistant*, using the Guiding Comprehension questions to apply *realism and fantasy* and *monitor and fix up*. DAY 2 *268-283*

Main Selection—Fiction

❑ **Reader Response** Use the questions on Student Edition p. 284 to discuss the selection. DAY 3 *284g-285*

❑ **Skills and Strategies in Context** Read "Helping Hand," guiding children as they apply skills and strategies. DAY 4 *286-289*

Paired Selection— Nonfiction

❑ **Leveled Text** Apply *realism and fantasy* and *monitor and fix up* to read leveled text. DAY 4 *LR37-LR45*, DAY 5 *LR37-LR45*

Leveled Readers

❑ **Homework** Practice Book 2.2 pp. 94, 95. DAY 1 *264-265*, DAY 2 *266e*

ASSESS

❑ **Selection Test** Determine children's understanding of the main selection and assess their ability to recognize *realism and fantasy*. DAY 3

❑ **Story Reading** Have children read the passage "Sausages to Go." Ask questions that require them to use *realism and fantasy*. Then have them retell. DAY 5 *290e-290g*

RETEACH/REVIEW

❑ **Reteach Lesson** If necessary, reteach *realism and fantasy*. DAY 5 *DI· 68*

FLUENCY

SKILL READ WITH APPROPRIATE PHRASING Appropriate phrasing means pausing at the right places when you read. Punctuation marks, such as commas and periods, signal the right places to pause.

REREAD FOR FLUENCY

❑ **Oral Rereading** Have children read orally from Decodable Reader 25 or another text at their independent reading level. Listen as children read and provide corrective feedback regarding their oral reading and their use of the blending strategy. DAY 1 *264q*

❑ **Paired Reading** Have pairs of children read orally from the main selection or another text at their independent reading level. Listen as children read and provide corrective feedback regarding oral reading and their use of the blending strategy. DAY 2 *282-283*

TEACH

❑ **Model** Use passages from *The Signmaker's Assistant* to model reading with appropriate phrasing. DAY 3 *284f*, DAY 4 *289a*

PRACTICE/APPLY

❑ **Choral Reading** Have groups choral read parts from *The Signmaker's Assistant*. Monitor progress and provide feedback regarding children's phrasing. DAY 3 *284f*

❑ **Paired Reading** Have partners read passages from "Helping Hand," switching who reads first at the beginning of each page. Monitor progress and provide feedback regarding children's phrasing. DAY 4 *289a*

❑ **Listening Center** Have children follow along with the AudioText for this week's selections. ANY DAY *264j*

❑ **Reading/Library Center** Have children build fluency by rereading Leveled Readers, Decodable Readers, or other text at their independent level. ANY DAY *264j*

❑ **Fluency Coach** Have children use Fluency Coach to listen to fluent reading or to practice reading on their own. ANY DAY

ASSESS

❑ **Story Reading** Take a one-minute timed sample of children's oral reading. Use the passage "Sausages to Go." DAY 5 *290e-290g*

❶ Use assessment data to determine your instructional focus.

❷ Preview this week's instruction by strand.

❸ Choose instructional activities that meet the needs of your classroom.

WRITING

Trait of the Week

SENTENCES Sentences should make sense. A mix of short and long sentences creates rhythm and style.

TEACH

☐ **Write Together** Engage children in writing activities that develop language, grammar, and writing skills. Include independent writing as an extension of group writing activities.

> **Shared Writing** DAY 1 *265a*
> **Interactive Writing** DAY 2 *283a*
> **Writing Across the Curriculum** DAY 4 *289b*

☐ **Trait of the Week** Introduce and model *sentences*. DAY 3 *285a*

PRACTICE/APPLY

☐ **Write Now** Examine the model on Student Edition pp. 290–291. Then have children write signs. DAY 5 *290-291*

Write Now

> **Prompt** In *The Signmaker's Assistant*, the signmaker put important messages on his signs. Think about important messages you want to tell people. Now write two messages on signs.

☐ **Daily Journal Writing** Have children write about concepts and literature in their journals. **EVERY DAY** *264d-264e*

☐ **Writing Center** Write an ad for a new assistant. **ANY DAY** *264k*

ASSESS

☐ **Scoring Rubric** Use a rubric to evaluate signs. DAY 5 *290-291*

RETEACH/REVIEW

☐ **The Grammar and Writing Book** Use pp. 194–199 of The Grammar and Writing Book to extend instruction. **ANY DAY**

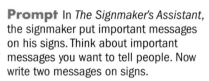
The Grammar and Writing Book

SPEAKING AND VIEWING

TEACH

☐ **Analyze Advertisements** Demonstrate how to analyze advertisements. Have children analyze advertisements they have seen, heard, or read. DAY 4 *289d*

GRAMMAR

SKILL CONTRACTIONS A contraction is a short way to put two words together. An apostrophe (') takes the place of one or more letters.

TEACH

☐ **Grammar Transparency 25** Use Grammar Transparency 25 to teach *contractions*. DAY 1 *265b*

Grammar Transparency 25

PRACTICE/APPLY

☐ **Develop the Concept** Review the concept of *contractions* and provide guided practice. DAY 2 *283b*

☐ **Apply to Writing** Have children use contractions in writing. DAY 3 *285b*

☐ **Define/Practice** Review *contractions*. Then have children fill in blanks using contractions. DAY 4 *289c*

☐ **Write Now** Discuss the grammar lesson on Student Edition p. 291. Have children use contractions in important messages. DAY 5 *290-291*

Write Now

☐ **Daily Fix-It** Have children find and correct errors in grammar, spelling, and punctuation. DAY 1 *265b*, DAY 2 *283b*, DAY 3 *285a*, DAY 4 *289c*, DAY 5 *290-291*

☐ **Homework** The Grammar and Writing Practice Book pp. 97–100. DAY 2 *283b*, DAY 3 *285b*, DAY 4 *289c*, DAY 5 *290-291*

RETEACH/REVIEW

☐ **The Grammar and Writing Book** Use pp. 194–197 of The Grammar and Writing Book to extend instruction. **ANY DAY**

The Grammar and Writing Book

RESEARCH/INQUIRY

TEACH

☐ **Evaluate Online Sources** Model evaluating an online source. Have children compare and evaluate two Web sites. DAY 5 *291a*

☐ **Unit Inquiry** Have children present their posters. **ANY DAY** *153*

Resources for
Differentiated Instruction

LEVELED READERS

▶ **Comprehension**
- ⦿ **Skill** Realism and Fantasy
- ⦿ **Strategy** Monitor/Fix Up

▶ **Lesson Vocabulary**
- ⦿ Word Structure

idea	important
blame	signmaker
townspeople	afternoon

▶ **Social Studies Standards**
- **Rights and Responsibilities**
- **Laws**
- **Goods and Services**
- **Technology/Communication**

ONLINE
PearsonSuccessNet.com

Use the Online Database of over 600 books to
- Download and print additional copies of this week's leveled readers
- Listen to the readers being read online
- Search for more titles focused on this week's skills, topic, and content

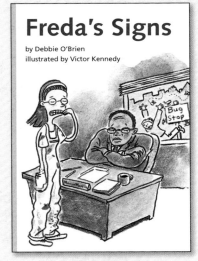

Freda's Signs
by Debbie O'Brien
illustrated by Victor Kennedy

On-Level Reader

Realism and Fantasy
Read the list of the things that happened in the story. Think about if they could or could not have happened. Then, circle the answer.

What Happened
1. The people of Midvale needed new signs.
(could)   could not have happened
2. Freda made mistakes on the signs.
(could)   could not have happened
3. The ants lined up at the sign.
could   (could not have happened)
4. The dogs talked about the sign.
could   (could not have happened)

Possible response given.
5. Think about the things that happened in the story. Write a sentence that tells if the story is a realistic story or a fantasy and why. What are the fantasy parts of this story?

This is a fantasy because dogs
do not talk.

⦿ **On-Level Practice** TE p. LR41

Vocabulary
Read the words in the first column below.
Then read the words in the second column.
Draw lines to connect the words and make compound words found in the story.

1. sign — c. maker
2. towns — a. people
3. after — b. noon

4. Write a sentence with the word *blame*. Possible responses given.
The townspeople did not blame
Freda for her mistake.

5. Write a sentence with the words *idea* and *important*.
People listen when you have
an important idea.

On-Level Practice TE p. LR42

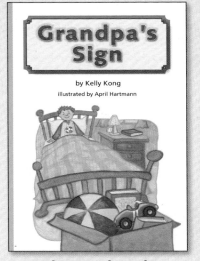

Grandpa's Sign
by Kelly Kong
illustrated by April Hartmann

Below-Level Reader

Realism and Fantasy
Read each question below. Then circle your answer.
1. Are there things in the story that could not really happen?
yes   (no)
2. Is there magic in the story?
yes   (no)
3. Could things in the story really happen?
(yes)   no
4. Do the people in the story do and say things like people I know?
(yes)   no

Possible response given.
5. Write one sentence that tells if the story *Grandpa's Sign* is a realistic story or fantasy. Tell how you know.

This is a realistic story because
it could really happen.

⦿ **Below-Level Practice** TE p. LR38

Vocabulary
Draw a line to match the word parts and make words from the story.

1. idea — a. maker
2. impor — b. tant
3. sign — c. noon
4. towns — d. people
5. after — e. s

6. Write a sentence with the word *blame*. Possible response given.
Andrew blamed himself for not
telling about the sign.

Below-Level Practice TE p. LR39

Advanced

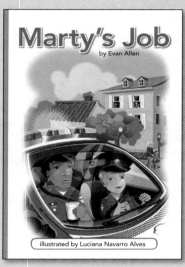

Marty's Job
by Evan Allen

illustrated by Luciana Navarro Alves

Advanced Reader

Realism and Fantasy

Read the list of the things that happened in the story. Think about if they could or could not have happened. Then, circle the answer.

What Happened
1. Marty Apple wanted a job.
   (could)   could not have happened

2. Marty got a job as a firefighter.
   could   (could not have happened)

3. Marty got a job as a police officer.
   could   (could not have happened)

4. Marty promises not to forget about his chores at home.
   (could)   could not have happened

   Possible response given.
5. Answer the question below.
   What are the fantasy parts of this story?

   The fantasy parts of the story
   are when Marty imagines
   himself as a firefighter or a
   police officer.

Advanced Practice TE p. LR44

Vocabulary

Words can be broken into two parts. Find the word ending that was added to the base word to make the vocabulary word. Write the answer on the line.

1. judge + **ment** = judgment

2. neglect + **ing** = neglecting

3. responsible + **ity** = responsibility

4. apology + **ize** = apologize

Possible response given.
5. Write a sentence with the words *citizen* and *volunteering*.

   Every volunteering citizen will
   get an award.

Advanced Practice TE p. LR45

Three Little Kittens Learn a Lesson
by Bethany Lyons
Illustrated by Janet Skiles

ELL Reader

ELL Poster 25

Teacher's Edition Notes

ELL notes throughout this lesson support instruction and reference additional resources at point of use.

ELL Teaching Guide pp. 169–175, 260–261

- Multilingual summaries of the main selection
- Comprehension lesson
- Vocabulary strategies and word cards
- ELL Reader 25 lesson

ELL and Transition Handbook

Ten Important Sentences

- Key ideas from every selection in the Student Edition
- Activities to build sentence power

More Reading

Readers' Theater Anthology
- Fluency practice
- Five scripts to build fluency
- Poetry for oral interpretation

Leveled Trade Books

- Extend reading tied to the unit concept
- Lessons in Trade Book Library Teaching Guide

School + Home

Homework
- Family Times Newsletter
- ELL Multilingual Selection Summaries

Take-Home Books
- Decodable Readers
- Leveled Readers

Literacy Centers

Listening

Let's Read
Along

MATERIALS `SINGLES`
CD player, headphones, print copies of recorded pieces

LISTEN TO LITERATURE As children listen to the following recordings, have them follow along or read along in the print version.

AudioText
The Signmaker's Assistant
"Helping Hand"

Sing with Me/Background Building Audio
"Best Judgment"

Phonics Songs and Rhymes Audio
"Tall Paul"

Tall Paul

Tall Paul thinks he is clever.
He plays small tricks to a fault.
Oh, he is so naughty
  and doesn't see
That his awful jokes
  make us so unhappy.

Oh, Tall Paul,
  please think it over.
If you pause and stop
  all these pranks,
We'll applaud you and
  call out your name
To give you thanks.

LUNCHROOM
Free Cake Today!

Audio CD **Phonics Songs and Rhymes Chart 25**

Reading/Library

Read It
Again!

MATERIALS `SINGLES` `PAIRS` `GROUPS`
collection of books for self-selected reading, reading logs

REREAD BOOKS Have children select previously read books from the appropriate book box and record titles of books they read in their logs. Use these previously read books:

- **Decodable Readers**
- **Leveled Readers**
- **ELL Readers**
- **Stories written by classmates**
- **Book from the library**

TEN IMPORTANT SENTENCES Have children read the Ten Important Sentences for *The Signmaker's Assistant* and locate the sentences in the Student Edition.

BOOK CLUB Use p. 285 of the Student Edition to set up an "Author Study" of Tedd Arnold. Encourage a group to share favorites.

Classroom Library

Word Work

Neighborhood
Walk

MATERIALS `PAIRS` `GROUPS`
neighborhood game board, number cube, game markers

VOWELS *aw, au, augh, al* Have two to four children play a game using words with vowels *aw, au, augh,* and *al.*

1. **Make a neighborhood game board that has spaces along a curved path. On each space, write a word. Write words with target vowels in red. Write short *a* words in blue.**
2. **Children take turns rolling the number cube and moving the appropriate number of spaces.**
3. **Children read the word on their space. If the word is red, they roll again. If the word is blue, they wait for their next turn.**
4. **Play continues until everyone has reached home.**

This interactive CD provides additional practice.

Scott Foresman Reading Street Centers Survival Kit

Use *The Signmaker's Assistant* materials
from the Reading Street Centers Survival Kit
to organize this week's centers.

Writing

Social Studies

Technology

Wanted: Signmaker

MATERIALS | **PAIRS**
paper, pencils

WRITE AN AD Recall that Norman was a signmaker's assistant who played tricks on people.

1. Ask partners to discuss qualities the signmaker might look for in a new assistant.
2. Have them write an ad for a new assistant.
3. Then have them share their ads with classmates.

LEVELED WRITING Encourage children to write at their own ability level. Some will write a simple ad with some attention to mechanics and spelling. Your better writers will write a clear, concise ad with greater detail and more attention to mechanics and spelling.

Wanted!

Honest assistant to help signmaker paint important signs. No jokers wanted.

Funny SIGNS

MATERIALS | **PAIRS**
cut-up posterboard, markers

MAKE SIGNS Children create funny signs.

1. Have pairs discuss funny signs they would like to see in their homes, classroom, or neighborhood.
2. Have children create their own signs.
3. Then partners can display their signs around the classroom.

Eat dessert first!

Wear your pjs to school.

Evaluating Sources

MATERIALS | **PAIRS**
computer with Internet access, paper, pencils

EVALUATE A WEB SITE Have pairs of children decide if a Web site is reliable.

1. Have children turn the computer on and open a search engine.
2. Ask pairs to search for information about one of the unit authors: Angela Royston, Hazel Hutchins, Barbara Abercrombie, James Howe, or Tedd Arnold.
3. When children find a Web site with information, they should decide if it is a good source of information. Have them explain why or why not.

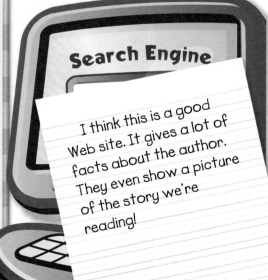

Search Engine

I think this is a good Web site. It gives a lot of facts about the author. They even show a picture of the story we're reading!

ALL CENTERS

Oral Vocabulary
"Best Judgment" 25

Phonics
Vowels *aw, au, augh, al*

Spelling Pretest:
Words with Vowels *aw, au, augh, al*

Read Apply Phonics **Word Wall**

Group Time < Differentiated Instruction

Listening Comprehension
Skill Realism and Fantasy
Strategy Monitor and Fix Up

Shared Writing
Sign

Grammar
Contractions

Materials

- *Sing with Me Big Book*
- Sound-Spelling Card 4
- Letter Tiles
- Decodable Reader 25
- Student Edition 264–265
- Graphic Organizer 25
- Skill Transparency 25
- Writing Transparency 25
- Grammar Transparency 25

Take It to the NET
ONLINE
Professional Development
To learn more about reading aloud, go to PearsonSuccessNet.com and read the article "Reading Aloud to Bulid Comprehension" by J. Gold and A. Gibson.

Morning Warm-Up!

We are taught to do the right thing. Sometimes it's hard though. What happens when we do the wrong thing?

QUESTION OF THE WEEK Tell children they will talk, sing, read, and write about what happens when we do the wrong thing. Write and read the message and discuss the question.

CONNECT CONCEPTS Ask questions to connect to other Unit 5 selections.

- What wrong thing did Horace and Morris do? What happened because of what they did?

- The Goalers like playing soccer. What happens when you do the wrong thing in a game or a sport?

REVIEW HIGH-FREQUENCY WORDS

- Circle the high-frequency words *taught* and *though* in the message.

- Have volunteers write the words on the board, and then have the whole class say the words together.

Build Background Use the Day 1 instruction on ELL Poster 25 to assess knowledge and develop concepts.

ELL Poster 25

Oral Vocabulary

SHARE LITERATURE Display p. 25 of the *Sing with Me Big Book*. Tell children that the class is going to sing a song about what to do if you've done something wrong. Ask the class to listen for the Amazing Words **apologize, citizen,** and **judgment** as you sing. Then ask for volunteers to use the Amazing Words to describe what's happening in the picture. Sing the song again, encouraging the class to sing along.

**Sing with Me/
Background Building Audio**

BUILD BACKGROUND Remind children of the question of the week.

- What happens when we do the wrong thing?

Draw a T-chart or use Graphic Organizer 25. Head the left column Rules and the right column If We Break the Rules. Ask children to suggest rules from home, the classroom, and the community to fill in the left column. Then ask them to describe what happens when each of these rules is broken. Display the chart for use throughout the week.

- What are some rules we have to follow in our neighborhood? (crossing the street at the light, not littering)
- What happens when we don't follow the rules? (we could get hurt, we could upset our neighbors)

Rules	**If We Break the Rules**

Best Judgment

We all try to use our best judgment.
Each citizen tries to be good.
But all of us make mistakes sometimes,
And don't do the things that we should.

When that happens,
Be responsible and be wise.
Tell what you did,
And then apologize.

Sing with Me Big Book

Amazing Words to build oral vocabulary

MONITOR PROGRESS

apologize
citizen
judgment
hoard
scold
interrupt
protest
troublemaker

If... children lack oral vocabulary experiences about the concept Responsibility.

then... use the Oral Vocabulary Routine below to teach *apologize*.

Oral Vocabulary ROUTINE

1. **Introduce the Word** Relate the word *apologize* to the song. Supply a child-friendly definition. Have children say the word. Example: When you say you are sorry for something, you apologize.

2. **Demonstrate** Provide an example to show meaning. She will apologize to her mom for not putting her toys away.

3. **Apply** Have children demonstrate their understanding. Which would you most likely *apologize* for—saying something mean or feeding the dog?

4. **Display the Word/Word Parts** Write the word on a card. Display it. Run your hand under the word parts in a-pol-o-gize as you read the word. See p. DI·7 to teach *citizen* and *judgment*.

Build Oral Vocabulary Help children understand the word *mistake*. Point out that the last line of the first verse helps explain what mistakes are. Encourage them to give examples.

Signmaker's Assistant **264m**

OBJECTIVES

- Associate the sound /ȯ/ with the *aw, au, augh, al* spelling patterns.
- Blend, read, and build *aw, au, augh,* and *al* words.

Skills Trace

Vowels *aw, au, augh, al*

Introduce/Teach	TE: 2.5 264n–o
Practice	TE: 2.5 264q, 266c–d; PB: 2.2 93, 108; DR25
Reteach/Review	TE: 2.5 290c, DI·68; 2.6 314c
Assess/Test	TE: 2.5 290e–g

Generalizations

Vowels *aw, au, augh, al* The letters *au, aw,* and *a* followed by *l* or *ll* can stand for the vowel sound in *ball,* /ȯ/.

When *au* is followed by *gh, au* may stand for the vowel sound in *ball,* /ȯ/, and the letters *gh* are silent.

Strategic Intervention

Use **Monitor Progress,** p. 264o, during Group Time after children have had more practice with vowels *aw, au, augh, al.*

Advanced

Use **Monitor Progress,** p. 264o, as a preassessment to determine whether this group of children would benefit from this instruction on vowels *aw, au, augh,* and *al.*

Support Phonics English language learners may need help with *augh* words such as *caught* and *taught,* in which the *gh* digraph is silent. Have them practice these words along with *au* words such as *auto* and *sauce.*

See the Phonics Transition Lessons in the ELL and Transition Handbook.

Vowels *aw, au, augh, al*

TEACH/MODEL

Blending Strategy

ROUTINE

1 **Connect** Write *saw.* What do you know about reading this word? (The letters *aw* stand for the sound /ȯ/) Today we will study the different spellings that stand for the sound /ȯ/.

2 **Use Sound-Spelling Card** Display Card 4. This is *audience.* The letters *au* stand for the vowel sound /ȯ/. Say it with me: /ȯ/. The letters *aw, augh,* and *al* also stand for the vowel sound /ȯ/

au

Sound-Spelling Card 4

3 **Model** Write *caught.* The letters *augh* stand for the vowel sound /ȯ/ in *caught.* Listen as I blend this word. Blend the sounds across the word in a continuous flow. Let's blend this word together: /cȯt/, *caught.* Repeat steps 2 and 3 with *salt, sauce,* and *yawn.*

4 **Group Practice** Continue blending sounds across the word with *paw, chalk, vault, taught, crawl, talk.*

5 **Review** What do you know about reading these words? The letters *aw, au, augh,* and· *al* can all stand for the sound /ȯ/.

c a u g h t

s a l t

s a u c e

y a w n

BLEND WORDS

INDIVIDUALS BLEND *aw, au, augh,* AND *al* WORDS Call on individuals to blend *fault, ball, fawn, talk, bald, cause, naughty.* Have them tell what they know about each word before reading it. For feedback, refer to step five of the Blending Strategy Routine.

SORT WORDS

INDIVIDUALS SORT *aw, au, augh,* AND *al* WORDS Distribute word cards for *aw, au, augh,* and *al* words. Write *aw, au, augh,* and *al* as headings. Have children read their words and place their word cards under the appropriate heading. Then have individuals read the words under each heading. Provide feedback if necessary.

aw	*au*	*augh*	*al*
awful	fault	taught	scald
lawn	haul	naughty	palm
hawk	pause	caught	always

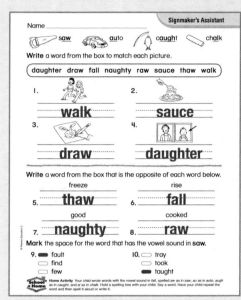

▲ **Practice Book 2.2** p. 93, Vowels *aw, au, augh, al*

Monitor Progress Check Word Reading Vowels *aw, au, augh, al*

Write the following words and have individuals read them.

auto	taught	sauce	jaunt	daughter
malt	bawl	raw	waltz	awful
rail	today	walk	applaud	main

If... children cannot blend words with *aw, au, augh,* and *al* at this point,

then... continue to monitor their progress using other instructional opportunities during the week so that they can be successful with the Day 5 Assessment. See the Skills Trace on p. 264n.

SUCCESS PREDICTOR

Spiral REVIEW

● Row 3 reviews long *a: ai, ay.*

▶ **Day 1 Check Word Reading**	**Day 2** Check Lesson Vocabulary/High-Frequency Words	**Day 3** Check Retelling	**Day 4** Check Fluency	**Day 5** Assess Progress

SUCCESS PREDICTOR

OBJECTIVES

- Segment sounds to spell words.
- Spell words with vowels *aw*, *au*, *augh*, *al*.

Spelling Words

Vowels *aw*, *au*, *augh*, *al*

1. talk
2. because
3. August
4. caught
5. draw
6. walk
7. chalk
8. auto
9. taught
10. thaw
11. fault*
12. launch

Challenge Words

13. applause
14. audience
15. awkward

* Words from the Selection

Vowel Sound in *fall*

Generalization The vowel sound in *fall* can be spelled *aw*, *au*, *augh*, and *al*: *draw*, *auto*, *caught*, and *talk*.

Sort the words by *aw*, *au*, *augh*, and *al*.

aw		augh	
1. draw		8. caught	
2. thaw		9. taught	
au		**al**	
3. because		10. talk	
4. August		11. walk	
5. auto		12. chalk	
6. fault			
7. launch			

Spelling Words
1. talk
2. because
3. August
4. caught
5. draw
6. walk
7. chalk
8. auto
9. taught
10. thaw
11. fault
12. launch
Challenge Words
13. applause
14. audience
15. awkward

Challenge Words

aw		au	
13. awkward		14. applause	
		15. audience	

School + Home Home Activity Your child is learning words with the vowel sound in fall spelled aw, au, augh, and al. To practice at home, have your child say the word, study the spelling of the vowel sound, and then write the word.

▲ **Spelling Practice Book** p. 97

Support Spelling Before giving the spelling pretest, clarify the meaning of each spelling word with examples, such as pointing to or writing with a piece or chalk for *chalk*, and demonstrating the meaning of *auto* by holding up a picture of a car.

Spelling

PRETEST VOWELS *aw*, *au*, *augh*, *al*

MODEL WRITING FOR SOUNDS Each spelling word has a vowel sound /ò/. Before administering the spelling pretest, model how to segment *aw*, *au*, *augh*, and *al* words to spell them.

- What sounds do you hear in *fraud*? (/f /r/ /ò/ /d/)
- What are the letters for /fr/? Write *fr.* Continue with the *f/f/*, *r/r/*, and *d/d/*.
- What letters stand for /o/? There are so many ways to spell /o/, that we have to learn the correct spelling of /o/ for each word. In *fraud*, /o/ is spelled *au*.
- What is the letter for /d/?
- Repeat with *fawn, caught, salt*.

PRETEST Dictate the spelling words. Segment the words for children if necessary. Have children check their pretests and correct misspelled words.

HOMEWORK Spelling Practice Book, p. 97

Justice Ruth Bader Ginsburg

Being on a jury is part of being a citizen. The people on a jury sit in a special area of a court room. They listen to people talk about something that happened and decide if a person is innocent or guilty of committing a crime. They pass judgment.

The person in charge of the court room is a judge. The judge makes sure everyone in the court room obeys the rules. Ruth Bader Ginsburg is a judge, but she is a very special kind of judge. She is a Supreme Court judge. The Supreme Court

Group Time

DAY 1

On-Level	Strategic Intervention	Advanced
Read Decodable Reader 25.	**Read** Decodable Reader 25.	**Read** Advanced Selection 25.
• Use p. 264q.	• Use the **Routine** on p. DI•54.	• Use the **Routine** on p. DI•55.

(E)(L)(L) Place English language learners in the groups that correspond to their reading abilities in English.

ⓘ Independent Activities

Fluency Reading Pair children to reread Leveled Readers or the ELL Reader from the previous week or other text at children's independent level.

Journal Writing Write a paragraph about a time when you had to apologize to someone. Share writing.

Independent Reading See p. 264j for Reading/Library activities and suggestions.

Literacy Centers To practice vowels *aw*, *au*, *augh*, *al*, you may use Word Work, p. 264j.

Practice Book 2.2 Vowels *aw*, *au*, *augh*, *al*, p. 93; Realism and Fantasy, p. 94

Break into small groups after Spelling and before the Comprehension lesson.

Apply Phonics

PRACTICE Vowels *aw, au, augh, al*

HIGH-FREQUENCY WORDS Review *again, because,* and *through.*

READ DECODABLE READER 25

• Pages 74–75 Read aloud quietly with the group.

• Pages 76–77 Have the group read aloud without you.

• Pages 78–80 Select individuals to read aloud.

CHECK COMPREHENSION AND DECODING Have children retell the story to include characters, setting, and plot. Then have children locate *aw, au, augh,* and *al* words in the story. Review *aw, au, augh,* and *al* spelling patterns. Sort words according to their spelling patterns.

aw	au	augh	al
thaw	August	caught	all
	launch		always
			baseball
			fall
			falls
			taller
			walk

HOMEWORK Take-Home Decodable Reader 25

REREAD FOR FLUENCY

Oral Rereading

ROUTINE

1 Read Have children read the entire book orally.

2 Reread To achieve optimal fluency, children should reread three or four times.

3 Provide Feedback Listen as children read and provide corrective feedback regarding their oral reading and their use of the blending strategy.

Monitor Progress

Decoding

If... children have difficulty decoding a word,	then... prompt them to blend the word.
	• What is the new word? • Is the new word a word you know? • Does it make sense in the story?

Access Content

Beginning Preview the story *Fun in the Summer Sun,* identifying and naming fun things in the pictures and print, such as *baseball* and *fishing.*

Intermediate Preview *Fun in the Summer Sun* and provide synonyms for unfamiliar words, such as *send off* and *melt* for *launch* and *thaw.*

Advanced After reading *Fun in the Summer Sun,* have partners take turns telling each other what they like to do in the summer for fun.

Skills Trace

🕙 Realism and Fantasy

Introduce/Teach	TE: 2.1 129a–b, 130e; 2.2 191a–b, 192e; 2.5 264r, 264–265
Practice	TE: 2.1 134–135; 2.2 196–197; 2.5 280–281; PB: 2.1 44–45, 64–65; 2.2 94–95
Reteach/Review	TE: 2.1 78–79, DI·68; 2.2 240–241, 266–267, DI·65; 2.5 DI·68; PB: 2.1 27, 77, 87
Test	TE: 2.1 156e–g; 2.2 216e–g; 2.5 290e–g; Selection Tests: 2.1 17–20; 2.2 29-32; Benchmark Test: Units 1, 2

One Fine Afternoon

What a boring day! Alex's good friend was sick. His other good friend had gone away on a trip. Alex missed his friends. He went into his room and closed the door.

His dog Rags sat on the rug and thumped his tail. Dancer the cat watched Alex sit on his bed and sigh.

"Bored?" Rags asked.

"What?" Alex's eyes grew big as he looked at his dog.

"He asked if you are bored?" Dancer repeated.

"You—you can talk!"

"Of course," Rags said.

"Always could," Dancer told Alex. "You just never listened."

Alex was a little surprised to hear his pets speak like people. He asked softly, "So, you think maybe we could all play?"

"Thought you'd never ask!" Rags said and carried a ball over to Alex. "Let's play!"

> **Strategy** Ask yourself, "Do I understand what's going on?" If not, read on. See if things begin to make sense.

> **Skill** Is this real? Can pets really talk to you like people do?

Unit 5 The Signmaker's Assistant · Skill Transparency 25

▲ **Skill Transparency 25**

Access Content

Beginning/Intermediate For a Picture It! lesson on realism and fantasy, see the ELL Teaching Guide, pp. 169–170.

Advanced Before children read "One Fine Afternoon" make sure they know the meanings of *thumped, sigh,* and *bored*.

🕙 Realism and Fantasy
🕙 Monitor and Fix Up

TEACH/MODEL

INTRODUCE Recall *Horace and Morris but mostly Dolores*. Have students tell what kinds of animals the characters are and some of the things they do. (Possible response: The characters are mice. They joined clubs for boy mice and girl mice before making their own club that included both.)

- Can animals really talk and join clubs? Could this story really happen?

Read p. 264 with children. Explain the following:

- A realistic story tells about something that could really happen. In a realistic story, people are like people I know. They say and do things like real people.

- A fantasy is make-believe. In a fantasy, animals might talk. Impossible things might happen.

- We can keep track of how well we understand a story by stopping when something doesn't make sense. Then we can "fix" what we don't understand by changing how we read or by asking questions.

Use Skill Transparency 25 to teach realism and fantasy and monitor and fix-up.

SKILL Use the first half of the selection to model distinguishing realism and fantasy.

 MODEL When Rags asked, "Bored?" I was surprised. I know animals can't talk. Then Dancer talked. I know this story is fantasy because this couldn't really happen.

STRATEGY Continue with the second half of the selection to model using fix-up strategies.

 MODEL I am a little confused because Alex is a real boy. So how can his pets talk? I want to make sure I understand. I will reread part of the story to make sure I have it right. **Reread paragraphs 3-6 aloud.** Yes, the animals do talk. I will read on to see if I can learn more about why they talk and what happens.

Comprehension

Skill
Realism
and Fantasy

Strategy
Monitor
and Fix Up

Realism and Fantasy

- A realistic story tells about things that could happen.
- A fantasy is a story that tells about things that could never happen.

What's Real	What's Not

Strategy: Monitor and Fix Up

Active readers make sure they understand what they are reading. If during reading you do not understand what's happening, go back and reread part of the story. Did you find something that makes the story clearer? Then read on.

Write to Read

1. Read "One Fine Afternoon." Make a graphic organizer like the one above. Write what is real and what is not.

2. As you read, write questions about what is happening in the story. Answer those questions by rereading or by reading on.

264

One Fine Afternoon

What a boring day! Alex's good friend was sick. His other good friend had gone away on a trip. Alex missed his friends. He went into his room and closed the door.

His dog Rags sat on the rug and thumped his tail. Dancer the cat watched Alex sit on his bed and sigh.

"Bored?" Rags asked.

"What?" Alex's eyes grew big as he looked at his dog.

"He asked if you are bored," Dancer repeated.

"You—you can talk!"

"Of course," Rags said.

"Always could," Dancer told Alex. "You just never listened."

Alex was a little surprised to hear his pets speak like people. He asked softly, "So, you think maybe we could all play?"

"Thought you'd never ask!" Rags said and carried a ball over to Alex. "Let's play!"

Strategy Ask yourself, "Do I understand what's going on?" If not, read on. See if things begin to make sense.

Skill Is this real? Can pets really talk to you like people do?

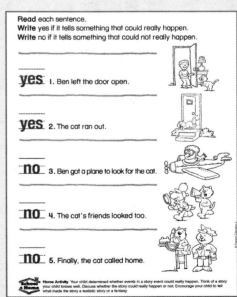

265

WRITE Work with children to fill in the boxes in the Write activity. Have children use the completed graphic organizer to decide whether the story is realism or fantasy.

Monitor Progress	**Realism and Fantasy**
If... children are unable to complete **Write** on p. 264,	**then...** use Practice Book 2.2, p. 94, for additional practice.

CONNECT TO READING Encourage children to ask themselves these questions when they read.

- Do I stop to check that I understand what I am reading?
- Do I look at illustrations to find clues about what is happening?
- Do I go back and reread if I do not understand what is happening?

Read each sentence.
Write yes if it tells something that could really happen.
Write no if it tells something that could not really happen.

yes 1. Ben left the door open.

yes 2. The cat ran out.

no 3. Ben got a plane to look for the cat.

no 4. The cat's friends looked too.

no 5. Finally, the cat called home.

Home Activity Your child determined whether events in a story event could really happen. Think of a story your child knows well. Discuss whether the story could really happen or not. Encourage your child to tell what made the story a realistic story or a fantasy.

▲ **Practice Book 2.2** p. 94, Realism and Fantasy

Shared Writing

WRITE Sign

GENERATE IDEAS Ask children to imagine they can put a message on a highway billboard. What advice would they give to people? What could they say to persuade people to follow their advice?

WRITE A DESCRIPTION Explain that the class will write a sign that tries to persuade people to do something that the class thinks is important.

 COMPREHENSION SKILL Have children think about a realistic message for a highway billboard.

- Display Writing Transparency 25 and read the title.
- Read the first prompt.
- As children give suggestions for completing the prompt; record their responses.

HANDWRITING While writing, model the letter forms as shown on pp. TR14–17.

READ THE SIGN Have children read the completed sign aloud as you track the print.

Read This!

Possible answer:
Here is some good advice.

You should **listen to your kids** because **you need to know what they are thinking.**

Unit 5 The Signmaker's Assistant   Writing Model **25**

▲ **Writing Transparency 25**

INDEPENDENT WRITING

WRITE A SIGN Have children write their own sign that might persuade people to believe something that could not be real. Encourage them to use words from the Word Wall and the Amazing Words board. Let children illustrate their writing. You may gather children's work to display on a classroom bulletin board.

ADDITIONAL PRACTICE For additional practice, use pp. 194–199 in the Grammar and Writing Book.

OBJECTIVE

● Write a sign.

DAILY FIX-IT

1. I have a foto of a dolfin.
I have a photo of a dolphin.

2. it was tuff to take a picture.
It was tough to take a picture.

This week's practice sentences appear on Daily Fix-It Transparency 25.

Strategic Intervention

Children who are not able to write independently may design a sign and add labels to it to explain their message.

Advanced

Have children write a sign that advertises something they feel is really important to their class-mates' lives, such as a homework helpline.

ELL

Support Writing Before writing a sign that tries to persuade others to believe in something that is not real, have children work in pairs to tell each other what they are planning to write about.

▲ **The Grammar and Writing Book**
For more instruction and practice, use pp. 194–199.

Grammar

TEACH/MODEL Contractions

REVIEW CONTRACTIONS Recall with children that a contraction is a short way to put two words together.

IDENTIFY CONTRACTIONS Display Grammar Transparency 25. Read the definition aloud.

- *Do not* can be shortened into one word, or a contraction. An apostrophe will take the place of the letter *o* in the word *not*.
- Many contractions like *don't* are formed with verbs and the word *not*.

Continue modeling with items 2–6.

PRACTICE

SUBSTITUTING WITH CONTRACTIONS Have children shorten words into contractions.

- What contraction can be made from the words *we will?*
- What two words make up the contraction *he's?*
- What contraction can be made from the words *they are?*

 VOWELS aw, au, augh, al Write *draw* and ask children what letters together represent the vowel sound. (*aw*) Have children name other words that are spelled with the *aw* vowel pattern.

 SPELLING VOWELS aw, au, augh, al Have children name the letters for each sound in *fault*. Write the letters as children write them in the air. Continue with *thaw* and *launch*.

 REALISM/FANTASY To help children recognize that some things in stories could happen while other things could not, ask: Could the pets in "One Fine Afternoon" really have a conversation with Alex? Could they really play? Why or why not?

LET'S TALK ABOUT IT Recall that in a fantasy some strange things could happen. What do you think could happen if Alex and his pets did the wrong thing and played a real ballgame in his room? (They would probably break windows and lamps, knock over furniture and books, and make a real mess of things.)

 HOMEWORK Send home this week's Family Times newsletter.

PREVIEW Day 2

Tell children that tomorrow the class will read about a signmaker's assistant and how he helps out or doesn't help out.

Day 2
AT A GLANCE

Share Literature
The Hoot and Holler Hat Dance

Phonics and Spelling

Vowels *aw, au, augh, al*
Spelling: Words with Vowels *aw, au, augh, al*

Build Background
Purpose of Signs

Lesson Vocabulary
*idea   important   blame
signmaker   townspeople
afternoon*
More Words to Know
assistant   wisdom   feverishly

Vocabulary
Skill Compound Words
Strategy Word Structure

Read

Group Time < Differentiated Instruction

The Signmaker's Assistant

Interactive Writing
Business Letter

Grammar
Contractions

Materials

- *Sing with Me Big Book*
- *Read Aloud Anthology*
- Phonics Songs and Rhymes Chart 25
- Background Building Audio
- Graphic Organizer 14
- Student Edition 266–283
- Tested Word Cards

Morning Warm-Up!

Today we will read all about Norman.

Norman makes an awful mistake and causes everybody to get upset.

Have you ever caused someone to be upset?

QUESTION OF THE DAY Encourage children to sing "Best Judgment" from the *Sing with Me Big Book* as you gather. Write and read the message and discuss the question.

REVIEW VOWEL SOUNDS

- Read the message again. Have children raise their hands when they hear a word with the sound /ȯ/. (*all, awful, causes, caused*)

- Have the class say each of the /ȯ/ words aloud. Then ask children what letters in each word make the /ȯ/ sound. (*a followed by l (l), aw, au*)

Build Background Use the Day 2 instruction on ELL Poster 25 to preview high-frequency words.

ELL Poster 25

Share Literature

BUILD CONCEPTS

FOLK TALE Point out the subtitle of "The Hoot and Holler Hat Dance." (a folk tale from Ghana) Tell children that Ghana is a country in Africa. Explain that a folk tale is a story that has been told for many, many years, and that it often explains why something in nature is the way it is.

BUILD ORAL VOCABULARY Introduce the Amazing Word **hoard,** and tell children that it means "to save and store away." Suggest that as you read, children listen to find out what kind of character Anansi is.

MONITOR LISTENING COMPREHENSION

- What words would you use to describe Anansi? (Possible responses: lazy, greedy, hungry)

- How do you know Anansi is greedy? (Possible responses: He hoards everything in sight, and he eats spoonful after spoonful of Mama's bean stew.)

- Why do you think the author wrote this story? (Possible responses: to explain why spiders hide, to tell the reader not to be greedy)

Read Aloud Anthology
The Hoot and Holler Hat Dance

OBJECTIVES

- Identify purpose of a folktale.
- Set purpose for listening.
- Build oral vocabulary.

Amazing Words to build oral vocabulary

	MONITOR PROGRESS
apologize citizen judgment hoard scold interrupt protest troublemaker	**If...** children lack oral vocabulary experiences about the concept Responsibility, **then...** use the Oral Vocabulary Routine. See p. DI·7 to teach *hoard*.

Build Concepts Explain the concept of harvest time to children. Tell them that people who plant fruit or vegetable seeds in the spring have to *harvest* their crops in the fall. This means they go into the fields and pick the fruit or vegetables they planted. If they don't harvest, the crops will go bad and won't be useful. Ask children what Anansi is picking (*corn*) and what he's putting it in (*basket*).

Vowels *aw, au, augh, al*

TEACH/MODEL

Fluent Word Reading

ROUTINE

1 **Connect** Write *daughter.* You can read this word because you know how to read words with the /ȯ/ sound. What sound does augh make? (/ȯ/) What's the word? *(daughter)* Do the same with *awful, salty,* and *haunt.*

2 **Model** When you come to new word, look at the letters from left to right and think about the vowel sounds. Say the sounds in the word to yourself and then read the word. **Model reading *almost, law, sausage, haughty.*** When you come to a new word, what are you going to do?

3 **Group Practice** Write *slaughter, laundry, walnut, squawk.* Read these words. Look at the letters in each word, think about the vowel sounds, say the sounds to yourself, and then read the word aloud together. Allow 2–3 seconds previewing time.

WORD READING

PHONICS SONGS AND RHYMES CHART 25 Frame each of the following words on Phonics Songs and Rhymes Chart 25. Call on individuals to read them. Guide children in previewing.

awful	**fault**	**tall**	**small**	**pause**
all	**naughty**	**Paul**	**call**	**applaud**

Sing "Tall Paul" to the tune of "Take Me Out to the Ball Game," or play the CD. Have children follow along on the chart as they sing. Then have individuals take turns circling *aw, au, augh,* and *al* words on the chart.

 **Phonics Songs and Rhymes Audio**

Phonics Songs and Rhymes Chart 25

SORT WORDS

INDIVIDUALS SORT *aw, au, augh,* **and** *al* **Words** Write the four /ȯ/ spelling patterns as heads for four columns. Have individuals write /ȯ/ words from the Phonics Chart under the appropriate headings and circle the letters that stand for the /ȯ/ sound. Have children complete the activity on paper. Ask individuals to read the words. Provide feedback as necessary.

aw	*au*	*augh*	*al*
awful	author	caught	bald
gnaw	haul	naughty	waltz
scrawl	because	daughter	false

Spelling

PRACTICE Vowels *aw, au, augh, al*

WRITE DICTATION SENTENCES Have children write these sentences. Repeat words slowly, allowing children to hear each sound. Children may use the Word Wall to help with spelling high-frequency words. **Word Wall**

> **In August I like to draw on the walk with chalk.**
> **I like Ann because she likes to talk.**
> **Do not launch the toy near the auto!**
> **I caught the football the way Dad taught me.**

HOMEWORK Spelling Practice Book, p. 98

HOMEWORK Spelling Practice Book, p. 98

Spelling Words

Vowels aw, au, augh, al

1. **talk**		7. **chalk**
2. **because**		8. **auto**
3. **August**		9. **taught**
4. **caught**		10. **thaw**
5. **draw**		11. **fault***
6. **walk**		12. **launch**

Challenge Words

13. **applause**
14. **audience**
15. **awkward**

* Words from the Selection

Vowel Sound in *fall*

Spelling Words					
talk	because	August	caught	draw	walk
chalk	auto	taught	thaw	fault	launch

Read the word. **Write** a related list word.

1. blackboard: **chalk** 2. mouth: **talk**
3. teach: **taught** 4. road: **auto**
5. month: **August** 6. artist: **draw**
7. path: **walk** 8. warm: **thaw**

Write the missing list words.

9. Let's **launch** the boat!
10. It was his **fault** that we missed the bus.
11. I am happy **because** I won the game.
12. She **caught** three fish.

Home Activity Your child wrote words with the vowel sound in fall spelled aw, au, augh, and al. Ask your child how all the list words are the same. (All have the vowel sound found in fall; all have an a in combination with other letters.)

▲ **Spelling Practice Book** p. 98

Build Background

DISCUSS THE PURPOSE OF SIGNS Display or draw pictures of familiar signs. Show a stop sign, a sale sign, or signs around your school. Initiate discussion by asking children what other signs they have seen.

● What signs do you see at school or on your way to school?
● How are these signs helpful?

BACKGROUND BUILDING AUDIO Have children listen to the CD and share the new information they learned about the purpose of signs.

**Sing with Me
Background Building Audio**

COMPLETE A WEB Draw a web or display Graphic Organizer 14 and add circles to the radiating arms. Write *Purpose of Signs* in the center circle. Ask children to suggest the purposes of signs they see and write their responses in the other circles.

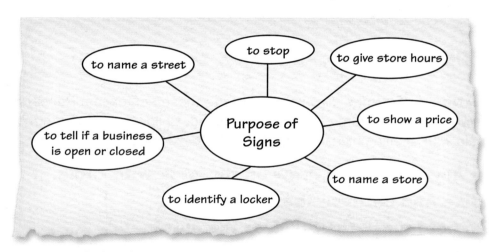

▲ **Graphic Organizer 14**

CONNECT TO SELECTION Connect background information to *The Signmaker's Assistant.*

Signs are important. They help us know where we are, what the rules are, and what to do. In this story, Norman helps a signmaker make signs. Let's find out what happens when the signmaker goes away overnight and Norman uses bad judgment and makes his own signs.

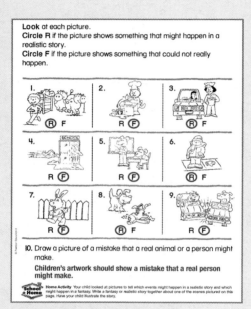

Look at each picture.
Circle R if the picture shows something that might happen in a realistic story.
Circle F if the picture shows something that could not really happen.

10. Draw a picture of a mistake that a real animal or a person might make.

Children's artwork should show a mistake that a real person might make.

 **Home Activity** Your child looked at pictures to tell which events might happen in a realistic story and which might happen in a fantasy. Write a fantasy or realistic story together about one of the scenes pictured on this page. Have your child illustrate the story.

▲ **Practice Book 2.2** p. 95,
Realism and Fantasy

ELL

Activate Prior Knowledge Show students pictures of important signs. Read the signs with them and discuss the meaning of the words.

Vocabulary

LESSON VOCABULARY

DISCUSS THE VOCABULARY Share the lesson vocabulary with children. Have them locate each word in their glossaries and note each word's pronunciation and meaning.

WORDS TO KNOW

T **idea** thought or opinion

T **important** taken seriously

T **blame** to say that something is someone's fault

T **signmaker** someone who makes signs or public notices that give information

T **townspeople** people who live in a town

T **afternoon** the time of day between noon and night

MORE WORDS TO KNOW

assistant someone who helps someone else do a job

wisdom knowledge based on experience

feverishly done with great excitement or activity

T = Tested Word

- Children should be able to decode all words except *feverishly*. To read *feverishly*, divide the word into syllables. *(fe/ver/ish/ly)*. Tell children that this word has two suffixes, *ish* and *ly*. Have children blend the syllables with you.

- Ask children to show the meanings of the words. Use questions, such as *What is an example of an idea? What is an example of something important? What is an example of something a signmaker makes?*

Pick a word from the box to match each clue.
Write the letters of the word on the blanks.
The boxed letters spell two words.

| afternoon   blame   idea   important |
| signmaker   townspeople |

1. between lunch and dinner   a f <u>t</u> e r n o o n

2. having great meaning   i m p <u>o</u> r t a n t

3. those who live in the city   t <u>o</u> w n s p e o p l e

4. to hold at fault   <u>b</u> l a m e

5. one who makes signs   s i g n m <u>a</u> k e r

6. what you think up   i <u>d</u> e a

What can you say if something goes wrong?
HINT: Find the words hidden in the boxes above.

___ **too** ___ **bad**

School + Home Home Activity Your child used word clues to identify vocabulary words. Challenge your child to use some of this week's vocabulary words to make up a story about something that goes wrong. Work with your child to write the story. Then ask your child to read it aloud to you.

▲ **Practice Book 2.2** p. 96, Lesson Vocabulary

Monitor Progress | Check Lesson Vocabulary

Point to the following words and have individuals read them.

idea	important	blame	signmaker	townspeople
afternoon	tomorrow	couldn't	door	sign
sorry	school	work	watch(ed)	

If... children cannot read these words,

then... have them practice in pairs with word cards before reading the selection. Monitor their fluency with these words during reading, and provide additional practice opportunities before the Day 5 Assessment.

SUCCESS PREDICTOR

Spiral REVIEW

- Reviews previously taught high-frequency words and lesson vocabulary.

Day 1 Check Word Reading

▶ **Day 2** Check Lesson Vocabulary/High-Frequency Words

Day 3 Check Retelling

Day 4 Check Fluency

Day 5 Assess Progress

Word Reading

SUCCESS PREDICTOR

2

Student Pages 266–267

Words to Know

signmaker

townspeople

afternoon

blame

important

idea

Remember

Try the strategy. Then, if you need more help, use your glossary or a dictionary.

Vocabulary Strategy
for Compound Words

Word Structure When you are reading, you may come to a long word. Do you see two small words in it? Then it could be a compound word. You may be able to use the two small words to help you figure out the meaning of the compound word. For example, a *mailbox* is a box in which we put our mail.

1. Divide the compound word into its two small words.

2. Think of the meaning of each small word. Put the two meanings together. Does this help you understand the meaning of the compound word?

3. Try the meaning in the sentence. Does it make sense?

Read "Sigmund's Sign." Use the meanings of the small words in a compound word to help you understand its meaning.

266

Sigmund's Sign

Sigmund was a signmaker. Every shop, every building, and every house in the town had one of Sigmund's signs. The signs told what was sold in the shop (Toys) or who worked in the building (Police) or who lived in the house (The Guntersons). The signs were very useful. They helped the townspeople find their way around the town.

But Sigmund thought that signs could do much more than that. One afternoon a large sign appeared in the town square. It said, "Don't blame them." People stopped to read the sign. Then they talked to one another about the sign. They wondered what the sign meant. They thought about their own actions. Had they blamed someone? Had they been unfair?

Sitting in his signmaking shop, Sigmund smiled. He knew that a sign could do more than help people find their way around. A sign could make people think about an important idea. Sigmund began to paint another large sign.

Words to Write

What sign do you think Sigmund painted next? Write about it. Use words from the Words to Know list.

267

OBJECTIVE

● Use the smaller words in a compound word to determine its meaning.

Access Content Use ELL Poster 25 and reinforce the words with the vocabulary activities and word cards in the ELL Teaching Guide, pp. 171–172. Choose from the following to meet children's language proficiency levels.

Beginning If children are unfamiliar with the words *signmaker, townspeople,* and *afternoon,* break each word into the two smaller words and help children define the smaller words.

Intermediate Point out to Spanish speakers that *important* and *ideas* have Spanish cognates: *importante* and *ideas.*

Advanced Teach the lesson on pp. 266–267. Children can say the words for *afternoon, blame, important,* and *ideas* in their home languages.

Vocabulary Strategy

TEACH/MODEL Word Structure

CONNECT Remind children of strategies to use when they come across words they don't understand.

● Sometimes we can get the meaning from word parts. We may understand the base word and prefix *(untie, the opposite of tie)* or suffixes. *(happily, in a happy way)*

● We can look for the shorter words in a compound. Today we will learn more about compounds.

266–267 Responsibility • Week 5

INTRODUCE THE STRATEGY

- Read and discuss the steps for figuring out the meanings of compound words on p. 266.

- Have children read "Sigmund's Sign," paying attention to the two smaller words in each highlighted compound word.

- Model figuring out the meaning of unfamiliar compound words using the word *signmaker*.

 Think Aloud

MODEL The word *signmaker* is a compound word. If I say it slowly, I can hear the two words *sign* and *maker*. I know a *sign* is something that tells me information, and *maker* is someone who makes things. So a *signmaker* must be someone who makes signs.

PRACTICE

- Have children determine the meanings of highlighted words in "Sigmund's Sign" and explain how they used the two small words in each compound word to figure out the meanings.

- Point out that sometimes the meanings of the smaller words, such as those in *butterfly*, do not help with meaning.

WRITE Children's writing should include lesson vocabulary in a description of what sign Sigmund painted next.

CONNECT TO READING Encourage children to use these strategies to determine the meaning of an unknown word.

- Look for the two or more words in a compound word.

- Use endings added to base words.

- Use the glossary or a dictionary.

Group Time

On-Level	Strategic Intervention	Advanced
Read *The Signmaker's Assistant.*	**Read** SI Decodable Reader 25.	**Read** *The Signmaker's Assistant.*
• Use pp. 268–283.	• Read or listen to *The Signmaker's Assistant.*	• Use the Routine on p. DI•57.
	• Use the Routine on p. DI•56.	

 ELL Place English language learners in the groups that correspond to their reading abilities in English.

(i) Independent Activities

Independent Reading See p. 264j for Reading/Library activities and suggestions.

Journal Writing Write about a time when a sign helped you know where to go. Share writing.

Literacy Centers To provide experiences with *The Signmaker's Assistant,* you may use the Listening Center on p. 264j.

Practice Book 2.2 Realism and Fantasy, p. 95; Lesson Vocabulary, p. 96; Author's Purpose, p. 97

DAY 2

Break into small groups after Vocabulary and before Writing.

2

THE SIGNMAKER'S ASSISTANT
by Tedd Arnold

Genre

Humorous fiction is a funny story about imaginary people and events. Look for the funny things that happen in this story.

268

How will the signmaker's assistant fix the problems he causes?

269

AudioText

Read
Prereading Strategies

PREVIEW AND PREDICT Have children read the title. Identify Norman as the boy in the picture. He is the signmaker's assistant. Identify the author. Do a picture walk of pp. 270–273. Ask children what they think this story will be about.

DISCUSS HUMOROUS FICTION Explain that fiction is a story about imaginary people or things. Make sure children understand that there are many funny events in this story that could not really happen. Remind children that a funny story about imaginary people and events is called humorous fiction. Read the definition of humorous fiction on p. 268 of the Student Edition.

SET PURPOSE Read the question on p. 269. Ask children to read to find out what kinds of problems the signmaker's assistant causes.

Access Content Before reading, review the story summary in English and/or the home language. See the ELL Teaching Guide, pp. 173–175.

_____ Vowels *aw, au, augh, al*   ☐ lesson/tested vocabulary

Everyone in town agreed. The old signmaker did the finest work for miles around. Under his brush, ordinary letters became beautiful words—words of wisdom, words of warning, or words that simply said which door to use.

When he painted STOP, people stopped because the sign looked so important. When he painted PLEASE KEEP OFF THE GRASS, they kept off because the sign was polite and sensible. When he painted

270

GOOD FOOD, they just naturally became hungry.

People thanked the signmaker and paid him well. But the kind old man never failed to say, "I couldn't have done it without Norman's help."

271

Guiding Comprehension

Prior Knowledge • Inferential

- *Text to World* **Why do people use signs?**
Signs give people directions and information about where to go or what to do.

Predict • Inferential

- **How do you think Norman helps the signmaker?**
Children may respond that he probably helps paint or put up signs.

▲ **Pages 270–271**
Have children read to find out what people do when they read the sign-maker's signs.

Monitor Progress	
Read New Words	
If... children come to a word they don't know,	**then...** remind them to: 1. Blend the word. 2. Decide if the word makes sense. 3. Look in a dictionary for more help.

Norman was the signmaker's assistant. Each day after school he cut wood, mixed colors, and painted simple signs.

"Soon I will have a shop of my own," said Norman.

"Perhaps," answered the signmaker, "but not before you clean these brushes."

One day, after his work was done, Norman stood at a window over the sign shop and watched people. They stopped at the STOP sign. They entered at the ENTER sign. They ate under the GOOD FOOD sign.

272

"They do whatever the signs say!" said Norman to himself. "I wonder. . ." He crept into the shop while the signmaker napped. With brush and board he painted a sign of his own.

Early the next morning he put up the sign, then ran back to his window to watch.

"No school?" muttered the principal. "How could I forget such a thing?"

"No one informed me," said the teacher.

"Hooray!" cheered the children, and everyone went home.

273

▲ **Pages 272–273**
Have children read to find out how Norman assists the signmaker.

EXTEND SKILLS

Dialogue

For instruction in dialogue, discuss the following:

• The author uses quotation marks to tell us characters are talking.

Point to the quotation marks around a character's words.

• What does the character say?

Assess Have children look for other examples of dialogue in the story and point out the quotation marks.

Guiding Comprehension

Detail • Literal

• **How does Norman assist the signmaker?**
He cuts wood, mixes colors, and paints some signs.

Draw Conclusions • Critical

• **Why does Norman make a sign that says "NO SCHOOL TODAY"?**
He thinks the children will enjoy not having to go to school, and he sees that people do whatever the signs say.

Make Judgments • Critical

• **Do you think Norman was right to make the sign? Why or why not?**
Children may respond that Norman shouldn't have made the sign because children are supposed to go to school.

_____ Vowels *aw, au, augh, al*   ☐ lesson/tested vocabular·

OPEN FOR SWIMMING

"This is great!" cried Norman. He looked around town for another idea. "Oh," he said at last, "there is something I have always wanted to do."

The following day Norman jumped from the top of the fountain in the park. As he swam, he thought to himself, *I can do lots of things with signs.* Ideas filled his head.

That afternoon when Norman went to work, the signmaker said, "I must drive to the next town and paint a large sign on a storefront. I'll return tomorrow evening, so please lock up the shop tonight."

274

As soon as the signmaker was gone, Norman started making signs. He painted for hours and hours and hours.

In the morning people discovered new signs all around town.

BANK CLOSED
DEPOSIT MONEY HERE

EAT YOUR HAT

TOY SHOP
BUY NORMAN A PRESENT

275

Strategies in Context
⊚ MONITOR AND FIX UP

▲ **Pages 274–275**
Have children read to find out what Norman has always wanted to do.

• **What has Norman always wanted to do?**
Norman has always wanted to swim in the fountain.

Monitor Progress	**Monitor and Fix Up**
If... children have difficulty answering the questions,	**then...** model how to go back to look at illustrations and reread the text.

MODEL If I don't understand something, I reread. I reread the first paragraph and noticed that after Norman says there is something he has always wanted to do, he goes swimming in the fountain. The pictures show that he made a sign that said the fountain was open for swimming. Now I understand that swimming in the fountain is what Norman wanted to do.

ASSESS Have children practice going back to reread and study the pictures to answer questions.

Communi-cation

Time for **SOCIAL STUDIES**

Some signs tell us about laws—not to litter, what the speed limit is, when to stop, and where we can park our cars. Others warn us about dangers such as falling rocks or wet floors. Some products are packaged with warning labels. Some signs provide information such as what a store sells or when a store is open for business. Have children tell about other signs or warning labels they have seen. Provide examples for children to read.

Norman watched it all
and laughed until tears came
to his eyes. But soon he saw
people becoming angry.

276

277

▲ **Pages 276–277**
Have children read to find out what
happens when Norman makes more
signs.

Have children ask themselves these
questions to check their reading.

Vocabulary Strategy
• Do I look for the two or more
  words in a compound word?
• Do I look for endings added
  to base words?
• Do I use the glossary or a
  dictionary?

Monitor and Fix Up
• Do I stop to check that I
  understand what I am reading?
• Do I look at illustrations to find
  clues about what is happening?
• Do I go back and reread if I do not
  understand what is happening?

Guiding Comprehension

Draw Conclusions • Inferential
• **Why does Norman laugh when he sees citizens doing what his signs say
  to do?**
  His signs make them do silly things.

Character • Critical
• **What kind of a person do you think Norman is?**
  Children may respond that Norman is mean and doesn't care about others or
  that he thinks it's fun to play tricks on people.

Summarize • Inferential
• **What has happened in the story so far?**
  Norman helped the signmaker make good signs. Then he started making signs
  of his own that told people to do silly things, and people started getting angry.

___ Vowels *aw, au, augh, al*

☐ lesson/tested vocabulary

278

"The signmaker is playing tricks," they shouted. "He has made fools of us!"

The teacher tore down the NO SCHOOL TODAY sign. Suddenly people were tearing down all the signs—not just the new ones but every sign the signmaker had ever painted.

279

Skills in Context

REVIEW AUTHOR'S PURPOSE

- **Why do you think the author included the pictures on p. 278?**
  The author wanted us to understand the bad things that happened when people did what Norman's signs told them to do.

Monitor Progress	Author's Purpose
If... children are unable to determine the author's purpose,	**then...** model how to use the illustrations to determine the author's purpose.

 Think Aloud

MODEL The pictures show many bad things happening because of Norman's signs. I think the author included these pictures so I could understand the bad things that happened because of Norman's signs.

ASSESS Have children discuss the purpose of the picture on p. 279. (The author wanted to show that people are angry about Norman's signs.)

▲ **Pages 278–279**
Have children look at the illustrations and read to find out what problems Norman causes.

Read the story.
Follow the directions.

The Rabbit and the Turtle
by Aesop

One day Rabbit and Turtle agreed to race. Soon Rabbit was far in front of Turtle. Rabbit was sure he would win so he sat down to rest. Rabbit was soon asleep. Turtle kept on walking. In time he passed the sleeping Rabbit and won the race. When Rabbit woke up he got a big surprise!

1. Circle the author's name.

2. Circle the word below that tells what Rabbit and Turtle were doing.

   sleeping   racing   talking

3. Circle the part of the story that tells why Rabbit sat down.

4. Underline the part of the story that tells why Turtle won the race.

5. Write a sentence that tells why you think the author wrote this story.

   Possible answer: The author wanted to teach a lesson about the importance of working hard.

School + Home Home Activity Your child answered questions about a fable and explained why the author wrote it. Read or tell a fairy tale or fable. Ask your child what he or she learned from the story. Discuss why authors sometimes use stories to teach important lessons.

▲ **Practice Book 2.2** p. 97, Author's Purpose

Signmaker's Assistant **278–279**

Then the real trouble started. Without store signs, shoppers became confused. Without stop signs, drivers didn't know when to stop. Without street signs, firemen became lost.

280

In the evening when the signmaker returned from his work in the next town, he knew nothing of Norman's tricks. An angry crowd of people met him at the back door of his shop and chased him into the woods.

As Norman watched, he suddenly realized that without signs and without the signmaker, the town was in danger.

"It's <u>all</u> my <u>fault</u>!"cried Norman, but no one was listening.

281

▲ **Pages 280–281**
Ask children to read to think about which things could and couldn't happen as they read.

Goods and Services
Time for **SOCIAL STUDIES**

A good is something that is made or grown and then sold. A service is a job that one person does for another. The toys sold at the toy shop and the signs Norman and the signmaker sell are goods. Firefighters put out fires, and teachers teach others. They both perform services.

Skills in Context

↻ REALISM AND FANTASY

- **So far, which things could really happen and which could not?**
  A signmaker could really make signs. People would never obey signs that told them to do things like put money in a trash can.

Monitor Progress	**Realism and Fantasy**
If... children are unable to identify realism and fantasy,	**then...** model how to distinguish between what could and could not really happen.

Think Aloud

MODEL To figure out if something could really happen or not, I think about what I already know. It is realistic that drivers wouldn't know where to stop without stop signs, but people wouldn't really follow a detour sign and drive through someone's house.

ASSESS Have children identify fantastic situations in stories they have read so far.

Late that night the signmaker returned and saw a light on in his shop. Norman was feverishly painting.

While the town slept and the signmaker watched, Norman put up stop signs, shop signs, street signs, danger signs, and welcome signs; in and out signs, large and small signs, new and beautiful signs. He returned all his presents and cleared away the garbage at the grocery store. It was morning when he finished putting up his last sign for the entire town to see.

Then Norman packed his things and locked up the shop. But as he turned to go, he discovered the signmaker and all the townspeople gathered at the door.

282

"I know you're angry with me for what I did," said Norman with downcast eyes, "so I'm leaving."

"Oh, we were angry all right!" answered the school principal. "But we were also fools for obeying signs without thinking."

"You told us you are sorry," said the signmaker, "and you fixed your mistakes. So stay and work hard. One day this shop may be yours."

"Perhaps," answered Norman, hugging the old man, "but not before I finish cleaning those brushes."

283

Guiding Comprehension

Character • Inferential
- **What did Norman learn by the end of the story?**
Possible response: He learned that it's important to fix your mistakes and apologize for them.

Make Judgments • Critical
- *Text to World* **What do you think are some important signs? Why?**
Children might say that traffic signs are important because they keep people safe or that street signs are important because they tell people where they are.

Pages 282–283
Have children read to find out how the story ends.

Reread For Fluency · ROUTINE

1. **Reader 1 Begins** Children read the entire book, switching readers at the end of each page.

2. **Reader 2 Begins** Have partners reread; now the other partner begins.

3. **Reread** For optimal fluency, children should reread three or four times.

4. **Provide Feedback** Listen to children read and provide corrective feedback regarding their oral reading and their use of blending.

2

Strategic Intervention

Have children copy a portion of the letter, writing at least one of the ways they could be of assistance. They can then illustrate their writing.

Advanced

Have children who are able to write complete sentences independently write their own business letter responding to the letter.

Writing Support Before writing, children might share ideas in their home languages.

Beginning Pair children with more proficient English speakers. A more proficient speaker can help the partner write a letter.

Intermediate Help children orally practice ways they can be of help before they write.

Advanced Encourage children to write and read aloud their business letters.

Support Grammar Some languages such as the Romance languages include contractions. If possible, provide examples of contractions in the home language. (In Spanish, *a* + *el* = *al* and *de* + *el* = *del*; in Portuguese, *de* + *as* = *das*.) Explain that in English contractions use an apostrophe to replace the missing letters. See the Grammar Transition lessons in the ELL and Transition Handbook.

Interactive Writing

WRITE Business Letter

MAKE A WEB Use *The Signmaker's Assistant* to create a word web about what a signmaker's assistant does.

SHARE THE PEN Have children participate in writing a business letter to the signmaker asking him for a job as his assistant. Have a child suggest the greeting, inviting individuals to capitalize *Dear* and *Signmaker.* Ask questions such as:

- Where should we put the date? (top right)
- Where could we look to spell the word *assistant?* (in the book or a dictionary)
- What closing should we use for our letter?

Continue to have individuals make contributions. Frequently reread what has been written while tracking the print.

READ THE BUSINESS LETTER Read the completed letter aloud, having children echo you.

April 18

Dear Signmaker,

    I would like to be your assistant. I could help you paint your signs. I could help you hang your signs. I could help you cut wood for your signs.

Sincerely,

Lillie Kaplan

INDEPENDENT WRITING

WRITE A BUSINESS LETTER Have children write their own business letters asking for a job at a place they would like to work. Let children address an envelope to go with the letter. Remind them that the return address goes on the top left corner, the stamp goes on the top right corner, and the address of the person (or company) to whom the letter is being sent goes in the middle of the envelope. The envelope should be addressed to the recipient, using Mr., Mrs., or Ms. before the name, and envelopes should always include a ZIP code.

Grammar

DEVELOP THE CONCEPT Contractions

IDENTIFY CONTRACTIONS Write *did* and *not* on the board. Point to each word as you read it. Ask children to combine the words into a contraction. (*didn't*) Continue with *they* and *will*.

A contraction is a short way to put two words together. What symbol takes the place of one or more letters when those words are combined? (an apostrophe)

PRACTICE

SUGGEST CONTRACTIONS Write the sentence above on the board. Then underline *teacher is* and *We will*.

 MODEL I can shorten *she is* to the contraction *she's*. Write *teacher's*. I can shorten *we will* to *we'll* as well. Write *we'll*.

Have children suggest other sentences that include words that can be shortened into contractions. Write the sentences children provide.

DAILY FIX-IT

3. It was a rough hike to the clif?
   It was a rough hike to the cli**ff**.

4. The fone sounded phunny.
   The **ph**one sounded **f**unny.

Contractions

A **contraction** is a short way to put two words together. An **apostrophe** (') takes the place of one or more letters. Contractions can be formed by putting together a pronoun and another word, such as *will*, *are*, or *is*.

    I will get some flowers. **I'll** get some flowers.
Many contractions are formed with verbs and the word *not*.
    Otto **did not** read the sign. Otto **didn't** read the sign.

Replace the underlined words with a contraction from the box.

He'll	he's	aren't	shouldn't	I'm

1. "Signs <u>are not</u> important," Otto said.   **aren't**

2. Otto said, "<u>I am</u> going to pick flowers."   **I'm**

3. People said he <u>should not</u> pick them.   **shouldn't**

4. Now <u>he is</u> just looking at the flowers.   **he's**

Home Activity Your child learned about contractions. Say sentences using the contractions on this page and ask your child to identify the contraction and the two words that make up the contraction.

▲ **Grammar and Writing Practice Book** p. 97

Wrap Up Your Day!

 LESSON VOCABULARY Write the following sentence. *The signmaker was not to blame for the ideas on the newest signs.* Ask children to read the sentence and identify the vocabulary words *signmaker, blame, ideas.*

 MONITOR AND FIX UP Recall the first sign Norman put up that made him realize people would follow not-so-good ideas. How did you know what the sign said? (The sign was in the illustration.) What else can you do when you don't understand what you read? (Reread sentences or paragraphs you read before.)

LET'S TALK ABOUT IT Recall what happened when people tore down all the signs. Ask: What happened to the town when all the signs were thrown away? (Everyone got confused.) Discuss with children why it is not always a good idea to throw away, destroy, or stop doing something when one thing goes wrong. Talk about how Norman fixed the problem and ways other problems can be fixed.

 PREVIEW Day 3

Tell children tomorrow they will hear about a spider who learns a lesson.

Day 3

AT A GLANCE

Share Literature
The Hoot and Holler Hat Dance

Phonics and Spelling
REVIEW *ph, gh/f/*
Spelling: Words with Vowels *aw, au, augh, al*

Vocabulary
Skill Compound Words

Fluency
Read with Appropriate Phrasing

Writing Trait
Sentences

Grammar
Contractions

Materials

- *Sing with Me Big Book*
- *Read Aloud Anthology*
- Student Edition 284–285

Morning Warm-Up!

Today we'll read more about Anansi.
His mama says, "Don't eat my stew!"
Anansi doesn't obey her though.
Why do we have rules to obey?

QUESTION OF THE DAY Encourage children to sing "Best Judgment" from the *Sing with Me Big Book* as you gather. Write and read the message and discuss the question.

REVIEW CONTRACTIONS

- Read the message again. Have volunteers circle the contractions. (*we'll, don't, doesn't*)

- Review that *we'll* is a shorter way of saying *we will.* Ask children to tell you what the other two contractions mean. (*do not, does not*)

Build Background Use the Day 3 instruction on ELL Poster 25 to support children's use of English to communicate about Lesson Concepts.

ELL Poster 25

Share Literature

LISTEN AND RESPOND

CAPITALIZATION Ask children the names of the cat (*Okra*) and the dog (*Kraman*) in "The Hoot and Holler Hat Dance." Write these names on the board and remind children that names start with capital letters. Write the title and point out that in titles, all the important words have capitals.

BUILD ORAL VOCABULARY Introduce the Amazing Word **scold.** Tell children it means "to speak in an angry way." Review that yesterday the class listened to the story to find out what kind of character Anansi is. Ask that children listen today to find out what happens when Anansi disobeys his mother.

MONITOR LISTENING COMPREHENSION

- What did Mama tell Anansi to do before he could have stew? **(finish picking the corn)**

- What did Anansi do when the cat caught him eating stew? **(Anansi put on his hat, which was filled with beans; then he smiled.)**

- What happened to Anansi because of his greediness? **(The beans burned him, and he lost all of his hair.)**

- Do you think Mama scolded Anansi when she found out he had disobeyed her? Why do you think that? **(Possible response: No, because Anansi was punished enough by having the beans burn his hair off.)**

Read Aloud Anthology
The Hoot and Holler Hat Dance

OBJECTIVES
- Discuss uses of capitalization.
- Set purpose for listening.
- Build oral vocabulary.

Amazing Words
to build oral vocabulary

	MONITOR PROGRESS
apologize citizen judgment hoard scold interrupt protest troublemaker	**If...** children lack oral vocabulary experiences about the concept Responsibility, **then...** use the Oral Vocabulary Routine. See p. DI·7 to teach *scold.*

Listen and Respond Help children visualize the dance in "The Hoot and Holler Hat Dance." Make sure they understand the meaning of the words *shook, jumped, danced,* and *jiggled* by showing them actions for each verb. Reread the last part of the story. As you read, have children pantomime Anansi's actions.

3

Review Phonics

REVIEW *ph, gh/f/*

READ *ph, gh* WORDS Write *phrase* and *laugh.* Look at these words. You can read these words because you know that *ph* and *gh* can stand for the sound /f/. What sound can *ph* and *gh* stand for? (/f/) What are the words?

BUILD WORDS Write these sentences. Have children read the sentences and identify the word in each that has the sound /f/. Have them circle the letters that stand for /f/. Then have them choose one of the *ph* or *gh* words in the chart and use it in a sentence.

What is your phone number?

Rick has a cold and a cough.

Mom took many photos on our trip.

Have you studied enough?

We learned about graphs in math.

ph	gh
phone	cough
photo	rough
phase	tough
graph	enough

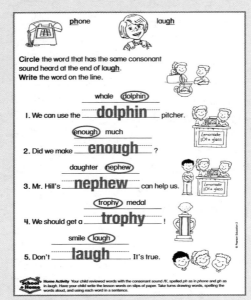

▲ Practice Book 2.2 p. 98, *ph, gh/f/*

Lesson Vocabulary

PRACTICE

ANSWER QUESTIONS Write questions using lesson vocabulary words on the board and underline the lesson vocabulary words. Have children read the questions and write one-sentence answers, using the lesson vocabulary words.

- What good <u>idea</u> might help you get up on time in the morning?
- What is the most <u>important</u> thing you have learned today?
- Would you take the <u>blame</u> for something?
- When might you need to hire a <u>signmaker</u>?
- Who are some <u>townspeople</u> you know?
- What things can you do in the <u>afternoon</u> that you can't do in the morning or at night?

Spelling

PRACTICE *Vowels aw, au, augh, al*

WRITE ILLUSTRATED SENTENCES Have children practice the spelling words by writing and illustrating sentences.

- Ask children to write sentences that use each of the spelling words.
- Have children draw pictures that illustrate their sentences.
- Gather all sentences together in a class reference book.

HOMEWORK Spelling Practice Book, p. 99

Pick a word from the box to finish the sentence. Write the word on the line.

afternoon blame idea important
signmaker townspeople

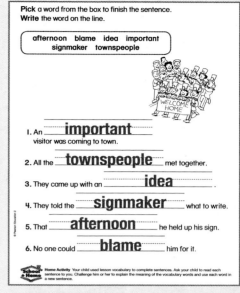

1. An **important** visitor was coming to town.
2. All the **townspeople** met together.
3. They came up with an **idea** .
4. They told the **signmaker** what to write.
5. That **afternoon** he held up his sign.
6. No one could **blame** him for it.

Home Activity Your child used lesson vocabulary to complete sentences. Ask your child to read each sentence to you. Challenge him or her to explain the meaning of the vocabulary words and use each word in a new sentence.

▲ **Practice Book 2.2** p. 99, Lesson Vocabulary

Spelling Words

Vowels *aw, au, augh, al*

1. talk
2. because
3. August
4. caught
5. draw
6. walk
7. chalk
8. auto
9. taught
10. thaw
11. fault*
12. launch

Challenge Words

13. applause
14. audience
15. awkward

* **Word from the Selection**

Vowel Sound in *fall*
Read the letter. **Circle** three spelling mistakes and a word that needs a capital letter. **Write** the words correctly.

August 5

Dear (aunt) Helen,
    Thank you for the big box of (chauk) I used it to (drawe) pictures all over the walk. Everyone (thot) they were beautiful!
            Love,
            Janie

Spelling Words	
talk	chalk
because	auto
August	taught
caught	thaw
draw	fault
walk	launch

Frequently Misspelled Words
thought
caught

1. **chalk** 2. **draw**
3. **thought** 4. **Aunt**

Circle the misspelled list word. **Write** each word correctly.

5. The ice will (thau).   5. **thaw**
6. Who (taut) you how to swim? 6. **taught**
7. I left (becus) I felt sick.   7. **because**
8. He runs an (aughto) repair shop. 8. **auto**

Home Activity Your child identified misspelled words with the vowel sound in fall spelled aw, au, augh, and al. Give clues about a spelling word. Ask your child to guess and spell it.

▲ **Spelling Practice Book** p. 99

Signmaker's Assistant   **284d**

OBJECTIVES

● Discuss compound words.
● Create compound words.

Vocabulary

COMPOUND WORDS

DISCUSS COMPOUND WORDS Point to the word *signmaker* on p. 269. Ask children what they notice about the word. Explain that it is made up of two separate words: *sign* and *maker.* Tell them that words that are made up of two or more words put together are called *compound words.* Explain that they can sometimes figure out what a compound word means if they know the meanings of the words that make up the compound word. A *signmaker* is a person who makes signs. Ask children to list other compound words and tell what they mean.

EXPAND LESSON VOCABULARY Write the following words on the board: *sign, towns, noon, after, people, maker.* Call on volunteers to come to the board to create a compound word using two of the words listed. Discuss with children if the new word is a real word. If not, erase the word.

Strategic Intervention

Have children choose a compound word from the lesson to illustrate. They should draw two pictures: one for each word in the compound word. Ask them to share their pictures while the rest of the class tries to guess the compound word.

Advanced

Have children make up a list of compound words. They can use a dictionary if they need help. Ask them to break up each word into individual words and then write each word on an index card. Then have them play a compound word matching game. With the cards face down on a desk, children should take turns turning over two cards at a time. When children turn over two cards that make a compound word, they keep the cards and take another turn.

Extend Language Help children understand that they can predict the meaning of a compound word by using the meaning of the individual words. Carefully review the meaning of each individual word in the lesson.

Group Time

DAY 3

On-Level

Read *The Signmaker's Assistant.*

• Use pp. 268–285.

Strategic Intervention

Read or listen to *The Signmaker's Assistant.*

• Use the **Routine** on p. DI•58.

Advanced

Read Self-Selected Reading.

• Use the **Routine** on p. DI•59.

 Place English language learners in the groups that correspond to their reading abilities in English.

ⓘ Independent Activities

Independent Reading See p. 264j for Reading/Library activities and suggestions.

Journal Writing Write a journal entry about a practical joke or magic trick you have done. Share writing.

Literacy Centers To provide experiences with *The Signmaker's Assistant,* you may use the Writing Center on p. 264k.

Practice Book 2.2 *ph, gh*/f/, p. 98; Lesson Vocabulary, p. 99

Break into small groups after Vocabulary and before Writing.

Fluency

READ WITH APPROPRIATE PHRASING

MODEL READING WITH APPROPRIATE PHRASING Use *The Signmaker's Assistant.*

- Point to the text on p. 270. There is quite a bit of punctuation in this story, so I want to be sure I group words appropriately. For example, I will take a short pause when I come to commas and dashes. I will also take a short pause when I get to the words in all capital letters, as these are the words that appear on signs in the story.

- Ask children to follow along as you read the page with appropriate phrasing.

- Have children read the page after you. Encourage them to read with appropriate phrasing by grouping words appropriately. Continue in the same way with pp. 271–272.

REREAD FOR FLUENCY

Choral Reading

ROUTINE

1. **Select a Passage** For *The Signmaker's Assistant,* use the entire story, dividing it into equal sections for the number of groups you have.

2. **Divide into Groups** Assign each person in each group a part to read. For this story, use these parts: the narrator, Norman, the signmaker, the principal, the crowd of people.

3. **Model** Have children track the print as you read.

4. **Read Together** Have children read along with you.

5. **Independent Readings** Have the groups read aloud without you. Monitor progress and provide feedback. For optimal fluency, children should reread three to four times.

Monitor Progress	Fluency
If... children have difficulty reading with appropriate phrasing,	**then...** prompt: • What do you do when you see a comma? • What do you do when you see a period?
If... the class cannot read fluently without you,	**then...** continue to have them read along with you.

OBJECTIVE

● Read aloud fluently with appropriate phrasing.

Options for Oral Reading

Use *The Signmaker's Assistant* or one of the following Leveled Readers.

On-Level

Freda's Signs

Strategic Intervention

Grandpa's Sign

Advanced

Marty's Job

E L L

Model reading *The Three Little Kittens Learn What to Do* or *The Signmaker's Assistant* with appropriate phrasing for English language learners by attending to punctuation. Have children echo what you read, grouping words appropriately.

 **Fluency Coach CD** To develop fluent readers, use Fluency Coach.

Retelling Plan

☑ Week 1 assess Strategic Intervention students.

☑ Week 2 assess Advanced students.

☑ Week 3 assess Strategic Intervention students.

☑ Week 4 assess On-Level students.

☐ **This week assess any students you have not yet checked during this unit.**

Look Back and Write Point out information from the text that answers the question. Then have children write a response to the question. For test practice, assign a 10–15 minute time limit. For assessment, see the Scoring Rubric at the bottom of this page.

Assessment Let beginning English learners listen to other retellings before attempting their own. For more ideas on assessing comprehension, see the ELL and Transition Handbook.

Reader Response

TALK ABOUT IT Model a response. I will tell him that he should only make signs to help people, not ones that tell people to do silly or dangerous things.

1. RETELL Have children use the retelling strip in the Student Edition to retell the selection.

Monitor Progress	**Check Retelling** Rubric 4 3 2 1

Have children retell *The Signmaker's Assistant.*

If... children have difficulty retelling the story,

then... use the Retelling Cards and the Scoring Rubric for Retelling on pp. 284–285 to help them move toward fluent retelling.

SUCCESS PREDICTOR

Day 1 Check Word Reading

Day 2 Check Lesson Vocabulary/High-Frequency Words

▶ **Day 3** Check Retelling

Day 4 Check Fluency

Day 5 Assess Progress

2. REALISM AND FANTASY Model a response. People in real life would think before following any sign they read. Norman couldn't make new signs for the whole town in only one night.

3. PRIOR KNOWLEDGE Model a response. Not many of the signs I see are hand-painted by a signmaker. That tells me this is a make-believe story.

LOOK BACK AND WRITE Read the writing prompt on p. 284 and model your thinking. I'll look back at page 273. I'll read what happens after Norman says, "I wonder...." What Norman does next might show what he is trying to figure out. Then I'll write my response. **Have children write their responses.**

Scoring Rubric	**Look Back and Write**

Top-Score Response A top-score response will use details from p. 273 and later pages of the selection to tell what Norman wondered and what he later found out.

Example of a Top-Score Response Norman wondered if people would really do whatever signs tell them to do. He found out that people do follow signs. He also learned that you shouldn't trick people because it makes them angry.

For additional rubrics, see p. WA10.

Reader Response

Open for Discussion Suppose Norman asks to come and work in your community. What will you say to him?

1. Use the pictures below to help retell the story. Which picture from the story would you put in the last box to show the ending? Retell

2. Why couldn't this story happen in real life? Realism/Fantasy

3. Think about the signs you see every day. How does this help you know that *The Signmaker's Assistant* is a make-believe story? Fix Up

 Look Back and Write On page 273, Norman says, "They do whatever the signs say!" Then he says, "I wonder. . . ." Write what Norman wondered and what he later found out.

Meet the Author and Illustrator

Tedd Arnold

Here are two more books written or illustrated by Tedd Arnold.

No More Water in the Tub

Tracks

The library is one of Tedd Arnold's favorite places to go. He gets ideas there. Once he rode a bus through a town and noticed all the store signs. The signs were nice, and he thought about the person who painted them. The signmaker told people where to go. He controlled what the neighborhood looked like. Mr. Arnold said, "I began to wonder how else a signmaker might have control. Of course, I started thinking of silly signs that could control people and make them do goofy things. That's how the story got started!"

Retelling Strip

284

285

Scoring Rubric Narrative Retelling

Rubric 4 3 2 1	4	3	2	1
Connections	Makes connections and generalizes beyond the text	Makes connections to other events, stories, or experiences	Makes a limited connection to another event, story, or experience	Makes no connection to another event, story, or experience
Author's Purpose	Elaborates on author's purpose	Tells author's purpose with some clarity	Makes some connection to author's purpose	Makes no connection to author's purpose
Characters	Describes the main character(s) and any character development	Identifies the main character(s) and gives some information about them	Inaccurately identifies some characters or gives little information about them	Inaccurately identifies the characters or gives no information about them
Setting	Describes the time and location	Identifies the time and location	Omits details of time or location	Is unable to identify time or location
Plot	Describes the events in sequence, using rich detail	Tells the plot with some errors in sequence that do not affect meaning	Tells parts of plot with gaps that affect meaning	Retelling has no sense of story

Use the Retelling Chart on p. TR20 to record retelling.

Selection Test To assess with *The Signmaker's Assistant,* use Selection Tests, pp. 97–100.

Fresh Reads for Differentiated Test Practice For weekly leveled practice, use pp. 145–150.

Retelling

SUCCESS PREDICTOR

OBJECTIVE

● Recognize and use varied sentences in writing.

DAILY FIX-IT

5. bill playyed a joke on her.
   <u>Bill</u> pla<u>y</u>ed a joke on her.

6. She would'nt talk to he all day.
   She would<u>n't</u> talk to <u>him</u> all day.

Connect to Unit Writing

Writing Trait

Have children use strategies for developing **sentences** when they write a persuasive letter in the Unit Writing Workshop, pp. WA2–WA9.

Sentences Read imperative, exclamatory, and interrogative sentences aloud to English learners, using tone to show how these sentences add excitement to writing. Add think-aloud comments to explain how punctuation helps readers understand sentences.

Writing Trait of the Week

INTRODUCE Sentences

TALK ABOUT SENTENCES Explain to children that good writers use both long and short sentences. They also use different words to begin sentences. This gives the writing rhythm and style. Ask children to think about the lengths and beginnings of sentences used in *The Signmaker's Assistant*. Then model your thinking.

MODEL Some stories are dull because the writer uses many short sentences or many long sentences or because too many sentences begin with words such as *the* and *he*. *The Signmaker's Assistant* is fun to read aloud because the sentences flow together. This is because the writer uses both short and long sentences and different sentence beginnings. Here are sentences from the story.

> **Everyone in town agreed. The old signmaker did the finest work for miles around. Under his brush, ordinary letters became beautiful words—words of wisdom, words of warning, or words that simply said which door to use.**

I notice that the first sentence is short. The second is medium-long. The last is very long. Together, the three sentences flow and have rhythm. I also see that each sentence begins with a different word.

STRATEGY FOR DEVELOPING SENTENCES Write the following sentences on the board. Ask children to rearrange words in each sentence so that it does not begin with *He*. Each new sentence should begin with the underlined phrase.

He stood at the door <u>one day</u>. (One day he stood at the door.)

He cut wood and mixed colors <u>after school</u>. (After school he cut wood and mixed colors.)

He painted signs <u>for hours</u>. (For hours he painted signs.)

PRACTICE

APPLY THE STRATEGY Ask children to make a sign that advertises a product, such as toothpaste or shoes, or an event, such as a school play. Remind them to include short and long sentences and sentences that begin with different words.

Grammar

APPLY TO WRITING Contractions

IMPROVE WRITING WITH CONTRACTIONS Do you think Norman should or should not have used signs to trick people? (should not) Write *should not* and *shouldn't* on the board. Explain that *shouldn't* and *should not* mean exactly the same thing, but the contraction *shouldn't* is shorter and it sounds less formal. Point out that writers sometimes use contractions to make their writing sound less formal or more like real speech. Remind children to use contractions correctly in their own writing.

Ask volunteers to tell something they will do, and write the sentences on the board, using contractions. Invite them to tell about things they do not do or should not do.

I'll practice the piano today.
I don't watch television.
I shouldn't tease animals.

PRACTICE

WRITE WITH CONTRACTIONS Write additional contractions on the board, such as *aren't, isn't, wouldn't, couldn't, he's, she's, it's, didn't, wasn't, we're, we've,* and *you'll.* Call on individuals to make up sentences using these contractions. Write the sentences on the board, underlining the contractions.

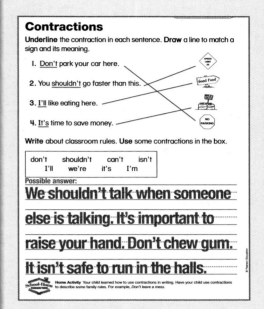

▲ **Grammar and Writing Practice Book** p. 98

Wrap Up Your Day!

✓ **REALISM AND FANTASY** If "The Signmaker's Assistant" were a realistic story, what do you think would have happened when Norman displayed his signs? (Children might suggest that someone would have just taken them down.) Do you think the story would have been as funny? (Children may recognize that much of the story's humor comes from its fantasy elements.)

✓ **FLUENCY** Call on individuals to read aloud their favorite parts of the story. Remind them to use appropriate phrasing.

LET'S TALK ABOUT IT Lead a discussion about how people should behave when they've done something wrong. When Norman saw the trouble he'd caused, he fixed all the signs. Then he apologized. Do you think it's enough to fix something you did wrong? Do you think it's enough to apologize? Do you need to do both?

PREVIEW Day 4

Tell children that tomorrow they will read about children who started groups that help other people.

Day 4
AT A GLANCE

Share Literature
Troublemaker

Phonics and Spelling
 Vowels *aw, au, augh, al*

Spelling: Words with Vowels *aw, au, augh, al*

Read

Group Time < Differentiated Instruction

"Helping Hand"

Fluency
Read with Appropriate Phrasing

Writing Across the Curriculum
Signs

Grammar
Contractions

Speaking and Listening
Understand Advertising

Materials

- *Sing with Me Big Book*
- *Read Aloud Anthology*
- Student Edition 286–289

Morning Warm-Up!

Today we will read about some young people and their ideas. They started some important groups that made a difference.

How can you make a difference?

QUESTION OF THE DAY Encourage children to sing "Best Judgment" from the *Sing with Me Big Book* as you gather. Write and read the message and discuss the question.

REVIEW LESSON VOCABULARY

- Circle the words *ideas* and *important* in the message. Review what each word means, recalling the story *The Signmaker's Assistant*.

- Ask children if they think the young people referred to in the message have *wisdom,* reviewing the meaning if necessary. Then ask if the young people might need an *assistant.* Encourage children to explain their thinking.

ELL

Extend Language Use the Day 4 instruction on ELL Poster 25 to extend and enrich language.

ELL Poster 25

Share Literature

CONNECT CONCEPTS

ACTIVATE PRIOR KNOWLEDGE Recall Norman and Anansi and the trouble they got into. Explain that you will read another story about someone who often gets into trouble—"Troublemaker" by Jodi Wheeler.

Read Aloud Anthology
Troublemaker

BUILD ORAL VOCABULARY Introduce the Amazing Words **interrupt, protest,** and **troublemaker.** Explain that *interrupt* means "to speak while someone else is speaking," *to protest* means "to argue," and a *troublemaker* is "someone who causes problems." Ask that children listen to the story to find out why Justin protested.

REVIEW ORAL VOCABULARY After reading, review all the Amazing Words for the week. Have children take turns using them in sentences that tell about the concept for the week. Then talk about Amazing Words they learned in other weeks and connect them to the concept, as well. For example, ask:

- Can you **predict** what might happen if we don't **respect** other people's property?

- What would you do if someone in your **community** wrongly accused you of bad **behavior?**

- How might you **reprimand** someone who has done something wrong?

MONITOR LISTENING COMPREHENSION

- What did everyone think of Justin and why? (They thought he was a troublemaker because he got into arguments and because he ran through the halls.)

- What did Mrs. Richardson do when Ray and some other kids started laughing at Justin? (She interrupted them and said she hoped Justin would share some poetry soon.)

- Why did Justin protest when Mrs. Richardson told him to move his desk? (because he didn't throw the paper ball at Nieka—Ray did)

- Why do you think Justin was able to write his first poem? (Possible response: because he needed to tell Mrs. Richardson how he felt)

Amazing Words to build oral vocabulary

	MONITOR PROGRESS
apologize citizen judgment hoard scold **interrupt** **protest** **troublemaker**	**If...** children lack oral vocabulary experiences about the concept Responsibility, **then...** use the Oral Vocabulary Routine. See p. DI•7 to teach *interrupt, protest,* and *troublemaker.*

Connect Concepts Help children understand that what Justin wrote was indeed a poem. Tell them that this kind of poem is called an acrostic. It is a poem in which the first letters of the lines, read downwards, form a word. Ask them what word is formed in Justin's poem. (*mad*) Encourage students to write their own acrostic.

4

Spiral **REVIEW**

- Reviews silent consonants *kn, wr, gn, mb.*
- Reviews consonant + *le.*
- Reviews high-frequency words *behind, brought, door, every-body, minute, promise,* and *sorry.*

Sentence Reading

REVIEW WORDS IN CONTEXT

READ DECODABLE AND HIGH-FREQUENCY WORDS IN CONTEXT Write these sentences. Call on individuals to read a sentence. Then randomly point to words and have them read. To help you monitor word reading, high-frequency words are underlined and decodable words are circled.

I (knew) the (plumber) would close the <u>door</u> <u>behind</u> him.

Dad <u>brought</u> a thick (cable) to hang the (sign).

I <u>promise</u> I will not (giggle) (mumble) (talk), or (wriggle).

I must (wrap) my (knee) with a (little) tape the <u>minute</u> I get home.

<u>Sorry</u>, I forgot the (knife) for cutting the (limb) that was (caught) on the roof.

Put the (gnome) and the (wreath) in the yard by the (auto) so <u>everybody</u> will see them.

Monitor Progress	Word Reading
If... children are unable to read an underlined word,	**then...** read the word for them and spell it, having them echo you.
If... children are unable to read a circled word,	**then...** have them use the blending strategy they have learned for that word type.

Support Phonics For additional review, see the phonics activities in the ELL and Transition Handbook.

Spelling

PARTNER REVIEW Vowels *aw, au, augh, al*

READ AND WRITE Supply pairs of children with index cards on which the spelling words have been written. Have one child read a word while the other writes it. Then have children switch roles. Have them use the cards to check their spelling.

HOMEWORK Spelling Practice Book, p. 100

Group Time

On-Level	Strategic Intervention	Advanced
Read "Helping Hand." • Use pp. 286–289.	**Read** or listen to "Helping Hand." • Use the Routine on p. DI•60.	**Read** "Helping Hand." • Use the Routine on p. DI•61.

 Place English language learners in the groups that correspond to their reading abilities in English.

(i) Independent Activities

Fluency Reading Pair children to reread *The Signmaker's Assistant.*

Journal Writing Write a story about a time you had to make a difficult decision. Share writing.

Spelling Partner Review

Independent Reading See p.264j for Reading/Library activities and suggestions.

Literacy Centers To provide listening opportunities, you may use the Listening Center on p. 264j. To extend social studies concepts, you may use the Social Studies Center on p. 264k.

Break into small groups after Spelling and before Fluency.

Vowel Sound in *fall*

Spelling Words					
talk	because	August	caught	draw	walk
chalk	auto	taught	thaw	fault	launch

Finish the list words in the box. Each word has been started.

1. launch	2. because	3. August
4. draw	5. thaw	6. walk
7. fault	8. auto	9. chalk

Unscramble the list word. Write it.

10. augh t t   **taught**

   t augh c   **caught**

   k t al   **talk**

School + Home Home Activity Your child has been learning words with the vowel sound in fall spelled aw, au, augh, and al. Toss a coin onto the box above and read the word. Can your child correctly spell the word without looking? Take turns tossing the coin and spelling words.

▲ **Spelling Practice Book** p. 100

Reading Online

New Literacies: PearsonSuccessNet.com

Evaluating Sources

Genre
- You can find information fast on the Internet.
- You need to decide what is good information and what's not.

Text Features
- The addresses of Web sites you can count on often end in *.gov*, *.edu*, or *.org*.
- Web sites that end in *.com* may also be useful, but you must check them carefully. The description with the address can help you choose.

Link to Social Studies
Find out about a volunteer group in your area. Report about it.

Helping Hand

The signmaker learned about being responsible. You can do an Internet search to find out how you can help your neighbors. Use a search engine and type in the keyword *volunteer*. Here are two topics you might find listed. Which one would tell you about volunteer work? To choose, look carefully at both the source and the description.

For more practice
Take It to the Net
PearsonSuccessNet.com

286

> This is a .com Web site. A .com site often sells things. It may or may not be a good source.

File Edit View Favorites Tools Help

http://www.url.here

Show Your Colors. T-shirts, bumper stickers, decals, and other items can show your loyalty to a group that you support.

Save the Whales!

Organizations Started by Kids. Think you're too young to start your own organization? Hmm . . . maybe you'll change your mind after seeing what these kids have done.

WE RECYCLE

> This is a .org Web site. A .org site is usually a good source.

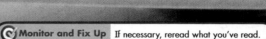
Monitor and Fix Up If necessary, reread what you've read.

287

AudioText

Time for
SOCIAL STUDIES

Internet
Lead children in a discussion about the Internet. Ask them how this technology has changed the way that people communicate. Lead them to conclude that people can communicate quickly by e-mail and instant messaging. Point out that more information is available to people as well.

Read
Reading Online

PREVIEW AND PREDICT Read the title. Have children preview the article and discuss what they notice. (computer screen, art) Then ask them to predict what they will learn about in this article. Have children read to find out how to search the Internet for good information.

INFORMATIONAL TEXT Review that selections about real people doing real things are called nonfiction. Point out that the text that appears on the computer screen gives information about community organizations. The text in boxes outside the screen gives information about reading online sources.

VOCABULARY/SUFFIX -ly Remind children that the word part *-ly* can be added to the end of some describing words to mean "in a __ way." Point out the word *carefully* on p. 286 and *currently* on p. 288. Take away the word part *-ly*. What word do you have? What does it mean?

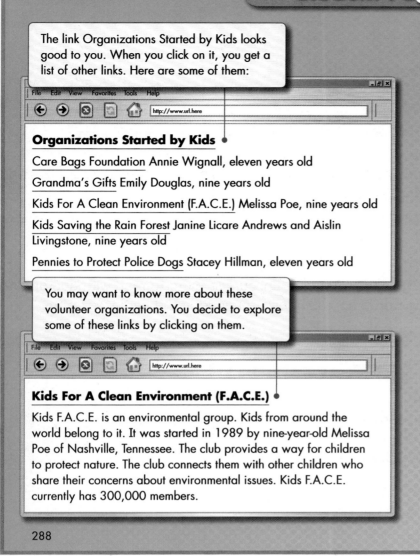

The link Organizations Started by Kids looks good to you. When you click on it, you get a list of other links. Here are some of them:

File Edit View Favorites Tools Help

http://www.url.here

Organizations Started by Kids

Care Bags Foundation Annie Wignall, eleven years old

Grandma's Gifts Emily Douglas, nine years old

Kids For A Clean Environment (F.A.C.E.) Melissa Poe, nine years old

Kids Saving the Rain Forest Janine Licare Andrews and Aislin Livingstone, nine years old

Pennies to Protect Police Dogs Stacey Hillman, eleven years old

You may want to know more about these volunteer organizations. You decide to explore some of these links by clicking on them.

File Edit View Favorites Tools Help

http://www.url.here

Kids For A Clean Environment (F.A.C.E.)

Kids F.A.C.E. is an environmental group. Kids from around the world belong to it. It was started in 1989 by nine-year-old Melissa Poe of Nashville, Tennessee. The club provides a way for children to protect nature. The club connects them with other children who share their concerns about environmental issues. Kids F.A.C.E. currently has 300,000 members.

288

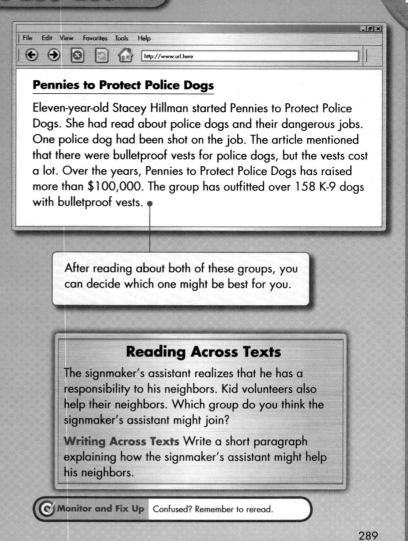

File Edit View Favorites Tools Help

http://www.url.here

Pennies to Protect Police Dogs

Eleven-year-old Stacey Hillman started Pennies to Protect Police Dogs. She had read about police dogs and their dangerous jobs. One police dog had been shot on the job. The article mentioned that there were bulletproof vests for police dogs, but the vests cost a lot. Over the years, Pennies to Protect Police Dogs has raised more than $100,000. The group has outfitted over 158 K-9 dogs with bulletproof vests.

After reading about both of these groups, you can decide which one might be best for you.

Reading Across Texts

The signmaker's assistant realizes that he has a responsibility to his neighbors. Kid volunteers also help their neighbors. Which group do you think the signmaker's assistant might join?

Writing Across Texts Write a short paragraph explaining how the signmaker's assistant might help his neighbors.

Monitor and Fix Up Confused? Remember to reread.

289

BUILD CONCEPTS

Classify • Inferential

- **What can you tell about all the groups listed on the screen on p. 287?**
  They are all organizations started by kids.

Draw Conclusions • Critical

- **How are members of Kids F.A.C.E. and Pennies to Protect Police Dogs being responsible?**
  Members of these groups help protect nature and help protect police dogs. This shows a responsibility to the needs of their communities.

CONNECT TEXT TO TEXT

What do you know about the signmaker's assistant that can help you say which volunteer group he might join?

Have children review the story *The Signmaker's Assistant* to get clues about the group that might best fit the assistant.

Remind children to begin their paragraph by identifying the group they chose. They can then support their choice with examples and reasons they concluded from the story.

Activate Prior Knowledge Ask: What neighborhood and community groups do you know about? Supply the names of service organizations in your area, such as scouting groups, neighborhood watch groups, and others as necessary.

Options for Oral Reading

Use *The Signmaker's Assistant* or one of the following Leveled Readers.

On-Level

Freda's Signs

Strategic Intervention

Grandpa's Sign

Advanced

Marty's Job

Provide opportunities for children to echo read, repeating a passage phrase-by-phrase as each phrase is read aloud by the teacher, aide, or another skilled reader such as a proficient student.

To develop fluent readers, use Fluency Coach.

Fluency

READ WITH APPROPRIATE PHRASING

MODEL READING WITH APPROPRIATE PHRASING Use *The Signmaker's Assistant.*

- Review that good readers group words appropriately. When I read, I group words together. I do not read word-by-word. I read at a good pace and pause at the commas.

- Ask children to follow along as you read p. 273 with appropriate phrasing.

- Have children read the page after you. Encourage them to read with appropriate phrasing by grouping words appropriately. Continue in the same way with pp. 274–275.

REREAD FOR FLUENCY

Paired Reading

ROUTINE

1. **Select a Passage** For "Helping Hand," use pp. 286–289.

2. **Reader 1 Begins** Have children read, switching who reads first at the end of each page.

3. **Reader 2 Begins** Have partners reread; now the other partner begins.

4. **Reread** For optimal fluency, children should reread three or four times with attention to accuracy, pace, and expression/intonation.

5. **Provide Feedback** Listen as children read and provide corrective feedback regarding their oral reading and their use of the blending strategy.

Monitor Progress | Check Fluency WCPM

As children reread, monitor their progress toward their individual fluency goals. Current Goal: 82–92 words correct per minute. End-of-Year Goal: 90 words correct per minute.

If... children cannot read fluently at a rate of 82–92 words correct per minute,

then... make sure children practice with text at their independent level. Provide additional fluency practice, pairing nonfluent readers with fluent readers.

If... children already read at 90 words correct per minute,

then... they do not need to reread three to four times.

SUCCESS PREDICTOR

Day 1 Check Word Reading

Day 2 Check Lesson Vocabulary/High-Frequency Words

Day 3 Check Retelling

▶ **Day 4 Check Fluency**

Day 5 Assess Progress

Writing Across the Curriculum

WRITE Signs

BRAINSTORM Have children look at the illustration on p. 279. Which signs pictured here do you think are important for the safety and well-being of people? (Children should mention the stop sign and may suggest the detour, parking, and street name signs or others.) Ask children to explain why they think each sign is important.

SHARE THE PEN Have children participate in creating signs. To begin, have a volunteer draw a stop sign, including the word *STOP*. Explain that signs give information briefly and visually. Point out that the color and shape of a sign gives people clues to its meaning. Have children create a display of different important signs. Call on individuals to name a sign. Discuss any special shape the sign might have. Write the sign's text, inviting individuals to help spell the message by writing familiar letter-sounds. Ask questions, such as the following:

- Are these signs written in full sentences? (not usually)

- How can you tell? (They may be missing subjects, verbs, or end marks.)

- Why do you think this is so? (It is important to convey messages quickly and briefly.)

Continue having individuals contribute to writing signs. Frequently reread the signs.

OBJECTIVE

● Identify contractions.

DAILY FIX-IT

7. The auto accident was he's
   fawlt.

The auto accident was <u>his</u> <u>fau</u>lt.

8. He did n't read those sign.

He di<u>dn</u>'t read <u>the</u> sign.

Contractions

Underline the contraction in each sentence. Draw a line to match a sign and its meaning.

1. <u>Don't</u> park your car here.

2. You <u>shouldn't</u> go faster than this.

3. <u>I'll</u> like eating here.

4. <u>It's</u> time to save money.

Write about classroom rules. Use some contractions in the box.

| don't | shouldn't | can't | isn't |
| I'll | we're | it's | I'm |

Possible answer:

We shouldn't talk when someone
else is talking. It's important to
raise your hand. Don't chew gum.
It isn't safe to run in the halls.

Home Activity Your child learned how to use contractions in writing. Have your child use contractions to describe some family rules. For example, *Don't leave a mess.*

▲ **Grammar and Writing
Practice Book** p. 98

Grammar

REVIEW Contractions

DEFINE CONTRACTIONS

● What is a contraction? (a short way to put two words together)

● What symbol takes the place of one or more letters when a contraction is formed? (an apostrophe)

PRACTICE

SUPPLY CONTRACTIONS Write these sentences on the board.

_____ see the movie.

_____ give me a ride.

_____ want to bake a cake.

_____ in a play.

_____ be home soon.

Have individuals fill in the blanks, using contractions. Point out that each blank could be filled in many different ways.

<u>I can't</u> see the movie.
<u>He wouldn't</u> give me a ride.
<u>She doesn't</u> want to bake a cake.
<u>I'm</u> in a play.
<u>They'll</u> be home soon.

Viewing and Speaking

ANALYZE ADVERTISEMENTS

DEMONSTRATE VIEWING AND SPEAKING Show children some advertisements clipped from newspapers or magazines. What is the purpose of advertisements? (to sell something) Have children discuss how an advertisement sells products and services. Do advertisers use facts? Do they use opinions? How do they try to make you feel about their product? About yourself?

TAKE A SURVEY Ask children to tell about an advertisement they have seen on television, heard on the radio, or read in a magazine or a newspaper. Ask them to describe the advertisement, tell how it tried to make them think or feel, and tell whether it made them want to try the product.

I saw a TV commercial for "Lemon Flakes" cereal. The announcer said it was the most popular new cereal. Everybody is trying it. All the kids in the commercial were smiling and saying "Yum!" I thought it must taste pretty good. I wanted to try it.

Wrap Up Your Day!

☑ **MAKING CONNECTIONS** Remind students about the organizations they read about in "Helping Hand." Would you like to start an organization to help people? If so, what would your organization do?

LET'S TALK ABOUT IT Remind children of the Question of the Week: What happens when we do the wrong thing? Then ask them to think about the organizations in "Helping Hand." Ask them to answer the opposite question: What happens when we do the right thing? Is it always easy to do the right thing?

PREVIEW Day 5

Remind children that they read a story about a signmaker's assistant who got into trouble. Tell them that tomorrow they will read about Norman again.

Day 5
AT A GLANCE

Share Literature
"Troublemaker"

Phonics and Spelling
 Review Vowels *aw, au, augh, al*

Lesson Vocabulary
idea   important   blame
signmaker   townspeople
   afternoon
More Words to Know
assistant   wisdom   feverishly

Monitor Progress
Spelling Test: Words with Vowels
  aw, au, augh, al

Group Time < Differentiated
Assessment

Writing and Grammar
Trait: Sentences
Contractions

Research and Study Skills
Evaluate Online Sources

Materials

- *Sing with Me Big Book*
- *Read Aloud Anthology*
- Reproducible Pages TE 290f–290g
- Student Edition 290–291
- Graphic Organizer 25

Morning Warm-Up!

This week we read about troublemakers.

They often use bad judgment and do the wrong thing. What can you do when you make a mistake?

QUESTION OF THE DAY Encourage children to sing "Best Judgment" from the *Sing with Me Big Book* as you gather. Write and read the message and discuss the question.

REVIEW ORAL VOCABULARY Have children name the characters from this week's readings who

- were troublemakers
- used bad judgment
- got scolded
- apologized
- caused someone to protest

ELL

Assess Vocabulary Use the Day 5 instruction on ELL Poster 25 to monitor children's progress with oral vocabulary.

ELL Poster 25

Share Literature

LISTEN AND RESPOND

USE PRIOR KNOWLEDGE Review that yesterday the class listened to "Troublemaker" to find out why Justin protested. Suggest that today the class listen to find out how Justin protested.

MONITOR LISTENING COMPREHENSION

- Why did Mrs. Richardson think that Justin had thrown the paper ball at Nieka? (Possible responses: because it had come from near him, and everybody thought he was a troublemaker)

- How did Justin feel about moving his desk? (He was mad.)

- How does Justin tell Mrs. Richardson that he didn't throw the paper ball? (He writes a letter to her with a poem in it; the poem says he didn't do it.)

Read Aloud Anthology
Troublemaker

BUILD ORAL VOCABULARY

GENERATE DISCUSSION Recall how Justin responded to being blamed for something he didn't do. (He kept quiet and wrote a poem to his teacher.) Have children discuss different ways people can react when they are being blamed for something they didn't do. Then talk about ways people can respond when blamed for something they *did* do. Have children use some of this week's Amazing Words as they share their ideas.

Monitor Progress | Check Oral Vocabulary

Remind children of the unit concept—Responsibility. Ask them to tell you about the concept using some of this week's Amazing Words: *apologize, citizen, judgment, hoard, scold, interrupt, protest,* and *troublemaker.*

If... children have difficulty using the Amazing Words,

then... ask more questions about the Read Aloud selection or the concept using the Amazing Words. Note which questions children can respond to. Reteach unknown words using the Oral Vocabulary routine on p. DI·1.

SUCCESS PREDICTOR

| **Day 1** Check Word Reading | **Day 2** Check Lesson Vocabulary/High-Frequency Words | **Day 3** Check Retelling | **Day 4** Check Fluency | ▶ **Day 5** Check Oral Vocabulary/ Assess Progress |

Amazing Words to build oral vocabulary

apologize	scold
citizen	interrupt
judgment	protest
hoard	troublemaker

ELL

Extend Language Explain to children that often the meaning of a compound word is very different from the meanings of its two parts. Write the words *butter* and *fly,* and ask children what each word means. Then ask them what a *butterfly* is, and help them see that this word's meaning changes when it becomes a compound. Do the same with *strawberry* and *handsome.*

Oral Vocabulary

SUCCESS PREDICTOR

OBJECTIVES

- Review *aw, au, augh,* and *al* words.
- Review lesson vocabulary.

Vowels *aw, au, augh, al*

REVIEW

IDENTIFY *aw, au, augh,* AND *al* WORDS Write these sentences. Have children read each one aloud. Call on individuals to name and underline the *aw, au, augh,* and *al* words and identify the vowel sounds.

Did you see the <u>bald</u> man <u>waltz</u> with his <u>daughter</u>?

I <u>paused</u> and <u>caught</u> a look at the little <u>fawn</u>.

She drove her <u>auto</u> <u>because</u> she had to get a <u>malt</u>.

I put some <u>salt</u> and <u>sauce</u> on the <u>raw</u> meat.

Lesson Vocabulary

REVIEW

MEANING CLUES Read the following clues for children. Have children write a Word to Know from p. 266 for each clue. Then reread clues and answers together.

This is a job in which someone makes something with words and messages. (signmaker)

This comes between morning and evening. (afternoon)

These fill your head when you are thinking. (ideas)

These individuals live together in a town. (townspeople)

It is a word that means "fault." (blame)

This word means the opposite of *small* or *little*. (important)

Vocabulary For additional practice with the lesson vocabulary, use the vocabulary strategies and word cards in the ELL Teaching Guide, pp. 171–172.

SPELLING TEST Vowels *aw, au, augh, al*

DICTATION SENTENCES Use these sentences to assess this week's spelling words.

1. Grandma will come visit in <u>August</u>.
2. I saw the rocket <u>launch</u> into space.
3. Did you <u>talk</u> to Pete today?
4. That red <u>auto</u> belongs to Max.
5. It is not your <u>fault</u> that we are late.
6. I drew pictures with <u>chalk</u>.
7. She <u>caught</u> the ball!
8. Please <u>walk</u> to the park with me.
9. Our teacher <u>taught</u> us about the stars.
10. The ice will <u>thaw</u> when winter ends.
11. Did you <u>draw</u> that pretty picture?
12. The vase broke <u>because</u> it fell off the table.

CHALLENGE WORDS

13. The <u>audience</u> loves our show!
14. It is <u>awkward</u> for me to walk in big shoes!
15. The <u>applause</u> after the play was loud.

ASSESS

● Spell words with *au, aw, augh, al.*

Spelling Words

Vowels *aw, au, augh, al*

1.	talk	7.	chalk
2.	because	8.	auto
3.	August	9.	taught
4.	caught	10.	thaw
5.	draw	11.	fault*
6.	walk	12.	launch

Challenge Words

13.	applause	15.	awkward
14.	audience		

* Words from the Selection

Group Time

On-Level	**Strategic Intervention**	**Advanced**
Read Set B Sentences and Story for rechecking.	**Read** Set A Sentences and Story for rechecking.	**Read** Set C Sentences and Story for rechecking.
• Use pp. 290e–290g.	• Use pp. 290e–290g.	• Use pp. 290e–290g.
	• Use the Routine on p. DI•62.	• Use the Routine on p. DI•63.

ELL Place English language learners in the groups that correspond to their reading abilities in English.

DAY **5**

(*i*) Independent Activities

Fluency Reading Children reread selections at their independent level.

Journal Writing Write about a signmaker who makes a very unusual sign. Share writing.

Independent Reading See p. 264j for Reading/Library activities and suggestions.

Literacy Centers You may use the Technology Center on p. 264k to support this week's concepts and reading.

Practice Book 2.2 Evaluate Online Sources, p. 100

Break into small groups after Spelling and before Grammar and Writing.

ASSESS

- Decode vowels *aw, au, augh, al.*
- Read lesson vocabulary.
- Read aloud with appropriate speed and accuracy.
- Distinguish between realism and fantasy.
- Retell a story.

Differentiated Assessment

On-Level

Set B

Strategic Intervention

Set A

Advanced

Set C

Fluency Assessment Plan

☑ Week 1 assess Advanced students.

☑ Week 2 assess Strategic Intervention students.

☑ Week 3 assess On-Level students.

☑ Week 4 assess Strategic Intervention students.

☑ **This week assess any students you have not yet checked during this unit.**

Set individual fluency goals for children to enable them to reach the end-of-year goal.

- Current Goal: 82–92 wcpm
- End-of-Year Goal: 90 wcpm
- **ELL** An informal method of assessing oral reading fluency is to simply listen to a child reading orally and judge how clear the reading is.

SENTENCE READING

ASSESS VOWELS *aw, au, augh, al* AND LESSON VOCABULARY Use one of the reproducible lists on p. 290f to assess children's ability to read words with vowels *aw, au, augh, al* and lesson vocabulary. Call on individuals to read two sentences aloud. Have each child in the group read different sentences. Start over with sentence one if necessary.

RECORD SCORES Use the Sentence Reading Chart for this unit on p. WA19.

Monitor Progress	Vowels *aw, au, augh, al*
If... children have trouble reading vowels *aw, au, augh, al,*	**then...** use the Reteach Lessons on p. DI•68.
Lesson Vocabulary	
If... children cannot read a lesson vocabulary word,	**then...** mark the missed words on a lesson vocabulary list and send the list home for additional word reading practice or have the child practice with a fluent reader.

FLUENCY AND COMPREHENSION

ASSESS FLUENCY Take a one-minute sample of children's oral reading. See Monitoring Fluency, p. WA17. Have children read "Sausages to Go," the on-level fluency passage on p. 290g.

RECORD SCORES Record the number of words read correctly in a minute on the child's Fluency Progress Chart.

ASSESS COMPREHENSION Have the child read to the end of the passage. (If the child had difficulty with the passage, you may read it aloud.) Ask questions about what could really happen and what could not really happen and have the child retell the passage. Use the Retelling Rubric on p. 284–285 to evaluate the child's retelling.

Monitor Progress	Fluency
If... a child does not achieve the fluency goal on the timed reading,	**then...** copy the passage and send it home with the child for additional fluency practice or have the child practice with a fluent reader.
Realism and Fantasy	
If... a child cannot distinguish realism and fantasy,	**then...** use the Reteach Lesson on p. DI•68.

READ THE SENTENCES

Set A

1. The townspeople cut down tall stalks of corn.
2. The signmaker taught Paul how to make letters.
3. It is important that the straw be here by dawn.
4. We will talk about the law this afternoon.
5. Do not blame him because the mall was closed.
6. Draw a picture of your ideas for the wall.

Set B

1. The plumber took the blame for the flaw in the faucet.
2. We saw a hawk high in a tree in the afternoon.
3. It is important to add only a little salt to the sauce.
4. The signmaker painted a small sign for the lawn.
5. Saul had ideas about how to do the laundry better.
6. The townspeople met at the city hall in August.

Set C

1. Paula's plans caught the attention of the townspeople.
2. The author scrawled her ideas on the chalkboard.
3. It is important to walk fast so we don't miss the rocket launch.
4. The signmaker will draw pictures of steaks and sausages on the meat market's sign.
5. Ann wore her shawl in the chilly autumn afternoon.
6. Blame the icy roads for the auto wreck because the driver was not at fault.

REPRODUCIBLE PAGE • See also Assessment Handbook, p. 353

© Pearson Education

Monitor Progress | Vowels *aw, au, augh, al*
Lesson Vocabulary

290f

SUCCESS PREDICTOR

Sausages to Go

Every August the town of Smallville had a	8
sausage contest to see who could make the best	17
sausages. The people cooked from dawn to dusk.	25
They used salt and pepper and other spices.	33
Some made fine sauces too. Then people walked	41
from stall to stall and ate sausages all day.	50
One year a sly hawk wanted some meat to	59
gnaw on. He thought, "It will be easy to grab	69
sausages in my claws." So the hawk stole link	78
after link. The people were at a meeting and didn't	88
see him. But a little boy named Claude caught the	98
hawk in the act.	102
When the people came back, they all blamed	110
each other for stealing their sausages. The little	118
boy yelled out, "It's not your fault. I saw the hawk	129
do it!"	131
That taught everyone a lesson. From then on,	139
the town always had a "Hawk Watch." Thanks to	148
Claude no one's sausages were ever stolen again.	156

See also Assessment Handbook, p. 354 • REPRODUCIBLE PAGE

Write Now
Writing and Grammar

Sign

Prompt

In *The Signmaker's Assistant*, the signmaker put important messages on his signs.
Think about important messages you want to tell people.
Now write two messages on signs.

Writing Trait

You can use different kinds of **sentences** on your signs.

Student Model

Writer speaks directly to reader as *you*.

Messages are short and clear.

> Show respect for others. You'll be glad you did because they'll show respect for you.

Sentences are statements, a command, and an exclamation.

> It's wise to count to ten when you're angry. You don't want to say something you shouldn't!

290

Writer's Checklist

- ✔ **Focus** Does each sign stick to one idea?
- ✔ **Organization** Are sentences in a clear order?
- ✔ **Support** Does each sign make its point?
- ✔ **Conventions** Are contractions written correctly?

Grammar

Contractions

A **contraction** is a short way to put two words together. Contractions can combine a pronoun and a verb, such as *will*, *are*, or *is*, or a verb and the word *not*. An **apostrophe (')** takes the place of one or more letters.

> **I'll** close the shop. *(I + will)*
> Please **don't** leave. *(do + not)*

....

Look at the signs. Write the contractions. Then write the two words used to make each contraction.

291

Writing and Grammar

LOOK AT THE PROMPT Read p. 290 aloud. Have children select and discuss key words or phrases in the prompt. *(important messages you want to tell people, two messages on signs)*

STRATEGIES TO DEVELOP SENTENCES Have children

- find examples of different kinds of sentences in a story.
- rewrite commands as statements. Which makes a bigger impact?
- include more than one sentence in a message, each a different kind.

See Scoring Rubric on p. WA11. **Rubric 4 3 2 1**

HINTS FOR BETTER WRITING Read p. 291 aloud. Use the checklist to help children revise their signs. Write a list on the board of contractions and the two words that make each of them: *don't (do + not), can't (can + not), shouldn't (should + not), I'll (I + will), you'll (you + will), they'll (they + will), it's (it + is).* Then discuss the grammar lesson. (Answers: *You'll, You will; they'll, they will; It's, It is; you're, you are; don't, do not; shouldn't, should not*) Have children use contractions correctly on their signs.

DAILY FIX-IT

9. I useed chawk to draw a sign.
   I us<u>ed</u> ch<u>al</u>k to draw a sign.

10. They goed the write way.
    They <u>went</u> the <u>right</u> way.

Contractions

Replace the underlined words with a contraction from the box.

wasn't	didn't	wouldn't

1. Hannah <u>did not</u> spill the paint.   **didn't**

2. She <u>would not</u> drip water on Alex.   **wouldn't**

3. Hannah <u>was not</u> sure about the lost key.   **wasn't**

Circle the contraction that means the same as the underlined words. **Write** each sentence. **Use** the contraction you circled.

4. <u>It is</u> a bad day for Hannah. (It'll, (It's))

   It's a bad day for Hannah.

5. Today <u>she is</u> unhappy. ((she's) she'd)

   Today she's unhappy.

6. <u>We will</u> all help her. (We've, (We'll))

   We'll all help her.

Home Activity Your child reviewed contractions. Look through a storybook together. Ask your child to point out contractions and to tell what two words make up each contraction.

▲ **Grammar and Writing Practice Book** p. 100

Signmaker's Assistant **290-291**

Research/Study Skills

TEACH/MODEL Evaluate Online Sources

MODEL EVALUATING ONLINE SOURCES Explain that many Web sites contain useful information, but that some are not accurate or reliable. Anyone can put a Web site online. Children need to decide which are good sources of information. Write these common domains on the board and review their meanings: *.edu, .gov, .org, .com.* Then model how to evaluate a Web site.

 MODEL If a Web site address contains .edu or .gov, I know it's from a school or government and is likely to be reliable. However, even an .edu address may belong to an individual college student and may not be completely reliable. If the address contains .org or .com, I know it's from an organization or business that might present just one side of an issue. So I look to see if the information is balanced and complete. I also check to see if it is up to date and if the writer is an expert in the subject.

IDENTIFY SIGNS OF RELIABILITY Discuss with children the following Web site content. Have them decide which are reliable and which are unreliable sources: advertisements, background information on the author or sponsoring organization, dates indicating when the content was last updated, requests for money or personal information, list of sources used, facts and statistics, clear text.

PRACTICE

COMPARE ONLINE SOURCES Have groups of children compare two different Web sites on similar topics. One site should be a nonprofit or educational site. The other site should be a commercial site designed to sell products. Have each group report on whether its site would be a reliable source of information. Have them give at least two reasons for their answers.

Read Ana's Internet search results.
Write the answer to each question.

Search | painting

1 Painter's Supply
Paint, brushes, buckets. We sell **painting** supplies.
2 100 Masters of Painting
Take an online tour. See some of the world's best **paintings**.
3 Long Painters
No **painting** job too small—from one room to the entire house.
4 Brush Up Your Paint Skills
Simple **painting** lessons that anyone can master.

1. What keyword did Ana enter? **painting**

2. Is Painter's Supply more likely to have a Web address that ends with **.com** or **.edu**? Explain.

It will end with .com because they are selling things.

3. At which Web site could Ana learn to paint?

Brush Up Your Paint Skills

4. How does 100 Masters of Painting differ from Long Painters?

One tells about artists, and one is a painting company.

School + Home Activity Your child learned how to evaluate information from online sources. Ask your child to tell you about the different kinds of information available on the Internet. If possible, work with your child to gain access to the Internet and search for information on a topic of interest to your child.

▲ **Practice Book 2.2** p. 100, Online Sources

Access Content Explain to English language learners that domain names are abbreviations, or shortened forms, of words. Tell them that the domain name *.edu* is short for *education,* so when they see that they should think of a school or some other educational organization, Do the same for other domain names such as *.gov* and *.org*.

Wrap Up Your Week!

LET'S TALK ABOUT Responsibility

QUESTION OF THE WEEK Recall this week's question.

- What happens when we do the wrong thing?

Display Graphic Organizer 25 or the T-chart you made earlier. Ask children to try to add one or more new rules to the chart. Then ask what rules they would make if they were in charge at school or at home. Have them tell what might happen if their rules were broken.

Rules	If We Break the Rules
crossing the street at the light	We could get hurt.
not littering	Our neighborhood would be dirty.
bedtime at a certain time	We could get tired.

▲ Graphic Organizer 25

CONNECT Use questions such as these to prompt a discussion.

- What should a troublemaker do besides apologize and say, "I'm sorry"?
- A citizen can protest in different ways. If you disagreed with a rule, what would be a good way to protest it?
- What do you think should happen to someone who makes a mistake in judgment? Should that person be scolded or taught how to look at the situation correctly? Give a reason for your answer.

ELL

Build Background Use ELL Poster 26 to support the Preview activity.

You've learned **008** Amazing Words this week!	You've learned **201** Amazing Words so far this year!

PREVIEW Tell children that next week they will meet some American heroes and also read about some important traditions.

PREVIEW Next Week

Assessment Checkpoints *for the Week*

Selection Assessment

Use pp. 97–100 of Selection Tests to check:

 Selection Understanding

  Comprehension Skill *Realism and Fantasy*

 Selection Vocabulary
afternoon
blame
idea
important
signmaker
townspeople

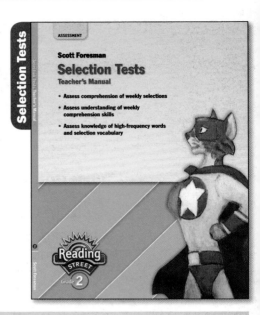

Leveled Assessment

- On-Level
- Strategic Intervention
- Advanced

Use pp. 145–150 of Fresh Reads for Differentiated Test Practice to check:

 Comprehension Skill *Realism and Fantasy*

 REVIEW **Comprehension Skill** *Author's Purpose*

 Fluency *Words Correct Per Minute*

Managing Assessment

Use Assessment Handbook for:

 Weekly Assessment Blackline Masters for Monitoring Progress

☑ **Observation Checklists**

☑ **Record-Keeping Forms**

☑ **Portfolio Assessment**

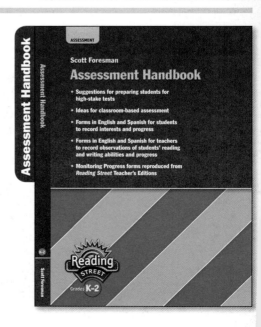

Unit 5
Concept Wrap-Up

Children are ready to express their understanding of the unit concept question through discussion and wrap-up activities and to take the Unit 5 Benchmark Test.

Unit Wrap-Up

Use the Unit Wrap-Up on pp. 292–293 to discuss the unit theme, Responsibility, and to have children show their understanding of the theme through cross-curricular activities.

Unit Project

On p. 153 you assigned children a unit-long inquiry project, to research ways that people are responsible in the community. Children have investigated, analyzed, and synthesized information during the course of the unit as they prepared their posters. Schedule time for children to present their projects. The project rubric can be found below.

Unit Inquiry Project Rubric

4	3	2	1
• Child participates in brainstorming. Research is complete and relevant to inquiry. Research is organized and list of resources is useful. • Illustrations complement text. Poster is legible, instructive, and organized.	• Child participates in brainstorming. Research is accurate but not as thorough. Most sources are relevant to inquiry question. • Poster contains information, but could be more organized and legible.	• Child does not participate in brainstorming. Research is not accurate and contains little information. • Poster has little information and is not focused on the subject.	• Research is not organized and does not relate to inquiry question. Child does not participate in brainstorming. • Poster is not complete or helpful.

Unit 5
Wrap-Up

OBJECTIVES

- Discuss the unit theme.
- Connect content across selections.
- Combine content and skills in meaningful activities that build literacy.
- Respond to unit selections through a variety of modalities.

RESPONSIBILITY

Discuss the Big Idea

What does it mean to be responsible?

Help children relate the theme question for this unit to the selections and their own experiences. Write the questions and prompt discussion with questions such as the following. Then assign the Wrap-Up activities.

- How are people in the selections responsible? (Possible answers: *Firefighter!* Firefighters work hard to keep our communities safe from fire. *One Dark Night* Jonathan helped a stray cat and her kittens during a storm. *Bad Dog, Dodger!* Sam took responsibility to train his dog so that Dodger would not get into so much trouble. *Horace and Morris but mostly Dolores* Dolores took responsibility for forming a fun club that both boys and girls could join. *The Signmaker's Assistant* Norman learned that people respect a signmaker when he or she acts responsibly.)

- Why is following rules an important part of being responsible? (Possible response: Without rules people could get hurt.) Have children generate a list of rules or procedures for the classroom. Post the rules in a visible spot for everyone to follow.

- Do you think being responsible is always easy? Why or why not? (Answers will vary.)

Job Chart

connect to SOCIAL STUDIES

In Unit 5, you read about people who are responsible in different ways. Each person in a certain role or job needs to have special skills and training to do a job well. Make a chart. Show each job or role you read about. List a few important skills for doing the job well.

Job	Skill
Firefighter	Strong

292

What does it mean to be responsible?

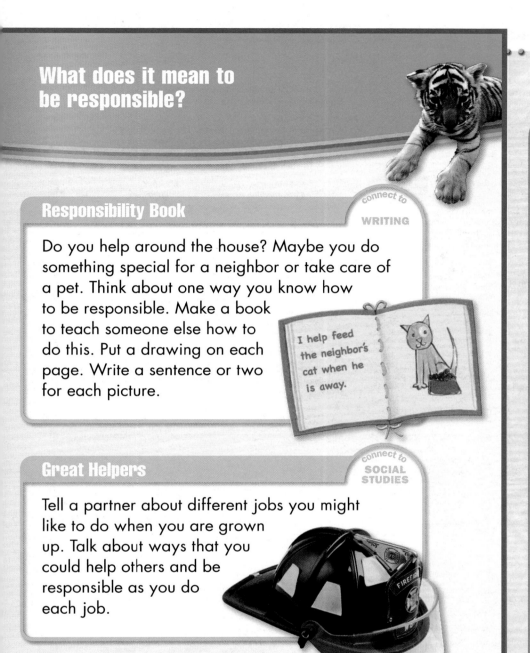

Responsibility Book

connect to WRITING

Do you help around the house? Maybe you do something special for a neighbor or take care of a pet. Think about one way you know how to be responsible. Make a book to teach someone else how to do this. Put a drawing on each page. Write a sentence or two for each picture.

I help feed the neighbor's cat when he is away.

Great Helpers

connect to SOCIAL STUDIES

Tell a partner about different jobs you might like to do when you are grown up. Talk about ways that you could help others and be responsible as you do each job.

293

ACTIVITIES

Job Chart

Make a Chart To get children started, you can model the skills needed for your own job as a teacher. As children suggest ideas, remind them to reread the text and look at things each character did to show responsibility.

Responsibility Book

Write and Draw Before children write, have them brainstorm ways they can help others. Encourage them to draw pictures that show how they help and then write captions for the pictures. Tell them to make sure the book can give other children ideas on how to help others.

Great Helpers

Discuss Make sure that partners pay special attention to one another as they discuss the jobs they might like to have. Tell them that as they listen, they should look directly at the speaker and sit quietly without fidgeting.

Glossary

Glossary

Aa

adventure (uhd VEN cher) An **adventure** is an exciting or unusual thing to do: Riding a raft down the river was a great **adventure**. *NOUN*

afternoon (af ter NOON) The **afternoon** is the part of the day between morning and evening: On Saturday we played all **afternoon**. *NOUN*

America (uh MAIR uh kuh) **America** is another name for North **America**. Some people use the name **America** to mean the United States. *NOUN*

America

American Revolution (uh MAIR uh kuhn rev uh LOO shuhn) The **American Revolution** was a series of protests and acts of American colonists from 1763 to 1783 against England. It is also known as the Revolutionary War.

angry (ANG gree) If you are **angry**, you feel upset or mad: Dad was **angry** when he saw the broken car window. *ADJECTIVE*

assistant (uh SIS tuhnt) An **assistant** is a helper: I was her **assistant** in the library. *NOUN*

aunt (ANT or AHNT) Your **aunt** is your father's sister, your mother's sister, or your uncle's wife. *NOUN*

Bb

bank¹ (BANK) A **bank** is a place where people keep their money: My brother has a **bank** for nickels and pennies. *NOUN*

436

bank² (BANK) The **bank** of a river or lake is the ground beside it: He sat on the river **bank**. *NOUN*

bases (BAY sez)
1. A **base** is the bottom of something: The metal **bases** of the floor lamps might scratch the floor. *NOUN*
2. A **base** is also an object in some games: After hitting a home run, the player ran the **bases**. *NOUN*

basket (BAS kuht)
1. A **basket** is something to carry or store things in. **Baskets** are made of straw, plastic, or strips of wood. *NOUN*
2. In basketball a **basket** is used as a goal. The **basket** is made of a metal ring with a net hanging from it. *NOUN*

basket

bellowed (BELL ohd) To **bellow** is to make a loud, deep noise: The moose **bellowed** angrily at the man. *VERB*

birthday (BERTH day) A **birthday** is the day that a person was born or something was started: Our country's **birthday** is July 4th. *NOUN*

blame (BLAYM) To **blame** is to hold someone responsible for something bad or wrong. *VERB*

blankets (BLANG kuhts) **Blankets** are soft, warm coverings for beds: We bought new, wool **blankets**. *NOUN*

437

bleachers (BLEE cherz) **Bleachers** are benches for people attending games or other outdoor events. *NOUN*

block (BLOK)
1. A **block** is a thick piece of wood or plastic: My little brother held one green **block** and two blue ones. *NOUN*
2. If you **block** something, you fill it so that nothing can pass by: I saw a large truck **block** traffic. *VERB*
3. A **block** is also an area of a city that has a street on each side: I walked down the **block** to my friend's house. *NOUN*

borrow (BAR oh or BOR oh) If you **borrow** something, you get it from a person or place just for a while: I like to **borrow** books from the library. *VERB*

branches (BRANCH ez)
1. **Branches** are the part of the tree that grow out from the trunk: Swings hung from the tree's **branches**. *NOUN*
2. **Branches** are small parts of something: The **branches** of the river had quiet water. *NOUN*

brooding (BROOD ing) **Brooding** is to hang over as if to cover: The **brooding** storm clouds settled over the town. *ADJECTIVE*

building (BIL ding) A **building** is something that has been built. A **building** has walls and a roof. Schools, houses, and barns are **buildings**. *NOUN*

building

438

bulges (BUHL jez) **Bulges** are an outward swelling: The air in the man's jaws made **bulges** in his cheeks. *NOUN*

bumpy (BUHM pee) If something is **bumpy**, it is rough or has a lot of bumps: This street is too **bumpy** to skate on. *ADJECTIVE*

burning (BERN ing) **Burning** means to be on fire: Dad carefully watched the **burning** leaves. *ADJECTIVE*

Cc

campfire (KAMP fyr) A **campfire** is an outdoor fire used for cooking or staying warm. *NOUN*

cattle (KAT uhl) **Cattle** are animals raised for their meat, milk, or skins. Cows and bulls are **cattle**. *NOUN PLURAL*

chased (CHAYST) When you **chase** someone or something, you run after them: The children **chased** the ball down the hill. *VERB*

cheers (CHEERZ) When you **cheer**, you call out or yell loudly to show you like something: She **cheers** for her team. *VERB*

chewing

chewing (CHOO ing) When you **chew** something, you crush it with your teeth: He was **chewing** the nuts. *VERB*

chuckle (CHUK uhl) When you **chuckle**, you laugh softly: She will **chuckle** when she sees her gift. *VERB*

439

Glossary

chuckwagon (CHUK WAG uhn) A **chuckwagon** is a wagon or truck that carries food and cooking equipment for cowhands. *NOUN*

clattering (KLAT tuhr ing) **Clattering** is having a loud, rattling noise: The **clattering** dishes woke me up. *ADJECTIVE*

climbed (KLYMD) When you **climb**, you go up something, usually by using your hands and feet: The children **climbed** into the bus. *VERB*

clubhouse (KLUB HOWSS) A **clubhouse** is a building used by a group of people joined together for some special reason. *NOUN*

clung (KLUNG)
1. If you **clung**, you held tightly to someone or something: He **clung** to his father's hand. *VERB*
2. **Clung** means to have stuck to something: The vine **clung** to the wall. *VERB*

collects (kuh LEKTS) If you **collect** things, you bring them together or gather them together: The student **collects** the crayons. *VERB*

colonies (KOL uh neez) A **colony** is a group of people who leave their own country to settle in another land but who still remain citizens of their own country: The thirteen British **colonies** became the United States of America. *NOUN*

cowboy

Congress (KONG gris) **Congress** is the national legislative body of the United States. **Congress** has two parts, the Senate and the House of Representatives. *NOUN*

cowboy (KOW boi) A **cowboy** is a person who works on a cattle ranch. **Cowboys** also take part in rodeos. *NOUN*

crawls (KRAWLZ) When you **crawl** you move on your hands and knees or with your body close to the ground: The lizard **crawls** across the floor. *VERB*

cycle (SY kuhl) A **cycle** is a series of events that repeats itself in the same order over and over again: A frog's life **cycle** begins as an egg. *NOUN*

Dd

dripping

downhearted (DOWN HART id) To be **downhearted** is to be depressed or discouraged: The team was **downhearted** because we lost the last game. *ADJECTIVE*

dripping (DRIP ing) When something **drips**, it falls in drops: The rain was **dripping** on the roof. *VERB*

drum (DRUHM) A **drum** is a musical instrument that makes a sound when it is beaten. A **drum** is hollow with a cover stretched tight over each end. *NOUN*

drum

440

441

---

dugout (DUHG OWT) A **dugout** is a small shelter at the side of a baseball field, used by players not on the field: The team sat in the **dugout** while the batters took turns. *NOUN*

Ee

exploring (ek SPLOR ing) When you are **exploring**, you are traveling to discover new areas: Astronauts are **exploring** outer space. *VERB*

Ff

fair[1] (FAIR) If you are **fair**, you go by the rules. People who are **fair** treat everyone the same: Try to be **fair** in everything you do. *ADJECTIVE*

fair[2] (FAIR) A **fair** is an outdoor show of farm animals and other things: We enjoyed ourselves at the county **fair**. *NOUN*

fair

favorite (FAY ver it)
1. Your **favorite** thing is the one you like better than all the others: What is your **favorite** color? *ADJECTIVE*
2. A **favorite** is a person or thing that you like very much: Pizza is a **favorite** with me. *NOUN*

feverishly (FEE vuhr ish lee) When something is done **feverishly**, it is done in an excited or restless way: We packed **feverishly** for the trip. *ADVERB*

field (FEE uhld) A **field** is a piece of land used for a special purpose: The football **field** needs to be mowed. *NOUN*

fierce (FEERS) When something is **fierce**, it is very great or strong: A **fierce** wind blew the tree house down. *ADJECTIVE*

fingers (FING gerz) Your **fingers** are the five end parts of your hand. *NOUN*

fireproof (FYR proof) A thing that is **fireproof** is almost impossible to burn: Steel and concrete are **fireproof**. *ADJECTIVE*

fingers

flag (FLAG) A **flag** is a piece of colored cloth with stars or other symbols on it. Every country and state has its own **flag**. *NOUN*

flag

flashes (FLASH ez) To **flash** is to give a light or flame: The light **flashes** on and off. *VERB*

forties (FOR teez) The **forties** are the 1940s: My granddad was born in the **forties**. *NOUN*

freedom (FREE duhm) **Freedom** is not being under someone else's control or rule. *NOUN*

fruit (FROOT) **Fruit** is the part of a tree, bush, or vine that has seeds in it and is good to eat. Apples, oranges, strawberries, and bananas are **fruit**. *NOUN*

fruit

Gg

galloped (GAL uhpt) To **gallop** is to run very fast: The horse **galloped** down the road. *VERB*

442

443

Glossary

giant

giant (JY uhnt)
1. In stories, a **giant** is a person who is very large. *NOUN*
2. If something is **giant**, it is much bigger than usual: We made a **giant** sandwich for lunch. *ADJECTIVE*

glee (GLEE) **Glee** is a feeling of great delight or lively joy: The children at the party laughed with **glee** at the clown. *NOUN*

grabbed (GRABD) When you **grab** something, you take it suddenly: The dog **grabbed** the bone. *VERB*

greatest (GRAYT est) If something is the **greatest**, it is the best and most important: He thought it was the **greatest** book he had ever read. *ADJECTIVE*

Hh

harvest (HAR vist)
1. A **harvest** is the ripe crops that are picked after the growing season is over: The corn **harvest** was poor after the hot, dry summer. *NOUN*
2. When you **harvest**, you gather in the crops and store them: We **harvest** the apples in late fall. *VERB*

hatchet (HACH it) A **hatchet** is a small ax with a handle about a foot long, for use with one hand: Dad chopped the log with a **hatchet**. *NOUN*

herd

herd (HERD) A **herd** is a group of the same kind of animals: We saw a **herd** of cows when we drove through the country. *NOUN*

444

hydrant (HY druhnt) A **hydrant** is a large water pipe that sticks up out of the ground. It has places where firefighters can connect hoses. *NOUN*

Ii

ideas (eye DEE uhz) **Ideas** are thoughts or plans: The class had different **ideas** on how to spend the money. *NOUN*

important (im PORT uhnt) Something that is **important** has a lot of meaning or worth: Learning to read is **important**. *ADJECTIVE*

insect

insects (IN sekts) **Insects** are small animals with six legs and bodies that have three parts. Most **insects** have four wings. Flies, bees, butterflies, and mosquitoes are **insects**. *NOUN*

Jj

jingle (JING uhl)
1. To **jingle** is to make or cause a sound like little bells. *VERB*
2. A **jingle** is a cone-shaped piece of tin sewn in rows onto a Native American dress. *NOUN*

Ll

lightning (LYT ning) **Lightning** is a flash of electricity in the sky. The sound that usually comes after a flash of **lightning** is thunder. *NOUN*

445

Louisville slugger (LOO ee vil SLUG ger) A **Louisville slugger** is one kind of a baseball bat. *NOUN*

Mm

masks (MASKS) **Masks** are coverings that hide or protect your face: The firefighters wear gas **masks**. *NOUN*

moccasins

moccasins (MOK uh suhnz) A **moccasin** is a soft leather shoe or sandal, often without an attached heel. Many Native Americans wore **moccasins**, often made of deer hide. *NOUN*

Nn

nicknames (NIK naymz) **Nicknames** are names used instead of real names: Ed is a **nickname** for Edward. *NOUN*

ninetieth (NYN tee ith) **Ninetieth** is next after the 89th: Great-grandmother celebrated her **ninetieth** birthday. *ADJECTIVE*

nudging (NUJ ing) **Nudging** means to give a slight push: The mother cat was **nudging** her kittens along. *VERB*

Oo

outrigger (OWT RIG er) An **outrigger** is a framework that sticks out from the side of a light boat, canoe, or other vehicle to keep it from turning over: The **outrigger** helped to steady the fire truck. *NOUN*

446

Pp

patchwork (PACH werk) **Patchwork** is pieces of cloth of various colors or shapes sewed together: Mother made the quilt from **patchwork**. *NOUN*

picnic (PIK nik) A **picnic** is a party with a meal outdoors: Our class had a **picnic** at the park. *NOUN*

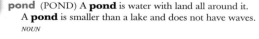
piñata

piñata (pee NYAH tuh) A **piñata** is a decorated shape filled with candy, fruit, and small toys and hung at holiday time in Mexico and other Latin American countries. Blindfolded children swing sticks in order to break the **piñata** to get what is inside. *NOUN*

plate (PLAYT)
1. A **plate** is a dish that is almost flat and is usually round. We eat food from **plates**. *NOUN*
2. A **plate** is a hard rubber slab that a baseball player stands beside to hit the ball. *NOUN*

pond

pond (POND) A **pond** is water with land all around it. A **pond** is smaller than a lake and does not have waves. *NOUN*

pounds (POWNDZ) To **pound** is to hit something hard again and again: She **pounds** the door with her fist. *VERB*

pours (PORZ) When it **pours**, it rains a lot: The rain **pours** down on the city. *VERB*

447

Glossary

powerful (POW er fuhl) **Powerful** is being strong and having great force: The runner had **powerful** legs. *ADJECTIVE*

practice (PRAK tiss) A **practice** is a training session: Coach says that to play the game, you must go to **practice**. *NOUN*

present[1] (PREZ uhnt) Another word for **present** is *here*. If you are **present**, you are not absent: Every member of the class is **present** today. *ADJECTIVE*

present[2] (PREZ uhnt) A **present** is a gift. A **present** is something that someone gives you or that you give someone: His uncle sent him a birthday **present**. *NOUN*

pressing (PRESS ing)
1. **Pressing** is pushing something in a steady way: The child is **pressing** the elevator button. *VERB*
2. When you **press** clothes, you make them smooth with a hot iron: I was **pressing** my shirt to get out the wrinkles. *VERB*

pretended (pri TEND ed) To **pretend** is to make believe that something is real when it is not: We **pretended** that we were camping. *VERB*

present

Qq

quickly (KWIK lee) **Quickly** means in a short time: When I asked him a question, he answered **quickly**. *ADVERB*

448

quilt (KWILT) A **quilt** is a soft covering for a bed. A **quilt** is usually made from two pieces of cloth sewn together with soft material between them. *NOUN*

quilt

Rr

railroad (RAYL rohd) A **railroad** is a road or track of two steel rails. Trains run on **railroads**. *NOUN*

regalia (ri GAY lee uh) **Regalia** are the decorations of any society: He wore the **regalia** of the Lakota Indians. *NOUN*

roar (ROR) A **roar** is a loud, deep sound: The **roar** of the lion frightened some people at the zoo. *NOUN*

rolling (ROHL ling) **Rolling** is making deep loud sounds: The **rolling** thunder woke the baby. *ADJECTIVE*

root (ROOT)
1. The **root** is the part of a plant that grows underground. A plant gets food and water through its **roots**. *NOUN*
2. A **root** is also a word from which other words are made. In the words *rounder* and *roundest*, the **root** is *round*. *NOUN*

roundup (ROWND up) A **roundup** is the act of driving or bringing cattle together from long distances. *NOUN*

Ss

sailed (SAYLD) When something **sails**, it travels on the water or through the air: The ball **sailed** out of the ballpark. *VERB*

449

scent (SENT) A **scent** is a nice smell: Helen loved the **scent** of freshly baked cookies. *NOUN*

sewer (SOO er) A **sewer** is an underground drain that carries away waste water and trash. *NOUN*

shed (SHED) To **shed** is to let hair, skin, or fur fall off: The dog **shed** on the rug. *VERB*

shuffled (SHUF uhld) To **shuffle** is to scrape or drag your feet while walking: We **shuffled** along the slippery sidewalk. *VERB*

signmaker (SYN mayk er) A **signmaker** makes marks or words on a sign that tell you what to do or not to do. *NOUN*

silver (SIL ver) **Silver** is a shiny white metal. **Silver** is used to make coins, jewelry, and other things. *NOUN*

skin (SKIN) **Skin** is the outside covering of human and animal bodies, plants, fruits, and seeds: Her **skin** was red from too much sun. *NOUN*

smooth (SMOOTH) When something is **smooth**, it has an even surface. Something that is **smooth** is not bumpy or rough: The road was very **smooth**. *ADJECTIVE*

soar (SOR) To **soar** is to fly at a great height: Did you see the kite **soar** in the air? *VERB*

soar

450

soil

soil[1] (SOIL) **Soil** is the top layer of the earth. **Soil** is dirt: Our garden has such rich **soil** that almost anything will grow in it. *NOUN*

soil[2] (SOIL) If you **soil** something, you make it dirty: The dust will **soil** her white gloves. *VERB*

spawn (SPAWN) **Spawn** is the eggs of fish, frogs, shellfish, and other animals growing or living in water. *NOUN*

special (SPESH uhl)
1. If something is **special**, it is unusual or different in some way: Your birthday is a **special** day. *ADJECTIVE*
2. A **special** is a TV show produced for one showing: I saw a TV **special** on wolves. *NOUN*

spectators (SPEK tay ters) A **spectator** is someone who looks on without taking part. There were many **spectators** at the ball game. *NOUN*

stars (STARZ)
1. **Stars** are the very bright points of light that shine in the sky at night: On a clear night, the **stars** are very bright. *NOUN*
2. **Stars** are also shapes that have five or six points: I drew **stars** on the paper. *NOUN*

451

Glossary

station (STAY shuhn) A **station** is a building or place used for a special reason: The man went to the police **station**. *NOUN*

stitched (STICHT) To **stitch** is to sew or fasten something with **stitches**: Mom **stitched** the hole in my sweater. *VERB*

storm

storm (STORM) A **storm** is a strong wind with rain, snow, or hail. Some **storms** have lightning and thunder. *NOUN*

stray (STRAY) A **stray** is a lost animal: That cat is a **stray** that we took in. *NOUN*

stripes (STRYPS) **Stripes** are long, narrow bands of color: Our flag has seven red **stripes** and six white **stripes**. *NOUN*

strong (STRAWNG) Something that is **strong** has power. A **strong** person can lift and carry things that are heavy. **Strong** means not weak: A **strong** wind blew down the tree. *ADJECTIVE*

stuffing (STUF ing) **Stuffing** is material used to fill or pack something: The **stuffing** is coming out of the pillow. *NOUN*

Tt

tantrum (TAN truhm) A **tantrum** is a sudden, childish outburst of bad temper or ill humor: The girl had a **tantrum** when she couldn't get her way. *NOUN*

452

tears (TEERZ) **Tears** are drops of salty water that come from your eye. **Tears** fall when you cry. *NOUN*

tendrils

tendrils (TEN druhls) A **tendril** is the thin, curling part of a climbing plant that attaches itself to something and helps support the plant: The ivy plant sent out long, thin **tendrils**. *NOUN*

threw (THROO) When you **threw** something, you sent it through the air: She **threw** the ball back to him. *VERB*

thunder (THUHN der) **Thunder** is the loud noise from the sky that comes after a flash of lightning. *NOUN*

tía (TEE uh) **Tía** is the Spanish word for aunt: My **tía** is my mother's sister. *NOUN*

tightly (TYT lee) When something is tied **tightly**, it is firmly tied: The rope was tied **tightly**. *ADVERB*

townspeople (TOWNZ pee puhl) **Townspeople** are the men, women, and children who live in a village or town: The **townspeople** enjoyed the fair. *NOUN*

trails (TRAYLZ) **Trails** are paths across fields or through the woods: Two **trails** led to the river. *NOUN*

treat (TREET) A **treat** is a gift of food, drink, a free ticket, or the like: She gave us **treats** on the last day of school. *NOUN*

453

trouble (TRUHB uhl)
1. **Trouble** is something that makes you upset, bothers you, or gives you pain: I had a lot of **trouble** working those math problems. *NOUN*
2. If you are in **trouble**, people are angry or upset with you: You will be in **trouble** if you knock that can of paint over. *NOUN*

truest (TROO ist) To be **true** is to be faithful and loyal: She is the **truest** friend I have. *ADJECTIVE*

trunks

trunks (TRUHNGKS) **Trunks** are large boxes for carrying clothes. *NOUN*

Uu

unpacked (uhn PAKT) To **unpack** is to take things out that were packed in a box, trunk, or other container: He **unpacked** his clothes. *VERB*

usually (YOO zhoo uhl lee) **Usually** tells how something is seen, found, or happening most of the time: We **usually** eat at six o'clock. *ADVERB*

Vv

vegetarians (vej uh TAIR ee uhns) A **vegetarian** is someone who eats vegetables but no meat: **Vegetarians** like to eat fruit. *NOUN*

vine (VYN) A **vine** is a plant that grows along the ground. Some **vines** climb up walls and fences. Pumpkins, melons, and grapes grow on **vines**. *NOUN*

454

voice (VOISS) Your **voice** is the sound you make with your mouth. You use your **voice** when you speak, sing, or shout. *NOUN*

Ww

wagged (WAGD) To **wag** is to move from side to side or up and down: The dog **wagged** her tail. *VERB*

wisdom (WIZ duhm) **Wisdom** is knowledge and good judgment based on experience: The leader's **wisdom** guided the group through the woods. *NOUN*

wither (WITH er) To **wither** is to make or become dry and lifeless; dry up: The hot sun will **wither** the plants. *VERB*

wondered (WUHN derd) When you **wondered** about something, you wanted to know about it: He **wondered** what time it was. *VERB*

wrapped

wonderful (WUHN der fuhl) If something is **wonderful**, you like it very much: The ocean was a **wonderful** sight. *ADJECTIVE*

wrapped (RAPT) When you **wrap** something, you cover it up, usually with paper: We **wrapped** presents all morning. *VERB*

455

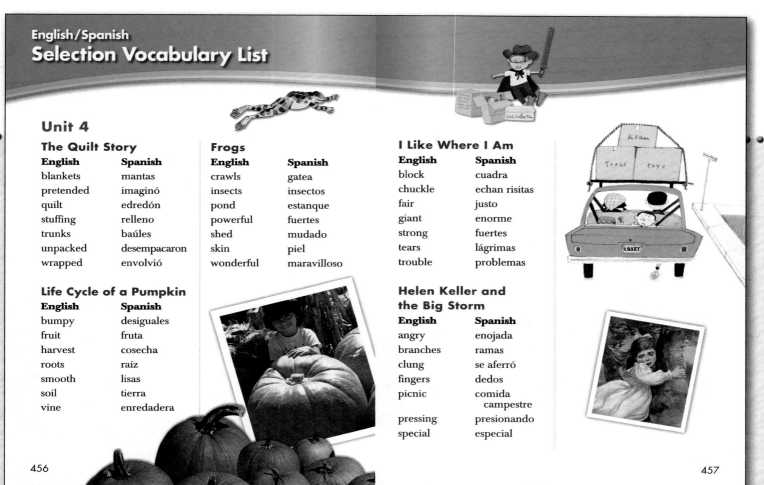

English/Spanish
Selection Vocabulary List

Unit 4

The Quilt Story

English	Spanish
blankets	mantas
pretended	imaginó
quilt	edredón
stuffing	relleno
trunks	baúles
unpacked	desempacaron
wrapped	envolvió

Life Cycle of a Pumpkin

English	Spanish
bumpy	desiguales
fruit	fruta
harvest	cosecha
roots	raíz
smooth	lisas
soil	tierra
vine	enredadera

Frogs

English	Spanish
crawls	gatea
insects	insectos
pond	estanque
powerful	fuertes
shed	mudado
skin	piel
wonderful	maravilloso

I Like Where I Am

English	Spanish
block	cuadra
chuckle	echan risitas
fair	justo
giant	enorme
strong	fuertes
tears	lágrimas
trouble	problemas

Helen Keller and the Big Storm

English	Spanish
angry	enojada
branches	ramas
clung	se aferró
fingers	dedos
picnic	comida campestre
pressing	presionando
special	especial

456

457

Unit 5

Firefighter!

English	Spanish
building	edificio
burning	ardiente
masks	máscaras
quickly	rápidamente
roar	rugido
station	estación
tightly	bien

One Dark Night

English	Spanish
lightning	relámpago
flashes	destella
pounds	golpea
pours	llueve a cántaros
rolling	retumbando
storm	tormenta
thunder	truenos

Bad Dog, Dodger!

English	Spanish
chased	persiguieron
chewing	mordiendo
dripping	goteando
grabbed	agarró
practice	entrenamiento
treat	galletas (de perro)
wagged	meneó

Horace and Morris but mostly Dolores

English	Spanish
adventure	aventura
climbed	subieron
clubhouse	casa del club
exploring	explorando
greatest	mejores
truest	más verdaderos
wondered	se preguntaba

The Signmaker's Assistant

English	Spanish
afternoon	tarde
blame	culpen
ideas	idea
important	importante
signmaker	rotulista
townspeople	ciudadanos

458

459

ELL Glossary

Unit 6

Just Like Josh Gibson

English	Spanish
bases	bases
cheers	gritos de entusiasmo
field	campo
plate	base meta
sailed	volaban
threw	tiró

Red, White, and Blue: The Story of the American Flag

English	Spanish
America	Estados Unidos
birthday	cumpleaños
flag	bandera
freedom	libertad
nicknames	apodos
stars	estrellas
stripes	franjas

A Birthday Basket for Tía

English	Spanish
aunt	tía
bank	alcancía
basket	cesta
collects	recoge
favorite	favorito
present	regalo

Cowboys

English	Spanish
campfire	fuego (de campamento)
cattle	ganado
cowboy	vaquero
galloped	galoparon
herd	manada
railroad	ferrocarril
trails	sendas

Jingle Dancer

English	Spanish
borrow	pedir prestado
clattering	ruidosos
drum	tambor
jingle	cascabeles
silver	plata
voice	voz

460

461

Acknowledgments

Text

Page 16: *The Quilt Story* by Tony Johnston and illustrated by Tomie dePaola. Text Copyright © Tony Johnston, 1985. Illustrations Copyright © Tomie dePaola, 1985. Published by arrangement with G.P. Putnam's Sons, a division of Penguin Young Readers Group, a member of Penguin Group (USA) Inc. All rights reserved.

Page 46: *The Life Cycle of a Pumpkin* by Ron Fridell and Patricia Walsh. Harcourt Global Library, art of Harcourt Education Ltd. Reprinted by permission.

Page 62: From *Where Fish Go in Winter And Other Great Mysteries* by Amy Goldman Koss, copyright © 1987 by Amy Goldman Koss, text. Used by permission of Dial Books for Young Readers, A Division of Penguin Young Readers Group, A Member of Penguin Group (USA) Inc., 345 Hudson Street, New York, NY 10014. All rights reserved.

Page 70: From *Frogs* by Gail Gibbons. Copyright © 1993 by Gail Gibbons. All rights reserved. Reprinted from *Frogs* by permission of Holiday House, Inc.

Page 90: From *Life Cycles* by Michael Elsohn Ross; illustrated by Gustav Moore. Text copyright © 2001 by Michael Elsohn Ross; illustrations copyright © 2001 by Gustav Moore. Used by permission of Millbrook Press, a division of Lerner Publishing Group. All rights reserved.

Page 100: *I Like Where I Am* by Jessica Harper and illustrated by Brian Karas. Text Copyright © Jessica Harper 2004. Illustrations Copyright © Brian Karas, 2004 Published by arrangement with G.P. Putnam's Sons, a division of Penguin Young Readers Group, a member of Penguin Group (USA) Inc. All rights reserved.

Page 128: Reprinted with the permission of Aladdin Paperbacks, an imprint of Simon & Schuster Children's Publishing Division from *Helen Keller and the Big Storm* by Patricia Lakin. Copyright © 2002 Patricia Lakin.

Page 144: Reprinted with the permission of Aladdin Paperbacks, an imprint of Simon & Schuster Children's Publishing Division from *Wind* by Marion Dane Bauer. Copyright © 2003 Marion Dane Bauer.

Page 158: *Fire Fighter!* by Angela Royston. Copyright © 1998 Dorling Kindersley Limited, London. Reprinted by permission.

Page 184: *One Dark Night* written by Hazel Hutchins and illustrations by Susan Hartung. Text copyright © 2001 by Hazel Hutchins. Illustrations copyright © 2001 by Susan Hartung. Published by arrangement with Viking Children's Books, a division of Penguin Young Readers Group, a member of Penguin Group (USA) Inc.

Page 204: Isabel Joshlin Glaser for "Adoption". Reprinted from *Y ou and Me* by Salley Mavor, 1997. Reprinted by permission of Isabel Joshlin Glaser.

Page 205: *"The Stray Cat"* by Eve Merriam. Used by permission of Marian Reiner.

Page 212: Reprinted with the permission of Margaret K. McElderry Books, an imprint of Simon & Schuster Children's Publishing Division from *Bad Dog, Dodger!* by Barbara Abercrombie. Text copyright © 2002 Barbara Abercrombie.

Page 238: From *Horace and Morris but Mostly Dolores.* Text copyright © 1999 by James Howe. Illustrations copyright © 1999 by Amy Walrod. Reprinted with permission of Atheneum Books for Young Readers, Simon & Schuster Children's Publishing Division. All rights reserved.

Page 268: *The Signmaker's Assistant* by Tedd Arnold. Copyright © 1992 by Tedd Arnold. Published by arrangement with Dial Books for Young Readers, a division of Penguin Young Readers Group, a member of Penguin Group (USA) Inc..

Page 286: Action Without Borders Web site, www.idealist.org/kt/youthorgs.html. Reprinted by permission.

Page 300: From *Just Like Josh Gibson.* Text copyright © 2004 by Angela Johnson. Illustrations copyright © 2004 by Beth Peck. Reprinted with permission of Simon & Schuster Books for Young Readers, Simon & Schuster Children's Publishing Division. All rights reserved.

Page 326: *Red, White, And Blue* by John Herman, and illustrated by Robin Roraback. Text Copyright © John Herman, 1998. Illustration Copyright © Robin Roraback, 1998. Published by arrangement with Grosset & Dunlap, a division of Penguin Young Readers Group, a member of Penguin Group (USA) Inc. All rights reserved.

Page 354: From *A Birthday Basket for Tía.* Text copyright © 1992 by Pat Mora. Illustrations copyright © 1992 by Cecily Lang. Reprinted with permission of Simon & Schuster Books for Young Readers, Simon & Schuster Children's Publishing Division. All rights reserved.

Page 370: From www.kidparties.com/traditions.htm. Reprinted by permission.

Page 380: *Cowboys* by Lucille Recht Penner, illustrated by Ben Carter, Grosset & Dunlap, 1996.

Page 404: From *The Cowboy's Handbook* by Tod Cody, copyright © 1996 by Breslich & Foss, entire text and compilation of illustrations. Used by permission of Cobblehill Books, an affiliate of Dutton Children's Books, A Division of Penguin Young Readers Group, A Member of Penguin Group (USA) Inc., 345 Hudson Street, New York, NY 10014. All rights reserved.

Page 412: *Jingle Dancer* by Cynthia Leitich Smith, illustrated by Cornelius Van Wright and Ying-Hwa Hu. Text copyright © 2000 by Cynthia Leitich Smith. Illustrations copyright © 2000 by Cornelius Van Wright and Ying-Hwa Hu.

Page 428: From "Celebrating the Buffalo Days" from *Buffalo Days* by Diane Hoyt-Goldsmith, Photographs by Lawrence Migdale, Illustrations by Ted Furlo. Text copyright © 1997 by Diane Hoyt-Goldsmith. Photographs copyright © 1997 by Lawrence Migdale. All rights reserved. Reprinted from *Buffalo Days* by permission of Holiday House, Inc.

Illustrations

89, 117, 129, 150-151, 174-177, 212-225, 250, 292-293, 345, 403, 434-435 Laura Ovresat; **128-140** Troy Howell; **206** Jui Ishida; **214-226** Diane Greenseid; **316-319** Clint Hansen; **326-336, 340-342** Shannan Stirnweiss; **338, 400-401** Derek Grinnell

Photographs

Every effort has been made to secure permission and provide appropriate credit for photographic material. The publisher deeply regrets any omission and pledges to correct errors called to its attention in subsequent editions.

Unless otherwise acknowledged, all photographs are the property of Scott Foresman, a division of Pearson Education.

Photo locators denoted as follows: Top (T), Center (C), Bottom (B), Left (L), Right (R), Background (Bkgd).

10 Man on the Moon (A Day in the Life of Bob). ©2002 Simon Bartram. First published in Great Britain by Templar Publishing. Reproduced by permission of the publisher/Candlewick Press, Inc., Cambridge, MA; **13** Corbis; **15** ©Michael Boys/Corbis; **34** Getty Images; **35** (CR, BR) Getty Images, (TR) ©Cape Cod Travel; **36** (TR, BR) ©Cape Cod Travel; **37** ©Lee Snider/Corbis; **38** ©Amy Dykens/Cape Cod Travel; **39** ©Cape Cod Travel; **43** ©Renee Lynn/Corbis; **45** (TR, BR) Getty Images; **46** (Bkgd) Getty Images, (TR) ©Royalty-Free/Corbis; **48** (CR) ©Royalty-Free/Corbis, (TC) ©Ben Klaffe; **49** (TL) Getty Images, (TR) ©Dwight R. Kuhn; **50** (TL, TR) ©Dwight R. Kuhn; **51** (TC) ©Shmuel Thaler/Index Stock Imagery, (CR) ©Dwight R. Kuhn; **52** (T) ©Steve Solum/Index Stock Imagery, (CR) ©Ben Klaffe; **53** (T, TR) ©Dwight R. Kuhn; **54** (T, BR) ©Ben Klaffe; **55** (T) ©Reuters/Corbis, (CR) ©Dwight R. Kuhn; **56** (T) ©Dwight R. Kuhn, (CR) Getty Images; **57** (T) ©Barry Lewis/Corbis, (CR) ©Matthew Klein/Corbis; **58** (TL) ©Tony Freeman/PhotoEdit, (TR) ©Royalty-Free/Corbis; **59** ©Richard Hamilton Smith/Corbis; **60** ©Dwight R. Kuhn; **61** (BL) ©Dwight R. Kuhn, (BR) ©Ben Klaffe, (TL) ©Matthew Klein/Corbis, (TC) ©Royalty-Free/Corbis, (BC) Getty Images, (CL) ©Alex Cohn; **63** ©David Aubrey/Corbis; **65** ©Royalty-Free/Corbis; **67** (BL) ©Royalty-Free/Corbis, (BC) ©Richard Cummins/Corbis; **68-69** Getty Images; **97** ©Royalty-Free/Corbis; **99** (TR) Corbis, (CR, BR) Getty Images; **118** ©Craig Aurness/Corbis; **125** ©DK Images; **126-127** ©G.K. & Vikki Hart/ PhotoDisc; **130** (BL) Getty Images, (TR) ©Royalty-Free/Corbis; **131** ©Bettmann/Corbis; **132** (TL) Getty Images, (C) ©Bettmann/ Corbis; **133** (TL) ©Bettman/ Corbis, (TR) ©Siede Preis/Getty Images, (T) Getty Images; **135** ©Royalty-Free/Corbis; **141** (TC) ©Royalty-Free/Corbis, (R) Getty Images, (C) Corbis; **142** (BR) ©Bettmann/Corbis, (TL) Getty Images; **143** (TR) ©Siede Preis/Getty Images, (BR) ©Royalty-Free/Corbis, (BC) ©Bettman/Corbis, (T) Getty Images, (B) ©First Light/Corbis; **144** ©Kevin Anthony Horgan/Getty Images; **145** (BL) ©Martin Barraud/Getty Images, (CR) ©Geostock/Getty Images; **146** (TC) ©Guy Grenier/ Masterfile Corporation, (TL) ©Michael Melford/ Getty Images, (TR) Getty Images, (CL) ©Alan R. Moller/Getty Images, (BL) ©Guy Motil/Corbis, (BR) ©Randy Faris/Corbis; **147** (TR) ©Stan Osolinski/Getty Images, (CL) ©World Perspectives/ Getty Images, (CR) Getty Images, (Bkgd) ©Stephen Frink/Getty Images; **148** ©Bettman/Corbis; **151** ©Geostock/Getty Images; **152** ©Jim Sugar/Corbis; **155** ©DK Images; **157-158** ©Tim Ross/Index Stock Imagery; **159** (Bkgd) ©Mark Barrett/Index Stock Imagery, (B) ©Walter Bibikow/Index Stock Imagery; **160** (BL) ©Royalty-Free/ Corbis, (TL) ©Roberts Company, Inc., (TR) Lynton Gardiner/©DK Images, (BL) Michal Heron/©DK Images, (R) Richard Leeney/©DK Images; **161** (BC) Getty Images, (TL) Michal Heron/©DK Images, (R) ©DK Images; **162** (TR, BR) ©DK Images; **163** (TR) Lynton Gardiner/ ©DK Images; **164** ©Jim Pickerell/Stock Connection; **165** Lynton Gardiner/©DK Images; **166** ©James McLoughlin; **167** (BR) ©Rubberball Productions/Getty Images, (BC) Corbis; **168** Getty Images; **169-170** ©Lynton Gardiner/©DK Images; **171** Getty Images; **172** ©Roberts Company, Inc.; **173** (B) ©Richard Leeney/ ©DK Images, (TR) Corbis; **174** (TC) ©Roberts Company, Inc., (Bkgd) ©Comstock Images/Getty Images; **175** ©Royalty-Free/ Corbis; **176** ©Comstock Images/Getty Images; **179** ©DK Images; **181** Getty Images; **183** ©Rob Matheson/Corbis; **203** ©Pat Doyle/ Corbis; **209, 211** Getty Images; **227** (TL) ©Comstock Inc., (BC) ©Robert Dowling/Corbis; **229** (BL) ©Jim Craigmyle/Corbis, (BR) ©Tracy Morgan/©DK Images, (TR) ©Cydney Conger/Corbis; **230** (BC) ©Burke/Triolo Productions/FoodPix, (TR) ©Jim Craigmyle/ Corbis; **231** (B) ©Tracy Morgan/©DK Images, (T) ©Jim Craigmyle/ Corbis; **235** (BL, BR) Getty Images; **237** Getty Images; **257** (TL) ©Hans Neleman/Getty Images, (T) Photo of James Howe used with permission of Simon & Schuster, Inc. ©John Maggiotto, (BL) Getty Images; **258** (BR) Getty Images, (C) ©Bob Thomas/Getty Images; **259** (TR) ©Lori Adamski Peek/Getty Images, (BR) ©Bob Gomel/ Corbis; **260** (TR) ©Tim Pannell/Corbis, (BR) ©Charles Gupton/ Corbis; **261** ©Lori Adamski Peek/Getty Images; **265** (TR, BC) Getty Images; **267** ©Royalty-Free/Corbis; **286** ©Tom Stewart/Corbis; **287** (TR) Getty Images, (CR) Jacob Taposchaner/Taxi/Getty Images; **292** ©Tom Brakefield/Corbis; **293** (T) ©Joseph Van Os/Getty Images, (BR) Getty Images; **294** ©Ariel Skelley/Corbis; **297** ©Royalty-Free/ Corbis; **299** (T) ©Royalty-Free/Corbis, (BR) ©Ariel Skelley/Corbis; **315** Illustration Works, Inc.; **317** Library of Congress; **323** (TR) ©Royalty-Free/Corbis, (BR) ©Jim Cummins/Corbis; **325** (CR) Corbis, (BR) ©Jerry Tobias/Corbis; **330** (BL) Stock Montage Inc., (TR) ©Bettmann/ Corbis, (CR) ©PoodlesRock/Corbis; **334** (T) Composite photograph of the 190 year-old Star-Spangled Banner, the flag that inspired the national anthem. Smithsonian's National Museum of American History, ©2002/Smithsonian Institution; **335** Corbis; **336** (T) The Granger Collection, NY; **338** ©Bjorn G. Bolstad/Photo Researchers, Inc.; **340** (BL) Corbis; **343** Digital Vision; **347** ©Terence Beddis/Getty Images; **348** (BR) ©Bettmann/ Corbis, (BL) Stock Montage Inc.; **349** Digital Vision; **353** (BR) Brand X Pictures, (TR) Getty Images; **369** Corbis; **370** ©Jose L. Pelaez/Corbis; **372** Getty Images; **377** Corbis; **379** (TR) ©Jules Frazier/Getty Images, (BR) ©Macduff Everton/Corbis; **380** ©Guillaud Jean Michel/Sygma/Corbis; **382** Getty Images; **400** (TR) ©Jules Frazier/Getty Images, (B) Getty Images; **401-402** ©Jules Frazier/Getty Images; **403** Getty Images; **404** (B, TR) Getty Images, (TR) ©C Squared Studios/Getty Images, (BR) Brand X Pictures; **405** Getty Images; **409** ©Lindsay Hebberd/Corbis; **411** (T) ©Werner Forman/Corbis, (B) Getty Images; **428** (L, T) ©Lawrence Migdale, (C) Getty Images, (BC) ©C Squared Studios/Getty Images; **429** ©Lawrence Migdale; **431** ©Lawrence Migdale; **434** ©Ariel Skelley/ Corbis; **435** Getty Images; **436** ©Ira Rubin/Getty Images; **437** ©Thinkstock/Getty Images; **438** ©Craig Aurness/Corbis; **439** image100; **441** (BR) Getty Images, (BL) ©Richard H. Johnston/ Getty Images; **442** ©Patrick Ward/Corbis; **443** (CL) Corbis, (BL, TR) Getty Images; **444** (BL) Getty Images, (TL) ©Brian Hagiwara/ Getty Images; **445** ©G.K. & Vikki Hart/PhotoDisc; **446** ©Werner Forman/Corbis; **447** (CL) ©Betsie Van der Meer/Getty Images, (CL) ©R. Derek Smith/Getty Images; **448-449** Getty Images; **450** ©Guy Grenier/Masterfile Corporation; **451** ©David Aubrey/Corbis; **452** ©Alan R. Moller/Getty Images; **453** ©Kevin Schafer/Corbis; **454** Corbis; **455** ©Jose Luis Pelaez, Inc./Corbis

Glossary

The contents of this glossary have been adapted from *My First Dictionary*. Copyright © 2000, Pearson Education, Inc.

Writing

Writing Trait of the Week

Writing Workshop

Unit 1   A Story About Me (Personal Narrative)
Unit 2   How-to Report
Unit 3   Compare and Contrast Essay
Unit 4   Description

Unit 6   Research Report

Rubrics

Rubric
4 3 2 1

Assessment

Assessment

Student Tips for Making Top Scores in Writing Tests

❶ Use words such as these to connect ideas, sentences, or paragraphs.

first	last	before	now
next	finally	after	then

❷ Write a good beginning. Make readers want to read more.
- I peeked in the room and screamed.
- Never try to mess with an angry bee.
- When I was four, I saw a purple dog.
- Have you ever heard of a talking tree?

❸ Focus on the topic.
If a word or sentence is not about the topic, get rid of it.

❹ Organize your ideas.
Have a plan in mind before you start writing. Your plan can be a list or a web. Your writing will go faster if you spend time planning first.

❺ Support your ideas.
- Use examples and details to make your ideas clear.
- Use vivid words that create pictures.
- Try not to use dull *(get, go, say),* unclear *(thing, stuff, lots of),* or overused *(really, very)* words.
- Use a voice that your readers will understand.

❻ Make writing conventions as error-free as possible.
Proofread your work carefully. Read it three times. Look for correct punctuation, then capitalization, and finally spelling.

❼ Write an ending that wraps things up. "The end" is not a good ending.
- That's why I don't eat grapes anymore.
- I still think Chip is the best cat ever.
- My bedroom was never the same again.
- Next time I'll wear my raincoat.

Focus/Ideas

Organization/ Paragraphs

Voice

Word Choice

Sentences

Conventions

Writing Traits

- **Focus/Ideas** refers to the main purpose for writing and the details that make the subject clear and interesting. It includes development of ideas through support and elaboration.

- **Organization/Paragraphs** refers to the overall structure of a piece of writing that guides readers. Within that structure, transitions show how ideas, sentences, and paragraphs are connected.

- **Voice** shows the writer's unique personality and establishes a connection between writer and reader. Voice, which contributes to style, should be suited to the audience and the purpose for writing.

- **Word Choice** is the use of precise, vivid words to communicate effectively and naturally. It helps create style through the use of specific nouns, lively verbs and adjectives, and accurate, well-placed modifiers.

- **Sentences** covers strong, well-built sentences that vary in length and type. Skillfully written sentences have pleasing rhythms and flow fluently.

- **Rules** refers to mechanical correctness and includes grammar, usage, spelling, punctuation, capitalization, and paragraphing.

Writing Workshop

Persuasive Letter

OBJECTIVES

- Develop an understanding of persuasive writing.
- Use the letter format.
- Use processes and strategies that good writers use.

Key Features
Persuasive Letter

A persuasive letter uses facts and opinions to get readers to do something.

- Is written in correct letter format
- Uses persuasive words, such as *must* or *best*
- Uses reasons, facts, and examples to make a point
- Often organizes facts in order of importance

Connect to Weekly Writing

Writing Transparencies 21–25

Strategic Intervention

See Differentiated Instruction p. WA8.

Advanced

See Differentiated Instruction p. WA9.

ELL

See Differentiated Instruction p. WA9.

Additional Resource for Writing
Writing Rubrics and Anchor Papers, pp. 19–22

WA2   *Persuasive Letter*

Writing Prompt: Responsibility
What is something that you think a family member should do or not do? Write a letter to the family member. Give reasons why the action you are suggesting would be the responsible thing to do.
Purpose: Persuade
Audience: A family member

READ LIKE A WRITER

Ask children to look back at *Horace and Morris but mostly Dolores.* Remind them how Dolores tries to persuade the girl mice that it's fun to go exploring and to explore with the boys. Tell children that they will write a letter to persuade someone to do something.

SHOW THE MODEL AND RUBRIC

GUIDED WRITING Read the model aloud. Point out persuasive words *(need, please, promise, best)*.

- Read aloud the last sentence. Point out that the writer gives the best reason—the one that is most likely to convince a parent—last.
- Discuss how the model reflects traits of good writing.

April 2, 2007

Dear Mom,

    I need a picture of my favorite place, so I want to take a photo of the park. The picture will go with an essay I'm writing for school. May I please use your camera? I promise I will follow all the instructions you gave me. Keep the strap on your wrist. Carry the camera in its case. Hold the camera by the sides.

    I could draw a picture of the park, but you know I'm not very good at drawing! A photo would be the best way to show exactly what I like about the park.

            Your son,

            Tyler

Unit 5 A Letter to Persuade • PREWRITE   Writing Process **25**

▲ **Writing Transparency** WP25

Traits of a Good Letter to Persuade

Focus/Ideas	Letter sticks to the topic and gives reasons.
Organization/ Paragraphs	Writer saves best reason for last.
Voice	Letter is serious. Writer communicates request clearly.
Word Choice	Writer uses persuasive words. (*need, please, promise, best*)
Sentences	Writer uses different kinds and lengths of sentences.
Conventions	Writer uses good grammar, capitalization, and spelling.

Unit 5 A Letter to Persuade • PREWRITE   Writing Process **26**

▲ **Writing Transparency** WP26

FINDING A TOPIC

TALK WITH A PARTNER Have pairs of children discuss things they could ask family members to do.

NARROW THE CHOICE Have children ask questions about the ideas they have chosen. They might ask: What do I want a family member to do? Can I think of good reasons why a family member should do what I ask?

Topic Ideas

go to Krim Park
get Grandpa to recycle
give me a camera

Think Aloud

MODEL We went to Krim Park last week. I don't think I can convince anyone to go again this week. I'd love to get a camera, but it is expensive and I'm supposed to be saving money so I can buy one for myself. Grandpa doesn't recycle paper. I think if he knew how easy and important it is, he would do it. I'm going to write a letter to Grandpa.

PREWRITING STRATEGY

USE A PERSUASION CHART Use Writing Transparency WP27 to show how to organize reasons to persuade someone to do something.

Think Aloud

MODEL

• Grandpa is the *audience*. The *purpose* of the letter is to get Grandpa to start recycling paper.

• These are five good reasons for recycling paper.

• The most important reasons are that recycling helps prevent air and land pollution and that the grandfather loves his granddaughter and therefore will want to do what she asks.

PREWRITING ACTIVITY Have children use the Persuasion Chart graphic organizer on the Grammar and Writing Practice Book p. 176 to help them organize their ideas.

Persuasion Chart
Fill out this persuasion chart to help you organize your ideas.

Topic   I want __Grandpa__ to __recycle paper__.
                    (audience)   (purpose)

Brainstorm reasons here.

easy to do
make new paper
no air pollution
no landfills
you love me

Organize your reasons here.

Least important	Most important
easy to do	no air pollution
make new paper	no landfills
	you love me

Unit 5 A Letter to Persuade • PREWRITE   Writing Process **27**

▲ **Writing Transparency** WP27

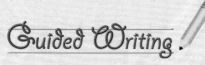
Guided Writing

Some children will need additional guidance as they plan and write their letters. You might give these children the option of writing a group letter under your supervision or pair them with a more able writer.

Persuasion Chart
Fill out this persuasion chart to help you organize your ideas.

Topic   I want _____ to _____
                    (audience)   (purpose)

Brainstorm reasons here.
Answers will vary.

Organize your reasons here.

Least important	Most important
Answers will vary.	

▲ **Grammar and Writing Practice Book** p. 176

Writing Workshop

Think Like a Writer

Know Your Audience Ask children who will get their letter. How can they get this person to do what they want? For example, if their brother hates sports, then they will have a hard time convincing him to go to a soccer game. If their mother enjoys cooking, they might convince her to try a recipe they found.

ELL

Support Writing Help children focus on presenting good reasons and on word choice. Omit the advice about saving the best reason until last. As appropriate, explain the persuasive words.

WRITING THE FIRST DRAFT

GUIDED WRITING Have children review their Persuasion Chart to help them organize their ideas as they write their first drafts. Remind them to do the following.

- Present good reasons.
- Save the best reason until last.
- Use persuasive words.
- Keep their purpose and audience in mind.

USE PERSUASIVE WORDS List the persuasive words on the board. Explain that these words can help convince readers to think or act in a certain way. Have children use the words in sentences about something they want. For example, *I need a better computer. It is important that a computer is up to date. The worst thing is a computer that is old and slow.* Remind children to use some of these words in their letters.

DRAFTING STRATEGIES

WRITE WHAT YOU WOULD SAY Point out to children that a letter is like a one-way conversation. Have children imagine that they are talking to a family member and asking him or her to do something. In the first draft, children should get their reasons on paper quickly. They can worry about spelling and punctuation later.

PRACTICE USING PERSUASIVE WORDS Have children use Grammar and Writing Practice Book p. 177 to practice using persuasive words. Draw attention to the letter format.

Persuasive Words

best

worst

must

should

important

need

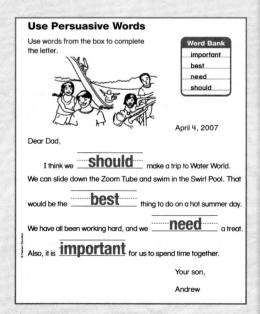

Use Persuasive Words

Use words from the box to complete the letter.

Word Bank
important
best
need
should

April 4, 2007

Dear Dad,

I think we **should** make a trip to Water World.
We can slide down the Zoom Tube and swim in the Swirl Pool. That
would be the **best** thing to do on a hot summer day.
We have all been working hard, and we **need** a treat.
Also, it is **important** for us to spend time together.

Your son,

Andrew

▲ **Grammar and Writing Practice Book** p. 177

REVISING STRATEGIES

GUIDED WRITING Use Writing Transparency WP28 to model how to revise a persuasive letter.

MODEL This is the correct format for a friendly letter. The first two sentences clearly state the purpose of the letter. The writer keeps her reasons in order and saves her most powerful reason for the last paragraph. Twice the writer changes the weak verb *put* to another, more vivid action verb, *drop* and *set*. She also adds detail to one of her reasons to make the connection clearer. Finally, she changes the vague adjective *nice* to two stronger adjectives, *clean, healthy*.

Revising Marks	
Add	^
Take Out	⌐

October 13, 2007

Dear Grandpa,

I need your help, and the Earth needs your help too. You can help we both by recycling paper.

drop
Its easy to do. Just put your newspapers,
Set
magazines, and junk mail into a recycling bin. Put the bin on the curb on friday. That old paper will be picked up and made into new paper.

Recycling is better than burning. Smoke pollutes the air. Recycling is also better than throwing paper
goes into landfills and
away becuz trash pollutes the land.
clean, healthy
I know you love me and want me to live on a nice planet. Please recycle.

Love,

Kelsey

Unit 5 A Letter to Persuade • REVISE   Writing Process 28

▲ **Writing Transparency** WP28

WRITER'S CRAFT Word Choice

ELABORATION Remind children that good writers choose words that make their writing lively and interesting. Write the following sentences on the board. Ask children to make the sentences more interesting by changing and adding words.

She has a pretty scarf.

I got a nice sweater.

Help children brainstorm ways to change the sentences. For example, She wears (or puts on) a bright (or colorful) scarf. I bought (or received) a warm (or orange or fluffy) sweater.

ADDITIONAL SUPPORT Point out how changing the weak verbs and adjective improved the writing model on Writing Transparency WP28.

Use Grammar and Writing Practice Book p. 178 to improve word choice.

APPLY WRITER'S CRAFT Have children examine word choice in their writing.

- Encourage them to look for places where they can add or change words to make their writing more interesting.

- Write the Revising Checklist on the board or make copies to distribute. Children can use this checklist to revise their letters.

Revising Checklist

✔ Does the letter tell what I want someone to do?

✔ Have I included good reasons?

✔ Did I save the best reason until last?

✔ Did I use persuasive words?

ELL

Extend Language To help children think of persuasive words to use in their writing, work with them to make a list of persuasive words. Begin with *need, must,* and *should.* Encourage children to find other words in their reading and add the words to the list. (*best, worst, better, important, safe*)

Writing Trait: Word Choice

Underline the sentence in each pair that sounds more interesting.

Snow was in the yard.
Snow blanketed the yard.

The boy whispered his name.
The boy said his name.

Those flowers are pretty.
Those roses are bright red.

Rewrite the following sentences to make them more interesting. You can change and add words. Possible answers:

1. The dog was nice.

The brown dog was friendly.

2. I rode on my bike.

I raced on my old blue bike.

▲ **Grammar and Writing Practice Book** p. 178

Monitor Progress

Differentiated Instruction

If... children have trouble using different kinds of pronouns,	**then...** review the grammar lesson on p. 235b.

Editing Checklist

✔ Did I spell words correctly, including those with the vowel sound in *fall?*

✔ Did I use the correct pronouns?

✔ Does each sentence begin with a capital letter and end with a punctuation mark?

EDITING STRATEGY

LINE BY LINE Show children how to place a sheet of paper or an index card under a line of text to help them focus on finding errors. Model this strategy using Writing Transparency WP29.

Think Aloud **MODEL** First, I check to see that the letter has all its parts. Date, greeting, body, closing, and signature are all in the right places. Now I will look at the letter line by line. I see an incorrect pronoun. *We* should be *us* because it follows an action verb. *Its* is a contraction, so it needs an apostrophe between the *t* and the *s*. *Friday* should begin with a capital letter because it is the name of a day of the week. I see a misspelled word, *becuz*. It should be *because*.

Write the Editing Checklist on the board or make copies to distribute. Children can use this checklist to edit their descriptions.

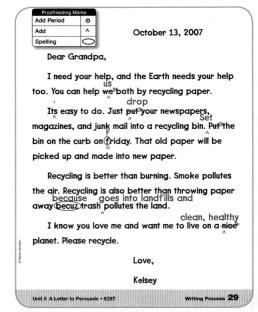

▲ **Writing Transparency** WP29

Tech Talk ONLINE If children are using a computer to type their letter, they may find these tips useful.

- If your program has a print preview or a page layout feature, you may wish to use this to see how your letter will appear on the page when it is printed. You can check the format of your letter.

- Print out a copy of your letter. It is easier to find errors on a paper than on a computer screen. Mark the errors on the paper and then fix them on the screen.

SELF-EVALUATION

Prepare children to fill out a Self-Evaluation Guide. Display Writing Transparency WP30 to model the self-evaluation process.

Think Aloud — **MODEL** I used good persuading words, adjectives and exact words. I would mark *Yes* for numbers 1, 2 and 3. My favorite part is the opening sentence. I think it gets the reader's attention. If I wrote this letter again, I would add that I'd help Grandpa pack things into the recycle bin. This would show that I really wanted to help and wasn't just giving him advice.

Assign Grammar and Writing Practice Book p. 179. Children can save their Self-Evaluation Guides and their work in a portfolio to monitor their development as writers. Encourage them to build on their skills and note areas to improve.

October 13, 2007

Dear Grandpa,

I need your help, and the Earth needs your help too. You can help us both by recycling paper.

It's easy to do. Just drop your newspapers, magazines, and junk mail into a recycling bin. Set the bin on the curb on Friday. That old paper will be picked up and made into new paper.

Recycling is better than burning. Smoke pollutes the air. Recycling is also better than throwing paper away because trash goes into landfills and pollutes the land.

I know you love me and want me to live on a clean, healthy planet. Please recycle.

Love,

Kelsey

Unit 5 A Letter to Persuade • PUBLISH   Writing Process **30**

▲ **Writing Transparency** WP30

Ideas for Publishing

E-mail Letters If access to e-mail is available, children can send their letters to the family member they are addressing.

Illustrated Letters Children can illustrate their letter with a picture cut out of a magazine or with their own artwork.

Self-Evaluation Guide

Check *Yes* or *No* about word choice in your letter.

	Yes	No
1. I used one or more words to persuade.		
2. I used one or more good adjectives to describe.		
3. I used exact words instead of vague ones such as *nice*.		

Answer the questions.

4. What is the best part of your letter?

Answers will vary.

5. What is one thing you would change about this letter if you could write it again?

Answers will vary.

▲ **Grammar and Writing Practice Book** p. 179

Scoring Rubric   Persuasive Letter

Rubric 4 3 2 1	4	3	2	1
Focus/Ideas	Persuasive letter strongly focused; clear, developed ideas	Persuasive letter generally focused; good ideas	Persuasive letter that strays off topic; unclear ideas	Persuasive letter with no focus; confusing ideas
Organization/ Paragraphs	Strong reasons in order, with most important one last	Reasons in order, with most important one last	Reasons in no apparent order	Few reasons in no order
Voice	Clearly shows writer's feelings about topic	Shows some of writer's feelings about topic	Little sense of writer's feelings about topic	Writer not involved
Word Choice	Uses persuasive words effectively	Uses some persuasive words	Uses few persuasive words	Uses no persuasive words
Sentences	Complete, varied sentences	Complete sentences	Some incomplete or unclear sentences	Incomplete or unclear sentences
Conventions	Understands writing conventions	Understands most writing conventions	Understands some writing conventions	Makes serious errors that detract from writing

For 6-, 5-, and 3-point Scoring Rubrics, see pp. WA13–WA16.

Writing Workshop

Persuasive Letter
Differentiated Instruction

WRITING PROMPT: Responsibility

What is something that you think a family member should do or not do? Write a letter to the family member. Give reasons why the action you are suggesting would be the responsible thing to do.

Purpose: Persuade

Audience: A family member

MODIFY INSTRUCTION

Pick One

ALTERNATIVE PROMPTS

ALTERNATIVE PROMPT: Persuasive Writing

Strategic Intervention Think of a place that you want someone to take you to. Write a note to your mom, dad, or another family member. Tell him or her about the place. Give one good reason why both of you should go there.

On-Level Think of an activity you want to do with a friend. Write a letter to your friend. Tell him or her about the activity. Persuade your friend to do this activity with you. Include three good reasons.

Advanced Think of something that you and your classmates could do to help your neighborhood, school, or community. Write a letter to your classmates. Tell them what your idea is and give them at least three reasons why it is a good idea.

Strategic Intervention

MODIFY THE PROMPT

Help emerging writers focus on important words in the prompt. Write the prompt on the board and underline key words such as *something, family member, should do or not do, letter, reasons,* and *responsible.* Discuss the meanings of these key words, and make sure children understand what they are expected to do.

1 PREWRITE **2** DRAFT **3** REVISE **4** EDIT **5** PUBLISH

PREWRITING SUPPORT

- Tell children about something you might ask a family member to do, such as asking your grandmother to give you a special family recipe or asking your brother to help you plant a garden. Ask children to help you think of good reasons you could use.

- Review the parts of a friendly letter: date, greeting, body, closing, signature. Draw a letter form on the board for children to use as their model.

- Let children dictate to you what they want to say in their letters. Record their ideas and point out whether they have included good reasons that support their request. Help them think of reasons they can add.

OPTIONS

- Give children the option of writing a group letter under your supervision.

CHECK PROGRESS Segment the assignment into manageable pieces. Check work at intervals, such as graphic organizers and first drafts, to make sure writing is on track.

Advanced

MODIFY THE PROMPT

Expect advanced writers to produce a letter that shows they understand the purpose of their letter and stay focused on that purpose. They should use persuasive words and strong reasons that convince the reader to act as they wish. Their letters should have a serious tone and follow the correct format for a letter.

APPLY SKILLS

- As children edit their work, have them consider some ways to improve it.

  Make sure they have included all the parts of a friendly letter.

  Check that they have used the correct verb forms with singular and plural pronouns.

  Make sure they have included apostrophes in contractions.

OPTIONS

- Work with children to create their own class rubrics. Follow these steps:

  1. Read examples of class letters and rank them 1–4, with 4 the highest.

  2. Discuss how they arrived at each rank.

  3. Isolate the six traits and make a rubric based on them.

CHECK PROGRESS Discuss children's Self-Evaluation Guides. Work with children to monitor their growth and identify their strengths and weaknesses as writers.

ELL

MODIFY THE PROMPT

Help beginning speakers by providing the framework of a friendly letter with partial sentences that children can complete. For example, write Dear ____ , and let children add the name; write We should ____ and have children complete the sentence.

BUILD BACKGROUND

- Write the word *persuade* on the board. Explain that when we persuade someone, we win the person over to do or believe what we want them to do or believe. The best way to do this is to give the person good reasons. Discuss the list of Key Features of a persuasive letter that appears in the left column of p. WA2.

OPTIONS

- As children write their letters, guide them toward books, magazines, or Web sites that provide comprehension support through features such as the following.

  persuasive articles

  friendly letters

  text in the home-language

- For more suggestions on scaffolding the Writing Workshop, see the ELL and Transition Handbook.

CHECK PROGRESS You may need to explain certain traits and help children fill out their Self-Evaluation Guides. Downplay conventions and focus more on ideas. Recognize examples of vocabulary growth and efforts to use language in more complex ways.

Scoring Rubric | Look Back and Write

2 points The response indicates that the student has a complete understanding of the reading concept embodied in the task. The response is accurate, complete, and fulfills all the requirements of the task. Necessary support and/or examples are included, and the information given is clearly text-based.

1 point The response indicates that the student has a partial understanding of the reading concept embodied in the task. The response includes information that is essentially correct and text-based, but the information is too general or too simplistic. Some of the support and/or examples may be incomplete or omitted.

0 points The response indicates that the student does not demonstrate an understanding of the reading concept embodied in the task. The student has either failed to respond or has provided a response that is inaccurate or has insufficient information.

Scoring Rubric | Look Back and Write

4 points The response indicates that the student has a thorough understanding of the reading concept embodied in the task. The response is accurate, complete, and fulfills all the requirements of the task. Necessary support and/or examples are included, and the information is clearly text-based.

3 points The response indicates that the student has an understanding of the reading concept embodied in the task. The response is accurate and fulfills all the requirements of the task, but the required support and/or details are not complete or clearly text-based.

2 points The response indicates that the student has a partial understanding of the reading concept embodied in the task. The response that includes information is essentially correct and text-based, but the information is too general or too simplistic. Some of the support and/or examples and requirements of the task may be incomplete or omitted.

1 point The response indicates that the student has a very limited understanding of the reading concept embodied in the task. The response is incomplete, may exhibit many flaws, and may not address all requirements of the task.

0 points The response indicates that the student does not demonstrate an understanding of the reading concept embodied in the task. The student has either failed to respond or has provided a response that is inaccurate or has insufficient information.

Writing Trait Rubric — *Firefighter!*, p. 178–179

	4	3	2	1
Word Choice	Vivid style created by use of exact nouns, strong verbs, and exciting adjectives	Some style created by strong and precise words	Little style created by strong, precise words; some lack of clarity	Word choice vague or incorrect
	Uses strong, specific words that make report unusually clear and lively	Uses some specific words that make report clear	Needs more precise word choice to create style and clarity in report	Report made dull or unclear by poor word choice

Writing Trait Rubric — *One Dark Night*, p. 206–207

	4	3	2	1
Voice	Excellent sense of writer's attitude toward topic; strongly engages audience and speaks directly to them	Clear sense of how writer feels and thinks; engages audience	Some sense of how writer feels and thinks; weak attempt to engage audience	No sense of how writer feels and thinks about topic; no attempt to engage audience
	Uses well-chosen words in reasons to clearly show feelings toward topic	Uses words in reasons that show some feelings about topic	Needs to use more words in reasons that show feelings about topic	Uses no words in reasons that show feelings about topic

Writing Trait Rubric — *Bad Dog, Dodger!*, p. 232–233

	4	3	2	1
Voice	Excellent sense of writer's attitude toward topic; writer unusually aware of audience and purpose	Clear sense of how writer feels and thinks; writer aware of audience and purpose	Some sense of how writer feels and thinks; writer somewhat involved with topic	No sense of how writer feels and thinks about topic; writer not involved with topic
	Uses well-chosen words in rules to clearly show feelings toward topic	Uses words in rules that show some feelings about topic	Needs to use more words in rules that show feelings about topic	Uses no words in rules that show feelings about topic

Writing Trait Rubric — *Horace and Morris, p. 262–263*

	4	3	2	1
Focus/Ideas	Excellent focus with many vivid supporting details; nothing superfluous	Clear focus with some supporting details; nothing superfluous	Limited focus with a few supporting details; some unrelated details	Unfocused with little support and many unrelated details
	Excellent advice with interesting, well-supported main idea	Advice with adequately supported main idea	Sharper focus on main idea needed in advice	Advice with no clear focus or main idea

Writing Trait Rubric — *The Signmaker's Assistant, p. 290–291*

	4	3	2	1
Sentence	Interest, style, and clarity created in sentences	Clear sentences	Most sentences clear	Most sentences unclear
	Uses good variety of types and lengths of sentences in sign	Uses some different types and lengths of sentences in sign	Needs more sentence variety to add interest to sign	Sentences of one type and length leading to dull sign

Scoring Rubric | Narrative Writing

	6	5	4	3	2	1
Focus/Ideas	Excellent, focused narrative; well elaborated with quality details	Good, focused narrative; elaborated with telling details	Narrative focused; adequate elaboration	Generally focused narrative; some supporting details	Sometimes unfocused narrative; needs more supporting details	Rambling narrative; lacks development and detail
Organization/ Paragraphs	Strong beginning, middle, and end; appropriate order words	Coherent beginning, middle, and end; some order words	Beginning, middle, and end easily identifiable	Recognizable beginning, middle, and end; some order words	Little direction from beginning to end; few order words	Lacks beginning, middle, end; incorrect or no order words
Voice	Writer closely involved; engaging personality	Reveals personality	Pleasant but not compelling voice	Sincere voice but not fully engaged	Little writer involvement, personality	Careless writing with no feeling
Word Choice	Vivid, precise words that bring story to life	Clear words to bring story to life	Some specific word pictures	Language adequate but lacks color	Generally limited or redundant language	Vague, dull, or misused words
Sentences	Excellent variety of sentences; natural rhythm	Varied lengths, styles; generally smooth	Correct sentences with some variations in style	Correctly constructed sentences; some variety	May have simple, awkward, or wordy sentences; little variety	Choppy; many incomplete or run-on sentences
Conventions	Excellent control; few or no errors	No serious errors to affect understanding	General mastery of conventions but some errors	Reasonable control; few distracting errors	Weak control; enough errors to affect understanding	Many errors that prevent understanding

Scoring Rubric | Narrative Writing

	5	4	3	2	1
Focus/Ideas	Excellent, focused narrative; well elaborated with quality details	Good, focused narrative; elaborated with telling details	Generally focused narrative; some supporting details	Sometimes unfocused narrative; needs more supporting details	Rambling narrative; lacks development and detail
Organization/ Paragraphs	Strong beginning, middle, and end; appropriate order words	Coherent beginning, middle, and end; some order words	Recognizable beginning, middle, and end; some order words	Little direction from beginning to end; few order words	Lacks beginning, middle, end; incorrect or no order words
Voice	Writer closely involved; engaging personality	Reveals personality	Sincere voice but not fully engaged	Little writer involvement, personality	Careless writing with no feeling
Word Choice	Vivid, precise words that bring story to life	Clear words to bring story to life	Language adequate but lacks color	Generally limited or redundant language	Vague, dull, or misused words
Sentences	Excellent variety of sentences; natural rhythm	Varied lengths, styles; generally smooth	Correctly constructed sentences; some variety	May have simple, awkward, or wordy sentences; little variety	Choppy; many incomplete or run-on sentences
Conventions	Excellent control; few or no errors	No serious errors to affect understanding	Reasonable control; few distracting errors	Weak control; enough errors to affect understanding	Many errors that prevent understanding

Scoring Rubric | Narrative Writing

	3	2	1
Focus/Ideas	Excellent, focused narrative; well elaborated with quality details	Generally focused narrative; some supporting details	Rambling narrative; lacks development and detail
Organization/ Paragraphs	Strong beginning, middle, and end; appropriate order words	Recognizable beginning, middle, and end; some order words	Lacks beginning, middle, end; incorrect or no order words
Voice	Writer closely involved; engaging personality	Sincere voice but not fully engaged	Careless writing with no feeling
Word Choice	Vivid, precise words that bring story to life	Language adequate but lacks color	Vague, dull, or misused words
Sentences	Excellent variety of sentences; natural rhythm	Correctly constructed sentences; some variety	Choppy; many incomplete or run-on sentences
Conventions	Excellent control; few or no errors	Reasonable control; few distracting errors	Many errors that prevent understanding

Scoring Rubric — Descriptive Writing

	6	5	4	3	2	1
Focus/Ideas	Excellent, focused description; well elaborated with quality details	Good, focused description; elaborated with telling details	Description focused; good elaboration	Generally focused description; some supporting details	Sometimes unfocused description; needs more supporting details	Rambling description; lac development and detail
Organization/ Paragraphs	Compelling ideas enhanced by order, structure, and transitions	Appealing order, structure, and transitions	Structure identifiable and suitable; transitions used	Adequate order, structure, and some transitions to guide reader	Little direction from beginning to end; few transitions	Lacks direction and identifiable structure; no transitions
Voice	Writer closely involved; engaging personality	Reveals personality	Pleasant but not compelling voice	Sincere voice but not fully engaged	Little writer involvement, personality	Careless writing with no feeling
Word Choice	Vivid, precise words that create memorable pictures	Clear, interesting words to bring description to life	Some specific word pictures	Language adequate; appeals to senses	Generally limited or redundant language	Vague, dull, or misused words
Sentences	Excellent variety of sentences; natural rhythm	Varied lengths, styles; generally smooth	Correct sentences with variations in style	Correctly constructed sentences; some variety	May have simple, awkward, or wordy sentences; little variety	Choppy; many incomplete run-on sentences
Conventions	Excellent control; few or no errors	No serious errors to affect understanding	General mastery of conventions but some errors	Reasonable control; few distracting errors	Weak control; enough errors to affect understanding	Many errors that prevent understanding

Scoring Rubric — Descriptive Writing

	5	4	3	2	1
Focus/Ideas	Excellent, focused description; well elaborated with quality details	Good, focused description; elaborated with telling details	Generally focused description; some supporting details	Sometimes unfocused description; needs more supporting details	Rambling description; lacks development and detail
Organization/ Paragraphs	Compelling ideas enhanced by order, structure, and transitions	Appealing order, structure, and transitions	Adequate order, structure, and some transitions to guide reader	Little direction from beginning to end; few transitions	Lacks direction and identifiable structure; no transitions
Voice	Writer closely involved; engaging personality	Reveals personality	Sincere voice but not fully engaged	Little writer involvement, personality	Careless writing with no feeling
Word Choice	Vivid, precise words that create memorable pictures	Clear, interesting words to bring description to life	Language adequate; appeals to senses	Generally limited or redundant language	Vague, dull, or misused words
Sentences	Excellent variety of sentences; natural rhythm	Varied lengths, styles; generally smooth	Correctly constructed sentences; some variety	May have simple, awkward, or wordy sentences; little variety	Choppy; many incomplete or run-on sentences
Conventions	Excellent control; few or no errors	No serious errors to affect understanding	Reasonable control; few distracting errors	Weak control; enough errors to affect understanding	Many errors that prevent understanding

Scoring Rubric — Descriptive Writing

	3	2	1
Focus/Ideas	Excellent, focused description; well elaborated with quality details	Generally focused description; some supporting details	Rambling description; lacks development and detail
Organization/ Paragraphs	Compelling ideas enhanced by order, structure, and transitions	Adequate order, structure, and some transitions to guide reader	Lacks direction and identifiable structure; no transitions
Voice	Writer closely involved; engaging personality	Sincere voice but not fully engaged	Careless writing with no feeling
Word Choice	Vivid, precise words that create memorable pictures	Language adequate; appeals to senses	Vague, dull, or misused words
Sentences	Excellent variety of sentences; natural rhythm	Correctly constructed sentences; some variety	Choppy; many incomplete or run-on sentences
Conventions	Excellent control; few or no errors	Reasonable control; few distracting errors	Many errors that prevent understanding

Scoring Rubric — Persuasive Writing

	6	5	4	3	2	1
Focus/Ideas	Persuasive argument carefully built with quality details	Persuasive argument well supported with details	Persuasive argument focused; good elaboration	Persuasive argument with one or two convincing details	Persuasive piece sometimes unfocused; needs more support	Rambling persuasive argument; lacks development and detail
Organization/ Paragraphs	Information chosen and arranged for maximum effect	Evident progression of persuasive ideas	Progression and structure evident	Information arranged in a logical way with some lapses	Little structure or direction	No identifiable structure
Voice	Writer closely involved; persuasive but not overbearing	Maintains persuasive tone	Persuasive but not compelling voice	Sometimes uses persuasive voice	Little writer involvement, personality	Shows little conviction
Word Choice	Persuasive words carefully chosen for impact	Argument supported by persuasive language	Uses some persuasive words	Occasional persuasive language	Generally limited or redundant language	Vague, dull, or misused words; no persuasive words
Sentences	Excellent variety of sentences; natural rhythm	Varied lengths, styles; generally smooth	Correct sentences with variations in style	Carefully constructed sentences; some variety	Simple, awkward, or wordy sentences; little variety	Choppy; many incomplete or run-on sentences
Conventions	Excellent control; few or no errors	No serious errors to affect understanding	General mastery of conventions but some errors	Reasonable control; few distracting errors	Weak control; enough errors to affect understanding	Many errors that prevent understanding

Scoring Rubric — Persuasive Writing

	5	4	3	2	1
Focus/Ideas	Persuasive argument carefully built with quality details	Persuasive argument well supported with details	Persuasive argument with one or two convincing details	Persuasive piece sometimes unfocused; needs more support	Rambling persuasive argument; lacks development and detail
Organization/ Paragraphs	Information chosen and arranged for maximum effect	Evident progression of persuasive ideas	Information arranged in a logical way with some lapses	Little structure or direction	No identifiable structure
Voice	Writer closely involved; persuasive but not overbearing	Maintains persuasive tone	Sometimes uses persuasive voice	Little writer involvement, personality	Shows little conviction
Word Choice	Persuasive words carefully chosen for impact	Argument supported by persuasive language	Occasional persuasive language	Generally limited or redundant language	Vague, dull, or misused words; no persuasive words
Sentences	Excellent variety of sentences; natural rhythm	Varied lengths, styles; generally smooth	Carefully constructed sentences; some variety	Simple, awkward, or wordy sentences; little variety	Choppy; many incomplete or run-on sentences
Conventions	Excellent control; few or no errors	No serious errors to affect understanding	Reasonable control; few distracting errors	Weak control; enough errors to affect understanding	Many errors that prevent understanding

Scoring Rubric — Persuasive Writing

	3	2	1
Focus/Ideas	Persuasive argument carefully built with quality details	Persuasive argument with one or two convincing details	Rambling persuasive argument; lacks development and detail
Organization/ Paragraphs	Information chosen and arranged for maximum effect	Information arranged in a logical way with some lapses	No identifiable structure
Voice	Writer closely involved; persuasive but not overbearing	Sometimes uses persuasive voice	Shows little conviction
Word Choice	Persuasive words carefully chosen for impact	Occasional persuasive language	Vague, dull, or misused words; no persuasive words
Sentences	Excellent variety of sentences; natural rhythm	Carefully constructed sentences; some variety	Choppy; many incomplete or run-on sentences
Conventions	Excellent control; few or no errors	Reasonable control; few distracting errors	Many errors that prevent understanding

Scoring Rubric — Expository Writing

	6	5	4	3	2	1
Focus/Ideas	Insightful, focused exposition; well elaborated with quality details	Informed, focused exposition; elaborated with telling details	Exposition focused, good elaboration	Generally focused exposition; some supporting details	Sometimes unfocused exposition needs more supporting details	Rambling exposition; lacks development and detail
Organization/ Paragraphs	Logical, consistent flow of ideas; good transitions	Logical sequencing of ideas; uses transitions	Ideas sequenced with some transitions	Sequenced ideas with some transitions	Little direction from beginning to end; few order words	Lacks structure and transitions
Voice	Writer closely involved; informative voice well suited to topic	Reveals personality; voice suited to topic	Pleasant but not compelling voice	Sincere voice suited to topic	Little writer involvement, personality	Careless writing with no feeling
Word Choice	Vivid, precise words to express ideas	Clear words to express ideas	Words correct and adequate	Language adequate but may lack precision	Generally limited or redundant language	Vague, dull, or misused words
Sentences	Strong topic sentence; fluent, varied structures	Good topic sentence; smooth sentence structure	Correct sentences that are sometimes fluent	Topic sentence correctly constructed; some sentence variety	Topic sentence unclear or missing; wordy, awkward sentences	No topic sentence; many incomplete or run-on sentences
Conventions	Excellent control; few or no errors	No serious errors to affect understanding	General mastery of conventions but some errors	Reasonable control; few distracting errors	Weak control; enough errors to affect understanding	Many errors that prevent understanding

Scoring Rubric — Expository Writing

	5	4	3	2	1
Focus/Ideas	Insightful, focused exposition; well elaborated with quality details	Informed, focused exposition; elaborated with telling details	Generally focused exposition; some supporting details	Sometimes unfocused exposition needs more supporting details	Rambling exposition; lacks development and detail
Organization/ Paragraphs	Logical, consistent flow of ideas; good transitions	Logical sequencing of ideas; uses transitions	Sequenced ideas with some transitions	Little direction from beginning to end; few order words	Lacks structure and transitions
Voice	Writer closely involved; informative voice well suited to topic	Reveals personality; voice suited to topic	Language adequate but may lack precision	Little writer involvement, personality	Careless writing with no feeling
Word Choice	Vivid, precise words to express ideas	Clear words to express ideas	Topic sentence correctly constructed; some sentence variety	Generally limited or redundant language	Vague, dull, or misused words
Sentences	Strong topic sentence; fluent, varied structures	Good topic sentence; smooth sentence structure	Sincere voice suited to topic	Topic sentence unclear or missing; wordy, awkward sentences	No topic sentence; many incomplete or run-on sentences
Conventions	Excellent control; few or no errors	No serious errors to affect understanding	Reasonable control; few distracting errors	Weak control; enough errors to affect understanding	Many errors that prevent understanding

Scoring Rubric — Expository Writing

	3	2	1
Focus/Ideas	Insightful, focused exposition; well elaborated with quality details	Generally focused exposition; some supporting details	Rambling exposition; lacks development and detail
Organization/ Paragraphs	Logical, consistent flow of ideas; good transitions	Sequenced ideas with some transitions	Lacks structure and transitions
Voice	Writer closely involved; informative voice well suited to topic	Sincere voice suited to topic	Careless writing with no feeling
Word Choice	Vivid, precise words to express ideas	Language adequate but may lack precision	Vague, dull, or misused words
Sentences	Strong topic sentence; fluent, varied structures	Topic sentence correctly constructed; some sentence variety	No topic sentence; many incomplete or run-on sentences
Conventions	Excellent control; few or no errors	Reasonable control; few distracting errors	Many errors that prevent understanding

Monitoring Fluency

Ongoing assessment of a child's reading fluency is one of the most valuable measures we have of children's reading skills. One of the most effective ways to assess fluency is taking timed samples of children's oral reading and measuring the number of words correct per minute (WCPM).

How to Measure Words Correct Per Minute—WCPM

Choose a Text
Start by choosing a text for the child to read. The text should be:
- narrative
- unfamiliar
- on grade level

Make a copy of the text for yourself and have one for the child.

Timed Reading of the Text
Tell the child: As you read this aloud, I want you to do your best reading and to read as quickly as you can. That doesn't mean it's a race. Just do your best, fast reading. When I say begin, start reading.

As the child reads, follow along in your copy. Mark words that are read incorrectly.

Incorrect	Correct
• omissions	• self-corrections within 3 seconds
• substitutions	• repeated words
• mispronunciations	
• reversals	

After One Minute
At the end of one minute, draw a line after the last word that was read. Have the child finish reading but don't count any words beyond one minute. Arrive at the words correct per minute—WCPM—by counting the total number of words that the child read correctly in one minute.

Fluency Goals
Grade 2 End-of-Year Goal = 90 WCPM

Target goals by unit

Unit 1 50 to 60 WCPM	**Unit 4** 74 to 84 WCPM
Unit 2 58 to 68 WCPM	**Unit 5** 82 to 92 WCPM
Unit 3 66 to 76 WCPM	**Unit 6** 90 to 100 WCPM

More Frequent Monitoring
You may want to monitor some children more frequently because they are falling far below grade-level benchmarks or they have a result that doesn't seem to align with their previous performance. Follow the same steps above, but choose 2 or 3 additional texts.

Fluency Progress Chart Copy the chart on the next page. Use it to record each child's progress across the year.

Fluency Progress Chart, Grade 2

Name _____

WCPM

	1	2	3	4	5	6	7	8	9	10	11	12	13	14	15	16	17	18	19	20	21	22	23	24	25	26	27	28	29	30
125																														
120																														
115																														
110																														
105																														
100																														
95																														
90																														
85																														
80																														
75																														
70																														
65																														
60																														
55																														
50																														
45																														
40																														
35																														
30																														

Timed Reading

Sentence Reading Chart

Unit 5

	Phonics		Lesson Vocabulary		Reteach ✓	Reassess: Words Correct
	Total Words	Words Correct	Total Words	Words Correct		
Week 1 *Firefighter!* A B C						
Suffixes *-ly, -ful, -er, -or*	4					
Lesson Vocabulary			2			
Week 2 *One Dark Night* A B C						
Prefixes *un-, re-, pre-, dis*	4					
Lesson Vocabulary			2			
Week 3 *Bad Dog, Dodger!* A B C						
Silent Consonants	4					
Lesson Vocabulary			2			
Week 4 *Horace and Morris but mostly Dolores* A B C						
ph, gh/f/	4					
Lesson Vocabulary			2			
Week 5 *The Signmaker's Assistant* A B C						
Vowels *aw, au, augh, al*	4					
Lesson Vocabulary			2			
Unit Scores	20		10			

- **RECORD SCORES** Use this chart to record scores for the Day 5 Sentence Reading Assessment. Circle A, B, or C to record which set of sentences was used.
- **RETEACH PHONICS SKILLS** If the child is unable to read all the tested phonics words, then reteach the phonics skills using the Reteach lessons on pp. DI·64–DI·68.

- **PRACTICE LESSON VOCABULARY** If the child is unable to read all the tested high-frequency words, then provide additional practice for the week's words. See pp. 178e, 206e, 232e, 262e, and 290e.
- **REASSESS** Use the same set of sentences or an easier set for reassessment.

Unit 5
Assess and Regroup

FYI In Grade 2 there are opportunities for regrouping every five weeks—at the end of Units 2, 3, 4, and 5. These options offer sensitivity to each child's progress, although some teachers may prefer to regroup less frequently.

Regroup for Unit 6

To make regrouping decisions at the end of Unit 5, consider children's end-of-unit scores for
- Unit 5 Sentence Reading (Day 5 Assessments)
- Fluency (wcpm)
- Unit 5 Benchmark Test

Group Time

On-Level	Strategic Intervention	Advanced
To continue On-Level or to move into the On-Level group, children should	**Children would benefit from Strategic Intervention if they**	**To move to the Advanced group, children should**
• score 80% or better on their cumulative Unit Scores for Sentence Reading for phonics and lesson vocabulary	• score 60% or lower on their cumulative Unit Scores for Sentence Reading for phonics and lesson vocabulary, regardless of their fluency scores	• score 100% on their cumulative Unit Scores for Sentence Reading for phonics and lesson vocabulary
• meet the current benchmark for fluency (82–92 wcpm), reading On-Level text such as Student Edition selections	• do not meet the current benchmark for fluency (82–92 wcpm)	• score 95% on the Unit 5 Benchmark Test
• score 80% or better on the Unit 5 Benchmark Test	• score below 80% on their cumulative Unit Scores for Sentence Reading for phonics and lesson vocabulary AND have fluency scores below the current benchmark of 82–92 wcpm	• read above grade-level material (82–92 wcpm) with speed, accuracy, and expression. You may try them out on one of the Advanced Selections.
• be capable of working in the On-Level group based on teacher judgment	• score below 60% on the Unit 5 Benchmark Test	• use expansive vocabulary and ease of language in retelling
	• are struggling to keep up with the On-Level group based on teacher judgment	• be capable of handling the problem solving and the investigative work of the Advanced group based on teacher judgment

QUESTIONS TO CONSIDER

- What types of test questions did the child miss? Are they specific to a particular skill or strategy?
- Does the child have adequate background knowledge to understand the test passages or selections for retelling?
- Has the child's performance met expectations for daily lessons and assessments with little or no reteaching?
- Is the child performing more like children in another group?
- Does the child read for enjoyment, different purposes, and with varied interests?

Benchmark Fluency Scores

Current Goal: 82–92 wcpm

End-of-Year Goal: 90 wcpm

Unit Scores for Sentence Reading

Phonics	Lesson Vocabulary
100% = **20**	100% = **10**
80% = **16**	80% = **8**
60% = **12**	60% = **6**

Leveled Readers

Table of Contents

LR

Leveled Readers

Community Helpers

Community Helpers
by Marianne Lenihan

◉ **MAIN IDEA**

◉ **TEXT STRUCTURE**

LESSON VOCABULARY buildings, burning, masks, quickly, roar, station, tightly

SUMMARY Many people live and work in a community. From police officers to firefighters, from teachers to doctors and mail carriers, the people who work in a community help each other and other people who live in the community.

INTRODUCE THE BOOK

BUILD BACKGROUND Say the word *community,* and ask children to say the first words that pop into their minds. Record children's ideas on chart paper. Help children conclude that communities are places where people live and work.

PREVIEW/TAKE A PICTURE WALK Encourage children to identify the tools that each community worker uses. For example, on page 5, which police officer's tool do children see? What firefighter's tool do they see on pages 6–7?

TEACH/REVIEW VOCABULARY Write the words on the board and read them with the class. Invite children to suggest sentences for each word. Have children explain the meaning of each word, based on the way they used it in the sentence.

ELL Try to find a picture of a burning building to share with children. Label parts of the picture to introduce the vocabulary words, such as *building, burning,* and *masks* worn by firefighters. Act out other words, such as *quickly, roar,* and *tightly.*

TARGET SKILL AND STRATEGY

◉ **MAIN IDEA** Review with children that the *main idea* of a book is the big idea the book is trying to get across. Read page 3 with the group and ask children to identify the main idea of this text. (what is a community?)

◉ **TEXT STRUCTURE** Share with children that *text structure* is the way information is organized. In this reader, information is organized according to the different roles community workers play. Have students cite examples to show why this is so.

READ THE BOOK

Use the following questions to support comprehension.

PAGE 4 What is the main idea of this page? *(Communities need people to help the community.)*

PAGE 8 What might be the sequence of events for this teacher during one day? *(The teacher gets up, goes to school, prepares for class, teaches the children, grades papers, goes home, eats dinner.)*

PAGE 10 Why do communities need first-aid workers? *(To help people who are hurt or sick.)*

TALK ABOUT THE BOOK

READER RESPONSE
1. Possible responses: Community workers help people who live in a community.
2. Possible responses: First, the firefighters get their masks and hoses. Then, they jump into their fire truck. They drive to the fire. They rescue people and put out the fire.
3. Possible responses: police station, fire station, library, school, hospital, post office
4. Possible responses: helmet, protective jacket and pants, truck with crane and ladder

RESPONSE OPTIONS

WRITING Ask children to choose one job in this book that interests them. Have children write a few sentences that explains why they might someday like to do this job.

CONTENT CONNECTIONS

Time for SOCIAL STUDIES

SOCIAL STUDIES Divide the class into groups, one for each worker in this book. Have children research the training each job requires. Guide their research in books or over the Internet. Invite groups to report their findings back to the class.

Name _____

Main Idea

Read the paragraph below.

> Police officers patrol their communities using cars, bicycles, or horses. They make sure everyone is safe. Some police officers direct traffic. Police officers help the people in a community live together in peace.

What is the main idea of this paragraph? Write your ideas below.

_____
- -
_____
_____
- -
_____
_____
- -
_____
_____
- -
_____
_____
- -
_____

94

Name _____

Vocabulary

Choose a word from the box that best fits in each sentence.

> **Words to Know**
>
> buildings   burning   masks   quickly
> roar   station   tightly

1. The alarm went off at the fire _____ .

2. The firemen dressed _____ and rushed to the fire engine.

3. The fire spread to three apartment _____ .

4. The firemen wore _____ on their faces to help them breathe.

5. They gripped the hose _____ .

6. People could hear the fire _____ .

7. The firemen rushed into the _____ building.

95

Who Can Help?

Who Can Help?

SUMMARY When help is needed in a community, a team of emergency workers work together. From the 911 operator to the firefighting team to the EMTs and police officers, and ultimately doctors and nurses, people work together in a community when people need help.

INTRODUCE THE BOOK

BUILD BACKGROUND Suggest to children that a small fire broke out in the school. Ask children which community workers would come to their school to help. Confirm that firefighters and police officers would probably arrive, as well as people in ambulances in case someone was hurt.

PREVIEW/TAKE A PICTURE WALK Have children leaf through the book, and encourage them to look for the emergency workers mentioned in the above discussion— firefighters, police officers, EMTs. Ask children to identify other emergency workers they see.

TEACH/REVIEW VOCABULARY As children look through the book, have them apply the vocabulary words to the various pictures. For example, the 911 operator works at a telephone *station.* The operator works *quickly* to alert others about the emergency.

ELL Invite children to role-play being firefighters as they use the vocabulary. For example, children can pretend to slip on *masks,* work *quickly,* leave the *station,* and approach a *burning building,* holding onto their hoses *tightly.*

TARGET SKILL AND STRATEGY

🎯 **MAIN IDEA** Review with children that the *main idea* of a book is the *big* idea the book is trying to get across. Read page 3 with the group, and ask children to identify the main idea of this text. (Some community workers help people who are in danger.)

🎯 **TEXT STRUCTURE** Explain that *text structure* is the way information is organized. Have children consider the chronology of a 911 operator's job. As they list the sequence, have them consider the main idea of this sequence too.

READ THE BOOK

Use the following questions to support comprehension.

PAGE 5 What is the main idea of this page? *(This page describes what EMTs do.)*

PAGE 15 What is the sequence of events on this page? *(EMTs call the nurses. Nurses and doctors wait for the ambulance. They rush people to the emergency room once they arrive.)*

PAGE 15 What might happen if a community worker did not do his or her job? *(People might not be saved. The emergency could get worse.)*

TALK ABOUT THE BOOK

READER RESPONSE

1. Possible response: Some community workers help people during an emergency.
2. They told me what kind of worker I would learn about in each section. The information was organized according to types of community workers.
3. Sentences will vary, but should use *quickly* and *tightly* as adverbs.
4. Answers will vary.

RESPONSE OPTIONS

WRITING Have children write an ad, looking for people to be community helpers. Tell children to write why the jobs are important and why community helpers are needed.

CONTENT CONNECTIONS

SOCIAL STUDIES Invite a community helper from your area to speak to the class. Ahead of time, have children create a list of questions to ask the community helper. Encourage children to ask their questions at the appropriate time.

Time for **SOCIAL STUDIES**

Name _____

Main Idea

Read the paragraph below.

> Emergency line operators, or 911 operators, answer phone calls from people in danger. They keep the caller calm and ask the right questions. They make sure help gets sent out quickly. The 911 operators make sure that other people in the emergency team know everything they need to know to help.

What is the main idea of this paragraph? **Write** your ideas below.

_____
_____
_____
_____
_____
_____
_____
_____
_____
_____
_____
_____

94

Name _____

Vocabulary

The paragraph below tells about an emergency, but some words are missing. **Read** the paragraph and fill in the correct missing words from the box.

Hint: The part of speech has been given to help you.

Words to Know			
buildings	burning	masks	quickly
roar	station	tightly	

A fire erupted last night at the Townville apartment (noun)

_____   _____

_____. Firefighters (adverb) _____

responded to the call from the emergency operators. They could

_____

hear the (noun) _____ of the fire as they approached.

_____

The firefighters pulled their (noun) _____ over their faces
to protect themselves. They then ran toward the (adjective)

_____   _____

_____ buildings, holding (adverb) _____ to
their hoses. They worked steadily for one hour, and the fire was

_____

extinguished. They returned to the fire (noun) _____
weary but glad that no one had been injured.

95

Goods and Services

Goods and Services
by Megan Litwin

SUMMARY People in a community depend on each other as consumers and producers. Some people provide goods or services; they are the producers. The people who pay for these goods or services are the consumers.

INTRODUCE THE BOOK

BUILD BACKGROUND Hold up a simple classroom object, such as a pencil, and ask children where pencils come from. Let children freely exchange ideas. Then explain that the person who makes the pencil is called a producer. The people who buy the pencil are consumers.

PREVIEW/TAKE A PICTURE WALK Invite children to flip through the book to become familiar with the book's format and some of the vocabulary. Have children read headings. Also call attention to graphic elements, such as the arrows that connect the pictures on pages 6 and 7. Speculate what these arrows could represent.

TEACH/PREVIEW VOCABULARY Arrange the words in a word web. Place the word *community* in the center of the web, then write the remaining words in circles around the center. Help children make the connection that consumers and producers work together in a *community.*

ⒺⓁⓁ Write each word on the board, and break it apart by syllables. Help children read each word as syllables. Then help them role-play being consumers and producers to understand the words' meanings.

TARGET SKILL AND STRATEGY

🎯 **MAIN IDEA** Review with children that the *main idea* of a book is the "big idea" the book is trying to get across. Read the first paragraph on page 3 with the group, and ask children to identify the main idea. *(what are goods)*

🎯 **TEXT STRUCTURE** Share with children that *text structure* is the way information is organized. Explain that sometimes information is organized in sequence, or in chronological order. Have children look at the graphic on page 4, and encourage them to explain this sequence. Have them consider the main idea of this sequence. *(how shelves are produced)*

READ THE BOOK

Use the following questions to support comprehension.

PAGES 6–10 What is the main idea of these pages? *(how producers and consumers depend on each other; how banana bread is produced)*

PAGE 11 What might be the sequence of events for setting up a lemonade stand? *(buy ingredients; make lemonade; set up the stand; sell the lemonade)*

PAGE 12 What is the difference between goods and services? *(Goods are things people make to sell; services are things people do.)*

TALK ABOUT THE BOOK

READER RESPONSE
1. Possible responses: A community needs both producers and consumers; they need each other.
2. Possible responses: Buy bananas and flour from other producers; make the bread; sell the bread.
3. Possible responses: haircuts; medical care; dental care; dry cleaning; transportation
4. Possible response: in the Glossary

RESPONSE OPTIONS

WRITING Have children think of a product they enjoy. Encourage children to write a radio ad about the product, telling consumers why they should buy it.

CONTENT CONNECTIONS

SOCIAL STUDIES Divide the class into groups. Have the groups choose a food they like and then learn how it is produced. Invite children to share what they learn by role-playing the different producers needed to bring the food to consumers.

Time for **SOCIAL STUDIES**

Name _____

Main Idea

Read the paragraphs below.

> Sometimes we don't need to buy something, but we need to pay someone to help us get something done. If you need a haircut, you might go to a hairdresser. You wouldn't ask the baker who sold you banana bread to cut your hair! You would want help from someone who knows how to cut hair. When a person with special training gives you help, it is called a service.
>
> Goods and services are similar. The people who provide services are also producers. The people who pay for their services are consumers.

What is the main idea of this paragraph? **Write** your ideas below.

_____

- -

_____

- -

_____

_____

- -

_____

94

Name _____

Vocabulary

Choose a word from the Word Box that best fits in each sentence.

Words to Know

community   consumers   goods   producers
responsible   service   teamwork

_____
----
1. _____ are things that people buy.
   Which do you like? Which would you try?

_____
----
2. _____ make the things we need.
   Like clothes and books and cars with speed.

_____
----
3. _____ buy what a producer makes.
   Like shoes and cookies, freshly baked.

4. Need a haircut? Get one here!
   _____

   We provide _____ throughout the year.

5. Consumers, producers, services, too.
   _____

   Are in your _____ to help you.

95

Horse Rescue!

SUMMARY The U.S. Coast Guard is mostly known for rescuing people from the sea. On March 7, 2001, the Coast Guard was called in to rescue 16 horses trapped by floodwaters in Louisiana. This book takes readers through that daring rescue.

INTRODUCE THE BOOK

BUILD BACKGROUND Invite children to share their knowledge of horses. Ask children if they consider horses to be land animals or water animals. Ask children what might happen, then, if horses became stuck in rising waters from a flood.

PREVIEW/USE TEXT FEATURES Invite children to look through the book and to point out images that surprise them. For example, children might be surprised to see the horse and the helicopter on pages 10 and 11. Have children explain why this image is surprising.

ELL Ask children to draw a picture of a rain storm, with dark clouds and lightning. Help children label parts of their pictures with vocabulary words. Demonstrate the verbs *pours, pounds,* and *flashes* through hand motions.

TEACH/REVIEW VOCABULARY Say the words for the class, and ask children what images come to mind. Write the words on the board for children to read, and invite children to use the words in sentences to tell about storms they've experienced or imagined.

TARGET SKILL AND STRATEGY

◎ **SEQUENCE** Share with children that *sequence* is the order in which things happen. Have children read the text on page 3. Talk about the sequence of events that would prompt the Coast Guard to rescue someone.

◎ **GRAPHIC ORGANIZERS** Share some graphic organizers that children already use, such as word webs, Venn diagrams, and flow charts. Explain that a time line is a graphic organizer that shows a sequence. Work with children to complete a time line for the sequence they described on page 3.

READ THE BOOK

Use the following questions to support comprehension.

PAGE 5 What sequence is being described on this page? *(How the land flooded and the horses became trapped.)*

PAGE 5 Use a time line to show the sequence of events on this page. *(It rained for a long time. The rivers filled up. Then, water came onto the land. The land began to flood. The farmers tried to rescue the horses. The horses became trapped.)*

PAGE 6 Why did the farmers call the Coast Guard? *(To rescue the horses; because they knew the Coast Guard were experts at water rescue.)*

TALK ABOUT THE BOOK

READER RESPONSE
1. It rained for so long that the rivers overflowed and flooded the land.
2. They flew over the horses. A person went into the water to place a sling around each horse. The helicopters lifted the horses to dry land.
3. Possible response: bursts of lightning
4. Possible response: The illustration shows what the sling is like.

RESPONSE OPTIONS

WRITING Tell children to imagine they are interviewing the Coast Guards members who saved the horses. What questions might they ask? How might the Coast Guard answer? Ask children to write questions and answers, using information from the book.

CONTENT CONNECTIONS

SCIENCE Remind children that most horses are domesticated animals, meaning people raise and care for them. Ask children what kind of shelter they think would be best for horses, and have children explain their ideas.

Name _____

Sequence

Number the sentences below from 1 to 7 to show the sequence of the horse rescue.

Hint: Look for clue words, like **first** and **finally**.

_____

_____ Next, the Coast Guard lowered a person down to each big horse.

_____

_____ Helicopters flew to the place where the horses were last seen.

_____

_____ Finally, an animal doctor checked the horses.

_____

_____ The Coast Guard loaded the smaller horses onto a boat.

_____

_____ Then the person put a sling around the big horse.

_____

_____ First, the farmers called the U.S. Coast Guard for help.

_____

_____ The helicopters flew the big horses to safety.

© Pearson Education 2

98

Name _____

Vocabulary

Find these words in the puzzle. They can be across, up, or down.

flashes	lightning	pounded	poured
rolling	storm	thunder	

```
L  I  G  H  T  N  I  N  G
F  L  A  S  H  E  S  L  N
O  O  P  O  U  R  E  D  I
K  P  O  U  N  D  E  D  L
A  T  T  H  D  E  S  K  L
Y  H  O  R  E  S  E  S  O
F  S  T  O  R  M  L  Y  R
```

Now write the leftover letters in order on the lines below to reveal a secret message.

__ __ __ __   __ __   __ __ __

__ __ __ !

__ __ __ __ __ __   __ __ __ !

99

Unit 5 Week 2

◉ **SEQUENCE**

◉ **GRAPHIC ORGANIZERS**

LESSON VOCABULARY flashes, lightning, pounds, pours, rolling, storm, thunder

Animal Shelters

SUMMARY Animals need shelters to protect them from harsh weather. Some animals, like those that live on a farm, are cared for by people. Their owners provide shelter, like barns. Other animals, like bees and birds, live in the wild. They build their own shelters.

INTRODUCE THE BOOK

BUILD BACKGROUND Encourage children to think about animals that live with people, such as cats, dogs, perhaps even a classroom pet. Have children explain how people protect and care for these animals. Ask children if animals in the wild need the same kind of care. Lead children to the idea of shelter—protection from the weather.

PREVIEW/USE TEXT FEATURES Ask children to look through the book and identify the animal shelters. For example, what animal shelter is on page 3? *(a nest)* On pages 4 and 5? *(barns and birdhouses)* List the words for these shelters on the board to prepare for reading.

ELL Show children pictures of a rainstorm, and say the vocabulary words. Use hand motions to help children learn the meanings of the words.

TEACH/REVIEW VOCABULARY Write the words on the board, and read them with the class. Ask children what images these words evoke, and agree that these words make them think of bad weather. Ask children why these words might appear in a book about animal shelters.

TARGET SKILL STRATEGY

◉ **SEQUENCE** Share with children that *sequence* is the order in which things happen. Have children read the text on page 3. Encourage children to tell the sequence of a storm. For example, at first dark clouds roll in. Then, they might hear thunder. A raindrop might fall. Ask: What might happen next?

◉ **GRAPHIC ORGANIZERS** Share some graphic organizers that children already use. Explain that a flow chart is a graphic organizer that shows a sequence. Work with children to complete a flow chart for the sequence of a storm.

READ THE BOOK

Use the following questions to support comprehension.

PAGE 5 Which type of animal and animal shelters do you read about first? *(farm animals and shelters for farm animals)*

PAGES 6–8 What type of graphic organizer could help you compare the similar yet different shelter needs of pigs and cows? *(a Venn diagram)*

PAGE 11 How are wild animals different from farm animals? *(Farm animals are cared for by people; people build shelters for them. Wild animals take care of themselves; they build their own shelters.)*

TALK ABOUT THE BOOK

READER RESPONSE
1. Possible responses: Farm Animals: pigs, cows, sheep, chickens; Wild Animals: bees, birds; Pets: guinea pigs, hamsters, fish, lizards
2. Possible responses: barns, pens, coops, hives, nests, birdhouses
3. Sudden bursts of light
4. Possible response: The pictures show that shelters are places animals feel safe.

RESPONSE OPTIONS

WRITING Have children write sentences that explain why all animals need shelter.

CONTENT CONNECTIONS

SCIENCE Write the words "Farm Animals" and "Wild Animals" above the two outer circles of a Venn diagram. Invite children to explain the different needs of each type of animal. Help children conclude that both domesticated and wild, animals need food and shelter to protect them from harsh weather.

TIME FOR Science

Name _____

Sequence

Complete the chart below. Write the animals in the order in which they appeared in the book.

Farm Animal Shelter

1. _____   3. _____

2. _____   4. _____

Wild Animal Shelter

1. _____   2. _____

Shelter for Pets

1. _____   3. _____

2. _____   4. _____

98

Name _____

Vocabulary

Finish the poem below. Think about what makes sense and what words rhyme. The words below each rhyme tell you the part of speech.

flashes   lightning   pounds   pours
rolling   storm   thunder

_____   _____
- -

Lightning _____. _____ pounds.
              (verb)   (noun)
- -

Rain _____ down, and down and down.
         (verb)
- -

The _____ is bursting, all around,
      (noun)
- -

_____ with a scary sound.
        (verb)

Think about the words you wrote and their parts of speech. Make any changes. Compare poems with a classmate.

99

A Day in the Life of a Vet

A Day in the Life of a Vet
by Kristin Cashore
illustrated by Aleksey Ivanov

◎ **SEQUENCE**

◎ **GRAPHIC ORGANIZERS**

LESSON VOCABULARY growth, llama, protect, survive, veterinarian, yak

SUMMARY Vets take care of sick or injured animals. Some vets care for small animals, like pets, while others care for large animals, like cows and horses. There are vets who work at zoos and vets who care for wild animals.

INTRODUCE THE BOOK

BUILD BACKGROUND Ask children where people go when they are sick or injured. Share with children that veterinarians, or vets, are doctors who care for animals. Add that vets specialize in the types of animals they care for.

PREVIEW/TAKE A PICTURE WALK Let children flip through the book to become familiar with its format and content. Have them pause on page 3, and encourage children to identify the animals they see. Ask children if they think one type of vet takes care of all these different animals.

ELL Ask children to write the nouns *llama, veterinarian,* and *yak* on self-stick notes. Have them say the words, then show them which pictures in the book illustrate these words. Have children place the self-stick notes on the pictures.

TEACH/PREVIEW VOCABULARY Review with children which words are nouns (*growth, llama, veterinarian, yak*) and which are verbs (*protect, survive*). Have children look through the book to find pictures that show a llama, a vet, and a yak.

TARGET SKILL AND STRATEGY

◎ **SEQUENCE** Share with children that *sequence* is the order in which things happen. Suggest to children that a classroom pet must visit a vet. Discuss the order in which events might occur.

◎ **GRAPHIC ORGANIZERS** Share some graphic organizers that children already use, such as word webs, Venn diagrams, and flow charts. Explain that a time line is a graphic organizer that shows a sequence. Work with children to complete a time line for the sequence of events of discovering a pet is sick and then taking it to the vet.

READ THE BOOK

Use the following questions to support comprehension.

PAGE 4 Which type of vet do we read about first in the book? *(a small animal vet)*

PAGES 4–5 Use a word web to show the four types of vets you read about in this book. *(Center Circle: Types of Vets; Outer Circles: small animal vet; large animal vet; wildlife vet; zoo vet)*

PAGE 11 Why do wildlife vets work all over the world? *(Wild animals live all over the world. Wildlife vets go where they are needed.)*

TALK ABOUT THE BOOK

READER RESPONSE
1. Possible responses: the yak, the elephant, the crocodile; he visited the animals in order of urgency; in the order of appointments; according to the location of their zoo habitats.
2. Answers will vary, but should reflect an understanding of both the question and the work of the different veterinarians.
3. Possible response: to help it continue to live
4. Possible responses: They resemble cows; they have long fur; they have horns.

RESPONSE OPTIONS

WRITING Encourage children to consider which type of vet they think has the most interesting job. Have children write a few sentences that explain their ideas.

CONTENT CONNECTIONS

TIME FOR Science

SCIENCE Invite a local veterinarian to speak to your class. Ahead of time, have children write questions to ask the vet. Then, have the vet explain to children the training and responsibilities of being a vet. At the appropriate time, have children ask their questions.

Sequence

Write the names of the vets in the box in the order in which we met them in the book.

Dr. Billings and Dr. Mor—Wildlife Vets

Dr. Hopkins—A Small Animal Vet

Dr. Jung—A Zoo Vet

Dr. Martinez—A Large Animal Vet

1. _____

2. _____

3. _____

4. _____

Choose one of the vets from *A Day in the Life of a Vet*.
Fill in the schedule below to show the order in which he or she examined patients.

First patient: _____

Second patient: _____

Third patient: _____

Last patient: _____

98

Name _____

Vocabulary

Read the report below. It was written by an animal doctor.
Complete the report with the missing words from the box.

Words to Know

growth   llama   protect   survive   yak   veterinarian

January 14

I have completed my morning rounds. I checked on the

_____ of a newborn giraffe. I had a report that

something was tangled around a _____'s horns.

I also stopped by the pen of a _____ whose

nails were recently trimmed. I am worried about our newest

addition, a crocodile. If the crocodile is to _____

the winter, we'll need to _____ it from cold

weather. Ah! The job of a _____ is never done.

What kind of vet wrote this report? Write your idea below.

_____

_____

_____

_____

99

Sally and the Wild Puppy

Sally and the Wild Puppy
by Evan Allen
illustrated by Bob Brugger

Unit 5 Week 3

◉ **THEME AND PLOT**

◉ **PRIOR KNOWLEDGE**

LESSON VOCABULARY chased, chewing, dripping, grabbed, practice, treat, wagged

SUMMARY This story is about Sally and her new puppy, Sparks. At first, Sparks is very wild, but after some training and practice, he begins to learn how to behave.

INTRODUCE THE BOOK

BUILD BACKGROUND Engage children in a discussion of puppies and invite them to share what they know. Ask: What are the different things that puppies do? Why do puppies get in trouble?

PREVIEW/TAKE A PICTURE WALK Have children preview the book by looking at the illustrations. Invite them to describe what is happening on each page and predict what the text will be about. Ask: What is the puppy doing here? Is he being good or bad? How does the girl, Sally, feel about her puppy? What tells you this?

TEACH/REVIEW VOCABULARY Play a game of charades by having children take turns acting out and guessing the vocabulary words. As children guess each word correctly, help them write it down on their own paper. To aid comprehension, offer a few different sentences using each word.

TARGET SKILL AND STRATEGY

◉ **THEME AND PLOT** Explain to the children that every story has a "big idea" or a *theme*. Before reading, invite children to predict what the story is all about, or what we might learn about. Remind them to think about what the "big idea" might be as they read. Tell children that keeping track of the main events of the story will help them determine the theme.

◉ **PRIOR KNOWLEDGE** Before reading, use your discussion of puppies to encourage children to activate their existing knowledge of the subject. Ask: What do you know about puppies that might help you better understand this story? How did you use your knowledge of puppies to understand what the author meant by the "wild" puppy?

ELL Have children describe or act out the meaning of *wild* for greater comprehension. As they do so, encourage children to say the word in English as well as in their native languages.

READ THE BOOK

Use the following questions to support comprehension.

PAGE 3 What does the grandmother mean by "a special treat"? *(a surprise or present)*

PAGE 8 Why do you think Sally gives Sparks hugs when he obeys? *(because Sally is happy with Sparks, wants to encourage him, wants him to continue to obey)*

PAGE 11 Why was Sparks so good by the end of the story? *(because Sally had practiced with him and he learned how to behave and obey)*

TALK ABOUT THE BOOK

READER RESPONSE

1. Theme: Training a puppy. Beginning: Sally gets a new puppy; Middle: Sparks is disobedient; End: Sally trains Sparks.

2. Responses will vary but children should be encouraged to activate their prior knowledge about practicing.

3. A *treat* is a small gift or reward. Sally might give her puppy a bone.

4. Answers should reflect comprehension of plot.

RESPONSE OPTIONS

SPEAKING Help children retell the story by recalling the main events from the beginning, middle, and end of the book. Use a graphic organizer and write down these main events for children to use as a reference.

CONTENT CONNECTIONS

ART Have children illustrate two events from the story by choosing one good thing and one bad thing that Sparks did. Children can label their illustrations with *good* and *bad* and post their drawings to share with the rest of the class.

Theme and Plot

Sally and the Wild Puppy is all about training a puppy. Circle the three events from the story that best relate to training a puppy. Then write "beginning," "middle," or "end" next to the circled events to tell when they happened in the story.

_____

_____   1. Sparks learned to obey and became a
                                       good listener.

_____

_____

_____   2. Grandma gave Sally a puppy.

_____

_____

_____   3. Sparks made a big mess.

_____

_____

_____   4. Sally practiced with Sparks.

_____

_____

_____   5. Sally was happy to get a puppy.

In the space below, draw a picture that shows the theme of *Sally and the Wild Puppy.*

102

Name _____

Vocabulary

Choose a word from the box that best fits in each sentence.

Words to Know
chased   chewing   dripping   grabbed
practice   treat   wagged

1. Grandma said she had a special _____ for Sally.

2. Sally's puppy was _____ everything in sight.

3. The puppy's tail _____ so hard that it was blurry.

4. Sally wanted Sparks to _____ to become the perfect puppy.

5. Sparks _____ after Sally.

6. Sally _____ Sparks as he ran out the door.

7. Sparks liked to give sloppy, _____ licks.

© Pearson Education 2

103

Hubert and Frankie

🎯 **THEME AND PLOT**

🎯 **PRIOR KNOWLEDGE**

LESSON VOCABULARY chased, chewing, dripping, grabbed, practice, treat, wagged

SUMMARY This fiction book tells the story of the Kent family's new puppy, Frankie. Frankie has trouble listening and behaving, so Hubert, the older family dog, helps him learn.

INTRODUCE THE BOOK

BUILD BACKGROUND Engage children in a discussion of pets and puppies. Invite those who have puppies, dogs, or other pets at home to share their experiences. Encourage them to describe both good and bad things about having pets.

PREVIEW/TAKE A PICTURE WALK Have children preview the book, looking at the illustrations. Ask children to describe what they see happening on each page and predict what the text might be about. Ask: What is the puppy doing here? How do you think the family feels about it?

TEACH/REVIEW VOCABULARY Have children write down each of the vocabulary words and discuss the definitions. Assist the children in writing sentences using each of the words.

ELL Use pantomime to help English language learners understand the meanings of the vocabulary words.

TARGET SKILL AND STRATEGY

🎯 **THEME AND PLOT** Prior to reading, tell the children that every story has a "big idea" called a *theme*. Explain that this big idea is what the story is all about. As they read, encourage children to take note of the different events that can help tell us what the *big idea* of the story might be.

🎯 **PRIOR KNOWLEDGE** Before reading, use your discussion of puppies and other pets to encourage children to activate their existing knowledge of the subject. Ask: What do you know about puppies and dogs that might help you better understand this story?

READ THE BOOK

Use the following questions to support comprehension.

PAGE 3 Why do you think Hubert thought Frankie was trouble? *(because Frankie misbehaved by chasing the cat and chewing on shoes)*

PAGE 7 What does Hubert remember? Why does this make him think he might be able to help? *(He remembers how hard it was to listen and behave when he was a puppy. He can help because he remembers and understands how hard it is for Frankie.)*

PAGE 12 Why does Frankie stop reaching for the hamburger when Madeline says, "No, Frankie!"? *(Because he has learned his name and how to listen.)*

TALK ABOUT THE BOOK

READER RESPONSE

1. Theme: Learning the rules. Plot/events: Kents get Frankie; Frankie misbehaves; Hubert teaches Frankie the rules; Madeline's hamburger falls to the ground; the two dogs show their owners what they have worked on; everyone is happy and the two dogs get a treat.
2. Responses will vary.
3. run, walk, rush, race, crawl, etc.
4. Responses will vary. Make sure children use reasons to support their answers.

RESPONSE OPTIONS

WRITING Ask children to write a short paragraph about the story from Frankie's point of view. Ask: If Frankie could talk to the family, what do you think he would say?

CONTENT CONNECTIONS

SOCIAL STUDIES Engage children in a discussion of responsibilities. Ask them to describe what things they need to do at home or school to show that they are responsible. Discuss why we all need to be responsible.

Time for **SOCIAL STUDIES**

Name _____

Theme and Plot

Hubert and Frankie is all about learning the rules. Circle the three events from the story that best relate to learning and the rules. Then write "beginning," "middle," or "end" next to the circled events to tell when they happened in the story.

_____

- -

_____   1. Hubert taught Frankie to listen and what the words *no* and *stop* meant.

_____

- -

_____   2. Madeline tried and tried to teach Frankie to sit, but he would not listen.

_____

- -

_____   3. Hubert had lived with the Kent family for a long time and Frankie was the new puppy.

_____

- -

_____   4. Hubert thought Frankie was trouble.

_____

- -

_____   5. Frankie showed the Kents that he knew how to sit.

© Pearson Education 2

102

Name _____

Vocabulary

Choose a word from the Word Box that best fits in each sentence.

Words to Know
chased   chewing   dripping   grabbed
practice   treat   wagged

1. To show he was happy, Frankie _____ his tail.

2. Frankie _____ the baseball glove.

3. Frankie liked _____ on bones.

4. After splashing in the puddle, Frankie was _____ wet.

5. Hubert helped Frankie _____ how to behave.

6. Both Frankie and Hubert got a _____ when they were good.

7. Frankie still _____ the cat sometimes.

103

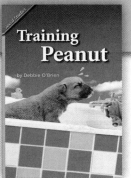

Training Peanut

- ⊙ **THEME AND PLOT**
- ⊙ **PRIOR KNOWLEDGE**
- **LESSON VOCABULARY** behavior, command, naughty, obey, patient, praise

---

SUMMARY This story is about Tomás and Sofía and their family's new puppy, Peanut.

INTRODUCE THE BOOK

BUILD BACKGROUND Invite children to share what they know about puppies (or dogs) and training. Ask: Why do puppies and dogs need to be trained? What would happen if people didn't train their dogs?

PREVIEW/TAKE A PICTURE WALK Have the children preview the book by looking at the photographs. Ask children to think about the title, *Training Peanut,* in relation to the photographs and to make predictions about the text.

TEACH/PREVIEW VOCABULARY Put children into pairs or small groups and assign one word to each. Have children skim the book to find their word and then read the sentence aloud to the class. Based on the sentences from the book, help children determine the meanings of the words.

ELL Pair less-proficient speakers with more-proficient speakers for this activity. Encourage English language learners to repeat the sentences after their partners.

TARGET SKILL AND STRATEGY

⊙ **THEME AND PLOT** Remind children that each story has a "big idea" called a *theme.* The big idea is what the story is all about. It might be something that the characters learn or even something that we learn from reading the story. Also remind children that events in the story can help us determine the theme.

⊙ **PRIOR KNOWLEDGE** Pause after reading page 3, and point out Mom's words. Ask: What are some of the things Mom says you have to do when you have a puppy? How do you think she knows this? Encourage children to connect their own knowledge and experience to the story. Ask: What do you know about caring for a puppy? Is Mom right? How do you know?

READ THE BOOK

Use the following questions to support comprehension.

PAGE 3 What are some of the reasons Tomás and Sofía give for getting a puppy? *(Cousin Luis has one; three neighbors have dogs so the puppy would have playmates.)*

PAGE 10–11 Why do you think the instructor tells the owners to give their puppies treats when they behave? *(as a reward; to encourage the puppies to continue to behave)*

PAGE 18 Why is it important for the students to practice with their puppies every day? *(So they can grow up to be well-behaved dog.)*

TALK ABOUT THE BOOK

READER RESPONSE

1. Theme: Training a puppy takes work but is worthwhile. Beginning: Peanut misbehaves. Middle: Tomás and Sofía take Peanut to training. End: Peanut learns to obey.
2. Responses will vary. Encourage children to tell what they know about puppies and connect that information to the text.
3. Responses will vary but should indicate a comprehension of vocabulary.
4. Possible response: Yes, because now Peanut knows how to behave.

RESPONSE OPTIONS

WRITING Using their own experience as well as what they have read in the book, have children write a story about caring for a puppy. Ask: What would your puppy look like and what would you name him or her? What things would you have to do to care for your puppy? How would you train your puppy to behave?

CONTENT CONNECTIONS

SOCIAL STUDIES Talk about the different activities offered by the community center in the book.

Name _____

Theme and Plot

The theme of *Training Peanut* is that training a puppy takes work but is worthwhile. Circle the three events from the story that best relate to this theme. Then write "beginning," "middle," or "end" next to the circled events to tell when they happened in the story.

_____

_____ 1. When the puppy training course was over, Peanut had learned how to behave better. The family decided to take her to the advanced course for more training.

_____

_____ 2. Tomás and Sofía wanted a puppy more than anything else and asked Mom every day about getting one.

_____

_____ 3. At the first puppy training class, Mom, Sofía, and Tomás learned how to give the sit command. They practiced all week with Peanut.

_____

_____ 4. In a few weeks, Mr. Sanders taught the puppies how to lie down, stay, and heel. He told the families to go on many walks with their puppies to practice these commands.

_____

_____ 5. The family plans to take other classes at the community center too. Sofía and Tomás might even take swimming lessons.

102

© Pearson Education 2

Name _____

Vocabulary

Draw a line to match each word with its meaning.

1. behavior   **a.** behaving badly

2. command   **b.** to do what you are told

3. naughty   **c.** the way someone or something acts

4. obey   **d.** word or acts that show approval

5. patient   **e.** to be calm and wait

6. praise   **f.** an order

103

What an Adventure!

What an Adventure!
by Jessica Quilty

⊙ **AUTHOR'S PURPOSE**

⊙ **ASK QUESTIONS**

LESSON VOCABULARY adventure, climbed, clubhouses, exploring, greatest, truest, wondered

SUMMARY This nonfiction book describes how children can express friendship through an adventure club. It supports and extends the lesson concept of being a good friend and neighbor.

INTRODUCE THE BOOK

BUILD BACKGROUND Have children give examples of an adventure. Ask: Have you ever had an adventure with a friend? Invite children to share their experiences.

PREVIEW/TAKE A PICTURE WALK Have children preview the photos, captions, and labels. Ask them to discuss how they relate to the book's title.

TEACH/REVIEW VOCABULARY Give children sets of vocabulary word cards. Have them sort the words into groups of three-syllable (adventure, exploring), two-syllable (clubhouse, greatest, truest, wondered), and one-syllable (climbed) words.

ELL Invite children to play a riddle game. Have children place vocabulary word cards face down. They take turns picking up a card and making up a riddle for the others to guess. Have them use this pattern: This word starts with the letter(s) _____.

TARGET SKILL AND STRATEGY

⊙ **AUTHOR'S PURPOSE** Do not use the term *author's purpose*. During the preview, ask: Who wrote this book? What do you think the book will be about? Why? Do you think you will like the book? What do you think the book will be like—funny, sad, serious, exciting? Why? During reading, ask: Were you right about what the book is about? Also ask questions about specific parts: On page 8, why does the author include a picture of rafting? Finally, ask questions that relate to the theme: Why does the author talk directly to you?

⊙ **ASK QUESTIONS** Remind children that good readers ask questions about what they are reading to understand, find information, and think about what they have learned. Model: Before: I wonder what this will be about?/I really

want to know about . . . . During: I wonder what this means. I'll read it again to find out./I like this. How did the author make it so exciting? After: What did I like best?/The author didn't cover everything. I wonder where I can learn more about . . . . Encourage children to use a KWL chart to generate questions about this book. help children learn to use the chart by filling in the "K" section as a class.

READ THE BOOK

PAGE 4 Why else would you join an adventure club? (Possible response: to have fun.)

PAGE 7 Why is sailing included in a book about adventures? (Possible response: It is unusual and exciting.)

PAGE 10 Why does the author tell you about city clubs? (Possible response: She wants city kids to know they can have adventures at home.)

TALK ABOUT THE BOOK

READER RESPONSE
1. She wants you to join an adventure club.
2. Possible response: K: You do it in a river. W: What is white water rafting like? L: White water rafting is exciting.
3. Possible response: *club* and *house*; A clubhouse is a place where club members feel at home.
4. Possible response: Teamwork is important in group adventure activities.

RESPONSE OPTIONS

VIEWING Have children look at the photos and describe what skills are needed for each activity.

CONTENT CONNECTIONS

Time for SOCIAL STUDIES

SOCIAL STUDIES Have groups of children draw up a plan for an adventure club. Have them consider the club's purpose, and how they can get adults to help.

Name_____

Author's Purpose

Think about why the author wrote *What an Adventure!* Read each question below. Then underline the best answer.

1. Why does the author say that you can join an adventure club?
   a. to get you to do something
   b. to show how to do something
   c. to make you feel good

2. Why does the author show you camping tools?
   a. to get you to buy them
   b. to tell you about camping
   c. to teach you about the tools

3. Why does the author say that sailing is a lot of fun?
   a. to prove that sailing is better than camping
   b. to teach us about sailing
   c. to get us excited about sailing

4. Why does the author describe what adventure clubs do?
   a. to prove they are the best clubs
   b. to teach us about them
   c. to make us feel bad

5. Why did the author write this book?
   a. to get us to try an adventure club
   b. to make us laugh
   c. to help us take a test

106

Name_____

Vocabulary

Draw a line to match each word with its clue.

1. adventure	**a.** places to meet
2. climbed	**b.** most loyal
3. clubhouses	**c.** went up
4. exploring	**d.** an exciting time
5. greatest	**e.** had a question
6. truest	**f.** the most
7. wondered	**g.** looking for new things

107

You Can Make A Difference!

You Can Make A Difference!
by Laura Crawford
illustrated by Aleksey Ivanov

AUTHOR'S PURPOSE

ASK QUESTIONS

LESSON VOCABULARY adventure, climbed, clubhouse, exploring, greatest, truest, wondered

SUMMARY This nonfiction book describes how children can protect the environment together. It supports the lesson concept of being a good friend and neighbor.

INTRODUCE THE BOOK

BUILD BACKGROUND Have children share their experiences of helping out at home. Ask and discuss: How could you help your neighborhood?

PREVIEW/TAKE A PICTURE WALK Have children preview the pictures, headings, bullet list, and labels. Discuss how the headings help them to read this book by showing when a new topic begins. Ask: Why are there labels in the picture on page 6?

TEACH/REVIEW VOCABULARY Give sets of vocabulary word cards to children. Write the following words on the chalkboard, and read them aloud: searching, highest, questioned, meeting place, most dependable, trip, went up. Ask children to show the word card that best matches each.

ELL Use pictures, objects, or gestures to explain these words from the book: litterbug, wetlands, vet, vaccination, reusable, contract, aluminum.

TARGET SKILL AND STRATEGY

AUTHOR'S PURPOSE Do not use the term *author's purpose*. During the preview, ask: Who wrote this book? What do you think the book will be about? Why? Do you think you will like the book? Why? During reading, ask: Were you right about what the book is about? Ask about specific parts: On page 3, why does the author say it's your job to protect the environment? Finally, ask: Why does the author give so many examples of children protecting the environment?

ASK QUESTIONS Remind children that good readers ask questions about what they are reading to understand, find information, and think about what they have learned. Model: Before: I wonder what this will be about? / I really want to know about . . . . During: I wonder what this

means. I'll read it again to find out. / I like this. How did the author make it so exciting? After: What did I like best? / The author didn't cover everything. I wonder where I can learn more about . . . . Encourage children to use a KWL chart to generate questions about this book. Help children learn to use the chart by filling in the "K" section as a class.

READ THE BOOK

PAGE 4 Why is it important to protect the environment? *(Possible response: We need it to live.)*

PAGE 12 Why does the author include a picture of a contract? *(Possible response: She wants you to believe it is very important to keep a promise about protecting the environment.)*

PAGE 15 Why should your friends be ready to help you? *(Possible response: They care about me, so they care about what I care about.)*

TALK ABOUT THE BOOK

READER RESPONSE
1. She hopes we will help the EPA.
2. Possible responses: How did the club start? Are there dues? How often does it meet?
3. Answers will vary.
4. Answers will vary.

RESPONSE OPTIONS

WRITING Have children write a short letter to the editor about an environmental problem in their community and what should be done about it.

CONTENT CONNECTIONS

SOCIAL STUDIES Have small groups of children make a plan for helping the EPA. Suggest that they get ideas, with an adult's help, at the EPA's "For Kids" page at www.epa.gov.

Time for SOCIAL STUDIES

Name_____

Author's Purpose

Think about why the author wrote *You Can Make A Difference!* Read each question below. Then underline the best answer.

1. Why does the author say that every person needs to think about the environment?
   a. to make us angry
   b. to tell us what she believes
   c. to make us feel ashamed

2. Why does the author describe the EPA?
   a. to explain what the EPA does
   b. to get us to join the EPA
   c. to make us excited

3. Why does the author describe how students helped protect the wetlands?
   a. to compare wetlands to parks
   b. to tell how students can make a difference
   c. to teach us how to plant trees

4. Why does the author list everyday things we can do to make a difference?
   a. to get us to do something
   b. to help us feel good
   c. to fill up the page

5. Why did the author write this book?
   a. to give us a good time
   b. to describe the environment
   c. to get us to make a difference

106

© Pearson Education 2

Vocabulary

Write a word from the box that best fits into each sentence.

Words to Know

adventure   climbed   clubhouse
exploring   greatest   truest   wondered

1. We built a _____ for our bird club to meet in.

2. The person who picked up the most litter did the

   _____

   _____ job.

3. We _____ how many cans we collected.

4. They _____ the ladder to the treehouse.

5. Your _____ friends will help you keep the park clean.

6. Helping on a recyling project can be a big

   _____ .

7. _____ new places can be fun.

107

Taking Care of the Earth

TAKING CARE OF THE EARTH

by Jessica Quilty

◉ **AUTHOR'S PURPOSE**

◉ **ASK QUESTIONS**

LESSON VOCABULARY friendships, interests, landfill, litter, pollution, recycle, respect

SUMMARY This nonfiction book describes what you can do to help protect your environment. It supports the lesson concept of being a good friend and neighbor.

INTRODUCE THE BOOK

BUILD BACKGROUND Have children discuss how they conserve energy and water at home and what they know about recycling.

PREVIEW/TAKE A PICTURE WALK Have children look at the photos, captions, headings, and bullet list in the book before reading. Discuss how the photos and captions help to explain and supplement the text.

TEACH/PREVIEW VOCABULARY Invite children to flip through the book to become familiar with its format. Have children read headings. Call attention to the photo on page 3. Does it suggest a vocabulary word children might already know?

TARGET SKILL AND STRATEGY

◉ **AUTHOR'S PURPOSE** Do not use the term *author's purpose.* Instead, during the preview, ask children: Who wrote this book? What do you think the book will be about? Why? Do you think you will like the book? Why? During reading, ask follow-up questions: Were you right about what the book is about? Also ask questions about specific parts: On page 3, why does the author say it is important to protect the environment? Finally, ask questions that relate to the theme: Why does the author give examples of children protecting the environment?

◉ **ASK QUESTIONS** Remind children that good readers ask questions about what they are reading to understand, find information, and think about what they have learned. Model: Before: I wonder what this will be about?/I really want to know about . . . . During: I wonder what this means. I'll read it again to find out./I like this. How did the author make it so exciting? After: What did I like best? / The author didn't cover everything. I wonder where I can learn more about . . . . Encourage children to use a K-W-L chart to generate questions about this

book. Help children learn to use the chart by filling in one "K" section as a class.

ELL Use reciprocal teaching to model how to ask questions and to have children ask their own questions. Read a section of the text, ask questions, have children answer, then summarize the text. Then have children repeat your role.

READ THE BOOK

PAGE 3 Why does the author talk directly to you, the reader? *(Possible response: She wants to get her readers to take action.)*

PAGE 12 What could you do to not waste water? *(Possible response: Don't run water while brushing your teeth. Take short showers.)*

PAGE 17 Why are friendships a great way to build a recycling club? *(Possible response: It's easier to work with people you know.)*

TALK ABOUT THE BOOK

READER RESPONSE

1. She wants us to help protect the environment.
2. Possible responses: How many cans do you collect each week? What else does the club do?
3. Possible response: Recycle, because it helps the environment; littering hurts it.
4. Possible response: There is a lot of work, so many people are needed.

RESPONSE OPTIONS

WRITING Have children write a list of everyday things they can do to protect the environment.

CONTENT CONNECTIONS

Time for **SOCIAL STUDIES**

SOCIAL STUDIES Have children identify a pollution problem in their community. Have them draw up a plan to help solve the problem, based on the examples in this book.

Author's Purpose

Think about why the author wrote *Taking Care of the Earth*.
Read each question below. Then underline the best answer.

1. Why does the author say that it is important to protect the environment?
   a. to tell us what she believes
   b. to make us happy
   c. to describe the environment

2. Why does the author say that trash is taken to a landfill?
   a. to explain what landfills are used for
   b. to prove that landfills are bad
   c. to tell us how she feels

3. Why does the author tell us to reduce the amount of plastic we use?
   a. to explain what plastic is
   b. to make us angry
   c. to get us to do something

4. Why does the author list things we can do to respect Earth?
   a. to help us feel good
   b. to get us to do something
   c. to give us something to copy

5. Why did the author write this book?
   a. to explain how to recycle
   b. to show us how to protect the air
   c. to get us to protect the environment

© Pearson Education 2

106

Vocabulary

Write the words from the box to complete the paragraph.

> **Words to Know**
>
> **friendships   interests   landfill   litter
> pollution   recycle   respect**

There are many things you can do to show your

_____ for the environment. You can throw

your trash in a garbage can instead of dropping _____

_____ in the street. You can _____

paper, glass, and plastic to keep them from going to a

_____. When you work with people who share your

_____ to help reduce _____,

you may form lasting _____. Then you'll

help both the planet and yourself!

107

Grandpa's Sign
by Kelly Kong
illustrated by April Hartmann

◉ **REALISM AND FANTASY**

◉ **MONITOR AND FIX UP**

LESSON VOCABULARY ideas, important, blame, signmaker, townspeople, afternoon

Grandpa's Sign

SUMMARY Andrew breaks a sign his grandfather made, and then tries to hide the pieces. When his father finds the broken pieces, Andrew confesses and promises to be more careful, and more honest, next time.

INTRODUCE THE BOOK

BUILD BACKGROUND Invite children to talk about their experiences with doing something they know is wrong. Ask: How did you feel? What happened afterwards? What did you learn from your mistakes?

PREVIEW/TAKE A PICTURE WALK As children preview the book, have them notice the illustrations and the feature with the photo on page 12. Ask them to make predictions about what the story will be about, based on these text features.

TEACH/REVIEW VOCABULARY Have children look up the meaning of the word *blame*. Invite them to use the word in a sentence. Continue in a similar fashion with the remaining vocabulary words.

TARGET SKILL AND STRATEGY

◉ **REALISM AND FANTASY** Remind children that a *realistic* story tells about something that could happen. A *fantasy* is a story about something that could not happen. Invite them to look for details as they read that help them decide whether it is a realistic story or a fantasy.

ELL Page through the story and point to details in the illustrations. Invite children to identify objects on pages 3–5. Invite them to explain what happens on pages 6–9. Invite them to read the signs in the picture on pages 10–11.

◉ **MONITOR AND FIX UP** Remind children that a good reader knows reading has to make sense. Tell them to think about these questions as they read: Who is the story about? Where does the story happen? When does it happen? Explain that these questions can also help them determine whether the story is a realistic one or a fantasy.

READ THE BOOK

Use the following questions to support comprehension.

PAGE 4 Why was Andrew excited? *(He wanted to earn money by selling some of his old toys.)*

PAGE 5 What did Andrew's grandfather use to paint his signs on? *(glass)*

PAGE 6 Could what happens on this page really happen in real life? *(yes)*

PAGE 7 How did Andrew feel about hiding the broken sign? *(bad)*

PAGE 9 Why do you think Andrew didn't tell anyone about breaking Grandpa's sign? *(Possible response: He didn't want to get blamed or punished.)*

TALK ABOUT THE BOOK

READER RESPONSE
1. Possible response: Yes, I think the story could really happen, because people do have yard sales.
2. Answers should include Andrew looking at sign; noticing a customer; dropping sign on table; sign sliding off table and smashing.
3. No one would know who was responsible.
4. Answers will vary. Encourage children to empathize with Andrew's plight while acknowledging that being careful and honest is important.

RESPONSE OPTIONS

SPEAKING Invite children to tell the big idea of this story. Challenge them to put their idea into one sentence and support it with details from the story.

CONTENT CONNECTIONS

ART Children may wish to write their own realistic stories about a time when they did something they knew was wrong. Challenge them to "make a book" and to illustrate the pages. Have them tell what happened and how they felt about it.

Name _____

Realism and Fantasy

Read each question below. Then circle your answer.

1. Are there things in the story that could not really happen?

   yes   no

   _____

2. Is there magic in the story?

   yes   no

   _____

3. Could things in the story really happen?

   yes   no

   _____

4. Do the people in the story do and say things like people I know?

   yes   no

   _____

5. Write one sentence that tells if the story *Grandpa's Sign* is a realistic story or fantasy. Tell how you know.

   _____
   -
   _____
   _____
   -
   _____
   _____
   -
   _____
   _____
   -
   _____

© Pearson Education 2

110

Name _____

Vocabulary

Draw a line to match the word parts and make words from the story.

1. idea   a. maker

2. impor   b. tant

3. sign   c. noon

4. towns   d. people

5. after   e. s

6. Write a sentence with the word *blame*.

_____

- -

_____

- -

_____

- -

_____

111

Freda's Signs
by Debbie O'Brien
illustrated by Victor Kennedy

Unit 5 Week 5

🎯 **REALISM AND FANTASY**

🎯 **MONITOR AND FIX UP**

LESSON VOCABULARY idea, important, blame, signmaker, townspeople, afternoo...

Freda's Signs

SUMMARY Freda volunteers to make signs for the town of Midvale, but forgets to bring along a list of what the signs are supposed to say. This fantasy selection tells the story of what happens when we are forgetful and not responsible for our jobs.

INTRODUCE THE BOOK

BUILD BACKGROUND Invite children to tell about times they have forgotten things. Remind children that we all forget things from time to time, but that it is important to learn ways we can help ourselves remember better.

PREVIEW/TAKE A PICTURE WALK As children preview the book, have them notice the illustrations and the feature with the photo on page 16. Ask them to make predictions about what the story will be about, based on these text features.

TEACH/REVIEW VOCABULARY Create a vocabulary word wall by printing each word on a sentence strip card and placing cards backwards in a pocket chart. Choose one word at a time to display, focus on, define and discuss. Tell children one page each word appears on. Invite children to skim the text to locate each word in context.

TARGET SKILL AND STRATEGY

🎯 **REALISM AND FANTASY** Remind children that a realistic story tells about something that could happen. A fantasy is a story about something that could not happen. Invite them to look for details as they read that help them decide whether it is a realistic story or a fantasy.

🎯 **MONITOR AND FIX UP** Offer students the first detail in the book: *The people of Midvale needed new signs.* Then, have students take turns retelling additional story details in sequence until they have completed the story. Record their offerings on chart paper. If they are confused about any part of the story, have them reread the text to find the information they need.

READ THE BOOK

Use the following questions to support comprehension.

PAGE 3 What was Freda's biggest problem? *(She was very forgetful.)*

PAGES 6–7 Look at the picture on these pages. What do you notice about the picture that shows you this story is a fantasy? *(bugs seem to be arguing; bugs cannot really argue.)*

PAGE 13 What did Freda do when Mayor Martin asked her if she used the list he gave her for the signs? *(She told him the truth that she had forgotten the list.)*

TALK ABOUT THE BOOK

READER RESPONSE
1. Could Happen: mayor hiring signmaker who gets the signs wrong; Could Not Happen: bugs and dogs reading and obeying signs.
2. Freda made mistakes on three signs; She wrote *bug* for *bus, on* for *off,* and *barking* for *parking.*
3. Mayor Martin, the park ranger
4. Possible response: She could have gone back for the list.

RESPONSE OPTIONS

WRITING Have children take a walk to see signs in and around school. Invite children to make temporary replacement signs that read the opposite of the originals. Ask: How would these mistakes affect the school day?

ELL Invite children to read signs in the classroom. Have them compare terminology in English and another language.

CONTENT CONNECTIONS

SOCIAL STUDIES Ask children to imagine what would happen if various community and school helpers did not do their jobs or forgot what they needed to do.

Time for **SOCIAL STUDIES**

Name _____

Realism and Fantasy

Read the list of the things that happened in the story. Think about if they could or could not have happened. Then, circle the answer.

What Happened

1. The people of Midvale needed new signs.

   could   could not have happened

2. Freda made mistakes on the signs.

   could   could not have happened

3. The ants lined up at the sign.

   could   could not have happened

4. The dogs talked about the sign.

   could   could not have happened

5. Think about the things that happened in the story. Write a sentence that tells if the story is a realistic story or a fantasy and why. What are the fantasy parts of this story?

_____

- -

_____

_____

- -

_____

_____

- -

_____

110

Name _____

Vocabulary

Read the words in the first column below.
Then read the words in the second column.
Draw lines to connect the words and make compound words found
in the story.

1. sign   a. people

2. towns   b. noon

3. after   c. maker

4. Write a sentence with the word *blame*.

_____

_____
_____

_____

5. Write a sentence with the words *idea* and *important*.

_____

_____
_____

_____

111

Marty's Job
by Evan Allen

illustrated by Luciana Navarro Alves

- **REALISM AND FANTASY**
- **MONITOR AND FIX UP**

LESSON VOCABULARY apology, citizen, judgment, neglecting, responsibility, volunteering

---

SUMMARY Marty loves his volunteer job at the hospital, but his mother notices that he starts to neglect his responsibilities at home. This realistic story includes some fantasy elements and tells what happens when we take on too many responsibilities.

INTRODUCE THE BOOK

BUILD BACKGROUND Invite children to tell about times they have tried to do too many things. Maybe they have had too many activities or too many choices. Ask them to say how these situations made them feel.

PREVIEW/TAKE A PICTURE WALK Have children preview the book by first looking at the illustrations and saying what they believe the book is about. Based on the illustrations, ask them whether they think this story is realistic or if it is a fantasy. Invite them to explain their reasoning.

TEACH/PREVIEW VOCABULARY Have children look up the definitions for each of the vocabulary words. Have them make up a sentence for each word.

TARGET SKILL AND STRATEGY

REALISM AND FANTASY Remind children that a *realistic* story tells about something that could happen. A *fantasy* is a story about something that could not happen. Explain that sometimes a realistic story can have elements of a fantasy, or vice versa. Invite children to look for realistic and fantasy elements as they read.

MONITOR AND FIX UP Remind children that good readers learn to recognize when they don't understand what they are reading. They also know some fix-up strategies to use when reading stops making sense. Invite the children to record self-generated questions as they read. Then have them go back and find the answers to their questions in the story. Explain that asking and answering questions may also help them identify realistic and fantasy elements in the story.

READ THE BOOK

Use the following questions to support comprehension.

PAGE 5 What did Marty realize about his first idea for a job? *(It was a fantasy: no one would hire an eight-year-old to be a firefighter.)*

PAGE 9 What does Marty promise his mother? *(He won't forget to do his chores.)*

PAGE 13 What happened at the end of his first day of volunteering? *(Marty was so tired that he stumbled past his pajamas on the floor and tumbled into bed.)*

TALK ABOUT THE BOOK

READER RESPONSE
1. Answers will vary but should show understanding of realism and fantasy.
2. He thought she meant he could be a doctor, but he knew he was too young.
3. Marty began to trust that his mother might be right.
4. Answers will vary.

RESPONSE OPTIONS

WRITING Have children write their own real-life stories of having too many responsibilities or of their attempts to balance activities. They may wish to illustrate their stories.

ELL Invite students to interview each other about their responsibilities at home or at school. Encourage them to talk about how they manage their time.

CONTENT CONNECTIONS

Time for **SOCIAL STUDIES**

SOCIAL STUDIES Ask children to talk about what happens when people take on too many responsibilities. Ask them if they have ever been in a crowded setting where the workers seem to have too much to do and the children must wait a long time to be helped.

Realism and Fantasy

Read the list of the things that happened in the story. Think about if they could or could not have happened. Then, circle the answer.

What Happened

1. Marty Apple wanted a job.

   could   could not have happened

   _____

2. Marty got a job as a firefighter.

   could   could not have happened

   _____

3. Marty got a job as a police officer.

   could   could not have happened

   _____

4. Marty promises not to forget about his chores at home.

   could   could not have happened

   _____

5. Answer the question below.
   What are the fantasy parts of this story?

   _____
   -
   _____
   _____
   -
   _____
   _____
   -
   _____

© Pearson Education 2

110

Name _____

Vocabulary

Words can be broken into two parts. Find the word ending that was added to the base word to make the vocabulary word. Write the answer on the line.

_____
- - - - - - - - - - - - - - - - - - - -
1. judge + _____ = judgment

_____
- - - - - - - - - - - - - - - - -
2. neglect + _____ = neglecting

_____
- - - - - - - - - - - - - - - - - -
3. responsible + _____ = responsibility

_____
- - - - - - - - - - - - - - - - - -
4. apology + _____ = apologize

5. Write a sentence with the words *citizen* and *volunteering*.

_____
- -
_____
_____
- -
_____

111

Answer Key for Below-Level Reader Practice

Community Helpers   LR1

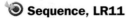 **Main Idea, LR2**

Police officers help the people in a community live together in peace.

Vocabulary, LR3

1. station **2.** quickly **3.** buildings **4.** masks **5.** tightly **6.** roar **7.** burning

Horse Rescue!   LR10

Sequence, LR11

4, 2, 7, 3, 5, 1, 6

Vocabulary, LR12

lightning, flashes, poured, pounded, storm, thunder, rolling. Look at the sky! Horses fly!

Sally and the Wild Puppy   LR19

Theme and Plot, LR20

1. end **3.** beginning **4.** middle

Vocabulary, LR21

1. treat **2.** chewing **3.** wagged **4.** practice **5.** chased **6.** grabbed **7.** dripping

What an Adventure!   LR28

Author's Purpose, LR29

1. a **2.** c **3.** c **4.** b **5.** a

Vocabulary, LR30

1. d **2.** c **3.** a **4.** g **5.** f **6.** b **7.** e

Grandpa's Sign   LR37

Realism and Fantasy, LR38

1. no **2.** no **3.** yes **4.** yes **5.** Possible response given. This is a realistic story because it could really happen.

Vocabulary, LR39

1. e **2.** b **3.** a **4.** d **5.** c **6.** Possible response given. Andrew blamed himself for not telling about the sign.

Answer Key for On-Level Reader Practice

Who Can Help? LR4

Main Idea, LR5
911 operators help people in danger.

Vocabulary, LR6
buildings, quickly, roar, masks, burning, tightly, station

Animal Shelters LR13

Sequence, LR14
Farm Animal Shelter **1.** pigs **2.** cows **3.** sheep **4.** chickens; Wild Animal Shelter **1.** bees **2.** birds; Shelter for Pets **1.** pigs **2.** hamsters **3.** fish **4.** lizard

Vocabulary, LR15
flashes, Thunder, pours, storm, rolling

Hubert and Frankie LR22

Theme and Plot, LR23
Circled: 1, 2, 5. **1.** middle **2.** beginning **5.** end

Vocabulary, LR24
1. wagged **2.** grabbed **3.** chewing **4.** dripping **5.** practice **6.** treat **7.** chased

You Can Make a Difference! LR31

Author's Purpose, LR32
1. b **2.** a **3.** b **4.** a **5.** c

Vocabulary, LR33
1. clubhouse **2.** greatest **3.** wondered **4.** climbed **5.** truest **6.** adventure **7.** Exploring

Freda's Signs LR40

Realism/Fantasy, LR41
1. could **2.** could **3.** could not have happened **4.** could not have happened. Possible response given. **5.** This is a fantasy because dogs do not talk.

Vocabulary, LR42
1. c **2.** a **3.** b. Possible response: **4.** The townspeople did not blame Freda for her mistake. **5.** People listen when you have an important idea.

Answer Key for Advanced-Level Reader Practice

Goods and Services   LR7

Main Idea, LR8
A service is when a person with special training gives you help.

Vocabulary, LR9
1. Goods 2. producers 3. consumers 4. service 5. community

A Day in the Life of a Vet   LR16

Sequence, LR17
1. Dr. Hopkins 2. Dr. Martinez 3. Dr. Billings, Dr. Mor;
4. Dr. Jung. Responses will vary.

Vocabulary, LR18
growth, yak, llama, survive, protect, veterinarian; a zoo vet

Training Peanut   LR25

Theme and Plot, LR26
1. end 3. beginning 4. middle

Vocabulary, LR27
1. c 2. f 3. a 4. b 5. e 6. d

Taking Care of the Earth   LR34

Author's Purpose, LR35
1. a 2. a 3. c 4. b 5. c

Vocabulary, LR36
respect, litter, recycle, landfill, interests, pollution, friendships

Marty's Job   LR43

Realism and Fantasy, LR44
1. could 2. could not have happened 3. could not have happened
4. could 5. Possible response: The fantasy parts of the story are when Marty imagines himself as a firefighter or a police officer.

Vocabulary, LR45
1. ment 2. ing 3. ty 4. ize 5. Possible response: Every volunteering citizen will get an award.

Differentiated Instruction

Table of Contents

Advanced Selections for Group Time

Daily Group Time Lessons

Continued on back of tab

Daily Group Time Lessons, continued

Let's Learn Amazing Words

TEACH/MODEL

Amazing Words to build oral vocabulary

Use the Oral Vocabulary Routine along with the definitions, examples, letter-sounds, and word parts that are provided on the following pages to introduce each Amazing Word.

ABOUT ORAL VOCABULARY A child's oral vocabulary development is a predictor of future reading success. Oral vocabulary development now boosts children's comprehension as they become fluent readers. Oral vocabulary is informally assessed.

Oral Vocabulary

ROUTINE

1 Introduce the Word Relate the word to the song or story in which it appears. Supply a child-friendly definition. Have children say the word. Example:

- In the song Anna is *responsible* for hooking up the hose. If someone is *responsible*, that person must do a job or take charge of something that others are counting on. Say the word *responsible* with me, *responsible*.

2 Demonstrate Provide familiar examples to demonstrate meaning. When possible, use gestures to help convey meaning. Examples:

- I am *responsible* for teaching this class. Jason is *responsible* for feeding his dog every day. Maria is *responsible* for completing her homework each night.

3 Apply Have children demonstrate understanding with a simple activity. Suggestions for step 3 activities appear on the next page. Example:

- Tell me something that you are *responsible* for. What would happen if you did not do a job for which you were *responsible*?

4 Display the Word/Letter-Sounds Write the word on a card and display it on a classroom Amazing Words board. Have children identify some familiar letter-sounds or word parts. Example:

- This word is *responsible.* Run your hand under the word parts *re-spon-si-ble* as you read it.

ACTIVITIES

To allow children to demonstrate understanding of the Amazing Words, use activities such as these in step 3 of the Routine.

ANSWER QUESTIONS Would you prefer to have a *festive* day or an *ordinary* day? Why?

CREATE EXAMPLES What is something a good *citizen* might do?

MAKE CHOICES If any of the things I name can *hatch*, say *hatch*; if not, say nothing: a train, a chicken, a jar of jam, a snake, a tadpole, a horse.

PANTOMIME Show me how an eagle *soars*, a rocket, an airplane.

PERSONAL CONTEXT Some people are *fond* of fishing. Tell about something you are *fond* of. Use the word *fond* when you tell about it.

SYNONYMS AND ANTONYMS Name a word that means the opposite of *genuine*; name a word that means about the same as *genuine*.

Monitor Progress | Check Oral Vocabulary

To monitor understanding of concepts and vocabulary that have been explicitly taught each week:

- Display the week's paired selection in the Student Edition. (In some cases you may prefer to use the opening pages of the first selection.)
- Remind the child of the concept that the class has been talking about that week.
- Ask the child to tell you about the paired selection illustrations using some of the week's Amazing Words.

If... a child has difficulty using the Amazing Words,
then... ask questions about the illustration using the Amazing Words. Note which questions the child can respond to. Reteach unknown words using the Oral Vocabulary Routine.

SUCCESS PREDICTOR

to build oral vocabulary

USE WITH

DAY 1

1 **COMMUNITY** The people who live around you are your *community*.

2 **Examples:** The *community* pitched in to clean up the empty lot. Our *community* has a fitness center.

4 **Word Parts:** Run your hand under the word parts in *com-mu-ni-ty* as you read it.

1 **RESPONSIBLE** If someone is *responsible*, that person must do a job or take charge of something that others are counting on.

2 **Examples:** I am *responsible* for teaching this class. Jason is *responsible* for feeding his dog every day.

4 **Word Parts:** Run your hand under the word parts in *re-spon-si-ble* as you read it.

1 **TEAMWORK** It is *teamwork* when a group of people put a lot of effort into doing something together.

2 **Examples:** The band made money for uniforms by using *teamwork* to wash cars. We need *teamwork* to clean the garage in one day.

4 **Word Parts:** Point out the two smaller words in the compound word *team-work*.

DAY 2

1 **OPERATION** When a doctor or vet opens the body to fix something, it is called an *operation*.

2 **Examples:** My dog had an *operation* to fix her ear. I had an *operation* to repair a broken leg.

4 **Word Parts:** Point out that *operate* is the base word in *operation*.

DAY 3

1 **INSTRUMENT** Any tool used by doctors and vets to help them examine a patient, to help them fix an injury, or to repair a part of the body is called an *instrument*.

2 **Examples:** The doctor used an *instrument* called a stethoscope to listen to my heart. The vet used an *instrument* to see inside my dog's ears.

4 **Word Parts:** Clap the syllables in *in-stru-ment* as you read it.

DAY 4

1 **CARETAKER** A *caretaker* is a person, like a custodian or janitor, who makes sure that everything on the inside and outside of a building is clean and in working order.

2 **Examples:** The *caretaker* will fix the broken lock on the door. Ask the *caretaker* if he will clean the front window.

4 **Word Parts:** Point out the two smaller words in the compound word *care-taker*.

1 **LUG** If you *lug* something, you carry or pull something that is very heavy or clumsy.

2 **Examples:** Please help me *lug* the suitcases up the stairs. He will *lug* the garbage cans out to the street.

4 **Letter-Sounds:** Children can decode the word *lug*.

1 **SUPPLIES** *Supplies* are the things you need to do a particular job or activity, such as cleaning *supplies*.

2 **Examples:** All of the washing *supplies* are on a shelf in the laundry room. The store sells many kinds of art *supplies*, including paint and chalk.

4 **Word Parts:** Point out that *supply* is the base word for *supplies*.

Definitions, examples, and **letter-sounds** to use with Oral Vocabulary Routine on p. DI•1

Amazing Words **to build oral vocabulary**

USE WITH

DAY 1

1 **CONCERN** When you have a reason to worry about something, you have *concern* about it. Or something can *concern* you by giving you an uneasy feeling.

2 **Examples:** Mom has *concern* about us crossing the street at the busy intersection.

4 **Letter-Sounds** Point out the hard and soft sounds of *c*.

1 **GROWTH** *Growth* is the process of something getting bigger or *developing*.

2 **Examples:** My brother had a *growth* spurt of two inches last year. I'd like to see more *growth* in our vegetable plants.

4 **Letter-Sounds** Children can decode *growth*.

1 **PROTECTION** If you keep something from being harmed or damaged, you give it *protection*.

2 **Examples:** The basement gives us *protection* from tornadoes. The citizens get *protection* from the police.

4 **Word Parts:** Point out the base word *protect*.

DAY 2

1 **FRAGILE** If something can break or be damaged easily, it is *fragile*.

2 **Examples:** The delicate wings of a butterfly are *fragile*. If you knock over the *fragile* vase, it will break. A spider web looks *fragile*, but it is quite strong.

4 **Letter-Sounds:** Point out the g/j/ sound.

DAY 3

1 **PELLETS** *Pellets* are small balls of material pressed together, very often a kind of animal feed.

2 **Examples:** Tony poured the *pellets* into the rabbit's bowl. My dog likes dog food made from beef-flavored *pellets*.

4 **Letter-Sounds:** Children can decode *pellets*.

DAY 4

1 **LITTER** *Litter* is scraps or pieces of trash left around.

2 **Examples:** There was *litter* in the stands after the football game. We picked up *litter* around our school yard.

4 **Letter-Sounds:** Children can decode *litter*.

1 **POLLUTE** When someone damages the air, soil, or water by making it dirty with harmful substances, we say they *pollute* it.

2 **Examples:** Oil spills from ships can *pollute* the water. Smoke from the factory *polluted* the air around us.

4 **Word Parts:** Run your hand under the two word parts in *pol-lute* as you read the word.

1 **RELEASE** If you *release* something, you set it free or let it go.

2 **Examples:** When the young raccoon's foot is healed, the vet will *release* it into the wild. We will *release* the baby birds as soon as they can fly.

4 **Word Parts:** Run your hand under the two word parts in *re-lease* as you read the word.

Amazing Words

to build oral vocabulary

Definitions, examples, and letter-sounds to use with Oral Vocabulary Routine on p. DI·1

USE WITH

DAY 1

1 BEHAVIOR The way people and animals act or behave is called their *behavior*.

2 Examples: The children had good *behavior* during the assembly. The dog's *behavior* improved after we trained her. We enjoy watching the birds' *behavior* at the feeders.

4 Word Parts Point out the base word *behave* in *behavior*.

1 COOPERATE When people or animals work together to accomplish a goal, they *cooperate* with each other.

2 Examples: The children will *cooperate* to paint a mural on the wall. The dog will *cooperate* with its owner to learn new tricks. The workers *cooperated* to build the house.

4 Word Parts: Clap the syllables in *co-op-er-ate* as you read the word.

1 OBEDIENT When a person or an animal is willing to do what they are told to do, he or she is *obedient*.

2 Examples: The *obedient* children did what their parents asked them to do. The dog was *obedient* when he stopped jumping on people.

4 Word Parts: Run your hand under the word parts in *o-be-di-ent* as you read the word.

DAY 2

1 COMPANION A *companion* is a person or animal who spends time with you, as a friend.

2 Examples: My grandfather lives alone but has a little dog for a *companion*. The toddler has *companions* who like to play together. The kitten is a *companion* for the older dog.

4 Letter-Sounds: Clap out the syllables in *com-pan-ion*.

1 CONSIDER When you *consider* something, you think about it very carefully before making a decision.

2 Examples: Mom will *consider* allowing me to get a pet cat. I had to *consider* whether I wanted to take piano lessons or not.

4 Word Parts: Run your hand under the three word parts in *con-sid-er* as you read the word.

DAY 3

1 REPRIMAND If you get a *reprimand*, that means you get a talking to, a warning, or a scolding for doing something wrong.

2 Examples: He got a *reprimand* for being late for school so many times. Mom gave me a *reprimand* for walking across the carpet with muddy shoes.

4 Word Parts: Run your hand under the three word parts in *rep-ri-mand* as you read the word.

DAY 4

1 CONFIDENT If animals or people are sure about things or are certain they have the ability to do something, then they will be *confident* in themselves.

2 Examples: Nate felt *confident* he would do well on the math test. I patted my dog's head so he would feel *confident* he was behaving properly.

4 Letter-Sounds: Children should be able to decode *confident*.

1 PROPERLY When something is done in a correct way, it is done *properly*.

2 Examples: I learned to form all my cursive letters *properly*. Mom said we needed to behave *properly* when we visited her friend. A *properly* trained dog will not tug on its leash.

4 Word Parts: Point out the base word *proper* and the *-ly* suffix in *properly*.

Oral Vocabulary

SUCCESS PREDICTOR

Definitions, examples, and letter-sounds to use with Oral Vocabulary Routine on p. DI·1

Amazing Words to build oral vocabulary

USE WITH

DAY 1

1 **APPRECIATE** When you *appreciate* something, you feel grateful or thankful for something. You can also *appreciate*, or like, the things in people that make them special.

2 **Examples:** We *appreciate* how hard our mother works. I *appreciate* having a friend who is always nice to me. We *appreciate* the gifts we get for our birthdays.

4 **Word Parts:** Run your hand under the four word parts in *ap-pre-ci-ate*.

1 **COMMUNICATE** If you *communicate* with a person, you talk to each other or keep in touch in other ways such as writing or sign language.

2 **Examples:** My friends and I *communicate* with each other every day during lunch. I *communicate* with my grandmother by e-mail. Jane *communicates* with her hearing-impaired friend by using sign language.

4 **Word Parts:** Run your hand under the four word parts in *com-mu-ni-cate* as you read the word.

1 **RESPECT** *Respect* is a feeling of high regard you have for another person. If you *respect* someone, you admire that person and think a lot of him or her.

2 **Examples:** Our principal has the *respect* of all the students in the school. Children should *respect* their parents. I *respect* the mayor for making our city a better place to live.

4 **Word Parts:** Run your hand under the two word parts in *re-spect* as you read the word.

DAY 2

1 **DEMAND** If you order someone to do something, you *demand* that he or she does it.

2 **Examples:** My friend asked me nicely to help him fix his bike, but he did not *demand* that I do it. Mom *demanded* that I clean my room on Saturday. The police *demanded* that we move our car to a different parking space.

4 **Word Parts:** Run your hand under the two word parts in *de-mand* as you read the word.

1 **FIRMLY** When you say something *firmly*, you say it in a determined way that shows you won't change.

2 **Examples:** Mom *firmly* told me I could not go outside until I cleaned my room. I speak nicely, but *firmly,* when I give commands to my dog.

4 **Word Parts:** Identify the base word *firm* and suffix *-ly*.

DAY 3

1 **ADVANTAGE** If you have an *advantage*, you are in a better or more favorable position than someone else.

2 **Examples:** Jason ran faster than the others, so he had an *advantage* in the race. Bob had an *advantage* over Ray in getting the job because he had two years of experience.

4 **Word Parts:** Run your hand under the three word parts in *ad-van-tage* as you read the word.

DAY 4

1 **DEFIANT** If someone is openly disobedient or challenging to someone else, that person is *defiant*.

2 **Examples:** My *defiant* dog would not get off the chair. My baby brother was *defiant* and wouldn't go to bed.

4 **Word Parts**: Run your hand under the three word parts in *de-fi-ant* as you read the word.

1 **FEROCIOUS** When something is powerful, violent, or fierce, it is *ferocious*.

2 **Examples:** The *ferocious* lion looked for food to eat. The bear had a *ferocious* growl.

4 **Word Parts:** Clap the syllables in *fe-ro-cious*.

Amazing Words to build oral vocabulary

Definitions, **examples**, and **letter-sounds** to use with Oral Vocabulary Routine on p. DI•1

USE WITH

DAY 1

① APOLOGIZE When you say you are sorry for doing or saying something that has upset someone, you *apologize* to that person.

② Examples: I will *apologize* to my friend for speaking in a mean tone. I will *apologize* to my mom for not putting my toys away.

④ Word Parts: Run your hand under the four word parts *a-pol-o-gize* as you read the word.

① CITIZEN You are a *citizen* of a country if you were born there or if you are legally accepted by a country to be a *citizen*.

② Examples: My friend goes to school in the United States but is a *citizen* of Spain. You must be a *citizen* in order to vote.

④ Letter-Sounds Children can decode *citizen*.

① JUDGMENT When people make decisions about what is sensible, they use their *judgment*.

② Examples: Use good *judgment* when you decide what color to paint the room. When you tell the truth, you use good *judgment*.

④ Letter-Sounds Children can decode *judgment*.

DAY 2

① HOARD If you *hoard* something, you collect it and store it away. Often this can be food or money, and sometimes it is done secretly.

② Examples: My brother likes to *hoard* candy in his room. My dog hoards bones in his doghouse. The king liked to *hoard* gold coins.

④ Letter-Sounds: Point out that *hoard* rhymes with board and has the same vowel spelling.

DAY 3

① SCOLD If you *scold* people, you tell them off or discipline them.

② Examples: I know Mom will *scold* me for eating cookies before a meal. My teacher *scolded* me for not doing my homework.

④ Letter-Sounds: Children can decode *scold*.

DAY 4

① INTERRUPT When you *interrupt*, you stop someone who is talking or you stop something that is happening.

② Examples: Do not *interrupt* other people while they are talking. She *interrupted* the speaker with a question.

④ Word Parts: Run your hand under the three word parts *in-ter-rupt* as you read the word.

① PROTEST If you *protest*, you tell or show how you disagree about something you think is not right.

② Examples: He tried to *protest* when his parents grounded him. The neighbors *protested* the building of a nearby factory.

④ Word Parts: Run your hand under the two word parts in *pro-test* as you read the word.

① TROUBLEMAKER A *troublemaker* often intentionally causes difficulties or problems.

② Examples: The *troublemaker* threw the ball over the fence. The *troublemaker* cut in line in front of me.

④ Word Parts: Point out the two words that make up the compound word *trouble-maker*.

Grade 2
Oral Vocabulary Words

UNIT 1 · UNIT 2 · UNIT 3 · UNIT 4 · UNIT 5 · UNIT 6

Exploration	Working Together	Creative Ideas	Our Changing World	Responsibility	Traditions

DEVELOP LANGUAGE

Exploration	Working Together	Creative Ideas	Our Changing World	Responsibility	Traditions
brittle	avalanche	construct	concentration	caretaker	athlete
creature	blustery	contraption	frown	community	challenge
dart	courageous	daydream	homeland	instrument	champion
decision	fast-paced	foolproof	patient	lug	dainty
investigate	hazard	project	preserve	operation	disguise
rural	instinct	scrap	represent	responsible	effort
underground	rescue	sidekick	tough	supplies	professional
urban	skittish	unique	valuable	teamwork	shortstop
ascend	actuate	correspond	adapt	concern	allegiance
descend	aloft	cove	ancient	fragile	frayed
enormous	compete	deaf	annual	growth	history
journey	contribute	footprint	bury	litter	independence
launch	deserve	imitate	massive	pellets	indivisible
meteorite	mope	postage	nutrients	pollute	patriotic
orbit	recreation	sign language	sprout	protection	symbol
universe	tinker	transport	undisturbed	release	unfurl
detective	coax	boast	appearance	behavior	angle
fascinating	conflict	consume	canopy	companion	brilliant
galaxy	inhabit	contentment	forage	confident	celebration
identify	ramp	cure	forepaw	consider	create
slimy	resolve	gloat	pursue	cooperate	custom
tranquil	serape	incident	restless	obedient	inspect
underneath	startle	prey	stage	properly	snapshot
wildlife	vacation	shrewd	transform	reprimand	tradition
		snicker			
arid	depend	abundant	accent	advantage	buckaroo
discovery	familiar	assist	adjust	appreciate	climate
dunes	insist	beam	foreign	communicate	drover
forbidding	miserable	dismay	forlorn	defiant	lariat
haven	partnership	efficient	landmark	demand	legend
landform	solution	forever	quiver	ferocious	livestock
ledge	struggle	generous	tease	firmly	occupation
precipitation	survival	situation	unexpected	respect	rawhide
delicate	banquet	accomplish	breeze	apologize	ceremony
exhibit	decorate	excel	condition	citizen	compliment
genius	dine	opportunity	funnel	hoard	culture
inquire	flare	original	predict	interrupt	evergreen
resist	glimmer	process	sparkle	judgment	festival
satisfaction	holiday	research	swirl	protest	fidget
stun	participate	scientist	terrifying	scold	multicolored
sturdy	whispery	unusual	whip	troublemaker	sash

REMEMBER that oral vocabulary is informally assessed.

Teamwork Works

"Class," said Mrs. Landers, "here is our job for Community Day. We must pack twenty boxes of food for families. We must also make twenty lunches for the drivers who will deliver the food."

Mrs. Landers divided the class into teams. Five children would make lunches. Twenty children would pack boxes.

The lunch team set up an assembly line. Two made turkey sandwiches. One packed carrot sticks. Another packed cookies. The fifth member washed and dried fresh apples.

When the food was ready, each child on the team took turns filling the lunch bags. Each bag got a sandwich, a bag of carrots, two cookies, and an apple. The children worked as a team and finished their work quickly.

The box team was having trouble. Some boxes had lots of canned fruit but no canned vegetables. Everyone was rushing around, but not one box was ready to go.

"Time out, class!" Mrs. Landers said. "We need a plan, or we will never get done! We must work as a team."

"I think I have a plan," Jamie said. "First, we empty the boxes and sort the foods into groups, such as canned fruits and canned vegetables. Next, we assign one box to each person on the team. Then, we pack one of each kind of food so each box will have a variety."

The class followed the plan, and the work got done. "Hurray for teamwork!" shouted the class.

ADVANCED SELECTION 21   **VOCABULARY:** community, teamwork

A Rescue Zoo

There is a zoo in Austin, Texas. Like many zoos, it has tigers, monkeys, bears, and other animals. There is a train ride and a store that sells T-shirts and toy animals. However, this zoo is different from most other zoos.

Most zoos have baby animals that are born at the zoo, but the Austin Zoo does not. All the animals at the Austin Zoo were rescued.

The Austin Zoo started as a family ranch. The family took in a few unwanted animals, but there were more animals that needed homes. So the zoo grew bigger to accommodate them.

Some people buy a wild animal as baby, but they soon learn that it does not make a good pet. An animal's normal growth can make it too difficult and dangerous to take care of later on. Other animals need protection because they are not getting proper care. The zoo provides a safe place for these animals.

The community gives money and supplies to the zoo. This helps the zoo build more homes for the many animals that need care. The Austin Zoo is doing its best to help.

ADVANCED SELECTION 22   VOCABULARY: growth, protection

Puppy Kindergarten

New puppies are cute. They jump up. They chew things. Many new owners do not mind because the puppies are small. However, bad puppy behavior can turn into bad dog behavior. That can be a big problem for both the owner and the dog.

It's better to start training a dog when it is still a puppy. Puppy kindergarten is a good start. It is a class for owners and their puppies. Puppies learn to sit and stay. They also learn to get along with other puppies and owners. Puppy owners learn a lot too. They learn how to train their dog.

Puppies can start class as young as seven or eight weeks old. Many puppies start later than that, but it is a good idea to train a puppy while it is still very young. That way, the puppy knows the right way to do things from the beginning, and puppies don't get into the wrong habits.

Owners often bring dog treats to class to reward the puppy for being obedient. Owners are also expected to clean up after their puppies and keep them healthy. Working together brings dogs and their owners closer.

ADVANCED SELECTION 23   VOCABULARY: behavior, obedient

The Bike-a-thon

"Sara, there's a phone call for you! It's Mrs. Jackson from the food bank. She's calling about the bike-a-thon," said Sara's mother as she handed the phone to Sara.

"Hello, Sara," said Mrs. Jackson. "I just wanted to tell you how much we appreciate what you are doing to help the food bank."

Sara had signed up to ride her bike four miles to help raise money for the food bank in her community. Friends and family were giving five dollars for every mile she rode. That money would help buy food for the food bank.

Sara wished that her best friend, Kim, was riding with her, but Kim was participating in a bike race today.

Sara ran to the garage to get her bike and saw that the back tire was flat! She tried to fix it with the air pump, but it didn't work.

"Mom!" she yelled. "What's wrong with this tire?"

"Oh, Sara," said Mom. "It must be the inner tube, and the bike shop's not open until Monday."

"But the bike-a-thon is today!" Sara cried.

Just then, Kim stopped by to wish Sara luck, and Sara told her friend about the tire.

"Here," Kim said. "You can borrow my bike. The race is not as important as the bike-a-thon."

As Sara crossed the finish line, Kim was waiting to congratulate her. "You did great!" said Kim.

"Thanks for being a good friend," said Sara.

ADVANCED SELECTION 24   VOCABULARY: appreciate

Justice Ruth Bader Ginsburg

Being on a jury is part of being a citizen. The people on a jury sit in a special area of a court room. They listen to people talk about something that happened and decide if a person is innocent or guilty of committing a crime. They pass judgment.

The person in charge of the court room is a judge. The judge makes sure everyone in the court room obeys the rules. Ruth Bader Ginsburg is a judge, but she is a very special kind of judge. She is a Supreme Court judge. The Supreme Court is the top court in the United States.

Justice Ginsburg did not start out as a judge. First she was a law student at the top of her class. However, when she finished school, she did not get the best jobs. At that time, lawyers and judges were all men. These men did not want to hire women.

Ruth Bader Ginsburg did not let this stop her. She worked hard to make sure that women had the same rights as men. Six of her cases were presented before the Supreme Court. These were very important cases, and she won five of them. These wins helped women's rights.

Ruth Bader Ginsburg was appointed to the U.S. Supreme Court by President Clinton in 1993 and continues to work for justice.

ADVANCED SELECTION 25 **VOCABULARY:** citizen, judgment

Group Time

Strategic Intervention

ROUTINE

1 Word Work

SUFFIXES *-ly, -ful, -er, -or* Reteach p. 154n. Additional words to blend:

| reader | actor | joyful | harshly |

Then have children sort the following words with suffixes *-ly, -ful, -er,* and *-or* and circle the letters that stand for the suffix.

| hopeful | firmly | sailor | singer | tenderly |
| quietly | helper | colorful | conductor | smoothly |

SPELLING Reteach p. 154p. Model spelling *visitor* and *quickly*. You may wish to give children fewer words to learn.

2 Read Decodable Reader 21

BEFORE READING Review the words with suffixes *-ly, -ful, -er,* and *-or* on p. 154q and have children blend these story words: *boastful, bravely, peaceful, storyteller, finished, hobbies, gardener, paintings.* Be sure children understand meanings of words such as *boastful.*

DURING READING Use p. 154q.

Monitor Progress	Word and Story Reading
If... children have difficulty with any of these words,	**then...** reteach them by modeling. Have children practice the words, with feedback from you, until they can read them independently.
If... children have difficulty reading the story individually,	**then...** read a page aloud as children follow along. Then have the group reread the page. Continue reading in this way before children read individually.

3 Reread for Fluency

Use the Oral Rereading Routine, p. 154q, and text at each child's independent reading level.

Decodable Reader 21

Hobbies
Written by Dennis Michaels
Illustrated by Tom Hurst

MORE READING FOR
Group Time

Use this Leveled Reader or other text at children's instructional level.

Below-Level

Reviews
• Lesson vocabulary *building, burning, masks, quickly, roar, station, tightly*
• Main idea/Supporting details

Check this database for additional titles.

Leveled Reader
Database
ONLINE
PearsonSuccessNet.com

Advanced

1 Word Work

⏺ **SUFFIXES** Practice with words ending in *-ly, -ful, -er,* and *-or.* If children know the words on first read, they may need no further practice. Practice items:

fully	**operator**	**joker**	**writer**	**joyful**
fearful	**happily**	**creator**	**actively**	**powerful**
actor	**dancer**	**computer**	**timidly**	**photographer**

Have children write the words on cards and sort by suffixes. Then have individuals choose several words to use in a sentence.

2 Read Advanced Selection 21

BEFORE READING Have children identify these oral vocabulary words: *community, teamwork.*

DURING READING Children may read silently. Provide guidance as needed.

AFTER READING Have children recall the two most important ideas in the selection. (Dividing tasks among groups and working together as a team helps get a job done quickly.) Ask:

- What is an assembly line? How does it work?
- What have you worked on as part of a team? Tell about it.

On the back of the selection page have children write some instructions for a sport that involves teamwork.

3 Extend Concepts Through Inquiry

IDENTIFY QUESTIONS Have children develop a project based on the power of teamwork. During the week, they should learn more about teamwork from reading, studying pictures, and talking with adults or older children. On Day 5 they will share what they learned. Guide children in brainstorming possible choices.

- Think about a project that would be best accomplished through teamwork. How would the project be different if only one person worked on it?

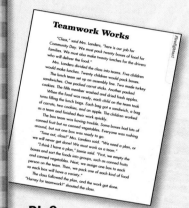

DI•9

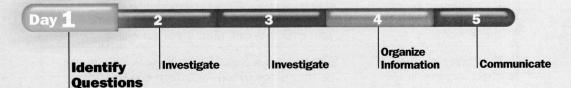

Day 1	2	3	4	5
Identify Questions	**Investigate**	**Investigate**	**Organize Information**	**Communicate**

MORE READING FOR
Group Time

Use this Leveled Reader or other text at children's instructional level.

Advanced

Reviews
- Concept vocabulary
- Main idea/Supporting details

Firefighter!
Group Time

DAY **2**

AudioText

ROUTINE

1 Word Work

SUFFIXES -ly, -ful, -er, -or Reteach p. 156c–156d. Additional words to blend:

gardener	editor	helpful	loudly
weekly	softly	storyteller	cheerful

LESSON VOCABULARY Reteach p. 156f. Have individuals practice reading the words from tested vocabulary cards.

2 Read Strategic Intervention Decodable Reader 21

BEFORE READING Before reading, review *building, burning, masks, quickly, roar, station,* and *tightly.* Lead children on a picture walk through "A Day in the Garden."

AFTER READING Check comprehension by having children retell the story, including the characters, setting, and plot.

Have children locate and list words with suffixes *-ly, -ful, -er,* and *-or.* Have children sort the words they found.

-ly: *brightly, closely, fondly, gently, hardly, quickly, sweetly, tightly, weekly*

-ful: *helpful, hopeful, peaceful, skillful, thankful*

-er: *helper, gardener, teacher*

-or: *visitor*

3 Read Firefighter!

BEFORE READING Have children practice the words below—first as a group and then individually. Then use Guiding Comprehension, pp. 158–171, to monitor understanding.

polishing	cushions	sirens	scenes
spreading	hydrant	telescope	chief

Monitor Progress	Word and Story Reading
If... children have difficulty with any of these words,	**then...** reteach them by modeling. Have children practice the words, with feedback from you, until they can read them independently.
If... children have difficulty reading the story individually,	**then...** have them follow along in their books as they listen to the AudioText. You may also have them read pages of the selection aloud together, first with you and then without you, before reading individually.

Advanced

DAY 2

1 **Read** *Firefighter!*

DURING READING Have children read silently to p. 163. Provide guidance as needed. Ask:
- Why is it important for the firefighters to check their equipment?
- What do you think the firefighters will do once they arrive at the burning house?

Have children read silently to p. 171. Then ask:
- Why does fire spread so quickly in a house?
- When do firefighters have time to rest and eat?

MAIN IDEA/SUPPORTING DETAILS Have children recall the most important idea of the story. (Firefighters work together to put out fires.) Discuss what kinds of things firefighters do to work together.
- Why does it take more than one firefighter to put out a fire?
- What would you do if you smelled smoke in your house?

Children can work together to complete Graphic Organizer 16 (Main Idea/Supporting Details Chart) and identify the main idea and supporting details.

Main Idea
Firefighters work together to put out fires.

Supporting Details

| The firefighters check their equipment to make sure it's working properly. | The firefighters drive to the burning house together. | Each firefighter works to help put out the fire. |

▲ Graphic Organizer 16

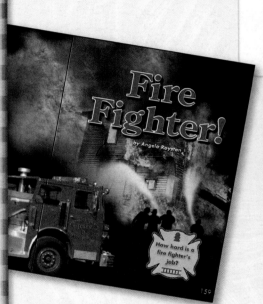

  AudioText

TEXT STRUCTURE Children can work with a partner to discuss the beginning, middle, and end of the story.

RESPONSE Ask children to devise escape routes for their homes in case of a fire. Have them draw pictures of their home and add escape routes in red.

2 **Extend Concepts Through Inquiry**

INVESTIGATE Guide children in choosing material at their independent reading level to explore their topic. Some books that may be appropriate are *Teamwork* by Ann Morris or *Working Together* by Elena Martin and Dwight Herold.

| 1 | Day 2 | 3 | 4 | 5 |

Identify Questions

Investigate

Investigate

Organize Information

Communicate

Firefighter!
Group Time

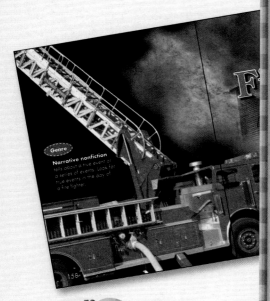

Audio CD AudioText

Strategic Intervention

1 Word Work

REVIEW **VOWEL PATTERNS *oo, ue, ew, ui*** Review p. 172c, using these additional words. Have children sort the words into *oo, ue, ew,* and *ui* lists.

pool	cool	juice	Sue	tooth	room
goose	flew	food	new	blue	suit

REVIEW **SENTENCE READING** Have individuals read these sentences to review decoding skills.

> I sat by the pool and had a glass of cool juice.
> Sue said she lost her tooth in the other room.
> The goose flew down to the lake to find food.
> Carl put on his new blue suit and went to work.

2 Comprehension

MAIN IDEA AND SUPPORTING DETAILS/TEXT STRUCTURE Reteach pp. 154r and 154–155. Have children respond to the Connect to Reading questions after completing step 3 Reread for Fluency.

• Now read the story again quietly. When you have finished, I'd like you to tell me what the story is mainly about and the order in which the events happen.

3 Reread for Fluency

READ SILENTLY WITH FLUENCY/ACCURACY Teach p. 172f using text at children's independent level. Reading options include Student Edition selections, Decodable Readers, Strategic Intervention Decodable Readers, and Leveled Readers.

Monitor Progress	Fluency
If... children have difficulty reading silently with fluency and accuracy,	then... have children read as if speaking and provide additional modeling. Have them listen to your model and then read aloud together, first with you and then without you, before reading silently.

MORE READING FOR
Group Time

Use this Leveled Reader or other text at children's instructional level.

Below-Level

Reviews
• Lesson vocabulary *building, burning, masks, quickly, roar, station, tightly*
• Main idea/Supporting details

Advanced

ROUTINE

1 Read Self-Selected Reading

BEFORE READING Have children select a trade book or Leveled Reader to read independently. Guide children in selecting books of appropriate difficulty.

AFTER READING When they have finished, have each child select an interesting event to discuss with a partner.

2 Extend Concepts Through Inquiry

INVESTIGATE Give children time to investigate the project they are thinking of and to begin preparing their information.

1	2	Day 3	4	5
Identify Questions	Investigate	**Investigate**	Organize Information	Communicate

---

DAY 3

Trade Books for Self-Selected Reading

TEAMWORK by Ann Morris, HarperCollins Publishers, 1999

WORKING TOGETHER by Elena Martin and Dwight Herold, Yellow Umbrella Books, 2004

MORE READING FOR
Group Time

Use this Leveled Reader or other text at children's instructional level.

Advanced

Reviews
• Concept vocabulary
• Main idea/Supporting details

Firefighter!
Group Time

Drama in Reading

Play

Genre
- A play is a story that is acted out.
- A play has characters who each have their own speaking parts.

Text Features
- A character's name appears before each speaking part.
- Directions to the actors sometimes appear in parentheses. These tell the actors how to move, where to go, or what to do.

Link to Reading
Use the library to find other plays to read. Choose one or two to read together as a Readers Theater.

174

AudioText

ROUTINE

1 Read "Firefighting Teamwork"

BEFORE READING Have children practice the words below—first as a group and then individually. Then use Drama in Reading, pp. 174–177.

inspection   council   location   alarm

Monitor Progress	Word and Selection Reading
If... children have difficulty with any of these words,	**then...** have them practice in pairs, reading word cards before reading the selection.
If... children have difficulty reading the selection individually,	**then...** have them follow along in their books as they listen to the AudioText. You may also have them read pages of the selection aloud together, first with you and then without you, before reading individually.

2 Reread for Fluency

Preteach p. 177a, using text at children's independent reading level. Reading options include Student Edition selections, Decodable Readers, Strategic Intervention Decodable Readers, and Leveled Readers.

3 Build Concepts

Use the Oral Vocabulary Routine, p. DI·1–DI·3, and the Oral Vocabulary Words on p. DI·8.

MORE READING FOR
Group Time

Use this Leveled Reader or other text at children's instructional level.

Below-Level

Reviews
- Lesson vocabulary *building, burning, masks, quickly, roar, station, tightly*
- Main idea/Supporting details

Advanced

DAY 4

1 Read "Firefighting Teamwork"

AFTER READING Ask:
- What are other chores the firefighters might do in the fire station?
- Why does the city council have to inspect the fire station?
- Why must firefighters stop what they're doing and immediately respond to the fire alarm?

2 Vocabulary

Extend vocabulary with questions such as these:
- How can you show that you are a *responsible* member of your *community*?
- Can you think of a sport that does not require *teamwork*?
- What kinds of *instruments* does a doctor use to perform an *operation*?
- What *supplies* do you use at school?

Encourage children to use the words in their writing.

3 Extend Concepts Through Inquiry

ORGANIZE INFORMATION Give children time to continue reading about their project. Remind them that tomorrow they will share their information. By now they should have begun putting the information in a presentation format.

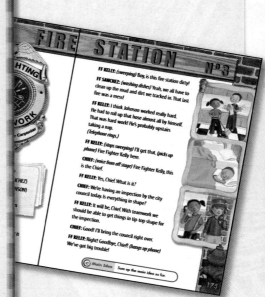

   AudioText

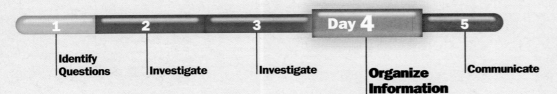

1	2	3	**Day 4**	5
Identify Questions	Investigate	Investigate	Organize Information	Communicate

MORE READING FOR
Group Time

Use this Leveled Reader or other text at children's instructional level.

Advanced

Reviews
- Concept vocabulary
- Main idea/Supporting details

Firefighter!
Group Time

Strategic Intervention

1 Word Work

SUFFIXES -ly, -ful, -er, -or Have children read aloud as you track the print. Call on individuals to blend the underlined words.

The <u>kindly</u> <u>editor</u> was very <u>helpful</u> to me.
The <u>wonderful</u> <u>singer</u> was a <u>visitor</u> from France.
The <u>sailor</u> stepped <u>lightly</u> and <u>carefully</u> onto the deck.
The <u>teacher</u> <u>quietly</u> said my artwork was <u>colorful</u>.

LESSON VOCABULARY Use p. 156f to review *building, burning, masks, quickly, roar, station, tightly.*

Monitor Progress	Vocabulary
If... children have difficulty with any of these words,	**then...** reteach them by modeling. Have children practice the words, with feedback from you, until they can read them independently.

2 Monitor Progress

SENTENCE READING SET A Use Set A on reproducible p. 178f to assess children's ability to read decodable and lesson vocabulary words in sentences.

COMPREHENSION To assess comprehension, have each child read Strategic Intervention Decodable Reader 21 or other text at the child's independent level. Ask what the story is mostly about (main idea) and have the child retell the story.

MORE READING FOR
Group Time

Use this Leveled Reader or other text at children's instructional level.

Below-Level

Reviews
• Lesson vocabulary *building, burning, masks, quickly, roar, station, tightly*
• Main idea/Supporting details

Advanced

1 Monitor Progress

SENTENCE READING SET C Use Set C on reproducible p. 178f to assess children's ability to read decodable and lesson vocabulary words in sentences. If you have any question about whether children have mastered this week's skills, have them read the Set B sentences.

COMPREHENSION Have each child read "Happy Campers at Bat" on reproducible p. 178g. Ask what the most important idea of the passage is (main idea), and have the child retell the passage. Use the Retelling Rubric on p. 202–203 to evaluate the child's retelling.

2 Extend Concepts Through **Inquiry**

COMMUNICATE Have children share their project about teamwork.

1	2	3	4	Day **5**
Identify Questions	Investigate	Investigate	Organize Information	

Communicate

ROUTINE

MORE READING FOR

Group Time

Use this Leveled Reader or other text at children's instructional level.

Advanced

Reviews
- Concept vocabulary
- Main idea/Supporting details

Group Time

DAY 1

ROUTINE

① Word Work

PREFIXES *un-, re-, pre-, dis-* Reteach p. 180n. Additional words to blend:

| unfinished | remake | displeased | preread | unseen |

Then have children sort the following words with prefixes *un-, re-, pre-,* and *dis-* and circle the letters that stand for the prefix.

| uneasy | discount | prewash | repave | disjoint |
| rewire | rerun | pretreat | unfrozen | preteen |

SPELLING Reteach p. 180p. Model spelling *preheat* and *unlock*. You may wish to give children fewer words to learn.

② Read Decodable Reader 22

BEFORE READING Review the words with prefixes *un-, re-, pre-,* and *dis-* on p. 180q and have children blend these story words: *relight, precooked, unpacks, unties, campsite, litter, sleeping, family.* Be sure children understand meanings of words such as *campsite*.

DURING READING Use p. 180q.

Monitor Progress	Word and Story Reading
If… children have difficulty with any of these words,	**then…** reteach them by modeling. Have children practice the words, with feedback from you, until they can read them independently.
If… children have difficulty reading the story individually,	**then…** read a page aloud as children follow along. Then have the group reread the page. Continue reading in this way before children read individually.

③ Reread for Fluency

Use the Paired Reading Routine, p. 180q, and text at each child's independent reading level.

MORE READING FOR

Group Time

Use this Leveled Reader or other text at children's instructional level.

Below-Level

Reviews
- Lesson vocabulary *flashes, lightning, pounds, pours, rolling, storm, thunder*
- Sequence

Check this database for additional titles.

Leveled Reader Database

ONLINE

PearsonSuccessNet.com

DAY 1

Advanced

ROUTINE

1 Word Work

PREFIXES Practice with words beginning with *un-, re-, pre-,* and *dis-.* If children know the words on first read, they may need no further practice. Practice items:

unable	**discover**	**prejudge**	**refresh**	**unnatural**
refill	**uncover**	**display**	**precaution**	**recharge**
uneasy	**recite**	**disgrace**	**disinfect**	**prehistoric**

Have children say the words again and sort by prefix. Then have individuals choose several words to use in a sentence.

2 Read Advanced Selection 22

BEFORE READING Have children identify these oral vocabulary words: *growth, protection.*

DURING READING Children may read silently. Provide guidance as needed.

AFTER READING Have children recall the events of the story. (The Austin Zoo started small. The zoo takes in unwanted animals. There is a learning center at the zoo. People give money and supplies to the zoo.) Ask:

• Why do you think there are so many animals that need help?
• Have you ever helped rescue an animal? Tell about it.

On the back of the selection page have children create an advertisement for the zoo.

A Rescue Zoo

There is a zoo in Austin, Texas. Like many zoos, it has tigers, monkeys, bears, and other animals. There is a train ride and a store that sells t-shirts and toy animals. However, this zoo is different from most other zoos.

Most zoos have baby animals that are born at the zoo, but the Austin Zoo does not. All the animals at the Austin Zoo were rescued.

The Austin Zoo started as a family ranch. The family took in a few unwanted animals, but there were more animals that needed homes. So the zoo grew bigger to accommodate them.

Some people buy a wild animal as baby, but they soon learn that it does not make a good pet. An animal's normal growth can make it too difficult and dangerous to take care of later on. Other animals need protection because they are not getting proper care. The zoo provides a safe place for these animals.

The community gives money and supplies to the zoo. This helps the zoo build more homes for the many animals that need care. The Austin Zoo is doing its best to help.

DI•10

3 Extend Concepts Through Inquiry

IDENTIFY QUESTIONS Have children choose another place that helps take care of animals. During the week, they should learn more about their choices from reading, studying pictures, and talking with adults or older children. On Day 5 they will share what they learned. Guide children in brainstorming possible choices.

• Think about a different type of place that helps animals. How is it different from the Austin Zoo?

Day 1	2	3	4	5
Identify Questions	Investigate	Investigate	Organize Information	Communicate

MORE READING FOR
Group Time

Use this Leveled Reader or other text at children's instructional level.

A Day in the Life of a Vet

Advanced

Reviews
• Concept vocabulary
• Sequence

One Dark Night
Group Time

Strategic Intervention

1 Word Work

PREFIXES *un-, re-, pre-, dis-* Reteach pp. 182c–182d. Additional words to blend:

unroll	resize	preorder	dislocate
disinfect	preflight	unplug	rewrap

LESSON VOCABULARY Reteach p. 182f. Have individuals practice reading the words from word cards.

2 **Read** Strategic Intervention Decodable Reader 22

BEFORE READING Before reading, review *flashes, lightning, pounds, pours, rolling, storm,* and *thunder* on the Word Wall. Preview the story with children and have them predict what they think Jon and Jack will do.

AFTER READING Check comprehension by having children retell the story, including the characters, setting, and plot.

Have children locate words beginning with prefixes *un-, re-, pre-,* and *dis-* in the story. List words children name. Review the prefix spelling patterns. Have children sort the words they found below *unable* and *reacts.*

unable	reacts
unhappy	reclose
unlocks	replay
unmasks	reuse
	rewind

3 **Read** *One Dark Night*

BEFORE READING Have children practice the words below—first as a group and then individually. Then use Guiding Comprehension, pp. 184–201, to monitor understanding.

already	whispers	brooding	snuggles
carrying	echo	hurtles	nudging

Monitor Progress	Word and Story Reading
If... children have difficulty with any of these words,	**then...** reteach them by modeling. Have children practice the words, with feedback from you, until they can read them independently.
If... children have difficulty reading the story individually,	**then...** have them follow along in their books as they listen to the AudioText. You may also have them read pages of the selection aloud together, first with you and then without you, before reading individually.

Audio CD AudioText

MORE READING FOR
Group Time

Use this Leveled Reader or other text at children's instructional level.

Below-Level

Reviews
- Lesson vocabulary *flashes, lightning, pounds, pours, rolling, storm, thunder*
- Sequence

Advanced

ROUTINE

1 Read *One Dark Night*

DURING READING Have children read silently to p. 193. Ask:
- What is one way to tell if a storm is getting closer?
- Why do you think the stray cat ran back outside?

Have children read silently to p. 200. Then ask:
- Why does the stray cat carry her kittens in her mouth?
- Do you think Jonathan's robe made a good bed? Why or why not?

SEQUENCE Have children recall the events of the story. (Jonathan helped a stray cat bring her kittens out of the storm and into the house.)
- What color was the first kitten the stray cat brought in the house?
- Does Grandfather pull the screen door shut before or after the stray cat brings in the second kitten?

GRAPHIC ORGANIZERS Children can work with a partner on story sequence. Draw a chart or distribute copies of Graphic Organizer 8.

RESPONSE Ask children to suppose that they are the stray cat in the story. Have them act out the sequence of events.

Title One Dark Night

Characters Jonathan, a stray cat, Grandfather, Grandmother, a gray kitten, a white kitten, and a black kitten

Setting a house

Events 1. First: There is a summer storm. 2. Next: A stray cat brings a kitten out of the storm and into the house. Jonathan warms the kitten in his bathrobe. 3. Then: The stray cat brings another kitten out of the storm and into the house. 4. Last: Jonathan helps the stray cat bring one more kitten into the house. They are all safe in the house.

▲ Graphic Organizer 8

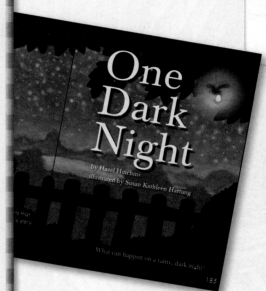

DAY **2**

Audio CD   AudioText

2 Extend Concepts Through Inquiry

INVESTIGATE Guide children in choosing appropriate material at their independent reading level, such as the books *One Day at Wood Green Animal Shelter* by Patricia Casey or *Helping Our Animal Friends (Books for Young Explorers)* by Judith E. Rinard and Susan McElhinney.

Help children decide how they will present their information. Children may use a graphic organizer, photographs, drawings, or models.

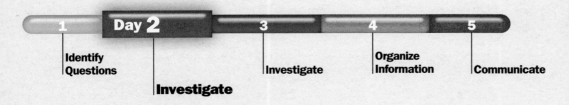

1	**Day 2**	3	4	5
Identify Questions	Investigate	Investigate	Organize Information	Communicate

MORE READING FOR
Group Time

Use this Leveled Reader or other text at children's instructional level.

Advanced

Reviews
- Concept vocabulary
- Sequence

One Dark Night

Group Time

Genre Realistic fiction

Audio CD AudioText

1 Word Work

REVIEW **SUFFIXES -ly, -ful, -er, -or** Review p. 202c, using these additional words. Have children sort the words into -ly, -ful, -er, and -or lists.

director	actor	clearly	driver	hopeful	powerful
writer	slowly	closely	skillful	visitor	gently

REVIEW **SENTENCE READING** Have individuals read these sentences to review decoding skills.

The director told the actor to say his lines slowly and clearly.
The driver was hopeful that his car was powerful enough to win.
The writer has to read very closely to catch every mistake.
The visitor moved my package.

2 Comprehension

SEQUENCE/GRAPHIC ORGANIZERS: ORDER OF EVENTS Reteach pp. 180r and 180–181. Have children respond to the Connect to Reading questions after completing step 3 Reread for Fluency.

• Now read the story again quietly. When you have finished, I'd like you to tell me the order in which the events happen and how you could order these events in a graphic organizer.

3 Reread for Fluency

READ WITH ACCURACY AND APPROPRIATE PACE/RATE Teach p. 202f using text at children's independent level. Reading options include Student Edition selections, Decodable Readers, Strategic Intervention Decodable Readers, and Leveled Readers.

Monitor Progress	Fluency
If... children have difficulty reading with accuracy and appropriate pace/rate,	**then...** discuss with them how to scan for unfamiliar words and provide additional modeling. Have them listen to your model and then read aloud together, first with you and then without you, before reading individually.

MORE READING FOR
Group Time

Use this Leveled Reader or other text at children's instructional level.

Below-Level

Reviews
• Lesson vocabulary *flashes, lightning, pounds, pours, rolling, storm, thunder*
• Sequence

Advanced

1 **Read** Self-Selected Reading

BEFORE READING Have children select a trade book or Leveled Reader to read independently. Guide children in selecting books of appropriate difficulty.

AFTER READING When they have finished, have each child select five interesting words to write and define.

2 Extend Concepts Through **Inquiry**

INVESTIGATE Give children time to investigate their topics and to begin preparing their information.

1	2	**Day 3**	4	5
Identify Questions	Investigate	Investigate	Organize Information	Communicate

DAY 3

Trade Books for Self-Selected Reading

ONE DAY AT WOOD GREEN ANIMAL SHELTER by Patricia Casey, Candlewick Press, 2001

HELPING OUR ANIMAL FRIENDS (BOOKS FOR YOUNG EXPLORERS) by Judith E. Rinard and Susan McElhinney, National Geographic Society, 1985

MORE READING FOR
Group Time

Use this Leveled Reader or other text at children's instructional level.

Advanced

Reviews
- Concept vocabulary
- Sequence

One Dark Night
Group Time

AudioText

Strategic Intervention

ROUTINE

① Read "Adoption"/"The Stray Cat"

BEFORE READING Have children practice the words below— first as a group and then individually. Then use Poetry in Reading, pp. 204–205.

creature	wrapped	heartbeat	alley
followed	tread	elegant	splotchy

Monitor Progress	Word and Selection Reading
If… children have difficulty with any of these words,	**then…** have them practice in pairs reading word cards before reading the selection.
If… children have difficulty reading the selection individually,	**then…** have them follow along in their books as they listen to the AudioText. You may also have them read pages of the selection aloud together, first with you and then without you, before reading individually.

② Reread for Fluency

Preteach p. 205a, using text at children's independent reading level. Reading options include Student Edition selections, Decodable Readers, Strategic Intervention Decodable Readers, and Leveled Readers.

③ Build Concepts

Use the Oral Vocabulary Routine, pp. DI·1–DI·2, DI·4, and the Oral Vocabulary Words on p. DI·8.

Advanced

ROUTINE

1 Read Poetry

AFTER READING Ask:

- What other animals might you see at a city pound?
- Where else could you find animals that need help?
- Is it possible for each person who finds a stray animal to keep it? Why or why not?

2 Vocabulary

Extend vocabulary with questions such as these:

- Which would you describe as fragile, an egg or an apple? Why?
- Can litter pollute a river? How?
- When you show concern, are you happy or worried? What concerns might a second grader have?

Encourage children to use the words in their writing.

3 Extend Concepts Through Inquiry

ORGANIZE INFORMATION Give children time to continue reading about their topic. Remind them that tomorrow they will share their information. By now they should have begun putting the information in a presentation format.

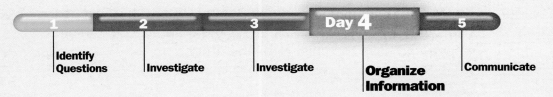

1	2	3	Day 4	5
Identify Questions	Investigate	Investigate	Organize Information	Communicate

The Stray Cat
Eve Merriam

It's just an old alley cat
that has followed us all the way home.
It hasn't a star on its forehead,
or a silky satiny coat.

No proud tiger stripes, no dainty tread,
no elegant velvet throat.

It's a splotchy, blotchy
city cat, not pretty cat,
a rough little tough little bag of old bones.

"Beauty," we shall call you.
"Beauty, come in."

Reading Across Texts
The cats in *One Dark Night* and in these two poems are homeless. Where was each cat was found? **Writing Across Texts** Write a sentence welcoming each cat to its new home.

Visualize As you read, create a picture of these cats in your mind.

 AudioText

MORE READING FOR

Group Time

Use this Leveled Reader or other text at children's instructional level.

A Day in the Life of a Vet

Advanced

Reviews
- Concept vocabulary
- Sequence

One Dark Night
Group Time

ROUTINE

DAY 5

1 Word Work

➤ **PREFIXES *un-, re-, pre-, dis-*** Have children read aloud as you track the print. Call on individuals to blend the underlined words.

I <u>redrew</u> my <u>unfinished</u> tree because I <u>disliked</u> the first one.
I <u>unlocked</u> the door, <u>preheated</u> the oven, and <u>reheated</u> a snack.
Mom was <u>disappointed</u> when the <u>preschool</u> <u>replaced</u> a teacher.
"I will <u>rewind</u> the tape so we can see the <u>previews</u>," I <u>repeated</u>.

LESSON VOCABULARY Use p. 182f to review *flashes, lightning, pounds, pours, rolling, storm, thunder.*

Monitor Progress	Vocabulary
If... children have difficulty with any of these words,	**then...** reteach them by modeling. Have children practice the words, with feedback from you, until they can read them independently.

2 Monitor Progress

SENTENCE READING SET A Use Set A on reproducible p. 206f to assess children's ability to read decodable and lesson vocabulary words in sentences.

COMPREHENSION To assess comprehension, have each child read Strategic Intervention Decodable Reader 22 or other text at the child's independent level. Ask about the order in which things happen and have the child retell the story.

MORE READING FOR
Group Time

Use this Leveled Reader or other text at children's instructional level.

Below-Level

Reviews
• Lesson vocabulary *flashes, lightning, pounds, pours, rolling, storm, thunder*
• Sequence

Advanced

DAY 5

1 Monitor Progress

SENTENCE READING SET C Use Set C on reproducible p. 206f to assess children's ability to read decodable and lesson vocabulary words in sentences. If you have any question about whether children have mastered this week's skills, have them read the Set B sentences.

COMPREHENSION Have each child read "Doghouse Redo" on reproducible p. 206g. Ask what the order of events are in the story (sequence), and have the child retell the passage. Use the Retelling Rubric on p. 172–173 to evaluate the child's retelling.

2 Extend Concepts Through INQUIRY

COMMUNICATE Have children share their information about another kind of place that helps animals.

1	2	3	4	Day 5
Identify Questions	Investigate	Investigate	Organize Information	

Communicate

MORE READING FOR
Group Time

Use this Leveled Reader or other text at children's instructional level.

Advanced

Reviews
• Concept vocabulary
• Sequence

Bad Dog, Dodger!

Group Time

DAY 1

Strategic Intervention

1 Word Work

 SILENT CONSONANTS *kn, wr, gn, mb* Reteach p. 208n. Additional words to blend:

| gnaw | kneel | wrong | sign | tomb |

Then have children sort the following words with silent consonants *kn, wr, gn,* and *mb* and circle the silent letters.

| climb | knobby | wringing | numb | resign |
| wrap | gnat | design | wrinkle | knuckle |

SPELLING Reteach p. 208p. Model spelling *write* and *knob*. You may wish to give children fewer words to learn.

2 Read Decodable Reader 23

BEFORE READING Review the *kn, wr, gn,* and *mb* words on p. 208q and have children blend these story words: *climbed, knights, knots, numb, wrapped, signed, thumb, knit, writing.* Be sure children understand meanings of words such as *numb.*

DURING READING Use p. 208q.

Monitor Progress	Word and Story Reading
If... children have difficulty with any of these words,	**then...** reteach them by modeling. Have children practice the words, with feedback from you, until they can read them independently.
If... children have difficulty reading the story individually,	**then...** read a page aloud as children follow along. Then have the group reread the page. Continue reading in this way before children read individually.

3 Reread for Fluency

Use the Oral Rereading Routine, p. 208q, and text at each child's independent reading level.

MORE READING FOR
Group Time

 Use this Leveled Reader or other text at children's instructional level.

Below-Level

Reviews
- Lesson vocabulary *chased, chewing, dripping, grabbed, practice, treat, wagged*
- Plot and theme

Check this database for additional titles.

Leveled Reader Database ONLINE
PearsonSuccessNet.com

Advanced

1 Word Work

SILENT CONSONANTS Practice with words that use the silent consonants *kn, wr, gn,* and *mb.* If children know the words on first read, they may need no further practice. Practice items:

knack	wrapper	combed	lambskin	plumbing
wrangle	knead	wrench	writer	knapsack
gnaw	gnarl	designer	climber	signage

Have children write the silent consonants on cards and use them to make other words. Then have individuals choose several words to use in a sentence.

2 Read Advanced Selection 23

BEFORE READING Have children identify this oral vocabulary word: *behavior*.

DURING READING Children may read silently. Provide guidance as needed.

AFTER READING Have children recall the events in the selection. (Puppies are cute, but they should be trained. Owners can take them to puppy kindergarten. This helps owners get to know their puppies better. Ask:
- Why can't puppies start classes when they are born?
- Have you ever helped train an animal? Tell about it.

On the back of the selection page have children write some things that puppies need to learn.

3 Extend Concepts Through Inquiry

IDENTIFY QUESTIONS Have children create a class for training an animal. During the week, they should learn more about training animals from reading, studying pictures, and talking with adults or older children. On Day 5 they will share what they learned. Guide children in brainstorming possible choices.
- Think about other animals that can be trained. How are these animals different from puppies?

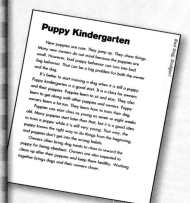

Puppy Kindergarten

New puppies are cute. They jump up. They chew things. Many new owners do not mind because the puppies are small. However, bad puppy behavior can turn into bad dog behavior. That can be a big problem for both the owner and the dog.

It's better to start training a dog when it is still a puppy. Puppy kindergarten is a good start. It is a class for owners and their puppies. Puppies learn to sit and stay. They also learn to get along with other puppies and owners. Puppy owners learn a lot too. They learn how to train their dog.

Puppies can start class as young as seven or eight weeks old. Many puppies start later than that, but it is a good idea to train a puppy while it is still very young. That way, the puppy knows the right way to do things from the beginning, and puppies don't get into the wrong habits.

Owners often bring dog treats to class to reward the puppy for being obedient. Owners are also expected to clean up after their puppies and keep them healthy. Working together brings dogs and their owners closer.

DI•11

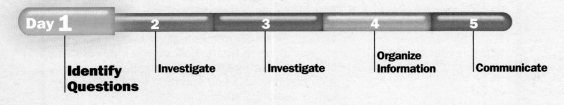

Day 1	2	3	4	5
Identify Questions	Investigate	Investigate	Organize Information	Communicate

MORE READING FOR
Group Time

Use this Leveled Reader or other text at children's instructional level.

Advanced

Reviews
- Concept vocabulary
- Plot and theme

Group Time

Audio CD AudioText

Strategic Intervention

ROUTINE

1 Word Work

🔊 **SILENT CONSONANTS *kn, wr, gn, mb*** Reteach pp. 210c–210d. Additional words to blend:

writing	knickers	lamb	gnaw
design	comb	wrapped	knowing

LESSON VOCABULARY Reteach p. 210f. Have individuals practice reading the words from tested word cards.

2 Read Strategic Intervention Decodable Reader 23

BEFORE READING Before reading, review *chased, chewing, dripping, grabbed, practice, treat,* and *wagged.* Preview the story with children, pointing and naming people, places, and things in the pictures.

AFTER READING Check comprehension by having children retell the story, including the characters, setting, and plot.

Have children locate *kn, wr, gn,* and *mb* words in the story. List words children name. Have children sort the words they found beside *kn, wr, gn,* and *mb.*

kn: *knee, kneeled, knob, knocked, knocking, know*

wr: *wrapped, wreath, wrench(es), wrist, wrong*

gn: *sign*

mb: *lamb*

3 Read *Bad Dog, Dodger!*

BEFORE READING Have children practice the words below—first as a group and then individually. Then use Guiding Comprehension, pp. 212–225, to monitor understanding.

broccoli	spectators	ninth	watched
nibbled	curtains	league	meant

Monitor Progress	Word and Story Reading
If... children have difficulty with any of these words,	**then...** reteach them by modeling. Have children practice the words, with feedback from you, until they can read them independently.
If... children have difficulty reading the story individually,	**then...** have them follow along in their books as they listen to the AudioText. You may also have them read pages of the selection aloud together, first with you and then without you, before reading individually.

Advanced

ROUTINE

1 Read *Bad Dog, Dodger!*

DURING READING Have children read silently to p. 219. Provide guidance as needed. Ask:

- Why was Dodger misbehaving?
- What do you think Dodger is going to do next?

Have children read silently to p. 225. Then ask:

- Do you think Sam did a good job of training Dodger? Explain.
- Do animals always listen to their owners? Why might this be?

PLOT AND THEME Have children recall the events of the story, the problem, and the solution. (Sam got a puppy named Dodger. Dodger was getting into trouble. Sam trained Dodger.) Discuss why it is important for the owner to train an animal.

- Was Dodger misbehaving on purpose? How could you tell?
- What else could Sam have done to solve the problem?

Children can work with a partner to complete Graphic Organizer 20.

Problem

Dodger was misbehaving, and the family was getting upset.
Why did this happen?

↓

Solution

Sam trained Dodger so that he would follow directions.
What happened?

▲ **Graphic Organizer 20**

Audio CD **AudioText**

PRIOR KNOWLEDGE Children can work with a partner to discuss what they already know about training an animal.

RESPONSE Ask children to suppose they are chefs who specialize in making dog treats. Have them write a recipe for their best-selling treat.

2 Extend Concepts Through Inquiry

INVESTIGATE Guide children in choosing material at their independent reading level to explore the class they are creating. Some books that may be appropriate are *Kids Training Puppies in 5 Minutes* by JoAnne Dehan or *Kitten Training and Critters, Too!* by Judy Petersen-Fleming and Bill Fleming.

Help children decide how they will present their information. Children may create a brochure, a commercial, or a newspaper to advertise.

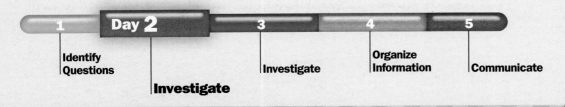

1 Identify Questions | **Day 2** Investigate | 3 Investigate | 4 Organize Information | 5 Communicate

Bad Dog, Dodger!

Group Time

DAY 3

ROUTINE

① Word Work

REVIEW **PREFIXES *un-, re-, pre-, dis-*** Review p. 226c, using these additional words. Have children sort the words into *un-, re-, pre-,* and *dis-* lists.

disappointed	unable	retie	dislikes	unkind	unfair
distrust	disagree	reunion	unfold	refold	uneven

REVIEW **SENTENCE READING** Have individuals read these sentences to review decoding skills.

Ann was disappointed when she was unable to retie her shoes.
My teacher dislikes seeing anyone acting unkind or unfair.
I didn't distrust or disagree with the man at the reunion.
Unfold the paper and then refold it so the edges aren't uneven.

② Comprehension

PLOT AND THEME/PRIOR KNOWLEDGE Reteach pp. 208r and 208–209. Have children respond to the Connect to Reading questions after completing step 3 Reread for Fluency.

• Now read the story again quietly and think about what you already know about the plot. When you have finished, I'd like you to tell me what happens in the beginning, middle, and end of the story and what you learned from the story.

③ Reread for Fluency

READ WITH EXPRESSION AND INTONATION Teach p. 226f, using text at children's independent level. Reading options include Student Edition selections, Decodable Readers, Strategic Intervention Decodable Readers, and Leveled Readers.

Monitor Progress	Fluency
If... children have difficulty reading with expression and intonation,	**then...** discuss with them the appropriate expression and intonation to be used with each passage and provide additional modeling. Have them listen to your model and then read aloud together, first with you and then without you, before reading individually.

212

Audio CD **AudioText**

MORE READING FOR
Group Time

Use this Leveled Reader or other text at children's instructional level.

Below-Level

Reviews
• Lesson vocabulary *chased, chewing, dripping, grabbed, practice, treat, wagged*
• Plot and theme

Advanced

DAY 3

1 Read Self-Selected Reading

BEFORE READING Have children select a trade book or Leveled Reader to read independently. Guide children in selecting books of appropriate difficulty.

AFTER READING When they have finished, have each child select an interesting animal fact to read aloud to a partner.

2 Extend Concepts Through Inquiry

INVESTIGATE Give children time to investigate the class they are creating and to begin preparing their information.

1	2	**Day 3**	4	5
Identify Questions	Investigate	Investigate	Organize Information	Communicate

Trade Books for Self-Selected Reading

KIDS TRAINING PUPPIES IN 5 MINUTES by JoAnne Dehan, Cork Hill Press, 2004

KITTEN TRAINING AND CRITTERS, TOO! by Judy Petersen-Fleming and Bill Fleming, Tambourine, 1996

MORE READING FOR
Group Time

Use this Leveled Reader or other text at children's instructional level.

Advanced

Reviews
- Concept vocabulary
- Plot and theme

Group Time

DAY 4

Strategic Intervention

1 Read "How to Train Your Puppy"

BEFORE READING Have children practice the words below— first as a group and then individually. Then use Science in Reading, pp. 228–231.

command   loosely   praise   friendship

Monitor Progress	Word and Selection Reading
If... children have difficulty with any of these words,	**then...** have them practice in pairs reading word cards before reading the selection.
If... children have difficulty reading the selection individually,	**then...** have them follow along in their books as they listen to the AudioText. You may also have them read pages of the selection aloud together, first with you and then without you, before reading individually.

2 Reread for Fluency

Preteach p. 231a, using text at children's independent reading level. Reading options include Student Edition selections, Decodable Readers, Strategic Intervention Decodable Readers, and Leveled Readers.

3 Build Concepts

Use the Oral Vocabulary Routine, pp. DI·1–DI·2, DI·5, and the Oral Vocabulary Words on p. DI·8.

228

AudioText

MORE READING FOR
Group Time

Use this Leveled Reader or other text at children's instructional level.

Below-Level

Reviews
- Lesson vocabulary *chased, chewing, dripping, grabbed, practice, treat, wagged*
- Plot and theme

Advanced

1 Read "How to Train Your Puppy"

AFTER READING Ask:

- Why should a puppy be trained to do only one new thing at a time?
- What kinds of treats are safe for puppies?
- How long do you think it takes to train a puppy?

2 Vocabulary

Extend vocabulary with questions such as these:

- Describe an *obedient* puppy.
- When someone gives you a *reprimand*, how does it make you feel? Why?
- Why should you *cooperate* when asked to do something *properly*?
- Why would you feel *confident* if someone said you did a good job?

Encourage children to use the words in their writing.

3 Extend Concepts Through **Inquiry**

ORGANIZE INFORMATION Give children time to continue reading about the class they are creating. Remind them that tomorrow they will share their information. By now they should have begun putting the information in a presentation format.

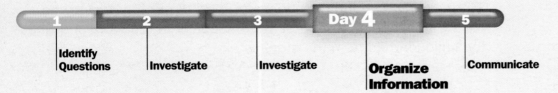

1	2	3	Day 4	5
Identify Questions	Investigate	Investigate	Organize Information	Communicate

229

AudioText

MORE READING FOR
Group Time

Training Peanut

Use this Leveled Reader or other text at children's instructional level.

Advanced

Reviews
- Concept vocabulary
- Plot and theme

Group Time

DAY 5

ROUTINE

1 Word Work

SILENT CONSONANTS *kn, wr, gn, mb* Have children read aloud as you track the print. Call on individuals to blend the underlined words.

Someone <u>knocked</u> over the <u>gnome</u> and the <u>sign</u> in our garden.
I <u>know</u> how to <u>climb</u> the ladder without making it <u>wriggle</u> or shake.
I will <u>design</u> the <u>knight</u> costume if you will <u>write</u> the script for the play.
Dad used the <u>wrong</u> <u>knife</u> to cut the <u>lamb</u> chops.

LESSON VOCABULARY Use p. 210f to review *chased, chewing, dripping, grabbed, practice, treat, wagged.*

Monitor Progress	Lesson Vocabulary
If... children have difficulty with any of these words,	**then...** reteach them by modeling. Have children practice the words, with feedback from you, until they can read them independently.

2 Monitor Progress

SENTENCE READING SET A Use Set A on reproducible p. 232f to assess children's ability to read decodable and lesson vocabulary words in sentences.

COMPREHENSION To assess comprehension, have each child read Strategic Intervention Decodable Reader 23 or other text at the child's independent level. Ask what happens in the story and what the child learned from the story.

MORE READING FOR
Group Time

Use this Leveled Reader or other text at children's instructional level.

Below-Level

Reviews
• Lesson vocabulary *chased, chewing, dripping, grabbed, practice, treat, wagged*
• Plot and theme

Advanced

ROUTINE

DAY 5

① Monitor Progress

SENTENCE READING SET C Use Set C on reproducible p. 232f to assess children's ability to read decodable and lesson vocabulary words in sentences. If you have any question about whether children have mastered this week's skills, have them read the Set B sentences.

COMPREHENSION Have each child read "Needles or Knots" on reproducible p. 232g. Ask about the events of the story, the problem, and the solution (plot and theme), and have the child retell the passage. Use the Retelling Rubric on p. 226–227 to evaluate the child's retelling.

② Extend Concepts Through INQUIRY

COMMUNICATE Have children share the information about the animal training class they created.

1	2	3	4	Day 5
Identify Questions	Investigate	Investigate	Organize Information	

Communicate

MORE READING FOR
Group Time

Use this Leveled Reader or other text at children's instructional level.

Advanced

Reviews
- Concept vocabulary
- Plot and theme

Group Time

ROUTINE

DAY 1

1 Word Work

DIGRAPHS *ph, gh*/f/ Reteach p. 234n. Additional words to blend:

phony	**enough**	**laugh**	**graph**	**dolphin**

Then have children sort the following words with digraphs *ph* and *gh* and circle the letters that stand for the sound /f/.

phantom	**coughing**	**gopher**	**laughed**
alphabet	**roughly**	**nephew**	**tough**

SPELLING Reteach p. 234p. Model spelling *laugh* and *tough*. You may wish to give children fewer words to learn.

2 Read Decodable Reader 24

Decodable Reader 24

Phil's Zoo Fun
Written by Alex Gardner
Illustrated by Nancy Peters

BEFORE READING Review the *ph* and *gh* words on p. 234q and have children blend these story words: *dolphin(s), enough, graph, laughs, photos, phrase, getting, hippos, puffer.* Be sure children understand meanings of words such as *graph* and *phrase*.

DURING READING Use p. 234q.

Monitor Progress	Word and Story Reading
If... children have difficulty with any of these words,	**then...** reteach them by modeling. Have children practice the words, with feedback from you, until they can read them independently.
If... children have difficulty reading the story individually,	**then...** read a page aloud as children follow along. Then have the group reread the page. Continue reading in this way before children read individually.

3 Reread for Fluency

Use the Paired Reading Routine, p. 234q, and text at each child's independent reading level.

MORE READING FOR
Group Time

Use this Leveled Reader or other text at children's instructional level.

Below-Level

Reviews
- Lesson vocabulary *adventure, climbed, clubhouse, exploring, greatest, truest, wondered*
- Author's purpose

Check this database for additional titles.

Leveled Reader Database ONLINE

PearsonSuccessNet.com

Advanced

1 Word Work

DIGRAPHS *ph, gh*/f/ Practice with words that contain *ph, gh*/f/. If children know the words on first read, they may need no further practice. Practice items:

phantom	**trough**	**phobia**	**pheasant**
laughing	**triumph**	**geography**	**toughen**
pharmacy	**physical**	**coughing**	**phonics**

Have children write the words on cards and sort by *ph* and *gh* spellings. Then have individuals choose several words to use in a sentence.

2 Read Advanced Selection 24

BEFORE READING Have children identify this oral vocabulary word: *appreciate*.

DURING READING Children may read silently. Provide guidance as needed.

AFTER READING Have children think about why the author wrote this selection. (The author wanted to share a story about friendship.) Ask:

- What is a food bank?
- What else could Sara have done to still participate in the bike-a-thon?

On the back of the selection page have children write a poem about a bike-a-thon.

The Bike-a-thon

DI•12

3 Extend Concepts Through Inquiry

IDENTIFY QUESTIONS Have children choose a cause for which they could raise money. During the week, they should learn more about their causes from reading, studying pictures, and talking with adults or older children. On Day 5 they will share what they learned. Guide children in brainstorming possible choices.

- Think about people or places that need donations. Do they accept donations other than money?

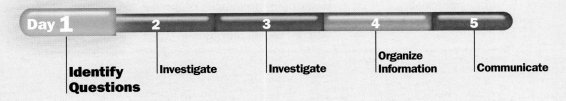

Day 1	2	3	4	5
Identify Questions	Investigate	Investigate	Organize Information	Communicate

MORE READING FOR
Group Time

Use this Leveled Reader or other text at children's instructional level.

Advanced

Reviews
- Concept vocabulary
- Author's purpose

Group Time

ROUTINE

DAY 2

Audio CD AudioText

1 Word Work

🔄 **DIGRAPHS *ph, gh/f/*** Reteach pp. 236c–236d. Additional words to blend:

photo	orphan	phone	rough
enough	telegraph	phrase	coughing

LESSON VOCABULARY Reteach p. 236f. Have individuals practice reading the words from word cards.

2 Read Strategic Intervention Decodable Reader 24

BEFORE READING Before reading, review *adventure, climbed, clubhouse, exploring, greatest, truest,* and *wondered.* Lead children on a picture walk through *Big Brother Ted* and have them name the things you point to in the pictures.

AFTER READING Check comprehension by having children retell the story, including the characters, setting, and plot.

Have children locate *ph* and *gh* words in the story. List words children name. Review the *ph* and *gh* spelling patterns. Have children sort the words they found below *enough* and *graphs.*

enough	graphs
laugh	phone
	photos
	phrases

3 Read *Horace and Morris*

BEFORE READING Have children practice the words below—first as a group and then individually. Then use Guiding Comprehension, pp. 238–255, to monitor understanding.

sewers	decision	allow	wondered
downhearted	friendship	announced	exploring

Monitor Progress	Word and Story Reading
If... children have difficulty with any of these words,	**then...** reteach them by modeling. Have children practice the words, with feedback from you, until they can read them independently.
If... children have difficulty reading the story individually,	**then...** have them follow along in their books as they listen to the AudioText. You may also have them read pages of the selection aloud together, first with you and then without you, before reading individually.

Within the extracted images:

Big Brother Ted
Written by Grace Peterson
Illustrated by Tracey Binder
Strategic Intervention Decodable Reader 24
Phonics Skill
/f/ph, gh
phone photos graphs laugh phrases

Horace and Morris
Genre **Fantasy** stories are make-believe stories because they couldn't really happen. What makes this story a fantasy?

Advanced

1 Read *Horace and Morris*

DURING READING Have children read silently to p. 247. Ask:
- Is Mount Ever-Rust a real place? How do you know?
- Do you think Horace and Morris should have joined an all-boys club? Why or why not?

Have children read silently to p. 255. Then ask:
- Why was Dolores bored at the clubhouse?
- Do you think more mice will join the new clubhouse? Explain.

⊙ **AUTHOR'S PURPOSE** Have children think about why the author chose the names in the story. (Horace, Morris, Dolores, Chloris, and Boris are all rhyming names.) Discuss author's choices.
- Why do you think the author named the clubhouses Mega-Mice and Cheese Puffs?
- How do you think the author thought of The Frisky Whisker Club?

⊙ **ASK QUESTIONS** Have children work with a partner to complete a questions web. Draw a web or distribute copies of Graphic Organizer 14. Have children draw a circle at the end of each spoke.

RESPONSE Ask children to design a clubhouse for their friends. They can draw a picture of it and make a sign for it.

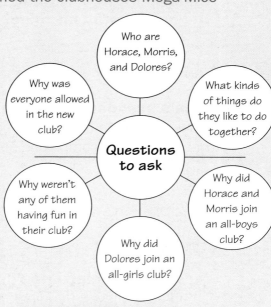

Who are Horace, Morris, and Dolores?

Why was everyone allowed in the new club?

What kinds of things do they like to do together?

Questions to ask

Why weren't any of them having fun in their club?

Why did Horace and Morris join an all-boys club?

Why did Dolores join an all-girls club?

▲ Graphic Organizer 14

2 Extend Concepts Through Inquiry

INVESTIGATE Guide children in choosing material at their independent reading level to explore various causes. Some books that may be appropriate are *Charities—Do They Work?* by Alison Brownlie or *Learning About Charity from the Life of Princess Diana* by Caroline M. Levchuck.

Help children decide how they will present their information.

Identify Questions

Day 2

Investigate

3 Investigate

4 Organize Information

5 Communicate

but mostly Dolores

by James Howe
illustrated by Amy Walrod

Will Horace, Morris, and Dolores remain very good friends?

239

AudioText

MORE READING FOR

Group Time

Use this Leveled Reader or other text at children's instructional level.

Advanced

Reviews
- Concept vocabulary
- Author's purpose

Horace and Morris
Group Time

Audio CD **AudioText**

ROUTINE

1 Word Work

REVIEW SILENT CONSONANTS *kn, wr, gn, mb* Review p. 256c, using these additional words. Have children sort the words into *kn, wr, gn,* and *mb* lists.

knight	knelt	knee	sign	gnu	gnats
knew	comb	knots	wrap	thumb	knife

REVIEW SENTENCE READING Have individuals read these sentences to review decoding skills.

The knight knelt down on one knee as a sign of respect.
A gnu was bothered by all the gnats buzzing around.
Mom knew how to comb the knots out of my hair.
He had to wrap his thumb after he cut it with a knife.

2 Comprehension

AUTHOR'S PURPOSE/ASK QUESTIONS Reteach pp. 234r and 234–235. Have children respond to the Connect to Reading questions after completing step 3 Reread for Fluency.

• Now read the story again quietly and ask yourself questions about the story as you read. When you have finished, I'd like you to tell me why you think the author wrote this story.

3 Reread for Fluency

EXPRESS CHARACTERIZATION Teach p. 256f using text at children's independent level. Reading options include Student Edition selections, Decodable Readers, Strategic Intervention Decodable Readers, and Leveled Readers.

Monitor Progress	Fluency
If... children have difficulty reading dialogue,	**then...** have them determine who is speaking and provide additional modeling. Have them listen to your model and then read aloud together, first with you and then without you, before reading individually.

MORE READING FOR
Group Time

Use this Leveled Reader or other text at children's instructional level.

Below-Level

Reviews
• Lesson vocabulary *adventure, climbed, clubhouse, exploring, greatest, truest, wondered*
• Author's purpose

Advanced

DAY 3

1 **Read** Self-Selected Reading

BEFORE READING Have children select a trade book or Leveled Reader to read independently. Guide children in selecting books of appropriate difficulty.

AFTER READING When they have finished, have each child select an interesting charity to discuss with a partner.

2 Extend Concepts Through **Inquiry**

INVESTIGATE Give children time to investigate the causes they are considering and to begin preparing their information.

1	2	Day 3	4	5
Identify Questions	Investigate	Investigate	Organize Information	Communicate

---

Trade Books for Self-Selected Reading

CHARITIES—DO THEY WORK? by Alison Brownlie, Raintree, 1999

LEARNING ABOUT CHARITY FROM THE LIFE OF PRINCESS DIANA by Caroline M. Levchuck, PowerKids Press, 1999

MORE READING FOR

Group Time

Use this Leveled Reader or other text at children's instructional level.

Advanced

Reviews
- Concept vocabulary
- Author's purpose

DAY 4

Social Studies in Reading

Good Kicking
by Rich Richardson
Staff Writer

Newspaper Article

Genre
• Newspaper articles may cover news about the city, the nation, or the world.

Text Features
• Newspaper articles usually have catchy headlines that grab the reader's attention.
• Photographs and captions give more information.
• Quotes from a real person help the reader know that the article is true and factual.

Link to Social Studies
Find out more about famous soccer players. Make a poster to report your findings.

258

Audio CD AudioText

Strategic Intervention

ROUTINE

1 Read "Good Kicking"

BEFORE READING Have children practice the words below— first as a group and then individually. Then use Social Studies in Reading, pp. 258–261.

soccer   importantly   responsibility   teammates

Monitor Progress	Word and Selection Reading
If... children have difficulty with any of these words,	**then...** have them practice in pairs reading word cards before reading the selection.
If... children have difficulty reading the selection individually,	**then...** have them follow along in their books as they listen to the AudioText. You may also have them read pages of the selection aloud together, first with you and then without you, before reading individually.

2 Reread for Fluency

Preteach p. 261a, using text at children's independent reading level. Reading options include Student Edition selections, Decodable Readers, Strategic Intervention Decodable Readers, and Leveled Readers.

3 Build Concepts

Use the Oral Vocabulary Routine, pp. DI·1–DI·2, DI·6, and the Oral Vocabulary Words on p. DI·8.

MORE READING FOR
Group Time

Use this Leveled Reader or other text at children's instructional level.

What an Adventure!

Below-Level

Reviews
• Lesson vocabulary *adventure, climbed, clubhouse, exploring, greatest, truest, wondered*
• Author's purpose

DAY
4

Advanced

ROUTINE

1 **Read** "Good Kicking"

AFTER READING Ask:
- What do you know about soccer? Tell about it.
- Can a team still have fun if it always loses? Why or why not?
- What are some other sports that depend heavily on teamwork?

2 **Vocabulary**

Extend vocabulary with questions such as these:
- If you *demand* something from someone, do you speak *firmly*?
- How can you *communicate* other than by talking?
- Would you be scared of a *ferocious* dog? Why or why not?
- If you are *defiant*, are you obeying the rules?

Encourage children to use the words in their writing.

3 **Extend Concepts Through Inquiry**

ORGANIZE INFORMATION Give children time to continue reading about the cause they are learning about. Remind them that tomorrow they will share their information. By now they should have begun putting the information in a presentation format.

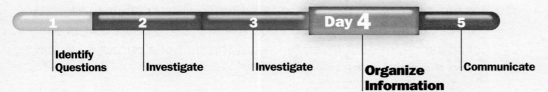

1	2	3	**Day 4**	5
Identify Questions	Investigate	Investigate	Organize Information	Communicate

 Audio CD   AudioText

Horace and Morris
Group Time

Strategic Intervention

ROUTINE

1 Word Work

↻ **DIGRAPHS** *ph, gh/f/* Have children read aloud as you track the print. Call on individuals to blend the underlined words.

I try not to <u>cough</u> or <u>laugh</u> when I'm on the <u>phone</u>.
She took <u>enough</u> <u>photos</u> of her <u>nephews</u>.
The <u>pheasant</u> flew near the <u>rough</u> rocks.
I had a <u>tough</u> time saying the <u>phrase</u> in Spanish.

LESSON VOCABULARY Use p. 236f to review *adventure, climbed, clubhouse, exploring, greatest, truest, wondered*.

Monitor Progress	Vocabulary
If... children have difficulty with any of these words,	**then...** reteach them by modeling. Have children practice the words, with feedback from you, until they can read them independently.

2 Monitor Progress

SENTENCE READING SET A Use Set A on reproducible p. 262f to assess children's ability to read decodable and lesson vocabulary words in sentences.

COMPREHENSION To assess comprehension, have each child read Strategic Intervention Decodable Reader 24 or other text at the child's independent level. Ask what the author's purpose is, and have the child retell the story.

MORE READING FOR
Group Time

Use this Leveled Reader or other text at children's instructional level.

Below-Level

Reviews
- Lesson vocabulary *adventure, climbed, clubhouse, exploring, greatest, truest, wondered*
- Author's purpose

Advanced

ROUTINE

DAY 5

1 Monitor Progress

SENTENCE READING SET C Use Set C on reproducible p. 262f to assess children's ability to read decodable and lesson vocabulary words in sentences. If you have any question about whether children have mastered this week's skills, have them read the Set B sentences.

COMPREHENSION Have each child read "A Dolphin, an Elephant, and a Gopher" on reproducible p. 262g. Ask why the author wrote this story (author's purpose), and have the child retell the passage. Use the Retelling Rubric on p. 256–257 to evaluate the child's retelling.

2 Extend Concepts Through **Inquiry**

COMMUNICATE Have children share the cause for which they chose to raise money.

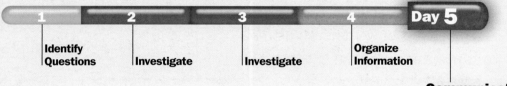

1	2	3	4	Day 5
Identify Questions	Investigate	Investigate	Organize Information	

Communicate

Group Time

DAY 1

Strategic Intervention

ROUTINE

1 Word Work

VOWELS *aw, au, augh, al* Reteach p. 264n. Additional words to blend:

| salt | brawny | fault | pause | tall |

Then have children sort the following *aw, au, augh,* and *al* words and circle the letters that stand for the sound /ȯ/.

| bald | vault | awful | naught | calling |
| sauce | slaughter | jaunt | hall | drawn |

SPELLING Reteach p. 264p. Model spelling *auto* and *chalk*. You may wish to give children fewer words to learn.

2 Read Decodable Reader 25

BEFORE READING Review the *aw, au, augh,* and *al* words on p. 264q and have children blend these story words: *always, August, caught, launch, thaw, cooler,* and *ground.* Be sure children understand meanings of words such as *thaw.*

DURING READING Use p. 264q.

Monitor Progress	Word and Story Reading
If... children have difficulty with any of these words,	**then**... reteach them by modeling. Have children practice the words, with feedback from you, until they can read them independently.
If... children have difficulty reading the story individually,	**then**... read a page aloud as children follow along. Then have the group reread the page. Continue reading in this way before children read individually.

3 Reread for Fluency

Use the Oral Rereading Routine, p. 264q, and text at each child's independent reading level.

MORE READING FOR
Group Time

Use this Leveled Reader or other text at children's instructional level.

Below-Level

Reviews
- Lesson vocabulary *afternoon, blame, idea, important, signmaker, townspeople*
- Realism and fantasy

Check this database for additional titles.

Leveled Reader Database ONLINE

PearsonSuccessNet.com

Advanced

ROUTINE

DAY 1

1 Word Work

VOWELS *aw, au, augh, al* Practice with words that contain *aw, au, augh,* and *al.* If children know the words on first read, they may need no further practice. Practice items:

crawdad	falsify	taught	walker	automatic
daughter	drawn	balk	drawing	awfully
naught	auction	altogether	already	awning

Have children write the words on cards and sort by vowel spellings. Then have individuals choose several words to use in a sentence.

2 **Read** Advanced Selection 25

BEFORE READING Have children identify these oral vocabulary words: *citizen, judgment.*

DURING READING Children may read silently. Provide guidance as needed.

AFTER READING Have children decide if this selection is fiction or nonfiction. (This selection describes the life of a real person, so it is nonfiction.) Ask:

- Why do you think the President of the United States chooses the justices for the Supreme Court?
- What are equal rights?

On the back of the selection page have children write some rules that people in a courtroom have to follow.

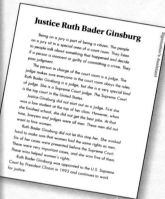

Justice Ruth Bader Ginsburg

DI•13

3 Extend Concepts Through **Inquiry**

IDENTIFY QUESTIONS Have children research two important political figures. During the week, they should learn more about those people from reading, studying pictures, and talking with adults or older children. On Day 5 they will share what they learned. Guide children in brainstorming possible choices.

- Think about people who have made a difference. What sorts of things have they accomplished? How are these people alike? How are they different?

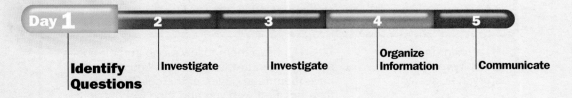

Day **1**	**2**	**3**	**4**	**5**
Identify Questions	Investigate	Investigate	**Organize Information**	Communicate

MORE READING FOR
Group Time

Marty's Job

Use this Leveled Reader or other text at children's instructional level.

Advanced

Reviews
- Concept vocabulary
- Realism and fantasy

Signmaker's Assistant
Group Time

ROUTINE

DAY 2

Audio **CD** **AudioText**

1 Word Work

VOWELS *aw, au, augh, al* Reteach pp. 266c–266d. Additional words to blend:

taught	crawl	auto	malt
launch	false	shawl	daughter

LESSON VOCABULARY Reteach p. 266f. Have individuals practice reading the words from word cards.

2 Read Strategic Intervention Decodable Reader 25

BEFORE READING Before reading, review *afternoon, blame, idea, important, signmaker,* and *townspeople.* Lead children on a picture walk through *A Job for Paul* and point out what Paul and Rex are doing in each picture.

AFTER READING Check comprehension by having children retell the story, including the characters, setting, and plot.

Have children locate *aw, au, augh,* and *al* words in the story. List words children name. Review the *aw, au, augh,* and *al* spelling patterns. Have children sort the words they found below *almost, awful, caught,* and *cause.*

almost	awful	caught	cause
calm	paw	naughty	Paul
small	paws	taught	
tall			
walk			

3 Read *The Signmaker's Assistant*

BEFORE READING Have children practice the words below—first as a group and then individually. Then use Guiding Comprehension, pp. 268–283, to monitor understanding.

ordinary	sensible	naturally	board
discovered	tearing	listening	feverishly

Monitor Progress	Word and Story Reading
If... children have difficulty with any of these words,	**then...** reteach them by modeling. Have children practice the words, with feedback from you, until they can read them independently.
If... children have difficulty reading the story individually,	**then...** have them follow along in their books as they listen to the AudioText. You may also have them read pages of the selection aloud together, first with you and then without you, before reading individually.

Advanced

ROUTINE

1 Read *The Signmaker's Assistant*

DURING READING Have children read silently to p. 275. Provide guidance as needed. Ask:
- Do you think Norman enjoys his job? Why or why not?
- How are people going to feel about Norman's signs?

Have children read silently to p. 283. Then ask:
- Do you think Norman meant to make people angry?
- Will Norman make a good signmaker someday?

DAY 2

REALISM/FANTASY Have children decide whether this story is real or fantasy. (fantasy) Children can work with a partner to complete Graphic Organizer 25 (T-Chart) to help decide which parts of the story could be real and which parts could only be fantasy.

MONITOR AND FIX UP Children can work with a partner to reread difficult sentences.

RESPONSE Ask children to suppose they are the signmaker's assistant. Have them draw a silly sign that would make people laugh but wouldn't make them angry.

Real	Fantasy
1. The signmaker painted signs.	1. The principal thought he forgot that there was no school.
2. The signmaker appreciated Norman's help.	2. People put their money in a garbage can instead of the bank.
3. People were confused without signs.	3. People took bites out of their hats.
4. Norman felt bad and put up new signs.	4. People knocked heads.
5. Norman apologized to the people.	5. People dumped garbage at the grocery store.

▲ Graphic Organizer 25

THE SIGNMAKER'S ASSISTANT
by Tedd Arnold

How will the signmaker's assistant fix the problems he causes?

 AudioText

2 Extend Concepts Through Inquiry

INVESTIGATE Guide children in choosing material at their independent reading level to explore their topic. Some books that may be appropriate are shown on DI•59.

Help children decide how they will present their information.

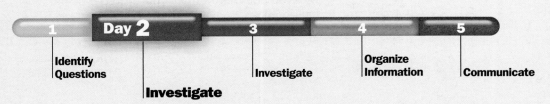

1	Day 2	3	4	5
Identify Questions	Investigate	Investigate	Organize Information	Communicate

MORE READING FOR
Group Time

Marty's Job

Use this Leveled Reader or other text at children's instructional level.

Advanced

Reviews
- Concept vocabulary
- Realism and fantasy

Signmaker's Assistant
Group Time

AudioText

DAY 3

1 Word Work

REVIEW **DIGRAPHS ph, gh/f/** Review p. 284c, using these additional words. Have children sort the words into *ph* and *gh* lists.

nephew	laughed	elephant	Phil	cough	phone
enough	photo	dolphin	sphere	phase	graph

REVIEW **SENTENCE READING** Have individuals read these sentences to review decoding skills.

My nephew laughed when the elephant sprayed water.
Phil started to cough while he was on the phone.
Can you get close enough to take a photo of the dolphin?
The sphere is one phase of this project that you can graph.

2 Comprehension

REALISM AND FANTASY/MONITOR AND FIX UP Reteach pp. 264r and 264–265. Have children respond to the Connect to Reading questions after completing step 3 Reread for Fluency.

• Now read the story again quietly and keep track of how well you understand what you are reading by stopping when something doesn't make sense. When you have finished, I'd like you to tell me whether the things that happen in the story are impossible or if they could really happen.

3 Reread for Fluency

READ WITH APPROPRIATE PHRASING Teach p. 284f, using text at children's independent level. Reading options include Student Edition selections, Decodable Readers, Strategic Intervention Decodable Readers, and Leveled Readers.

Monitor Progress	Fluency
If... children have difficulty reading with expression,	then... discuss with them the appropriate expression to be used with each passage and provide additional modeling. Have them listen to your model and then read aloud together, first with you and then without you, before reading individually.

MORE READING FOR
Group Time

Use this Leveled Reader or other text at children's instructional level.

Below-Level

Reviews
• Lesson vocabulary *afternoon, blame, idea, important, signmaker, townspeople*
• Realism and fantasy

Advanced

ROUTINE

DAY 3

1 Read Self-Selected Reading

BEFORE READING Have children select a trade book or Leveled Reader to read independently. Guide children in selecting books of appropriate difficulty.

AFTER READING When they have finished, have each child select an interesting person to read about to a partner.

2 Extend Concepts Through Inquiry

INVESTIGATE Give children time to investigate the people they are learning about and to begin preparing their information.

1	2	Day 3	4	5
Identify Questions	Investigate		Organize Information	Communicate
		Investigate		

Trade Books for Self-Selected Reading

PRESIDENTS' DAY by David F. Marx, Children's Press, 2002

MADAM PRESIDENT: THE EXTRAORDINARY, TRUE (AND EVOLVING) STORY OF WOMEN IN POLITICS by Catherine Thimmesh, Houghton Mifflin, 2004

MORE READING FOR
Group Time

Use this Leveled Reader or other text at children's instructional level.

Advanced

Reviews
- Concept vocabulary
- Realism and fantasy

Signmaker's Assistant
Group Time

AudioText

DAY 4

---

1 Read "Helping Hand"

BEFORE READING Have children practice the words below—first as a group and then individually. Then use Reading Online, pp. 286–289.

volunteer	source	description
decals	loyalty	organizations

Monitor Progress	Word and Selection Reading
If... children have difficulty with any of these words,	**then...** have them practice in pairs reading word cards before reading the selection.
If... children have difficulty reading the selection individually,	**then...** have them follow along in their books as they listen to the AudioText. You may also have them read pages of the selection aloud together, first with you and then without you, before reading individually.

2 Reread for Fluency

Preteach p. 289a, using text at children's independent reading level. Reading options include Student Edition selections, Decodable Readers, Strategic Intervention Decodable Readers, and Leveled Readers.

3 Build Concepts

Use the Oral Vocabulary Routine, pp. DI·1–DI·2, DI·7, and the Oral Vocabulary Words on p. DI·8.

MORE READING FOR
Group Time

Use this Leveled Reader or other text at children's instructional level.

Below-Level

Reviews
- Lesson vocabulary *afternoon, blame, idea, important, signmaker, townspeople*
- Realism and fantasy

Advanced

ROUTINE

1 Read "Helping Hand"

AFTER READING Ask:
- Would you be interested in joining either of these organizations? Why or why not?
- If you started your own organization, what would it be?
- In what ways do you already help your neighbors?

2 Vocabulary

Extend vocabulary with questions such as these:
- Would a *troublemaker* make a good friend? Why or why not?
- If you *interrupted* someone, would you *apologize*? Why?
- Have you ever been *scolded* for something you didn't do? How did that make you feel?
- If someone *hoarded* all of the snacks, would they be sharing?

Encourage children to use the words in their writing.

3 Extend Concepts Through INQUIRY

ORGANIZE INFORMATION Give children time to continue reading about the people they are studying. Remind them that tomorrow they will share their information. By now they should have begun putting the information in a presentation format.

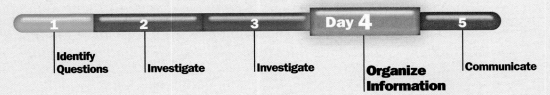

1	2	3	Day 4	5
Identify Questions	Investigate	Investigate	Organize Information	Communicate

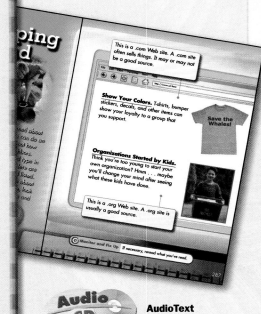

This is a .com Web site. A .com site often sells things. It may or may not be a good source.

Show Your Colors. T-shirts, bumper stickers, decals, and other items can show your loyalty to a group that you support.

Save the Whales!

Organizations Started by Kids. Think you're too young to start your own organization? Hmm . . . maybe you'll change your mind after seeing what these kids have done.

This is a .org Web site. A .org site is usually a good source.

Audio CD   AudioText

MORE READING FOR
Group Time

Marty's Job

Use this Leveled Reader or other text at children's instructional level.

Advanced

Reviews
- Concept vocabulary
- Realism and fantasy

Signmaker's Assistant

Group Time

Strategic Intervention

ROUTINE

1 Word Work

VOWELS *aw, au, augh, al* Have children read aloud as you track the print. Call on individuals to blend the underlined words.

I <u>caught</u> an <u>awful</u> cold in <u>August</u>.
The man and his <u>daughter</u> <u>waltzed</u> at the <u>ball</u>.
Our teacher <u>taught</u> us about <u>all</u> the <u>laws</u>.
It was my <u>fault</u> that the dog <u>crawled</u> on the sofa and <u>clawed</u> at it.

LESSON VOCABULARY Use p. 266f to review *afternoon, blame, idea, important, signmaker, townspeople.*

Monitor Progress	Lesson Vocabulary
If... children have difficulty with any of these words,	**then...** reteach them by modeling. Have children practice the words, with feedback from you, until they can read them independently.

2 Monitor Progress

SENTENCE READING SET A Use Set A on reproducible p. 290f to assess children's ability to read decodable and lesson vocabulary words in sentences.

COMPREHENSION To assess comprehension, have each child read Strategic Intervention Decodable Reader 25 or other text at the child's independent level. Ask which parts were realism or fantasy, and have the child retell the story.

MORE READING FOR
Group Time

Use this Leveled Reader or other text at children's instructional level.

Below-Level

Reviews
• Lesson vocabulary *afternoon, blame, idea, important, signmaker, townspeople*
• Realism and fantasy

Advanced

ROUTINE

1 Monitor Progress

SENTENCE READING SET C Use Set C on reproducible p. 290f to assess children's ability to read decodable and lesson vocabulary words in sentences. If you have any questions about whether children have mastered this week's skills, have them read Set B sentences.

COMPREHENSION Have each child read "Sausages to Go" on reproducible p. 290g. Ask if this story could really happen (realism/fantasy), and have the child retell the passage. Use the Retelling Rubric on p. 284–285 to evaluate the child's retelling.

2 Extend Concepts Through Inquiry

COMMUNICATE Have children share their information about two political figures.

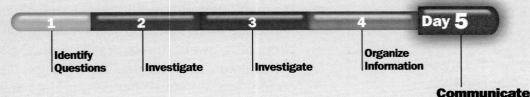

1	2	3	4	Day 5
Identify Questions	Investigate	Investigate	Organize Information	

Communicate

MORE READING FOR

Group Time

Use this Leveled Reader or other text at children's instructional level.

Advanced

Reviews
• Concept vocabulary
• Realism and fantasy

Firefighter!

Suffixes *-ly, -ful, -er, -or*

1 TEACH

Write on the board these suffixes:

-ly   -ful   -er   -or

Say: These are suffixes that can be added to base words. Sometimes they change the meaning of the word or how the word is used. They always add a syllable to the base word.

Write this sentence on the board with the words underlined as shown:

Our <u>teacher</u> talks <u>softly,</u> and she is a <u>wonderful</u> <u>actor</u>.

Tell children that each underlined word is made up of a base word and a suffix. Underline the base word in each. *(teach, soft, wonder, act)* Circle the suffix.

Explain that when a word ends in a consonant followed by *y*, the *y* is changed to *i* before adding the suffix *-ly*. Write happy and happily on the board to demonstrate.

Tell children that the suffix *-ful* means "full of." Explain that when *-er* or *-or* is added to a word, the new word may mean "someone or something that _____."

2 PRACTICE AND ASSESS

Write the following words on the board:

peaceful	quickly	sailor
teacher	careful	loudly
slowly	actor	rancher

Have volunteers underline the base word and circle the suffix in each. Then have them tell what each word means. Ask volunteers to use each word in an oral sentence.

Firefighter!

Main Idea

1 TEACH

Remind children that the main idea is the most important idea in a selection, or what the selection is mainly about. Read the following paragraph aloud:

Our trip to Washington, D.C., was wonderful. We saw the White House and the Capitol. We visited many historic landmarks. My favorite was the Smithsonian Museum. I could have stayed there for a whole week!

Make an idea web on the board. Ask children to name the main idea and write it in the middle circle of the web. (trip to Washington, D.C.) Then ask children to name details. Write the details on the web. Remind children that details give information about the main idea. Reread the paragraph, if necessary.

2 PRACTICE AND ASSESS

Recall with children the story *Firefighter!* Ask children to name things they learned in the selection. Write responses on the board. If children don't include the main idea, say: I learned something too. I learned that a firefighter has an important job. Write that idea on the board.

Then ask if any of the ideas on the board tell the main idea. Remind children that the selection includes many small bits of information, or details. Guide children in recognizing that the main idea is that a firefighter has an important job.

Have pairs of children choose a book to read together. Tell children to identify the main idea and details on a favorite page of the book.

One Dark Night

Prefixes *un-*, *re-*, *pre-*, *dis-*

1 TEACH

Write *dis-*, *un-*, *re-*, and *pre-* on the board.

Say: These word parts are called prefixes. A prefix is added to the beginning of a word. A prefix can change the meaning of a word.

Under *dis-* write *agree,* under *un-* write *true,* under *re-* write *write,* and under *pre-* write *view.* Help children add the prefix to each word under it. Write each new word. Have children explain what the base word means and how adding the prefix changed the meaning of the word.

2 PRACTICE AND ASSESS

Write these words on the board. Ask children what was added to each word to make the second word.

play	tie	connect	heat
replay	untie	disconnect	preheat

Have children use each word pair in a sentence to show meaning.

One Dark Night

Sequence

1 TEACH

Remind children that events in a story happen in a certain order. Tell children that if they understand the order events happen, they will better understand what they are reading.

Write the clue words *first, second, next, then, last,* and *finally* on the board and review them with children. Ask how these words help make it easier to retell events in a story.

Write the following on the board. Ask children to add a clue word to each line to tell the order of events.

Beth forgot to set her alarm clock so she overslept.
She missed the bus.
She got to school thirty minutes late.

2 PRACTICE AND ASSESS

Write the following on sentence strips:

First, Jon made posters about his lost puppy.
Next, he put the posters on trees and poles near his house.
Then, he went home and hoped for the best.
Finally, someone called with good news about his puppy.

Place all the sentence strips in a bowl and mix them up. Ask children to pull sentence strips from the bowl, one at a time, and read them aloud. Have them place the sentence strips in the correct order, using the clue words as a guide.

Have children choose a favorite story or movie and write four events in order. Encourage them to use time-order clue words: *first, next, then, last.* If time permits, have children read their ordered events and let others identify the story or movie they are describing.

Bad Dog, Dodger!

Silent Consonants

1 TEACH

Write the sentences below on the board:

The knight knew to climb the ladder.
Can you write a sign?

Read the first sentence with children. Point out the word *knight* and have children repeat it. Frame *knight* and ask children what beginning sound *knight* has, and what letter children see at the beginning. (/n/, *k*) Explain that when a word begins with *kn,* the *k* is silent. Have children find another silent *k* word. *(knew)*

Next, frame *climb.* Have children say it and listen for the ending sound. Ask what sound children hear at the end of *climb.* (/m/) Point out that the word ends with the letters *mb.* Tell children that when a word ends with *mb,* the *b* is silent.

Then read the second sentence with children. Point to *write* and ask which letter is silent. *(w)* Do the same with *sign.* Explain that *w* can be silent when it comes before *r,* and *g* can be silent when it comes before *n.*

2 PRACTICE AND ASSESS

Write the rhyme below on the board.

Does a gnat have knees?
Can it knock on a door?
Can it gnaw on a crumb
that it finds on the floor?
Can it wriggle its wrist?
Can it climb up a tree?
Can a gnat wrap a box
and send it to me?

With children, read aloud the poem. Have them tell what sound each set of circled letters stands for.

Bad Dog, Dodger!

Plot and Theme

1 TEACH

Remind children that a plot is what happens in the beginning, middle, and end of a story. Explain that a story usually has a problem, events that lead to solving the problem, and a solution to the problem. **Say:** A story map shows the plot of a story. Let's use a story map to show the plot of *Bad Dog, Dodger!*

Beginning
Sam gets a dog for his birthday. He names the dog Dodger.

Middle
Dodger gets into all kinds of trouble. The family doesn't know what to do.

End
Sam spends more time with Dodger and trains him. Dodger learns to do what Sam tells him.

Remind children that each part of the story map tells important ideas, not small ideas.

Then remind children that the theme of a story is the big idea. Ask children to identify the theme of *Bad Dog, Dodger!* Guide children to understand that the theme of this story is that if you take the time to train a pet, good things will happen.

2 PRACTICE AND ASSESS

Place children in small groups and give each group the name of a story they have read. Have children make a story map like the one from **Teach.** Tell children to record the most important ideas of each part of the story. Have children write the theme of the story on the bottom of the page. Ask groups to share and discuss their story plots and themes.

Horace and Morris but mostly Dolores

ph, gh/f/

1 TEACH

Write this sentence on the board and read it with children:

The photo shows a cowgirl laughing.

Pronounce /f/ and have children raise a hand each time they hear a word with /f/ as you reread the sentence. Underline the words *photo* and *laughing* as children identify them. Circle the *ph* in *photo* and the *gh* in *laughing* and explain that these letters together usually stand for /f/.

2 PRACTICE AND ASSESS

Write the rhymes below on the board.

If you're strong and tough,
you'll laugh when things get rough.

My nephew Phil
won a trophy for his skill.

Read aloud each rhyme, and have children repeat it. Invite volunteers to identify the words that have /f/ and ask them to circle the letters in each word that stand for /f/.

Horace and Morris but mostly Dolores

Author's Purpose

1 TEACH

Remind children that an author always has a purpose for writing a book. Say: When I read a book I ask myself why the author wrote it. I know that the author must have had a purpose in mind. Was it to tell a good story? Was it to give me information? Was it to persuade me that something is important?

Display fiction and nonfiction stories that children have read. Hold up each book and review with children what the book is about. Then discuss the author's purpose with children. Guide children to understand that often fiction stories were written to entertain and nonfiction stories were written to give information.

2 PRACTICE AND ASSESS

Give each child a book that he or she can read. Tell children to read the title and flip through the pages, reading and looking at the pictures. Ask children to decide the author's purpose for the book. Then have children put the books in two piles—one pile for books that tell a good story and the other pile for books that give information.

Hold up the books, one at a time, and give a general synopsis of the book. Ask children if they agree that each book is in the appropriate pile.

Tell children to review the selections in *Responsibility* and decide the author's purpose for each. Ask children to share their ideas.

The Signmaker's Assistant

Vowels *aw, au, augh, al*

1 TEACH

Write this sentence on the board:

The naughty puppy paused when he saw a walnut fall from the tree.

Read the sentence aloud and underline the words *naughty, paused, saw,* and *walnut.* Say: These four words all have something in common, the vowel sound /ȯ/.

Have children say the words aloud as you circle the *augh, au, aw,* and *al.* Then say: The letter combinations *aw, au, augh,* and *al* usually stand for /ȯ/.

2 PRACTICE AND ASSESS

Write the following words on self-stick notes: *paw, claw, toy, jaw, draw, straw, book, haunt, pause, because, town, launch, false, walk, talk, take, caught, catch, taught, daughter, band, luck.*

Have children take turns selecting a word and reading it aloud. If the word has the /ȯ/ sound, they should stick it to the board or to chart paper. When all the /ȯ/ words have been identified, have children sort them into four groups according to their spelling. Have volunteers read the words in each group.

Children can choose two or more words to write sentences about a favorite toy, story, or movie.

The Signmaker's Assistant

Realism and Fantasy

1 TEACH

Remind children that some stories tell about real characters and actions and some stories tell about make-believe characters and actions. Explain that stories that could really happen are called realistic stories. Stories that couldn't really happen are called fantasies.

Tell children you will say some story titles. If the story could be real, children should stand up. If the story is fantasy, children should sit down. Say the following story titles aloud:

Keisha's Trip to the Moon (fantasy)

Bobby Bear's Birthday Party (fantasy)

A Pet Hamster for Martin (real)

There's a Dinosaur in My Backyard (fantasy)

Fun at the Zoo (real)

2 PRACTICE AND ASSESS

Write the titles above on the board, as well as the words in parentheses. Read the first title aloud and ask children why this story would be fantasy. (because a little girl couldn't really go to the moon) **Ask:** How could I change the title so the story would be about something real? (Possible responses: *Keisha's Trip to Chicago* or *An Astronaut's Trip to the Moon.*)

Continue the routine with the remaining titles.

Then have children name favorite real and fantasy stories. Discuss why each could or could not really happen.

Providing children with reading materials they can and want to read is an important step toward developing fluent readers. A running record allows you to determine each child's instructional and independent reading level. Information on how to take a running record is provided on pp. DI•71–DI•72.

Instructional Reading Level

Only approximately 1 in 10 words will be difficult when reading a selection from the Student Edition for children who are at grade level. (A typical second-grader reads approximately 90–100 words correct per minute.)

- Children reading at grade level should read regularly from the Student Edition and On-Level Leveled Readers, with teacher support as suggested in the Teacher's Editions.
- Children reading below grade level can read the Strategic Intervention Leveled Readers and the Decodable Readers. Instructional plans can be found in the Teacher's Edition and th Leveled Reader Teaching Guide.
- Children who are reading above grade level can use the Advanced Leveled Readers and the Advanced Selection in the Teacher's Edition. Instructional plans can be found in the Teacher's Edition and the Leveled Reader Teaching Guide.

Independent Reading Level

Children should read regularly in independent-level texts in which no more than approximately 1 in 20 words is difficult for the reader. Other factors that make a book easy to read include the child's interest in the topic, the amount of text on a page, how well illustrations support meaning, and the complexity and familiarity of the concepts. Suggested books for self-selected reading are provided for each lesson on p. TR18 in this Teacher's Edition.

Guide children in learning how to self-select books at their independent reading level. As you talk about a book with children, discuss the challenging concepts in it, list new words children find in sampling the book, and ask children about their familiarity with the topic. A blackline master to help children evaluate books for independent reading is provided on p. DI•70.

Self-Selected/Independent Reading

While oral reading allows you to assess children's reading level and fluency, independent reading is of crucial importance to children's futures as readers and learners. Children need to develop their ability to read independently for increasing amounts of time.

- Schedule a regular time for sustained independent reading in your classroom. During the year, gradually increase the amount of time devoted to independent reading.
- More fluent readers may choose to read silently during independent reading time. Other children might read to a partner, to a stuffed animal, or to an adult volunteer.
- Help children track the amount of time they read independently and the number of pages they read in a given amount of time. Tracking will help motivate them to gradually increase their duration and speed. Blackline masters for tracking independent reading are provided on pp. DI•70 and TR19.

Choosing a Book to Read by Yourself

These questions can help you pick a book to read.

_____ 1. Is this book about something that I like?

_____ 2. This book may be about a real person, about facts, or a made-up story.
Do I like reading this kind of book?

_____ 3. Have I read other things by this author? Do I like the author?

If you say "yes" to question 1, 2, or 3, go on.

_____ 4. Were there fewer than 5 hard words on the first page?

_____ 5. Does the number of words on a page look about right to me?

If you say "yes" to questions 4 and 5, the book is right for you.

Silent Reading

Write the date, the title of the book, and the number of minutes you read.

Date	Title	Minutes

Taking a Running Record

A running record is an assessment of a child's oral reading accuracy and oral reading fluency. Reading accuracy is based on the number of words read correctly. Reading fluency is based on the reading rate (the number of words correct per minute) and the degree to which a child reads with a "natural flow."

How to Measure Reading Accuracy

1. Choose a grade-level text of about 80 to 120 words that is unfamiliar to the child.
2. Make a copy of the text for yourself. Make a copy for the child or have the child read aloud from a book.
3. Give the child the text and have the child read aloud. (You may wish to record the child's reading for later evaluation.)
4. On your copy of the text, mark any miscues or errors the child makes while reading. See the running record sample on page DI•72, which shows how to identify and mark miscues.
5. Count the total number of words in the text and the total number of errors made by the child. Note: If a child makes the same error more than once, such as mispronouncing the same word multiple times, count it as one error. Self-corrections do not count as actual errors. Use the following formula to calculate the percentage score, or accuracy rate:

$$\frac{\text{Total Number of Words} - \text{Total Number of Errors}}{\text{Total Number of Words}} \times 100 = \text{percentage score}$$

Interpreting the Results

- A child who reads **95–100%** of the words correctly is reading at an **independent level** and may need more challenging text.
- A child who reads **90–94%** of the words correctly is reading at an **instructional level** and will likely benefit from guided instruction.
- A child who reads **89%** or fewer of the words correctly is reading at a **frustrational level** and may benefit most from targeted instruction with lower-level texts and intervention.

How to Measure Reading Rate (wcpm)

1. Follow Steps 1–3 above.
2. Note the exact times when the child begins and finishes reading.
3. Use the following formula to calculate the number of words correct per minute (wcpm):

$$\frac{\text{Total Number of Words Read Correctly}}{\text{Total Number of Seconds}} \times 60 = \text{words correct per minute}$$

Interpreting the Results

An appropriate reading rate for a second-grader is 90–100 (wcpm).

Running Record Sample

Running Record Sample

Symbols

Just then a fly crawled near Fred.
Fred's long, sticky tongue shot out in a
flash and caught the tiny insect.

"Delicious! I'm full now," he said
loudly. He had already eaten three other
insects and a worm in the past hour.

Frankie overheard Fred and climbed
down a few branches. He moved quickly
and easily without falling.

"What are you doing, Fred?" he
asked in a friendly voice.

"I was just finishing up my lunch,"
Fred answered. "How is life up high
today, my friend?"

—From *Frog Friends*
On-Level Reader 2.4.3

Accurate Reading
The student reads the word correctly.

Insertion
The student inserts words or parts of words that are not in the text.

Mispronunciation/Misreading
The student pronounces or reads a word incorrectly.

Hesitation
The student hesitates over a word, and the teacher provides the word. Wait several seconds before telling the student what the word is.

Self-Correction
The student reads a word incorrectly but then corrects the error. Do not count self-corrections as actual errors. However, noting self-corrections will help you identify words the student finds difficult.

Omission
The student omits words or word parts.

Substitution
The student substitutes words or parts of words for the words in the text.

Running Record Results   ▶   **Reading Accuracy**   ▶   **Reading Rate—WCPM**

Total Number of Words: **86**

Number of Errors: **5**

$$\frac{86 - 5}{86} \times 100 = 94.18 = 94\%$$

$$\frac{81}{64} \times 60 = 75.9 = 76 \text{ words correct per minute}$$

Reading Time: **64 seconds**

Accuracy Percentage Score: **94%**

Reading Rate: **76 WCPM**

Teacher Resources

Table of Contents

TR

Teacher Resources

Bookmarks

Fiction

- Who are the characters?

- Where does the story take place?

- When does the story take place?

- What happens . . .
  at the beginning?
  in the middle?
  at the end?

Nonfiction

- What did I learn?

- What is this mainly about?

Iris and Walter

Short Vowels; Short e: ea

add	pack	peck	pink	knock	junk
ask	pan	red	quick	lock	just
back	pat	sled	rib	lots	luck
band	plan	speck	ring	pond	lump
bang	rang	step	rip	rock	mug
bank	sack	tell	sick	shock	must
black	sad	them	sing	slop	run
bland	sang	well	sink	sock	rust
brand	sank	went	six	sod	sung
camp	sat	when	slim	stock	truck
cap	slap	yell	sling	stop	trunk
cat	stack	big	slip	tock	tub
crack	tag	bring	still	top	tuck
drank	tank	cling	swing	bunk	tug
fast	track	crib	think	but	bread
grab	van	fill	thing	chunk	breath
grand	bed	fist	this	cup	dead
grass	bell	fit	tip	cut	dread
hand	bend	fix	will	drum	feather
hat	best	hill	win	duck	head
jag	check	his	wing	dunk	leather
lack	deck	hit	box	dust	meadow
land	desk	kid	clock	fun	read
last	dress	king	dock	gum	ready
man	end	lick	frog	hug	spread
map	get	list	got	hum	sweater
mask	less	mist	honk	hung	thread
mat	let	pick	jog	jump	weather

Spelling Words

chop
desk
drum
dust
job
list
mess
pack
rib
rock
sack
sad
tag

High-Frequency/ Tested Words

beautiful
country
friend*
front
someone
somewhere

Selection Words

amazing
ladder
meadow
roller-skate

Exploring Space with an Astronaut

Long Vowels CVCe; c/s/, g/j/, s/z/

age	pace	exercise	ride	lone	tube
airplane	page	file	ripe	nose	tune
ate	place	fine	shines	note	use
bake	plane	hike	size	poke	
brave	plate	ice	slice	pose	
cage	race	inside	spice	rode	
cake	rage	kite	time	rose	
cape	rake	lice	twice	telescope	
date	safe	life	white	those	
drape	sage	like	wide	tone	
erase	shake	lime	wise	vote	
face	space	mice	bone	confuse	
game	spaceship	miles	broke	cube	
gape	stage	mime	chose	cute	
lace	take	mine	close	fuse	
lake	tame	nice	code	huge	
lane	wage	outside	dose	mule	
late	bite	pile	home	mute	
made	bride	price	hope	plume	
make	dice	quite	hose	rude	
mane	dime	rice	joke	rule	

Spelling Words

blaze
cube
fine
home
late
mice
nose
page
size
space
tune
vote

High-Frequency/ Tested Words

everywhere
live*
machines
move
woman
work*
world

Selection Words

astronaut
experiment
gravity
shuttle
telescope

* = reviewed high-frequen[cy]
word from Grade 1

Henry and Mudge and the Starry Night

Consonant Blends

ct	bride	croak	flock	land	pride	small	stars	tent
ant	bring	crows	flop	last	prop	smelly	state	trace
ask	brisk	crust	flute	long	raft	smile	step	track
and	broke	drank	fly	lost	scrape	snack	stick	tree
est	brush	dread	frame	mask	screech	snake	stink	tribe
lack	bust	dreams	frog	milk	scrub	snap	stone	trip
blades	camp	drink	front	must	send	snuck	strand	trunk
blame	clam	drool	glad	nest	skate	snuggle	strap	trust
blank	clamp	drop	glide	next	skills	sound	stream	tusk
blast	clank	drove	grace	past	skit	space	stress	twice
blew	clap	dump	grand	pest	sky	splat	stretch	twigs
blond	clean	dusk	grass	place	slat	splint	strict	twin
bluebird	close	dust	gray	plan	sleep	split	stride	went
brake	crackers	dwell	grind	plank	slept	spread	strike	west
branch	craft	fast	groan	plant	slide	spring	string	wind
brand	cramp	felt	hand	plate	slippery	spruce	stripe	
brave	crate	flake	help	plug	slope	stage	strong	
bread	crept	flat	jump	plump	slow	stamp	stump	
breeze	crest	flex	just	pond	slump	stand	stung	

Spelling Words

ask
brave
breeze
clip
hand
mask
nest
state
stop
strap
stream
twin

High-Frequency/ Tested Words

bear
build
couldn't
father
love*
mother
straight

Selection Words

drooled
lanterns
shivered
snuggled

A Walk in the Desert

Base Words and Endings -s, -ed, -ing

-s		-ed			-ing		
amazes	pecks	dragged	peeled		amazing	playing	
asks	pretends	dropped	petted		asking	racing	
bakes	protects	filled	placed		bugging	riding	
calls	races	gagged	raced		carving	rubbing	
chips	rubs	gobbled	rested		confusing	running	
cools	runs	grabbed	rubbed		dining	scaring	
drags	seems	grinned	saved		dragging	shaking	
eats	smiles	happened	smiled		hiding	sleeping	
gets	uses	hiked	snapped		hiking	sliding	
grows	wags	hopped	tagged		hopping	smiling	
hikes	walks	hugged	traded		jumping	soaring	
howls	wipes	jogged	wagged		lifting	sunning	
jumps		jumped	walked		looking	trading	
lies	-ed	lifted	watched		making	wagging	
lives	added	looked	wiped		opening	walking	
makes	amazed	nodded	yelled		patting	winning	
	asked	patted					

Spelling Words

dropped
dropping
excited
exciting
hugged
hugging
lifted
lifting
smiled
smiling
talked
talking

High-Frequency/ Tested Words

animals
early*
eyes*
full
water*
warm

Selection Words

cactus
climate
coyote
desert
harsh

The Strongest One

Consonant Digraphs

ch	crouch	fresh	shrimp	teeth	together	stretch
arch	each	fish	shrubs	than		watch
bench	lunch	hush	shut	thank	tch	
branches	much	mash	shy	that	batch	wh
bunch	pinch	mush	splash	them	catch	elsewhere
chalk	such	shack	trash	then	clutch	whale
chase	teach	shake	wash	there	crutch	when
chat	watch	shape	wish	they	ditch	where
check	which	shell		thick	fetch	which
chest		shin	th	thin	hatch	while
chick	sh	shine	bath	think	hutch	whim
chicken	bash	ship	everything	things	itch	whip
chimp	blush	shirt	forth	third	latch	whirl
chin	brush	shone	fourth	thirsty	match	whisk
chip	bushes	shop	math	those	patch	whistle
chop	crush	shore	mouth	thud	pitch	white
chose	dash	shot	path	thumb	scratched	
church	dish	show	something	thump	stitch	

Spelling Words

bunch
chase
itch
match
patch
shape
that
them
whale
what
when
wish

High-Frequency/ Tested Words

gone
learn*
often
pieces
though
together*
very*

Selection Words

dangerous
gnaws
narrator
relatives

* = reviewed high-frequency word from Grade 1

Tara and Tiree, Fearless Friends

r-Controlled ar, or, ore; Syllables VCCV

ar	dark	shark	fork	**ore**	belly	packet
alarm	darling	smart	form	adore	bucket	panda
armies	far	star	fort	before	carpet	pepper
armor	farm	start	horse	bore	chicken	picnic
art	garden	target	morning	chore	corner	pocket
artist	hard	yard	north	more	correct	pompom
barber	harm		orbit	score	darling	problem
bark	harp	**or**	order	shore	distant	puppet
barn	jars	border	porch	sore	enlist	rabbits
car	lark	born	short	store	forget	ribbon
carp	mark	corn	sport	stories	gimmick	socket
carpet	market	corner	stork	therefore	insect	target
cart	parched	correct	storm		kitten	until
cartoon	part	forget	stormy	**VCCV**	mitten	winter
charm	party	forgot	thorn	basket	muffin	

Spelling Words

before, born, chore, corn, farm, hard, horse, more, part, porch, score, smart

High-Frequency/Tested Words

break, family*, heard, listen, once*, pull*

Selection Words

brave, collar, slipped

Ronald Morgan Goes to Bat

Contractions

aren't	don't	how's	it's	that's	who's
can't	hadn't	I'll	let's	there's	won't
couldn't	haven't	I'm	she's	they'll	you'll
didn't	he's	isn't	she'll	wasn't	
doesn't	he'll	it'll	shouldn't	we'll	

Spelling Words

didn't, hadn't, hasn't, he's, I'll, I'm, isn't, it's, she's, wasn't, we'll, who'll

High-Frequency/Tested Words

certainly, either, great*, laugh*, second, worst, you're

Selection Words

clutched, spirit, terrific

Turtle's Race with Beaver

r-Controlled er, ir, ur; Syllables VCCV

er	swerve	flirt	curl	turtle	corner	surface
certain	term	shirk	curler	urge	curler	survive
clerk	verse	shirt	disturb	urn	dirty	tender
fern		skirt	fur		disturb	thirty
germ	**ir**	squirrel	furry	**VCCV**	enter	turkey
her	birch	stir	hurry	after	gotten	under
herd	bird	third	hurt	almost	happens	until
herself	birdbath	thirsty	murmur	arrive	happy	winter
jerk	birth	thirty	nurse	batter	hurry	wonder
kernel	birthday	twirl	purple	better	kernel	
nerve	chirp		purse	border	murmur	
perch	circus	**ur**	return	bottom	perfect	
perfect	confirm	blurt	spurt	burger	plenty	
perk	dirt	burden	surf	butter	rabbit	
person	dirty	burger	surface	certain	sherbet	
pert	girl	burn	survive	challenge	sister	
serve	girth	burst	Thursday	chipmunk	splendid	
sherbet	firm	church	turkey	circus	squirrel	
stern	first	curb	turn	confirm	summer	

Spelling Words

birth, curb, curl, dirt, her, nurse, person, purse, serve, skirt, turn, turtle

High-Frequency/Tested Words

above*, ago, enough*, toward*, whole, word

Selection Words

buried, challenge, dam, embarrassed, halfway, lodge

* = reviewed high-frequency word from Grade 1

The Bremen Town Musicians

Plurals -s, -es, -ies

-s

animals	drinks	monsters	towns	dishes	**-ies**
bags	ducklings	nails	toys	ditches	armies
cases	ducks	nickels	tunes	dresses	babies
baskets	experts	notes	twigs	foxes	berries
bikes	farms	orders	vases	glasses	buddies
bins	forests	papers	years	kisses	bunnies
books	friends	pencils		lashes	candies
boys	gerbils	piles	**-es**	leashes	cherries
cages	germs	places	ashes	lunches	cities
cards	girls	planes	batches	matches	daddies
centers	globes	plates	beaches	messes	families
cents	grapes	pockets	benches	mixes	flies
chores	hands	purses	boxes	patches	jellies
classmates	heels	races	branches	peaches	ladies
corners	holes	robbers	brushes	perches	lilies
crafts	homes	rocks	bunches	ranches	mommies
crops	hoses	roses	buses	scratches	nannies
cups	hours	spices	bushes	switches	parties
dancers	houses	stamps	churches	watches	pennies
desks	jobs	stands	classes	wishes	ponies
dimes	kittens	stars	circuses		puppies
dogs	lamps	stores	crashes		stories
	lots	things	crutches		supplies

Spelling Words

babies
baby
lunch
lunches
note
notes
stories
story
switch
switches
tune
tunes

High-Frequency/ Tested Words

bought
people*
pleasant
probably
scared
shall
sign*

Selection Words

excitement
mill
monsters
musicians
robbers

A Turkey for Thanksgiving

Long a: a, ai, ay; Syllables VCV

a	claim	pain	**ay**	ray	ever
acorns	explain	paint	away	say	famous
agent	fail	quail	bay	spray	holiday
apron	faint	rail	day	stay	lady
baby	frail	rain	dismay	stray	lazy
famous	gain	raised	gray	sway	paper
lady	grain	sail	fray	today	visit
lazy	hail	snail	hay	stay	
paper	laid	stain	holiday	way	
table	maid	tail	lay		
	mail	train	may	**VCV**	
ai	main	waist	okay	acorn	
aim	nail	wait	pay	agent	
braid	paid		play	baby	
brain	pail		pray	began	

Spelling Words

away
brain
main
paint
play
raise
say
stay
tail
today
tray
wait

High-Frequency/ Tested Words

behind*
brought
door*
everybody
minute
promise
sorry

Selection Words

hooves
lumbered
riverbank
Thanksgiving

* = reviewed high-frequency
word from Grade 1

Pearl and Wagner: Two Good Friends

Long e: e, ee, ea, y; Syllabels VCV

e	greet	beam	please	lady
be	jeep	bean	read	lazy
detail	keep	beat	readers	leafy
equal	meet	bleach	seal	lucky
even	need	cheap	seat	only
he	screech	clean	squeak	party
maybe	seed	cream	stream	pony
me	seek	crease	teach	pretty
meter	seems	dreamed	teacher	ready
recess	sleep	each	team	really
secret	sleet	ease	tease	shaky
she	speech	easel	treat	silly
we	steep	easy		story
	street	eating	**y**	windy
ee	succeed	feast	any	
agree	sweeping	heal	anything	**VCV**
bee	sweet	heap	baby	city
beet	teeth	leafy	bunny	detail
breeze	three	leaping	city	electric
creep	tree	leave	cozy	even
deep	weed	mean	dirty	meter
feed	week	meat	everyone	recess
feel	wheel	neat	everywhere	remember
feet		pea	funny	robins
fifteen	**ea**	peach	happy	
green	beach	peak	jolly	

Spelling Words

deep
easy
feel
leave
party
read
seat
sleep
team
teeth
wheel
windy

guess
pretty
science*
shoe*
village
watch
won

Selection Words

electricity
robot
trash
wad

Dear Juno

Long o: o, oa, ow; Syllables VCV

o	open	croak	blown	thrown
almost	over	float	bowl	window
bold	photograph	foamy	flow	yellow
cold	post	goal	flown	
colt	postcard	goat	follow	**VCV**
donate	rotate	loaf	glow	donate
fold	scold	loan	grow	favor
gold	so	moat	grown	hero
hello	soda	oat	growth	locate
hero	sold	oath	know	moment
hold	strolled	road	mow	noticed
host	told	roam	mower	open
locate	unfolded	roast	own	photograph
mold		throat	owner	robot
moment	**oa**	toad	row	soda
most	boast	toast	show	
noticed	boat		shown	
notion	coach	**ow**	slow	
ocean	coast	below	snow	
old	coat	blow	throw	

Spelling Words

ago
bowl
float
goat
hold
most
open
show
slow
toad
toast
told

answer*
company
faraway
parents
picture*
school*
wash

Selection Words

envelope
persimmons
photograph
smudged

* = reviewed high-frequent
word from Grade 1

Anansi Goes Fishing

Compound Words

afternoon	carpool	grandpa	mailman	railroad	sunrise
airline	catfish	grandparents	maybe	raindrop	sunscreen
airplane	cowboy	grandson	myself	rainstorm	sunshine
airport	cupcake	grasshoppers	nearby	rainbow	suntan
anything	daylight	haircut	netmaker	riverbank	supermarket
babysit	daytime	halfway	network	riverboat	teacup
backpack	dishpan	haystack	nobody	rowboat	teammates
backyard	driveway	himself	nothing	sailboat	teardrop
baseball	drugstore	homemade	nowhere	sandpaper	thunderstorm
bathtub	everybody	homework	nutshell	schoolyard	treehouse
bedroom	everyone	inside	oatmeal	seashore	watermelon
bedtime	everything	landlord	outside	seaweed	weekend
beehive	everywhere	laptop	pancake	shortstop	whatever
birthday	faraway	ladybug	paycheck	snowflake	wherever
blackbird	fireplace	lipstick	peanuts	snowstorm	wildflower
brainstorm	flashlight	lookout	pinecone	someone	worksheet
breakfast	forever	lunchbox	pitchfork	something	yourself
buttermilk	goldfish	lunchtime	playmate	starfish	
cannot	granddad	mailbag	playoff	streetcar	
carefree	grandma	mailbox	popcorn	sunflowers	

Spelling Words

backyard
basketball
bathtub
bedtime
birthday
driveway
mailbox
raindrop
riverbank
someone
something
weekend

High-Frequency/Tested Words

been
believe
caught
finally
today*
tomorrow
whatever

Selection Words

delicious
justice
lazy
weave

Rosa and Blanca

Long i: i, ie, igh, y

i	spider	lied	nightlight	fly
behind	wild	pie	right	hydrant
bind	tiger	tie	sigh	July
blind	tiny	tried	sight	myself
child	title		slight	nylon
cider		*igh*	thigh	shy
climb	*ie*	bright	tight	sky
find	cried	flight		sly
kind	cries	fright	*y*	try
lilac	die	high	by	why
mild	dried	knight	cry	
mind	flies	light	cycle	
pilot	fries	might	cyclone	
sign	lie	night	dry	

Spelling Words

blind
bright
child
cry
find
flight
fly
myself
right
sky
spider
wild

High-Frequency/Tested Words

alone
buy
daughters
half
many*
their*
youngest

Selection Words

chiles
luckiest
tortillas

A Weed Is a Flower

Comparative Endings

-er	harsher	softer	-est	happiest	saddest
bigger	heavier	sooner	biggest	heaviest	silliest
brighter	hotter	stranger	bravest	highest	slowest
colder	higher	taller	brightest	hottest	smallest
fairer	lazier	thicker	busiest	latest	smartest
fancier	littler	thinner	closest	laziest	softest
faster	longer	tighter	coldest	lightest	sweetest
finer	nicer	tinier	cutest	littlest	tallest
friendlier	prettier	uglier	fairest	longest	thinnest
greener	redder	weaker	fastest	nicest	tiniest
happier	sillier	wider	finest	prettiest	ugliest
harder	slower		friendliest	reddest	weakest
			fullest	ripest	widest

Spelling Words

busier
busiest
fatter
fattest
happier
happiest
hotter
hottest
smaller
smallest
sooner
soonest

High-Frequency/Tested Words

clothes
hours
money
neighbor
only*
question
taught

Selection Words

agriculture
college
greenhouse
laboratory

* = reviewed high-frequency
word from Grade 1

The Quilt Story

Syllables: Consonant +*le*

able	cradle	maple	rattle	stable	twinkle
ankle	cuddle	middle	riddle	staple	uncle
apple	dimple	mumble	rifle	startle	whistle
bottle	fable	nibble	ripple	struggle	wiggle
bubble	giggle	noble	sample	stumble	wobble
bugle	gobble	paddle	scribble	table	
bundle	handle	pickle	simple	tickle	
cable	jumble	puddle	snuggle	title	
candle	ladle	purple	sparkle	trouble	
cattle	little	puzzle	sprinkle	tumble	

Spelling Words

able, ankle, apple, bubble, bugle, bundle, cable, giggle, purple, sparkle, tickle, title

Vocabulary/Tested Words

blankets, pretended, quilt, stuffing, trunks, unpacked, wrapped

High-Frequency Words

beautiful, country, friend, front, someone, somewhere

Life Cycle of a Pumpkin

Vowels *oo, u*

oo				*u*	
book	foot	nook	took	bull	bushy
bookbag	football	notebook	understood	bulldog	full
brook	footstep	overlook	wood	bullet	fully
cook	good	root	wooden	bullfrog	pudding
cookbook	hood	shook	woodpile	bully	pull
cookie	hoof	soot	wool	bush	pulley
crook	hook	stood		bushel	push
	look	textbook			put

Spelling Words

brook, cook, full, hood, hook, July, pull, push, put, shook, stood, wood

Vocabulary/Tested Words

bumpy, fruit, harvest, root, smooth, soil, vine

High-Frequency Words

everywhere, live, machines, move, woman, work, world

Frogs

Vowel Diphthongs *ou, ow/ou/*

ou				*ow*		
about	house	proud	round	allow	flower	towel
aloud	loud	round	scout	bow	frown	towers
amounts	mouse	scout	shout	brown	gown	town
around	mouth	shout	sound	clown	growl	vow
bounce	ouch	sound	south	cow	how	vowel
bound	ounce	south	sprout	cowboy	howl	
cloud	our	sprout	stout	crowd	now	
count	out	stout	trout	crown	owl	
crouch	outside	trout	voucher	down	plow	
found	pouch	voucher	without	downtown	powder	
grouch	pounce	without		drown	powerful	
ground	pound			drowsy	rowdy	
	pout				shower	

Spelling Words

about, around, crown, downtown, flower, gown, ground, howl, mouse, pound, south

Vocabulary/Tested Words

crawls, insects, pond, powerful, shed, skin, wonderful

High-Frequency Words

bear, build, couldn't, father, love, mother, straight

Like Where I Am

Vowel Diphthongs oi, oy/oi/

oi			oy	
avoid	joint	point	annoy	joy
boil	joist	poise	boy	loyal
broil	hoist	poison	boyhood	oyster
choice	loiter	rejoice	cowboy	ploy
coil	moist	sirloin	coy	royal
coin	noise	soil	destroy	soy
foil	noisy	spoil	employ	toy
join	oily	toil	enjoy	voyage
	ointment	voice		

Spelling Words

broil
cowboy
destroy
enjoy
foil
joint
joy
loyal
moist
noise
royal
spoil

Vocabulary/ Tested Words

block
chuckle
fair
giant
strong
tears
trouble

High-Frequency Words

animals
early
eyes
full
water

Helen Keller and the Big Storm

Vowels oo, ew, ue, ui

oo			ew	ue	ui
bathroom	moo	spool	blew	blue	bruise
bloom	mood	spoon	brew	clue	cruise
boot	moon	stoop	chew	cue	fruit
broom	noon	too	crew	due	juice
classroom	pool	tool	drew	glue	nuisance
cool	proof	tooth	few	hue	recruit
food	raccoon	troop	flew	true	suit
goose	room	zoo	grew		
hoop	school	zoom	knew		
hoot	scoop		new		
loop	smooth		stew		
loose	snoop		threw		
	soon				

Spelling Words

blue
clue
cool
drew
flew
fruit
juice
new
spoon
suit
too
true

Vocabulary/ Tested Words

angry
branches
clung
fingers
picnic
pressing
special

High-Frequency Words

gone
learn
often
pieces
though
together
very

Firefighter!

Suffixes -ly, -ful, -er, -or

-ly
boldly
bravely
brightly
carefully
clearly
closely
finally
firmly
fondly
gently
gladly
hardly
harshly
kindly

lightly
loudly
lovely
proudly
quickly
quietly
slowly
smoothly
softly
suddenly
sweetly
tenderly
tightly
weekly

-ful
boastful
careful
cheerful
colorful
eventful
graceful
harmful
helpful
hopeful
joyful
peaceful
playful
powerful
restful

skillful
thankful
wonderful

-er
computer
dancer
driver
farmer
fighter
firefighter
gardener
helper
hiker
leader

painter
player
rancher
reader
singer
storyteller
teacher
vacationer
waiter
writer

-or
actor
calculator
conductor

creditor
director
editor
inventor
refrigerator
sailor
supervisor
visitor

Spelling Words

cheerful
fighter
graceful
hardly
helper
quickly
sailor
slowly
teacher
visitor
weekly
yearly

Vocabulary/Tested Words

building
burning
masks
quickly
roar
station
tightly

High-Frequency Words

break
family
heard

listen
once
pull

One Dark Night

Prefixes un-, re-, pre-, dis-

un-
unable
unclasp
undisturbed
uneasy
uneven
unfair
unfinished
unfold
unfrozen
unglue
unhappy
unhook
unkind
unlatch
unload
unlock

unmasks
unpack
unplug
unroll
unsafe
unseen
untie
untrue

re-
react
reclose
redrew
refilled
refold
reheated
relight

remake
repack
repaint
repave
replace
replaced
replay
rerun
resize
rethink
reuse
rewind
rewire
rework
rewrite

pre-
precooked
predate
preflight
preheat
preorder
prepaid
preread
preschool
preteen
pretest
pretreat
preview
prewash

dis-
disagree
disappear
disappointed
disapprove
disconnect
discount
disinfect
disjoint
dislike
dislocate
displace
displease
disprove
distrust

Spelling Words

disagree
disappear
preheat
preschool
regroup
rerun
retie
rewind
unlock
unpack
unplug
unsafe

Vocabulary/Tested Words

flashes
lightning
pounds
pours
rolling
storm
thunder

High-Frequency Words

certainly
either
great
laugh
second

worst
you're

Bad Dog, Dodger!

Silent Consonants: kn, wr, gn, mb

kn
knee
kneecap
kneel
knew
knickers
knife
knight
knit
knob
knock

knot
know
knuckle

wr
wrap
wreath
wreck
wren
wrench
wrestle

wriggle
wringing
wrinkle
wrist
write
wrong
wrote

gn
design
gnat
gnaw
gnome
gnu
resign
sign

mb
climb
comb
crumb
dumb
lamb
limb
numb
plumber
thumb
tomb

Spelling Words

climb
comb
gnat
knee
knob
knock
lamb
sign
wrap
wren
write
wrong

Vocabulary/Tested Words

chased
chewing
dripping
grabbed
practice
treat
wagged

High-Frequency Words

above
ago
enough
toward
whole
word

orace and Morris but mostly Dolores

h, gh/f/

phabet	phantom	sphere	laugh
olphin	phase	telegraph	rough
ephant	pheasant	trophy	roughly
opher	phone		tough
aph	phony	**gh**	
ephew	phooey	autograph	
rphan	photo	cough	
	phrase	enough	

Spelling Words

cliff
cough
enough
giraffe
graph
laugh
phone
photo
puff
rough
stuff
tough

Vocabulary/ Tested Words

adventure
climbed
clubhouse
exploring
greatest
truest
wondered

High-Frequency Words

bought	scared
people	shall
pleasant	sign
probably	

The Signmaker's Assistant

Vowels aw, au, augh, al

aw	raw	cause	haughty	false
awful	saw	fault	naughty	malt
bawl	scrawl	haul	slaughter	salt
brawny	shawl	haunt	taught	small
claw	squawk	jaunt		talk
crawl	straw	launch	**al**	taller
draw	thaw	laundry	all	walk
drawn	yawn	pause	also	wall
fawn		sauce	always	walnut
gnaw	**au**	sausage	bald	waltz
hawk	applaud	vault	ball	
law	August		baseball	
raw	author	**augh**	call	
lawn	auto	caught	chalk	
paw	because	daughter	fall	

Spelling Words

August
auto
because
caught
chalk
draw
fault
launch
talk
taught
thaw
walk

Vocabulary/ Tested Words

afternoon
blame
idea
important
signmaker
townspeople

High-Frequency Words

behind	minute
brought	promise
door	sorry
everybody	

Just Like Josh Gibson

Contractions

could've	she'd	we're	you'd
don't	should've	we've	you're
he'd	they'd	where'd	you've
I'd	they're	won't	
I've	they've	would've	

Spelling Words

can't
don't
he'd
I'd
I've
she'd
they'd
they're
we're
we've
won't
you're

Vocabulary/Tested Words

bases
cheers
field
plate
sailed
threw

High-Frequency Words

guess	village
pretty	watch
science	won
shoe	

Red, White, and Blue: The Story of the American Flag

Base Words and Endings

added	cries	having	pinches	spotted
baking	crossed	heading	places	started
beginning	crying	helped	planning	stepped
belonged	danced	hiking	plans	stepping
bigger	dancing	hoped	pointed	steps
biggest	decided	hopes	pouncing	stopped
bombed	discovered	hoping	pounds	stopping
bounced	dropped	hopped	prepays	stops
bounces	drops	hopping	prettiest	streets
bouncing	drumming	hugged	propping	stripes
braver	ended	hurried	purred	talking
burned	erupted	jogging	reapplied	thanks
called	excited	joking	replied	thinking
carried	faster	judging	returns	thornier
carries	fastest	knows	richest	tied
carrying	fighting	landed	rides	tried
changes	fitted	loneliest	rolling	tries
chokes	flies	longest	rubbed	trying
cleaned	floated	luckier	rubbing	unhappier
cleaning	floating	luckiest	rushed	unluckiest
cleared	floats	making	sadder	used
clearer	flying	marched	sailed	visits
clearest	fried	minded	scampered	wanted
clearing	friendlier	moved	scared	watched
clears	funnier	named	sewing	waved
climbed	funniest	needed	shouted	waving
closed	glued	nicer	showed	wider
coming	going	nicest	singing	widest
continued	hammered	nodded	skipping	wishes
cooking	happened	opened	sleepiest	
crazier	happier	owned	smarter	
craziest	happiest	peeking	smiles	
cried	hardest	picked	spiciest	

Spelling Words

cried
crying
hiked
hiking
liked
liking
planned
planning
skipped
skipping
tried
trying

Vocabulary/Tested Words

America
birthday
flag
freedom
nicknames
stars
stripes

High-Frequency Words

answer	picture
company	school
faraway	wash
parents	

Birthday Basket for Tía

Syllables *tion, ture*

tion
fraction
location
lotion
mention
motion
nation
portion
position
potion
recreation

section
station
suction
tuitions
vacation

ture
adventure
capture
creature
culture
feature
fixture
fracture
furniture
future

lecturing
mixture
moisture
nature
picture
puncture
sculpture
vulture

Spelling Words

action
caution
feature
fixture
future
mixture
motion
nation
nature
picture
section
station

Vocabulary/Tested Words

aunt
bank
basket
collects
favorite
present

High-Frequency Words

been	today
believe	tomorrow
caught	whatever
finally	

Cowboys

Suffixes *-ness, -less*

-ness
awareness
cheerfulness
brightness
darkness
emptiness
fairness
fitness
fondness
friendliness
fullness
gentleness
goodness
greatness
happiness

illness
kindness
lateness
laziness
loneliness
loudness
madness
quickness
redness
rudeness
sadness
sickness
soreness
stillness
suddenness

sweetness
tenderness
usefulness
watchfulness
weakness
weariness

-less
ageless
bottomless
careless
cloudless
colorless
cordless
countless

fearless
flightless
friendless
harmless
heartless
helpless
hopeless
hopelessly
jobless
joyless
meatless
mindless
painless
penniless
pointless

restless
shameless
shapeless
sleepless
speechless
spotless
thankless
thoughtless
tireless
toothless
useless
worthless

Spelling Words

careless
darkness
fearless
fitness
goodness
helpless
kindness
sadness
sickness
thankless
useless
weakness

Vocabulary/Tested Words

campfire
cattle
cowboy
galloped
herd
railroad
trails

High-Frequency Words

alone	many
buy	their
daughters	youngest
half	

Jingle Dancer

Prefixes *mis-, mid-*

-mis
misbehave
misbehavior
miscompute
misconduct
miscopy
misdeed
misdirect
misfile
misfit

misguided
misinform
misjudge
mislabel
mislaid
mislead
misleading
mismatch
misplace
misprint

misquote
misread
misreport
misshape
misspoke
misstep
mistreat
mistype
misunderstood

-mid
midafternoon
midair
midcircle
midday
midlife
midline
midnight
midpoint
midsentence

midship
midsize
midstream
midsummer
midtown
midway
midweek
midyear

Spelling Words

midair
midday
midway
midweek
midyear
misbehave
misdeed
mislead
mismatch
misplace
misprint
mistake

Vocabulary/Tested Words

borrow
clattering
drum
jingles
silver
voice

High-Frequency Words

clothes	only
hours	question
money	taught
neighbor	

Position for Writing

Left-handed and right-handed writers slant their papers differently from one another, but they sit and hold their pencils the same way.

Body Position

- Children should sit tall, with both feet flat on the floor and arms relaxed on a table or desk.

- Children should hold their papers with their non-writing hand.

Paper Slant

- Paper should be positioned at a slant that is approximately parallel to the writing arm.

- For left-handed children, the paper should slant from the right at the top to the left at the bottom.

- Right-handed children should slant the paper from the left at the top to the right at the bottom.

Pencil Grip

- Children should grasp the pencil lightly between the thumb and index finger, usually about an inch above the pencil point.

- For a child who grasps the pencil too close to the point, a simple remedy is to wrap a rubber band around the pencil about an inch above the point. Have the child hold the pencil above the rubber band.

Legibility

Legibility should be the goal of handwriting instruction. Children should be praised for writing legibly, even though their writing may deviate from a perfect model. Legibility is based on flexible but standard criteria for letter form, size, and slant, and for letter and word spacing.

Letter Form

- Standards for letter form enable each letter to be distinguished clearly from other letters.

- In the letter *a*, for example, the round part of the letter must be open, and the letter must be closed at the top. The letter *a* must not be confused with *u, d,* or *o.*

- The letters *t* and *f* must be crossed; the letters *i* and *j* dotted.

Letter Size

- Small letters sit on the bottom line and touch the middle line.

- Tall letters sit on the bottom line and touch the top line.

- Letters with descenders have tails that go down under the bottom line and touch the line below.

Letter Slant

- Letter slant should be consistent.

- All letters may slant to the right, to the left, or be straight up and down.

Letter and Word Spacing

- Letters in a word should be evenly spaced. They should not be written too close together or too far apart.

- There should be more space between words in a sentence than between letters in a word. This allows each word to stand out.

D'Nealian™ Alphabet

a b c d e f g h i

j k l m n o p q r s t

u v w x y z

A B C D E F G

H I J K L M N O

P Q R S T U V

W X Y Z . , ' ?

1 2 3 4 5 6

7 8 9 10

Manuscript Alphabet

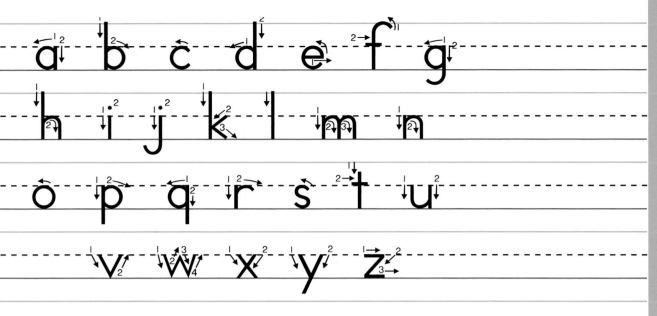

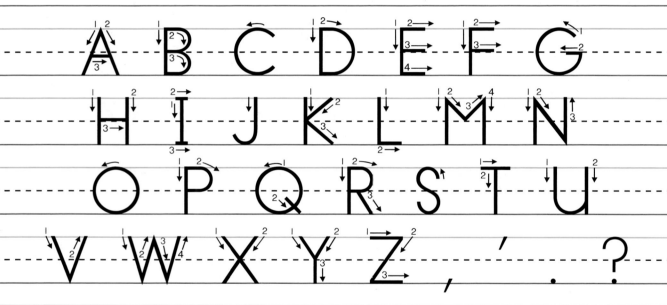

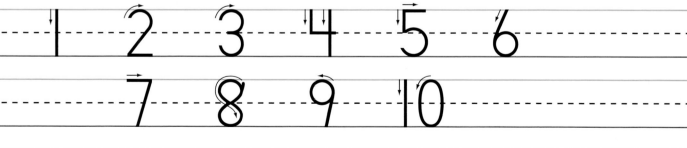

D'Nealian™ Cursive Alphabet

a b c d e f g

h i j k l m n

o p q r s t u

v w x y z

A B C D E F G

H I J K L M N

O P Q R S T U

V W X Y Z . , ' ?

1 2 3 4 5 6

7 8 9 10

Unit 5 *Responsibility*

	Below-Level	**On-Level**	**Advanced**

Firefighter!

To Read Aloud!
A Day in the Life of a Zookeeper
by Nate Leboutillier (First Fact Books, 2004) Beautiful full-color photographs highlight this interesting profession.

Aero and Officer Mike: Police Partners

by Joan Plummer Russell (Caroline House Boyds Mills Press, 2001) The real-life inspiration for the Officer Buckle and Gloria books, this book describes the daily life of a police officer and his dog.

How It Happens at the Post Office

by Dawn Frederick (Clara House Books, 2001) This book gives an insightful look at what happens to the mail once it has been posted.

My Hometown Library

by William Jaspersohn (Houghton Mifflin, 1994) The Guilford Free Library in Connecticut is highlighted in this picture book about how libraries are run and used.

One Dark Night

To Read Aloud!
Carlotta's Kittens and the Club of Mysteries
by Phyllis Reynolds Naylor (Atheneum Books, 2000) This is a book about a group of cats who leave their homes to meet in a garage for companionship and adventure.

Biscuit Wants to Play

by Alyssa Satin Capucilli (HarperCollins, 2001) When two kittens get stuck in a tree after chasing a butterfly, Biscuit comes to the rescue.

The Dog Who Had Kittens

by Polly Robertus (Holiday House, 1991) Baxter the dog is not a fan of cats, especially Eloise, but when Eloise has kittens and Baxter does not like her way of parenting, he takes over.

Everything Cat: What Kids Really Want to Know about Cats

by Marty Crisp (Northword Press, 2003) This book answers kids' questions about cats in an informal and chatty style that makes for easy and entertaining reading.

Bad Dog, Dodger!

To Read Aloud!
Lucy Comes to Stay
by Rosemary Wells (Dial, 1994) Lucy, a tiny puppy, learns the ropes from her new owner Mary Elizabeth in this gentle and warm picture book.

A Home for Mindy

by F.R. Robinson (Rigby, 2001) A story that explores the answer to how a lost dog finds a new home where it can be healthy and happy.

Henry and Mudge and the Best Day of All

by Cynthia Rylant (Macmillan, 1995) Henry and his dog Mudge celebrate Henry's birthday.

Martha Calling

by Susan Meddaugh (Houghton Mifflin, 1996) Martha the talking dog is back! This time, her family disguises her as their grandmother in order to sneak her into an inn.

Horace and Morris but mostly Dolores

To Read Aloud!
The Boys Start the War
by Phyllis Reynolds Naylor (Yearling, 2002) When a family of all boys finds out a family of all girls is moving next door, they start a campaign to get the girls out of their neighborhood.

Shy Charles

by Rosemary Wells (Dial, 1988) A painfully shy young mouse rescues his babysitter in an emergency situation.

Shrinking Mouse

by Pat Hutchins (Greenwillow, 1997) Four animal friends figure out that the size of something in the distance depends on how close they are to it.

Horrible Harry's Secret

by Suzy Kline (Viking Kestrel, 1990) Harry's best friend Doug finds out it's not easy being friends with someone who thinks he's in love with a girl.

The Signmaker's Assistant

To Read Aloud!
I Did It. I'm Sorry.
by Caralyn Buehner (Dial, 1998) Each double-page spread in this book presents the reader with three choices for how an animal should behave, two obviously wrong and amusing and one right.

Paper Lanterns

by Stefan Czernecki (2001) Old Chen is tired of making the beautiful paper lanterns he is known for. When a child shows up full of awe, Chen decides to teach him the craft.

If I Were In Charge of the World and Other Worries...

by Judith Viorst (Aladdin Paperbacks, 1984) Forty-one humorous and poignant poems highlight ordinary things in unusual ways.

Antonio's Apprenticeship: Painting a Fresco in Renaissance Italy

by Taylor Morrison (Holiday House, 1996) This book follows Antonio through his days as a painter's apprentice in 1478.

Unit 5 Reading Log

Name _____

Dates Read	Title and Author	What is it about?	How would you rate it?	Explain your rating.
From ____ to ____			Great 5 4 3 2 1 Awful	
From ____ to ____			Great 5 4 3 2 1 Awful	
From ____ to ____			Great 5 4 3 2 1 Awful	
From ____ to ____			Great 5 4 3 2 1 Awful	
From ____ to ____			Great 5 4 3 2 1 Awful	

Unit 5 Narrative Retelling Chart

Selection Title _____   Name _____   Date _____

Retelling Criteria/Teacher Prompt	Teacher-Aided Response	Student-Generated Response	Rubric Score (Circle one.)
Connections Does this story remind you of anything else?			4　3　2　1
Author's Purpose Why do you think the author wrote this story? What was the author trying to tell us?			4　3　2　1
Characters What can you tell me about _____ (use character's name)?			4　3　2　1
Setting Where and when did the story happen?			4　3　2　1
Plot What happened in the story?			4　3　2　1

Summative Retelling Score 4　3　2　1 _____

Comments _____

_____

Unit 5 Expository Retelling Chart

Name _____ **Date** _____

Selection Title _____

Retelling Criteria/Teacher Prompt	Teacher-Aided Response	Student-Generated Response	Rubric Score (Circle one.)
Connections Did this selection make you think about something else you have read? What did you learn about as you read this selection?			4 3 2 1
Author's Purpose Why do you think the author wrote this selection?			4 3 2 1
Topic What was the selection mostly about?			4 3 2 1
Important Ideas What is important for me to know about _____ (topic)?			4 3 2 1
Conclusions What did you learn from reading this selection?			4 3 2 1

Summative Retelling Score 4 3 2 1

Comments _____

_____

Reading

Concepts of Print and Print Awareness	Pre-K	K	1	2	3	4	5
Develop awareness that print represents spoken language and conveys and preserves meaning	•	•	•				
Recognize familiar books by their covers; hold book right side up	•	•					
Identify parts of a book and their functions (front cover, title page/title, back cover, page numbers)	•	•	•				
Understand the concepts of letter, word, sentence, paragraph, and story	•	•	•				
Track print (front to back of book, top to bottom of page, left to right on line, sweep back left for next line)	•	•	•				
Match spoken to printed words	•	•	•				
Know capital and lowercase letter names and match them	•	• T	•				
Know the order of the alphabet	•	•	•				
Recognize first name in print	•	•	•				
Recognize the uses of capitalization and punctuation		•	•				
Value print as a means of gaining information	•	•	•				

Phonological and Phonemic Awareness	Pre-K	K	1	2	3	4	5
Phonological Awareness							
Recognize and produce rhyming words	•	•	•				
Track and count each word in a spoken sentence and each syllable in a spoken word	•	•	•				
Segment and blend syllables in spoken words			•				
Segment and blend onset and rime in one-syllable words		•	•				
Recognize and produce words beginning with the same sound	•	•	•				
Identify beginning, middle, and/or ending sounds that are the same or different	•	•	•				
Understand that spoken words are made of sequences of sounds	•	•	•				
Phonemic Awareness							
Identify the position of sounds in words		•	•				
Identify and isolate initial, final, and medial sounds in spoken words	•	•	•				
Blend sounds orally to make words or syllables		•	•				
Segment a word or syllable into sounds; count phonemes in spoken words or syllables		•	•				
Manipulate sounds in words (add, delete, and/or substitute phonemes)	•	•	•				

Phonics and Decoding	Pre-K	K	1	2	3	4	5
Phonics							
Understand and apply the **alphabetic principle** that spoken words are composed of sounds that are represented by letters	•	•	•				
Know letter-sound relationships	•	• T	• T	• T			
Blend sounds of letters to decode		•	• T	• T	• T		
Consonants, consonant blends, and consonant digraphs		•	• T	• T	• T		
Short, long, and r-controlled vowels; vowel digraphs; diphthongs; common vowel patterns			• T	• T	• T		
Phonograms/word families		•	•	•	•		
Word Structure							
Decode words with common word parts		•	• T	• T	• T	•	•
Base words and inflected endings			• T	• T	•	•	•
Contractions and compound words			• T	• T	• T	•	•
Suffixes and prefixes			• T	• T	• T	•	•
Greek and Latin roots						•	•
Blend syllables to decode words			• T	• T	• T	•	•
Decoding Strategies							
Blending strategy: Apply knowledge of letter-sound relationships to decode unfamiliar words		•	•	•	•		
Apply knowledge of word structure to decode unfamiliar words		•	•	•	•	•	•
Use context and syntax along with letter-sound relationships and word structure to decode	•	•	•	•	•	•	•
Self-correct			•	•	•	•	•

Fluency	Pre-K	K	1	2	3	4	5
Read aloud fluently with accuracy, comprehension, appropriate pace/rate; with expression/intonation (prosody); with attention to punctuation and appropriate phrasing			• T	• T	• T	• T	• T
Practice fluency in a variety of ways, including choral reading, partner/paired reading, Readers' Theater, repeated oral reading, and tape-assisted reading		•	•	•	•	•	•

• instructional opportunity   **T** tested in standardized test

Reading (Oral and Written)	Pre-K	K	1	2	3	4	5	6
toward appropriate fluency goals by the end of each grade			•T	•T	•T	•T	•T	•T
regularly in independent-level material			•	•	•	•	•	•
silently for increasing periods of time			•	•	•	•	•	•

abulary (Oral and Written)

	Pre-K	K	1	2	3	4	5	6
d Recognition								
gnize regular and irregular high-frequency words	•	•	•T	•T				
gnize and understand selection vocabulary		•	•	•T	•	•	•	•
rstand content-area vocabulary and specialized, technical, or topical words			•	•	•	•	•	•
d Learning Strategies								
op vocabulary through direct instruction, concrete experiences, reading, listening to text read aloud	•	•	•	•	•	•	•	•
knowledge of word structure to figure out meanings of words			•	•T	•T	•T	•T	•T
context clues for meanings of unfamiliar words, multiple-meaning words, homonyms, homographs			•	•T	•T	•T	•T	•T
grade-appropriate reference sources to learn word meanings	•	•	•	•	•T	•T	•T	•T
picture clues to help determine word meanings	•	•	•	•				
new words in a variety of contexts	•	•	•	•	•	•	•	•
mine word usage and effectiveness		•	•	•	•	•	•	•
te and use graphic organizers to group, study, and retain vocabulary			•	•	•	•	•	•
end Concepts and Word Knowledge								
emic language	•	•	•	•	•	•	•	•
sify and categorize	•	•	•	•	•	•	•	•
nyms and synonyms			•	•T	•T	•T	•T	•T
ographs, homonyms, and homophones				•	•T	•T	•T	•T
iple-meaning words			•	•	•T	•T	•T	•T
ted words and derivations					•	•	•	•
ogies					•		•	
notation/denotation						•	•	•
rative language and idioms			•	•	•	•	•	•
scriptive words (location, size, color, shape, number, ideas, feelings)	•	•	•	•	•	•	•	•
utility words (shapes, colors, question words, position/directional words, and so on)	•	•	•	•				
e and order words	•	•	•	•	•	•	•	•
sition words						•	•	•
d origins: Etymologies/word histories; words from other languages, regions, or cultures					•	•	•	•
rtened forms: abbreviations, acronyms, clipped words			•	•	•	•	•T	

xt Comprehension

	Pre-K	K	1	2	3	4	5	6
mprehension Strategies								
view the text and formulate questions	•	•	•	•	•	•	•	•
and monitor purpose for reading and listening	•	•	•	•	•	•	•	•
vate and use prior knowledge	•	•	•	•	•	•	•	•
ke predictions	•	•	•	•	•	•	•	•
nitor comprehension and use fix-up strategies to resolve difficulties in meaning: adjust reading rate, ead and read on, seek help from reference sources and/or other people, skim and scan, summarize, text features				•	•	•	•	•
ate and use graphic and semantic organizers		•	•	•	•	•	•	•
wer questions (text explicit, text implicit, scriptal), including *who, what, when, where, why, what if, how*	•	•	•	•	•	•	•	•
ook back in text for answers				•	•	•	•	•
nswer test-like questions				•	•	•	•	•
nerate clarifying questions, including *who, what, where, when, how, why,* and *what if*	•	•	•	•	•	•	•	•
cognize text structure: story and informational (cause/effect, chronological, compare/contrast, scription, problem/solution, proposition/support)	•	•	•	•	•	•	•	•
mmarize text		•	•	•	•	•	•	•
ecall and retell stories		•	•	•	•	•	•	•
dentify and retell important/main ideas (nonfiction)	•	•	•	•	•	•	•	•
dentify and retell new information			•	•	•	•	•	•
ualize; use mental imagery		•	•	•	•	•	•	•
e strategies flexibly and in combination			•	•	•	•	•	•

Comprehension Skills

	Pre-K	K	1	2	3	4	5
Author's purpose			• T	• T	• T	• T	• T
Author's viewpoint/bias/perspective					•	•	•
Categorize and classify	•	•	•	•			
Cause and effect		•	• T	• T	• T	• T	• T
Compare and contrast		•	• T	• T	• T	• T	• T
Details and facts		•	•	•	•	•	•
Draw conclusions		•	• T	• T	• T	• T	• T
Fact and opinion				• T	• T	• T	• T
Follow directions/steps in a process	•	•	•	•	•	•	•
Generalize					• T	• T	• T
Graphic sources		•	•	•	•	• T	• T
Main idea and supporting details		• T	• T	• T	• T	• T	• T
Paraphrase			•	•	•	•	•
Persuasive devices and propaganda				•	•	•	•
Realism/fantasy		•	• T	• T	• T	•	•
Sequence of events		• T	• T	• T	• T	• T	• T

Higher Order Thinking Skills

	Pre-K	K	1	2	3	4	5
Analyze				•	•	•	•
Describe and connect the essential ideas, arguments, and perspectives of a text			•	•	•	•	•
Draw inferences, conclusions, or generalizations, support them with textual evidence and prior knowledge	•		•	•	•	•	•
Evaluate and critique ideas and text			•	•	•	•	•
Hypothesize						•	•
Make judgments about ideas and text			•	•	•	•	•
Organize and synthesize ideas and information			•			•	•

Literary Analysis, Response, & Appreciation

	Pre-K	K	1	2	3	4	5
Genre and Its Characteristics							
Recognize characteristics of a variety of genre	•	•	•	•	•	•	•
Distinguish fiction from nonfiction		•	•	•	•	•	•
Identify characteristics of literary texts, including drama, fantasy, traditional tales		•	•	•	•	•	•
Identify characteristics of nonfiction texts, including biography, interviews, newspaper articles		•	•	•	•	•	•
Identify characteristics of poetry and song, including nursery rhymes, limericks, blank verse	•	•	•	•	•	•	•
Literary Elements and Story Structure							
Character	•	• T	• T	• T	• T	• T	• T
Recognize and describe traits, actions, feelings, and motives of characters		•	•	•	•	•	•
Analyze characters' relationships, changes, and points of view		•	•	•	•	•	•
Analyze characters' conflicts				•		•	•
Plot and plot structure	•	• T	• T	• T	• T	• T	• T
Beginning, middle, end	•	•	•	•	•		
Goal and outcome or problem and solution/resolution		•	•	•	•	•	•
Rising action, climax, and falling action/denouement; setbacks						•	•
Setting	•	• T	• T	• T	• T	• T	
Relate setting to problem/solution						•	•
Explain ways setting contributes to mood						•	•
Theme		•	• T	• T	•	•	•
Use Literary Elements and Story Structure	•	•	•	•	•	•	•
Analyze and evaluate author's use of setting, plot, character				•	•	•	•
Identify similarities and differences of characters, events, and settings within or across selections/cultures	•	•	•	•	•	•	•
Literary Devices							
Allusion							
Dialect						•	
Dialogue and narration	•	•	•	•	•	•	•
Exaggeration/hyperbole					•	•	•
Figurative language: idiom, jargon, metaphor, simile, slang			•	•	•	•	•

• instructional opportunity   T tested in standardized test f[or]

	Pre-K	K	1	2	3	4	5	6
back						•	•	•
hadowing							•	•
al and informal language				•	•	•	•	•
r					•	•	•	•
ery and sensory words			•	•	•	•	•	•
				•	•	•	•	•
nification				•	•	•	•	•
of view (first person, third person, omniscient)					•	•	•	•
and word play				•	•	•	•	•
d devices and poetic elements	•	•	•	•	•	•	•	•
teration, assonance, onomatopoeia	•	•	•	•	•	•	•	•
me, rhythm, repetition, and cadence	•	•	•	•	•	•	•	•
rd choice				•	•	•	•	•
olism				•	•	•	•	•
							•	•
hor's and Illustrator's Craft								
nguish the roles of author and illustrator	•	•	•	•				
ognize/analyze author's and illustrator's craft or style				•	•	•	•	•
erary Response								
llect, talk, and write about books	•	•	•	•	•	•	•	•
ect on reading and respond (through talk, movement, art, and so on)	•	•	•	•	•	•	•	•
k and answer questions about text	•	•	•	•	•	•	•	•
ite about what is read	•	•	•	•	•	•	•	•
e evidence from the text to support opinions, interpretations, or conclusions			•	•	•	•	•	•
pport ideas through reference to other texts and personal knowledge				•	•	•	•	•
cate materials on related topic, theme, or idea				•	•	•	•	•
enerate alternative endings to plots and identify the reason for, and the impact of, the alternatives	•	•	•	•	•	•	•	•
thesize and extend the literary experience through creative responses	•	•	•	•	•	•	•	•
e connections: text to self, text to text, text to world	•	•	•	•	•	•	•	•
uate and critique the quality of the literary experience				•	•	•	•	•
r observations, react, speculate in response to text				•	•	•	•	•
erary Appreciation/Motivation								
w an interest in books and reading; engage voluntarily in social interaction about books	•	•	•	•	•	•	•	•
ose text by drawing on personal interests, relying on knowledge of authors and genres, estimating text culty, and using recommendations of others	•	•	•	•	•	•	•	•
d a variety of grade-level appropriate narrative and expository texts			•	•	•	•	•	•
d from a wide variety of genres for a variety of purposes	•	•	•	•	•	•	•	•
d independently			•	•	•	•	•	•
ablish familiarity with a topic			•	•	•	•	•	•
ltural Awareness								
velop attitudes and abilities to interact with diverse groups and cultures	•	•	•	•	•	•	•	•
nnect experiences and ideas with those from a variety of languages, cultures, customs, perspectives	•	•	•	•	•	•	•	•
derstand how attitudes and values in a culture or during a period in time affect the writing from that ture or time period						•	•	•
mpare language and oral traditions (family stories) that reflect customs, regions, and cultures		•	•	•	•	•	•	•
cognize themes that cross cultures and bind them together in their common humanness						•	•	•

anguage Arts

riting	Pre-K	K	1	2	3	4	5	6
ncepts of Print for Writing								
velop gross and fine motor skills and hand/eye coordination	•	•	•					
t own name and other important words	•	•	•					
te using pictures, some letters, and transitional spelling to convey meaning	•	•	•					
tate messages or stories for others to write	•	•	•					

	Pre-K	K	1	2	3	4	5	6
Create own written texts for others to read; write left to right on a line and top to bottom on a page	•	•	•					
Participate in shared and interactive writing	•	•	•					

Traits of Writing

Focus/Ideas

	Pre-K	K	1	2	3	4	5	6
Maintain focus and sharpen ideas		•	•	•	•	•	•	
Use sensory details and concrete examples; elaborate		•	•	•	•	•	•	
Delete extraneous information			•	•	•	•	•	
Rearrange words and sentences to improve meaning and focus				•	•	•	•	
Use strategies, such as tone, style, consistent point of view, to achieve a sense of completeness						•	•	

Organization/Paragraphs

	Pre-K	K	1	2	3	4	5	6
Use graphic organizers to group ideas		•	•	•	•	•	•	
Write coherent paragraphs that develop a central idea			•	•	•	•	•	
Use transitions to connect sentences and paragraphs			•	•	•	•	•	
Select an organizational structure based on purpose, audience, length						•	•	
Organize ideas in a logical progression, such as chronological order or by order of importance		•	•	•	•	•	•	
Write introductory, supporting, and concluding paragraphs					•	•	•	
Write a multi-paragraph paper				•	•	•	•	

Voice

	Pre-K	K	1	2	3	4	5	6
Develop personal, identifiable voice and an individual tone/style			•	•	•	•	•	
Maintain consistent voice and point of view						•	•	
Use voice appropriate to audience, message, and purpose						•	•	

Word Choice

	Pre-K	K	1	2	3	4	5	6
Use clear, precise, appropriate language		•	•	•	•	•	•	
Use figurative language and vivid words				•	•	•		
Select effective vocabulary using word walls, dictionary, or thesaurus		•	•	•	•	•	•	

Sentences

	Pre-K	K	1	2	3	4	5	6
Combine, elaborate, and vary sentences		•	•	•	•	•	•	
Write topic sentence, supporting sentences with facts and details, and concluding sentence			•	•	•	•	•	
Use correct word order			•	•	•	•		
Use parallel structure in a sentence							•	

Conventions

	Pre-K	K	1	2	3	4	5	6
Use correct spelling and grammar; capitalize and punctuate correctly		•	•	•	•	•	•	
Correct sentence fragments and run-ons					•	•	•	
Use correct paragraph indention			•	•	•	•	•	

The Writing Process

	Pre-K	K	1	2	3	4	5	6
Prewrite using various strategies	•	•	•	•	•	•	•	
Develop first drafts of single- and multiple-paragraph compositions		•	•	•	•	•	•	
Revise drafts for varied purposes, including to clarify and to achieve purpose, sense of audience, precise word choice, vivid images, and elaboration		•	•	•	•	•	•	
Edit and proofread for correct spelling, grammar, usage, and mechanics		•	•	•	•	•	•	
Publish own work	•	•	•	•	•	•	•	

Types of Writing

	Pre-K	K	1	2	3	4	5	6
Narrative writing (such as personal narratives, stories, biographies, autobiographies)	•	•	•T	•T	•T	•T	•T	•
Expository writing (such as essays, directions, explanations, news stories, research reports, summaries)		•	•T	•T	•T	•T	•T	•
Descriptive writing (such as labels, captions, lists, plays, poems, response logs, songs)	•	•	•T	•T	•T	•T	•T	•
Persuasive writing (such as ads, editorials, essays, letters to the editor, opinions, posters)		•	•T	•T	•T	•T	•T	•

Writing Habits and Practices

	Pre-K	K	1	2	3	4	5	6
Write on a daily basis	•	•	•	•	•	•	•	•
Use writing as a tool for learning and self-discovery				•	•	•	•	•
Write independently for extended periods of time			•	•	•	•	•	•

ENGLISH LANGUAGE CONVENTIONS in WRITING and SPEAKING	Pre-K	K	1	2	3	4	5	6

Grammar and Usage in Speaking and Writing

Sentences

	Pre-K	K	1	2	3	4	5	6
Types (declarative, interrogative, exclamatory, imperative)	•	•	•T	•T	•T	•T	•T	•
Structure (simple, compound, complex, compound-complex)	•	•	•	•	•	•T	•T	•

• instructional opportunity   **T** tested in standardized test f[...]

	Pre-K	K	1	2	3	4	5	6
s (subjects/predicates: complete, simple, compound; phrases; clauses)				•T	•	•T	•T	•T
ments and run-on sentences		•	•	•	•	•	•	•
bine sentences, elaborate			•	•		•	•	•
of speech: nouns, verbs and verb tenses, adjectives, adverbs, pronouns and antecedents, ctions, prepositions, interjections		•	•T	•T	•T	•T	•T	•T
e								
ject-verb agreement		•	•T	•	•	•T	•T	•T
oun agreement/referents			•T	•	•	•T	•T	•T
placed modifiers						•	•T	•T
used words					•	•	•	•T
gatives; avoid double negatives					•	•	•	•

hanics in Writing

	Pre-K	K	1	2	3	4	5	6
alization (first word in sentence, proper nouns and adjectives, pronoun *I*, titles, and so on)	•	•	•T	•T	•T	•T	•T	•T
uation (apostrophe, comma, period, question mark, exclamation mark, quotation marks, and so on)		•	•T	•T	•T	•T	•T	•T

elling

	Pre-K	K	1	2	3	4	5	6
independently by using pre-phonetic knowledge, knowledge of letter names, sound-letter knowledge	•	•	•	•	•	•	•	•
sound-letter knowledge to spell	•	•	•	•	•	•	•	•
nsonants: single, double, blends, digraphs, silent letters, and unusual consonant spellings		•	•	•	•	•	•	•
vels: short, long, *r*-controlled, digraphs, diphthongs, less common vowel patterns, schwa		•	•	•	•	•	•	•
knowledge of word structure to spell			•	•	•	•	•	•
se words and affixes (inflections, prefixes, suffixes), possessives, contractions and compound words			•	•	•	•	•	•
eek and Latin roots, syllable patterns, multisyllabic words			•	•	•	•	•	•
high-frequency, irregular words		•	•	•	•	•	•	•
frequently misspelled words correctly, including homophones or homonyms			•	•	•	•	•	•
meaning relationships to spell					•	•	•	•

ndwriting

	Pre-K	K	1	2	3	4	5	6
increasing control of penmanship, including pencil grip, paper position, posture, stroke	•	•	•	•				
legibly, with control over letter size and form; letter slant; and letter, word, and sentence spacing		•	•	•	•	•	•	•
lowercase and capital letters	•	•	•	•				
anuscript	•	•	•	•	•	•	•	•
rsive				•	•	•	•	•
numerals	•	•	•					

tening and Speaking

	Pre-K	K	1	2	3	4	5	6
tening Skills and Strategies								
en to a variety of presentations attentively and politely	•	•	•	•	•	•	•	•
monitor comprehension while listening, using a variety of skills and strategies	•	•	•	•	•	•	•	•
en for a purpose								
r enjoyment and appreciation	•	•	•	•	•	•	•	•
expand vocabulary and concepts	•	•	•	•	•	•	•	•
obtain information and ideas	•	•	•	•	•	•	•	•
follow oral directions	•	•	•	•	•	•	•	•
answer questions and solve problems	•	•	•	•	•	•	•	•
participate in group discussions	•	•	•	•	•	•	•	•
identify and analyze the musical elements of literary language	•	•	•	•	•	•	•	•
gain knowledge of one's own culture, the culture of others, and the common elements of cultures	•	•	•	•	•	•	•	•
ognize formal and informal language			•	•	•	•	•	•
en critically to distinguish fact from opinion and to analyze and evaluate ideas, information, experiences		•		•	•	•	•	•
uate a speaker's delivery				•	•	•	•	•
rpret a speaker's purpose, perspective, persuasive techniques, verbal and nonverbal messages, and of rhetorical devices					•	•	•	•
eaking Skills and Strategies								
ak clearly, accurately, and fluently, using appropriate delivery for a variety of audiences, and purposes	•	•	•	•	•	•	•	•
proper intonation, volume, pitch, modulation, and phrasing		•	•	•	•	•	•	•
ak with a command of standard English conventions	•	•	•	•	•	•	•	•
appropriate language for formal and informal settings	•	•	•	•	•	•	•	•

Speak for a purpose	Pre-K	K	1	2	3	4	5
To ask and answer questions	•	•	•	•	•	•	•
To give directions and instructions	•	•	•	•	•	•	•
To retell, paraphrase, or explain information		•	•	•	•	•	•
To communicate needs and share ideas and experiences	•	•	•	•	•	•	•
To participate in conversations and discussions	•	•	•	•	•	•	•
To express an opinion	•	•	•	•	•	•	•
To deliver dramatic recitations, interpretations, or performances	•	•	•	•	•	•	•
To deliver presentations or oral reports (narrative, descriptive, persuasive, and informational)	•	•	•	•	•	•	•
Stay on topic	•	•	•	•	•		
Use appropriate verbal and nonverbal elements (such as facial expression, gestures, eye contact, posture)	•	•	•	•	•	•	•
Identify and/or demonstrate methods to manage or overcome communication anxiety						•	•

Viewing/Media	Pre-K	K	1	2	3	4	5
Interact with and respond to a variety of print and non-print media for a range of purposes	•	•	•	•	•	•	•
Compare and contrast print, visual, and electronic media					•	•	•
Analyze and evaluate media			•	•	•	•	•
Recognize purpose, bias, propaganda, and persuasive techniques in media messages			•	•	•	•	•

Research and Study Skills

Understand and Use Graphic Sources	Pre-K	K	1	2	3	4	5
Advertisement			•	•	•	•	•
Chart/table	•	•	•	•	•	•	•
Diagram/scale drawing			•	•	•	•	•
Graph (bar, circle, line, picture)		•	•	•	•	•	•
Illustration, photograph, caption, label	•	•	•	•	•	•	•
Map/globe	•	•	•	•	•	•	•
Order form/application						•	•
Poster/announcement	•	•	•	•	•	•	•
Schedule						•	•
Sign	•	•	•	•		•	
Time line				•	•	•	•

Understand and Use Reference Sources	Pre-K	K	1	2	3	4	5
Know and use parts of a book to locate information	•	•	•	•	•	•	•
Use alphabetical order			•	•	•	•	
Understand purpose, structure, and organization of reference sources (print, electronic, media, Internet)	•	•	•	•	•	•	•
Almanac						•	•
Atlas		•		•	•	•	•
Card catalog/library database				•	•	•	•
Dictionary/glossary		•	•	•	• T	• T	• T
Encyclopedia				•	•	•	•
Magazine/periodical				•	•	•	•
Newspaper and Newsletter				•	•	•	•
Readers' Guide to Periodical Literature						•	•
Technology (computer and non-computer electronic media)		•	•	•	•	•	•
Thesaurus				•	•	•	•

Study Skills and Strategies	Pre-K	K	1	2	3	4	5
Adjust reading rate			•	•	•	•	•
Clarify directions	•	•	•	•	•	•	•
Outline				•	•	•	•
Skim and scan			•	•	•	•	•
SQP3R						•	•
Summarize		•	•	•	•	•	•
Take notes, paraphrase, and synthesize			•	•	•	•	•
Use graphic and semantic organizers to organize information		•	•	•	•	•	•

• instructional opportunity   **T** tested in standardized test f

t-Taking Skills and Strategies	Pre-K	K	1	2	3	4	5	6
stand the question, the vocabulary of tests, and key words			•	•	•	•	•	•
er the question; use information from the text (stated or inferred)		•	•	•		•	•	•
across texts				•	•	•	•	•
lete the sentence				•	•	•	•	•

hnology/New Literacies	Pre-K	K	1	2	3	4	5	6

Computer Electronic Media

	Pre-K	K	1	2	3	4	5	6
tapes/CDs, video tapes/DVDs	•	•	•	•	•	•	•	
television, and radio		•	•	•	•	•	•	•

puter Programs and Services: Basic Operations and Concepts

	Pre-K	K	1	2	3	4	5	6
ccurate computer terminology	•	•	•	•	•	•	•	•
e, name, locate, open, save, delete, and organize files		•	•	•	•	•	•	•
nput and output devices (such as mouse, keyboard, monitor, printer, touch screen)	•	•	•	•	•	•	•	•
asic keyboarding skills		•	•	•	•	•	•	•

onsible Use of Technology Systems and Software

	Pre-K	K	1	2	3	4	5	6
cooperatively and collaboratively with others; follow acceptable use policies	•	•	•	•	•	•	•	•
gnize hazards of Internet searches			•	•	•	•	•	•
ect intellectual property					•	•	•	•

rmation and Communication Technologies: Information Acquisition

	Pre-K	K	1	2	3	4	5	6
electronic web (non-linear) navigation, online resources, databases, keyword searches			•	•	•	•	•	•
visual and non-textual features of online resources	•	•	•	•	•	•	•	•
net inquiry			•	•	•	•	•	•
entify questions			•	•	•	•	•	•
cate, select, and collect information			•	•	•	•	•	•
alyze information			•	•	•	•	•	•
Evaluate electronic information sources for accuracy, relevance, bias				•	•	•	•	•
Understand bias/subjectivity of electronic content (about this site, author search, date created)						•	•	•
nthesize information				•	•	•	•	•
mmunicate findings				•	•	•	•	•
fix-up strategies (such as clicking *Back, Forward,* or *Undo;* redoing a search; trimming the URL)			•	•	•	•	•	•

munication

	Pre-K	K	1	2	3	4	5	6
aborate, publish, present, and interact with others		•	•	•	•	•	•	•
online resources (e-mail, bulletin boards, newsgroups)			•	•	•	•	•	•
a variety of multimedia formats			•	•	•	•	•	•

blem Solving

	Pre-K	K	1	2	3	4	5	6
ect the appropriate software for the task	•	•	•	•	•	•	•	•
technology resources for solving problems and making informed decisions			•	•	•	•	•	•
ermine when technology is useful				•	•	•	•	•

e Research Process	Pre-K	K	1	2	3	4	5	6
ose and narrow the topic; frame and revise questions for inquiry		•	•	•	•	•	•	•
ose and evaluate appropriate reference sources			•	•	•	•	•	•
ate and collect information	•	•	•	•	•	•	•	•
e notes/record findings				•	•	•	•	•
bine and compare information				•	•	•	•	•
uate, interpret, and draw conclusions about key information		•	•	•	•	•	•	•
nmarize information		•	•	•	•	•	•	•
ke an outline				•	•	•	•	•
anize content systematically		•	•	•	•	•	•	•
mmunicate information		•	•	•	•	•	•	•
rite and present a report				•	•	•	•	•
Include citations						•	•	•
Respect intellectual property/plagiarism						•	•	•
elect and organize visual aids		•	•	•	•	•	•	•

Teacher's Edition

Text

KWL Strategy: The KWL Interactive Reading Strategy was developed and is used by permission of Donna Ogle, National-Louis University, Evanston, Illinois, co-author of *Reading Today and Tomorrow*, Holt, Rinehart & Winston Publishers, 1988. (See also *The Reading Teacher*, February 1986, pp. 564–570.)

Artists

Scott Gustafson: cover, page i